MOON

PACIFIC COAST HIGHWAY
Road Trip

VICTORIAH ARSENIAN

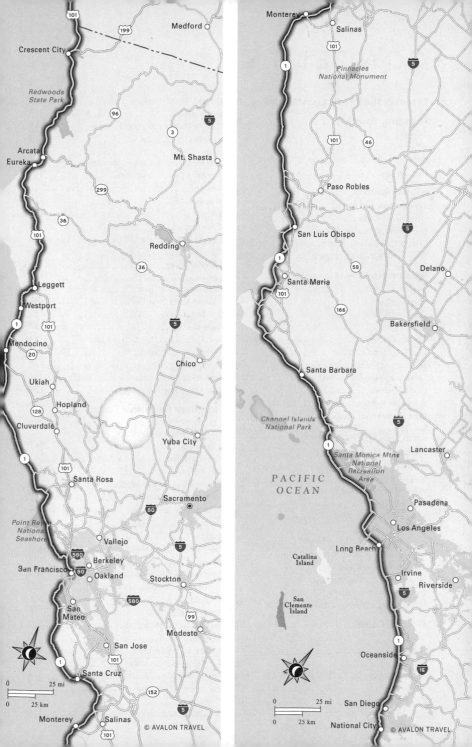

© AVALON TRAVEL

CONTENTS

DISCOVER
the Pacific
Coast Highway

The Pacific Coast Highway is an epic journey, offering up 1,700 astounding miles to those with playful hearts and the passion for adventure.

A spirit born of earth and water breathes over the Pacific Coast: across the western edge of Washington's glacier-carved Olympic Peninsula, along the delicately etched sea arches of Oregon, riding California's rocky northern shore south until it softens in the warm embrace of sunny southern skies.

Curving down from the Strait of Juan de Fuca, the highway rounds Olympic National Park, where Mount Olympus casts a shadow over mystical evergreen giants. Heading south past Washington's rough-and-tumble logging and fishing communities, the road keeps pace with cedar plank canoes used by Native Americans following the watery highway of their ancestors. The southernmost tip of Washington marks the end of Lewis and Clark's journey; their names are carved into a tree atop Cape Disappointment.

Much of Oregon's shoreline is publicly owned, including otherworldly features like basalt sea stacks and towering sand dunes. Wild winds choreograph the dance of colorful kites every summer, while caches of blown-glass floats gleam above the tide line.

Giant redwoods punch upward through a layer of fog at the start of California's 1,100-mile sprawl of coastline. The tallest and most majestic line the Avenue of the Giants, alongside the kitschiest: drive-through trees, drive-on trees, and

houses carved from trees. The phenomenal northern coastline is rivaled only by the drama of Big Sur farther south, beyond which stretch the endless summer beachfronts of Southern California. The land of beach boys and surfer girls really does exist.

Laced between and around these scenes lie cities built upon the dreams and the backs of those who believed. Seattle, Portland, San Francisco, Los Angeles, and San Diego are gateways to the landscapes that separate them, as well as destinations in their own right. Blue-collar ports alternate with vacation retreats along the way, adding a range of cafés, seafood grills, and bijou restaurants, as well as diverse places to stay, from lighthouse youth hostels to upscale new-age resorts.

What are you waiting for? PCH is calling.

PLANNING YOUR TRIP

Regions

Washington Coast

Looking for new experiences? Steeped in natural beauty from emerald forests to the wild Pacific Ocean, the **Olympic Peninsula** has them. Explore meandering trails. Wander beneath the lush canopy of **rain forests.** Go storm watching. But save time for an urban stopover in **Seattle,** where the fish fly at Pike Place Market and you can get the perfect cup of coffee any time of day.

Oregon Coast

With whimsical **arches** and **sea stacks,** towering **cliffs,** and seemingly endless **sand dunes,** Oregon's coast is both magnificent and mysterious. Just about anything is possible, from exploring otherworldly coastal caverns to navigating wild rivers. For a taste of urban living, Oregon-style, head to **Portland** for some of the best farm-to-table dining and craft beers in the state.

Northern California Coast

California, here we come! Drive through **giant redwoods**—in some cases quite literally. Find yourself on the **Lost Coast.** Sip a glass or two of pinot noir. Then cross the iconic Golden Gate Bridge into **San Francisco.** With some of the most famous sights and best dining along the entire West Coast, the City by the Bay is the heartbeat of Northern California.

Central California Coast

While it's not undiscovered, the Central Coast is still untamed. Artists, writers, and poets find inspiration in this wild, ever-changing landscape. There's much to do here: meet jellyfish in **Monterey,** tour **Hearst Castle,** sample the good life

in **Santa Barbara.** But first, stand on a bluff in **Big Sur** and discover why—without a word—central California defines "breathtaking."

Southern California Coast

As it continues south, California's coastline becomes soft and **sun-drenched.** Here you'll find the high times and easy living that define the Golden State's beach culture. Spot celebrities in **Hollywood** and legends in their own minds on the **Venice Boardwalk.** Go surfing in **Malibu,** snorkel in **La Jolla,** and bike along the shore in **San Diego.** You can even pal around with a cartoon mouse. SoCal has no limits!

When to Go

The best time for this road trip is **late spring to early fall,** when the weather is best.

The window for good weather is shorter in **Washington** and **Oregon;** it's best **June through September** when it's warm and dry with average temperatures of 80°F.

Part of **California**'s allure is in its relatively **mild weather year-round.** While the northern coast rarely hits 70°F in the summertime and can be rainy and foggy, the farther south you go, the warmer and sunnier it gets. In the San Francisco Bay Area, temperatures reach into the 70s and even 80s in summer and fall. Be prepared for the **chill of fog** in the evenings; even the warmest summer days often end with fog spilling over the Golden Gate into the city. From Santa Barbara south to San Diego, temperatures in the 80s are not unheard of even in January; summer temperatures can often hit the triple digits in inland Los Angeles.

If you drive PCH in the **high summer season,** expect heavier **traffic** and **crowds.** Hotels and rental-car reservations go fast, so make your arrangements in advance. Rates are also higher during

Clockwise from top left: Muir Woods National Monument; Seattle's Space Needle; Cannon Beach's Haystack Rock.

the summer. Port towns in Washington and Oregon can be hectic. Arrive early to the **ferry docks;** long lines form quickly and the wait can be two hours or more. Crowds and especially traffic intensify in California, especially on the freeways. Plan extra driving time and extra time along the way, especially at popular sights in big cities.

A **spring** or **fall** road trip will be less hectic, but the weather will be less reliable, especially in the Pacific Northwest, where you'll be certain to get some rain (and maybe even snow).

Before You Go

Getting There
Each region has a convenient **travel hub** in a metropolitan city: **Seattle** in Washington, **Portland** in Oregon, **San Francisco** in Northern California, **Los Angeles** and **San Diego** in Southern California. Smaller **regional airports** may also be helpful, including Eugene and North Bend in Oregon, Crescent City, Oakland, and San Jose in Northern California, Monterey and Santa Barbara in central California, and Burbank, Long Beach, and Ontario in Southern California.

Choose your travel hub based on which leg of the Pacific Coast Highway you want to explore. If you want to drive the entire almost 1,700-mile route, it's convenient to **fly into Seattle** at the north end and **fly out of San Diego** at the southern end. You can also drive the route south to north; however, it's worth noting that you will have the **best views** of the amazing coastal scenery along the way by driving north to south.

If you want to drive the entire coastal highway, you can return to your starting point via **I-5.** This roughly 1,300-mile route between Seattle and San Diego is **quicker (20 hours of driving),** but less scenic. It also offers few points of interest. You can also divert from the coast to I-5

at various points along the way to make up time. Keep in mind that I-5 and US-101 run parallel at the southern end of the route, near San Diego.

Reservations
High-season travelers should also plan ahead for the **big-name attractions.** If you have your heart set on visiting **Alcatraz** in San Francisco, purchase tickets at least two weeks in advance. You'll save money buying advance tickets for **Disneyland** online as well. Reservations are pretty much essential at **hotels** and **campgrounds,** especially in and around the popular resort towns. If you need a **rental car,** book it in advance, too.

Passports and Visas
Coming to the United States from abroad? You'll need your **passport** and possibly a **visa.**

What to Pack
Be prepared for foggy, rainy weather on the northern section of the route and hot, sunny weather more likely the farther south you drive. Fog and the chill that comes with it are possible anywhere along the coast. Bring **layered clothing.** No matter what, bring (and use!) **sunscreen;** that cold fog doesn't stop the rays from burning unwary beachcombers.

Driving Tips

Weather
The northern section of the Pacific Coast Highway endures **harsh weather** during **winter,** and gusty winds almost year-round. There can be delays even in the warmer spring and summer months due to **heavy traffic** or **roadwork.** Most of the road is a **two-lane highway,** but there are plenty of sections that allow for passing. It is just important to remember to take your time and enjoy the natural setting.

With the exception of Southern California, weather conditions change

Clockwise from top left: San Francisco's Golden Gate Bridge; Astoria Column; Mount Olympus in Washington.

rapidly along the Pacific Coast. Be prepared for weather extremes from blustery rainstorms to hot sunny days. Highways can be closed abruptly with some sections impassable, typically due to **heavy rains** and **mudslides.** In the event of a road closure, be prepared with alternative routes. **Winter snow** is a possibility in Washington and Oregon. Carry chains and know how to use them.

When warm inland air mixes with cool coastal temperatures, shazam! **Fog.** It's the most likely hazard along coastal highways. Keep your low beams on and drive *very* slowly. Use the pullouts as necessary.

Traffic

Expect **traffic delays** at major cities along the route; this is especially true of California travel hubs San Francisco, Los Angeles, and San Diego, where the rush hour commute can begin mid-afternoon and extend into late evening.

To receive reports on **traffic and road conditions, call 511.** If your phone carrier does not support 511, call toll-free 800/977-6368. There are also additional resources online: **Washington State Department of Transportation** (www.wsdot.com); **Oregon Department of Transportation** (www.oregonlive.com); and the **California Department of Transportation** (www.dot.ca.gov).

Fueling Up

Locating a **gas station** isn't hard throughout cities and towns en route; however, there are segments of the Pacific Coast Highway where nothing exists but trees, water, and local wildlife. Plan accordingly by knowing what time you will be arriving at your destination and whether there is a gas station available. Many stations in small towns (especially in Oregon) do not stay open late. Keep a full gas tank when you hit the road and refill whenever you have the opportunity.

HIT THE ROAD

Pack up the car, SUV, or family bus, fill up the tank, and start your engine. This world-class road trip will take you through nearly 1,700 miles of unparalleled landscape.

The full drive takes about **three weeks,** planning on **3-5 hours of driving each day.** Don't have time to see it all? No worries! You can start in the **travel hub** of your choice (Seattle, Portland, San Francisco, Los Angeles, or San Diego) and plan a **4-7-day trip** that works for you. Whatever section of this legendary highway you drive, your memories will last a lifetime.

For driving directions all along the way, see the *Getting There* sections in later chapters. All mileage and driving times are approximate, and will vary depending on weather, traffic, and road conditions.

Washington in 4 Days

Days 1-2
SEATTLE
Spend two days in **Seattle,** a city almost entirely surrounded by water. Stunning mountain views from every direction are best spied from the top of the soaring **Space Needle.** Explore rock 'n' roll history at the Frank Gehry–designed **Experience Music Project (EMP).** Then ride the Monorail downtown to **Pike Place Market** for lunch, shopping, and people-watching. Spend the afternoon exploring the city's past (and underground with a guided tour) at **Pioneer Square.** Enjoy dinner in Capitol Hill and spend the night downtown at

Paramount Hotel. For more ideas on how to spend your time in Seattle, see page 34.

Day 3
SEATTLE TO PORT ANGELES
82 mi / 132 km / 3 hrs
Cross Puget Sound on the **Seattle-Bainbridge Island Ferry** (depart from Pier 52). Take WA-305 North to WA-104 West, crossing the Hood Canal Bridge to connect with US-101. Spend the day exploring tiny villages and rustic scenery. Tour the **Olympic Game Farm** or **Dungeness Spit** in sunny Sequim, where you can also stop for lunch.

Spend your afternoon enjoying spectacular panoramic views while hiking along **Hurricane Ridge.** Then continue on US-101 to end your day in **Port Angeles.** Enjoy a hearty dinner before spending the night at charming **Colette's Bed & Breakfast.**

Day 4
PORT ANGELES TO LAKE QUINAULT
124 mi / 200 km / 3 hrs
Rise early to continue your journey on US-101. Stop at the sapphire waters of **Lake Crescent** for an easy hike to **Marymere Falls** or take a dip in steamy **Sol Duc Hot Springs.** Plan on lunch in **Forks,** with a quick look at the logging artifacts at the **Forks Timber Museum.**

Then head for the highlight of your day: **Hoh Rain Forest.** Wander the **Hall of Mosses** and **Spruce Nature Trails** through a lush, canopied wonderland or stroll driftwood-strewn **Ruby Beach,** taking in views of its sea stacks.

Head south on US-101 to **Lake Quinault** and the **Quinault Rain Forest,** exploring more trails as time allows before checking in at historic **Lake Quinault Lodge** for a relaxing evening.

Best Beaches

Washington

- **Dungeness Spit** (page 57) provides a sandy habitat for 250 bird species and is heaven for bird-watchers.

- **Rialto Beach** (page 72) offers sea stacks, tidepools, and, best of all, solitude.

Oregon

- **Cannon Beach** (page 109) is home to ever-popular, photogenic Haystack Rock. If it gets too crowded, head south to **Hug Point State Park** (page 113) for its mysterious caves and towering cliffs.

- **Oswald West State Park** (page 113) is home to driftwood-laden and surfer-friendly Short Sands Beach.

Northern California

- **Black Sands Beach** (page 163), composed of crumbly volcanic rock, is the most accessible sight on the remote Lost Coast.

- **Stinson Beach** (page 184) is the favorite destination for San Franciscans seeking some surf and sunshine.

Central California

- **Año Nuevo State Reserve** (page 214) is world famous as the winter home and breeding ground of once-endangered elephant seals.

- **Carmel Beach** (page 235) features soft sand, blue water, and dogs roaming freely.

- **Pfeiffer Beach** (page 244) is the best place to watch the sun set along the Big Sur coastline.

- **Moonstone Beach** (page 250) is known for breathtaking views and surf-smoothed stones.

Southern California

- **Zuma Beach** (page 281) is the site of classic beach parties as well as surfing, boogie boarding, and volleyball.

- **Malibu Surfriders Beach** (page 282) offers a pretty stretch of sugar-like sand and reliable waves.

- **Huntington City Beach** (page 313) is known as Surf City, USA for good reason.

- **La Jolla Cove** (page 322) has white sand, deep blue water, and sea caves inhabited by colorful marinelife.

Oregon in 5 Days

Day 5
LAKE QUINAULT TO CANNON BEACH
146 mi / 236 km / 3.5 hrs

Get an early start, following US-101 south along Willapa Bay. Then it's welcome to Oregon!

Stop in **Astoria** for lunch before climbing the 164-step spiral staircase to the top of the **Astoria Column** for the perfect view of the **Astoria Bridge.** Check out the **Columbia River Maritime Museum** (one of the state's best). Explore **Fort Clatsop,** the centerpiece of sprawling Lewis and Clark National Historical Park.

Continue past the little towns of Gearhart and Seaside before arriving at artsy **Cannon Beach**—home to impressive **Haystack Rock.** Stop for lunch before some shopping and gallery-hopping. Check in at enchanting **Stephanie Inn.** Enjoy a leisurely dinner before calling it a night.

Clockwise from top left: Oregon Dunes National Recreation Area; Heceta Head lighthouse; Devil's Punchbowl.

Days 6-7
EXCURSION TO PORTLAND
80 mi / 128 km / 1.5 hrs

From Cannon Beach, you can continue south down the coast toward Newport, or head east on US-26 for an inland excursion to **Portland.**

Take two days to explore the city of "mosts": most parks, most bikeable, most breweries, most indie coffee shops. Stop at famed **Powell's City of Books** and enjoy a one-of-a-kind treat at **Voodoo Doughnut.** Sip tea in the **Portland Japanese Garden** (most authentic outside of Japan) and ramble along the manicured trails in **Washington Park.** Ride a bike along the banks of the Willamette River, breaking to watch the sunset, and end your day with dinner in the **Pearl District.** For more ideas on how to spend your time in Portland, see page 92.

To return to the coast, take US-26 west back to **Cannon Beach.** Another option is to divert from US-26 onto OR-6 West to **Tillamook** (74 mi / 118 km / 1.5 hrs) and continue on US-101 South to Lincoln City, as described on Day 8 below.

Day 8
CANNON BEACH TO NEWPORT
125 mi / 202 km / 4 hrs

Set out early from Cannon Beach for a morning packed with memorable views. Begin just south of town at **Hug Point** before exploring the beautiful beaches at **Oswald West State Park.** Continue south to the **Three Capes Scenic Loop.** Try to spot migrating whales from the **Cape Meares** scenic viewpoint. Farther on, follow the trail at **Cape Lookout State Park** through the forest. Or wander mammoth-sized dunes at **Cape Kiwanda.**

Back on US-101, drive south, past Tillamook to **Lincoln City,** a good stop for lunch. If you're here during June or October, head to the beach to watch colorful soaring kites. Otherwise, continue south, making stops at **Otter Crest Loop** for 360-degree views of the coast and

Devil's Punchbowl, where sea and rock engage in an inconclusive battle.

Continue south to **Newport,** where you should bypass the tourist traps in favor of renowned **Oregon Coast Aquarium, Yaquina Bay Lighthouse,** and **Yaquina Head Lighthouse.** Head to quaint **Nye Beach** for dinner, followed by live music at **Nana's Irish Pub.** Stay at the literary-themed **Sylvia Beach Hotel,** which boasts astounding cliffside views.

Day 9
NEWPORT TO GOLD BEACH
192 mi / 310 km / 4.5 hrs

Fill up your tank and get back on the road, driving between the forested mountains of the coast range and the Pacific Ocean. Just past the historic **Heceta Head** lighthouse, spectacular windswept sand takes shape along the stretch of **Oregon Dunes National Recreation Area,** which stretches 47 miles from Florence in the north to North Bend on the south. Stop at **Old Town** in **Florence** for a bite to eat. Then put on a pair of goggles to surf the dunes riding an ATV.

Continue for another 125 miles, passing Lakeside, North Bend, and Coos Bay. Stop for photo-ops in **Bandon,** with its dramatic views of boulders, sea stacks, and **Cape Blanco Light,** the oldest lighthouse in Oregon.

Stop for the night in **Gold Beach,** reserving a room at **Tu Tu Tun Lodge,** set high above the Rogue River.

Northern California in 5 Days

Day 10
GOLD BEACH TO ARCATA
160 mi / 258 km / 4 hrs

Head south on US-101, crossing the Oregon/California border, driving through thick stands of giant redwoods. Stop in **Crescent City** for lunch, before continuing on to the **Trees of Mystery**

Best Views

Washington

* The **Space Needle** (page 38) in Seattle was built for 360-degree views of Puget Sound, while the **Seattle Great Wheel** (page 35) offers views of the city skyline that include the Space Needle.

* **Hurricane Ridge** (page 62) rises over 5,757 feet from the Strait of Juan de Fuca, with views stretching from the Cascades to the Olympic Peninsula and beyond.

* **Neah Bay** (page 69) offers the most dramatic shoreline drive in the state.

Oregon

* **Ecola State Park** (page 109) has the most photographed view on the Oregon coast, featuring iconic **Haystack Rock** (page 109).

* **Cape Perpetua** (page 124) yields 150-mile views of the coast from a rustic, WPA-built observation point.

Northern California

* **Crescent Beach Overlook** (page 152) in Redwood National Park offers views of the seascape that are hard to beat.

* **Bodega Head** (page 177) offers views of Pacific gray whales along their migration route.

* The **Marin Headlands** (page 186) have the best views of the San Francisco skyline and the Golden Gate Bridge, while the city's **Baker Beach** (page 199) offers the same view— bridge and headlands—from the opposite side.

Central California

* **Pfeiffer Beach** (page 244) showcases the best sunsets on the Big Sur coastline.

* **Julia Pfeiffer Burns State Park's Overlook Trail** (page 246) ends with a stunning view of McWay Falls cascading down the cliffside to a remote cove.

* **Gaviota Peak** (page 260) is at the end of a rugged three-mile trail that climaxes with stunning views of the Channel Islands.

Southern California

* **Point Dume State Beach** (page 281) has the best views of the Malibu coastline outside of a movie star's mega-mansion.

* **The Getty Center** (page 297) is a hilltop museum with unmatched views of the L.A. skyline and coastline.

* The **Hotel del Coronado** (page 332) capitalizes on some of the best seaside views in San Diego.

to ride the gondola and browse Native American art.

Exit US-101 to **Newton B. Drury Scenic Parkway** and explore **Prairie Creek Redwoods State Park.**

Return to US-101. After a few miles south, head west on Davison Road to **Gold Bluffs Beach.** Hike **Fern Canyon Trail,** marveling at the steep canyon dripping with green ferns—a vision of prehistoric times.

Continue south to **Arcata.** Get dinner before retiring for a good night's rest at the **Best Western Arcata Inn.**

Clockwise from top left: Santa Cruz Beach Boardwalk; San Francisco skyline; centuries old moss-covered cypress tree in Carmel.

Day 11
ARCATA TO MENDOCINO
152 mi / 245 km / 3 hrs
Drive US-101 South, rounding the east edge of Arcata Bay then curving inland to the **Avenue of the Giants,** which runs through magnificent redwoods. At the US-101 South/CA-1 split (just before Leggett), take CA-271 South to the admittedly cool tourist trap **Chandelier Drive-Thru Tree.**

Backtrack to CA-1, then head south to **Fort Bragg** for lunch along the harbor. Continuing south, stop at **Point Cabrillo Light Station State Historic Park** to explore the museum and marinelife exhibit. Don't forget to take a few pictures of the **Point Cabrillo Lighthouse.**

Continue on to Mendocino, where you'll spend the rest of the day strolling through art galleries and shops. Book a room at the charming **MacCallum House,** where you can dine in the restaurant, enjoy a cocktail at the bar, or soak in a hot tub.

Day 12
MENDOCINO TO SAN FRANCISCO
170 mi / 272 km / 4.5 hrs
After breakfast in the garden at MacCallum House, pack a picnic lunch and drive south along the coast to the rocky coves at **Salt Point State Park.** Continue on CA-1 South to **Bodega Head** (watch for the sign!), the best spot for bird-watching, whale-watching, and your picnic lunch. Hike along Bodega Head for panoramic views of the coast.

Follow CA-1 South to US-101 South. Stop in the Marin Headlands to enjoy the view of the iconic **Golden Gate Bridge** before crossing over it into San Francisco. Check into the Beatnik throwback **Hotel Boheme.** Greet the city with a 15-minute walk down Columbus Avenue to explore the waterfront shops. Dine with views of the bay in **Fisherman's Wharf** or along the **Embarcadero.**

Days 13-14
SAN FRANCISCO
Explore **Golden Gate Park.** Choose between the **de Young Museum, California Academy of Sciences,** or **Conservatory of Flowers,** all on-site at the park. Cross the bay for a fascinating tour of the island prison of **Alcatraz.** Shop in **Union Square** or ride the cable car to **Chinatown.** When the sun goes down, head to **North Beach** for an old world Italian dinner. Don't want the night to end? Put on your dancing shoes and head to **Ruby Skye** or catch a show at the historic **Golden Gate Theater.** For more ideas on how to spend your time in San Francisco, see page 190.

Central California in 3 Days

Day 15
SAN FRANCISCO TO BIG SUR
160 mi / 250 km / 4 hrs
Move out early and head down CA-1, rounding Monterey Bay. Choose stops along the way based on your interests. Stroll the boardwalk and ride the roller coaster in **Santa Cruz.** Tour **Monterey**'s famous aquarium. **Carmel** offers pristine white sand, cypress trees, and charming art galleries. All three towns have plenty of options for lunch.

The highway heading into **Big Sur** has some of the most scenic stretches in California. Be sure to snap some photographs, stopping or using pullouts only when it's safe. Enjoy astonishing views at the **Point Lobos State Reserve** and the **Bixby Bridge.** On the west side of CA-1, take Sycamore Canyon Road to **Pfeiffer Beach** to see impressive rock formations. Time your stop to enjoy the sunset.

Stop for dinner and a bed at historic **Deetjens Big Sur Inn,** nestled in the redwoods.

Clockwise from top left: California's Big Sur coastline; Rodeo Drive in Beverly Hills; Old Mission Santa Barbara.

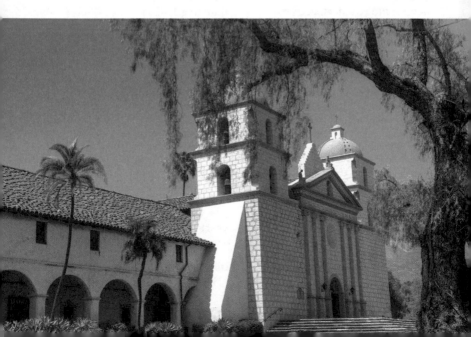

Day 16
BIG SUR TO SAN LUIS OBISPO
117 mi / 188 km / 3 hrs

Set out early in the morning, stopping along the way at **Julia Pfeiffer Burns State Park** to hike the short trail to the scenic overlook of McWay Falls. See the lighthouse and elephant seals at **Piedras Blancas.** Continue south to **San Simeon,** where you'll stop for lunch before touring the enchanting **Hearst Castle.**

At Morro Bay, CA-1 moves inland toward **San Luis Obispo,** a laid-back college town, where roadside attraction the **Madonna Inn** is worth a look around—or an overnight stay, depending on your appreciation for kitsch. Another option is to continue south to spend the night at the **Dolphin Bay Resort & Spa** at **Pismo Beach.**

Day 17
SAN LUIS OBISPO TO SANTA BARBARA
105 mi / 170 km / 2 hrs

Continue south on US-101 to **Gaviota State Park,** where you can hike to Gaviota Peak for stunning views of the Channel Islands. Less ambitious beachgoers may prefer spending the morning at scenic **El Capitán State Beach.**

Continue south to **Santa Barbara** to enjoy lunch along the water. Spend the afternoon diving into Santa Barbara's history and culture, visiting the **Old Mission Santa Barbara** or **Santa Barbara Museum of Art.** Do some window-shopping on **State Street,** which also offers plenty of dinner options. Get a room at the Spanish-style **Brisas del Mar Inn,** just a short walk from the beaches.

Southern California in 4 Days

Day 18
SANTA BARBARA TO SANTA MONICA
85 mi / 136 km / 2 hrs

Ease your way into the Los Angeles metro area, stopping along the way based on your interests (and need to take a break from the traffic). Take the US-101 South route toward **Ventura**'s picturesque harbor, the point of departure for the Channel Islands. About five miles out of Ventura, CA-1 splits from US-101 and heads southwest through Oxnard to **Point Mugu State Park** in the Santa Monica Mountains. Watch for surfers as you drive through **Malibu.** Lovers of art and history should consider a stop at the **Getty Villa.**

Once you reach **Santa Monica,** stop at the **Santa Monica Pier** for strolling, amusements, and plenty of options for sunset dining. Stay at the beachfront **Georgian Hotel.**

Day 19
LOS ANGELES

Sleep in a little to avoid the morning traffic. Then it's time for a classic L.A. drive up **Sunset Boulevard** to **Hollywood.** Wander the **Hollywood Walk of Fame** (corner of Gower Street and Hollywood Boulevard) and get an eyeful at the ornate **TCL Chinese Theatre.**

Enjoy some science along with views of the city from the **Griffith Observatory**—or take your views with a side of art at **The Getty Center.** Get a taste of Hollywood nightlife on the **Sunset Strip.** Or head back to the beach to wander quirky **Venice Beach Boardwalk.** Families may want to plan on an extra day for an excursion to **Disneyland Resort.** For more ideas on how to spend your time in Los Angeles, see page 291.

Day 20
SANTA MONICA TO SAN DIEGO
140 mi / 240 km / 3 hrs

Continue south down the coast, stopping along the way based on traffic and your interests. Stop in **Long Beach** to tour the *Queen Mary* or the **Aquarium of the Pacific.** Hit the sand or the waves at surf mecca **Huntington Beach.** Stop in any of the Orange County beach cities for lunch. For a less civilized beach experience,

Roadside Attractions

One person's tourist trap is another person's must-see. Here are attractions that will have you pulling over.

- **Marsh's Free Museum** (page 79) features exhibits like the world's largest frying pan and Jake the Alligator Man.

- The **Prehistoric Gardens** (page 138) is the only place you can see life-sized dinosaurs outside of Jurassic World.

- The **Trees of Mystery** (page 148) poses the question "Is that Paul Bunyan and Babe the Blue Ox striding through the California redwoods?" Yes, yes it is.

- The **Kinetic Grand Championship** is a race run between Arcata (page 157) and Eureka (page 160) that's more like a race between the swift and the ridiculous. Human-powered sculptures shaped like dinosaurs, donkeys, and dung beetles are in it to win it.

- **Drive-Thru Trees** (pages 164 and 166) are just what they sound like. How many times do you get to drive through a redwood tree? At least twice on this road trip.

- The **Madonna Inn** (page 253) is a roadside motel that shows that there's no limit to bad taste. Sleep in the Cave-Man Room or make a pit stop at the waterfall urinal.

- **Solvang** (page 259) is a faux-Danish village that might make you wonder if Hans Christian Andersen was born in California. He wasn't.

- The **Venice Beach Boardwalk** (page 287) hosts a wild parade of counterculture that proves people are the kitschiest attractions of all.

- **Sunny Jim Cave** (page 323) was once used by smugglers. It's the only sea cave on the West Coast with a staircase.

wander **Torrey Pines State Reserve,** one of the wildest stretches along the southern coastline.

The coast highway goes through a few transformations, becoming the San Diego Freeway, then County Road S-21 and Historic Route 101 in northern San Diego County. Upon arrival in **San Diego,** check into **Hotel Indigo.**

Day 21
SAN DIEGO

Visit **Balboa Park,** including the grand **Botanical Building.** Families will want to spend the day at the famous **San Diego Zoo.** Outdoor enthusiasts should head north to **La Jolla Cove** for some kayaking or snorkeling. Sun-worshippers should head to **Coronado** with its beachside shops and the legendary **Hotel del Coronado.** End your trip in the **Gaslamp Quarter** with a toast to PCH. For more ideas on how to spend your time in San Diego, see page 330.

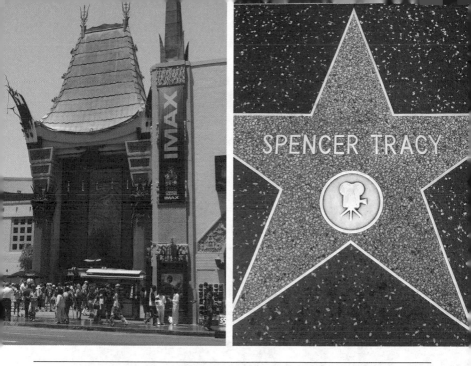

Clockwise from top left: TCL Chinese Theatre; Spencer Tracy's Hollywood Star; Torrey Pines State Reserve.

Washington Coast

The far western edge of Washington State is a scenic wonderland composed of some of the least touched natural areas in the country.

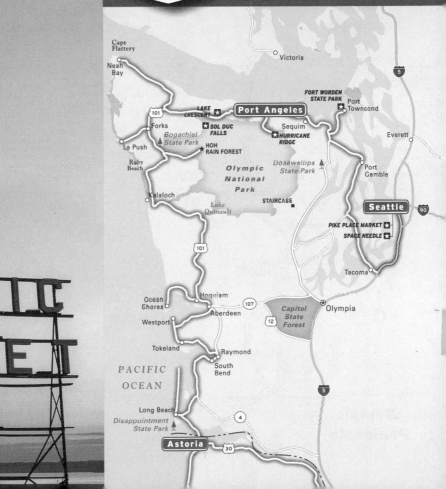

Cape Flattery

Neah Bay

Victoria

FORT WORDEN STATE PARK

101

LAKE CRESCENT

Port Angeles

Port Townsend

SOL DUC FALLS

Sequim

Everett

Forks

Bogachiel State Park

HURRICANE RIDGE

La Push

HOH RAIN FOREST

5

Ruby Beach

Olympic National Park

Dosewallips State Park

Port Gamble

Kalaloch

STAIRCASE

Seattle

90

Lake Quinault

PIKE PLACE MARKET

SPACE NEEDLE

101

Tacoma

Ocean Shores

Hoquiam

107

Capitol State Forest

Olympia

Westport

Aberdeen

12

Tokeland

Raymond

5

South Bend

PACIFIC OCEAN

Long Beach

Disappointment State Park

4

Astoria

30

Olympic
Peninsula

© AVALON TRAVEL

Highlights

★ **Pike Place Market:** Immerse yourself in the sights, sounds, and smells (both flowery and fishy) of the oldest continuously working market in the United States (page 31).

★ **Space Needle:** Built to celebrate the Space Age in 1962, the iconic tower is now synonymous with Seattle (page 38).

★ **Fort Worden State Park:** This decommissioned military base offers more than history; its sandy beaches and views of the Olympic Mountains make it worth a visit (page 51).

★ **Hurricane Ridge:** The most popular spot in Olympic National Park provides unmatched views of the gorgeous Strait of Juan de Fuca (page 62).

★ **Lake Crescent:** With its cold depths measured at more than 1,000 feet, this lake is a place of beauty and mystery—and the home of the Beardslee trout (page 64).

★ **Sol Duc Falls:** A one-mile hike through old-growth forest leads to these year-round falls (page 68).

Here you can explore massive old-growth forests, rich river valleys, and an abundant coastline.

Starting at charming Port Townsend, US-101 bends west around the north end of the Olympic National Forest, passing near the most northwesterly tip of the contiguous United States. Heavy rains (12-14 feet a year) feed the temperate rain forests and form mist around the small towns that dot the coastline.

The harbor town of Port Angeles is the access point to the Olympic Discovery Trail—an old Milwaukee Railroad line that follows the waterfront, and the Olympic National Park. Explore more than 600 miles of hiking trails; discover 1,000 year-old trees that tower over rivers and glacier-fed lakes; or gaze at awe-inspiring views of the Olympic Mountain Range. The possibilities are truly limitless.

Tracing the edges of a landscape carved out by ancient glaciers and the Pacific Ocean, the highway follows the curves of the brilliant blue waters of Lake Crescent, then descends southwest through wooded lowlands and beaches toward the resort town near Lake Quinault and the maritime seaport of Grays Harbor.

The city of Seattle is a 35-minute ferry ride across Puget Sound, making it a convenient access point to the Olympic Peninsula, which offers interesting sights of its own.

Planning Your Time

Plan at least four days to hit the main sights and two weeks to explore and take it all in, while making a couple of side trips.

The best places to stay are waterfront towns like Port Townsend, Port Angeles, Forks, and Grays Harbor. To make sure you don't get stuck without a room, book 4-6 months in advance.

It's roughly 330 miles from Seattle around the Olympic Peninsula and down to Long Beach on US-101. The

Best Hotels

★ **Ann Starrett Mansion:** This Port Townsend fixture enchants with a spiral staircase and ornate domed tower (page 55).

★ **Manresa Castle:** This medieval (and haunted?) 1892 mansion makes guests feel like royalty (page 55).

★ **Sequim Bay Lodge:** This conveniently located hotel is clean, comfortable, and surrounded by greenery (page 58).

★ **Lake Crescent Lodge:** Surrounded by fir trees, this historic lakeside retreat counts FDR among its many guests (page 66).

★ **Sol Duc Hot Springs Resort:** This retreat is built around its namesake bubbling mineral waters (page 68).

★ **Kalaloch Lodge:** The selling point of this lodge is access to nearby Ruby Beach (page 75).

★ **Lake Quinault Lodge:** This regal lodge benefits from its magnificent setting on the lake (page 76).

★ **Quinault Beach Resort and Casino:** Spacious rooms come with oceanfront views and gaming tables on the side (page 77).

Olympic Peninsula is a rural area connected by mostly two-lane highway, with long windy stretches between basic services, so fuel up and keep plenty of water, snacks, and an emergency kit in your vehicle.

Getting There
Car
Drivers enter from the north, over the Canadian border, east from Idaho, or south from Oregon. **I-5** is the major north-south route, extending from the Canadian border in the north to the Mexican border in the south. **I-90** is the best east-west route, but keep in mind that winter snow may close mountain passes.

Air
The **Seattle-Tacoma International Airport** (SEA, 800/544-1965 or 206/787-5388, www.portseattle.org/seatac) is the usual point of entry and is served by about two dozen airlines. Another option is **Portland International** (PDX, 7000 NE Airport Way, 877/739-4636, www.pdx.com), which is only a 2.5-hour drive from Seattle, over the Oregon border.

Train
Amtrak (800/872-7245, www.amtrak.com) provides transport service throughout the country to the Northwest. The **Coast Starlight** connects Seattle, Portland, Sacramento, Oakland, and Los Angeles. Amtrak also runs the **Cascade Line** (800/872-7245, www.amtrakcascades.com), which runs between Eugene, Oregon, and Vancouver, British Columbia, with stops in Portland and Seattle. International visitors can buy an unlimited travel USA Rail Pass good for 15, 30, or 45 days.

Bus
Greyhound (800/231-2222, www.greyhound.com) offers special discounts to students and seniors with routes and stops sticking to major highways and cities.

The **BoltBus** (648 SW Salmon St., 877/265-8287, www.boltbus.com) is the cheapest way to travel south from Vancouver, British Columbia, with stops in Seattle, Portland, and Eugene.

Fuel and Services
Services are limited inside Olympic National Park to minimize the environmental impact. Take advantage of the small towns that surround the park to gas up and stock up on supplies. Two of the state's lowest priced **gas stations** are along Washington's Pacific Coast route. **Union 76** (907 E 1st St.) is easy to find in

Best Restaurants

★ **Portage Bay Café:** Start your day with waffles and fresh berries at this Seattle favorite (page 38).

★ **The Wild Ginger:** This fusion of Asian favorites is the best in Seattle (page 38).

★ **Vios Café:** This Capitol Hill gem serves tasty Greek cuisine and a wonderful weekend brunch (page 39).

★ **Fountain Café:** Art lines the walls of this funky east-meets-west eatery in Port Townsend (page 53).

★ **The Oak Table Café:** This is the place to find a perfect cappuccino—not to mention Swedish pancakes—in Sequim (page 58).

★ **Toga's Soup House:** Three words: Dungeness Crab Panini (page 58).

Port Angeles. Fifty-seven miles farther southwest in Forks, **Ron's Food Mart** (170 N Forks Ave.) is a good source of area information, travel accessories, and snacks.

To receive reports on **road conditions**, call **511**. If your phone carrier does not support 511, call toll-free at 800/977-6368.

For **emergency assistance** and services call **911**.

Seattle

Dubbed the "Emerald City" and "Jet City," Seattle boasts an eclectic population of techies and ecofriendly outdoor enthusiasts who don't mind walking in the rain or drinking espresso in the middle of the afternoon. It's America's fastest growing city, both in populace and economically, but it's still small town at heart because Seattleites value their roots. This becomes obvious when you visit the century-old Pike Place Market or walk along the waterfront. Ride up the Space Needle to watch the sun set behind majestic snowcapped mountains. Gaze at the glimmering waters of an inlet sea as ferries sail across its surface. Breathe in the brisk air rejuvenated by rain-washed breezes. These moments will tell you all you need to know about why people find Seattle so livable.

Getting There and Around
Air
Seattle-Tacoma International Airport (SEA, 800/544-1965 or 206/787-5388, www.portseattle.org/seatac) is the gateway to the Pacific Northwest. It's only a 30-minute drive north on **I-5** from Sea-Tac to downtown Seattle. Rush hour traffic arrives like clockwork 5pm-7pm, but express lanes offer some relief. **WA-99** is a more scenic alternate drive that traverses the industrial district bounded by the Duwamish River and passes through the Alaskan Way Viaduct and the Battery Street Tunnel right into downtown Seattle.

orca whale pod passing through Puget Sound

Ferry

Ferries ride across the Puget Sound to the nearby islands of Bainbridge, Blake, and Vashon, as well as the Olympic Peninsula. The most convenient access point to the Washington Coast is **Pier 52** (801 Alaskan Way, 888/808-7977 or 206/464-6400, www.wsdot.wa.gov/ferries, $16 per car one-way, $8 per passengers and walk-ons), by way of the **Seattle-Bainbridge Island Ferry.** It's a 35-minute glide across the open Puget Sound waters with comfortable seating, snacks, and restrooms on the main deck.

The **Edmonds-Kingston Ferry** (888/808-7977 or 206/464-6400, www.wsdot.wa.gov/ferries, $16 per car one-way, $8 per passengers and walk-ons) is in quaint suburban Edmonds, a 20-minute drive north of Seattle on I-5; take Exit 177 and follow the signs to the ferry terminal. The crossing takes 30 minutes and the ferry departs every 40 minutes.

Public Transit

Seattle is an easy city to get around with most attractions concentrated in the walkable downtown area. The free-zone **King County Metro system** (206/553-3000, www.metro.kingcounty.gov, free) operates several lines throughout the city. The **Seattle Center Monorail** (5th Ave. and Pine St., www.seattlemonorail.com, 7:30am-11pm Mon.-Fri., 8:30am-11am Sat.-Sun., $2.25 adults, $1 children) links downtown with Seattle Center and the Space Needle. **Sound Transit light rail** (888/889-6368, www.soundtransit.org, from $2) connects all of downtown from Westlake Center to the International District.

Sights
Downtown
★ Pike Place Market

If it is possible to capture the essence of a city in one place, then **Pike Place Market** (Pike Pl. and Virginia St. btwn. 1st Ave. and Western Ave., 206/682-7453, www.pikeplacemarket.org, 6am-1:30am daily) is Seattle's true soul. Famous for fish-throwing and the original Starbucks, it's a mecca of fresh produce, good food, and street entertainment. The main market is a micro-economy of 700 or so butchers and fishmongers, produce and flower vendors, artists and craftspeople, restaurateurs and entrepreneurs. It's lined with street-level stalls and an underground maze of unique shops that descends to the waterfront.

Waterfront Park

From Pike Place Market, you can easily walk down to **Waterfront Park** (1301 Alaskan Way, 206/684-4075, www.seattle.gov/parks), which offers beautiful views of Puget Sound along with benches and tables from which to admire them. If that's not close enough to the water, board one of the **Argosy Cruises** (Pier 55, 1101 Alaskan Way, 206/623-1445 or 800/642-7816, www.argosycruises.com)

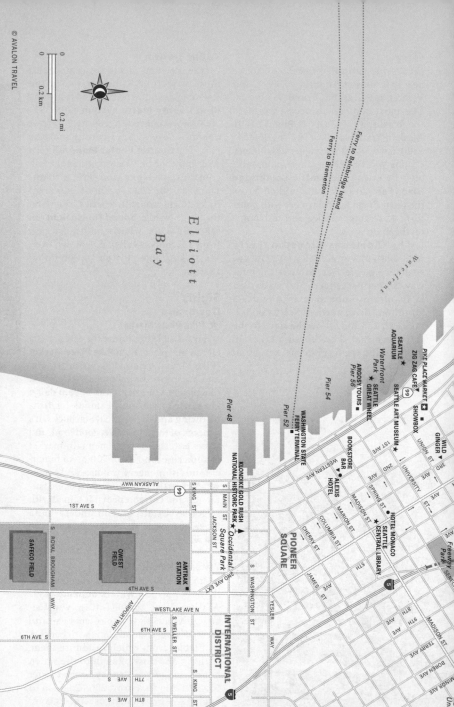

© AVALON TRAVEL

0
0.2 km

0
0.2 mi

Elliott Bay

Ferry to Bainbridge Island

Ferry to Bremerton

Waterfront

Pier 48

Pier 52

Pier 54

Pier 56

ARGOSY TOURS ★
SEATTLE ★
GREAT WHEEL

Waterfront
Park
SEATTLE ■
AQUARIUM

PIKE PLACE MARKET ■
SEATTLE ART MUSEUM ★

ZIG ZAG CAFE ▲

SHOWBOX ●
✚

WILD
GINGER ▼

99

WASHINGTON STATE
FERRY TERMINAL

ALASKAN WAY

99

1ST AVE S

S KING ST

S MAIN ST

JACKSON ST

Occidental
Square Park

KLONDIKE GOLD RUSH
NATIONAL HISTORIC PARK ★

BOOKSTORE
BAR ●

ALEXIS
HOTEL ●

WESTERN AVE

1ST AVE

2ND AVE

UNION ST

UNIVERSITY ST

SPRING ST

MADISON ST

3RD AVE

4TH AVE

MARION ST

COLUMBIA ST

CHERRY ST

JAMES ST

HOTEL
MONACO ●

SEATTLE ●
CENTRAL
LIBRARY

5TH AVE

PIONEER
SQUARE

S ROYAL BROUGHAM WAY

SAFECO
FIELD

QWEST
FIELD

AMTRAK
STATION

4TH AVE S

2ND AVE EXT

S WASHINGTON ST

YESLER WAY

WESTLAKE AVE N

AIRPORT WAY

S WELLER ST

6TH AVE S

6TH AVE S

S KING ST

S JACKSON ST

INTERNATIONAL
DISTRICT

5

7TH AVE S

8TH AVE S

Freeway
Park

SENECA ST

5

6TH AVE
7TH AVE
8TH AVE
9TH AVE

TERRY AVE
BOREN AVE

MADISON ST

MINOR AVE

University

BROADWAY

Ferry to San Juan Island
Ferry to Victoria, BC

Pier 70
VICTORIA CLIPPER
TO VICTORIA, BC

Pier 69

Myrtle Edwards Park

Olympic Sculpture Park

ALASKAN WAY

BELLTOWN

CITY HOSTEL SEATTLE

BATTERY ST TUNNEL

99

Victor

ELLIOTT AVE

WESTERN AVE

1ST AVE

BELL ST

BATTERY ST

2ND AVE

LENORA ST

3RD AVE

BLANCHARD ST

4TH AVE

5TH AVE

6TH AVE

VIRGINIA ST

7TH AVE

8TH AVE

STEWART ST

SOUTH LAKE UNION STREETCAR TERMINAL

GREYHOUND BUS DEPOT

OLIVE WAY

PINE ST

PIKE ST

PARAMOUNT HOTEL

A CONTEMPORARY
ACT
VISITOR INFORMATION

5

BROAD ST

CLAY ST

CEDAR ST

VINE ST

WALL ST

Downtown Seattle

4TH AVE W
3RDD AVE W
2ND AVE W
1ST AVE W
QUEEN ANNE AVE
1ST AVE N

DENNY WAY

JOHN ST

THOMAS ST

2ND AVE N

HARRISON ST

W REPUBLICAN ST

W OLYMPIC PL

W KINNEAR PL

W PROSPECT ST

W HIGHLAND ST

KERRY PARK

ROY ST

QUEEN ANNE

SEATTLE CENTER

★ SPACE NEEDLE
✚ CHIHULY GARDEN AND GLASS

MONORAIL TERMINAL

5TH AVE N

MERCER ST

ROY ST

VALLEY ST

ALOHA ST

WARD ST

PROSPECT ST

HIGHLAND DR

99

TAYLOR AVE

AURORA AVE

7TH AVE

Denny Park

DEXTER AVE

THOMAS ST

HARRISON ST

REPUBLICAN ST

8TH AVE N

WESTLAKE AVE N

9TH AVE N

WESTLAKE AVE N

TERRY AVE N

PORTAGE BAY CAFE

BOREN AVE N

JOHN ST

FAIRVIEW AVE N

MINOR AVE N

PONTIUS AVE N

YALE AVE N

EASTLAKE AVE N

CASCADE

VALLEY ST

Lake Union Park

Lake Union

FAIRVIEW AVE N

EASTLAKE AVE N

5

LAKEVIEW BLVD E

BELLEVUE AVE E

SUMMIT AVE E

E UNION ST

E PINE ST

BELMONT AVE E

E PIKE ST

E OLIVE ST

E HOWELL ST

Central Community College

BROADWAY

E PINE ST

E PIKE ST

E THOMAS ST

E HARRISON ST

E DENNY WY

E JOHN ST

E REPUBLICAN ST

E MERCER ST

E ROY ST

SUMMIT

BELMONT PL E

BOYLSTON AVE E

HARVARD AVE

BROADWAY

10TH AVE E

E ALOHA ST

E PROSPECT ST

CAPITOL HILL

Two Days in Seattle

Pioneer Square

Day 1

Put on a pair of comfortable walking shoes and grab your windbreaker to **Ride the Ducks of Seattle** (400 Pine St., 800/817-1116 or 206/441-3825, www. ridetheducksofseattle.com, 10am-4pm daily, $28 adults, plus tax, $17 children 3-12, plus tax). This tour via amphibious vehicle is a great starting point to get to know the city. Sit back and enjoy the sites while learning a few interesting city facts from a zany but sane driver.

After your tour, head west down Pine Street to **Pike Place Market** (page 31), the historic landmark where locals and tourists connect. Grab some lunch, browse the creative wares, and enjoy the quirky street performers. Cap off your visit with a ride to the top of the **Seattle Great Wheel** (page 35) to enjoy amazing views of Puget Sound.

Come down to earth to explore the underwater world of the **Seattle Aquarium** (page 35). If art is your passion, head a few blocks east to spend the afternoon at the **Seattle Art Museum** (page 35) instead.

End your day with dinner and a show at the **Pink Door** (page 39), where the cuisine may be accompanied by trapeze artists overhead.

Day 2

Begin your day with waffles at **Portage Bay Café** (page 38). Then head south five miles to **Pioneer Square** (page 36), a historic neighborhood of 19th-century buildings. Take **Bill Siedel's Underground Tour** (page 36) or visit the **Klondike Gold Rush National Historical Park Museum** (page 36). Grab lunch at **The Metropolitan Grill** (page 39).

Leave the past behind and head a mile to the future at the **Seattle Center** (page 38), where the trip to the top of the **Space Needle** (page 38) is worthwhile for 360-degree views of Puget Sound. If you prefer your views a little more down to earth, head farther north to Queen Anne Hill's **Kerry Park** (page 37) for incredible, camera-ready views of Elliott Bay, Bainbridge Island, and Mount Rainier. Kick back on the grass and watch the sunset with the perfect backdrop of the Space Needle and city skyline. End your day with dinner at **Olympia Pizza and Spaghetti House** (page 39).

that leave from Pier 55 for a one-hour spin around Elliott Bay.

At Pier 57, the **Seattle Great Wheel** (1301 Alaskan Way, 206/623-8600, www. seattlegreatwheel.com, 11am-10pm Mon.-Thurs., 11am-midnight Fri., 10am-midnight Sat., 10am-10pm Sun., shorter hours in winter, $13 adults, $11 seniors, $8.50 children 4-11, free children under 4) is the best seat in the city: 175 feet up in the sky. Opened in 2012, the newest city icon offers views that extend over the waterfront and out over Puget Sound and the surrounding islands and mountains.

Seattle Aquarium

Along the waterfront, the **Seattle Aquarium** (1483 Alaskan Way, 206/386-4320, www.seattleaquarium.org, 9:30am-5pm daily, $22 adults, $15 children 4-12, free children under 4) is the best way—short of donning scuba gear—to see the colorful underwater wildlife inhabiting Puget Sound's icy depths. Get your hands wet in tidepools and marvel at 350 species of aquatic animals on display, including harbor seals, sharks, giant Pacific octopuses, and sea otters. The 400,000-gallon Underwater Dome alone is worth the trip: Descend into a half-sphere to find scores of deep-sea creatures completely surrounding you.

Seattle Art Museum

The entrance to the **Seattle Art Museum (SAM)** (1300 1st Ave., 206/654-3100, www.seattleartmuseum.org, 10am-9pm Thurs., 10am-5pm Wed. and Fri.-Sun., closed Mon.-Tues., $19.50 adults, $12.50 youth 13-19, free children under 13) is marked by a 48-foot kinetic sculpture, *Hammering Man,* that towers over the sidewalk as though he's about to smash his hammer into the concrete. The museum is renowned for its cultural displays of Native American, Asian, and African

From top to bottom: Pike Place Market; Rachel the pig at Pike Place Market; the Seattle Center Monorail

36

American art. The spacious, three-level building includes a café and gift shop.

Central Library
The spectacular Rem Koolhaus-designed glass and steel of the **Central Library** (1000 4th Ave., 206/386-4636, www.spl.org/locations/central-library, 10am-8pm Mon.-Thurs., 10am-6pm Fri.-Sat., noon-6pm Sun.) adds character to an otherwise traditional cityscape. The very modern architecture matches the library's other state-of-the-art features, such as the talking book repository outside and the automated book circulation system that ferries materials from floor to floor using a series of conveyor belts. A must-see on a library visit is the Books Spiral, a long, gently sloping ramp that winds through four floors of materials. This innovative design allows the library's entire nonfiction collection to be accessed by anyone, without relying on stairs or elevators. The 10th floor holds the true reward: The view is spectacular,

if not dizzying, and worth braving weekend crowds for.

Pioneer Square
South of the downtown core lies the **Pioneer Square Historic District** (1st Ave. Yesler Way). Seattle's oldest neighborhood features 19th-century buildings nestled along modern art galleries, cafés, and nightclubs. Today, the square is the starting point of the **Bill Siedel's Underground Tour** (608 1st Ave., 206/682-4646, www.undergroundtour.com, $16 adults, $8 children), an entertaining excursion through the original streets beneath the current city. It's also the location of the **Klondike Gold Rush National Historical Park Museum** (319 2nd Ave. S., 206/553-7220, www.nps.gov/klse, 9am-5pm daily, free), which traces Seattle's gold rush history through educational exhibits, films, historic photos, and activities. There's even a free walking tour (10am daily mid-June to Labor Day weekend).

view of Seattle skyline and Puget Sound from Kerry Park

At night, revelers come to enjoy the square's many restaurants, bars, and clubs, especially when the Mariners or Seahawks are playing. Safeco Field, the Mariners' home base, sits a few blocks south of Pioneer Square.

Capitol Hill

Home to the city's counterculture communities and some of Seattle's more eclectic denizens, the Capitol Hill district is located on a steep hill just east of the central downtown area and Pike Place Market. Bustling daytime activities flow into a rich nightlife that can extend into the early morning hours and occasionally spills onto the streets.

Broadway is arguably the heart of the district and the reason Capitol Hill was once known as Broadway Hill. Walk down the street and you're bound to come across the engaging bronze *Dancers' Series: Steps* (eight locations along Broadway), a series of footprints of various dances embedded in the sidewalk by artist Jack Mackie in 1982. The year-round **Broadway Farmers Market** (Broadway Ave. E. and E. Pine St., 206/547-2278, www.seattlefarmersmarkets.org, 11am-3pm Sun.) draws shoppers looking for fresh vegetables, fruits, cheeses, and specialty treats.

Volunteer Park

New York has Central Park; San Francisco has Golden Gate Park; and Seattle has **Volunteer Park** (accessible from 4th or 5th Ave. E., 206/684-4743, www.seattle.gov/parks, 6am-10pm daily). Stroll the many trails framed in greenery to the conservatory, a glass building filled with rooms of blooming flowers and seasonal displays. A short walk to the other side of the park leads to a spiral staircase leading to the 75-foot water tower with sweeping city views.

Queen Anne Hill

Named for the architecture style of the mansions built on the hill by many of Seattle's founding elite, Queen Anne is boarded by Belltown (to the south), Lake Union (to the east), Lake Washington ship canal (to the north), and Magnolia (to the west.) Along its picturesque residential streets you will find some of Seattle's most historic homes, and as Queen Anne is considered the highest named hill in Seattle, you will also find some of the city's steepest streets.

Queen Anne is divided into two district areas: upper Queen Anne, a quieter more residential environment, and lower Queen Anne (also known as Uptown), the commercial heart of the district.

Kerry Park

A small, perfectly manicured lawn and a few benches is all you'll find in **Kerry Park** (corner of 2nd Ave. W. and W. Highland Dr., free), but people don't come here for the seating. If there is one place to see everything it's from the perch of this quiet neighborhood park. Amateur and professional photographers, locals, and tourists

all come here for the sweeping views of downtown Seattle, the Space Needle, Mount Rainier, the waterfront, and the best scene of all—the sunset.

Seattle Center

Adjacent to lower Queen Anne is the tourist mecca known as the **Seattle Center** (305 Harrison St., 206/684-7200, www.seattlecenter.com, 7am-9pm daily, free). Built for the 1962 World's Fair, it encompasses fairgrounds, the International Fountain, and a-year-round arts and entertainment center, as well as the Space Needle and the Experience Music Project. It's also the location of the north terminal of the Seattle Monorail, which transports visitors between Seattle Center and downtown approximately every 10 minutes.

★ Space Needle

First sketched on a napkin by artist Edward E. Carlson in a coffee shop, the **Space Needle** (400 Broad St., 206/905-2100, www.spaceneedle.com, 8am-midnight daily, $19-24 adults, $9.50-15 youth) dominated the 1962 Seattle World's Fair and has since become a celebrated Seattle icon enjoyed by locals and visitors alike. Traveling at a speed of 10 mph, the elevators glide 605 feet up to the observation deck, where panoramic, 360-degree views of the entire city and Puget Sound leave visitors breathless. With 25 lightning rods on its roof and elevators that reduce speed when winds reach 35 mph, the Needle was built to withstand the rough winds and thunderstorms that bless the Pacific Northwest.

Experience Music Project

The **Experience Music Project (EMP)** (325 5th Ave. N., 206/367-5483, www.empmuseum.org, 10am-5pm daily, $23) is also located in Seattle Center. The colorful, Frank Gehry-designed blob of a building is part rock-and-roll history museum (the space was initially envisioned as a showcase for Microsoft billionaire Paul

Allen's Jimi Hendrix memorabilia), part interactive musical adventure, and part live music venue.

Food

Downtown

Organic and fresh breakfast and lunch is always perfect at ★ **Portage Bay Café** (4130 Roosevelt Way NE, 206/547-8230, www.portagebaycafe.com, 7:30am-2pm daily, $11 and up) with delicious waffles and pancakes topped with colorful berries and fresh cream. The menu has home-style favorites with some new ones like their crab cakes benedict.

If fresh bread and baked treats is your desire, **Grand Central Bakery** (214 1st Ave. S., 206/622-3644, www.grandcentralbakery.com, 7am-5pm Mon.-Fri., 8am-4pm Sat., $15 and up) is a warm and natural environment that also offers breakfasts and soup and sandwiches for lunch. The cookies and assorted pastries are always sure to please, and the service is inviting.

★ **The Wild Ginger** (1401 3rd Ave., 206/623-4450, www.wildginger.net, 11:30am-3pm and 5pm-11pm Mon.-Fri., 11:30am-3pm and 4:30pm-11pm Sat., 4pm-9pm Sun., $18 and up) mixes diverse Asian flavors in Thai, Indonesian, and Szechuan dishes. The *satay* is the best you'll find in the city.

Before Seattle gained notoriety for serving up some of the best espressos and café lattes, it was known for delivering the freshest seafood right off the boat to your plate. **Elliott's Oyster House** (Pier 56, 1201 Alaskan Way, 206/623-4340, www.elliottsoysterhouse.com, 11am-10pm Sun.-Thurs., 11am-11pm Fri.-Sat., $9-38) still serves the freshest wild salmon and Dungeness crab, while giving shellfish lovers 40 different varieties of oysters. There is an extensive selection of wine, cocktails, and draft beers alongside the best waterfront view of Elliott Bay.

French-trained chef Chris Lobkovich uses his eclectic and minimalist style of cooking to create classic American dishes with a unique Northwest twist at **Bookstore Bar & Café** (1007 1st Ave., 206/624-3646, www.bookstorebar.com, 7am-10:30am, 11:30am-2pm, and 5pm-10pm Mon.-Fri., 8am-2pm brunch and 5pm-10pm Sat.-Sun., $15 and up). Newly expanded, the café features a warm and cozy environment with communal dining tables.

The **Metropolitan Grill** (820 2nd Ave., 206/624-3287, www.themetropolitangrill.com, 11am-10pm Mon.-Thurs., 11am-10:30pm Fri., 4pm-11pm Sat., 4pm-9pm Sun., $20 and up) is where the best steaks are served in an elegant atmosphere with private booths or, if you prefer, wide-open tables. The onion rings are thickly cut, making a great appetizer, and the crab cakes are perfect. Entrées include great steak choices, including seafood, and a tasty grilled portabello mushroom.

A rooftop terrace in the summer, comfortable dining room seating, and trapeze artists swinging overhead while you eat, that's the unique atmosphere and allure of the **Pink Door** (1919 Port Alley, Pike Place Market, 206/443-3341, www.thepinkdoor.com, 11:30am-3pm and 5pm-10pm Mon.-Sat., 4pm-10pm Sun., 11pm-1am Fri.-Sat., $25 and up), a favorite among Seattleites and visitors alike. American-Italian-style cooking is served for lunch and dinner.

Capitol Hill
Capitol Hill restaurants seem to serve up some of the tastiest dishes around in some of the most enjoyable foodie atmospheres. A neighborhood gem, ★ **Vios Café** (903 19th Ave. E., 206/329-3236, www.vioscafe.com, 11am-9pm Tues.-Fri., 10am-3pm and 5pm-9:30pm Sat., 10am-3pm Sun., $10 and up) serves a wonderful brunch on Saturdays and Sundays and delicious Greek dishes like souvlaki, moussaka, and tasty hummus every day. It's a wonderful environment for families with a friendly, warm atmosphere.

Once one of Seattle's best-kept secrets, **Volunteer Park Café** (1501 17th Ave. E., 206/328-3155, www.alwaysfreshgoodness.com, 7am-9pm Tues.-Fri., 8am-9pm Sat., 8am-4:30pm Sun., $12 and up) has been "discovered" and is now a favorite of many. Serving farm-fresh American cuisine for breakfast, lunch, and dinner, using local and seasonal ingredients from the Pacific Northwest, the café serves up meals that build community around the dinner table.

Barrio Mexican Kitchen & Bar (1420 12th Ave., 206/588-8105, www.barriorestaurant.com, 11am-midnight Mon.-Thurs., 11:30am-1am Fri., 10am-1am Sat., 10am-11pm Sun., $13-24) prepares delicious Latin classics like pork taquitos, tacos, and enchiladas with plenty of side dishes and great margaritas.

Altura (617 Broadway E., 206/402-6749, www.alturarestaurant.com, 5:30pm-10pm Tues.-Thurs., 5pm-10pm Fri.-Sat., $73 and up for three-course meal) serves fresh Pacific Northwest delectables with an Italian flare. It's fine dining at its best with a 10-15-course tasting menu prepared by talented chefs that celebrate seasonal cuisine. The wine selection is vast and the service is superb.

Queen Anne Hill
Several restaurants line the main avenue on the lower and upper neighborhood of Queen Anne, with some busier than others. **Olympia Pizza and Spaghetti House** (1500 Queen Anne Ave. N., 206/285-5550, www.olympiapizzaonqueenanne.com, 4pm-7pm Mon., 11:30am-10pm Tues.-Thurs., 11:30am-11pm Fri.-Sat., 11:30am-10pm Sun., $8 and up) has delicious pies, savory pastas, subs, and calzones, which will put a great big smile on your face. Their salads are topped with mozzarella cheese and black olives, and the avgolemono is made fresh daily. It's the best pizzeria to bring the kids or a late-night date. Enjoy a glass of wine or a draft beer, or have a pizza delivered to you.

Peso's (605 Queen Anne N., 206/283-9353, http://pesoskitchenandlounge.com, 10am-3pm and 5pm-1am Tues.-Fri., 9am-3pm and 5pm-1am Sat.-Sun., $10 and up) offers great Mexican fare at a good value. In the evening this hot spot tends to draw youthful crowds to its lounge.

Nightlife
Bars and Clubs

Seattle has a dynamic nightlife with party clubs like **Volume** (172 S. Washington St., 206/679-1744, www.volume.com, noon-2am daily, no cover), a DJ pounding, party-til-the-sun-comes-up kind of place that makes even the straitlaced go a little crazy.

Put some swank in your night with the glitz and glamour of **Ibiza** (529 2nd Ave., 206/381-9090, www.ibizaseattle.com, 4pm-11pm Wed.-Fri., cover varies). With a large open main floor and an intimate upper mezzanine, this place has it all: sophistication, VIP seating, and private events hosting!

A big club with an intimate atmosphere right in the heart of historic Pioneer Square, **Club Contour** (807 1st Ave., 206/447-7704, www.clubcontour.com, 3pm-2am daily, $5-10 cover) is the place for progressive dance music, DJ beats, and live entertainment. Its outdoor patio lets you appreciate warm summer nights while taking a break from the cozy dance floor.

There's never a dull moment at **Re-Bar** (1114 Howell St., 206/233-9873, www.rebarseattle.com, 6pm-2am Tues.-Sun., cover varies). They've got DJs, they've got burlesque, they've got karaoke, they've got glitter. Re-Bar's sparkle might grow on you—literally.

Here's something to check off your bucket list: Get jiggy in a tree house at the **Woods** (3rd Fl., 1512 11th Ave., 206/324-7467, www.grimseattle.com, 3pm-midnight Mon.-Fri., 10am-midnight Sat.-Sun., $5). The pulsating dance floor gets packed as the DJ spins a multi-genre mix.

Live Music

Seattle has the highest per-capita music and dance attendance in the country, with 80 live music clubs and 15 symphony orchestras. Its venues are eclectic, offering everything from jazz, blues, and pop to good old rock.

The Crocodile Café (2200 2nd Ave., 206/441-4618, www.thecrocodile.com, 3pm-2am daily, cover varies) is a "come as you are" venue with a stage that has seen the likes of big performers Nirvana and Mudhoney. There's a performance every night and great food downstairs in the café.

It's always the dives where great music is born. The **OK Hotel Café & Bar** (212 Alaskan Way S., 206/264-1688, www.theokhotel.com) has seen its share of legendary performers, from homegrown musical acts to poetry slams and the Earshot Jazz Festival.

There is always something different happening at the **Triple Door** (216 Union St., 206/838-4333, www.tripledoor.net, 4pm-2am daily, $10-30). With everything from blues, jazz, pop, and funk, it's a microcosm of good tunes, drinks, and food, all under the roof of the old Embassy Theatre.

Marked by the "Gum Wall" in Pike Place Market, the **Alibi Room** (85 Pike St. #410, 206/623-3180, www.seattlealibi.com, noon-2am daily) is like Batman—not what it seems. A great little food venue that serves cold beer and fantastic pizza by day, Alibi turns into a hip hot spot by night, where locals let their hair down in the ambiance of low lighting and artwork.

A Seattle "landmark," **The Showbox** (1426 1st Ave., 206/628-3151, www.showboxpresents.com) has been a fixture in the city's music scene for over 75 years, hosting bands like Dizzy Gillespie, Muddy Waters, Pearl Jam, and the Dave Matthews band. Sit back, have a drink, and enjoy up-and-comers or big-name acts belt it out on a phenomenal sound system and big stage.

Arts and Entertainment
Performing Arts
Built in the era of vaudeville and silent films, the exquisite **Paramount Theater** (911 Pine St., 206/902-5500, http://theater-seattle.com) is Seattle's surviving theater royalty. This lavish, intricately decorated theater has been the backdrop to decades of performances and the home of a priceless Wurlitzer organ, which can be viewed as part of a theater tour.

There's not a bad seat in the house at **ACT (A Contemporary Theatre)** (700 Union St., 206/292-7676, www.acttheatre.org). Each of its five theater stages draws the audience in for an intimate experience with year-round contemporary productions.

Galleries
You've heard of the glass slipper, but have you heard of the glass house? It's the centerpiece of **Chihuly Garden and Glass** (305 Harrison St., 206/753-4940, www.chihulygardenandglass.com, 10am-9pm Sun.-Thurs., 10am-10pm Fri.-Sat., $18 adults, $12 children 4-12, free children under 4, add $2/ticket if purchased at the door), an amazing gallery that pays tribute to the famous artist Dale Chihuly with an exhibition hall that includes eight galleries and three drawing walls, and a lush garden with four majestic sculptures. This glass house will overwhelm you.

Ghost Gallery (504 E. Denny Way, 206/832-6063, www.ghostgalleryart.com, 11am-7pm daily, free) isn't haunted by spirits, but it is hidden within a courtyard in the heart of the Capitol Hill neighborhood. Peruse local and national artist displays, a "petite works" room with miniature art, boutique wines, and a selection of handmade jewelry and vintage goods.

Follow the stairway under the ornate marquee by the **5th Avenue Theatre** (1308 5th Ave., 206/625-1900) to one of the best-kept secrets: the **Pedestrian Underground Concourse.** This isn't your typical art gallery. It's a three-block-long passage that chronicles the history of downtown Seattle through historic photos that line the walls.

At **Ancient Grounds** (1220 1st Ave., 206/749-0747, noon-6pm Tues.-Fri., 7:30am-4pm Sat.) you can enjoy a caffé latte in a beautiful setting surrounded by Asian tapestries and Native American prints. Ooh and aah at the faces on the tribal masks while they ooh and aah right back at you.

Shopping
Downtown
Pacific Place (600 Pine St., 206/405-2655, www.pacificplaceseattle.com, 10am-9pm daily) has great eats, a big cinema, a skybridge, lots of moderately priced shops, and some expensive boutiques and specialty stores like Brookstone and Trophy Cupcakes. During the holidays, snow falls through the center of the mall as nightly performances echo the spirit of the holidays.

Every nook and cranny at **Laguna Pottery** (116 S Washington St., 206/682-6162, www.lagunapottery.com, 10am-5:30pm daily) is overflowing with rare and vintage pottery. It's a hidden gem tucked in the corner of Occidental Park in Pioneer Square and a rainbow of ceramics.

Who wouldn't love a new stylish handbag, or stunning scarf, or beautiful jewelry? Or maybe you just forgot to pack that perfect accessory for a night out on the town. Don't worry—**Fini** (86 Pine St , 206/443-0563, www.ilovefini.com, 10am-6pm daily) has your back! With so many choices, you could spend all day trying to decide which funky wrapped bracelet you like best!

Ah, the "golden age" when ham was Spam and celebrities were cutouts. That's what you'll find at **The Golden Age** (1501 Pike Place Market, Ste. 401, 206/622-9799, www.goldenagecollectables.com, 9:30am-7pm daily), a throwback shop where just about everything is nostalgic from lunch boxes to bobbleheads. One step inside and you may rediscover your inner nerd.

Souvenir and antique shoppers are sure to find the perfect gift for that special someone at the **Raven's Nest** (85 Pike St., Ste. B, 206/343-0890, www.ravenstreasure.com, 9:30am-6pm Tues.-Sat., 10am-5pm Sun.), nestled behind MarketSpice in Pike Place Market. It's a treasure trove of Native American art, intricate carvings, unique statues, and beautiful jewelry.

Capitol Hill

Big in space and selection, **Elliott Bay Book Company** (1521 10th Ave., 206/624-6600, www.elliottbaybook.com, 10am-10pm daily) lacks nothing, not even great espresso or pastries! It's a great place to get lost in a book or in the shelves, browsing through the new and old.

Hip, funky, fabulous, and pink—there are all kinds of words to describe **Pretty Parlor** (119 Summit Ave. E., 206/405-2883, http://prettyparlor.com). With a

vast selection of clothing by local designers, this shop has fashionable apparel for women and men.

Melrose Market (1501 Melrose Ave., 206/405-2883, www.melrosemarketseattle.com, 11am-7pm daily) is the Pike Place Market of the Capitol Hill neighborhood. It's a community of shops that encompass the aroma of fresh flowers, local organic produce and craft vendors, and a 5,000-square-foot space for urban events.

Queen Anne Hill

The best place on Queen Anne Hill is **Four Winds Artful Living** (1521 Queen Anne Ave. N., 206/282-0472, 10:30am-6:30pm daily), an exotic import boutique with handmade silver jewelry, candles and oils, leather handbags, home decor, and clothing.

Chocolopolis (1527 Queen Anne Ave. N., 206/282-0776, www.chocolopis.com, 11am-7pm Mon.-Wed., 11am-9pm Thurs.-Sat., 11am-6pm Sun.) is not a

Safeco Field is the home of the Seattle Mariners.

mythical place but a real paradise. The unique artisan chocolate bars are worth every delicious nibble.

Recreation
Bicycling
Leg power and sweat is all you need to bicycle Seattle. The opportunities are numerous in and around the city. Rent a bike at **Seattle Cycling Tours** (714 Pike St., 206/356-5803, www.seattle-cycling-tours.com) or **The Bicycle Repair Shop** (928 Alaskan Way, 206/682-7057, www.thebicyclerepairshop.com, $9/hr), and give the **Cheshiahud Lake Union Loop,** a six-mile loop around Lake Union, a whirl. Interpretive signs along the trail provide insight into Seattle's Native American and maritime histories. There are plenty of grassy spots and picnic areas to stop for water breaks and snacks.

For a day ride that extends outside of Seattle, the **Burke-Gilman Trail** connects friendly, urban neighborhoods lined with restaurants, shops, and beautiful scenery. This is not a loop, so you will have to come back the way you came. Begin at the south end of Golden Gardens Park on Puget Sound and bike to the Ballard Locks (about 2 miles), a popular site where salmon can be seen at the fish ladder during spawning season in August. The trail ends here, but a short ride on the road (NW Market St. to Shilshole Ave. to NW 45th St.) picks up the trail at Gasworks Park, a 19-acre public park that sits on the former Seattle Gas Light Company plant along Lake Union, and traverses the campus of University of Washington. You can head back here, or continue east, passing crowds of picnickers and volleyball nets at several parks nestled along the path. The trail forks after crossing 96th Avenue NE: veer left toward the Sammamish River Trail (which continues another 11 miles to Marymoor Park in Redmond) or take the right fork, which crosses the Sammamish River and ends the route at Riverside Drive.

If huffing it on two wheels isn't your idea of fun, leave the pedaling to someone else. For a few bucks, **Seattle Pedicabs** (1937 Occidental Ave., 206/708-1726, www.seattlepedicabs.com) will show you around in a bright green cab fully equipped with seatbelts, comfortable seats, and hydraulic breaks. It's fun and a great way to enjoy the sites, get a little history, and avoid dragging a bike and yourself up the city's many hills.

Spectator Sports
The **Seattle Seahawks** (206/628-0888, www.seahawks.com) make their touchdowns at Quest Field, a 72,000-seat, open-air stadium that also plays host to the city's beloved Seattle Sounders soccer team.

The **Seattle Mariners** (206/346-4001 or 800/696-2746, www.mariners.mlb.com) run the bases right next door at Safeco Field, a state-of-the-art facility with seating for 47,000 fans, a retractable roof, kid zone, and several team shops and public

services. Ticket costs vary from cheap to expensive, but no seat is a bad seat at this stadium. You don't have to live here to enjoy a Mariners' ballgame, but you do have to try the garlic fries.

Events

One of the world's biggest entertainment festivals, **Bumbershoot** (www. bumbershoot.org, Labor Day weekend) does not disappoint with over 100 musical acts, endless rows of food vendors, the Indie Market of handmade crafts, one-of-a-kind designs and fine arts, and loads of fun! Expect huge crowds and walk, don't drive—it's always sunny for Bumbershoot!

Seafair (www.seafair.com) is an eight-week summer celebration of the Puget Sound lifestyle, with festivals, parades, triathlon, and the roaming Seafair Pirates! And if that's not enough, the two main events are the Seafair Cup hydroplane races and the Blue Angels' air shows.

Expect nonstop music, food, and fun at the **Northwest Folklife Festival** (www. nwfolklife.org). You don't have to be a local to appreciate the Northwest tradition that is folklife. There are plenty of family-friendly activities and a wonderful cultural art exhibit near the International Fountain Pavilion.

Accommodations

From comfy and affordable to lavish and upscale, there are plenty of places to stay in Seattle. Summer rates are the highest. Most hotels are located in walking distance of the free-zone Metro stops and on the link light rail, making it easy to get to and from your hotel without worrying about traffic, parking, and navigating.

Under $150

Cheap doesn't have to lack style, and you'll find both at **Hostel Seattle** (2327 2nd Ave., 206/706-3255, www.hostelseattle.com, $28 s, $78 d). With eccentric and artful motifs by local artists, it's been voted best hostel in the United States. Its location between the Space Needle and Pike Place Market makes it a geographic gem!

A well-known historical hotel, **Moore Hotel** (1926 2nd Ave., 206/448-4851 or 800/421-5508, www.moorehotel.com, $59 s, $71 d, $79 private bath) offers rooms with shared bathrooms located down the hall. For a little more money, you can get a room with a private bath.

$150-250

The **Best Western Pioneer Square Hotel** (77 Yesler Way, 206/340-1234 or 800/800-5514, www.pioneersquare.com, $160-350, $20 parking) is located in a restored building just a few blocks from the Seattle Mariners ballpark. They offer a continental breakfast and tasteful rooms.

A boutique hotel with modern panache, **Hotel Andra** (2000 4th Ave., 206/448-8600, www.hotelandra.com, $180 and up) is in the heart of downtown and perfectly set between Seattle's thriving retail hub and iconic attractions.

Seattle has a good collection of elegant and trendy hotels that make for a memorable stay. **Paramount Hotel** (724 Pine St., 206/292-9500 or 800/426-0670, www.westcoasthotels.com, $199-239) is located in the center of downtown Seattle, just minutes away from the city's sights. Its lobby is decorated in dark woods and deep reds and the rooms are tasteful and spacious.

Hotel Vintage Park (1100 5th Ave., 206/624-8000 or 800/853-3914, www. kimptonhotels.com, $189-239) is a beautiful boutique hotel with a 24-hour fitness center and nightly hosted wine hour that features local wine partners.

Over $250

Luxury and romance are what **Hotel Monaco Seattle** (1101 4th Ave., 206/621-1770, www.monaco-seattle.com, $289 and up) is all about. Your wish is their command. But with spacious rooms, pillow-top beds, complimentary wine tasting, and an in-room pet goldfish, what else would you wish for? You can walk from the hotel to Pike Place Market, Pioneer Square, and the world-famous Seattle Public Library.

The Alexis Hotel (1007 1st Ave., 206/624-4844 or 800/264-8482, www. alexishotel.com, $335-395) is where you want to hang your hat. With their 300-thread-count sheets, you may never get out of bed. The rooms feature themed art and plush furnishings. Complimentary wine is offered in the afternoons at the Library Bistro, which also serves Northwest cuisine. A full spa is available when you want to relax after a day of shopping.

A hotel with modern tastes, **Hotel 1000** (1000 1st Ave., 206/957-1000, www. hotel1000.com, $449-649, $39 parking) is one of the most upscale places to stay in the downtown Seattle area. The rooms feature waterfall showerheads, marbled bathrooms, and beautiful dark wood furnishings. One of the most unique features of the hotel is its virtual golf course where you can practice your swing.

Information and Services
Seattle Visitor Center and Concierge Services (866/732-2695 or 206/461-5840) provides accurate visitor information, and its location in the Washington State Convention Center lobby makes it easy to find.

Port Gamble

Settled on the shores of the Hood Canal River, Port Gamble (pop. 916) is a picturesque town reminiscent of a New England community with maple and elm trees lining the streets. It was founded in 1853 by two Maine businessmen, William Talbot and Andrew Pope, who, along with partners Josiah Keller and Charles Foster, formed the Puget

Mill Company to harvest lumber for the expanding West. The sand spit at the mouth of Gamble Bay proved to be the perfect location to log and ship timber, but it was already the site of an ancient S'Klallam village called Teekalet. Many of the S'Klallam had moved across the bay as more settlers arrived.

Though it's a tiny town (120 acres), Port Gamble warrants a stop to look out across the bay or to walk the original street laid over a century ago. The New England architecture marks a period in time when familiarity was important to East Coast migrants looking for a better life. The town was constructed to make workers feel at home by reflecting the communities they left behind. The **Port Gamble Historic Museum** (32400 Rainier Ave. NE, 360/297-7636, www.portgamble.com, 10am-5pm daily May 1-Sept. 30, 11am-4pm Fri.-Sun. Oct. 1-Apr. 30, $4 adults, $3 students and seniors, free children 6 and under) is filled with early 1800s photographs and town artifacts on the second floor of the General Store. There's no getting lost here: The town shops are all on a little two-block stretch on Rainier Avenue. The General Store is the last building on the right and sells a wide variety of merchandise and has a restaurant. Nearby shops include antiques stores, a trading company, featuring local artists, a truffle shop, and day spa. The **Olympic Outdoor Center** (32379 Rainier Ave., 360/297-4659, www.olympicoutdoorcenter.com, bike $15/hr, kayak $16/hr) rents bicycles and kayaks and offers Salmon Habitat tours. The regal **St. Paul's Church** sits south of the shops, across the bend on a hill surrounded by meticulously manicured lawns and a white picket fence. You won't find hotels here, but a few cottages and B&Bs are on offer, including the **Port Gamble Guest Houses** (32440 Puget Ave. NE, 360/447-8473, www.portgambleguesthouse.com, $200-500).

Olympic National Park

Olympic National Park stretches across much of the Olympic Peninsula's interior and coastline. You could spend eternity exploring Olympic National Park's breathtaking beauty and vast natural diversity; its sheer size is overwhelming (over 922,651 acres).

President Grover Cleveland designated these old-growth forests as a reserve in 1897. President Franklin Roosevelt established the area as a national park in 1938 to preserve its treasures for future generations. But it isn't just its intrinsic qualities that make this place memorable. It's the story that still lives within the landscape. Before the arrival of concrete and tire tracks, Native Americans forged the paths we still follow, hunting in the damp forests and fishing in the deep lake caverns. It was, and continues to be, a land embedded in tribal culture, exhibiting a spiritual understanding of the universe that unifies all living things. For Euro-Americans it was a place of opportunity, where the struggles and hardships of life were overcome by perseverance and hope.

There are three prominent ecosystems in the park: rugged coastline, snow-capped mountains, and temperate rain forests, containing record-sized trees. Wildlife thrive and can be seen throughout the park, especially Roosevelt elk, blacktailed deer, many species of birds along the coastline estuaries, and a variety of amazing butterflies (alongside wildflowers) in valley meadows and hillsides. Black bears roam the Quinault River valley.

Orientation

There are several access points into Olympic National Park. They are described as they appear, approaching from Seattle along US-101.

Eastern Olympic National Park

The little-visited eastern corner of the park, accessible from **Dosewallips** (see page 49) and **Staircase** (see page 50), is for adventurous travelers. Ancient stands of Douglas fir and cedar cloak the steep ridges of the wilderness valley. The wild waters of Skokomish River, awash with rainbow and bull trout, surge through the deep forest bed.

Northern Olympic National Park

The northern section of the park lies along the Strait of Juan de Fuca, one of the most beautiful places in the world. Frequent sightings of marine mammals, elk, deer, and even the occasional black bear make the region an animal haven. Not far from the town of Port Angeles is one of the most visited areas of the park: **Hurricane Ridge** (see page 62). Nearby, **Lake Crescent** (see page 64) is a deep, watery cavern popular for its Beardslee trout and for the shimmering cascades of Marymere Falls.

Western Olympic National Park

A lush green canopy of coniferous and deciduous species is found in the rainy western side of the Olympics. Mosses and ferns shroud the surface in shades of green as record-breaking trees cloak misty waterfalls, glacier-carved lakes, and an abundance of wildlife. This is where you'll find **Hoh Rain Forest** (see page 73) and **Lake Quinault** (see page 75), a favorite for outdoor activity.

Visiting the Park
Getting There

Olympic National Park is the center of the Olympic Peninsula, covering a 50-mile radius that includes most of the Pacific coastline. One major highway, **US-101,** loops around the park, following the northern edge of Lake Crescent to Lake Quinault's southwest edge. The central portion of the park is completely roadless, so it is not possible to drive through

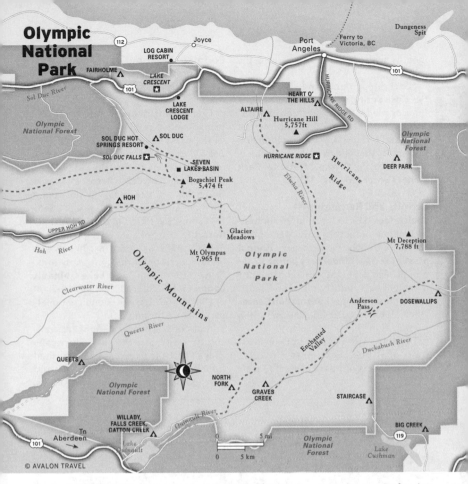

Olympic National Park

© AVALON TRAVEL

the park. Off US-101, **access roads** wind deeper into the park's interior; however, you will eventually have to return to US-101 to exit the park.

The highway can be dangerous in extremely **windy** areas at Morse Creek. As you drive through Port Angeles, the **name of the highway changes** (to Golf Course Rd., Front and 1st Sts., and Lincoln Ave.), which can be confusing, but well-placed signs help keep you on the right track.

Park Entrances

The coastal portion along the peninsula is accessible from US-101 at Kalaloch, La Push, Cape Alava, and Neah Bay. **Access Roads** run from US-101 into the park's interior at Hurricane Ridge (17 miles south of Port Angeles), Elwha (11 miles west of Port Angeles), Sol Duc (approx. 12 miles west of Lake Crescent), Hoh Rain Forest (31 miles east of Forks), and Quinault. Two access points allow for exploration of the remote east side at the Staircase (9 miles west of US-101 in Hoodsport) and Quilcene (north of the Hood Canal Bridge).

Seasons

Olympic National Park is open year-round, 24 hours a day. Expect **snow** in the winter and **rain** in spring and fall. Pack reliable rain gear and a few extra pairs of socks. **July, August,** and most of **September** are the **driest and warmest** months, with temperatures reaching the mid-70s.

Some campgrounds and visitor facilities **close during winter,** including some interior roads. Fires and flooding contribute to the temporary shutdown of roads and services. Up-to-date information on weather and available facilities is available at the **Olympic National Park Visitor Center** (360/565-3130).

Permits and Regulations

Vehicle fees ($15, $5 for children and visitors on foot or bicycle) cover park entry. All passes are good for seven days. **Annual passes** are $30. **Wilderness permits** ($5/ group, plus $2/night pp) required for overnight backcountry hikers are available at the **Wilderness Information Center** (3002 Mount Angeles Rd., 360/565-3100, www.nps.gov) in Port Angeles.

Dogs are allowed but not on most trails or in the backcountry. Trailers must be 21 feet or less (15 feet at Queets Campground).

Lodging, Camping, and Food

Places to stay vary, as do rates. Many resorts fill up fast. Make reservations ahead of time.

Concessionaire **Aramark** (www.olympicnationalparks.com) runs four lodges in the park: **Lake Crescent Lodge** (416 Lake Crescent Rd., 360/928-3211, www. olympicnationalparks.com, May-Dec., $125 and up), **Log Cabin Resort** (3183 East Beach Rd., 360/928-3325, www.olympicnationalparks.com, late May-Sept., $66-161 cabins, $40 RVs), **Sol Duc Hot Springs Resort** (12076 Sol Duc Hot Springs Rd., 360/327-3583 or 866/476-5382, www. olympicnationalparks.com, Apr.-mid-Oct., $173 and up), and **Lake Quinault Lodge** (345 S. Shore Rd., 360/288-2900 or 800/562-6672, www.olympicnational-parks.com, $109 and up).

Additional accommodations are available in towns near the park. Hurricane Ridge and Lake Crescent can be visited from Port Angeles; Hoh Rain Forest and Lake Quinault can be visited from Forks.

Hurricane Ridge

Campsites are available at 16 NPS-operated campgrounds in various areas of the park. Nearly all are first-come, first-served and do not take reservations. Kalaloch Campground takes individual reservations for the summer season, which can be made up to six months in advance. Sites can range from primitive to fairly modern and usually have picnic tables and a grill or a fire pit. Water, toilets, and garbage containers are found at most sites, however, you have to go into town for laundry, showers, and hookups.

RV Dump Stations ($5 per use) are located at Fairholm, Hoh, Kalaloch, Mora, and Sol Duc campsites.

Camp concessions are open seasonally and sell wood. If there's no store or if it's outside operating hours, collecting dead wood in the campgrounds is permitted.

In many parts of the park, it's best to bring your own food. The only restaurants within the national park boundaries are inside the park lodges. Bears, raccoons, and other critters are more than happy to clean up your campsite by eating all your goodies. Animal-resistant containers will keep your food safe, and many wilderness areas within the park require it.

Dosewallips

The 425-acre **Dosewallips State Park** (306996 US-101, approx. 45-minute drive from Staircase, 888/226-7688, 8am-10pm daily summer, 8am-5pm daily winter) is near the city of Brinnon, the site of the oldest Boy Scout camp, "Camp Parson," west of the Mississippi. The town of Brinnon is tiny and you may miss it if you blink while driving through. Though there is a market, it lacks in selection and is costly. Stop in Hoodsport (about one hour south) for groceries and gas. The park is about a minute north of Brinnon, sandwiched between the saltwater of Hood Canal and the freshwater Dosewallips River. There's a great viewing platform and large flats where clamming is popular seasonally with a permit. The Dosewallips River originates in two forks, which join about five miles from the headwaters near Mt. Anderson. There are several legends about how the river got its name; the Klallam Native American oral history tells of the Doquebatl "Great Changer," who transformed a Klallam chief into a mountain at the river's source.

Like many rivers throughout the region, the Dosewallips once teemed with salmon, but human tinkering of the landscape by logging and farming ultimately destroyed the salmon habitat. Restoration efforts led by the Port Gamble S'Klallam Tribe, Wild Fish Conservancy, and the Hood Canal Coordinating Council are working to reconnect the river to its original delta to improve salmon habitat. The entire Dosewallips River Estuary is located within Dosewallips State Park, where you can watch seasonal salmon spawning.

Recreation
Unmarked trails lead into the woods, but don't let this stop you from exploring. **Steam Donkey Loop Trail** (begins behind the park entrance) is an easy three-mile loop around the park through ferns and maple. It traverses many bridges onto the old Izett Railroad Grade before descending back to the main road. The **Rocky Brook Trail** is only accessible by hiking in since the road washed out over a decade ago, but the 229-foot waterfall that cascades from above is worth the trouble. The trail is very short and begins just after crossing Rocky Brook Bridge. Walk through wooded brush and green foliage before arriving at the spectacular waterfall.

Experienced mountain climbers will find **Mt. Anderson** (elevation 7,330 feet) and **Mt. Constance** (elevation 7,756 feet) both imposing and rewarding with steep jagged cliffs, areas of crumbling rock, and commanding views of forest treetops, the Cascade Range, and various waterways.

Camping
Dosewallips Campground (800/452-5687, www.nps.gov, free) has several rustic walk-in campsites located on both sides of the highway. There are picnic and day-use facilities, but no running water and only pit toilets.

Staircase

Roughly 30 miles southwest of Dosewallips, the Staircase area is the main entry into the southeast portion of Olympic National Park. Although this is the "forgotten" corner of the park, that doesn't mean there isn't anything worth seeing or doing. This is the place for adventurous explorers, as trails penetrate deep into the primitive forest, fringing the Skokomish and Dosewallips Rivers, passing Pacific rhododendrons (the state flower), vibrant mossy old growth, waterfalls, and small alpine lakes.

Storms sometimes cause road closures. Always check weather and road reports before venturing into this part of the park.

Recreation
Hidden in the shadow of Mt. Lincoln and behind popular Lake Cushman, Staircase offers a myriad of nature trails. To enter the park, follow the signs to Lake Cushman and turn left at the end of the road, twisting along the dirt road to Staircase Ranger Station. There are no stairs, but there were when an 1890 expedition built a cedar stairway to get over the rock bluff. **Shady Lane Trail** marks the location. The path is a short 1.5-mile stroll through mossy undergrowth and grand vistas of Mt. Rose and the North Fork of the Skokomish River, passing a few bridges and an abandoned mine along the way. If you want a good look at rapids, a longer trail runs alongside the Skokomish River in a complete loop. The **North Fork Skokomish Trail** is about a 4-mile trek to Flapjacks Lake; you can continue and make a complete 15-mile loop, passing a beautiful waterfall and rare views of the ragged Sawtooth Range of the Olympics. A steep three-mile climb to Wagonwheel Lake gains nearly 4,000 feet in subalpine forest, where bobcats, deer, and elk roam.

Camping
Staircase Campground (360/565-3131, www.nps.gov, $12/night) is in a deeply wooded area away from the river but a great point for starting hikes into the Skokomish River Valley. There are no RV hookups. Toilets and drinking water are only available in the summer.

Port Townsend

With roots seeded in maritime culture, Port Townsend (pop. 8,900) has transformed itself into a sophisticated city of the arts. It's one of the last of the Victorian-era seaports, a classic town of ornate 19th-century mansions that flourished until the 1890s when plans to extend the railroad failed and its booming economy dried up. The town was nearly abandoned until the development of artillery fortifications at Fort Worden and the paper mill moderately rekindled the economy. But it wasn't until the 1970s, when retirees and artists moved in, restoring the town's historic attributes and creating trendy shops, art galleries, and restaurants, that Port Townsend returned to its former glory.

Getting There

Port Townsend rests on the northwestern tip of the Olympic Peninsula. After crossing the Hood Canal Bridge, turn right on SR-19 (Beaver Valley Rd.) and drive 22 miles to SR-12, which joins WA-20. There are visible signs along the highway, but be aware that segments of the highway change to street names.

Sights

Port Townsend has a rich maritime heritage preserved by its continued marine trades industry and observed by its historic buildings and classic wooden boats. A good place to start is at the **Port Townsend Visitor Information Center** (440 12th St., 360/385-2722, www.enjoypt.com, 9am-5pm Mon.-Fri., 10am-4pm Sat., 11am-4pm Sun.) to pick up a tour map.

★ Fort Worden State Park

Perched above the northwest entrance of Puget Sound, **Fort Worden** (200 Battery Way, 360/344-4400, 11am-4pm daily, $2 adults, free children) was commissioned in 1902 as part of the U.S. Army's "Triangle of Fire" harbor defenses. The government spent $7.5 million on its completion, with strategically constructed barracks designed to confuse the aim of gunners firing offshore and 41 artillery pieces that were never fired in battle. After 51 years of service, it was decommissioned and operated as a state detention center before becoming a state park. The **Coast Artillery Museum** (Bldg. 201, Fort Worden, 360/385-0373, http://coastartillery.org, 10am-5pm Fri.-Sat., 11am-4pm Sun.-Thurs., May-Aug., limited hours Sept.-Apr.), barracks, and hangar once used for airships offer compelling insight into the fort's history. Much of the movie *An Officer and a Gentleman* was filmed here. Within the park's 434 acres, there are sandy beaches and views of the Olympic and Cascade Mountains. Hiking, kayaking, and biking are popular here. Guided tours operate seasonally.

Rothschild House

Head uptown to get a good look at maritime life in the Victorian era by touring the **Rothschild House** (418 Taylor St., 360/385-1003, 11am-4pm daily May-Sept., $4 adults, $1 children 3-12) and the remnants of the Kentucky Store. The store once sat on a pier that extended into Port Townsend Bay, where ships could directly load and unload their cargo, ranging from needles to anchors. The house's furnishings, from the mattresses to the wallpaper, are originals. The family photo album preserves photos of sailing shipmasters.

Maritime Sights

The **Marine Science Center** (532 Battery Way, 360/385-5582, www.ptmsc.org, 11am-5pm Wed.-Mon. summer, noon-5pm Fri.-Sun. spring, fall, and winter, $5 adults, $3 children 6-17, free children 5 and under) offers a chance to touch the interesting creatures that live in the cold waters of the Pacific.

Tour the **Point Wilson Lighthouse**

Port Townsend

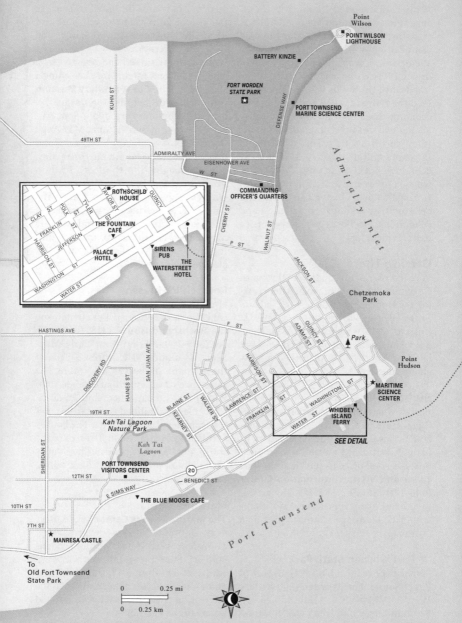

Point Wilson

POINT WILSON LIGHTHOUSE

BATTERY KINZIE

FORT WORDEN STATE PARK

DEFENSE WAY

PORT TOWNSEND MARINE SCIENCE CENTER

Admiralty Inlet

49TH ST

KUHN ST

ADMIRALTY AVE

EISENHOWER AVE

W ST

COMMANDING OFFICER'S QUARTERS

CHERRY ST

WALNUT ST

P ST

JACKSON ST

Chetzemoka Park

HASTINGS AVE

F ST

QUINCY ST

ADAMS ST

Park

Point Hudson

DISCOVERY RD

HAINES ST

SAN JUAN AVE

BLAINE ST

WALKER ST

KEARNEY ST

HARRISON ST

LAWRENCE ST

FRANKLIN ST

WASHINGTON ST

WATER ST

ST

MARITIME SCIENCE CENTER

WHIDBEY ISLAND FERRY

SEE DETAIL

19TH ST

Kah Tai Lagoon Nature Park

Kah Tai Lagoon

SHERIDAN ST

12TH ST

PORT TOWNSEND VISITORS CENTER

20

BENEDICT ST

E SIMS WAY

THE BLUE MOOSE CAFÉ

10TH ST

7TH ST

MANRESA CASTLE

To Old Fort Townsend State Park

Port Townsend

Detail

CLAY ST

POLK ST

TYLER ST

TAYLOR ST

QUINCY ST

FRANKLIN ST

HARRISON ST

JEFFERSON ST

WASHINGTON ST

WATER ST

ROTHSCHILD HOUSE

THE FOUNTAIN CAFÉ

PALACE HOTEL

SIRENS PUB

THE WATERSTREET HOTEL

0   0.25 mi
0   0.25 km

(10541 Flagler Rd., 360/385-3701, 1pm-4pm Sat. May-Sept.), named by Captain George Vancouver, who first sighted the point in 1792. The foghorn can be heard from over three miles away. Just three miles southeast, the 1888 Marrowstone Point Lighthouse standing at the entrance to Port Townsend Bay, is not open to the public.

Fort Flagler Museum (10541 Flagler Rd., 360/385-3701, open weekends, $2 donation) houses many coastal defense artifacts.

Visit **Northwest Maritime Center** (431 Water St., 360/385-3628, http://nwmaritime.org, call for hours), a beautiful two-story building where they show you how wooden boats are built as well as hold informational classes and workshops.

Food

Chic cafés and quaint restaurants are not hard to find, with the majority on the east end of town.

Art lovers will appreciate ★ **Fountain Café** (920 Washington St., 360/385-1364, 11am-3pm and 5pm-9pm daily, $8-17), a funky eatery with east Mediterranean influences and art-lined walls set inside a historic building. The 1950s-style **Nifty Fifty's Soda Fountain** (817 Water St., 360/385-1931, www.niftyfiftyspt.com, $5-12) brings back the era of thick burgers and thick milkshakes. Located in the center of Haven Shipyard, the **Blue Moose Café** (311 Haines Pl., 360/385-7339, 6:30am-2pm Mon.-Fri., 7:30am-2pm Sat.-Sun., $8-20, no credit cards) serves fluffy pancakes and famous corn beef and hash. The **Owl Sprit Café** (218 Polk St., 360/385-5275, 11am-8pm daily, $14 and up) serves up soups, sandwiches, and tasty local favorites like "haystack" fried onions.

If seafood is what you crave, the **Silverwater Café** (237 Taylor St., 360/385-6448, www.silverwatercafe.com, 11:30am-3pm and 5pm-10pm daily, $18 and up) takes Pacific Northwest cuisine to new heights with pan-seared halibut

in a rich hazelnut cream sauce or jumbo prawns with cilantro ginger lime. All the Italian classics are at **Lanza's Ristorante** (1020 Lawrence St., 360/379-1900, www.lanzaspt.com, 5pm-11pm Tues.-Sat., $20-30). Its authentic dishes and intimate atmosphere make it a perfect place for couples. Upscale **Sweet Laurette Café & Bistro** (1029 Lawrence St., 360/385-4886, www.sweetlaurette.com, 8am-5pm Wed., 8am-9pm Thurs.-Sat., 8am-3pm Sun., $15-30) offers French delights and coffees in its café and also serves entrées that could put any Parisian restaurant to shame.

Nightlife

Though Port Townsend isn't a "club" town, it does have some good wine bars and pubs, including a few where weekend bands perform. The **Cellar Door** (940 Water St., entrance on Tyler St., 360/385-6959, www.cellardoorpt.com, music Tues., Wed., and weekends, no cover) is a casual wine and cocktail bar decorated in classic furnishings with diverse live music 7pm-10pm. Every Friday and Saturday night **Sirens** (823 Water St., 360/379-1100, www.sirenspub.com, open daily) welcomes local music and offers guests a variety of drinks and food. Have a beer and play table tennis at the **Pourhouse** (2231 Washington St., 360/379-5586). Set in a warehouse, it has several local brews on tap and a beer garden. The **Uptown Pub** (1016 Lawrence St., 360/385-1530, music on weekends) has a laid-back atmosphere with pool tables, live music, and a dance floor.

Shopping

Port Townsend is known for its antiques, art galleries, eclectic shops, and used bookstores. The **Port Townsend Antique Mall** (802 Washington St., 360/379-8069, 10am-5:30pm Mon.-Fri., 10am-6pm Sat., 11am-5pm Sun.) is composed of several vendors stuffed to the brim with vintage and nautical collectibles.

Walk one block west to Water Street in

the downtown waterfront district where the popular **Gallery Walks** (first Sat. of every month) take place. Many galleries and shops stay open until 8:30pm; local artists are showcased and mingle with the public. **Forest Gems Gallery** (807 Washington St., 360/379-1713, www.forestgems.com) is a gallery of gorgeous, finely finished furniture carved from West Coast woods. Carefully navigate through this store and be mindful of the No Touching signs.

Despite the name, **The Green Eyeshade** (720 Water St., 360/385-3838, www.thegreeneyeshade.com, 10am-6pm daily) doesn't deal in cosmetics, but it does have lots of home decor items, handcrafted jewelry, and specialty gifts neatly laid out in this appropriately green building.

Jewelry is what you'll find at **Lila Drake Jewelry** (918 Water St., 360/379-2899, 10am-6pm daily) and you won't believe your eyes when you see their prices. There aren't many places where you can buy beautiful silver pieces for under $20. For fashion that's unusually theatrical and fun, **Expressions** (834 Water St., 360/385-5887, 10am-6pm daily) has reasonably priced clothing and accessories.

The **Northwest Man** (901 Water St., 360/385-6734, 10am-6pm daily) has everything the male of the species needs, from Pendleton wool plaid and sweaters to Cutter & Buck cardigans.

Bacon-flavored gumballs, wacky sunglasses, and an old photo booth to smile at and say "cheese!" is only the tip of the iceberg of what you'll find at **Sideshow Variety** (630 Water St., 360/379-4699, 10am-6pm daily).

Discover your inner-writer on the corner of Water and Taylor Streets at **The Writers' Workshoppe and Bookstore** (234 Taylor St., 360/379-2617, 10am-6pm daily), a tiny bookstore filled with fantasy, horror, and fun stuff, like T-shirts, coffee mugs, and classic typewriters. Step into another world at **Phoenix Rising** (696 Water St., 360/385-4464, 10am-6pm daily) and browse a huge selection of spiritual books, crystals, music, and fairies. The staff is helpful, but the store gets pretty busy. Plan to spend a little extra time in this place.

Recreation

From water sports and walking trails to bird-watching and picnicking, there are no shortage of activities. Pack a picnic basket and watch the natural side of life unfold at **Kah Tai Lagoon Nature Park** (access at 12th St. on the southeast end of the lagoon). The park borders the lagoon on 14th Street between Kearney and Haines Streets and is a protected sanctuary for waterfowl nesting and feeding. Trails meander along the edges of the lagoon and through the natural landscape.

To get your feet wet, head two miles north on Cherry Street to **Fort Worden State Park** (200 Battery Way), where you can swim, scuba dive, or play in the sand. The on-site Cable House Canteen store has all kinds of goodies, and restrooms are located across the street.

Events

Port Townsend hosts the largest **Wooden Boat Festival** (http://nwmaritime.org, Sept., one-day ticket $15 adults, $10 teens and seniors; multi-day ticket $30 adults, $20 teens and seniors) in the world with more than 300 wooden vessels, hundreds of indoor and outdoor presentations, exhibitors, musical performances, children's activities, and more. It's a three-day event held at the Point Hudson Marina entrance.

The town has also been the set of popular movies like *An Officer and a Gentleman* and *Snow Falling on Cedars*. Independent filmmakers and cinema lovers flock here in September to attend the **Port Townsend Film Festival** (downtown district, 360/379-1333, www.ptfilmfest.com, Sept.). There are five indoor and two outdoor theaters, numerous food venues, cocktail lounge, and ongoing mingling with producers, directors, and actors.

Early October brings the very odd **Kinetic Sculpture Race** (www.ptkineti-crace.org, Oct.), a themed contest of human-powered works of art that race over land and sea to the finish.

Accommodations

Embellished with antique furnishings and rich colors, ★ **Manresa Castle** (651 Cleveland St., 360/385-5750 or 800/732-1281, www.manresacastle.com, $109-229) makes every guest feel like royalty with luxurious rooms in a haunted castle that overlooks Port Townsend Bay and the Cascade Mountains. Stay in "Room 305" to be visited by the mansion's original 1892 owner, Kate Eisenbeis.

The ★ **Ann Starrett Mansion** (744 Clay St., 800/321-0644, www.starrett-mansion.com, $115-225) enchants guests with a three-tiered spiral staircase that rises 70 feet inside an ornately decorated domed tower that features a solar calendar. Rooms include water or mountain views and free WiFi.

The Waterstreet Hotel (635 Water St., 360/385-5467 or 800/735-9810, $50-140) is located in the renovated 1889 N.D. Hill Building. Rooms range from one-bed spaces with shared bath to suites with private decks overlooking the bay.

Built in 1889, the **Palace Hotel** (1004 Water St., 360/385-0773, www.palace-hotelpt.com, $59-109) is a beautifully restored boutique hotel with antique furnishings, high ceilings, and an old-world charm. Some rooms have a shared bath.

The **Bishop Victorian Hotel** (714 Washington St., 360/385-6122, www.bishopvictorian.com, $150 and up) is a turn-of-the-century building with 16 suites, each with its own cozy fireplace. It is located right in the heart of the historic downtown district and is in walking distance of the waterfront.

While some towns have a few old homes turned into B&Bs, Port Townsend seems to burst at the seams with wonderful homes from its late 19th-century glory days. One lovely Victorian B&B, **The Old Consulate Inn** (313 Walker St., 360/385-6753, www.oldconsulate.com, $120-230) overlooks Port Townsend from atop a high bluff, providing panoramic mountain and water views in comfortably elegant surroundings. The inn was built in 1889 by F. W. Hastings, son of Port Townsend's founding father Loren B. Hastings, and served as the office of the German Consul (hence the "Old Consulate" name) in the early part of the 20th century. Eight guest rooms all have private baths.

For less-pricey lodging, the **Port Townsend Inn** (2020 E. Washington St., 360/385-2211, www.porttownsendinn.com, $68-136) has comfortable rooms without all the frills and a nice indoor pool and hot tub. The **HI-Olympic Hostel** (Fort Worden, 360/385-0655, $22 per person) has dorm beds in the old army barracks at Fort Worden, on the coast two miles north of town.

The **Point Hudson Resort** (101 Hudson St., 360/385-2828, $30-52) is a private facility on the beach with full hookups for RVs. The **Jefferson County Fairgrounds** (4907 Landes St., 360/385-1013, www.jeffcofairgrounds.com, $7-20) provides year-round camping and RV parking without a reservation. It's a full-service facility with a bus stop located within the grounds.

Information and Services

The **Port Townsend Visitor Information Center** (440 12th St., 360/385-2722, www.enjoypt.com, 9am-5pm Mon.-Fri., 10am-4pm Sat., 11am-4pm Sun.) is a good resource for local events and activities. It is conveniently located right next to the Jefferson Transit Park-and-Ride, where you can catch a shuttle bus to downtown. Gasoline and small convenience stores are available within the town.

Jamestown S'Klallam Tribal Community

Twenty-five miles southwest of Port Townsend via WA-20 and US-101, the Jamestown S'Klallam "Strong People" Tribal Community looks out over Sequim Bay. Towering totem poles welcome visitors at the information kiosk pull-out west of the highway. These carved masterpieces reflect the Coastal Salish Indian traditions and legacies. Listen to timeless legends as you journey along numerous totem poles to the **House of Myths** (set behind a native art gallery), where each totem is carefully carved. It's a fascinating, tribally guided tour known as **Tour of the Totems.** For scenic views or a leisurely stroll, follow the stairway at the west end of the pullout down to the **Olympic Discovery Trail,** a path that traces the former railroad corridors that were constructed between Port Angeles and Discovery Bay in the early 1900s. Two short bridges cross the Jimmycomelately Creek and Estuary, a stream that flows from the Olympic Mountains and into Sequim Bay. The logging and farming of the late 1800s nearly decimated the stream and salmon beds; the S'Klallam Tribe has led restoration efforts to revive salmon runs and protect the stream. In the summer, you can watch as chum salmon fight their way to spawning grounds, and observe a variety of birds and wildlife.

There are no overnight accommodations, but a mile farther on US-101 in Blyn you'll find a restaurant inside the **Seven Cedars Casino** (270756 US-101, 360/683-7777, www.7cedarsresort.com) with a weekend buffet. The casino's **Longhouse Market & Deli** (360/681-7777) provides the perfect opportunity to fuel up on gasoline and snacks.

colorful lavender in Sequim

Sequim and the Dungeness Valley

Less than five minutes from the Jamestown S'Klallam Tribal Community on US-101, Sequim (pop. 6,624; pronounced "skwim") is a pleasantly dry patch on a peninsula famous for its rain. A typical year has 299 days of sunshine and just 17 inches of rain (comparable to rainfall in sunny Los Angeles). The agreeable climate has made this little town a popular retirement destination.

Sights

One block north of US-101 in Sequim, the **Museum and Arts Center** (175 W. Cedar St., 360/683-8110, www.macsequim. org, 11am-3pm Wed.-Sat., $2 donation) was built to store the 12,000-year-old tusks, bones, and artifacts unearthed at Sequim's famous Manis Mastodon Site, discovered in 1977 by Emanuel Manis,

a retired farmer. Archaeologists discovered a prehistoric spear point in the rib cage of one of the mastodons, some of the earliest evidence that humans hunted these elephantine beasts. Other displays include several fine old cedar bark baskets, pioneer farming displays, and timber exhibits.

The aptly named **Dungeness Spit** (the word "Dungeness" means sandy cape, closed to horses on weekends and holidays Apr. 15-Oct. 15) is a 5.5-mile-long stretch of sand that creates Dungeness Bay. The **Dungeness National Wildlife Refuge** (554 Voice of America Rd., 360/457-8451, $3 per family or group of up to four adults) provides habitat for 250 species of birds on the nation's longest natural sand spit. As many as 30,000 birds rest at this saltwater lagoon during their migratory journeys.

Built in 1857, the **New Dungeness Lighthouse** (at the tip of the spit, 360/683-6638, http://newdungenesslighthouse.com) is managed by volunteers and offers tours, but you'll have to hike a total of 11 miles out and back to see it. It's a good idea to check the tide charts before starting out. For an overview of the area, hike the 0.5-mile trail from the parking lot to a bluff overlooking Dungeness Bay. Clamming, fishing, and canoeing are permitted in this protected wildlife refuge, but no camping, dogs, firearms, or fires.

The **Olympic Game Farm** (1423 Ward Rd., 360/683-4295 or 800/778-4295, www.olygamefarm.com, $12 adults, $11 seniors and children 6-14, free children 5 and under), a vacation and retirement home for Hollywood stars, is a 90-acre preserve where over 200 animals, some of TV and movie fame, can be visited. Many of the Walt Disney nature specials were filmed here, along with parts of many feature movies. Follow the signs from Sequim five miles northwest to Ward Road.

Food

For the best French toast or Swedish pancakes, ★ **The Oak Table Café** (3rd and Bell Sts., 360/683-2179, www.oaktablecafe.com, 7am-3pm daily, $5-20) is where the locals go. The service is friendly, the cappuccinos perfect, and the prices will barely make a dent in your wallet.

For fast and well-prepared lunches, **Hi-Way 101 Diner** (392 W. Washington, 360/683-3388, $12) is a "fabulous fifties" family diner with the biggest local burgers. It's also a popular spot for breakfast.

Accommodations

Enjoy a room with a hot tub at ★ **Sequim Bay Lodge** (268522 US-101, 800/622-0691, www.sequimbaylodge.com, $120-200) conveniently located off US-101. It's not a glitzy hotel, but it's clean, comfortable, and surrounded by beautiful greenery.

For an intimate experience, **Groveland Cottage** (4861 Sequim-Dungeness Way, 360/683-3565, www.grovelandcottage.com, $100 and up) is a century-old house with a large lawn and pond. Inside are five guest rooms with private or shared baths.

Juan de Fuca Cottages (182 Marine Dr., 360/683-4433, www.juandefuca.com, $120 and up) offers suites and fully equipped housekeeping cottages overlooking Dungeness Spit.

Port Angeles

Port Angeles (pop. 19,100) was built on a 2,700-year-old Native American village and is one of only two municipalities designated as a federal city by President Abraham Lincoln—the other being Washington, D.C. It was once a booming logging community, but the preservation of endangered spotted owls forced paper and logging mills to close, uprooting generations of workers. Just as the phoenix rises from the ashes, so has this city, likely due to its prime position between the Strait of Juan de Fuca and the magnificent mountains of Olympic National Park. Port Angeles has become one of the Olympic Peninsula's most multi-faceted tourist destinations, with cultured wineries, year-round art and music festivals, and many recreational opportunities.

Getting There and Around

US-101 brings you right into downtown Port Angeles via East 1st and Front Streets to Lincoln Street. The public bus service connects all local towns, making the area fairly simply to get around. **Clallam Transit** (#20-26 buses, 360/452-4511 or 800/858-3747, www.clallamtransit.com, $1 single, plus $0.50 for additional zones, $2 day pass) offers service in and around Port Angeles to Forks, Neah Bay, La Push, and the Olympic National Park. **Olympic Bus Lines** (360/417-0700 or 800/457-4492, www.olympicbuslines.com) provides service to Seattle and Sea-Tac Airport.

Sights

Downtown Port Angeles was raised in the 1900s. **Port Angeles Historical Underground** (Port Angeles Chamber of Commerce, 360/452-2363, www.portangeles.org, 10am-2pm daily, $8-12) is a heritage tour through the past, uncovering the buildings lost beneath the city that remained forgotten for over a century before they were rediscovered.

The **Museum at the Carnegie** (207 S. Lincoln St., 360/452-6779, www.clallamhistoricalsociety.com, 1pm-4pm Wed.-Sat., donation $2 per adult, $5 per family) houses a modest collection of artifacts and exhibits on the town's logging history as well as local Native American culture.

Food

Soup and sandwiches is what ★ **Toga's Soup House** (122 W. Lauridsen Blvd., 360/452-1952, www.togassouphouse.com, Mon.-Fri. 10am-6pm, $10-30) does, but don't expect just grilled cheese! Try Dungeness crab panini, an Alaska salmon sandwich, or one of their many

Port Angeles

Strait of Juan de Fuca

Ediz Hook

Port Angeles Harbor

LIGHTHOUSE

Waterfront Trail
VISITOR CENTER
RAILROAD AVE
NEXT DOOR GASTROPUB
RED LION HOTEL
MICHAEL'S SEAFOOD AND STEAKHOUSE
KOKOPELLI GRILL
BELLA ITALIA
PORT ANGELES INN
OAK ST
E 3RD ST
FRONT
E 1ST ST

SEE DETAIL

Ferry to Victoria, BC

To Airport

To Forks

To Domaine Madeleine and Sequim

Olympic National Park
OLYMPIC NATIONAL PARK VISITOR CENTER

To Hurricane Ridge

© AVALON TRAVEL

homemade soups served in colorful bowls.

A bargain for the quality, **First Street Haven** (107 E. 1st St., 360/457-0352, $10-30) hits the spot! It's small but homey with delicious pastries and the perfect breakfast.

Right in front of the Red Lion Hotel downtown, **Kokopelli Grill** (203 Front St., 360/457-6040, www.kokopelli-grill.com, 11am-9pm Mon.-Thurs., 11am-10pm Fri.-Sat., 4pm-8pm Sun., $7-26) features Southwestern cooking in a warm, friendly space.

Bella Italia (118 E. 1st St., 360/457-5442, www.bellaitaliapa.com, 4pm-9pm daily, $12 and up) has all the Italian classics with an award-winning wine list.

Michael's Seafood & Steak (117 B E. 1st St., 360/417-6929, www.michaelsdining.com, $11 and up) is set in an underground location where the dress code is casual, the seafood is fresh, and the booths are cozy.

Enjoy the rustic elegance of **Bushwhackers** (1527 E. 1st St., 360/457-4113, www.bushwackerspa.com, 11:30am-9pm daily, $8-30), where there's something for the whole family.

There are a number of places to eat and drink by the ferry terminal, including the attractive **Smuggler's Landings Restaurant** (115 E. Railroad Ave., 360/457-6768, www.smugglerslanding.com, 6:30pm-9pm daily, $15 and up) with great fish-and-chips.

Nightlife and Entertainment

Most of the bars are on 1st and Front Streets.

DJs turns up the volume for a younger crowd at **BarN9NE** (229 W. 1st St., 360/797-1999, www.barn9nepa.com, 2pm-2am daily).

Beer, pool, and an old jukebox are what's up at **Zak's** (125 W. Front St., 360/452-7575, 4pm-2am daily). Don't expect swank at **Front Street Alibi** (1605 E. Front St., Ste. A., 360/797-1500, 10am-2am daily), just strong drinks, a DJ, dance floor, and interesting dive bar characters.

Joshua's Restaurant & Lounge (113 Del Guzzi Dr., 360/452-6545, 6am-9pm Mon.-Sat., 6am-8pm Sun.) serves live music along with its award-winning wines Thursday-Saturday nights.

A few blocks off the waterfront, **Next Door Gastropub** (113 W. 1st St., 360/504-2613, 11am-11pm Mon.-Thurs., 11am-2am Fri.-Sat., 10am-10pm Sun.) hosts live music and comedy acts on weekends.

Shopping

Follow the sculptures that line the west side of Railroad Avenue to 1st Street, the city's shopping hub of antiques, books, and hobby shops.

The Landing Mall (115 E. Railroad Ave., Ste. 112, 360/457-1427) is a tri-level building, ideally situated next to the city pier on Railroad Avenue, with several art galleries, eateries, and specialty gift shops.

Step into the past at **Port Angeles Antique Mall** (109 W. 1st St., 360/452-1693) and **Brocante** (105 W. 1st St., 360/452-6322, 11am-5pm Tues.-Fri., 10:30am-5pm Sat.), where heirlooms ornament the interior with mystery and charm.

Get InSpired! (124 W. 1st St. #B, 360/504-2590, 10:30am-5:30pm daily) by the whimsical and spiritual with books,

From top to bottom: Red Lion hotel in Port Angeles; Elwha River; seafront view from Port Angeles.

meditation supplies, and handcrafted soaps and lotions.

Unique gift items from jewelry to brass Buddhas make **Olympic Stained Glass** (112 N. Laurel St., 360/457-1090, 10am-5:30pm Mon.-Fri., 10am-5pm Sat.) a fun shop to browse.

Port Book and News (104 E. 1st St., 360/452-6367, 8am-8pm daily), **Odyssey Books** (114 W. Front St., 360/457-1045, 9am-7pm Mon.-Sat., 10am-5pm Sun.), and **Olympic Stationers** (112 E. Front St., 360/457-6111, 8:30am-5:30pm Mon.-Fri., 10am-3pm Sat.) all offer a wide selection of reading material.

Anime Kat (114 W. 1st St., 360/797-1313, 11am-7pm daily) sells collectible card games, board game players, and anime figures.

The **Port Angeles Farmers Market** (125 E. Front St., The Gateway Plaza, 360/417-4550, 10am-2pm Sat.) brings homegrown businesses together to present organic foods and fresh baked goods to the public.

Recreation

The west central route of the 30-mile **Olympic Discovery Trail** provides the perfect scenic stroll or bike ride on a maintained trail that begins at Port Angeles City Pier (Lincoln St. at W. Front St.) and extends across the Elwha River, along the coastal lowlands and Lake Crescent, to the top of Fairholm Hill.

Sound Bikes and Kayaks (120 E. Front St., 360/457-1240, 10am-6pm Mon.-Sat., bikes $10/hr or $45/day, kayaks $15/hr or $50/day) rents out whatever you need to pedal or paddle your way around.

Events

Every August bicyclists can **Ride The Hurricane** (www.portangeles.org, 6am-noon, $40 registration, spectators welcome) in a 24-36-mile recreational ride to Olympic National Park Hurricane Ridge Road free of motorists.

Bring a chair or blanket to **Concerts on the Pier** (www.portangeles.org, 6pm-8pm

Wed. June-Sept.), an outdoor festival of music for every melodic taste from Irish folk and jazz to country and rock. **Arts In Action** (early Sept., free) is an annual event downtown with sand sculpture contests, music, sidewalk sales, and local art.

Accommodations

Rates in Port Angeles vary with the season from cheap **Flagstone Motel** (415 E. 1st St., 360/457-9494, www.flagstonemotel.net, $40 s, $69 d) to modern **Best Western Olympic Lodge** (140 Del Guzzi Dr., 360/452-2993 or 800/600-2993, www.olympiclodge.com, $130-219).

Traveler's Motel (1133 E. 1st St., 360/452-2303 or 866/452-2301, www.travelersmotel.net, $39-100) and the **Aircrest Motel** (1006 E. Front St., 360/452-9255, www.aircrest.com, $48-78) are two cheap motels in Port Angeles.

The **Quality Inn Uptown** (101 E. 2nd St., 360/457-9434 or 800/858-3812, www.qualityinn.com, $80-299) and the **Port Angeles Inn** (111 E. 2nd St., 360/452-9285, www.portangelesinn.com, $59-195) offer open-space rooms with kitchenettes and bay views.

One block from the town center, the **Red Lion** (221 N. Lincoln St., 360/452-9215, www.redlion.com/portangeles, $109-259) overlooks the Strait of Juan de Fuca.

The best B&Bs are just east of the city and sit right on the waterfront. **Colette's Bed & Breakfast** (339 Finn Hall Rd., 360/457-9197, www.colettes.com, $150-375) is a favorite choice for romantic getaways with luxurious suites, an outdoor sanctuary, and magnificent oceanfront views. Down the road, the **George Washington Inn** (939 Finn Hall Rd., 360/452-5207, www.georgewashingtoninn.com, $175-250) is a picturesque colonial building with a white picket fence surrounded by lavender.

Campgrounds and RV parks are sprinkled around Olympic National Park and not within the city.

Ferries to Victoria, British Columbia

The MV *Coho* ferry crosses between Port Angeles and Victoria, B.C.

Port Angeles is a major transit point for travelers heading to or from Victoria, B.C., just 18 miles away across the Strait of Juan de Fuca. The **MV *Coho*** leaves Port Angeles for Victoria 3 times daily in summer (mid-May to mid-Sept.) and 1-2 times daily the rest of the year, except for a couple of winter weeks when the ferry is out for maintenance. The **Coho Ferry Terminal** (101 E. Railroad Ave., 360/457-4491, www.cohoferry.com, 1.5 hours, one-way $62 for car and driver, $17.50 adults, $8.75 children) is located at the foot of Laurel Street in Port Angeles. Departure times are listed by date on the website. Vehicle space is at a premium on summer weekends; reservations can be made for an additional fee. The *Coho* lands in Victoria, within walking distance of many picturesque sights. A car is not entirely necessary for a day trip. You can pick up a map of Victoria at the visitors center located near the ferry terminal in Port Angeles.

Information and Services

The **North Olympic Peninsula Visitors and Convention Bureau** (93 Beaver Valley Rd., 800/942-4042) is a good source for local attractions with a helpful staff, or stop by the **Port Angeles Chamber of Commerce** (121 E. Railroad Ave., 360/452-2363, www.cityofpa.com, 10am-4pm daily).

★ Hurricane Ridge

The most visited site in Olympic National Park, Hurricane Ridge rises over 5,757 feet from the Strait of Juan de Fuca, looking out over alpine meadows and a crescent of peaks. Picturesque meadows are populated by colorful wildflowers as well as mountain goats, deer, and Olympic marmots (found only in the Olympics).

The view is so vast that the U.S. military placed a lookout post here during World War II. Views to the north reveal the Strait of Juan de Fuca, Dungeness Spit, and Vancouver Island; dozens of glaciated and snowcapped peaks of the awe-inspiring Olympic Mountain range span across the south end; and to the east, Puget Sound, Hood Canal, and the Cascade Mountains stretch across the skyline.

The name comes from a Seattle Press Expedition in 1897. The winds blew so hard that the prospector declared the site Hurricane Ridge.

Getting There

Accessed via the Heart O' the Hills entrance, Hurricane Ridge is located about 17 miles south of Port Angeles and is reached by Hurricane Ridge Road, which turns off Mount Angeles Road at the Olympic National Park Visitor Center. During winter, the road shuts down Monday-Thursday, except holiday Mondays, and may be closed due to weather conditions at other times. Call **Northwest Avalanche Center** (360/565-3131) for up-to-date road status information.

Recreation
Hiking

Visitors can follow Hurricane Ridge's well-worn network of trails. From spring to early fall, there are vistas to enjoy and an abundance of wildlife and wildflowers to see. Keep your eyes peeled to catch deer and elk grazing along the green-sloped meadow valleys. Mountain goats are often spotted traversing the trails, but chances are they've spotted you first. Marmots, chipmunks, and other furry critters run freely, playing in the grassy meadows while butterflies swoon about.

The easiest hike is **Hurricane Hill Trail,** which begins at the parking lot at the end of Hurricane Ridge Road. The 1.6 miles lead to the top of the hill and 360-degree views of mountain peak vistas, Port Angeles, and the Strait of Juan de Fuca.

Hurricane Ridge also has a network of switchback trails accessed near the Hurricane Ridge Visitor Center. Start at the trailhead on the opposite end of the parking lot from the visitors center. The **Big Meadow Trail** (0.5 mile round-trip) is a short walk to the northern views of Hurricane Hill, the Strait of Juan de Fuca, and Vancouver Island. The **Cirque Rim Trail** (0.5 mile round-trip) leads through meadows of purple Broadleaf Lupine. The **High Ridge Trail** (1 mile round-trip) may be the best of the easy hikes,

offering panoramic views. It also leads to a spur trail that continues to a narrow crest aptly named **Sunrise Point.** The **Klahhane Ridge Trail** (5 miles round-trip) is a difficult but beautiful climb among colorful flowers and butterflies, mountain goats, and deer.

Winter Sports

During winter months, Hurricane Ridge becomes a cross-country and downhill skier dreamland. The **Hurricane Ridge Winter Sports Club** (rentals 10am-4pm Sat.-Sun. and holiday Mon.) operates two rope tows and a Poma lift that opens in December and continues until the end of March. It is the westernmost ski area in the contiguous United States, averaging 400 inches of snowfall a year. The sports facility is on a hill above the Hurricane Ridge Visitor Center, where you can obtain information.

Food and Accommodations

There are no options for lodging within Hurricane Ridge. The closest you'll find is 17 miles north in the town of Port Angeles, which has a wide range of B&Bs, motels, and RV parks.

Twelve miles north of Hurricane Ridge, **Heart O' the Hills** (Hurricane Ridge Rd., 360/565-3130, $12) offers 105 campsites in the old-growth forest year-round.

Food and beverage concessions, much like what you'd find at a ski resort, are located at the **Hurricane Ridge Visitor Center** (Hurricane Ridge Rd., 360/565-3131 www.nps.gov/olym, 9am-7pm daily in summer, 10am-4pm Sat.-Sun. late Dec.-Apr.).

Information and Services

Information is available at the **Hurricane Ridge Visitor Center** (Hurricane Ridge Rd., 360/565-3131, www.nps.gov/olym, 9am-7pm daily in summer, 10am-4pm Sat.-Sun. late Dec.-Apr.), which also houses exhibits, a gift shop, and a café and offers guided walks and outdoor programs (late June), as well as details on the surrounding winter-use area for skiing and sledding.

The **Olympic National Park Visitor Center** (3002 Mount Angeles Rd., 360/565-3130, 9am-4pm daily May-Sept., 10am-4pm daily Oct.-Apr.) offers maps; trail brochures; campground, weather, and road information; as well as area wildlife viewing locations. **Park entrance fees** run about $15 per car, or you purchase a yearly pass for $30. Weather dependent, the road generally opens to uphill traffic at 9am and closes to uphill traffic at 4pm.

The **Wilderness Information Center** (600 East Park Ave., 360/565-3100, www.nps.gov/olym, 7:30am-6pm daily late June-Labor Day; 7:30am-6pm Sun.-Thurs., 7:30am-7pm Fri.-Sat. rest of the year) is located directly behind the Olympic National Park Visitor Center and provides trail and safety information and up-to-date weather reports. It issues camping permits, handles campground reservations (where necessary), and rents animal-proof containers ($3).

★ Lake Crescent

A sparkling sapphire set amid high-forested mountains that seem to touch the sky, Lake Crescent is more than a place of beauty, it is a place of mystery. The cold depths of Lake Crescent and its ancient past have formed many of the myths that surround it. In 1970, surveys estimated the lake depth at around 624 feet, the maximum range of the instruments used, but recent measurements show depths in excess of 1,000 feet, shedding some light on its Loch Ness aura. The lake, named for its sickle shape, is also famous for its Beardslee trout, a 14-pound fish found only at Lake Crescent.

In the lore of the local S'Klallam and Quillieute peoples, Lake Crescent is the site of a conflict between two tribes that ended in destruction when the god

Lake Crescent is known for its brilliant blue waters.

Mountain Storm King (4,534 feet to the east of the lake) broke off part of his head and hurled it at the warriors, killing them all and splitting the lake in two, creating the upper Lake Sutherland.

Getting There

US-101 skirts the southern shore of alluring Lake Crescent, just 20 miles west of Port Angeles. The closest ranger station is Storm King. Accessing Lake Crescent from Hurricane Ridge by car requires driving out of the park and getting back on US-101.

Recreation
Hiking

The 90-foot Marymere Falls is a spectacular marvel, accessed via the **Marymere Falls Trail,** which starts at the Storm King Ranger Station, about 0.2 mile up from Lake Crescent Lodge. A flat path leads over Barnes Creek via footbridge, and from here stairs climb to the falls viewing area (0.85 mile), where the sheer force

of the falls creates a cool, thick mist. A complete two-mile loop can be done by taking the **Crescent Lake Lodge Trail.**

At 2.2 miles one-way, the **Mount Storm King Trail** at the Marymere Falls Trail split takes you to an elevated (over 3,000 feet) view of the lake.

The well-known **Spruce Railroad Trail** (4 miles) is accessed from North Shore Road or Lyre Road at the opposite ends of the lake. The trail follows a World War I rail bed built to extract large Sitka spruce for aircraft, but the war ended prior to its completion. Starting from the Spruce Railroad Trailhead on North Shore Road, the trail eases upward a half-mile to its crest, then descends to the lakeshore to Devil's Punchbowl Bridge. Across the bridge are open views of Mount Storm King rising from the southern shore. Working toward the northern end, the trail passes two old railroad tunnels that are closed to visitors due to dangerous conditions. The journey continues with views of the lake and Aurora Ridge emerging from behind the lodge. Inland, the trail ascends and meets the four-mile trailhead of the west side.

Water Sports

The lake's true depth is ultimately unknown, but its beauty is famous. You can rent a canoe or paddleboat at the **Fairholm General Store** (221121 US-101, 360/928-3020, $9-40) at the west end of the lake. The **Lake Crescent Lodge** (416 Lake Crescent Rd., 360/928-3211, www. lakecrescentlodge.com, $20/hr, $55 for 8-hour day) and **Log Cabin Resort** (Piedmont Rd., off US-101, 360/928-3325, www.olympicnationalparks.com, $20/hr, $55 for 8-hour day) rent kayaks, canoes, and paddleboats and offer guided kayaking tours (1 hour: $35 single, $45 double; 2 hours: $45 single, $60 double). The Lake Crescent Lodge also rents fishing rods (8-hour day: $12 adults, $10 children).

Boat launches are located at the east end. Motorboats are prohibited on the west side, which is reserved for swimmers. Lake Crescent is extremely cold due to its depth. Life jackets and protective clothing are suggested.

Lake Sutherland is warmer as it is shallower and hosts several water sports activities. Swimming is popular, as are sailing, windsurfing, waterskiing, tubing, and Jet Skiing.

East Beach Picnic Area (east end of Lake Crescent) is set on a grassy meadow overlooking Lake Crescent. It's a popular swimming spot with six picnic tables and vault toilets.

Lake Crescent is a catch-and-release recreational lake, with trout and salmon. Lake Sutherland is a premier spot for kokanee sockeye salmon, and cutthroat and rainbow trout. **Bob's Piscatorial Pursuits** (Forks, 866/347-4232, www.piscatorialpursuits.com) offers year-round fishing trips. A Washington punch card is required during salmon-spawning season; fishing regulations vary throughout the park. Always check with the National Park Service for information. Licenses are

available from sporting goods and outdoor supply stores around the peninsula.

Food and Accommodations

Built in 1916, ★ **Lake Crescent Lodge** (416 Lake Crescent Rd., 360/928-3211, www.olympicnationalparks.com, May-Dec., $125 and up) is a rustic lakeside retreat engulfed by hemlock and fir trees with inspiring sunset views. President Franklin D. Roosevelt, who stayed here in 1937, is one of the many guests who have rested at the lodge over the years. Sit on the porch for fine views of the mountains and Lake Crescent, or lounge in front of the big fireplace on a cool evening. The lodge has all sorts of accommodations, including lodge rooms (bath down the hall), cottages (some with fireplaces), and modern motel units. The on-site restaurant, appropriately named **The Lodge** (416 Lake Crescent Rd., 360/928-3211, May-mid-Oct., $12 and up), offers casual lakeside dining for breakfast, lunch, and dinner. Large bay windows look out

Sol Duc Falls

over the lake and feature gorgeous sunset views. Some of the menu favorites are wild salmon, filet mignon, glacier crab melt, grilled turkey sandwich, and an unforgettable clam chowder.

Log Cabin Resort (3183 E. Beach Rd., 360/928-3325, www.olympicnationalparks.com, late May-Sept., $66-161 cabins, $40 RVs), at the northeast end of the lake, is three miles from US-101. Lodging is available in rustic cabins, motel rooms, and waterfront A-frame chalets. Many of the buildings have stood here since the 1920s.

Fairholme Campground (western shore of Lake Crescent, May-Oct., campsites $12/night, plus $15 per vehicle park entry fee) has 88 campsites for tents and 21-foot RVs, and it has a boat launch. Campsites are available on a first-come, first-served basis.

Information and Services
Storm King Ranger Station (360/928-3380) is usually open in summer with information and books for sale, and it has accessible year-round restrooms.

Campgrounds have adjacent picnic areas with tables, limited shelters, and restrooms, but no cooking facilities. Drinking water is available at ranger stations, interpretive centers, and inside the campgrounds. Pets and bicycles are not permitted on trails, except on the Spruce Railroad Trail.

Sol Duc

South of Lake Crescent, the isolated Sol Duc Valley conceals hot springs, waterfalls, and alpine meadows, along with some of the best views of Mount Olympus. Nearly 50 miles of dense forest and rugged terrain separate the upper Soleduck (shimmering waters) from the Pacific Ocean and the high mountain ridges that lie to the north and south. Frequented for its superb fishing, the Sol Duc River is home to several species of salmon and trout.

Getting There
The Sol Duc Road, running southeast off US-101, takes you to Sol Duc, which lies 40 miles west of Port Angeles and 16 miles south of Lake Crescent. The Eagle Ranger Station (open in summer) is the closest National Park Service outpost.

Sights and Recreation
Sol Duc Road leads to the Sol Duc area. Spend the day exploring the nearby trails, then pamper yourself with a massage and fine dining at the resort.

It's important to check with the Olympic National Park Visitor Center on the correct fees and permits necessary. Backcountry wilderness permits are required for mountaineers.

Sol Duc Hot Springs
These bubbling mineral waters are captured in a spa-like outdoor pool area at the **Sol Duc Hot Springs Resort** (12076

Sol Duc Hot Springs Rd., 360/327-3583 or 866/476-5382, www.olympicnational-parks.com, $12.25 adults, $9.25 children 4-12). Relax and soak in the three mineral pools with approximate temperatures of 99°F, 101°F, and 104°F. There is a fresh-water pool, as well. Guests at the resort get free access to the pools, and day-use access is available for non-guests.

★ Sol Duc Falls

From Sol Duc Hot Springs Resort, a one-mile hike through old-growth western hemlocks and Douglas firs leads to well-known **Sol Duc Falls**. Along the way, you'll pass the 70-foot Salmon Cascades, where salmon fight their way upstream in late summer and fall. The falls themselves make for a pretty sight as the river navigates the change in terrain. For a longer stroll with or without your sweetheart, instead of going back the way you came, take the three-mile Lover's Lane Trail along the south side of the river to return to the hot springs.

Fishing

Trout and salmon from nearby streams flow into the Sol Duc River, attracting fishing enthusiasts; fly-fishing is a favorite pastime too. A Washington punch card is required during salmon-spawning season. Fishing regulations vary throughout the park, so always check with the National Park Service for information. Licenses are available from sporting goods and outdoor supply stores around the peninsula.

Food and Accommodations

In addition to the springs, ★ **Sol Duc Hot Springs Resort** (12076 Sol Duc Hot Springs Rd., 360/327-3583 or 866/476-5382, www.olympicnationalparks.com, Apr.-mid-Oct., $173 and up) has a restaurant, grocery store, and gift shop, plus cabins (some with kitchenettes). An RV campground is also available and reservations are advised.

Inside Sol Duc Hot Springs Resort, **The Springs Restaurant** (12076 Sol Duc

Cape Flattery, the northwesternmost point of the contiguous United States

Hot Springs Rd., 360/327-3583, $12 and up) serves Northwest cuisine, and the **Poolside Deli** (360/327-3583, $5-20) has lots of snacks, sandwiches, and cold drinks. There's also an espresso bar for a pick-me-up.

Sol Duc Campground (360/327-3534, $14) is open year-round and has 82 sites right along the river and a short walk away from the hot springs.

Information and Services
Eagle Ranger Station (Sol Duc Rd., 360/327-3534) is usually open in summer. **Sol Duc Hot Springs Resort** (12076 Sol Duc Hot Springs Rd., 360/327-3583 or 866/476-5382, www.olympicnational-parks.com) has a small store with snacks and basic personal items.

The **Fairholm General Store** (221121 US-101, 360/928-3020, www.fairholm-store.com) sells groceries and gasoline, and offers boat rentals (May-mid-Oct.). The store is easily found on the west side

of Lake Crescent. Restroom facilities are also available.

Campgrounds have adjacent picnic areas with tables, limited shelters, and restrooms, but no cooking facilities.

Drinking water is available at ranger stations, interpretive centers, and inside the campgrounds.

Pets and bicycles are not permitted on trails.

◈ WA-113 to WA-112: Neah Bay and Cape Flattery

Off US-101, WA-113 leads to WA-112 and the twin towns of Clallam Bay and Sekiu (SEE-kyoo), which are just a mile apart on the Strait of Juan de Fuca. These two towns offer basic services but not much else. Heading west from Sekiu on WA-112 is one of the most dramatic shoreline drives in Washington: The narrow road winds along cliff faces and past extraordinary views. At the end of the road, in virtual isolation, the 44-square-mile **Makah Indian Reservation** sits on Cape Flattery at the northwesternmost point of the contiguous United States. A **recreation permit** ($10-15 per car) is required to enter the reservation; it can be purchased at the Makah Cultural and Research Center, Makah Marina, Washburn's General Store, or Neah Bay Charter & Tackle.

Sights
In 1970, a powerful storm and the resulting tidal erosion unearthed an ancient Makah fishing village that had long been buried. Thousands of artifacts dating back 1,600-2,000 years were discovered, including harpoons, hooks, baskets, mats, cedar rope, paddles, carvings, and even full longhouse structures. Many of these artifacts are displayed at the **Makah Cultural and Research Center** (WA-112 and 1800 Bayview Ave., 360/645-2711,

www.makah.com, 10am-5pm daily, reservations required, $5 adults, $4 seniors and students). Private tours of the museum and the archaeological site can be arranged.

Recreation

Scenic hiking trails trace the coastline, offering gorgeous views. Head eight miles west along Bayview Avenue for one mile to Cape Flattery Road to access the **Cape Flattery Trail,** one of the most beautiful scenic hikes on the Makah Reservation. A 0.75-mile boardwalk leads down to the rocky coastline with views of the 1858 Cape Flattery Lighthouse on Tatoosh Island. A dump lies along the route, so beware of unpleasant odors especially on a warm summer day. Four observation decks offer breathtaking views of the Olympic Coast National Marine Sanctuary, which harbors a diverse collection of marinelife and wildlife, including over 239 species of birds. The trail continues around the cape in a 16-mile loop, passing a small waterfall on the way back to Neah Bay.

The **Ozette Triangle** is a remarkable day trip that connects the **Cape Alava Trail** to **Sand Point Loop.** Take WA-112 west to Sekiu. The road descends and winds its way toward Lake Ozette. Turn left on the Hoko-Ozette Road and take it to the end. Head to the Ozette Ranger Station, where restrooms and water are available, to reach the trailhead. Take the Cape Alava Trail through hemlock, cedar, and Sitka stands to a bridge. The trail climbs to a crest with views of a long abandoned homestead at Ahlstroms Prairie. At Cape Alava, enjoy views of Cannonball Island and Ozette Island offshore, where you may also see whales. Head south to the circular red-black symbol. To the right, ancient Makah petroglyphs can be seen carved into the large rock, Wedding Rock, depicting the large images of marine mammals. Continue on to Sand Point, then return three miles following the trail through the forest to Lake Ozette along nine-mile Sand Point Loop.

Camping

Stay overnight at **Ozette Campground** (21261 Hoko-Ozette Rd., 360/963-2725, $12-18/night), where tents and RVs are welcome, or head back to Neah Bay and relax in a beachfront cabin. Contact the **Olympic National Park Visitor Center** (3002 Mount Angeles Rd., 360/565-3100, www.nps.gov) for backcountry camping reservations, permits, and trail conditions.

Forks

The westernmost incorporated city in the Lower 48, Forks is the economic center and logging capital of the western Olympic Peninsula—a big handle for this little town with one main drag. Since the spotted-owl controversy began, logging in this area has been severely curtailed on Forest Service lands, and Forks went into something of a depression as loggers searched for alternate means of earning a living. In recent years the town has diversified, emphasizing the clean air, remote location, and abundance of recreational possibilities within a few miles in any direction at Olympic National Park or the Pacific Coast beaches. Tourism here has seen a boost thanks to author Stephanie Meyer, who chose Forks as the setting for her best-selling *Twilight* books.

Sights

The **Forks Timber Museum** (1421 S. Forks Ave./US-101, 360/374-9663, http://forkstimbermuseum.org, 10am-4pm daily mid-Apr.-Oct., free) has historical exhibits that include a steam donkey, a logging camp bunkhouse, old logging equipment, and various pioneer implements. The real surprise is a large 150-year-old canoe that was discovered by loggers in 1990. Out front is a memorial to loggers killed in the woods and a replica of a fire lookout tower.

While there's no dedicated *Twilight* museum for fans of the popular vampire series, the helpful **Forks Chamber of Commerce Visitor Center** (1411 S. Forks Ave., 360/374-2531 or 800/443-6757, www.forkswa.com, 9am-5pm daily in summer, 10am-4pm daily the rest of the year), located next to the timber museum, offers a map of *Twilight* points of interest, including Bella's old Chevy pick-up, for self-guided tours.

Food

Loggers stop for coffee and doughnuts at the **Forks Coffee Shop** (241 S. Forks Ave., 360/374-6769, $4-10), while friendly waitresses serve dependable food three meals a day. **The In Place** (320 S. Forks Ave., 360/374-4004, $6-10) is a good lunch spot, with deli sandwiches and great mushroom bacon burgers. They also serve pasta, steak, and seafood dinners.

Accommodations

Motels and bed-and-breakfasts make up the bulk of places to stay in Forks. **Pacific Inn Motel** (352 S. Forks Ave., 360/374-9400 or 800/235-7344, www.pacificinnmotel.com, from $89 d) offers clean, standard-issue rooms, as well as special red-and-black themed rooms for *Twilight* fans.

Located off South Forks Avenue, **Dew Drop Inn** (100 Fern Hill Rd., 360/374-4055 or 888/433-9376, www.dewdrop-innmotel.com, $94-149) has one- and two-bed rooms, each with a private balcony or patio.

Miller Tree Inn (654 E. Division, 360/374-6806, www.millertreeinn.com, $135-235 d) is a bed-and-breakfast with seven guest rooms (private or shared baths) in a beautiful three-story 1914 homestead set on a shady lot on the edge of town. The back deck has a large hot tub.

Information and Services

In addition to *Twilight* information, the **Forks Chamber of Commerce Visitor**

Center (1411 S. Forks Ave., 360/374-2531 or 800/443-6757, www.forkswa.com, 9am-5pm daily in summer, 10am-4pm daily the rest of the year) is a great resource for other area information.

The **Olympic National Forest and Park Recreation Information Office** (551 N. Forks Ave., 360/374-7566, 8:30am-12:30pm and 1:30pm-5:30pm daily in summer, Mon.-Fri. only the rest of the year) is housed in the transportation building in Forks. Stop here for recreation information, maps, and handouts, and to take a look at the big 3-D model of the Olympic Peninsula.

Bogachiel State Park

Six miles south of Forks on US-101, **Bogachiel State Park** (185983 US-101, 360/374-6356, www.parks.wa.gov) encompasses 123 acres on the usually clear Bogachiel River. (Bogachiel means muddy waters in the language of the local Quileute people.) Enjoy the short nature trail through a rain forest, or swim, paddle, or fish in the river—famous for its summer and winter steelhead, salmon, and trout. The park has **campsites** ($13 for tents, $19 for RV hookups) and is open year-round.

Right on the opposite side of the highway from the park entrance is Undi Road, which leads east five miles (the last two are gravel) to the **Bogachiel River Trailhead.** The trail follows the lush, infrequently visited valley of the Bogachiel River east for two miles through national forest land until reaching the edge of Olympic National Park, where the trail continues all the way up to Seven Lakes Basin (27 miles) or Sol Duc Hot Springs (27 miles). The lower section of trail in the rain forest is a lovely place for a day hike. Mountain bikers are allowed on the trail as far as the edge of the National Park, but it's a pretty soggy ride.

◈ WA-110: La Push and Rialto Beach

A short drive from US-101 via WA-110, Rialto Beach lies across the river from the small Quileute Indian village of La Push. A significant tourist destination, Rialto somehow remains mysteriously desolate. You can walk along the beach for miles without anyone around. Nearby, Mora Campground allows visitors to savor the many discoveries and activities along the seashore, like driftwood and sea stacks that rise from offshore. Low tide reveals wondrous tidepools. Surfers and kayakers love the powerful waves. Nature enthusiasts enjoy watching bald eagles and brown pelicans sail across the sky.

Recreation

Hikers can spend a few hours following the pathway from **First Beach** to **Second Beach** (0.75 mile), where a curious pointed stack resembling a needle can be seen, or spend the day continuing south to **Third Beach** and beyond, along the north end of the Hoh River. The 17-mile trail ends in Oil City, where 11 exploratory oil wells were drilled but abandoned when not much oil was found. Plans for a city dissolved, but the name didn't.

Food and Accommodations

The **Quileute Oceanside Resort** (330 Ocean Front Dr., 360/374-5267, www.quileuteoceanside.com, $63-280) offers several accommodation options from simple cabins to deluxe duplexes. There are also two full hookup RV parks and 20 beach campsites. In mid-July the tribe hosts **Quileute Days** with a traditional fish bake, canoe races, and fireworks.

There are no restaurants, grocery stores, or gas stations at La Push. The closest restaurant is six miles east at **Three Rivers Resort** (7765 La Push Rd.,

Hoh Rain Forest in Olympic National Park

360/374-5300, www.threeriversresortandguideservice.com, 11am-9pm), just outside of Forks.

Information and Services

For a tide chart or local hiking information, the **Mora Ranger Station** (360/374-5460) is staffed daily June-August.

Hoh Rain Forest

Olympic National Park is famous for the lush rain forests that carpet the western flanks of the mountains. The best known and most visited is Hoh Rain Forest, where annual rainfall averages over 10 feet. Vibrant foliage paints the dense landscape in an epic display of enormous Sitka spruce and Douglas fir trees that tower into the sky. Some of the towering conifers are over 200 feet tall and up to 10 feet wide. Mist lingers between the trees and along the banks of streaming rivers. Damp beds of moss

suck up moisture and spread across the ground and onto trees. Lacy ferns carpet the forest floor, and some even survive in the tops of the big-leaf and vine maples. Wandering into the Hoh Rain Forest is an adventure into another world, or so it would seem.

Getting There

One of the park's most famous sights is also one of its most remote. Fourteen miles south of Forks along US-101, the paved Upper Hoh Road heads east 19 miles into the Hoh Rain Forest.

Sights

A revered mountain of mystical creatures, **Mount Olympus** (7,828 ft.) is the centerpiece of the Olympic Peninsula. Though it's not the tallest mountain in western Washington, it does have a majestic allure that makes it a giant among higher peaks. In 1778, the British explorer John Meares said of the mountain, "If that not be the home where dwell the gods, it certainly is beautiful enough to be, and I therefore will call it Mount Olympus." But the mountain already had a name: the Quileute people called it "Oksy."

Mount Olympus is the first peak that storms encounter, resulting in high accumulations of snow and rain. Nestled around Olympus are several glaciers. The largest, Blue Glacier, covers over 5.31 kilometers; the longest, Hoh Glacier, is over 2 miles long. The mountain gets about 12 feet of rain each year along its west side and nearby valleys, which aids the growth of the temperate forest. Along the eastern side is a rain shadow that receives only 25 inches every year, creating a drier climate.

Recreation
Hiking

Three short interpretive trails lead through the lush, spikemoss-draped forests behind the visitors center. A paved wheelchair-accessible **mini-trail** (truly mini at 0.1 mile total) is directly behind the center, and the **Hall of Mosses Trail** offers an easy 0.8-mile loop. **Spruce Nature Trail** covers a 1.25-mile loop that crosses a crystalline spring-fed creek and then touches on the muddy, glacially fed Hoh River.

More adventurous folks can head out on the **Hoh River Trail,** an 18-mile path that ends at Blue Glacier and is used to climb Mount Olympus. Hikers heading into the wilderness need to pick up permits at the visitors center or the **Wilderness Information Center** (3002 Mount Angeles Rd., 360/565-3100, www.nps.gov) in Port Angeles.

Climbing

Mountain and ice climbing is a popular activity around Mount Olympus due to its triple peaks and glaciated surface. In good weather, climbing conditions are spectacular. But due to the heavily crevassed glaciers, winter months are considered very dangerous and weather changes occur without warning with heavy fog making it difficult to navigate. Climbing the mountain requires experience and tools such as rope, ice axe, crevasse rescue gear, and crampons. The most ventured trail to the dome of the mountain is a flat 13-mile trail along the Hoh River. Massive trees cluster together, some in diameter of 20 feet. The trail ascends to Glacier Meadows, where you can begin the ascent across Blue Glacier and onward to the summit. Guided expeditions are available through **Mountain Madness** (3018 SW Charlestown St., Seattle, 206/937-8389, www.mountainmadness. com, $950 and up).

Permits are required and group climbers must camp at designated group camping sites. Information on trailhead shuttles, camping, and backcountry permits are available at the **Wilderness Information Center** (3002 Mount Angeles Rd., Port Angeles, 360/565-3100, www.nps.gov).

Accommodations

Not far away from the visitors center, the **Hoh Rain Forest Campground** (360/452-4501, www.nps.gov, open year-round, $12/night) has 88 forested campsites nestled in the old-growth rain forest along Hoh River. Running water, toilets, and dump station are available.

There are **no restaurants or food options** in the Hoh Rain Forest area. Forks, about 30 miles away or a one-hour drive, offers more options for accommodations and food.

Information and Services

The **Hoh Rain Forest Visitor Center** (Upper Hoh Rd., 360/374-6925, 9am-7pm daily July-Aug., 9am-4pm Fri.-Tues. Apr.-June) offers interpretive exhibits and summertime guided walks and campfire programs. Stop by for brochures, information, books, and educational exhibits on the life of the forest and the climate.

Ruby Beach and Kalaloch

US-101 rejoins the coast at Ruby Beach, just south of the mouth of the Hoh River, and you quickly become aware that this part of Washington's coastline—from the state's northwest corner at Neah Bay to the Quinault Reservation—is a picture of how the Pacific Coast looks in brochures and calendar photos: pristine beaches, pounding waves, trees sculpted by relentless sea breezes.

A very popular trail leads down to beautiful sandy shoreline dotted with red pebbles (sadly not actual rubies), with piles of driftwood and the flat top of **Destruction Island** several miles offshore. The island is capped by a 94-foot lighthouse.

South of Ruby Beach, the highway cruises along the bluff, with five more trails dropping to shoreline beaches, creatively named Beach 6, Beach 5, and so on, to Beach 1. A massive western red cedar tree stands just off the highway near Beach 6.

Accommodations and Camping

Nine miles south of Ruby Beach, the ★ **Kalaloch Lodge** (157151 US-101, 360/962-2271, www.thekalalochlodge. com, $210-350 d) consists of a main lodge, cabins, and a motel. The only TV is in the common area sitting room. Some of the cabins have kitchens and offer waterside views. Make reservations far ahead for the nicest rooms or the bluff cabins; a year ahead of time is recommended for peak season (July-Aug.). The lodge also has a café, gift shop, and lounge. The on-site **Creekside Restaurant** (157151 US-101, 866/662-9928, www.thekalalochlodge.com, $6-32) has a great menu selection that ranges from French toast and omelets to burgers and king salmon.

The National Park Service's **Kalaloch Campground** (open year-round, $14-18) sits on a bluff overlooking the beach. It is also the only Olympic National Park campground that takes reservations for individual campsites (for summer only).

Information and Services

Across from the lodge is the Park Service's **Kalaloch Visitor Information Center** (360/962-2283, daily June-Sept.), where you'll find natural history books, maps, pamphlets, and tide charts.

Lake Quinault

Surrounded by steep mountains and dense rain forest, Lake Quinault is bordered on the northwest by Olympic National Park and on the southeast by Olympic National Forest; the lake itself and land to the southeast are part of the Quinault Reservation and subject to Quinault regulations. Located at the southwestern edge of Olympic National Park, Lake Quinault is a hub of outdoor activity during the summer months. This very scenic, tree-rimmed lake is surrounded by cozy lodges, and hiking trails provide a chance to get a taste of the rain forest that once covered vast stretches of the Olympic Peninsula.

The Quinault Rain Forest is one of three major rain forests that survive on the Peninsula. Here the annual average rainfall is 167 inches, resulting in enormous trees, lush vegetation, and moss-carpeted buildings. During the rainy winter months, bring your heavy rain gear and rubber boots, not just a nylon poncho and running shoes. If you're prepared, a hike in the rain provides a great chance to see this soggy and verdant place at its truest. July and August are the driest months, but even then it rains an average of three inches. Typical Decembers see 22 inches of precipitation.

Getting There

US-101 borders Lake Quinault, which is located approximately 70 miles south of Forks and 35 miles south of Kalaloch. To reach the Quinault Rain Forest Ranger Station, take the North Shore Road turnoff; to reach the U.S. Forest Services Ranger Station, take the South Shore Road turnoff.

Recreation
Hiking

The Quinault area is a hiker's paradise, with trails for all abilities snaking through a diversity of terrain. A good hike for those traveling with small children begins at North Fork Campground, following the Three Lakes Trail for the first mile to **Irely Lake.** The aptly named half-mile **Maple Glade Rain Forest Trail** begins at the Park Service's Quinault Rain Forest Ranger Station on North Fork Road and traverses a glade of maples.

Another easy jaunt is the **Cascading Terraces Trail,** a one-mile loop that begins at the Graves Creek Campground on the South Shore Road. From the same starting point, the **Enchanted Valley Trail** takes you through a wonderful rain forest along the South Fork of the Quinault River. Day hikers often go as far as Pony Bridge, 2.5 miles each way, but more ambitious folks can continue to Dosewallips, a one-way distance of 28 miles.

Food and Accommodations

Built in 1926 over a period of just 10 weeks, the rambling ★ **Lake Quinault Lodge** (345 S. Shore Rd., 360/288-2900 or 800/562-6672, www.olympicnationalparks.com, $109 and up) occupies a magnificent setting of grassy lawns bordering Lake Quinault. This is how a lodge should look, with a darkly regal interior, and a big central fireplace surrounded by comfortable couches and tables. Accommodations include a variety of rooms in the main lodge and in newer buildings nearby and include an indoor pool and sauna. Some of the rooms have kitchenettes. Call two months ahead to be sure of space in mid-summer. The **Roosevelt Dining Room** (345 S. Shore Rd., 360/288-2900, $8-30) in the lodge offers panoramic views of the mountains and lake, and a variety of menu items that will please, especially their homemade marionberry cobbler. Get groceries at the **Mercantile** (352 S. Shore Rd.) across the road, which also sells pizzas, burgers, milkshakes, espresso, and sandwiches.

Rain Forest Resort Village (S. Shore Rd., 360/288-2535 or 800/255-6936, www.rainforestresort.com, $119-245) has cabins with fireplaces (and some with kitchens). The resort also has a good **restaurant and lounge,** a general store, laundry, RV hookups, and canoe rentals. The world's largest Sitka spruce is on the resort grounds. This thousand-year-old behemoth is more than 19 feet in diameter and 191 feet tall.

Camping

Choose from a number of different public campgrounds in the Quinault Lake area. The Forest Service maintains three campgrounds on the south shore of Lake Quinault: **Falls Creek** (late

May-mid-Sept., $25, water); **Gatton Creek** (late May-mid-Sept., $20, walk-in only, no water); and **Willaby** (mid-Apr.-mid-Nov., $25, water), which has a boat ramp.

Olympic National Park campgrounds are more scattered. The spacious 30-site **Graves Creek** (near the end of S. Shore Rd., 360/565-3131, www.nps.gov, open year-round, $12) is 15 miles from the US-101 turnoff. The primitive **North Fork Campground** (end of N. Shore Rd., mid-May-late Sept., $10) does not have running water and is not recommended for RVs.

Park RVs at the private **Rain Forest Village Resort** (S. Shore Rd., 360/288-2535 or 800/255-6936, www.rainforestresort.com, $35), the only campground with showers.

Information and Services

The **U.S. Forest Services Ranger Station** (360/288-2525, daily Memorial Day-Labor Day, Mon.-Fri. the rest of the year) is next door to Quinault Lodge on the south side of the lake. They have informative handouts and offer guided nature walks and talks at the lodge in the summer.

Stop by the Olympic National Park's **Quinault Rain Forest Ranger Station** (5.5 miles up N. Fork Rd., Thurs.-Mon. June-Labor Day (funding dependent), open intermittently the rest of the year) for brochures, maps, and information on the park. The area around the station is a good place to see Roosevelt elk, especially in early summer and after September.

◆WA-109 to WA-115: Ocean Shores

Heading west from US-101, WA-109 hooks around the northern edge of North Bay, winding up at a forested bluff. There, at the southern tip of Lang Lake, WA-115 (milepost 16) continues south to Ocean Shores. This six-mile stretch of wide, sandy beaches backed by grassy dunes attracts resort-goers to build sandcastles, fly kites, surf, and, of course, sunbathe.

Recreation

Explore the beach by horseback with a friendly guide from **Honey Pearl Ranch Horseback Riding** (32 Humptulips Valley Rd., 360/987-2150, www.honeypearl. com, $20/hr, 10am-6pm daily in summer, seasonal hours rest of the year). If the thought of sand between your toes doesn't appeal to you, put on a pair of golf shoes at **Ocean Shores Golf Course** (500 Canal Dr. NE, 360/289-3357, www. oceanshoresgolf.com), an 18-hole championship course.

Food and Accommodations

The ★ **Quinault Beach Resort and Casino** (78 WA-115, 360/289-9466 or 888/461-2214, www.quinaultbeachresort. com, $179 d, $349-549 suites) offers spacious rooms with oceanfront views and has a full-service spa and fine dining. Get a good, affordable meal at **Alec's by the Sea** (131 E. Chance A La Mer NE, 360/289-4026, 4pm-9pm daily, $12-26). They have a big menu selection with great burgers, grilled steaks, pasta, salads, and steamed clams. Get a full kitchen suite at **Canterbury Inn** (643 Ocean Shores Blvd. NW, 360/289-3317, www.canterburyinn. com, $121 and up).

Information

For local information, **Ocean Shores Chamber of Commerce Visitor Information Center** (120-B W. Chance A La Mer, 360/289-2451, www.oceanshores. org, 9am-5pm Mon.-Fri., 10am-4pm Sat.-Sun.) provides brochures for all sorts of local activities, including area maps.

Grays Harbor: Aberdeen and Hoquiam

Aberdeen and Hoquiam (HO-qwee-um) are twin cities on the easterly tip of Grays Harbor, separated by the Hoquiam River.

Aberdeen is the larger of the two, with a population of 16,000, almost double the 9,000 of Hoquiam. The population is clustered along the eastern end of Grays Harbor, where the rivers meet the harbor.

Grays Harbor Historical Seaport (813 E. Heron St., 360/352-8611, www.historicalseaport.com) celebrates the area's maritime past with its full-scale replica of *Lady Washington*, the first American ship to sail around South America to reach the west coast of North America. When not visiting other ports, it and the *Hawaiian Chieftan*, which also calls Aberdeen home, are open for tours (free or $3 donation) and excellent 2-3-hour sailing trips ($75).

The 26-room mansion of the son of a wealthy lumber magnate is now the **Polson Museum** (1611 Riverside Ave., 360/533-5862, www.polsonmuseum.org, 11am-4pm Wed.-Sat., noon-4pm Sun., $4) in Hoquiam. The museum houses all sorts of memorabilia: a magnificent old grandfather clock, a fun model railroad, a model of an old logging camp, a two-man chainsaw, and even an old boxing bag. The adjacent park holds a rose garden, historic logging equipment, and a blacksmith shop.

➤ WA-105: Westport and Tokeland

Westport (pop. 2,000) once called itself "The Salmon Capital of the World," and it remains one of the most active ports in Washington. Charter services and commercial fishing and crabbing boats line the waterfront alongside the expected shops selling saltwater taffy, kites, and souvenir kitsch. Chain-smoking fishermen drive beat-up old pickups through town, and local life revolves around the crab cannery and seafood markets. This area is popular for sportfishing, but also offers long beaches, good surfing, and reasonably priced lodging.

Sights and Recreation

Two towers overlook the water. A tall observation tower provides a fine vantage point to view freighter activity, scenery, sunsets, or an occasional whale, while a lower ramp tower looks into the marina. In front of this is a small memorial to fishermen lost at sea.

Open for day-use only, **Westhaven State Park** (2700 Jetty Haul Rd., 360/268-9717, www.parks.wa.gov), on WA-105 just north of Westport, is popular with rock hounds, beachcombers, and divers. Surfers and sea kayakers find some of the most consistent waves in Washington here.

Westport Light State Park (1595 Ocean Ave., 360/268-9717, www.parks.wa.gov), about a mile south of Westhaven off WA-105 (continue straight when WA-105 goes left), is accessible on foot from Westhaven via a 1.3-mile paved boardwalk. This is another day-use park good for kite-flying, rock-hounding, and fishing for ocean perch, but there is no camping. The classic **lighthouse** inside the park—tallest on the West Coast—was built in 1898 and is visible from an observation platform on Ocean Avenue. The building is closed to the public. The lighthouse originally stood much closer to the water, but the accretion of sand has pushed the beachfront seaward.

On WA-105, two miles south of Westport, **Twin Harbors State Park** (3120 WA-105, 360/268-9717, www.parks.wa.gov, open year-round for day-use) has campsites, a 0.75-mile sand dune nature trail, picnic areas, and a playground. This is one of the most popular oceanside campgrounds, especially when razor clam harvesting is allowed (usually Mar. and Oct.).

Take a charter boat to find the best **fishing,** not to mention having your fish cleaned and ready to cook by the time you get back to shore. Wander along Westhaven Drive to check out the various charter companies, or get a listing of boats from the visitors center.

The charter services all charge about the same amount, so when you call for reservations be sure to check whether the price includes bait and tackle, cleaning, and sales tax. Note, however, that most departures are at the frightfully early hour of 6am, with a return around 3:30pm.

Many of the charter operators also provide **whale-watching trips** (Mar.-May) when the gray whales are heading north from their winter quarters off Baja California. The passenger ferry to Ocean Shores is an inexpensive way to watch for whales that periodically wander into Grays Harbor.

Food and Accommodations

Harbor Resort Motel (871 Neddie Rose Dr., 360/268-0169, www.harborresort.com, $89-169) has rooms with kitchenettes and cottages sleeping up to five. The cottages have private decks over the water. All rooms are decorated with antique furniture and nautical memorabilia. Many rooms have views over the harbor and marina.

In the tiny town of Tokeland, about 16 miles south of Westport off WA-105, is the **Tokeland Hotel** (100 Hotel Rd. at Kindred Rd., 360/267-7006, www.tokelandhotel.com, $65). Built in 1885, it's said to be the oldest resort hotel in Washington and is now on the National Register of Historic Places. The spacious front lawn, brick fireplace, and jigsaw puzzles provide an air of relaxation.

Because of the early morning departure of fishing charters, several local Westport cafés are already open at 5am, including the very popular café at the **Inn of the Westwind** (2119 N. Nyhus, 360/268-0677).

Buy freshly shucked oysters to go from **Brady's Oysters** (3714 Oyster Pl. E., 360/268-0077). They were the first to grow oysters on suspended lines, a method that many claim produces a more delicately flavored oyster.

Information

Westport-Grayland Chamber of Commerce Visitors Center (2985 N. Montesano St., 360/268-9422 or 800/345-6223, www.westportgrayland-chamber. org) provides maps, brochures, and tour and charter information.

Willapa Bay: Raymond and South Bend

East and south from Tokeland, Washington's coastline wraps around Willapa Bay, a 25-mile-long inlet protected by the Long Beach Peninsula. It is believed to be the cleanest and least developed estuary on the West Coast of the Lower 48 states. Locals posit that these waters produce the best-tasting oysters in the nation (a claim disputed by folks in Grays Harbor). WA-105 and US-101 skirt Willapa's scenic marshy shoreline, and tree farms carpet the surrounding hills.

From Aberdeen, US-101 continues south to the town of Raymond. There's not a lot to see, but the **Dennis Company** (146 5th St., 360/942-2427, www.denniscompany.com), a big, old-fashioned dry goods store, is worth a stop. In addition to hardware, clothing, and sporting goods, the store has many historic photos. A mural—said to be the largest in Washington—covering one wall of the building depicts the early days of logging. Across the street is a display of antique logging and farm equipment. Hikers and cyclists will enjoy the 3.5-mile **Rails to Trails** paved path that follows the river from Raymond to South Bend.

Just four miles west of Raymond, South Bend calls itself "The Oyster Capital of the West." Follow the signs up the hill to the 1910 **Pacific County Courthouse.** This "gilded palace of reckless extravagance" as it was called, was built in 1910 at the then-extravagant cost of $132,000. The immense stainedglass dome and mosaic-tile flooring are worth a look, but not everything is as it appears:

the marble columns are actually concrete painted to look like marble. A county jail inmate painted the columns and the decorative panels inside. The courthouse's grounds—complete with a stocked duck pond—offer views of the hills and the town below.

Long Beach Peninsula

The Long Beach Peninsula is a 28-mile-long strip of sand that locals call the "World's Longest Beach." Whether or not that claim is technically true, this is one *very* long stretch of sand, and a favorite getaway for folks from Seattle and Portland.

US-101 hits the southern end of the Long Beach Peninsula and junctions with WA-103 (a.k.a., Pacific Hwy.), which climbs north to Leadbetter Point State Park at the tip of the peninsula. From south to north, the settlements on the peninsula are Ilwaco, Seaview, the town of Long Beach, Klipsan Beach, and Ocean Park on the Pacific Ocean side. On the Willapa Bay side are Nahcotta and Oysterville.

Sights and Recreation

Contrary to expectations, the 28 miles of sandy beach on Long Beach Peninsula are not safe for swimming. Not only are there dangerous undertows and riptides, but rogue waves can occur, and there are no lifeguards. For kite enthusiasts, the beach at **Long Beach** is a delight. The walkable downtown offers little shops and souvenir joints.

It may be campy, but you definitely don't want to miss **Marsh's Free Museum** (409 Pacific Ave., 360/642-2188, www. marshfreemuseum.com), a huge souvenir shop in downtown Long Beach. Inside is a delightful collection of the tasteless and bizarre, much of it from old amusement parks, traveling shows, and attics. You'll find an impressive collection of glass fishing balls, the world's largest frying pan, a vampire bat skeleton, and a two-headed calf. Drop a nickel for a flapper-era peep show, pay a dime to test your passion factor on the "throne of love." And don't miss "Jake the Alligator Man," stuck in a back corner inside a glass aquarium.

The northern tip of Long Beach Peninsula is capped by two publicly owned natural areas. **Leadbetter Point State Park** (360/642-3078) has a 1.5-mile trail through the evergreen forest, connecting its two parking lots. From the north lot, you can enter **Willapa National Wildlife Refuge** and walk through stunted lodgepole pine forests to beachgrass-covered sand dunes along the Pacific Ocean.

This area is also a very important sanctuary for waterfowl, particularly during spring and fall migrations. Bird-watchers will see thousands (and sometimes hundreds of thousands) of black brant, Canada geese, dunlin, plover, sandpipers, and other birds in the marshes and beaches during these times. The northern end of Willapa National Wildlife Refuge is closed to all entry April-August to protect the threatened snowy plover that nests on the dunes here. No fires or camping are allowed.

Accommodations

Friendly with a funky sense of nostalgia, Seaview's **Sou'wester Lodge** (3728 J Pl., 360/642-2542, www.souwesterlodge. com, $95-138) is an offbeat haven for those who appreciate a place with simple comforts. The accommodations include rooms in the stately three-story lodge built in 1892 as a summer estate by Henry Winslow Corbett, a wealthy timber baron, banker, and U.S. senator from Oregon. Outside are beach cottages and even a hodgepodge of 1950s-era trailers. Tent and RV space are also available.

Seaview's acclaimed **Shelburne Inn** (4415 Pacific Way, 360/642-2442 or 800/466-1896, www.theshelburneinn.com, $139-199) is an elegant 1896 Victorian

building. The oldest continuously used lodging place in Washington, the inn is packed with tasteful antiques, stainedglass windows (from an old English church), and original artwork, but no televisions. A full country breakfast is included; for many, it's the highlight of their stay. Beware of the ghost who is rumored to wander the third floor on some nights.

Information

Get information at the **Long Beach Peninsula Visitors Bureau** (3914 Pacific Way, Seaview, 360/642-2400 or 800/451-2542, www.funbeach.com) at the junction of US-101 and WA-103.

◆ WA-100: Cape Disappointment State Park

Located 2.5 miles southwest of Ilwaco on Washington's southernmost point, **Cape Disappointment State Park** (244 Robert Gray Dr., Ilwaco, 360/642-3078, www. parks.wa.gov) is the peninsula's most scenic state park. The name originated in 1788, when British fur trader John Meares was searching for the fabled Northwest Passage. He had heard tales of an enormous river near here from a Spaniard, Bruno Heceta, who had noted it in 1775. Meares failed to find the river, hence the disappointment that gives the cape its name.

In the 1,882-acre park, you'll find a museum dedicated to Lewis and Clark, century-old military fortifications, historic lighthouses, old-growth forests, white beaches, and dramatic vistas across the mouth of the Columbia River. There are also excellent **campsites** (reservations 888/226-7688, $12-31 tents, $30-42 RVs).

The must-see **Lewis and Clark Interpretive Center** (360/642-3029, www. parks.wa.gov, 10am-5pm daily Apr.-Oct., 10am-5pm Wed.-Sun. Nov.-Mar., $5) is a fascinating introduction to the duo's historic 1804-1806 expedition. Exhibits detail

The Discovery Trail

The Discovery Trail (17 miles round-trip) on the Long Beach Peninsula traces the footsteps of the Lewis and Clark expedition after their West Coast arrival in 1805. The trail joins the towns of Long Beach on the north end of the peninsula and Ilwaco, near the mouth of the Columbia River to the south. Many bike and hike the trail to enjoy its sandy dunes, tall grasses, and marshes filled with dragonflies. Migrating trumpeter swans draw birdwatchers. Wooden boardwalks provide elevated views of migrating gray whales in spring and fall.

The trail's interpretive markers provide an opportunity to appreciate both the area's beauty and its historic significance.

"Clark's Tree," a bronze sculpture by Stanley Wanlass, commemorating the pine tree that Clark inscribed with the words, "William Clark. Nov. 19, 1805. By land from the U. States," stands beside the shore. Another sculpture appears two miles along the trail where a basalt monolith is inscribed with excerpts from Clark's journal. A 10-foot metal sturgeon, created by artist Jim Demetro, lies at the foot of a life-sized Clark, who gazes downward.

The trail does not continue to Cape Disappointment or to the Lewis and Clark Interpretive Center, but it is worth a side trip to gain a better perspective of the expedition. The Discovery Trail reaches its end at the Port of Ilwaco.

their trip up the Missouri River, over the Rockies, and then down the Columbia River. You'll learn about the various participants, the unusual air gun they used to impress local indigenous people, how they constructed dugout canoes, and the everyday experiences in their winter camp at Fort Clatsop. Expansive windows look out on Cape Disappointment Lighthouse, the Columbia River, and the mighty Pacific. You're certain to see ships plying the waters offshore.

Cape Disappointment Lighthouse is the Northwest's oldest, built in 1856. It offers great vistas across the mouth of the Columbia. Follow the quarter-mile trail from the interpretive center or a steep quarter-mile path from the Coast Guard Station to reach it.

More than 230 ships were wrecked or sunk on the Columbia bar before jetties were constructed to control the sand. The longest of these, **North Jetty,** reaches a half-mile out from the end of the cape and is a popular place to fish for salmon, rock cod, perch, and sea bass. Although the jetties succeeded in stabilizing the shifting Columbia bar, they also caused sand dunes to accumulate north of here and worsened an undertow that makes for dangerous swimming conditions.

Tiny **Waikiki Beach** is a favorite local spot for picnics and swimming in the summer (but no lifeguard). You can follow a trail uphill from Waikiki to the Lewis and Clark Interpretive Center, and then on to Cape Disappointment Lighthouse.

Oregon Coast

A myriad of dramatic scenery dominates the shores of Oregon, making it one of the most photographed coastlines in the country.

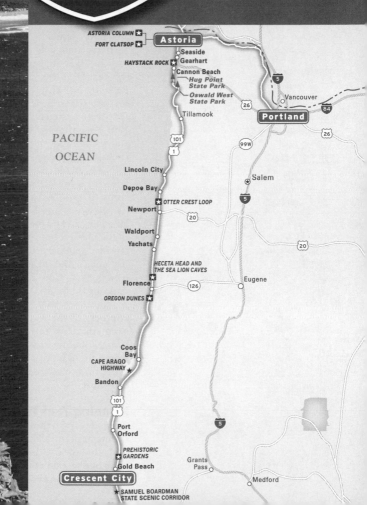

ASTORIA COLUMN ★
FORT CLATSOP ★
Astoria
Seaside
HAYSTACK ROCK ★ Gearhart
Cannon Beach
Hug Point State Park
Oswald West State Park
Tillamook
Vancouver
5
26
Portland
PACIFIC OCEAN
101
1
99W
26
Lincoln City
Salem
Depoe Bay
★ OTTER CREST LOOP
Newport
5
20
Waldport
Yachats
20
HECETA HEAD AND THE SEA LION CAVES
Florence
126
Eugene
OREGON DUNES ★
Coos Bay
CAPE ARAGO HIGHWAY ★
Bandon
101
1
5
Port Orford
PREHISTORIC GARDENS ★
Grants Pass
Gold Beach
Medford
Crescent City
★ SAMUEL BOARDMAN STATE SCENIC CORRIDOR

Coastal Oregon

WASHINGTON

PACIFIC OCEAN

Willapa Bay
Raymond
Chehalis
101
6
5
Castle Rock
Astoria
4
Columbia
Longview
30
River
Seaside
Gearhart
ASTORIA COLUMN
HAYSTOCK ROCK
FORT CLATSOP
Hug Point State Park
Cannon Beach
Oswald West State Park
26
30
Cape Falcon
6
Tillamook Bay
PORTLAND
Tillamook
Cape Lookout
Siuslaw National Forest
Neskowin
18
Lincoln City
SALEM
Depoe Bay
Willamette River
5
OTTER CREST LOOP
Newport
20
Albany
Waldport
101
Corvallis
Yachats
Siuslaw National Forest
Fern Ridge Lake
Cape Perpetua
HECETA HEAD AND THE SEA LION CAVES
126
Florence
Eugene
OREGON DUNES
Reedsport
Winchester Bay
Umpqua National Forest
North Bend
Coos Bay
Charleston
Coos Bay
CAPE ARAGO HIGHWAY
Bandon
42
Roseburg
Cape Blanco
101
Port Orford
Rogue River
PREHISTORIC GARDENS
Siskiyou National Forest
Gold Beach
Grants Pass
SAMUEL BOARDMAN STATE SCENIC CORRIDOR
Medford
Brookings
199
Ashland
Klamath National Forest
Crescent City
Redwood National Park
Yreka
CALIFORNIA

0   20 mi
0   20 km

© AVALON TRAVEL

These spirited towns and historic villages are gateways to wind-swept beaches, obscure sand dunes, massive rock arches, and towering sea cliffs—all sheathed in evergreen.

Oregon's North Coast stretches from the swift-flowing Columbia River at Astoria, one of the oldest American settlements west of the Rockies, to the rich dairy lands of Tillamook County. Scattered among the scenes of ship crossings and grazing cows are fragments of the past from the ruins of the famous *Peter Iredale* shipwreck to the replica of Fort Clatsop, where the Corps of Discovery waited out the harsh winter of 1805. Beachfront villages welcome weekend visitors and vacationers with unique shops, cafés, and galleries.

The Central Coast spans 60 miles from Lincoln City to Yachats, with stops in family-friendly beach towns like Newport and Florence in between. Heceta Head and the Sea Lion Caves lure in the masses, but you can still find less crowded spots, especially along the shifting sands of the Oregon Dunes, which extend down to Coos Bay.

Along the South Coast, stunning scenery continues from one dramatic cape to another, all the way through the most dramatic drive in the state, along the Samuel Boardman State Scenic Corridor. Along the way, you'll encounter everything from untamed rivers to life-sized dinosaurs.

Planning Your Time

A five-day trip will allow you to stop at all the major points of interest. Another option is to take five days to thoroughly explore one section of the coast: the North Coast, Astoria to Pacific City; the Central

Highlights

★ **Astoria Column:**
Climbing its 164 steps offers
views from the Cascades
south to Tillamook Head
(page 102).

★ **Fort Clatsop:** The centerpiece of Lewis and Clark
National Historical Park is a
reconstruction of the explorers' encampment during the
grueling winter of 1805-1806
(page 108).

★ **Haystack Rock:** This
icon of the Oregon coast

attracts seabirds, marinelife,
and photo-happy road-
trippers (page 109).

★ **Otter Crest Loop:**
This scenic drive on Cape
Foulweather climaxes with
the churning surf of the
Devil's Punchbowl (page
119).

★ **Heceta Head and the
Sea Lion Caves:** At 150 feet
above the ocean, a photogenic lighthouse stands watch

over the sea lion habitat
below (page 125).

★ **Oregon Dunes:** The
artistry of these crests of
sand—some as high as
500 feet—inspired Frank
Herbert's iconic sci-fi novel
(page 130).

★ **Prehistoric Gardens:** A
collection of dinosaur sculptures stand frozen in time at
this roadside attraction (page
138).

Coast, Lincoln City to Florence; or the South Coast, Reedsport to Brookings.

Although all towns along the coastline offer lodging, food, and fuel, larger towns and resort destinations such as Astoria, Cannon Beach, Newport, Florence, and Bandon have more travel-friendly options.

The Pacific Coast Highway through Oregon is well maintained. Numerous twists and sharp turns hugging the edges of high cliffs provide phenomenal views and treacherous driving. Allow extra time to safely navigate the roadway.

Getting There
Car
Interstate-5 (I-5), the major north-south artery of the West Coast, connects Oregon to Washington in the north and California in the south. The most viable highway for inbound travelers from the east is I-84, connecting Oregon to Idaho. I-84 extends west all the way to Portland.

The great Columbia River is the border between Oregon and Washington, linked together by the Astoria-Megler Bridge in the North Coast town of Astoria, and by the I-5 Bridge in Portland.

The Central Coast can be approached from Eugene via OR-126, which travels east to the seaside town of Florence.

The South Coast is easily accessed from Medford via US-199 south. The highway dips into Northern California and then curves up to the Oregon coast town of Brookings.

Air
Two international airports provide the main entry to the state. **Portland International** (PDX, 7000 NE Airport Way, 877/739-4636, www.pdx.com) offers regular nonstop flights. The other option is Seattle's **Seattle-Tacoma International Airport** (SEA, 800/544-1965 or 206/787-5388, www.portseattle.org/seatac), which is only a 2.5-hour drive from Portland, over the Washington border.

A few smaller regional airports offer limited domestic service. **Eugene** (EUG, 28801 Douglas Dr., 541/954-8344, www.eugene-or.gov), also known as Mahlon Sweet Field, provides service to a variety of metropolitan cities. Tiny **Southwest**

Best Hotels

★ **Hotel Vintage Plaza:** This landmark Portland hotel blends historic significance with modern-day elegance (page 101).

★ **The Cannery Pier Hotel:** Astoria's best hotel extends out onto the Columbia River for incomparable views (page 107).

★ **Stephanie Inn:** This enchanting Cannon Beach hotel is great for a romantic getaway (page 112).

★ **Sylvia Beach Hotel:** The literary decor of this Newport hotel, with rooms dedicated to authors like Jane Austen,

makes it perfect for curling up with a good book (page 123).

★ **Landmark Inn:** The hilltop location of this hotel in Florence not only affords it great views but also proximity to restaurants and shopping (page 129).

★ **Edwin K. B&B:** This elegant 1914 home now hosts guests and treats them to five-course breakfasts (page 129).

★ **Bandon Dunes Golf Resort:** This resort offers serenity amid the sand dunes and world-class golf greens (page 136).

Oregon Regional Airport/North Bend (OTH, 1100 Airport Ln., www.flyoth. com) is the gateway to the coast with limited flights to Portland and San Francisco. **Rogue Valley International/ Medford Airport** (1000 Terminal Loop Pkwy., 541/772-8068, www.jackson-countyor.org/airport) is the southern-most Oregon stop, located in Medford.

Train
Amtrak Coast Starlight (800 NW 6th Ave., 800/872-7245 or 503/273-4860, www.amtrak.com) train connects Portland with Seattle, San Francisco, Los Angeles, and San Diego. Amtrak also runs the **Cascade Line** (800/872-7245, www.amtrakcascades.com), which runs between Eugene, Oregon, and Vancouver, British Columbia, with stops in Portland and Seattle. International visitors can buy an unlimited travel USA Rail Pass, good for 15, 30, or 45 days.

Bus
Greyhound (550 NW 6th Ave., 800/231-2222 or 503/243-2361) buses provide service nationwide, and often work in tandem with Amtrak. Stations are located in downtown areas.

The BoltBus (648 SW Salmon St., 877/265-8287, www.boltbus.com) is the cheapest way to travel south from Vancouver, British Columbia, with stops in Seattle, Portland, and Eugene.

Fuel and Services
All **gas stations** in Oregon are **full service;** just pull up to a pump and an attendant will fill your tank for you. Oregon makes the top 10 list of most expensive states for gasoline—so expect to pay a little more.

There are 85 parks along US-101 with public facilities, rest stops (some have coffee), and roadside pullouts.

To receive reports on **road conditions,** call **511.** If your phone carrier does not support 511, call toll-free 800/977-6368.

For **emergency assistance** and services, call **911.**

Portland

Oregon's largest city is located inland from the coast, where the Willamette and Columbia Rivers meet.

If ever a city was obsessed with green spaces and trees, it's Portland! Its mountainous backdrop combined with the city's many parks and ecofriendly attitude have made it a hub for green thinking—a big change from the era when it was known as "Stumptown," a nickname earned by the hundreds of fir stumps

Best Restaurants

★ **Mother's Bistro & Bar:** There's nothing like a home-style meal at this Portland favorite (page 95).

★ **T Paul's Supper Club:** This Astoria hot spot is easygoing but a little bit swanky (page 105).

★ **Cannon Beach Café:** This Parisian-style eatery is the place for a fine meal in Cannon Beach (page 110).

★ **The Nelscott Café:** This old-school diner in Lincoln City does burgers right (page 116).

★ **Newport Café:** It's a reliable family restaurant with great breakfasts (page 122).

★ **Waterfront Depot:** Located in an old train station, this fine dining establishment in Florence has charm to spare (page 128).

left by loggers in the mid-19th century. Though railroad tracks and other heavy industrial remnants are still visible around town, Portland's riverfront park and numerous winding pathways keep the city livable.

This mini-metropolis values art, nature, and food—not always in that order. There's no shortage of culinary delights, fabulous brunch spots, award-winning microbrews, and coffee that rivals Seattle's sacred beans. Portland also has more movie theaters, restaurants, microbreweries, and bookstores per capita than any other U.S. city.

Getting There and Around
Air
Portland International (PDX) (7000 NE Airport Way, 877/739-4636, www.pdx. com) is located within 10 miles of downtown. The **MAX Light Rail system** connects to downtown; purchase your ticket from the kiosks located on the airport station platform and take the red line.

Public Transit
Getting around spirited Portland is a breeze thanks to an efficient, connected, multi-transportation system. **TriMet** (503/238-7433, www.trimet.org) serves most of the metro area with bus ($1 for 2 hours, $5 all day) and light-rail lines (every 15 minutes 5am-midnight daily, $2.50 adults, $1 seniors), which also connect with the **Portland Streetcar** (503/823-2900, www.port-landstreetcar.org).

Parking
SmartPark ($1.60/hr, $7 for 4 hours, rates subject to change) operates the most affordable parking garages in the city. Find them downtown at SW 10th and Yamhill, SW 4th and Yamhill, SW 3rd and Alder, SW 1st and Jefferson, and NW Naito and Davis.

Driving to the Coast
To get to the Oregon coast from Portland, take I-405 North from West

downtown Portland

Burnside Street to I-5 North; exit 36 connects with US-30 West. Route 30 follows the trail taken by the Lewis and Clark expedition. A two-lane road replaces the four-lane highway after about 25 miles, passing through sawmill towns, forested corridors, and alder trees. Following along the Columbia River and past the Lewis and Clark Wildlife Refuge, the highway arrives in Astoria.

Sights
Downtown
Downtown Portland is walkable, with compact blocks and narrow streets that are easily navigated via car, bike, and public transportation. Most of the city's municipal building and hotels are concentrated here, including a number of brand name and indie retailers. During the holidays, "Pop-Up" shops appear, adding another dimension to the city's original character.

Pioneer Courthouse Square
Smack in the center of downtown is **Pioneer Courthouse Square.** Affectionately referred to as "Portland's living room," it's a magnet for locals and visitors alike, featuring an elaborate fountain, bronze statue, and outdoor chess tables. Every day at noon lights flash and trumpets blare as the 33-foot-tall *Weather Machine* releases a cloud of mist followed by a series of objects that pop out from the top: the sun for clear weather, a heron for cloudy weather, and a dragon for rainy weather. The **Pioneer Courthouse** (700 SW 6th Ave.) itself is the oldest federal building in the Northwest. The square is also a venue for annual events, speeches, and political demonstrations.

Portland Art Museum
A hallmark to the city's visual arts culture, the **Portland Art Museum** (1219 SW Park Ave., 503/226-2811, www.portlandartmuseum.org, 10am-5pm Tues.-Sun., $15 adults, free children under 17) has been around since 1892, making it the oldest museum in the Pacific Northwest. Its vast collection takes visitors on a journey around the world and through time, spanning ancient to modern art. Notable exhibits include Vincent van Gogh's "The Ox-Cart" and an extensive treasury of Native American artifacts.

Oregon Maritime Museum
If sea-going vessels make you weak in the knees, climb aboard the stern-wheeler *Portland,* the last operating stern-wheel steamboat in the United States. Moored on the Willamette River at downtown's Waterfront Park, it's been converted into the **Oregon Maritime Museum** (115 SW Ash St., 503/224-7724, www.oregonmaritimemuseum.org, Mon., Wed., and Fri. 11am-4pm, $7 adults, $3 children), which preserves artifacts and memorabilia of the Northwest's seafaring past. There's a children's corner with nautical objects, a library with over 22,000 photographs that

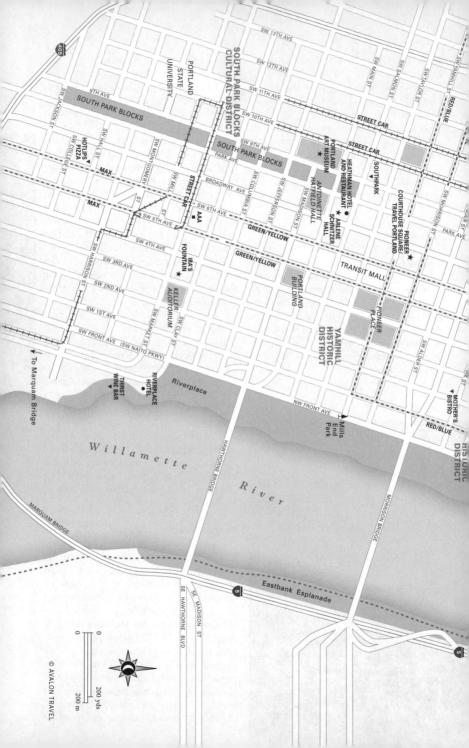

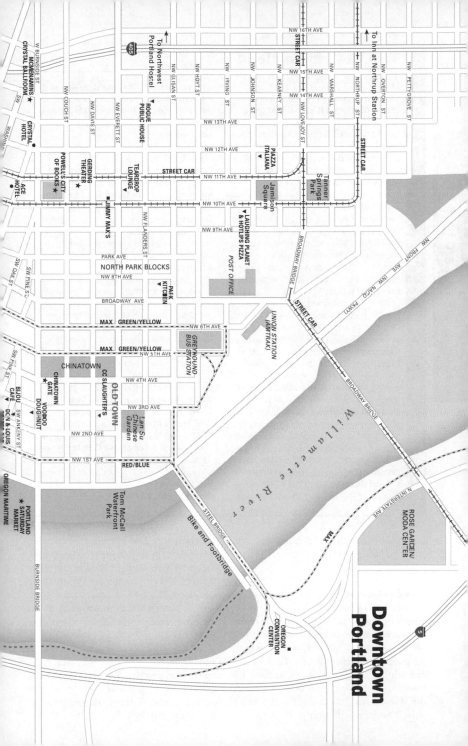

Two Days in Portland

Day 1

Start with a hearty breakfast at downtown's **Mother's Bistro & Bar** (page 95). If you're here on Saturday, peruse the **Portland Saturday Market** (page 101). Then follow the paved waterfront trail south to the stern-wheeler *Portland* and step aboard to tour the **Oregon Maritime Museum** (page 89).

Head to historic **Pioneer Courthouse Square** (page 89) at the corner of SW Broadway and Yamhill to catch the whimsical noon forecast of the *Weather Machine*. If skies are clear, eat lunch like the locals do: Head to SW 10th Avenue and Alder Street and grab a tasty bite from downtown's largest collection of **food carts** (page 96).

Next, ride the streetcar (Central Loop Line) to NW 10th and Johnson in the Pearl District. Shop the Pearl's many boutiques and art galleries, or explore the **Lan Su Chinese Garden** (page 94). Walk two blocks past the Old Town-Chinatown MAX light-rail station to the otherworldly **Hoodoo Antiques & Design** (page 100). Then walk a few blocks to **Voodoo Doughnut** (page 97) for a well-deserved sugar rush. Once you're re-energized, stroll the cobblestone streets of Ankeny Alley, then head north toward West Burnside to spend the afternoon browsing the endless aisles at **Powell's City of Books** (page 100). When you've had your fill of books, fill your stomach

with creative Pac Northwest cuisine at **Park Kitchen** (page 97). End the day with live music at **Jimmy Mak's** (page 99) and a nightcap at the **Teardrop Lounge** (page 98).

Day 2

Start with breakfast at the **Bijou Café** (page 97). Then it's off to spend the morning at the **Portland Art Museum** (page 89), followed by lunch at **Nel Centro** (page 96). If science is more to your interest, take a detour across the Hawthorne Bridge to the river's west bank and the **Oregon Museum of Science and Industry** (page 92).

The afternoon will take you to the west end of the city to explore Portland's greener side. First, follow the street signs off West Burnside to **Pittock Mansion** (page 95), worth a stop for its French-Renaissance architecture and panoramic views. Then it's off to **Washington Park** (page 94), where 160-plus acres and multiple attractions can occupy your time. Choose the **Oregon Zoo** (page 94), the **International Rose Test Garden** (page 95), the **Portland Children's Museum** (page 95), or all of the above. Plan to end your time in the park at the **Japanese Garden** (page 95) to enjoy its striking sunset views of Mount Hood. As night descends, head back downtown for a homemade Italian dinner at **Piazza Italia** (page 97).

catalogue the region's maritime history, and a gift shop to take a piece of the past home with you.

Oregon Museum of Science and Industry

Science comes to life at the **Oregon Museum of Science and Industry** (1945 SE Water Ave., 503/797-4000, www.omsi.edu, 9:30am-5:30pm Tues.-Sun., $13 adults, $9.50 children), across the Hawthorne Bridge from downtown, on the river's west bank. Four levels brim with hundreds of interactive exhibits

that challenge and entertain. Test your brainpower through hands-on lab exhibits, or watch a laser light show in the planetarium. There's even a real submarine to explore: The USS *Blueback* (SS-581) is the U.S. Navy's last non-nuclear, fast-attack submarine. It was the sub used in the movie *The Hunt for Red October*.

Pearl District

Located on Portland's northwest side, between West Burnside Street to the south and the Willamette River to the north, the historic Pearl District has transformed from its industrial, working-class roots into a neighborhood of trendy shops and eateries, art galleries, walking parks, and upscale condominiums.

With three public parks, there is plenty of open space to stroll or read a book. Jamison Square's simulated tidal pool fountain attracts families and people-watchers. Tanner Springs Park provides a walking trail and an opportunity to appreciate the renewed wetlands and creek. The largest park, Field's Park, lets dogs run free.

Powell's City of Books

The landmark **Powell's City of Books** (1005 W. Burnside St., 503/228-4651, www.powells.com, 11am-9pm daily) earns its name, with more than 1.5 million books taking up residence in an entire city block. A magnificent feat of literary enthusiasm, Powell's is so big it needs its own color-coded map. So grab a cup of your favorite bean concoction at the in-store café and plan a book-browsing route to adventure. If you don't like asking for directions—just dive in! This is the one place where getting lost isn't so bad. Plan to spend several hours or more browsing the endless aisles.

Old Town-Chinatown

Portland's oldest neighborhood is sandwiched between the Pearl District to the north and Downtown to the south. It encompasses the official historic districts of Skidmore-Old Town and Chinatown/Japantown. If the neon reindeer sign doesn't make it obvious that you've entered Old Town territory, you'll know for certain when you reach the 19th-century buildings lovingly converted into hip shops and notable eateries, and by the colorful characters (Old Town is home to many of the city's homeless).

From top to bottom: Powell's City of Books; the Pittock Mansion; Chinatown

Lan Su Chinese Garden

An incredible replication of Ming Dynasty landscaping, the **Lan Su Chinese Garden** (239 NW Everett St., 503/228-8131, www.lansugarden.org, $9.50 adults, $28 family) guides visitors through an oasis of prismatic landscapes, covered walkways, and pavilions, built by 65 artisans from Suzhou, China. The centerpiece of the garden is artificially constructed Lake Zither. Everywhere you look, there are a plethora of trees, bamboo, orchids, and fragrant gardenias, with over 400 different species of plant life in all.

Washington Park

In 1871, the City of Portland purchased undeveloped wilderness just west over the main highway (known as I-405). By the 1880s, German immigrant Charles M. Meyers had transformed the untamed land into a park, modeled by memories of his homeland. Today, visitors flock to **Washington Park** (1715 SW Skyline Blvd.,

503/823-2525, www.portlandonline.com, free, parking $3) for its sprawling 5,100 acres of trees, trails, and lively attractions. At its entrance stands a 34-foot granite memorial honoring the Lewis and Clark expedition (1804-1806) that traveled from St. Louis, Missouri, to the Pacific Coast. A nearby bronze statue of Sacajawea (Shoshone) holding her son Jean-Baptiste commemorates her significant role in aiding the explorers.

The park is easy to find. Get here via MAX Light Rail red or blue lines, or TriMet bus 63.

Oregon Zoo

Washington Park's east end is home to the **Oregon Zoo** (4001 SW Canyon Rd., 503/226-1561, www.oregonzoo.org, 9am-4pm daily spring-fall, 10am-4pm daily winter, $11.50 adults, $8.50 children), where endangered Asian elephants and African lions roam habitat grounds, and busy beavers can be seen chewing on river branches. Climb aboard the Zoo

the Japanese Garden in Washington Park

Railway for a scenic ride through the animal park.

Portland Children's Museum

At the west end of Washington Park, the **Portland Children's Museum** (4015 SW Canyon Rd., 503/223-6500, www.portlandcm.org, 9am-5pm daily, $10) inspires creative and interactive displays. But don't just stop at the exhibits; go outside and play on the outdoor eco-playground, which gives every child a chance to flex their sensory muscles.

International Rose Test Garden

Portland first became infatuated with roses when Georgiana Brown Pittock, wife of publisher Henry Pittock, founded the Portland Rose Society with a group of friends in 1889. The love affair continues today at the **International Rose Test Garden** (400 SW Kingston Ave., 503/823-3664, 7:30am-9pm daily), a fragrant wonderland of more than 550 colorful varieties. Free public tours are offered

at 1pm in the summer (Memorial Day weekend-Labor Day weekend).

Japanese Garden

The northern end of Washington Park includes the meditative **Japanese Garden** (611 SW Kingston Ave., 503/223-9233, www.japanesegarden.com/visit/tours, $8.50 adults, $3 children 6-17). Natural elements create the five distinct garden styles. Arbors, pagodas, bridges, ponds, and stone walkways complement the 5.5-acre landscape. Stop at any of the numerous benches to take in the serenity; close your eyes and listen to the trickling of the nearby streams. A gift shop and teahouse operate throughout the year and private tours are offered for groups of 10 or more (reservations required).

Pittock Mansion

Rising 1,000 feet from its perch above the city skyline, the century-old **Pittock Mansion** (3229 NW Pittock Dr., 503/823-3623, www.pittockmansion.org, 11am-4pm daily fall-spring, 10am-5pm daily summer, free, tours $9.50 adults and $6.50 children) boasts breathtaking panoramic views. A marvel of French-Renaissance architecture, it is a monument to Portland's transformation from a small lumber town into a prosperous city. A stroll through the 46-acre grounds reveals fragrant gardens, miles of hidden hiking trails, and commanding views of the city and snowcapped Cascade Mountain Range.

Food

Downtown Portland's many food venues are walking distance from hotels and area attractions. You'll find a mix of tasty and affordable fanfare to sophisticated and expensive dining throughout the city.

Downtown

"There's no place like home" or a home-style breakfast to start the day right at ★ **Mother's Bistro & Bar** (212 SW Stark

St., 503/464-1122, www.mothersbistro.com, 7am-2:30pm and 5:30pm-9pm Tues.-Fri., 8am-2:30pm and 5:30pm-10pm Sat., 8am-2:30pm Sun., $8-20). For Mom's meatloaf and gravy and chicken dumplings, stop in for lunch or dinner. In Downtown's west end, **Cheryl's on 12th** (1135 SW Washington St., 503/595-2252, www.cherylson12th.com, Mon.-Tues. 7am-4pm, Wed.-Fri. 7am-8pm, Sat. 8am-8pm, Sun. 8am-4pm, under $14) features a fantastic weekend brunch. Kids will love **Slappy Cakes** (4246 SE Belmont St., 503/477-4805, www.slappycakes.com, 8am-2pm daily, under $25), a popular pancake spot that lets you flip your own sweet masterpieces on a grill-installed table.

Bunk Sandwiches (211 SW 6th Ave., 503/972-8100, 8am-3pm Mon.-Fri., 9am-3pm Sat.-Sun., $8-11) specializes in satisfying meat and bread combinations; try the pulled pork or grilled Tillamook cheddar. Few can resist the spicy (or not) chicken and rice bowls at

Nong's Khao Man Gai (1003 SW Alder St., 971/255-3480, 10am-4pm Mon.-Fri., under $12). A few blocks east, the small **Portland Penny Diner** (410 SW Broadway, 503/228-7222, www.imperialpdx.com, 7am-3pm Mon.-Fri., under $8) gets its name from the penny-toss of 1845 that determined whether the city would be called Portland or Boston. It's a counter service diner, but the food mixes trendy Northwest flavors with a Native American twist.

Nel Centro (1408 SW 6th Ave., 503/484-1099, www.nelcentro.com, 6:30pm-9pm Sun.-Thurs., 7:30am-10pm Fri.-Sat., $12-30) dazzles sophisticated taste buds with classic dishes of the Riviera using only fresh, local ingredients. Sit near one of several cozy fireplaces or out in the open-air patio. Brunch is on Sundays 8am-2pm.

Want something to go? Head to SW 10th Avenue and Alder Street, where downtown's largest collection of **food carts** serves up tasty afternoon bites.

some of the creative delights served at Voodoo Doughnut

Pearl District

Byways Café (1212 NW Glisan St., 503/221-0011, www.bywayscafe.com, 7am-3pm daily, $8-16) serves all-American classics for breakfasts and lunch. The atmosphere is friendly, the decor a reminder of a roadside drive-in diner. Enjoy a mouthwatering pastry while streetcars glide by the big bay windows of **Lovejoy Bakers** (939 NW 10th Ave., 503/208-3113, 6am-6pm daily, $10-25), just north of Jamison Square. It's also a great stop for delicious sandwiches. For lattes and gelato, **Via Delizia** (1105 NW Marshall St., 503/225-9300, www.viadelizia.com, 7:30am-9:30pm daily, $5-25) is a charming spot, with the ambience of an Italian countryside villa.

Laughing Planet (721 NW 9th Ave. #175, 503/505-5020, www.laughingplanetcafe.com, 11am-9pm daily, under $10) takes healthy to delicious heights and makes it quick and affordable. Choose from fat-free burritos, cheesy quesadillas,

and zesty bowls of exotic flavors from around the world.

HotLips Pizza (721 NW 9th Ave. #150, 503/595-2342, www.hotlipspizza.com, 11am-10pm daily, $11-30) is legendary for locally grown, fresh ingredients and unique fruit sodas. Get it by the slice or devour a whole pie. Carnivores will love **Little Big Burger** (122 NW 10th Ave., 503/274-9008, www.littlebigburger.com, 11am-10pm daily, under $8) for its juicy quarter pounders on a brioche bun and fries at a bargain price.

Relish an authentic Italian diner at **Piazza Italia** (1129 NW Johnson St., 503/478-0619, www.pizzaportland.com, 11:30am-3pm and 5pm-10:30pm daily, $11-30), a small family-owned place with pastas and sauces made from scratch, and a nice wine selection.

Park Kitchen (422 NW 8th Ave., 503/223-7275, www.parkkitchen.com, 5pm-9pm daily, $30-60) has become a beacon for creative food. Try the fried beans with tarragon aioli, beef rib stuffed calamari, or buttermilk panna cotta with sugared pears.

Old Town-Chinatown

A morning staple, the **Bijou Café** (132 SW 3rd Ave., 503/222-3187, www.bijoucafepdx.com, 7am-2pm Sun.-Fri., 8am-2pm Sat., under $11) whips up famous oyster hash and delicious sausage and eggs daily. One block north, **Pink 'n' Black Waffle Shack** (231 SW Ankeny St., 5pm-2am daily, under $10) tops fluffy waffles, both savory and sweet, with every delicious cream, curd, berry, and crumble imaginable. It's the perfect spot for afternoon risers and those late-night breakfast cravings. Right next door, **Voodoo Doughnut** (22 SW 3rd Ave., 503/241-4704, www.voodoodoughnut.com, 24 hours daily, under $10) creates all kinds of inspired doughy treats to go with your cup of joe any time of day or night.

Red Robe Tea House & Café (310 NW Davis St., 503/227-8855, www.redrobeteahouse.com, 11am-8pm Mon.-Fri., noon-8pm Sat., under $15) serves good Asian-American fusion dishes in a setting reminiscent of contemporary China. The selection of traditional Chinese teas is exceptional. The owner often performs traditional tea ceremonies.

An Old Town fixture, world-famous **Dan & Louis Oyster Bar** (208 SW Ankeny St., 503/227-5906, www.danandlouis. com, 11am-9pm Sun.-Thurs., 11am-2pm Fri.-Sat., $20-29) has been serving its trademark seafood favorites for more than 100 years. Choose from pan-seared scallops or lightly breaded oysters or entrées like sockeye salmon or good old-fashioned steak.

Nightlife
Bars and Clubs
Above West Burnside Street in the northwest part of town, **Low Brow Lounge** (1036 NW Hoyt St., 503/226-0200, 3pm-2:30am daily) is a well-known dive bar that offers late-night drinks and fried food in a saloon setting. The lighting is dim, but the vibe is upbeat. A cool little basement bar in Old Town, **Shanghai Tunnels** (211 SW Ankeny Ave., 503/220-4001, 5pm-1:30am daily) is always busy during happy hour. Though it's dimly lit with hanging Chinese paper lanterns, it isn't a dingy dungeon. The drinks are cheap, and the food is pretty darn good; try the Udon noodles. There's a row of pinball machines and a pool table.

Chic sophistication with a modern euro-flair, **Vault Martini** (226 NW 12th Ave., 503/224-4909, 4pm-1am Mon.-Thurs., 4pm-2am Fri.-Sat., 4am-midnight Sun.) has a fantastic drink menu boasting its own house-fused vodka and 44 styles of martinis. Two blocks down the street, **Teardrop Lounge** (1015 NW Everett St., 503/445-8109, 4pm-close daily, happy hour 4pm-7pm Mon.-Fri.) caters to a trendy crowd with a nice selection of snazzy cocktails and light snacks.

Everyone's welcome at the cozy **Valentine's** (32 SW Ankeny St., 503/248-1600, 5pm-2:30am daily). This eclectic little gem hosts poetry slams, musical ensembles, and film discussions.

Upscale gay club **CC Slaughters Nightclub and Lounge** (219 NW Davis St., 503/248-9135, 3pm-2am daily) has it all: cheap drinks; phenomenal DJs; go-go dancers; a huge dance floor; and, the best part, no cover charge.

DJs turn it up at **Dirty NightLife** (35 NW 3rd Ave., 503/227-1898, 9pm-2:30am Wed.-Sat., no cover), a party palace of strobe lights and dance poles. Its dance floor and private dark corners attract a younger crowd.

Harvey's Comedy Club (436 NW 6th Ave., 503/241-0338, www.harveyscomedyclub.com, $11-30) plays host to some of the best national comedy acts. The food is basic bar fare and the drinks are pricy, but the atmosphere will always have you in good spirits.

On the east side of the river, across the Burnside Bridge, **APEX** (1216 SE Division St., 503/273-9227, www.apex. com, 11:30am-2:30am daily) is a cash-only taproom and outdoor beer garden with hundreds of brews. A mile north, the rooftop garden at **Noble Rot** (Leed-Platinum building, 111 E. Burnside St., 503/233-1999, 5pm-10pm daily) offers amazing sunset and night-sky views. Make selections from the vast wine list, yummy cocktails (they make a great pomegranate-lemon martini), and delicious small bites.

Live Music
The almighty **Crystal Ballroom** (1332 W. Burnside St., 503/225-0047, www. crystalballroompdx.com, $6-30) rules the downtown live music scene, hosting iconic musical talents (the Grateful Dead and James Brown played here back in the day) that fill its historic ballroom with the sounds of rock, country, swing, and hip-hop. Little Lola's Room downstairs showcases smaller acts.

Feel good jazz vibrations at **Brasserie Montmartre** (626 SW Park Ave., 503/236-3036, 11:30am-10pm Mon.-Thurs.,

11:30am-midnight Fri., 10am-midnight Sat., 10am-10pm Sun.), an intimate café with French-inspired fare. The music (Thurs.-Sat.) is free and the atmosphere warm and friendly.

Jimmy Mak's (221 NW 10th Ave., 503/295-6542, 5pm-midnight Mon.-Thurs., 5pm-1am Fri.-Sat., tickets $5-30, $15 food/drink minimum) hosts world-class jazz. Make reservations; stage-front tables fill up fast, but wherever you settle, every velvety note will be superb. Drinks and food are available.

Two blocks to the south, the **Splash Bar** (904 NW Couch St., 503/893-5551, 5pm-midnight Mon.-Sat., $10 cover) is an energetic, beach-themed club in the Pearl District with live bands Wednesday and Thursday nights and open jam sessions Saturdays at 10pm. There's also a decent dance floor, arcade games, and the usual bar grub.

In Old Town-Chinatown, **Ash Street Saloon** (225 SW Ash St., 503/226-0430, 4pm-2:30am daily, $5 cover) hosts international and local bands, playing everything from funk to punk. It can be a rough crowd depending on the genre. Housed in the historic Sinnot Building, **The Barrel Room** (105 NW 3rd Ave., 503/242-0700, 7pm-2:30am Fri.-Sat., $10) has multiple bars and a large covered outdoor dance space. It also hosts an all-request dueling piano show.

Arts and Entertainment
Performing Arts
Portland's Centers for the Arts (www.portland5.com) is a performance center that incorporates five venues in three buildings. Let's do the math. The 2,776-seat **Arlene Schnitzer Concert Hall** (1037 SW Broadway Ave., 503/248-4335, www.portland5.com), a restored late-1920s Italian Renaissance landmark, hosts the Oregon Symphony amid a rich variety of musical and theatrical performances. The courtyard-style **Winningstad Theatre** (Hatfield Hall building, 1111 SW Broadway Ave.) arranges floor seating, balconies, and the stage according to the creative whims of the performance, an innovative approach to set-design that ultimately shapes the experience of the audience for the better. The 1917 **Keller Auditorium** (222 SW Clay St.) has a capacity of 2,992 and hosts the Portland Opera, the Oregon Ballet Theatre, and touring Broadway shows. Each of the 880 seats at the Edwardian-style **Newmark Theater** (1111 SW Broadway Ave.) is the best in the house; none is farther than 65 feet from the stage. Many of the city's cultural events and modern dance performances take place here. The last of the five is the **Brunish Theatre** (1111 SW Broadway Ave.), which hosts private events.

In the Pearl District's historic Gerding Theater building, **Portland Center Stage** (128 NW 11th Ave., 503/445-3700, www.psc.org) features classic and modern plays, as well as popular musicals like *West Side Story* and *Dreamgirls*.

Galleries
In the Pearl District, **Blue Sky Gallery** (122 NW 8th Ave., 503/225-0210, www.blueskygallery.org, noon-5pm daily) features emerging and established photographers. An on-site reading room provides printed books of shows over the past 20 years. Nearby, **Quintana Galleries** (124 NW 9th Ave., 503/223-1729, www.quintanagalleries.com, 10:30am-5:30pm Tues.-Sat.) embodies the heartbeat of the Pacific Northwest through its beautiful collection of Native American art and artifacts.

West of the waterfront between SW Oak and SW Pine Streets, the **Attic Galley** (206 SW 1st Ave., 503/228-7830, www.atticgallery.com, 10am-5:30pm Mon.-Sat.) showcases original works by local artists. Exhibits change monthly. There are also beautiful Pendleton wool tapestries for purchase.

Shopping

A big perk to shopping in Portland (or anywhere in Oregon for that matter) is no sales tax.

Downtown

Find department stores, international retailers, boutiques, and specialty shops on the west end of Downtown.

Radish Underground (414 SW 10th Ave., 503/928-6435, www.radishunderground.com, 11am-7pm Mon.-Sat., noon-6pm Sun.) specializes in timeless quality clothing, jewelry, and artwork from local, independent designers and artists. Nearby, **Flora** (917 SW Washington St., 503/227-0586, www.florapdx.com, 11am-6pm daily) carries a wonderful collection of hand selected gifts, botanical scents and soaps, paraffin-free candles, and locally made jewelry. **Avalon Antiques & Vintage Clothes** (410 SW Oak St., 503/224-7156, 11am-6pm Mon.-Fri., noon-6pm Sat.-Sun.) has a large selection of consignment clothing and items that will add a little nostalgia to your wardrobe.

Arthur W. Erickson, Inc. Fine Arts & Unusual Antiques (1030 SW Taylor St., 503/227-4710, www.arthurwerickson.com, 11am-5pm Wed.) specializes in indigenous arts and artifacts, including basketry and pottery, beadwork and jewelry, rugs and blankets.

On the east side of the Willamette, **Music Millennium** (3158 E. Burnside St., 503/231-8926, 10am-10pm Mon.-Sat., 11am-9pm Sun.) is the oldest record store in the Pacific Northwest. It specializes in hard-to-find titles and underground music, and hosts in-store performances.

Union Way Arcade is a pedestrian alleyway that extends from downtown's Ace Hotel on Southwest Stark Street to Powell's City of Books in the Pearl District. Notable venues include designer clothier **Steven Alan** (1029 SW Stark St., 971/277-9585, www.stevenalan.com) and classic beauty boutique **Spruce Apothecary** (1022 W. Burnside St., 503/206-4022, www.spruceapothecary.com).

Pearl District

The Pearl District is a shopaholic's swank dream, with brand-name retailers and boutiques, most on or around West Burnside Street.

The big draw is **Powell's City of Books** (1005 W. Burnside St., 503/228-4651, www.powells.com, 11am-9pm daily), occupying an entire city block with 3,500 different sections.

The clothing lines at **Rachelle M. Rustic House of Fashion's** (132 NW 12th Ave., 971/319-6934, www.rachellem.com, 10am-7pm Mon.-Sat., 11am-6pm Sun.) reflect current fashion trends that meet every lifestyle and budget. Nearby, the products at **Thea's Vintage Living** (1204 NW Glisan St., 503/274-0275, 10am-6pm Mon.-Sat., 11am-5pm Sun.) date from the 1800s to mid-century, with an eclectic blend of furniture, accessories, and jewelry. A few blocks north, **FlairWalk** (1023 NW 11th Ave., 503/222-7750, www.flairwalk.com, 11am-6pm Mon.-Sat., noon-5pm Sun.) is a fashionista dream, with eye-catching cocktail evening and daywear, and the perfect handbags and jewelry to go with them.

Old Town-Chinatown

One of Portland's most intriguing places, **Hoodoo Antiques & Design** (122 NW Couch St., 503/360-3409, www.hoodooantiques.com, 11am-6pm Thurs.-Sun.) has eccentric and alluring curiosities clustered together throughout the store, creating an otherworldly aura. Browse vintage furnishings and unique art and decor from around the world.

Stop at the **Pendleton Home Store** (220 NW Broadway, 503/535-5444, 10am-7pm Mon.-Sat.) for Oregon-made wool blankets and clothing. Two blocks west, **Orox Leather Co.** (450 NW Couch St., 503/954-2593, www.oroxleather.com, 10am-5pm Mon.-Sat.) crafts quality leather products like sandals, wallets, and bags.

Events

The nation's largest weekly open-air market, happens every weekend March-December at the **Portland Saturday Market** (2 SW Naito Pkwy., 503/222-6072, www.portlandsaturdaymarket.com, 10am-5pm Sat., 11am-4:30pm Sun., free), which welcomes shoppers rain or shine. Rows of booths line Waterfront Park south of Burnside Bridge. Browse unique handcrafted arts and crafts from jewelry and home decor to cannabis paraphernalia. There are also food vendors and live music.

The **Portland Rose Festival** (503/227-2681, May-June, $30) originated in 1907, following the successful 1905 Lewis and Clark Exposition, which celebrated the centennial of the expedition. The civic festival begins with the glorious 4.3-mile **Grand Floral Parade** that begins inside the Memorial Coliseum and continues through Downtown. There's also a waterfront carnival, sing-off concerts, and an evening Starlight Parade.

Beneath the St. Johns Bridge, Cathedral Park's spacious lawns fill up for the annual three-day **Cathedral Park Jazz Festival** (8676 N. Crawford St., mid-July, free), the longest-running free jazz festival west of the Mississippi.

Accommodations
Under $150

★ **Hotel Vintage Plaza** (422 SW Broadway, 503/228-1212 and 800/263-2305, www.vintageplaza.com, $136 and up) is a restored landmark building that blends Pacific Northwest history with modern suaveness for a memorable stay in the heart of Downtown.

Located across the street from the legendary Crystal Ballroom, the **Crystal Hotel** (303 SW 12th Ave., 503/225-0047, www.mcmenamins.com/crystalhotel, $85-165) brings its rock and roll vibe and history to life through the decor in each of its 51 rooms. Richly painted walls highlight the artistry of the headboards, while black velvet drapery and animal print accents add a little Mick Jagger swagger. The hotel features a saltwater soaking pool, an upscale café that serves Northwest foods, and an adjoining bar with sidewalk seating that serves pub fare.

Portland has two conveniently located hostels. **Hawthorne Hostel** (3031 Hawthorne Blvd., 503/236-3380, www.portlandhostel.org, $25-31 shared room, $54-64 private) is an ecofriendly crashpad with 34 beds, including two private rooms and two co-ed dorm rooms. **Northwest Portland Hostel** (425 NW 18th Ave., 503/241-2783, www.nwportlandhostel.com, $25-34 shared room, $69 private) is housed in two historic buildings centrally located near popular restaurants and cafés and the city's vibrant nightlife.

$150-250

The impeccably restored **Heathman Hotel** (1009 SW Broadway, 503/241-4100 and 800/551-0011, $199 and up) is where the 50 Shades of Grey characters, Ms. Steele and Mr. Grey, frequently meet for a drink at the bar (try the "50 Shades Cocktail").

With a history dating back to 1915, the lovely **Hotel DeLuxe** (729 SW 15th Ave., 503/219-2094, www.hoteldeluxeportland.com, $150 and up) still projects old-fashioned glamor. It's an easy walk to Providence Park and the Pearl District.

Part of a boutique hotel chain, **Ace Hotel** (1022 SW. Stark St., 503/228-2277, www.acehotel.com, $200 and up) picks up on the Portland vice with vintage furniture, original art, complementary bicycles, and even Stumptown coffee. It's in the Pearl District, close to Powell's City of Books and a stone's throw away from the Portland streetcar.

Over $250

Conveniently located **Hotel Monaco Portland** (506 SW. Washington St., 503/222-0001, www.monaco-portland.com, $269 and up) is only a short walk away from Tom McCall Waterfront Park and downtown shopping. Large suites employ artful, eclectic decorative styles with whimsical accents. Extra-special amenities include a hosted wine reception, spa service, complementary bicycles, and even goldfish companions on request.

Rich in art, architecture, and history, the **Sentinel** (614 SW 11th Ave., 503/224-3400, www.sentinelhotel.com, $365 and up) is a timeless treasure. Housed in two historic downtown buildings (the east wing completed in 1909, and its west wing in 1926), it manages to be both luxurious and inviting.

Information and Services

The **Travel Oregon Visitor Information Center** (701 SW 6th Ave., Pioneer Courthouse Square, 503/275-8355 and 877/678-5263) is the best resource for local information and itinerary suggestions.

Astoria

The oldest American city west of the Rocky Mountains, Astoria was founded in 1811 by fur-trade tycoon John Jacob Astor. The town protected the tenuous American claim to the Pacific Coast until the opening of the Oregon Trail brought substantial settlement. By the turn of the 20th century, Astoria was still Oregon's second-largest city, gaining additional notoriety with the construction of the Astoria Bridge, which connects the states of Washington and Oregon.

Today, Astoria (pop. 9,510) is an enclave of historic haunts, fishing vessels, charming cafés, and grand views of where the Columbia River meets the Pacific Ocean. Its late-Victorian-period homes showcase the Queen Anne architectural style, which have made it a picturesque backdrop for Hollywood movies like *The Goonies* (1985). Astoria supports an active commercial fishing fleet. Dozens of tugboats guide tankers and container ships around treacherous sandbars. The most notorious is the three-mile wide Columbia River Bar, which has claimed some 2,000 large ships. One such shipwreck is the Liverpool sailing ship *Peter Iredale,* still visible at low tide.

Getting There and Around

From Portland, the west end of US-30 meets US-101 at the famous Astoria Bridge. The bridge marks the northern boundary of the city of Astoria. The historic **trolley** (480 Industry St., 503/861-5365, www.old300.org, $1 per boarding or $2 all day), lovingly dubbed "Old 300," is the best way to get around. The conductor narrates the town's history as the trolley makes its way around. If you don't mind walking, follow the **Astoria Riverwalk,** a 5.1-mile paved trail that runs along the waterfront between the Port of Astoria and 40th Street.

Sights

★ Astoria Column

Rising 125 feet, the **Astoria Column** (1 Coxcomb Dr., 503/325-2963, 9am-5:30pm Mon.-Fri., 9am-5pm Sat.-Sun., free, parking $2) sits atop Coxcomb Hill, overlooking the mouth of the Columbia River, showcasing expansive views from the coastal plain south to Tillamook Head, and on to the snowcapped Cascade Range. On a clear day you can see Mount St. Helens to the east. Constructed in 1926, the column was modeled after Trajan's Column in Rome. A mural encases the exterior wall, recording influential events in the town's history.

Pick up a free wooden airplane at the base of the column, then climb the 164-step spiral staircase to send it soaring from the top!

The Flavel House

The Flavel House (441 8th St., 503/325-2203, 10am-5pm daily May-Sept., 11am-4pm Thurs.-Sat., Oct.-Apr., tours $6 adults, $2 children) is a Queen Anne mansion built in 1886 by a sea captain who made millions operating the first pilot service to guide ships across the Columbia River Bar. He built the house for his very young wife (at the time of their wedding, she was 14 to his 30), and they filled it with three children. The restored mansion is elegantly furnished and features 14-foot ceilings and beautiful Douglas fir wood throughout. The visitors center located behind the house features exhibits, including a video presentation, and a gift shop.

Oregon Film Museum

Housed in the old Clatsop County Jail, the **Oregon Film Museum** (732 Duane St., 503/325-2203, www.oregonfilmmuseum.org, 11am-4pm daily Oct.-Apr., 10am-5pm daily May-Sept., $6 adults, $2 children 6-17) celebrates Astoria's contributions to the film industry, which date back to 1908. Get your own mug shot or wander the jail, which is famously depicted in the opening jailbreak scene of *The Goonies* (1985). You can even shoot your own film using Goonie-type sets. Fans of the film may want to drive by the **Goonies House** (368 38th St.), where main character Mikey lived. It's privately owned and not open to the public, so be respectful and don't disturb the residents.

Columbia River Maritime Museum

On the north side of the waterfront, the acclaimed **Columbia River Maritime Museum** (1792 Marine Dr., 503/325-2323, 9:30am-5pm daily, $12 adults, $5 children 6-17) displays some 30,000 artifacts of fishing, shipping, and military history. Interactive exhibits tell the story of the Columbia River and its treacherous sandbar, which claimed over 2,000 vessels, enough to earn it the name "the Graveyard of the Pacific." Docked behind the museum, the *Lightship Columbia* is a National Historic Landmark that once served as a floating lighthouse, providing ships with safe navigation.

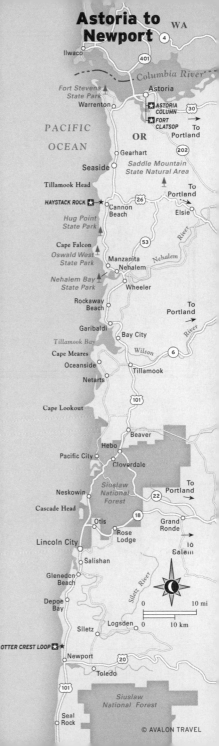

Astoria to Newport

© AVALON TRAVEL

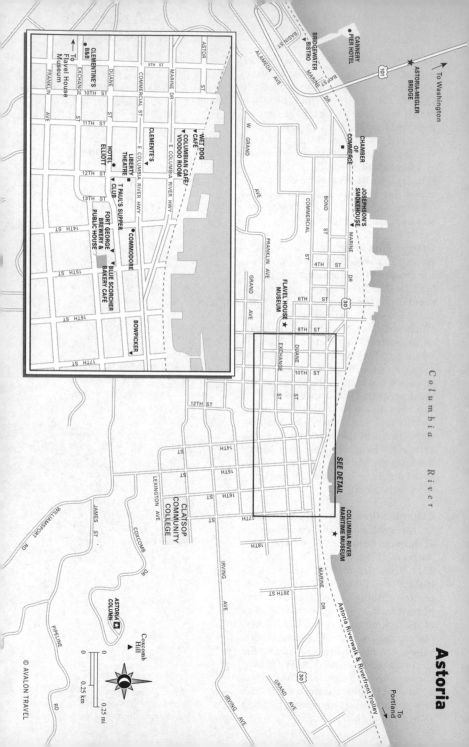

Astoria

Columbia River

To Washington

ASTORIA-MEGLER BRIDGE

101

CANNERY
PIER HOTEL

BRIDGEWATER
BISTRO

BASIN ST

ALAMEDA AVE

MARINE DR

CHAMBER OF COMMERCE

JOSEPHSON'S SMOKEHOUSE

MARINE DR

W GRAND AVE

COMMERCIAL ST

BOND ST

4TH ST

6TH ST

8TH ST

30

FLAVEL HOUSE MUSEUM ★

FRANKLIN AVE

GRAND AVE

EXCHANGE ST

DUANE ST

10TH ST

SEE DETAIL

COLUMBIA RIVER MARITIME MUSEUM ★

12TH ST

14TH ST

15TH ST

16TH ST

17TH ST

18TH ST

20TH ST

LEXINGTON AVE

CLATSOP COMMUNITY COLLEGE

COXCOMB DR

JAMES ST

WILLIAMSPORT RD

IRVING AVE

MARINE DR

Astoria Riverwalk & Riverfront Trolley

30

GRAND AVE

IRVING AVE

To Portland

ASTORIA COLUMN ✚

Coxcomb Hill ▲

PIPELINE RD

© AVALON TRAVEL

0   0.25 mi
0   0.25 km

Detail

To Flavel House Museum

CLEMENTINE'S B&B ●

EXCHANGE ST

DUANE ST

FRANKLIN AVE

ASTOR ST

9TH ST

COMMERCIAL ST

MARINE DR

10TH ST

11TH ST

CLEMENTE'S ■

HOTEL ELLIOTT

LIBERTY THEATRE ■

12TH ST

13TH ST

14TH ST

15TH ST

16TH ST

17TH ST

WET DOG CAFE ▼

COLUMBIAN CAFE/ VOODOO ROOM ▼

E COLUMBIA ST

E COLUMBIA RIVER HWY

T PAUL'S SUPPER CLUB ▼

COMMODORE ▼

FORT GEORGE BREWERY & PUBLIC HOUSE ●

BLUE SCORCHER BAKERY CAFE ▼

BOWPICKER ▼

Peter Iredale Shipwreck

The 275-foot British schooner *Peter Iredale* ran ashore on October 25, 1906, en route from Mexico to the Columbia River. All of the ship's crew members were rescued, but all efforts to recover the ship itself were unsuccessful. It was abandoned on the narrow Clatsop Spit near Fort Stevens. Today, you can still see the skeletal remains of the ship in **Fort Stevens State Park** (100 Peter Iredale Rd., 503/861-1671 or 800/551-6949, $5 day-use), 10 miles south of Astoria. At low tide, you can even walk right up to it—but be prepared to get wet!

Food

Directly across from the Elliot Hotel, ★ **T Paul's Supper Club** (360 12th St., 503/325-2545, www.tpaulssupperclub.com, 11am-9pm Mon.-Thurs., 11am-10pm Fri.-Sat., $12-26) adds a little swank to its easygoing atmosphere. The menu is laden with tempting choices like crab ravioli and mac 'n' cheese.

Enjoy a chic dining experience in the heart of historic downtown at **Clemente's Fresh Seafood Restaurant & Market** (1198 Commercial St., 503/325-1067, www.clementesrestaurant.com, 11am-3pm and 5pm-9pm Tues.-Sun., $7-20), which features seasonal menus based on local harvests and artwork by local artists.

For something quick and easy, head to the **Blue Scorcher Bakery Café** (1493 Duane St., 503/338-7473, www.bluescorcher.com, 8am-5pm daily, $3-8). It doubles as a bakery that sells fresh breads and pastries and a café that serves soups, pizza by the slice, and much more.

Join the long line outside the 48-foot boat across from the Columbia Maritime Museum, the home of **Bowpicker Fish & Chips** (1636 Duane St., 503/791-2942, www.bowpicker.com, 11am-6pm daily, $6-9). It's worth the wait for their famous lightly battered albacore tuna served with thickly cut steak fries. **Ship Inn** (1 2nd St., 503/325-0033, www.shipinn-astoria.com, 11:30am-9:30pm daily, under $18) serves fresh halibut-and-chips and other British specialties. Popular **Columbian Cafe** (1114 Marine Dr., 503/325-2233, 8am-2pm Wed.-Fri., 9am-2pm Sat.-Sun., 5pm-9pm Thurs.-Sat., under $12) is a good choice for fresh seafood, with large portions and reasonable prices.

Good food and fantastic views draws them in at the **Bridgewater Bistro** (20 Basin St., 503/325-6777, bridgewaterbistro.com, 11:30am-close daily, 11am-3pm Sun. brunch, under $34) on the Columbia River waterfront. The menu offers a diverse range from burgers to wild salmon and roasted duck; there's also Sunday brunch.

Pick up the best smoked salmon to go at commercial fish packers **Josephson's Smokehouse** (106 Marine Dr., 503/325-2190, 10am-5:30pm Mon.-Sat., 10am-5pm Sun., $12-18), a family-owned company for over 90 years.

Nightlife and Entertainment

If you think of food as a side dish to a prodigious beer, climb the spiral staircase to the **Fort George Brewery & Public House** (1483 Duane St., 503/325-7468, fortgeorgebrewery.com, call for hours, brewery tours 1pm-4pm Sat., $5-11), where the noble malted grain is always being perfected. The food, scenic views, and live music are great too!

Kick back and relax at the **Wet Dog Cafe & Astoria Brewing House** (144 11th St., 503/325-6975, 11am-10pm Mon.-Fri., 8am-10pm Sat.-Sun., happy hour 3pm-6pm Mon.-Fri.), just west of the Maritime Museum, or the **Rogue Public House** (100 39th St., 503/325-5964, 11am-9pm daily), inside the former Bumble Bee Tuna cannery on Pier 39. Both offer handcrafted ales and lagers and tasty happy hour menu specials.

Welcoming **Buoy Beer Company** (1 8th St., 503/325-4540, www.buoybeer.com, 11am-10pm Sun.-Thurs., 11am-midnight Fri.-Sat.) is housed in a 90-year-old cannery on the riverfront. Sample unique eats like the bison burger and "damn good beer," served with pride.

The self-proclaimed "oldest watering hole in the oldest American settlement west of the Rockies," **Astoria Portway Tavern** (422 W. Marine Dr., 503/325-2651, 11am-11pm Mon.-Tues., 11am-1am Wed.-Thurs., 11am-1:30am Fri.-Sat., noon- 9pm Sun.) offers great drink specials and bar grub as well as a variety of entertainment, including karaoke (Wed.-Sat.) and a resident ghost. The old-school **Desdemona Club** (2997 Marine Dr., 503/325-8540, 11am-close) serves affordable drinks and features three pool tables and a shuffleboard.

In its heyday, the 1920s **Liberty Theater** (1203 Commercial St., 503/325-5922, www.liberty-theater.org, $5-25) welcomed celebrities like Duke Ellington, Jack Benny, and presumably Al Capone. The impressive venue includes a Chinese lantern-style chandelier made of paper and cotton, and large Venetian paintings.

Enjoy plays, concerts, and the occasional apparition.

Shopping

The wonderful thing about shopping in Oregon is that it's tax-free. Browse and shop along Commercial Street, which is lined with diverse retail stores.

Terra Stones (951 Commercial St., 503/325-5548, 10am-6pm Mon.-Sat., 11am-4:30pm Sun.) carries unique art and gifts, jewelry-making supplies, and a large selection of beautiful beads. A block east, **A Gypsy's Whimsy Herbal** (1139 Commercial St., 503/338-4871, 11am-6pm Tues.-Sat.) is a mecca for organic herbs, teas, and metaphysical treasures. Head across the street for one-of-a-kind home decor and handcrafted gifts at **Foxgloves** (1124 Commercial St., 503/468-0700). A couple doors down, **Finn Ware** (1116 Commercial St., 800/851-3466 or 503/325-5720, www.finnware.com, 10am-5pm Mon.-Sat., noon-4pm Sun.) boasts stylish Norwegian products

The *Lightship Columbia* at the Columbia River Maritime Museum and authentic sauna aromas imported from Finland.

The two-story **Phog Bounders Antique Mall** (892 Marine Dr., 503/338-0101, www.phogbounders.com, 10am-5:30pm Mon.-Sat., 10am-5pm Sun.) brims with nostalgic items from bygone eras. Two blocks west, **Vintage Hardware** (380 14th St., 503/325-1313, www.astoriavintagehardware.com, 10am-5pm daily) is stocked with old-world wonders, from beautifully preserved furnishings to rare salvaged architecture.

From May to October, the **Astoria Sunday Market** (12th St., 503/325-1010) hosts regional artists, music, fresh produce, and culinary delights!

Events

Fisher Poets Gathering (www.fisherpoets.org, late Feb.) commemorates Astoria's maritime roots through art, music, and literature. The **Astoria Music Festival** (1271 Commercial St., 503/325-9896, www.astoriamusicfestival.org,

last weekend in June) highlights classical music and opera along with modern dance and ballet. The **Astoria Scandinavian Midsummer Festival** (Clatsop County Fairgrounds, 503/325-6136, 3rd weekend in June) celebrates that rich emigrant heritage with a parade, traditional music, dance, crafts, and foods.

Downtown's **Second Saturday Art Walk** (5pm-8pm every second Sat. of the month, free) celebrates Astoria's growing arts community with work by local artists and live entertainment. Maps are available at the **Astoria Chamber of Commerce** (111 W. Marine Dr., 503/325-6311).

Accommodations

Extending 600 feet out into the Columbia River, ★ **The Cannery Pier Hotel** (10 Basin St., 503/325-4996, www.cannerypierhotel.com, $418-1,150) is a rarity. Enjoy magnificent views of passing ships from your own private balcony. Complementary guest services include breakfast, wine-tasting, and day-use bicycles.

The **Crest Motel** (5366 Leif Erickson Dr., 503/325-3141, www.astoriacrest-hotel.com, $89 and up) overlooks the great Columbia River. Historic and stylish **Hotel Elliott** (357 12th St., 503/325-2222, www.hotelelliott.com, $132 and up) is located close to the Riverwalk.

You may never want to leave homey **Clementine's** (847 Exchange St., 503/325-2005, www.clementines-bb.com, $98-148), which boasts comfortable rooms and an amazing breakfast.

A charming boutique hotel located in the heart of downtown, the **Commodore Hotel** (258 14th St., 503/325-4747, $59 and up cabin, $149 and up deluxe suites) blends right in to the old-time feel of historic Astoria, and is walking distance from the Fort George Brewery and the Maritime Museum. It also offers European-style rooms with shared bathroom facilities or private bathroom suites. Go for a walk or run on the Astoria Riverwalk trail only a half block away.

The **Norblad Hotel and Hostel** (443 14th St., 503/325-6989, www.norbladhotel.com, $29 dorm, $59-89 private suite) is an affordable place to put your feet up after a long day of sightseeing.

The immaculate **Lewis & Clark Golf RV Park** (92294 Youngs River Rd., 503/338-3386, call for rates) has picnic tables, barbecues, and a large area for pets, nestled along a golf course.

Information and Services

The **Astoria Chamber of Commerce** (111 W. Marine Dr., 503/325-6311) provides a wide range of visitor information on local activities, restaurants, and accommodations.

★ Fort Clatsop

"Ocian in view! O! the joy" wrote Captain William Clark in his journal on November 7, 1805, when he first sighted the Pacific Ocean while standing at the mouth of the Columbia River. The 33-member Corps of Discovery, led by Clark and Meriwether Lewis, had traveled more than 4,000 miles across the North American continent to establish the most direct water route from the Missouri River to the unknown land of the Pacific. They waited out the grueling winter of 1805-1806 two miles upstream at the self-made Fort Clatsop (named for the local Indian tribe), passing the time by making 332 pairs of moccasins, producing 30 pounds of salt, creating maps, hunting elk, and fighting fleas.

Today, reconstruction of the encampment (the second built after the original was destroyed by fire in 2005) is the highlight of the **Fort Clatsop National Memorial** (92343 Fort Clatsop Rd., 503/861-2471, 9am-5pm daily Labor Day-mid-June, 9am-6pm daily mid-June-Labor Day, $5 peak season, $3 Labor Day-mid-June), as well as the focal point of the multiple sites that make up Lewis and Clark National Historical Park. A nearby visitors center houses historical items from the expedition and hosts costumed reenactments and historical demonstrations. Visitors can also trace the route the Lewis and Clark expedition took from Fort Clatsop to the Pacific Ocean, on the 6.5-mile **Fort to Sea Trail,** which crosses coastal rivers, lakes, and wondrous sand dunes.

Gearhart

Set between the buzz of Astoria and Seaside, **Gearhart** (pop. 1,488) seems like a quiet and uncrowded town. Its claim to fame is the culinary legacy of its former resident chef, TV personality and cookbook author James Beard. You can get a taste of Beard's famous crab cakes and other tasty Northwest cuisine at the **Pacific Way Bakery and Cafe** (601 Pacific Way, 503/738-0245, www.pacificwaybakery-cafe.com, bakery: 7am-1pm Thurs.-Mon., café: 11am-3:30pm and from 5pm Thurs.-Mon.), an eclectic place with an adjoining bakery that whips up delicious pastries and coffee.

Seaside

Seaside (pop. 6,441) is Oregon's oldest playground by the sea. Its first guesthouse was built in 1870 by Ben Holladay, a prominent land developer and railroad builder. Holladay envisioned an elegant summer resort for the wealthy and influential, but Seaside had already played host to a famous party some 65 years earlier: The Lewis and Clark Corps of Discovery. At the west end of Broadway, a bronze statue of Meriwether Lewis and William Clark (and Lewis' dog Seaman) marks the end of the Lewis and Clark Trail. Seaside's wide and sandy beaches are popular for beach biking, volleyball, kite flying, sand castles, and evening bonfires.

Apart from the saltwater taffy and

homemade ice cream shops on the Promenade, Seaside has several good eateries. Find morning bites and coffee at **Bagels by the Sea** (210 S. Holladay Dr., 503/717-9145, 6:30am-3pm daily, under $7), which also serves lunch. Grab a bucket of steamer clams at **Dundee's Bar & Grill** (414 Broadway, 503/738-7006, www.dundeeseaside.com, 7am-10pm daily, $6-18).

Book a room at **The Gilbert Inn** (341 Beach Dr., 800/507-2714, $85 and up), a classic Victorian built in 1892. Much of the original decor remains, including the parlor fireplace and groove ceilings.

The **Seaside Visitors Bureau** (7 N. Roosevelt Dr., 503/738-3097 or 888/306-2326, 9am-5pm Mon.-Sat., noon-4pm Sun.) is the best source for local information.

Cannon Beach

Cannon Beach (pop. 1,373) is one of the most picturesque destinations on the coast. Dozens of art galleries as well as charming restaurants and boutique shops line downtown's main drag, known as Hemlock Street. Walk along the long, sandy beach or just enjoy the view from the door of your beachfront suite; there are plenty of lodging choices. But no matter where you stay, Cannon Beach offers more awe-inspiring views than imaginable, making *National Geographic*'s list of "one of the world's 100 most beautiful places."

Getting Around
Sunset Empire Transit District (503/861-7433 or 866/811-1001, www.ridethebus.org, $1, runs hourly) operates the Cannon Beach Shuttle (Route 21), which runs a loop connecting Cannon Beach and Seaside.

Sights
★ Haystack Rock
Claimed as the third-tallest seashore formation in the state, the 235-foot-high **Haystack Rock** is also Cannon Beach's claim to fame, setting it apart from the other quaint seaside towns along this stretch of coastline. It's home to nesting seabirds in the summer and marine creatures year-round, in the tide pools that collect around its base. These creatures are protected as part of the Oregon Islands National Wildlife Refuge, which means no collecting, no harassment, and no climbing on the Rock. It's best admired from afar, or at least through a camera lens. It's one of Oregon's most popular photo ops, but it's not the only Haystack Rock along the coast—there are two other formations by that name at Cape Kiwanda and Bandon.

Ecola State Park
Just after Christmas Day in 1806, the Lewis and Clark Corps of Discovery scaled the rugged headlands and pushed through the thick shrubs and trees south to where a beached whale lay in what is now **Ecola State Park** (84318 Ecola State Park Rd., 503/436-2844, dawn-dusk daily, $5 per car). Today, it's a photographer's dream, with astonishing views. To the north, you can see Tillamook Rock Lighthouse, which guided its last ship in 1957. To the south, Haystack Rock and Cannon Beach rest in the shadow of Neahkahnie Mountain. The entire park encircles Tillamook Head, which rises 1,200 feet above the sea.

Cannon Beach History Center & Museum
Cannon Beach History Center & Museum (1387 S. Spruce St., 503/436-9301, www.cbhistory.org, call for hours, donation) houses a collection of artifacts and memorabilia, and an on-site gift and book shop.

Food
Get the day started with a morning cup of joe at **Sleepy Monk Coffee Roasters** (235 S. Hemlock St., 503/436-2796,

Cannon Beach

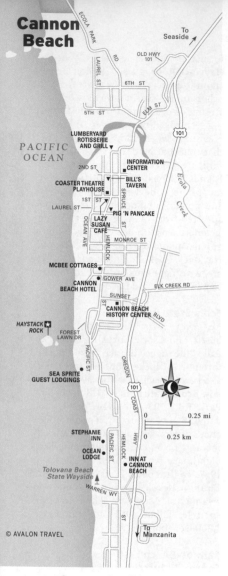

© AVALON TRAVEL

all sorts of delicious batters from blueberry to pecan. **Lazy Susan Café** (126 N. Hemlock St., 503/436-2816, www.lazy-susan-cafe.com, 8am-2:30pm Mon. and Wed.-Sun., $6-18) features delicious specialty omelets and endless coffee.

★ **Cannon Beach Café** (1116 S. Hemlock St., 503/436-1392, www.cannonbeachcafe.com, 11am-3pm daily, 5pm-9pm dinner Thurs.-Sun., $10-15) is a little gem inside the historic Cannon Beach Hotel. The menu has Parisian flair and the service will make you feel like family.

Ecola Seafoods (208 N. Spruce St., 503/436-9130, www.ecolaseafoods.com, 9am-9pm daily spring-fall, 10am-7pm daily winter, under $25) has been serving the best locally caught fish and shellfish for more than 37 years.

Castaways' Tini Tiki Hut (316 Fir St., 503/436-8777, 5pm-9pm daily, $11-30) is a little place with big Caribbean tastes like jerk chicken and jambalaya.

Nightlife and Entertainment

Bill's Tavern & Brewhouse (188 N. Hemlock St., 503/436-2202, www.billstavernandbrewhouse, 11:30am-10pm daily) offers a friendly neighborhood spirit, and good, strong craft beers, with a range of light to medium lagers. Enjoy the open rock fireplace, free pool tables, and low-key vibe at **The Lumberyard Rotisserie & Grill** (264 3rd St., 503/436-0285, www.thelumberyardgrill.com, noon-9pm Sun.-Thurs., noon-10pm Fri.-Sat.), which hosts live music Wednesday nights.

Sate your palate with superb Northwest wines at **The Wine Bar** (271 N. Hemlock St., 503/436-1539, www.thewinebarcannonbeach.com, 4pm-10pm Wed.-Thurs., 4pm-11pm Fri., 2pm-close Sat.-Sun.), which hosts Saturday night courtyard concerts.

The **Coaster Theatre Playhouse** (108 N. Hemlock St., 503/436-1242, www.coastertheatre.com, $15-23) stages a wide range of musicals and plays; there's not a bad seat in the house.

www.sleepymonkcoffee.com, 8am-2pm Mon.-Tues., 8am-4pm Fri.-Sun.). **Crepe Neptune** (175 E. 2nd St., 503/436-9200, www.crepeneptune.com, 9am-6pm daily summer, $5-10) specializes in generously stuffed savory or sweet French-style pancakes. They make pancakes à la American at **Pig 'N Pancake** (223 S. Hemlock St., 503/436-2851, www.pignpancake.com, 6am-8pm Sun.-Thurs., 6am-9pm Fri.-Sat., $7-14), stirring up

Shopping

Much of the charm of downtown Cannon Beach is due to the many local artists, galleries, and boutiques that are grouped into little courtyard plazas in the main shopping district along Hemlock Street.

Every piece of handcrafted jewelry made at **Golden Whale** (194 N. Hemlock St., 503/436-1166, www.goldenwhale-jewelry.com, 10am-5pm daily) is unique, imaginative, and affordable.

Upstairs in Sandpiper Square, **Primary Elements Gallery** (172 N. Hemlock St., 503/436-0220, www.primaryelements-gallery.com) has beautiful sculptures, woodcarvings, ceramics, and furniture. **Cannon Beach Treasure Co.** (148 N. Hemlock St., 503/436-1626) peddles artifacts salvaged from beneath the sea alongside one-of-a-kind artwork and jewelry. Expect the unexpected at **The Butler Did It** (124 N. Hemlock St., 503/436-2598, 11am-5pm daily), a whimsical little shop with kitchen accessories and vintage decor.

A few blocks south, **La Luna Loca** (382 12th St., 503/468-0788, 10am-6pm Tues.-Thurs., 10am-8pm Fri., 10am-4pm Sun.-Mon.) showcases artistry imported from around the world with clothing and jewelry that are colorful, comfortable, and fun.

Steidel's Art (116 S. Hemlock St., 503/436-1757, www.steidelart.com) enchants with colorfully brushed artworks and statuary. **DragonFire Studio and Gallery** (123 S. Hemlock St., Ste. 106, 503/436-1533, www.dragonfirestudio.com) makes exceptional yet affordable art pieces in media ranging from paint to fiber to metal. In the same building, **Dena's Shop on the Corner** (123 S. Hemlock St., 503/436-1275, www.denasshop.com, 10am-6pm Mon.-Sat., 10am-5pm Sun.) offers stylish and affordable women's clothing and accessories.

From top to bottom: The Cannon Beach History Center & Museum; Ecola State Park; the Coaster Theatre Playhouse.

Cannon Beach Surf (1088 S. Hemlock St., 503/436-0475, www.cannonbeachsurf.com, 8am-5pm Mon.-Fri., 8am-6pm Sat., 8am-5:30pm Sun.) carries everything for the beach: surfwear, sunglasses, even board rentals and surf lessons.

Browse artisanal products alongside local fresh fruit and vegetables at **The Cannon Beach Farmers Market** (163 E. Gower Ave., 503/436-8044, www.cannonbeachmarket.org, 1pm-5pm Tues. mid-June-Sept.).

Recreation

In Ecola State Park, the **Clatsop Loop Trail** (2.5 miles) begins at Indian Beach and travels to the southern end of Tillamook, allowing you to trace the steps of the Corps of Discovery. You'll pass interpretive signs, as well as salmonberry, large Sitka spruce, and salal along the pathway. Wildlife is easy to spot, especially during winter and spring when whales make their way along the coastline.

Stroll the boardwalk at **Sunset Beach State Park** (503/861-2471, $5 pp peak season, $3 pp off-season) for incredible views of Cape Disappointment and Ecola State Park. The beach is accessed from Sunset Beach Lane via US-101. Park entrance fees are paid at Fort Clatsop Visitor Center. The visitors center marks the western trailhead of the historic 6.5-mile **Fort to Sea Trail,** which traces the steps of Lewis and Clark.

Located on the south end of Cannon Beach, **Tolovana State Recreation Site** (800/551-6949) has lots of sandy oceanfront space for recreation.

Trot through the surf on horseback with **Sea Ranch Stables** (415 Fir St., 503/436-2815, www.searanchrv.com/stables, $70-130), which guides visitors along a southbound trail to Haystack Rock or northbound to Cove Beach. Riders must be at least 7 years old and reservations must be made in person.

Events

One of the oldest sandcastle contests in Oregon is **Sandcastle Day** (207 N. Spruce St., 503/436-2623), held annually in early June. Teams compete for cash, but you don't have to put your hands in the sand to have fun; watch as wondrous creations take shape before your eyes!

The annual **Stormy Weather Arts Festival** (207 N. Spruce St., 503/436-2623, free) is a three-day affair in November featuring exhibits and gallery shows, an auction, musical performances, and a special evening concert.

Accommodations

It's no surprise to find an enchanting hotel like ★ **Stephanie Inn** (2740 S. Pacific St., 800/633-3466, www.stephanieinn.com, $469 and up) in a magical place like Cannon Beach. It's the perfect getaway for couples and special occasions with afternoon wine-tasting, pampered services, and perfect views of Haystack Rock.

The Ocean Lodge (2864 S. Pacific St., 888/777-4047, www.theoceanlodge.com, $179-309) combines laid-back charm and quality service. The romantic **Inn at Cannon Beach** (3215 S. Hemlock St., 800/321-6304, www.innatcannonbeach.com, $139-195) is the perfect starting point for sunset strolls on the beach.

Just one block from the beach, **McBee Motel Cottages** (888 S. Hemlock St., 503/436-2569, $134 and up) is a refurbished vintage motor inn that welcomes guests and their pets. The charming oceanfront **Sea Sprite** (280 Nebesna St., 503/436-2266, seasprite.com, $184 and up) has beautifully appointed studios, suites, cottages, and vacation rentals with views of Haystack Rock.

Information and Services

The best source of complete information is the **Cannon Beach Visitor Center** (207 N. Spruce St., 503/436-2623, www.cannonbeach.org, 10am-5pm daily) in the heart of downtown Cannon Beach.

Hug Point State Park

Just five miles south of Cannon Beach, **Hug Point State Park** (800/551-6949) has beautiful, forested picnic areas, a magical seasonal waterfall, and mysterious caves carved into its towering cliffs. It's a good alternative to ever-popular Cannon Beach. But what's hidden beneath the waves make it a must-see: Old Stagecoach Road. Before the highway was built, carriages traveled along the shoreline, dashing between the incoming waves. At low tide, head north of the parking lot to see the rutted road left by these early pioneers, which is some 800 feet long.

Oswald West State Park

Ten miles south of Cannon Beach, the scenic coastline rises high above the ocean below, cutting into the mountains. The views are dominated by legendary **Neahkahnie Mountain,** which some say local Native Americans named "place of gods," no doubt for its transcendent views. But the mountain is also known for its hidden treasure, supposedly buried by the captain of a Spanish galleon that was shipwrecked at its base. Captain and crew hauled the treasure up the south side of Neahkahnie and concealed it in an unknown location. Though many have searched, no treasure has ever been found.

Neahkahnie is contained within the 2,484-acre rain forest of **Oswald West State Park** (Arch Cape, 800/551-6949). Here you can wander in the shade of cedar and spruce, ferns and salmonberry, or walk the half-mile trail beneath the highway to **Short Sands Beach,** a premier surfing destination.

A 13-mile segment of the **Oregon Coast Trail** winds through the entire park. In the spring, it's an unforgettable hike through wildflowers and old-growth forest that culminates at the Neahkahnie

summit for striking views of the coastline below.

Oswald West includes a well-sheltered **campground** (spring-fall, $15) with 29 campsites. Five miles south, **Nehalem Bay State Park** (503/368-5154 or 800/551-6949, open year-round, $24-54) has a large campground with hot showers.

Tillamook

US-101 curves inland past wetlands and dairy lands along Tillamook Bay (pronounced "Till-uh-muk," the name is a Salish word meaning "land of many waters"). Grazing cows come into view as you near the town of **Tillamook** (pop. 4,934), known for its cheese-making.

It's worth a stop to sample the creamy delights at the **Tillamook Cheese Factory** (4175 N. US-101, 503/815-1300, 8am-6pm daily Labor Day-mid-June, 8am-8pm daily mid-June-Labor Day, free self-guided tours) and watch how the curd is transformed into the many cheese varieties. A mile south, the **Blue Heron French Cheese Company** (2001 Blue Heron Rd., 503/842-8281) gives you a taste of their famous Blue Heron Brie. Their **Blue Heron Deli** (11am-4pm daily, under $16) is perfect for lunch, with fresh baked bread and homemade soups and salads.

The **Tillamook Air Museum** (6030 Hangar Rd., 503/842-1130, 10am-5pm daily, $9 adults, $5 children 6 and up) is housed in a former blimp hanger and one of the world's largest wooden structures, spanning seven acres. Its rare warbird collection includes MiG fighters, a twin-tailed P-38, and an F-14 Tomcat.

☞OR-131: Three Capes Scenic Route

Between Tillamook and Lincoln City, US-101 strays inland, losing sight of the Pacific Ocean. To continue along the

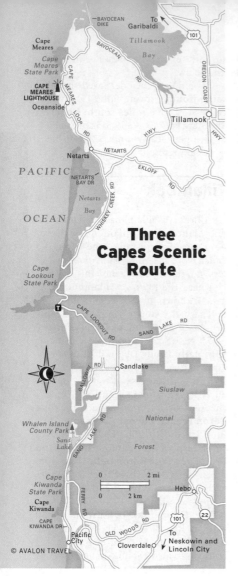

Three
Capes Scenic
Route

© AVALON TRAVEL

Cape Meares

On the south end of Tillamook Bay, **Cape Meares** (named for John Meares, a British explorer) forms a steep bluff where the historic Cape Meares Lighthouse and Sitka spruce trees sit atop its wind-beaten rock. The most famous Sitka spruce is the strangely twisted **Octopus Tree,** which rises some 105 feet. Believed to be several hundred years old, it has no central trunk and possibly owes its curious octopus-like shape to early Native Americans, who may have used the tree to hold ceremonial canoes. A scenic view-point overlooks the sea and rocky beach below. Whales can be seen in the spring and winter, along with sea lions and nesting sea birds.

A few miles south of Cape Meares, the coastal hamlets of **Oceanside** and **Netarts** provide opportunities to stop for gas and refreshments.

Cape Lookout

Roughly eight miles past Netarts, you'll reach **Cape Lookout.** Seventeen miles of trails wander through a forest of hemlock, alder, and fir trees, and along the sandy coastland. The Cape Trail (5 miles) encircles the cape, the South Trail heads down to a sandy beach and hidden cove, and the North Trail takes you to the tip of the cape. The campground at **Cape Lookout State Park** (503/842-4981) offers tent sites, yurts, and cabins with hot showers.

Continuing south, the loop briefly enters the Siuslaw National Forest, then enters an expanse of sweeping sand dunes, and the Sand Beach estuary. This ecological wonder includes woodlands, grasslands, wetlands, and dune sedgelands and serves as home to salmon, shorebirds, deer, otters, and even bears and cougars.

Cape Kiwanda

The route turns inland before winding south to **Cape Kiwanda,** notorious for some of the wildest surf in the state.

coast, head west on OR-131 and follow signs that point the way to the **Three Capes Scenic Route,** a worthy 35-mile side trip that strings together three captivating bluffs: Cape Meares, Cape Lookout, and Cape Kiwanda. The highway will take you through dairy land and second-growth forest. To enjoy the dramatic beauty of these capes, you'll need to get out of the car and hike along their trails.

Surfers, windsurfers, and kite flyers enjoy the shore winds, while hang gliders take advantage of the gusts from above. At its north end, a towering six-story-high sand dune juts out over the cape. A mile offshore, a second **Haystack Rock** (the more commonly known is in Cannon Beach) rises 327 feet from the seafloor.

Pacific City

South of Cape Kiwanda, the beach stretches eight miles toward the Nestucca Spit (which you'll have to cross) and on to the southernmost oceanfront settlement of **Pacific City.** You can grab a bite at the **Grateful Bread Bakery** (34805 Brooten Rd., 503/965-7337, 8am-3pm Thurs.-Mon., under $15), choosing between vegan dishes, sandwich wraps, breakfast scrambles, and delicious gluten-free breads.

Just past Pacific City, the route connects with US-101 at Lincoln City.

Lincoln City

Lincoln City (pop. 7,926) lies along the most developed section of US-101, a very busy and at times congested highway. Five fishing and logging towns were combined to form Lincoln City in the 1960s, which accounts for its larger size compared to most neighboring coastal towns.

Before early settlements infiltrated the region, it was inhabited by the Salish Indians, which included the Tillamook, Nehalem, and Siletz. Local rivers teemed with salmon, and homesteaders fished for extra income. By the 1920s, the numbers of fish had diminished and many turned to logging, which became the lifeblood of the town's economy, until it too dried up in the 1980s.

Today, Lincoln City has become a home to retirees and a destination for tourists seeking its beautiful 7.5-mile beach. From fall to spring caches of spherical blown-glass floats can be

spotted, reminiscent of the floats used by Japanese immigrants that, like so many, made their living on the sea.

Getting There and Around

Continue south via US-101 for 66 miles, passing through the small towns of Manzanita, Nehalem, and Wheeler to Lincoln City. The mostly two-lane highway becomes clogged with traffic just before entering the town.

Sights
Glass Floats

Lincoln City's main attraction is its beach, a mecca for beachcombing, kite flying, and sand-play. But its most intriguing sights are the colorful blown-glass floats seen above the tide line and below the beach embankment from mid-October through Memorial Day. These elegant glass orbs, emblematic of Northwestern coastal culture, are part of "Finders Keepers," a city-sponsored event where artist-signed and numbered floats are buried in the sand to be discovered and kept as souvenirs. If you find one, call the Visitor and Convention Bureau (800/452-2151 or 541/996-1274) and register your float to receive a certificate of authenticity.

You can also watch the 2,000-year-old art of glassblowing at the **Alder House III Glassblowing Studio** (611 Immonen Rd., 541/994-6485, www.alderhouse.com, 10am-5pm daily May-Oct.) or blow your own colorful spheres at **Jennifer L. Sears Glass Art Studio** (4821 SW US-101, 541/996-2569, $75 per float, call for appointment).

J. Marhoffer Shipwreck

In 1910, a gas explosion on board the wooden steam schooner *J. Marhoffer* set the 175-foot ship ablaze before it smashed into the craggy basalt lava rocks at Boiler Bay. The ship's boiler and driveshaft drifted ashore and are still visible at low tide. A large chunk of rusted steel sticks up from the bluff above, blown there by

LINCOLN CITY

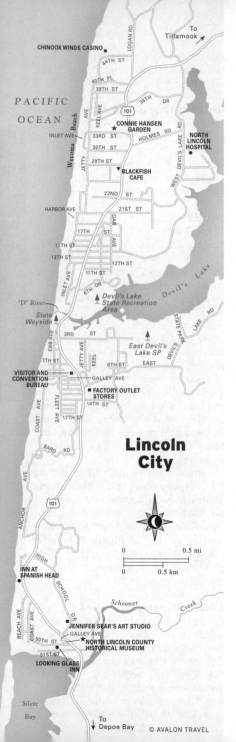

the force of the explosion and firmly embedded into the ground.

Connie Hansen Garden Conservancy

Enchanting pathways meander along lush greenery and colorful blooms at the **Connie Hansen Garden Conservancy** (1931 NW 33rd St., 541/994-633, www.conniehansengarden.com, dawn-dusk daily, free). A San Francisco artist who moved to Lincoln City in 1973 created it over a 20-year period—an amazing accomplishment considering the salt air and sandy soil. In the summertime, it bursts with color as everything is in bloom, including roses and rhododendrons. Rare trees and shrubbery can be seen throughout the year. Tours are available by appointment.

North Lincoln County Historical Museum

Local history and culture are preserved at the **North Lincoln County Historical Museum** (4907 SW US-101, 541/996-6614, noon-5pm Wed.-Sun. summer, noon-5pm Wed.-Sat. winter, free) with 19th- and 20th-century exhibits on the lives of early pioneers and homesteaders, and an amazing display of glass fishing floats.

Food

Enjoy delicious baked goods and gourmet coffee at **Beachtown Coffee** (2937 NW US-101, 541/994-4488, 7am-2pm Tues.-Sun., 7am-noon Mon., under $10) or start the day with a hearty breakfast at **The Otis Cafe** (1259 Salmon River Hwy., 541/994-2813, www.otiscafe.com, 7am-8pm daily, under $10), where large portions and affordable prices go hand in hand.

The 101 Burger (1266 SW 50th St., 541/418-2305, www.hwy101burger.com, 11am-7pm Mon.-Sat., 11am-4pm Sun., under $10) serves good old-fashioned burgers, thick and juicy, double or even quadruple. ★ **The Nelscott Café**

(3237 SW US-101, 541/994-6100, www. nelscottcafe.com, 9am-2pm Mon.-Fri., 8am-2pm Sat.-Sun., under $10) makes its burgers a little interesting with tasty sides like homemade pickle chips. If you stop in for breakfast, don't pass up the best stuffed French toast on the coast.

Blackfish Café (2733 NW US-101, 541/996-1007, www.blackfishcafe.com, 11:30am-9pm Wed.-Sun., $11-30) is known for its signature clam chowder, fish and chips, and breaded oysters. **J's Fish & Chips** (1800 SE US-101, 541/994-4445, 11am-7pm Mon.-Thurs., 11:30am-8pm Fri.-Sat., 11:30am-4:30pm Sun., $6-13) shucks then simmers clams in a creamy broth, and lightly coats and fries halibut to perfection.

Intimate dining doesn't get any better than **The Bay House** (5911 SW US-101, 541/996-3222, www.thebayhouse.org, call for hours, $23-34), a local favorite with views of the Pacific. Every dish is a culinary masterpiece, paired with fine wines for the ultimate in fine dining.

Only the finest regional ingredients reach your plate at **The Dining Room** (7760 US-101 N., 800/452-2300 or 541/764-3600, www.salishan.com, 5:30pm-9:30pm daily, under $38) at the Salishan Spa & Golf Resort. If that's not enough, the lodge's extensive wine cellars are the largest in the state. The five-star dining room overlooks Siletz Bay and the Salishan Spit.

Nightlife and Entertainment

The Nauti Mermaid Bar & Bistro (1343 NW US-101, 541/614-1001, 11am-2am daily) is a friendly neighborhood bar with mixed drinks, beer on tap, pool tables, and lottery games. **Old Oregon Tavern** (1604 NE US-101, 541/994-8515, 7am-2:30am daily) is a popular dive bar with cheap drinks, bar grub, and a big-screen TV. Across the street, **Maxwell's Restaurant & Lounge** (1643 NW US-101, 541/994-8100, www.maxwellslincolncity. com, 8am-2:30pm Fri.-Sun., 7am-2:30am Mon.-Thurs.) has pool tables, darts, golf, and karaoke.

At **Game Over Arcade Bar and Grill** (2821 NW US-101, 541/614-1150, www. gameover-arcade.com, 11am-midnight daily), a pocket full of quarters is all you need for a good time. It's for adults only (kids at heart), serving a variety of beer and wine amid the rows of old-school arcade games and pinball machines.

Entertainment abounds at **Chinook Winds Casino Resort** (1777 NW 44th St., 541/996-5825 and 888/244-6665, www. chinookwindscasino.com, open 24 hours daily), from slots, video poker machines, and table games to concerts and comedy acts. Situated above the fairways of the Chinook Winds golf course, **Aces Sports Bar & Grill** (541/994-8232) entertains with NFL games, UFC Pay per View, and the Pack 12 Network played on 14 screens.

Shopping

Along US-101 is a collection of galleries and souvenir and specialty shops. **101 Coastal Creations** (4840 SE US-101, 541/614-1525) specializes in blown glass, fine art, and handcrafted jewelry. **Cap'N Gulls Gift Place** (120 SE US-101, 541/994-7743) stocks glass floats, wind chimes, clothing, and specialty gifts. The **Oregon Surf Shop** (3001 SW US-101, 877/339-5672, www.oregonsurfshop.com, 10am-6pm Mon.-Sat., 1pm-5pm Sun.) is a one-stop shop for surf gear and beachwear. Browse handcrafted jewelry made from Pacific Northwest gems at **Rock Your World** (1423 NW US-101, 541/351-8423, 11am-6pm daily).

The Crystal Wizard (7150 Gleneden Beach Loop Rd., 541/764-7550, www. thecrystalwizard.com, 10am-5pm Wed.-Sun.) is a magical place stocked with metaphysical merchandise, carvings, statuary, books, and jewelry.

Lincoln City Farmers and Crafters Market (540 NE US-101, 541/921-5745, every Sun.) offers locally grown produce, baked goods, prepared foods, and handcrafted items from inside the Lincoln

City Cultural Center during the cold months, and outdoors when the sun is shining.

Tanger Outlet Center (1500 SE Devils Lake Rd., 541/996-5000, 10am-8pm Mon.-Sat., 10am-6pm Sun.) encompasses over 50 discount name-brand stores that will satisfy quality tastes without empting your wallet.

Recreation

Most people come to Lincoln City for a day at the beach. The favored access points are at the north and south ends of the city. The prettiest stretch of beach is on the north end of town at **Road's End State Wayside** (off US-101 on Logan Rd., open year-round, free). The cool sandy shore has interesting rock features and tide pools that reveal bright starfish and sea anemones at low tide.

A short drive north off Three Rocks Road, Knights Park marks the lower trailhead (open year-round, free) to the **Cascade Head Trail,** a moderate four-mile journey through old-growth fir and spruce, across streams and bridges, and butterfly meadows. Viewpoints extend down the coastline, exposing the Salmon River Estuary, Cape Foulweather, and Devil's Lake.

On the northeast side of US-101, **Devil's Lake State Park** (541/994-2002 and 800/551-6949, $5 per vehicle) offers summer recreation including fishing, boating ($10 moorage), and waterskiing. Boat launches are located on the west shore of the lake near the campground ($17-21 tents, $44 yurts, $27-31 RVs) and on the southern end at East Devil's Lake day-use park (205 NE East Devils Lake Rd.). **Blue Heron Landing Rentals** (4006 NE West Devils Lake Rd., 541/994-4708, www.blueheronlanding.net, 9am-7pm daily) rents canoes ($17/hr, $51/day) and kayaks ($13/hr, $39/day), and carries bait supplies and other fishing equipment.

To the south, across US-101, **Siletz Bay** is an estuary populated by many bird species, including great blue herons, hawks, and egrets. The sandy peninsula jutting out into the bay is the **Salishan Spit,** which provides both an easy and scenic 8.1-mile hike, passing spruce trees, crumbling sandstone ridges, and hundreds of lounging seals. The trailhead is accessed at Gleneden Beach State Park, off US-101 on Wesler Street.

Boiler Bay is popular with surfers despite its jagged lava-rimmed bay and strong currents; it is not a place for beginners. Sea-life is abundant, with whales seen off the bay year-round. At low tide, rich tide pools are revealed, as is the wreckage of the *J. Marhoffer.*

Events

Kites vie for sky space at Lincoln City's summer and fall **Kite Festivals** (D-River Wayside, late June and early Oct.). The weekend events feature demonstrations, kite-making activities, and some of the biggest, most colorful kites in the world.

Accommodations

Affordable yet charming, **Palace Inn and Suites** (550 SE US-101, 866/996-9466, www.thepalaceinn.com, $59 and up) has 51 spacious guest rooms in walking distance from the beach, restaurants, and shopping. The historic **Anchor Inn** (4417 SW US-101, 541/996-3810, www.historicanchorinn.com, $109 and up) surrounds you with 1940s nostalgia and nautical paraphernalia, and offers an on-site massage therapist. The **Inn at Wecoma** (2945 NW US-101, 541/994-2984 and 800/452-8981, www.innatwecoma.com, $108 and up) offers a hearty breakfast, spacious rooms, and special accommodations for pets. The **Looking Glass Inn** (861 SW 51st St., 541/996-3996 and 800/843-4940, www.lookingglass-inn.com, $115-155) sits on a driftwood-strewn beach, offering views of the Siletz River and Bay. Guest rooms include all the comforts of home.

Every room at **Inn At Spanish Head** (4009 SW US-101, 800/452-8127, www.spanishhead.com, $205 and up) offers floor-to-ceiling windows with unobstructed ocean views. You'll never miss a sunset at the **Nelscott Manor** (3037 SW Anchor Ave., 541/996-9300 or 800/972-6155, www.onthebeachfront.com, $129-425), which offers five oceanfront suites with whirlpool tubs.

Information and Services
Detailed information is available by contacting the **Lincoln City Visitor and Convention Bureau** (801 SW US-101, 800/452-2151, www.lincolncity.org, 8am-5pm Mon.-Fri.), located on the fourth floor of the City Hall building.

Depoe Bay

The tiny village of Depoe Bay boasts the "smallest harbor in the world," but its reigning title as the "Whale Watching Capital of the Oregon Coast" is more worthy of braggadocio. From March through December a resident pod of gray whales takes up residence offshore. But whales are not the only attraction blowing sea water into the air. Depoe Bay's coastline is riddled with lava beds that occasionally shoot water nearly 60 feet into the sky once enough pressure has built up. A huge sea wall runs along the entire length of downtown, where the ocean always remains in view.

Gracie's Sea Hag Restaurant & Lounge (58 US-101, 541/765-2734, www.the-seahag.com, 7am-9pm daily, under $15) is worth a stop for its homemade chowder. Gracie herself has become a local celebrity for playing "bottle music" behind the bar. There's more traditional live music Thursday-Sunday. Stay the night at the **Inn at Arch Rock** (70 NW Sunset St., 800/767-1835, http://innatarchrock.com,

$79-309), which offers spectacular views and easy access to the beach.

★ Otter Crest Loop: Cape Foulweather and the Devil's Punchbowl

During his voyage of discovery to the Sandwich Islands, Captain James Cook (circa 1778) first landed at **Cape Foulweather**, a basalt cliff that rises 500 feet above the Pacific, overlooking Otter Rock and Yaquina Head.

Between Depoe Bay and Newport, a sign on US-101 marks the turn-off to Otter Crest Access Loop Road, a twisting three-mile section of the old coastal highway, where the already rugged coastal bluffs become even more dramatic. It winds its way to the Otter Crest State Scenic Viewpoint, where there's a parking lot. Watch the crashing surf along the shore, sea lions basking in the sun, and migrating whales and ships passing on the horizon. The never-ending views are unforgettable. **The Lookout** (milepost 232.5, US-101, 541/765-2270, 10am-4pm Wed.-Sun.) is a small interpretive center and gift shop atop the bluff that is protected as a historic landmark.

At the south end of the Loop, the churning surf surges against a wave-sculpted basin appropriately named the **Devil's Punchbowl.** North of the Punchbowl, tide pools are revealed when the water recedes. To the south is a viewpoint with picnic tables. Still farther south is **Mo's West** (122 1st St., Otter Rock, 541/765-2442, www.moschowder.com, 11am-3pm Mon.-Fri., 11am-7pm Sat., 11am-6pm Sun.), where a hot cup of famous chowder hits the spot!

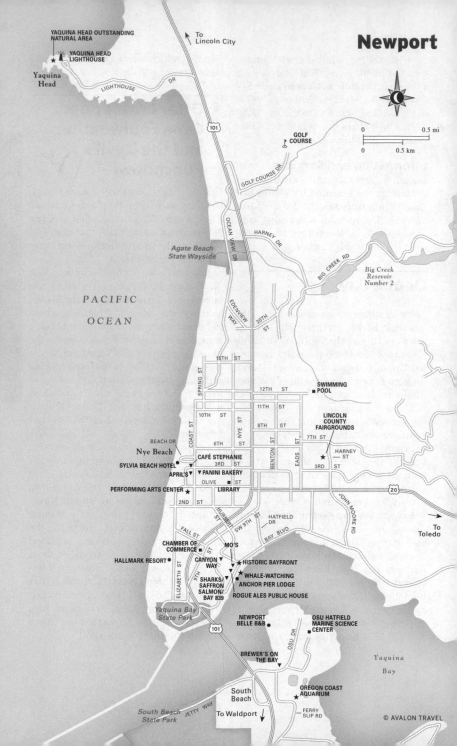

Newport

YAQUINA HEAD OUTSTANDING NATURAL AREA

YAQUINA HEAD LIGHTHOUSE

Yaquina Head

LIGHTHOUSE DR

To Lincoln City

101

GOLF COURSE

GOLF COURSE DR

OCEAN VIEW DR

HARNEY DR

Agate Beach State Wayside

PACIFIC OCEAN

BIG CREEK RD

Big Creek Resevoir Number 2

EDENVIEW WAY

20TH ST

15TH ST

12TH ST

SPRING ST

SWIMMING POOL

11TH ST

10TH ST

8TH ST

NYE ST

LINCOLN COUNTY FAIRGROUNDS

COAST ST

6TH ST

BENTON ST

EADS ST

7TH ST

HARNEY ST

3RD ST

BEACH DR

Nye Beach

SYLVIA BEACH HOTEL

CAFÉ STEPHANIE

3RD ST

APRIL'S

PANINI BAKERY

OLIVE ST

20

PERFORMING ARTS CENTER

LIBRARY

2ND ST

JOHN MOORE RD

To Toledo

HURBERT ST

SW 9TH ST

HATFIELD DR

FALL ST

BAY BLVD

CHAMBER OF COMMERCE

MO'S

HISTORIC BAYFRONT

HALLMARK RESORT

CANYON WAY

WHALE-WATCHING

ELIZABETH ST

9TH ST

SHARKS/ SAFFRON SALMON/ BAY 839

ANCHOR PIER LODGE

ROGUE ALES PUBLIC HOUSE

Yaquina Bay State Park

101

NEWPORT BELLE B&B

OSU DR

OSU HATFIELD MARINE SCIENCE CENTER

Yaquina Bay

BREWER'S ON THE BAY

South Beach

To Waldport

South Beach State Park

JETTY WAY

OREGON COAST AQUARIUM

FERRY SLIP RD

© AVALON TRAVEL

0   0.5 mi
0   0.5 km

Newport

The largest town on the Oregon coast, **Newport** (pop. 9,989) was founded in the 1860s largely due to the demand for its sweet Yaquina Bay oysters, which continue to be served in local restaurants. Summer tourists wander the shops, galleries, and attractions along the historic Bayfront and pack into the Oregon Coast Aquarium. In the distance, fishing boats bait the waters for the day's bounty, while sea lions lounge on the docks.

On the north side of town, charming **Nye Beach** was one of the first resort destinations on the coast. Old, 19th-century cottages remain as a testament to the town's early roots, scattered among neoteric hotels, vintage shops, and quaint cafés.

Getting There and Around

Newport sits at the junction of US-101 and US-20, 25 miles south of Lincoln City. Lincoln County provides daily bus service with the **Newport City Loop** (541/265-4900, www.co.lincoln.or.us, $1).

Sights
Bayfront

On the east side of US-101, Newport's historic **Bayfront** is Newport's tourist hub with saltwater taffy shops, souvenir stores, and overpriced attractions. **Mariner Square** (250 SW Bay Blvd., 541/265-2206, www.marinersquare. com, hours vary seasonally, 9am-8pm daily June-Sept., 10am-5pm Sat.-Sun. and 11am-4pm Mon.-Fri., Feb.-May, $12-25 adults, $7-15 children 5-12, free children 4 and under) marks the entrance to **The Wax Works, Ripley's Believe It or Not!,** and the **Undersea Gardens,** where Oregon's largest collection of local marinelife can be seen swimming through a kelp forest. Tickets can be purchased at Mariner Square per attraction or at a discount for all three. One of the biggest draws is the loitering sea lions sprawled out on floating docks near the Undersea Gardens. You can watch them from the pier, and listen to their incessant barking.

Oregon Coast Aquarium

Get a slimy handshake from the resident Giant Pacific Octopus at the **Oregon Coast Aquarium** (2820 SE Ferry Slip Rd., 541/867-3474, 10am-5pm daily winter, 9am-6pm daily summer, $20 adults, $18 seniors and children 13-17, $13 children 3-12), brought to the world's attention by its one-time main attraction the orca, Keiko, star of the 1993 hit movie *Free Willy*. Though Keiko is no longer here, the aquarium is still one of the top marine museums in the country, featuring outdoor exhibits of sea lions, tufted puffins, and other shorebirds cavorting in a simulated rockbound habitat, and an indoor aquatic aviary tunnel that allows for undersea viewing of sharks. The museum offers visual and interactive information on Pacific Coast ecosystems.

Nye Beach

Easily missed (if you don't know it's there), the little town of **Nye Beach** is tucked away along the shores of the Pacific, just north of Bayfront and west of US-101. It was one of the first beach resort towns in Oregon, and the first to erect all sorts of getaway abodes from motels and hotels to B&Bs to cottages. Nye is a great town to walk about (there is a car-free pedestrian street) and check out the quirky shops, charming cafés, and the captivating oceanfront views.

Lighthouses

Newport has two lighthouses, Yaquina Bay Lighthouse, built in 1871, and Yaquina Head Lighthouse, lit only a year later.

The oldest standing structure in Newport, **Yaquina Bay Lighthouse** (846 SW Government St., 541/265-5679, 11am-4pm daily in summer, noon-4pm daily rest of the year) sits above the mouth of the Yaquina River. It illuminated its oscillating light only for three years before it was decommissioned. The light tower sits above a two-story house, not the usual design for a watchtower, but it did serve as a residence and a guiding light to offshore vessels. In 1996, it was lovingly restored and its white light relit, now shining steadily from dusk to dawn. Visitors are welcome to explore the lighthouse on their own. Private tours can be arranged with Sylvia White (541/270-0131, fee may apply).

On the north side of town, **Yaquina Head Lighthouse** (750 NW Lighthouse Dr., 541/574-3100, parks and outdoor nature areas outside lighthouse 7am-sunset daily, $7 parking pass, good for three days) rises 93 feet from its basalt perch and is Oregon's tallest lighthouse. A tour guide paints a picture of the past dressed in 1800s attire and shares old tales, as you ascend the 114 spiraling steps to the top for a breathtaking view. Tours operate every hour (noon-3pm, Thurs.-Tues.). It's first-come, first-served and spaces are limited, so get there early. Even if you miss the tour, the 100-acre site offers visitors unprecedented views, an interpretive center, a gift shop, the Tide pool Loop Trail that leads through an old quarry, and abundant marine and wildlife.

Food

The family-friendly ★ **Newport Café** (534 N. Coast Hwy., 541/574-6847, www.thenewportcafe.com, open 24 hours daily, $4-15) serves big breakfasts at reasonable prices. The original **Mo's** (622 Bay Blvd., 541/265-2979, www.moschowder.com, 11am-8pm Sun.-Fri., 11am-9pm Sat., $4-22) started serving its famous clam chowder over 65 years ago. **Saffron Salmon** (859 SW Bay Blvd., 541/265-8921, 11:30am-2:15pm and 5pm-8:30pm Thurs.-Tues., $15-26) lures 'em in with fresh seafood; beefy burgers are on the menu, too.

The tiny district of Nye Beach dishes up some excellent grub! From its bright yellow exterior, **Cafe Stephanie** (411 NW Coast St., 541/265-8082, 7:30am-3pm daily, $8-14) is hard to pass up, and you won't want to miss their pastries galore, banana French toast, and omelets. **April's at Nye Beach** (749 NW 3rd St., 541/265-6855, www.aprilsatnyebeach.com, from 5pm Wed.-Sun., $16-18) keeps the ingredients and seafood fresh, with pastas and sauces all made from scratch. **Panini** (232 NW Coast St., 541/265-5033, 7am-7pm daily, under $20) makes fresh pizza in a woodfire oven and sells it by the slice. They also make great baked goods and the best lattes in town. Bright and cheery **Nye Beach Café** (526 NW Coast St., 541/574-1599, 8am-4pm Mon.-Thurs. and Sun., 8am-5pm Fri.-Sat., under $12) offers a mix of fresh, healthy fare, with gluten-free options and clam chowder that rivals Mo's.

On the southwest side of US-101, family-friendly **Georgie's Beachside Grill** (744 SW Elizabeth St., at Hallmark Resort, 541/265-9800, www.georgies-beachsidegrill.com, 7:30am-9pm daily, under $29) serves up fresh seafood, steak, pasta, and vegan dishes with a gorgeous ocean view.

Nightlife and Entertainment

On the Bayfront, **Port Dock One** (325 SW Bay Blvd., 541/265-2911) sits right on the dock overlooking Yaquina Bay. The lounge upstairs offers the best views and a full bar.

Artsy Nye Beach has a dynamic nightlife. **Nana's Irish Pub** (613 NW 3rd St., 541/574-8787, 11am-11pm Sun.-Thurs., 11am-midnight Fri.-Sat.) is a spirited meeting place with live music every Monday night (and sometimes weekends) with everything from traditional Irish music to rock and roll.

At upbeat, bohemian **Café Mundo** (209 NW Coast St., 541/574-8134, 11am-10pm Tues.-Thurs., 11am-midnight Fri.-Sat., 10am-4pm Sun.), the art is unique, the cocktails are perfect, and the music (jazz and folk) is always free. Maritime murals adorn the walls at **Bi-valve Bar** (740 W. Olive St., 541/264-8672, 11am-8:30pm Sun.-Thurs., 11am-close Fri.-Sat.). Kick back and enjoy spirits, imported wines, and local microbrews.

Newport Performing Arts Center (777 W. Olive St., 541/265-2787, www.coast-arts.org, box office: 9am-5pm Mon.-Fri., call for ticket pricing) hosts musical entertainment, Shakespearean plays, Broadway musicals, and dance productions year-round.

Shopping

The historic Bayfront is lined with a variety of art galleries and unique gift shops.

Located near the Undersea Gardens, **The Wind Drift Gallery II** (414 SW Bay Blvd., 541/265-7454, 10am-5:30pm daily) is filled with wind chimes, jewelry, home decor, and knickknacks. Next door, you'll find natural stone jewelry, exquisite glass art, and other crafts from Northwest artists at **Breach the Moon Gallery** (434 SW Bay Blvd., 541/265-9698, www.blue-herongallery.com). The art at **Latta's Fused Glass** (669 Bay Blvd., 541/265-9685, www.lattasfusedglass.com, 10am-5pm daily) ranges from the whimsical to sophisticated; every vase, plate, and platter has its own personality.

Forinash Gallery (856 SW Bay Blvd., 541/265-8483) showcases seascape photographs by award-winning photographer Chuck Forinash.

On a sea cliff west of US-101, Nye Beach has its own mix of stylish boutiques and quirky shops. **For ArtSake Gallery** (258 NW Coast St., 541/574-9070) displays paintings, pottery, leather handbags, jewelry, and glass art. **Things Rich & Strange** (255 NW Coast St., 541/265-3600) is an esoteric mix of crystals, books, incense, herbs, and custom jewelry. Make your own jewelry with help from **Nye Cottage Beads** (208 NW Coast St., 541/265-6262 or 866/592-5556, www.nyecottage.com, 10am-5pm daily), a little nook draped in wall-to-wall strands of color.

Pirates and sea creatures are scattered throughout clusters of colorful antique and specialty gift shops at **Aquarium Village** (3101 SE Ferry Slip Rd., 541/867-6531, www.aquariumvillage.org). There's also a climbable pirate ship for kids.

Recreation

On the south side of Yaquina Head, **Agate Beach** is a hot spot for surfers with good breaks at mid to high tide. The beach is easily accessed from the Agate Beach parking lot, located right past **Ossies's Surf Shop** (4860 N. Coast Hwy., 541/574-4634, 10am-5pm daily), which offers lessons ($80/two hrs), gear rentals, and kayak tours ($40 single 24 hrs, $55 double 24 hrs).

Crabbing and clamming around Yaquina Bay is also popular. Butter, cockle, and littleneck clams can all be found on the mud flats at **Sally's Bend,** accessed from Yaquina Bay Drive at low tide. Bring a shovel, bucket, and rubber boots. Red rock crabs are caught off the Abbey Street and Bay Street piers on the Newport Bay front. The required license can be purchased at local tackle shops, like **Harry's Bait & Tackle** (404 SW Bay Blvd., 541/265-2407), which also rents equipment ($25 deposit).

Events

The **Seafood and Wine Festival** (www.newportchamber.com, Feb.) is a gathering focused on culinary delights plucked from the sea, Pacific Northwest wines, and lovely artwork.

Writers, poets, playwrights, and songwriters perform at the monthly **Writers' Series** (777 NW Beach Dr., 541/563-6263, www.writersontheedge.org) in Nye Beach.

Accommodations

The ★ **Sylvia Beach Hotel** (267 NW Cliff St., 541/265-5428, www.sylviabeachhotel.com, $120 and up) has literary-themed rooms styled after authors like Jane Austen, Mark Twain, and J. K. Rowling, along with a library with large comfy chairs perfect for curling up with a good book. There's a two-night minimum stay, but you may never want to leave.

Agate Beach Motel (175 NW Gilbert Way, 541/265-8746 or 800/755-5674, www.agatebeachmotel.com, $115-179) offers cottage units with full kitchens, private decks, and easy beach access.

The romantic **Hallmark Resort** (744 SW Elizabeth St., 855/430-3279, www. hallmarkinns.com, $164 and up) has rooms with cozy fireplaces and spa tubs for two.

Little Nye Beach has several quaint places to stay. The **Inn at Yaquina Bay** (2633 S. Pacific Way, 541/867-7055, www. innatyaquinabay.com, $58 and up) is perfect for budget travelers, offering roomy accommodations with free WiFi and cable TV. The **Inn at Nye Beach** (729 NW Coast St., 541/265-2477 or 800/480-2477, www.innatnyebeach.com, $113-169) sits on a bluff connected by a staircase to the beach below. Sleep like a baby, wrapped in high thread-count linens, and wake up to fresh scones.

Information and Services

For further information on Newport attractions or for a complete list of hotels, contact the **Greater Newport Chamber of Commerce** (555 SW Coast Hwy., 541/265-8801, www.newportchamber. org, 8:30am-5pm Mon.-Fri.).

Waldport

Low-key **Waldport** offers an alternative to its bustling, tourist-hungry neighbors. Much of the town's economy still relies on fishing. The town's most popular activity is watching fishing boats, waterfowl, and seals in the Alsea Bay. **Alsea Bay Bridge Interpretive Center** (620 NW Spring St., 541/563-2002, 9am-4pm daily) offers clamming and crabbing demonstrations, bridge walk tours, and information on the local Alsea tribe.

The vintage **Cape Cod Cottages** (541/563-2106, www.capecodcottagesonline.com, $65-190) offers one- and two-bedroom rentals with full kitchens, located on a quiet sandy beach. **Beachside State Recreation Area** (541/563-3220) has a good-sized campground with all the amenities, including a coin-operated laundry.

Yachats

Eight miles south of Waldport, the charming, tiny village of **Yachats** (pop. 675; pronounced YA-hots) is an idyllic retreat in a remarkable natural setting at the mouth of the Yachats River and in the shadow of Cape Perpetua. You're more likely to find peace and quiet than crowds of beachgoers.

Along the beautiful one-mile loop around **Ocean Road State Natural Area,** you can see a spouting basalt blowhole and spot migrating whales. In and around town, there are artist galleries and gift shops, as well as a **Sunday Farmers Market** (4th St. next to Yachats Commons, 9am-2pm Sun. mid-May-mid-Oct.).

Overleaf Lodge & Spa (280 Overleaf Lodge Ln., 541/547-4880, $150 and up) looks out over the sea, offering sweeping views and relaxing spa treatments. **ONA Restaurant and Lounge** (131 US-101 N., 541/547-6627, 4pm-8:30pm Mon.-Fri., 11am-8:30pm Sat.-Sun., $15-30) is perfect for a romantic dinner, with views of the Yachats River and the Pacific Ocean.

Cape Perpetua

Cape Perpetua is a steep bluff rising above the Pacific Ocean, over 800 feet at its highest point. On a clear day, you can see nearly 70 miles of coastline from its ridge. It also includes 26 miles of hiking trails that meander through old-growth forests of Douglas fir, western hemlock, and spruce, including the 600-year-old Giant Spruce, which measures more than 185 feet tall.

As you enter, stop at the **visitors center** (2400 US-101, 541/547-3289, 10am-5pm daily mid-June-Aug., 10am-4pm daily Sept.-mid-June, $5/car) for hiking and driving tour maps. It also features an observation deck, natural history and cultural exhibits, a theater, and a small bookstore.

The driving tour will lead you to the summit. Once you've taken in the view, you can follow the half-mile loop **Whispering Spruce Trail,** which travels through the grounds of a Word War II Coast Guard station, built in 1933 by the Civilian Conservation Corps.

Down on the beach, you can make your way to Devil's Churn, Spouting Horn, and Thor's Well, basalt rock formations that spray sea water 50 feet into the air in strong surf.

Along the banks of Cape Creek, the **Cape Perpetua Campground** (2200 US-101, 877/444-6777, $22) is surrounded by trees. There are picnic tables, drinking water, and flush toilets, but no showers or hookups.

★ Heceta Head and the Sea Lion Caves

Perched at the top of 1,000-foot-high Heceta Head is one of the most visited and photographed lighthouses in the United States, drawing thousands of visitors each year. Built in 1893, it was named for a captain of the Royal Spanish Navy who made note of the headland in his journal when exploring the region. The masonry tower stands 56 feet tall and its light shines 21 miles out to sea—farther than any other on the Oregon coast.

The former light-keeper's house is today known as **Heceta House** (92072 US-101, 541/547-3696 or 866/547-3696, www.hecetalighthouse.com, free), which acts as an **interpretive center** (noon-5pm

Mon.-Thurs. Memorial Day-Labor day) and a quaint **bed-and-breakfast** ($133-315). Free guided tours are offered regularly during the summer and by appointment the rest of the year. Stories of strange activities and unexplained occurrences at Heceta House have collected over the years, winning it a place on lists of the 10 most-haunted houses in the United States. Public parking is located at the Heceta Head Lighthouse State Scenic Viewpoint ($5 per vehicle).

Just south of the lighthouse, the surge of the sea crashes into the vast **Sea Lion Caves** (91560 US-101, 541/547-3111, $18 adults, $8 children, 9am-5pm daily), one of the largest known sea caves in the world, and a dwelling place for thousands of Steller sea lions. You can ride the elevator down into the cavern and witness these enormous mammals (males can weigh over a ton, while females reach 600-800 pounds). Fall and winter are the best times to see them. When the sun comes out, you can see them playing in the ocean and basking on rocks from viewpoints along US-101.

Florence

Midway between the Oregon coastal cities of Newport and Coos Bay, **Florence** sits at the mouth of the Siuslaw River (pronounced sigh-YOU-slaw). It's an eclectic city of old and new, defined by its historic structures, natural setting, and commercial industries. The Siuslaw Indians originally lived around the estuary of the Siuslaw River, and taught early pioneers how to collect food and fish its

waters. Eventually "industry" took over with commercial fishing and timber mills, as the demand for wood increased throughout the West.

Along Bay Street's three blocks, you'll find a number of cafés and seafood restaurants, and all kinds of interesting boutiques and galleries with treasures to uncover. But the more interesting and somewhat curious wonders are found just south of Old Town.

Getting There and Around

Florence sits on US-101, separated by a 49-mile (70 minutes) stretch of highway that hugs the coastline, offering open views of the ocean.

Services and sights are spread out, so a car or bus service is best to get around.

The **Rhody Express** (541/902-2067, $1 one-way pass) is the public transportation service within the community, and operates a South (Dune Village, Old Town, Three Rivers Casino) and North (Grocery Outlet, Fred Meyer) loop in a

the Sea Lion Caves at Heceta Head

70-minute circuit. There are several stops along its route, each clearly visible.

Sights
Old Town
On the southern end of Florence, **Old Town** is nestled into the Port of Siuslaw. It's easy to miss from the highway and there is only one sign pointing the way, but that doesn't mean it's not worth stopping. It's a captivating fishing village, established in 1893, with narrow streets, historic buildings, and a meandering boardwalk. There's a lot to explore along Laurel and Bay Streets, where a collection of artful shops and eateries are found. Follow the brick path past the gazebo to the ferry landing overlook, a great spot for bird-watchers and for photos of the Siuslaw River Bridge.

Siuslaw River Bridge
Ferryboats were once the link across the Siuslaw River until 1936 when the **Siuslaw River Bridge** was completed.

Designed by Conde McCullough in the bascule style, the bridge has two 154-foot concrete tied arches and four art deco-style obelisks. Walking west on Bay Street brings you under the bridge to the **Interpretive Center** and viewing platform, which provides unobstructed views of the bridge and estuary. Walkways wander past benches where you can rest and take in the landscape, while interpretive signs give the history and geology of the site.

Siuslaw Pioneer Museum
Historic photographs and 19th-century artifacts fill **Siuslaw Pioneer Museum** (278 Maple St., 541/997-7884, noon-4pm Tues.-Sun., $3 adults), located in a renovated 1905 schoolhouse building. Upstairs, memorabilia from the Civil War and World Wars I and II share space with Native American relics, while downstairs exhibits focus on the logging, fishing, and maritime industries.

Darlingtonia State Natural Site
A visit to **Darlingtonia State Natural Site** (five miles north of Florence) might leave you uneasy once you realize what lives here: a carnivorous plant! No, it isn't Audrey II from the musical *Little Shop of Horrors;* it's Cobra Lily, a rare, hooded plant, also known as *Darlingtonia californica.* From the parking lot, a boardwalk trail with views of the Oregon Dunes leads to this botanical wonder that lures insects with sweet nectar from the opening beneath its yellowish-green leaves.

Jessie M. Honeyman Memorial State Park
Three miles south of Florence, **Jessie M. Honeyman Memorial State Park** (84505 US-101, 800/452-5687, www.oregonstateparks.org, $5 day-use) springs to life with vibrant rhododendrons in late April to the middle of May. But the park's main attractions are rows and rows of shifting **sand dunes** that stretch two miles along the coast. The Oregon Dunes National

Recreation Area adjoins the west side of the park.

Food

Housed in an old railroad station, ★ **Waterfront Depot** (1252 Bay St., 541/902-9100, www.thewaterfrontdepot. com, 4pm-10pm daily, under $28) serves great seafood and steaks in its dining room and outdoor patio, with picturesque views.

At the edge of Jessie M. Honeyman Memorial State Park, **Morgan's Country Kitchen** (85020 US-101, 541/997-6991, 8am-2pm daily, until 3pm in summer, $5-12) lives up to its down-home reputation with large portions and favorites like biscuits and gravy, home fries, and berry cobbler.

Big Dogs Donuts & Deli (1136 US-101, 541/997-8630, 5am-3pm Mon.-Sat., $1-9) is inside an old yellow gas station, but don't judge the food by the building. The fresh doughnuts here are legendary, and they know how to make a great sandwich, too.

For tastes with a little added spice, try family-owned **Rosa's Mexican Restaurant** (2825 US-101, 541/997-1144, $8-16), where the chips and salsa are homemade and the service is delightful.

Nature's Corner Café & Market (185 US-101, 541/997-0900, www.naturescornercafe.com, 8am-6pm Tues.-Fri., 8am-6:30pm Sat., 8am-3pm Sun., $4-21) serves everything organic and sometimes gluten-free, with everything from breakfast burritos and blueberry pancakes to fish tacos and burgers.

La Pomodori Ristorante (1415 7th St., 541/902-2525, www.lapomodori.com, 11:30am-2pm Tues.-Fri., 5pm-8pm Tues.-Sat., $6-22) fuses traditional Italian cooking with Northwest flavors. The pasta dishes and crab cakes are delicious, and the garlic bread is unbelievable.

The **ICM Restaurant** (1498 Bay St., 541/997-9646, www.icmrestaurant. com, 11am-9pm daily, $10-30) is easy to spot because of its giant mural of sea creatures. Inside, the bar and restaurant gleam with brass nautical fixtures and wood decor. The food is fantastic, with fresh seafood, wood-fired pizza, and award-winning clam chowder.

Colorful Asian bistro **Spice** (1269 Bay St., 541/997-1646, www.spiceinflorence. com, 3pm-8pm Tues.-Thurs., 3pm-9pm Fri.-Sat., $15-35) serves a variety of savory eastern dishes and Northwest favorites. Try the house favorite "Shellfish Madness"—so much seafood that it needs two bowls!

Nightlife and Entertainment

For over 50 years, the **Beachcomber Pub** (1355 Bay St., 541/997-6357, 7am-midnight Sun.-Thurs., 7am-1am Fri.-Sat.) has been a fixture in Old Town Florence, with over 100 bottled beers, a great selection of beers on tap, and live bands every Friday and Saturday night.

Despite its unassuming appearance, **Travelers Cove** (1362 Bay St., 541/997-6845, 9am-9pm daily, extended weekend hours) is a local favorite because of its well-priced drinks, eclectic musical entertainment, and the lively deck above the river.

Three Rivers Casino (5647 OR-126, 877/374-8377, www.threerivers.com) is packed with over 700 Vegas-style slots, video games, and table games. Inside the casino, **Ace's Sports Bar & Lounge** (10am-1:30am daily) serves a good selection of wine and specialty drinks, with live comedy and music on the weekend.

Enjoy an evening of theatrical delight attending a play or musical at the **Florence Playhouse** (208 Laurel St., 541/997-1675, www.florenceplayhouse. com), located in Old Town on Laurel and 1st Streets, just steps away from the Siuslaw River.

Shopping

Most shopping is in Old Town.

If you love beautiful things, stop by **Bonjour Boutique** (1336 Bay St., 541/997-8194, www.bonjourboutiqueonline.com,

10am-6pm daily) to explore exquisite clothing, jewelry, and gifts from around the world.

When they named it **All About Olives** (1367 Bay St., 541/997-3174, www.allaboutolives.net, 10am-5pm daily), they weren't kidding! This little shop is stuffed with unique and exotic varieties, as well as olive oils, balsamic vinegars, tapenades, and, best of all, free samples!

Aspiring chefs should head to **Balcony Gourmet** (1411 Bay St., 541/997-8003, 10am-5:30pm daily) and **Kitchen Klutter Inc.** (1258 Bay St., 541/997-6060, 10am-6pm daily). Both stores are furnished with everything you need to create your next culinary masterpiece.

Periwinkle Station (1308 Bay St., 541/902-7901, 10am-6pm) offers vintage games, lunch boxes, and books. Gaming is also the focus of **Wizard of Odds** (1384 Bay St., 541/902-0602, 10am-5:30pm daily), but in this case it involves sculpted pewter and resin dragons and fairies. **Treasure Bay** (125 Nopal St., 541/997-7300) stockpiles vintage collectibles, crafts, and jewelry.

An antiques district skirts US-101, north of the Siuslaw River Bridge. **Mon Ami Deli & Antiques** (490 US-101, 541/997-9234, 9:30am-4pm Mon.-Fri., 10am-4pm Sat.-Sun.) has all the usual and unusual old-world items, but what makes it different are its deli and espresso bar. Have a nibble while you shop. Across the street, **Brown Dog Antiques** (595 US-101, 541/902-7986, 10am-5pm daily) and **Florence Antiques** (494 US-101, 541/997-8104, 10am-5pm daily) are both treasure troves of fine china, art, and furniture.

Recreation

Inside Jessie M. Honeyman Memorial State Park are two natural freshwater lakes. **Cleawox Lake,** which occupies the park's west side, is a great place to swim, kayak, or canoe. At the larger **Woahink Lake,** on the east side, boating, waterskiing, and windsurfing are the popular activities. There are also camping

and bathroom facilities, and an on-site store with souvenirs and snacks open Memorial Day weekend-Labor Day. **Central Coast Watersports** (1901 US-101, 541/997-1812 and 800/789-3483, www.centralcoastwatersports.com) rents kayaks and canoes ($50-60 per day).

Eight miles north of Florence, **C&M Stables** (90241 US-101 N., 541/997-7540, www.oregonhorsebackriding.com, $55 and up) provides horseback riding tours along the beach.

Located just north of Three Rivers Casino, **Ocean Dunes Golf Links** (3345 Munsel Lake Rd., 541/997-3232, www.oceandunesgolf.com, $83-99 pp) is an 18-hole course with a par of 71 and a slope of 124.

Events

Florence holds the annual **Rhododendron Festival** (541/997-3128, www.florencechamber.com, $10-15) in Old Town the third weekend in May. It's the second-oldest flower festival in Oregon, showcasing a parade of flower-covered floats, a street fair, car show, and carnival.

Accommodations

Set on a hilltop with panoramic views of the river and sand dunes, the ★ **Landmark Inn** (1551 4th St., 800/822-7811, www.landmarkmotel.com, $75-150) is spacious, comfortable, and convenient to shopping and restaurants. The warm, family-friendly **Old Town Inn** (170 US-101, 800/301-6494 or 541/997-7131, www.old-town-inn.com, $84-109) is also well located, minutes away from popular sights and activities.

The elegantly restored 1914 ★ **Edwin K. B&B** (1155 Bay St., 541/997-8360, www.edwink.com, $135-240) has six spacious rooms with private baths. A five-course breakfast is served in the formal dining room. **Driftwood Shores** (88416 1st Ave., 541/997-8263 or 800/422-5091, www.driftwoodshores.com, $137-309) boasts magnificent oceanfront views. Rooms come with a full kitchen or refrigerator and microwave. There is an on-site swimming pool, restaurant, and bar.

Surrounded by the sandy seascape and wooded trails, **Three Rivers Casino & Hotel** (5647 OR-126, 877/374-8377, www. threeriverscasino.com, $228 and up) offers elegant rooms, free RV parking, and an electric car charging station.

Information and Services
The best source of information about the area is the **Florence Area Chamber of Commerce** (290 US-101, 541/997-3128).

★ Oregon Dunes

South of Florence, wind-sculpted sand dunes soar up to 500 feet above sea level, surrounded by clusters of trees, marshes, and beaches. This is the nearly 50-mile stretch of the **Oregon Dunes National Recreation Area,** the largest expanse of coastal sand dunes in North America. Formed by the weathering of inland mountains and volcanic eruption, these dunes are a testament to nature's artistry. "Tree Islands" remain as a reminder that before deposits of sand piled high onto the shore, a large forest covered the area. Travelers make pilgrimages here to see these ever-changing anomalies for themselves. Author Frank Herbert's famous science fiction novel *Dune* was inspired by these mountains of sand.

The geography is best explored at the dunes' midpoint, just south of the small town of **Reedsport.** Permits, required for day-use, hiking, and camping, are available at the **Reedsport Visitor Center** (855 US-101, 541/271-3611, 6am-10pm daily).

Recreation
Just off US-101, the **Oregon Dunes Overlook** is the trailhead for several loop hikes that lead through marshes, tree islands, forests, and dunes to the sea. The **John Dellenback Dunes Trail** is a moderate 2.7-mile trek that begins at Eel Creek Campground and continues through

evergreens and freshwater lakes before ending on the beach. The 3.5-mile loop to **Tahkenitch Creek** offers diverse flora and fauna, and glimpses of wildlife.

For a guided tour or to rent a dune buggy, head a few miles south of Florence to **Sandland Adventures** (85366 US-101 S., 541/997-8087) or **Sand Dunes Frontier** (83960 US-101 S., 541/997-5363). Tours generally cost up to $50, while dune buggy rentals run about $45 an hour.

For an even more exhilarating experience, try sandboarding down the dunes at Florence's **Sand Master Park** (87542 US-101 N., 541/997-6006, 10am-5pm Mon.-Tues. and Thurs.-Sat., noon-5pm Sun., $10-25). It's much like surfing—although you don't get wet!

Food and Accommodations
In the midst of the dunes, the line of motels and burger joints in the town of **Reedsport** seems a little surreal. **Maple Street Grille** (165 Maple St., 541/997-9811, 11am-9pm Tues.-Sat., under $18) cooks up good, old-fashioned dishes like pot roast, fried chicken burgers, and mac and cheese. Located just north of Reedsport, **Gardiner Guest House** (401 Front St., 541/543-0210, $75-95) offers a convenient stay in an elegant restored Victorian.

A number of campgrounds offer access points to the local dunes. **Eel Creek Campground** (72044 US-101, milepost 222), which offers flush toilets and drinking water, is the starting point of a moderate 2.7-mile trek through evergreens and freshwater lakes that ends on the beach.

Umpqua Lighthouse State Park
You can explore a mosaic of open sand dunes, ocean beach, freshwater lakes, and old-growth coniferous forests at **Umpqua Lighthouse State Park** (505 Lighthouse Rd., 800/551-6949, www. oregonstateparks.org, year-round, $5 day-use). The park was originally designated to preserve the forested basin of the small freshwater Lake Marie, which

lies between the headland and dune ridge formations. Swimming and fishing are popular activities. A one-mile hiking trail loops around Lake Marie, and a spur trail extends westward to an overlook at the edge of the forest above the sand dunes.

The **campground** (800/452-5687, 8am-5pm Mon.-Fri., $16-90) at Lake Marie has 44 campsites for both tents and RV; there are also yurts and log cabins. Showers are free and are centrally located near the restrooms.

The **Umpqua River Lighthouse** (1020 Lighthouse Rd., 541/271-4631, tours: 10am-4pm daily May-Oct., 10am-3pm Fri.-Sun. Mar.-Apr. and Nov.-Dec., $5 adults, $4 students and seniors) is adjacent to the park, an easy 0.6-mile hike from the campground, and offers panoramic views of the ocean, perfect for spotting California gray whales. The lighthouse was first constructed in 1857 along the Umpqua River, but strong winds and mountain runoff in 1861 caused severe damage and a few years later it collapsed. Rebuilt in 1864, the tower rises over the entrance of the Umpqua River with a focal plane of 165 feet above sea level. Guided tours are provided through the **Umpqua River Lighthouse Museum** (541/271-4631, Mar.-Dec., 10am-4:30pm daily May-Oct., free), located in the historic Coast Guard Station. There is no direct access to the dunes from Umpqua Lighthouse State Park.

Coos Bay

A thriving commercial harbor, **Coos Bay** (pop. 15,374) is home to the largest coastal deep-draft harbor between Puget Sound and San Francisco. It has the largest population on the Oregon coast. Several Native American tribes lived and fished along the bay for thousands of years, including Confederated Tribes of Coos, Lower Umpqua, and

Siuslaw Indians, and the Coquille Indians. In 1853, American settlers called the town Marshfield. Over a hundred years later, the name was changed to Coos Bay.

Downtown is the Old Marshfield district. You can tour the historic waterfront or walk along the **Coos Bay Boardwalk.**

Sharkbites Cafe (240 S. Broadway, 541/269-7475, 11am-9pm Mon.-Thurs., 11am-9:30pm Fri.-Sat., under $18) makes the best fish tacos in town, part of a menu that also includes award-winning fish and chips, seafood sandwiches, and juicy burgers.

If you can swing a room at the **Edgewater Inn** (275 E. Johnson Ave., 541/267-0423, $105 and up), you'll find that the view and locale are worth it! It's Coos Bay's only waterfront motel, located just one block off US-101 and only minutes from sand dunes, ocean beaches, and Shore Acres State Park. There are other lodging options as well, including chain motels and bed-and-breakfasts.

Cape Arago Highway: Shore Acres State Park

The Cape Arago Highway skirts the coastline for little more than 14 miles, providing access to beaches, sea caves, viewpoints, and uncrowded parks.

The crowning jewel of the South Coast, **Shore Acres State Park** (89039 Cape Arago Hwy., 9am-dusk daily, $5 day-use) sits high above the ocean swells on a wave-battered bluff. The park combines natural and artificially constructed features that pleasantly inspire those that make the journey. Wild spruce and pine trees encapsulate the meticulously manicured gardens with plant and flower varieties from around the world. There is an observation tower and paved trails that descend directly below to **Simpson Beach.** A winding path leads to more

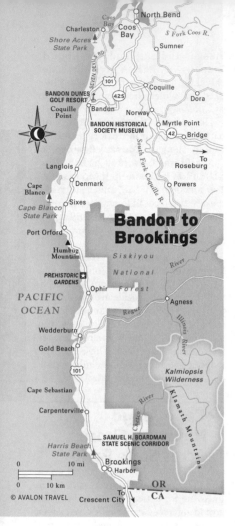

Bandon to
Brookings

seascape vistas, marinelife, and a secluded cove.

The highway culminates at **Cape
Arago State Park** (541/888-3778, $5
day-use). First sighted by Europeans
during Sir Francis Drake's expeditions in the 1500s, Cape Arago is a
good place to spot migrating whales
and other marine mammals. A north
trail leads to offshore views of sea
lions and seals at Shell Island (part of
the Oregon Islands National Wildlife
Refuge, closed Mar.-June), beachcombing, and fishing. The south trail takes

you to a sandy beach and tide pools
flowing with marinelife.

To return to US-101, you must backtrack six miles on Cape Arago Highway.
Turn right on Seven Devils Road to head
south for roughly six miles; then turn left
on West Beaver Hills Road to continue
south for another six miles to connect to
US-101.

Bandon

Roughly 30 miles south of Coos Bay,
Bandon (pop. 3,053) boasts a warmer,
almost Mediterranean climate along its
remote and stunning coastline. A Native
American village called Na-So-Mah existed here along the banks of the Coquille
(Ko-kwel) River some 3,500 years ago.
Euro-American settlers arrived in the
1850s and renamed the site Averill. The
name changed again to Bandon, which
felt more like home to a later wave of immigrants from Bandon, Ireland.

Bandon's economy is centered on wood
products, fishing, tourism, and agricul-
ture. It is also Oregon's cranberry capital.
In autumn, you can see cranberries floating at the top of flooded bogs, south of
town, awaiting harvest. An average of 30
million pounds are harvested each year.

Old Town's blocks are lined with galleries, craft shops, and fine restaurants.
A boardwalk runs along the waterfront,
linking the town with the historic lighthouse, and is often busy with visitor foot
traffic during warmer months. Bandon's
biggest feature is its natural wind-formed
monoliths. To get the full monty, drive
scenic **Beach Loop Road,** a two-plus-
mile waterfront route that passes a series
of offshore monoliths (the most famous
is **Face Rock**) with access to a couple of
photogenic viewpoints.

Getting There and Around
Bandon is on US-101 south of Coos Bay.
From the south, take I-5 north to OR-
42. **Coastal Express** (541/412-8806 and

800/921-2871, $4 per city segment) buses travel US-101 through Bandon, Coos Bay, and North Bend.

Sights
Face Rock

One mile south of Old Town, **Beach Loop** runs along a ridge overlooking a fantastic cluster of coastal monoliths and jagged Bandon Islands. The largest, **Face Rock** is easily identified by its human-like features. Its seemingly stoic silhouette gazes skyward, surrounded by the crashing of white-foamed waves and the wailing of gale winds. Both scientific theory and Native American storytelling explain the origins of the monoliths. The geologic story is riddled with volcanic eruptions, earthquakes, and erosion. The Coquille legend tells of the Indian princess Ewanua, who took her dog and pet raccoons down to the beach for a swim in the moonlight. The evil ocean spirit Seatco turned them all to stone. If you close your eyes and listen, you can hear Ewanua's voice in the wind.

The best place to see the face of the Indian princess is by following Beach Loop Road to **Face Rock State Scenic Viewpoint,** about a quarter-mile south of Old Town. A hiking trail leads down to the beach, where you can explore the rock and intertidal sea life, including starfish, sea anemone, and sea slugs at low tide. Beware of the tide as it rises, or you'll be swimming back to shore.

Bandon Historical Society Museum

In 1936, a wildfire swept through the region and lay waste to the downtown business district, destroying hundreds of shops and homes. This devastating event is preserved in the **Bandon Historical Society Museum** (270 Fillmore St., 541/347-2164, 10am-4pm Mon.-Sat., $2 adults). Other exhibits touch on the Native American culture of the Coquille people, whose legends and names are embedded in the landscape, as well as the

later maritime and cranberry industries that fueled the town's economy.

Coquille River Lighthouse

At the mouth of the Coquille River, the small **Coquille River Lighthouse** (800/551-6949, 11am-5pm daily May-mid-Oct.) is the only Oregon lighthouse to be struck by a ship when in 1903 an abandoned schooner smashed into it during a storm. During the devastating 1936 fire, the lighthouse was spared, touched only by ash. It was used as a temporary shelter for local hospital patients.

Westcoast Game Park Safari

Seven miles south of Bandon, the 129-acre **Westcoast Game Park Safari** (46914 US-101, 541/347-3106, 10am-4:30pm daily, $17.50 adults, $10 children 7-12, $7 children 2-6) is home to exotic animals that you can see, pet, and in some cases, actually hold. Several resident animals roam freely, mingling with visitors. The park houses endangered species, such as the snow leopard, part of the park's captive breeding program. All of the animals have been rescued, some from other zoos that can no longer take care of them.

Food

Get a hearty, affordable breakfast or brunch at the **Minute Café** (145 N. 2nd St., 541/347-2707, $4-10). If French croissants and pastries are more your style, **Bandon Baking Co & Deli** (160 2nd St. SE, 541/347-9440, www.bandonbakingco.com, 8am-4pm Tues.-Sat., $3-11) is a delicious choice. They also serve specialty sandwiches and hearty soups.

For fresh waterfront grub right on the boardwalk, stop at **Bandon Fish Market** (249 1st St., 541/347-4282, 11am-6pm Mon.-Sat., 11am-4pm Sun., $8-20). Or go for fish tacos, clam steamers, or Dungeness crab at **Tony's Crab Shack** (155 1st St., 541/347-2875, www.tonyscrabshack.com, 10am-6pm daily, under $20).

Grab a seat in the outdoor garden patio at **Sea Star Bistro** (230 2nd St. SE,

BANDON

541/290-1819, www.seastarbistro.com, 11am-4pm Tues.-Sat., under $13) for homemade chowder, sandwiches, and pasta dishes. They'll also happily pack a picnic lunch for you to enjoy at the beach.

The upscale **Lord Bennett's Restaurant and Lounge** (1695 Beach Loop Dr., 541/347-3663, www.lordbennett.com, 11am-2pm Fri.-Sat., 10am-2pm Sun., 5pm-9pm daily, $12-32) has spacious seating and gorgeous sunset views.

Watch the sun set over the Coquille River and lighthouse from **The Loft Restaurant & Bar** (315 1st St. SE, 541/329-0535, www.theloftofbandon.com, 5pm-9pm Wed.-Sat., $18-38), with the best views in town. The menu offers creative dishes with fresh, local ingredients.

Nightlife and Entertainment

Cheap, strong drinks draw a crowd at the no-frills **Arcade Bar** (135 Alabama Ave. SE, 541/347-3902, 10am-2am Mon.-Sat., 10am-midnight Sun.), a place with friendly service and decent bar fare.

The best bands and beers are at trendy **McFarlin's Bar & Grill** (325 2nd Ave. SE, 541/329-1200, 4pm-9pm Mon.-Fri., 11:30am-9pm Sat., noon-8pm Sun.), a friendly pub that also serves specialty pizzas and burgers. Sing along to karaoke Friday and Saturday nights at **Lloyd's Old Town Tavern** (219 2nd St. SE, 541/329-0280, 7am-10pm Sun. and Wed.-Thurs., 7am-2am Fri.-Sat.). It has a rustic feel and bargain-priced drinks and food.

Unwind with a glass of pinot noir and an appetizer at the charming **Alloro Wine Bar & Restaurant** (375 2nd St. SE, 541/347-1850, www.allorowinebar.com, 11am-9pm daily, $8-30).

Located downstairs in the lodge at Bandon Dunes Golf Resort, **The Bunker** (57744 Round Lake Dr., 888/345-6008, 6pm-1am daily, $8 and up) is a dapper man cave where you can shoot pool, play poker, smoke cigars, or have a glass of scotch.

Coquille River Lighthouse built in 1896

Shopping

In Old Town, **Big Wheel Farm Supply & General Store** (130 Baltimore St., 541/347-3719, 9am-5:30pm Mon.-Sat., 10am-5pm Sun.) offers a selection of T-shirts, myrtlewood gifts, and local jams. Perhaps best of all, it's the home of the **Fudge Factory,** which produces 26 varieties of the tasty treat. Upstairs, the **Bandon Driftwood Museum** (free) showcases both sculpted tree roots and fertilizer displays, epitomizing Bandon's back-to-the-land, hippie ethos. A block away, **2nd Street Gallery** (210 2nd St. SE, 541/347-4133, www.secondstreetgallery. net, 11am-close daily) displays sophisticated art, crafts, and original jewelry. **Gypsy Wagon** (175 2nd St. SE, 541/347-1775, www.shopgypsywagon.com, 11am-5pm daily) is a caravan of exotic clothing and gifts. **Devon's Boutique** (92 2nd St. SE, 541/347-8092, www.devonsboutique. com, 10am-5pm Mon.-Sat.) makes chic, unique, and comfortable apparel available for women.

Kimberly's Book Nook (175 2nd St. SE, 541/260-1343, 11am-4pm Mon.-Wed.) offers a mosaic of used books, while **WinterRiver Books** (170 2nd St. SE, 541/347-4111, 10am-6pm daily) stocks new titles and specialty items like Nepali singing bowls.

Shops along US-101 are also worth a look. **Bandon Glass Art Studio** (240 US-101, 541/347-4723, www.bandonglassart. com) is a remarkable gallery of intricately blown glass. **Truffles! Gift, Apparel, Home** (145 Fillmore Ave. SE, 541/347-3473, 10am-5:30pm Mon.-Sat., 10am-4pm Sun.) has everything from clothing to jewelry to home decor to furniture. The beautifully packaged, delicious jams and jellies at **Misty Meadows Jams** (48053 US-101, 888/795-1719) make perfect gifts.

Recreation

Explore the beach and view wildlife along the easy **Coquille Point Interpretive Trail,** a paved pathway winding over the headland, marked by a series of interpretive panels on local wildlife, history, and Coquille Indian sites. Access to the trail is at the Kronenberg County Park parking area, west of Beach Loop Drive.

Protecting a tidal salt marsh, the **Bandon Marsh National Wildlife Refuge** (W. Riverside Dr., 541/347-1470, sunset-sunrise daily, free) draws thousands of feather-gazers each year. Herons, falcons, and waterfowl can be seen from an elevated viewing platform located on the west side of Riverside Drive.

Just two miles north of Bandon, **Bullards Beach State Park** (52470 US-101, 541/347-2209, open year-round, $5 parking, $5 hiking) is a large, year-round park with 192 campsites ($28/night) and 13 yurts ($40/night), nestled in a forest of shore pines. Horse trails provide access to the beach and dunes for equestrian campers ($19/night). A public boat launch area includes a fish cleaning station, bathrooms, and picnic tables. It gets crowded during Chinook Salmon season (late summer-early fall).

The elite **Bandon Dunes Golf Resort** (57744 Round Lake Dr., 541/347-4380 or 888/345-6008, $75-250 greens fee) is set among massive dunes and pine trees, and is noted for its Scottish-style links. Surrounded by beautiful vistas, the affordable **Bandon Crossings Golf Course** (87530 Dew Valley Ln., 541/347-3232, www.bandoncrossings.com, $20-70) lets you play 18 holes in Bandon's "banana belt," which provides gentler weather for play.

Events

They say "the fresher the cranberry, the higher the bounce!" As Oregon's cranberry capital, Bandon does a lot of berry bouncing! The annual **Cranberry Festival** (Old Town, 541/347-9616, www. ouroregoncoast.com, second weekend in Sept.) celebrates the harvest with food, games, and craft booths. Activities include a parade, the Cranberry Bowl football game, a cranberry eating contest, and a petting zoo.

Accommodations

Find relaxation at the serene ★ **Bandon Dunes Golf Resort** (57744 Round Lake Dr., 888/345-6008, www.bandondunesgolf. com, $100-400), in the midst of sand dunes and forest. Options include single rooms, suites, and secluded multi-cottages. Guests receive discounts at the golf courses.

La Kris Inn (940 Oregon Ave. SE, 541/347-3610, www.lakrisinn.com, $55-100) is cheap, clean, and close to shops and eateries. The scenic **Bandon Inn** (355 US-101, 541/347-4417, $79-175) overlooks Old Town Bandon, the Coquille River, and the Pacific Ocean.

Two family-owned motels offer comfort and value. **The Table Rock Motel** (840 Beach Loop Dr., 541/347-2700, www. tablerockmotel.com, $50-140) is situated high on a bluff that overlooks the Pacific Ocean. Amenities include pillow-top mattresses, and the motel offers kitchenettes and pet-friendly rooms. On Coquille Point, **Bandon Beach Motel** (1090 Portland Ave., 866/945-0133, www.bandonbeachmotel.

Prehistoric Gardens

com, $85-175) is just steps away from tide pools, unique rock formations, and wildlife. Some rooms have fireplaces and patios; all have ocean views.

B&Bs are sprinkled along the Coquille waterfront. **The Sea Star Guest House** (370 1st St., 541/347-9632, www.seastarbandon.com, $60-125) offers rooms decorated in maritime themes. The tasteful **Lighthouse Bed & Breakfast** (650 Jetty Rd. SW, 541/347-9316, www.lighthouselodging.com, $140-245) provides both wonderful breakfasts and exceptional service.

Information and Services

For detailed information on local sights and visitor services, contact the **Bandon Chamber of Commerce** (300 2nd St. SE, 541/347-9616).

Cape Blanco

Jutting 1.5 miles out into the Pacific Ocean, **Cape Blanco** is the westernmost point in the state. Early Spanish explorers named it for its white-shelled cliff face.

To get a full appreciation of the cape's unabated beauty, follow the Oregon Coast Trail south from the Sixes River to the mouth of the Elk River. Depending on the time of year, the Elk River can be too treacherous to walk across, so use caution. It's about 8.5 miles round-trip along the sandy beach, past the cape and lighthouse, through dense woodlands with scenes of offshore rock formations, driftwood, and wildlife. North of the cape, you can see Gull Rock, Castle Rock, and Blacklock Point. To the south are views of Needle Rock, Blanco Reef, and Humbug Mountain.

Circa 1870, **Cape Blanco Light** (91100 Cape Blanco Rd., tours: 10am-3:30pm Wed.-Mon. Apr.-Oct., $2 adults, free children) is Oregon's oldest lighthouse. A mile away, **Hughes Historic House** (91816 Cape Blanco Rd., tours: 10am-3:30pm Wed.-Mon. Apr.-Oct., donation) is an 11-room, Victorian home built in 1898 by pioneers Patrick and Jane Hughes.

Port Orford and Humbug Mountain

US-101 moves inland along the 25-mile stretch between Bandon to **Port Orford** (pop. 1,198). Here, cranberry bogs, dairy and sheep farms, grasslands, and forest groves make up the changing landscape. The town has a rich history that includes fishing, mining, logging, and a notorious battle.

Captain William Tichenor arrived in June 1851 and left nine armed men to establish a European settlement right in the middle of Qua-to-mah Indian village. The newcomers were understandably not welcome. When conflict ensued, the men took refuge on a large rock at the edge of the beach, where they were besieged for two weeks before fleeing in the dark of night. Tichenor returned, better armed, with 70 men and succeeded in founding

his settlement. The Qua-to-mah village was lost, but the rock, dubbed **Battle Rock,** still remains.

Today, Port Orford has a collection of galleries, gift shops, cafés, and B&Bs.

Port Orford Wetland Interpretive Walkway (on the west side of US-101, 541/332-8055) is a 160-foot interpretive boardwalk that extends over a freshwater marsh. Viewing platforms provide an unhindered view of the wetlands' ecosystem, which supports birds, mammals, and amphibians. Interpretive signs explain the function of wetlands as a natural filtering system for runoff water before it flows into nearby lakes. The trailhead is accessed from 18th and Idaho Streets at a small parking lot.

Six miles south of Port Orford, US-101 rises into the lush rain forest before meeting the east edge of **Humbug Mountain.** At 1,756 feet in elevation, it's the highest peak on the coast. Adventurers can summit the mountain by way of a three-mile trail that begins at the highway near **Humbug State Park Campground** (541/332-6774, $14), which offers 101 campsites and shower facilities.

★ Prehistoric Gardens

Between Port Orford and Gold Beach, amid a lush rain forest of dewy mosses, large ferns, and imposing trees, lies one of the most unusual tourist traps on the Oregon coast: the **Prehistoric Gardens** (36848 US-101, 541/332-4463, 9am-6pm daily, $12 adults, $8 children 3-12). Here, a collection of vibrantly colored dinosaurs stand seemingly frozen in time within their jungle-like setting. They are the creation of amateur paleontologist E. V. Nelson, who sculpted his first of about two dozen life-sized replicas in 1953. Some stand at 40 feet high. While it's no *Jurassic World,* the mix of paleontology and kitsch is hard to beat. It's a must-see for anyone under the age of 10.

Gold Beach

Named for the gold once mined near the mouth of the Rogue River, **Gold Beach** today draws visitors seeking a different kind of treasure: salmon and steelhead.

Jerry's Rogue Jets (29985 Harbor Way, 541/247-4571 or 800/451-3645, www.roguejets.com, daily May-Oct., $50-75) has taken passengers upriver since 1958. The trip makes a 1.5-hour stop at **Agness,** a tiny town about 36 miles upstream, where lunch and dinner is served at a mountain lodge (food is not included in the tour price).

You'll find plenty of affordable motels right along US-101. For a more memorable stay, head for **Tu Tu Tun Lodge** (96550 North Bank Rogue, 541/247-6664 or 800/864-6357, www.tututun.com, $90 and up). Right on the banks of the Rogue River, the lodge is rustic yet luxurious, and, best of all, peaceful. Expect comfortable rooms and a great restaurant, which serves breakfast, lunch, and five-course dinners.

Samuel Boardman State Scenic Corridor

A small ribbon of land between the highway and sea, **Samuel Boardman State Scenic Corridor** is perhaps the most scenic drive on the entire Oregon coast. Allow extra driving time to stop for photo ops. Rugged cliffs tumbling dramatically to the violent sea, deep-water bays, endless sea stacks, and surreal rock arches are just some of the sights on this 12-mile segment of US-101. There are several parking areas and viewpoints, some with walking paths that connect to other lookouts.

The north end features the natural contours of **Arch Rock** just offshore; secluded **Secret Beach,** which is accessible by way of a steep trail; and the sandy beach at **Thunder Rock Cove.** Look for the small green **Thomas Creek Bridge** (the tallest bridge in Oregon at 345 feet) sign on the highway. At the south end is a turnout and viewpoint.

At the south end, the landscape shifts. The rocky cliffs are less steep, and conifer forests give way to a patchwork of woodlands and grassy bluffs. The most notable stop is **Whaleshead Beach,** named for the sea stack that resembles the head of a whale. When waves crash into the rock, its seawater sprays as if spurting from the whale's blowhole. A viewpoint and parking lot is located on US-101 about seven miles north of the town of Brookings. It's a good spot for pictures or for gazing out at the horizon. A trail heads down to the beach, but be cautious; it's steep.

There is no fee to park or walk the trails, and there are no facilities except for a few picnic areas.

Brookings: Harris Beach State Park

The southernmost town on the Oregon coast, **Brookings** is only five miles north of the California border. It offers warm, ocean breezes, unspoiled beaches, and saltwater fishing. Paddle a kayak on the mouth of Chetco River to catch fresh and saltwater fish, or paddle around exploring hidden coves, giant sea rocks, or, if you're lucky, behold the enormity of a passing whale.

In late spring and fall, colorful blooming azaleas blanket the 36-acre **Azalea Park** (640 Old County Rd., dawn-dusk daily), a popular gathering place for picnics, leisurely strolls, weddings, and summer concerts, like the annual **American Music Concert Series** (every other Sun. June-mid-Sept., free). If you enjoy beachcombing and evening sunsets, stay at **Lowden's** (14626 Wollam Rd., 541/469-7045 and 800/453-4768, $115 and up), a beachfront B&B with direct access to a crescent-shaped beach of sand and driftwood.

Harris Beach State Park is located just north of Brookings on US-101, adjacent to the Oregon Welcome Center. You'll find sandy beaches, rugged outcroppings, tide pools, and sea stacks. Just offshore, **Bird Island,** a National Wildlife Sanctuary, is a breeding ground for rare bird species. The park **campground** (800/551-6949, campsites $20-53) is open year-round and has flush toilets and hot showers.

A short drive southbound on US-101 brings you to the California border, where you'll enter Redwood National Park.

Northern California Coast

The contours of California's northern coast are framed not only by the dramatic seascape of the Pacific Ocean but by strands of ancient redwoods and magnificent mountains.

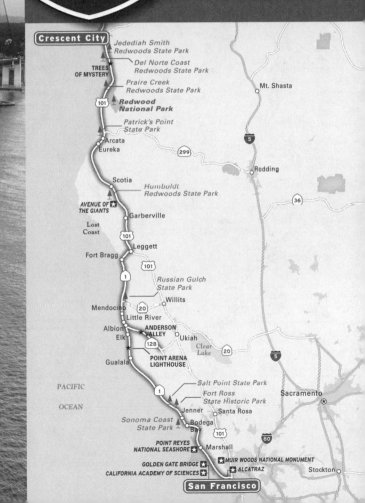

Crescent City
Jedediah Smith Redwoods State Park
TREES OF MYSTERY
Del Norte Coast Redwoods State Park
Prairie Creek Redwoods State Park
101
Redwood National Park
Patrick's Point State Park
Mt. Shasta
Arcata
Eureka
299
Redding
Scotia
Humboldt Redwoods State Park
AVENUE OF THE GIANTS
Garberville
36
Lost Coast
101
Leggett
Fort Bragg
101
1
Russian Gulch State Park
Willits
Mendocino
20
Little River
Albion
ANDERSON VALLEY
Elk
128
Ukiah
Clear Lake
20
Gualala
POINT ARENA LIGHTHOUSE
5
PACIFIC
1
Salt Point State Park
Fort Ross State Historic Park
OCEAN
Jenner
Santa Rosa
Sacramento
Sonoma Coast State Park
Bodega Bay
POINT REYES NATIONAL SEASHORE
101
Marshall
80
MUIR WOODS NATIONAL MONUMENT
ALCATRAZ
GOLDEN GATE BRIDGE
CALIFORNIA ACADEMY OF SCIENCES
Stockton
San Francisco

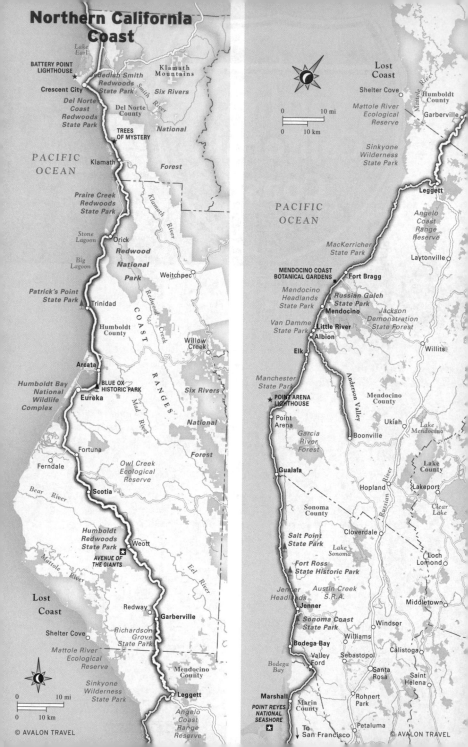

Northern California
Coast

BATTERY POINT
LIGHTHOUSE

Crescent City

Lake
Earl

Jedediah Smith
Redwoods
State Park

Klamath
Mountains

Del Norte
Coast
Redwoods
State Park

Del Norte
County

Six Rivers

PACIFIC
OCEAN

TREES
OF MYSTERY

National

Klamath

Forest

Prairie Creek
Redwoods
State Park

Stone
Lagoon

Orick

Redwood

Weitchpec

Big
Lagoon

National

Patrick's Point
State Park

Trinidad

Park

Humboldt
County

COAST

Willow
Creek

Arcata

Six Rivers

BLUE OX
HISTORIC PARK

Eureka

RANGES

National

Humboldt Bay
National
Wildlife
Complex

Fortuna

Forest

Ferndale

Owl Creek
Ecological
Reserve

Bear
River

Scotia

Humboldt
Redwoods
State Park

Weott

AVENUE OF
THE GIANTS

Eel River

Redway

Garberville

Mattole
River

Lost
Coast

Shelter Cove

Richardson
Grove
State Park

Mattole River
Ecological
Reserve

Mendocino
County

Sinkyone
Wilderness
State Park

Leggett

Angelo
Coast
Range
Reserve

0   10 mi

0   10 km

© AVALON TRAVEL

Lost
Coast

Shelter Cove

Mattole River
Ecological
Reserve

Garberville

Humboldt
County

0   10 mi

0   10 km

Sinkyone
Wilderness
State Park

Leggett

PACIFIC
OCEAN

Angelo
Coast
Range
Reserve

MacKerricher
State Park

Laytonville

MENDOCINO COAST
BOTANICAL GARDENS

Fort Bragg

Mendocino
Headlands
State Park

Russian Gulch
State Park

Jackson
Demonstration
State Forest

Mendocino

Van Damme
State Park

Little River

Albion

Willits

Elk

Anderson Valley

Mendocino
County

Manchester
State Park

POINT ARENA
LIGHTHOUSE

Ukiah

Lake
Mendocino

Point
Arena

Garcia
River
Forest

Boonville

Russian River

Gualala

Hopland

Lake
County

Lakeport

Salt Point
State Park

Sonoma
County

Lake
Sonoma

Cloverdale

Clear
Lake

Loch
Lomond

Fort Ross
State Historic Park

Austin Creek
S.R.A.

Middletown

Jenner
Headlands

Jenner

Sonoma Coast
State Park

Windsor

Williams

Calistoga

Bodega Bay

Bodega
Bay

Valley
Ford

Sebastopol

Santa
Rosa

Saint
Helena

Marshall

POINT REYES
NATIONAL
SEASHORE

Marin
County

Rohnert
Park

To
San Francisco

Petaluma

© AVALON TRAVEL

Highlights

★ **Avenue of the Giants:**
This aptly named scenic
drive parallels US-101 for 31
miles through Humboldt
Redwoods State Park and the
last remaining stands of virgin redwoods (page 164).

★ **Point Reyes National
Seashore:** Home to tule elk,
desolate beaches, dairy and
oyster farms, one of the oldest West Coast lighthouses,
and scores of remote wilderness trails, Point Reyes is one
of the most diverse parks in
the Bay Area (page 181).

★ **Muir Woods:** Stand
among trees nearly 1,000
years old and 200 feet tall in
one of the nation's earliest
national monuments (page
185).

★ **Golden Gate Bridge:**
Nothing beats the view from
one of the most famous and
fascinating bridges in the
country. Pick a fogless day for
a stroll or bike ride across the
span (page 186).

★ **Alcatraz:** Spend the
day in prison . . . at this
historically famous, former
maximum-security peniten-
tiary in the middle of the bay
(page 191).

★ **California Academy of
Sciences:** With a four-story
rain forest, a state-of-the-art
planetarium, and an underwater aquarium home to
38,000 animals, the Academy
of Sciences is a thrill for visitors of all ages (page 193).

Along this stretch you'll find a number of whistle-stops and old logging and fishing towns.

You'll pass through Crescent City and Eureka, and some of the oldest old-growth forests at Humboldt Redwoods State Park, before US-101 breaks away from the coast at Leggett. Here, CA-1 picks up the route, passing through the urbane town of Mendocino, briefly diverging from the coast to the town of Valley Ford before rejoining the sea near the mouth of Tomales Bay.

The highway runs by the beautiful 71,028-acre Point Reyes National Seashore, Muir Woods, and Golden Gate Bridge National Recreation Area before merging with US-101 to cross the famed Golden Gate Bridge to San Francisco. This spirited city birthed America's first counterculture and remains a hotbed of diversity.

Planning Your Time

Allow five days for exploration of the main sights along the northern coast, and a week to make the most of what Northern California's beaches, national forests, and historic cities have to offer.

Accommodations along the northern redwood coast are rustic but not hard to find. The towns from Fort Bragg south to San Francisco, including Mendocino, Bodega Bay, Point Reyes, and Stinson Beach, are popular getaways for city-dwellers; expect the charm and prices to rise accordingly.

It's just over 350 miles from Crescent City to San Francisco. If you plan to follow US-101 to CA-1, which hugs the coastline, navigate carefully around the bends and turns, planning extra driving time for scenic viewing and photo stops. Gas stations are well placed along the highway and within towns and cities.

Getting There
Car

From the north, US-101 provides a direct path from Oregon to Northern California, connecting to the northern coast and Eureka to the south. US-199 begins north of Crescent City and travels northeast to Grants Pass, Oregon. The junction of US-101 and US-199 is one of only two junctions of two U.S. routes in California.

US-101 and CA-1 (also known as Hwy-1, California 1, Shoreline Highway, Pacific Coast Highway, and PCH) are the best north-south routes,

Best Hotels

★ **Abigail's Elegant Victorian Mansion:** With an astonishing collection of antiques, this Eureka hotel is as Victorian as it gets (page 160).

★ **Cornelius Daly Inn:** Eureka's very Victorian inn includes turn-of-the-century antiques and lovely gardens (page 160).

★ **Olema Druids Hall & Cottage:** This restored 1885 meeting hall is a perfect base for exploring Point Reyes National Seashore (page 184).

★ **Hotel Boheme:** Decor from the best of the Beat era ensures a very San Francisco experience (page 201).

★ **Argonaut Hotel:** This boutique hotel has it all: history, classic style, and a prime San Francisco location (page 201).

providing a phenomenal scenic drive along most of California's Pacific coastline. CA-1 at times runs parallel to US-101. Its southern end is at I-5 near Dana Point and its northern end is at US-101 near Leggett.

Air
The major Northern California airport is **San Francisco International Airport** (SFO, 650/821-8211, www.flysfo.com), about 15 miles south of the city center. **Del Norte County Regional Airport** (707/464-7288) also known as Jack McNamara Field, is located three miles northwest of Crescent City, in Del Norte County, with service provided by SkyWest Airlines to Eureka/Arcata, Sacramento, and San Francisco.

Train or Bus
Amtrak (800/872-7245, www.amtrak.com, $135 and up) offers service on the **Coast Starlight** to Seattle, Portland, Sacramento, Oakland, and Los Angeles. International visitors can buy an unlimited travel USA Rail Pass, good for 15, 30, or 45 days.

Greyhound (800/231-2222, www.greyhound.com) offers special discounts to students and seniors with routes and stops sticking to major highways and cities.

Fuel and Services
Gas stations are all self-service and easily accessed off US-101 and CA-1. Service is sparser within national parks.

To receive reports on **road conditions**, call **511**. If your phone carrier does not support 511, call toll-free 800/977-6368.

For **emergency assistance** and services, call **911.**

Crescent City

This northernmost city on the California coast perches on the bay whose shape gave the town its name. Cool and windswept, Crescent City is a perfect place to put on a parka, stuff your hands deep in your pockets, and take a long contemplative walk along a wide, beautiful beach. Serious deep-sea fishing lovers will find fishing to their hearts' content, while lovely and uncrowded redwood forests beckon hikers. In 1964, much of Crescent City was destroyed in a tsunami caused by an Alaskan earthquake. In 2011, parts of the city were evacuated and the harbor was severely damaged after an earthquake hit Japan.

Sights
The sands of Crescent City are wide, flat expanses that invite strolling, running,

Best Restaurants

★ **Wildflower Café and Bakery:** This healthy choice in Arcata offers gourmet vegetarian fare (page 156).

★ **North Coast Brewing Company:** This classic brewpub in Fort Bragg was one of the pioneers of artisanal brewing (page 168).

★ **Station House Café:** The star of the Point Reyes restaurant scene is both casual and upscale (page 182).

★ **Mama's on Washington Square:** With 10 types of French toast on the menu, the only problem is choosing one (page 194).

★ **Trattoria Contadina:** San Francisco's North Beach is known for authentic Italian restaurants, and this is one of the best (page 195).

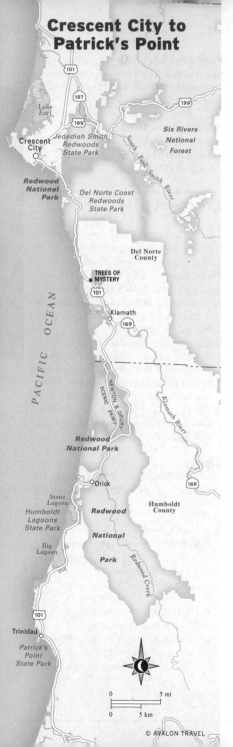

and just sitting to contemplate the endless crashing Pacific. **South Beach,** located, as advertised, at the south end of town, is perfect for a romantic stroll, so long as you're bundled up. Farther south, **Crescent Beach** and **Enderts Beach** offer picnic spots and tidepools.

Wild, lonely **Point St. George** (at the end of Washington Blvd.) epitomizes the glory of California's northern coast. Walk out onto the cliffs to take in the deep blue sea, wild salt- and flower-scented air, and craggy cliffs and beaches. On a clear day, you can see all the way to Oregon. Short, steep trails lead across wild beach prairie land down to broad, flat, nearly deserted beaches. In spring, wildflowers bloom on the cliffs, and swallows nest in the cluster of buildings on the point. On rare and special clear days, you can almost make out the St. George Reef Lighthouse, alone on its perch far out in the Pacific.

Are the kids bored despite all the scenery? A great family respite is **Ocean World** (304 US-101 S., 707/464-4900, www.oceanworldonline.com, 9am-9pm daily summer, 9am-5pm daily winter, $13 adults, $8 children). Tours of the small sea park depart about every 15 minutes and last about 40 minutes. Featured attractions are the shark petting tank and the 500,000-gallon aquarium.

Food and Accommodations

A top stop for the night is the popular **Curly Redwood Lodge** (701 S. Redwood Hwy., 707/464-2137, www.curlyredwoodlodge.com, $56-98), built entirely from a single sawn-up redwood tree. It isn't pet-friendly, but it is spacious and comfortable.

The **Good Harvest Café** (575 US-101 S., 707/465-6028, 7am-9pm Mon.-Sat., 8am-9am Sun., $7-10) offers a good range of options from diner food to fish tacos and seafood linguine.

🐾 US-199: Jedediah Smith Redwoods State Park

Jed Smith (US-199, nine miles east of Crescent City, 707/458-3018, www.parks. ca.gov, day-use $8 per vehicle), as it's known to locals, sits north of Crescent City along the Smith River, right next door to the immense Smith River National Recreation Area (US-199 west of Hiouchi). The state park visitors center sits on the east side of the park, doubling as the Hiouchi Information Center.

Sights
The best redwood grove in all of this old growth is **Stout Memorial Grove.** The coastal redwood trees are, as advertised, stout—though the grove was named for a Mr. Frank Stout, not for the size of the trees. Somehow spared the loggers' saws, these are some of the biggest and oldest trees on the north coast. The old giants make humans feel small. Its far-north latitude makes the grove harder to reach than many others, meaning there are often fewer tourists here.

Hiking
The trails running through the trees make for wonderful summer hiking that's cool and shady. Many trails run along the river and the creeks, offering a variety of ecosystems and plenty of lush scenery to enjoy. Just be sure that wherever you hike, you stay on the established trails. If you wander into the forest, you can stomp on the delicate and shallow redwood root systems, unintentionally damaging the very trees you're here to visit.

The **Simpson Reed Trail** (one mile, easy) takes you right from US-199 (six miles east of Crescent City) down to the banks of the Smith River.

To get a good view of the Smith River, hike the **Hiouchi Trail** (two miles, intermediate). From the visitors center and campgrounds, cross the Summer Footbridge, then follow the river north. The Hiouchi Trail then meets the Hatton Loop Trail and takes you away from the river and into the forest.

The **Mill Creek Trail** (7.5 miles round-trip, difficult) is a longer and more aggressive trek. A good place to start is at the Summer Footbridge. The trail then follows the creek down to the unpaved Howland Hill Road.

If it's redwoods you're looking for, take the **Boy Scout Tree Trail** (5.2 miles, difficult). It's more of a trek out to the trailhead along an unpaved road, but rumor has it that's part of the beauty of this hike.

Camping
The **Jedediah Smith campground** (US-199, Hiouchi, 800/444-7275, www.reserveamerica.com, $15-20 per night, $3 hike-in primitive sites) clusters near the river, with most sites near the River Beach Trail (immediately west of the visitors center). There are 106 RV and tent sites. Facilities include plenty of restrooms, fire pits, and coin-op showers. Reservations are advised in advance, especially for summer and holiday weekends.

Information and Services
Jed Smith has a **visitors center** (US-199, 1 mile west of Hiouchi) where you can get park information and purchase souvenirs and books. Ask for a schedule of nature programs and guided hikes.

Del Norte Coast Redwoods State Park

South of Crescent City, Del Norte Coast Redwoods State Park (US-101, accessible via Mill Creek Rd., 707/465-2146, www.parks.ca.gov) encompasses a variety of ecosystems, from eight miles of wild coastline to second-growth redwood forest to virgin old-growth forests. One of the largest in this system of parks, Del Norte is a great place to "get lost" in the backcountry with just your backpack and fishing rod, ready to camp and ply the waters of the meandering branches of Mill Creek.

Camping

Seven miles south of Crescent City, the **Mill Creek Campground** (707/465-7335 and 800/444-7275, www.parks.ca.gov, May 15-Oct. 31, $35 standard, $17.50 pass holders) has 145 sites to accommodate tents and RVs. Facilities include restrooms and hot showers.

Trees of Mystery

Generations of kids have loved spotting the gigantic wooden **Paul Bunyan** and his blue ox Babe from US-101. And the **Trees of Mystery** (15500 US-101 N., 707/482-2251 and 800/638-3389, www.treesof-mystery.net, 8am-7pm daily June-Aug., 9am-5pm daily Sept.-May, $15 adults, $8 children 6-12, free under 6) is a great

place to take a break from the road for some good cheesy fun. Enjoy the original Mystery Hike as well as the Skytrail gondola ride through the old-growth redwoods and the palatial gift shop. At the left end of the gift shop rests a little-known gem: the Native American museum. A large collection of artifacts from tribes across the country and native to the redwood forests grace several crowded galleries.

Just south of the Trees of Mystery, you'll find the northernmost of three drive-through trees. **Klamath Tour Thru Tree** (430 CA-169, 707/482-5971, $5 per vehicle) is over 725 years old.

◈ Prairie Creek Redwoods State Park

A gorgeous scenic cutoff through the redwoods, the **Newton B. Drury Scenic Parkway** (about 10 miles south of Trees of Mystery, cuts off US-101) features

Del Norte Coast Redwoods State Park

old-growth trees lining the roads, a close-up view of the redwood forest ecosystem, and a grove or trailhead about every hundred yards or so. Turn off the highway at the **Big Tree Wayside.** The namesake tree is only a short walk from the parking area, and several trails radiate from the little grove.

At the junction of the south end of the Newton B. Drury Scenic Parkway and US-101, **Prairie Creek Redwoods State Park** (25 miles south of Crescent City on Newton B. Drury Pkwy., 707/465-7347, www.parks.ca.gov) boasts large campgrounds and shady hiking trails through redwoods. Just beyond the entrance, the visitors center includes a small interpretive museum describing the history of the California redwood forests. A tiny bookshop adjoins the museum, well stocked with books describing the history, nature, and culture of the area. Many ranger-led programs originate at the visitors center.

One of the cool things that make a drive to Prairie Creek worth the effort is

the herd of **Roosevelt elk** that live there. The big guys with their huge racks hang out at—where else?—the Elk Prairie. This stretch of open grassland lies right along the highway. The best way to find the viewing platform is to watch for the road signs pointing you to the turnoff. The best times to see the elk out grazing in the field are early morning and around sunset. Please stay in the viewing area and let the elk enjoy their meals in peace.

Perhaps the single most famous hiking trail along the redwood coast is the 0.7-mile **Fern Canyon Trail** to Gold Bluffs Beach (trailhead at parking lot two miles off US-101 on Davison Rd.). This hike takes you through a narrow canyon carved by Home Creek. Ferns, mosses, and other water-loving plants grow thick up the sides of the canyon, creating a beautiful vertical carpet of green that made the perfect setting for Steven Spielberg's *Jurassic Park 2* and *The Return of the Jedi*.

A longer and tougher loop can take you from the visitors center on a more serious foot tour of the park. Start out on the **James Irvine Trail,** but don't follow it all the way to the coast. Instead, make a right onto the **Clintonia** and cut across to **Miner's Ridge.** The hike runs a total of about six miles.

Redwood National Park

Twenty million years ago, colossal giants thrived in the cool, continuously damp environment found only on the northernmost coast of what is today California. These conditions haven't changed, as the colossal giants are still here—we call them redwoods. Nobody really knows why these trees grow to such towering heights, and it may be this mystery, along with the area's magnificent beauty, that draws more than 400,000 people each year to Redwood National and State Parks. At one time, close to two million acres of old-growth redwoods blanketed

California's northern coast. Alas, massive logging left little more than 45 percent of the area's old-growth coast redwoods, half of which is found in the Redwood National and State Parks system.

In 1968, **Redwood National Park** was established to protect some 131,983 acres of redwood forest, of which 60,268 acres make up the adjacent Smith, Del Norte, and Prairie Creek State Parks. The trees preserved in the Redwood National Park section are not the oldest; they're second- or third-growth timber. However, these reddish-brown beauties still possess a magical sway that inspires awe among visitors.

Visiting the Park

Spanning a length of 50 miles from the Oregon border to the north and the Redwood Creek watershed near Orick, California, to the south, Redwood National Park is located on the northernmost coast of California. The cool, moist air created by the Pacific Ocean maintains the trees' moist habitat even during summer droughts.

Seasons

Redwood National Park is always open, welcoming visitors year-round. Visitors to the park should be prepared for all types of weather by dressing in layers to accommodate climate changes. Wear durable walking shoes or hiking boots with grip soles to avoid slipping on moist trails, logs, or rocks. Good rain gear and a water bottle are imperative.

Temperatures stay between the mid-40s to low-60s (Fahrenheit) with cooler, sometimes snowy winters. Warmer months bring moist fog that collects where the cold ocean and dry land meet, creating a damper interior. Rain averages 60-80 inches annually, with October-April as the rainier months. However, weather and climate cannot always be predicted.

The best time of year for hiking and outdoor activities is in summer. Cooler months (Dec.-Jan. and Mar.-Apr.) offer favorable opportunities to see migrating gray whales along the coast.

Weather can cause changes in both campground and trail access. Check for revised schedules before arrival.

Fog and strong winds can create difficult driving conditions and road closures. Check for updated highway reports with the California Department of Transportation.

Park Entrances

Many visitors are surprised to discover that there are no formal entrance stations, or even entrance fees at Redwood National Park. In fact, US-101 (known in these parts as the Redwood Highway) runs the entire length of the park.

Visitors Centers

There are two information centers and three visitors centers. The northernmost, **Crescent City Information Center** (1111 2nd St., 707/465-7335, 9am-5pm daily spring-fall, 9am-4pm daily winter) provides an array of useful materials, including maps and brochures, and has several great exhibits and live video feeds from the Castle Rock National Wildlife Refuge.

Less than 10 miles northeast of Crescent City, **Hiouchi Information Center** (US-199, 707/458-3294, 9am-5pm summer) operates only in the summer with ranger-led activities, exhibits, and public facilities.

The southernmost facility is the **Thomas H. Kuchel Visitor Center** (US-101, 707/465-7765, www.nps.gov/redw/planyourvisit/visitorcenters.htm, 9am-5pm spring-fall, 9am-4pm winter), which includes public facilities, as well as information, exhibits, beach access, and a bookstore.

All centers provide National Park passport stamps.

Permits and Regulations

There are no entrance fees for Redwood National Park. However, a $5 day-use fee is charged at the three adjoining state parks: Prairie Creek Redwoods State Park, Del Norte Coast Redwoods State Park, and Jedediah Smith Redwoods State Park.

A free permit for backcountry camping is required and is only available year-round from the Crescent City Information Center and Thomas H. Kuchel Visitor Center, and seasonally from Hiouchi Information Center.

A free permit is also required for "Tall Trees" access road and can be obtained at the Thomas H. Kuchel Visitor Center and Hiouchi Information Center (summer only). Please note that these permits are limited to only 50 per day and are on a first-come, first-served basis.

Special-use permits may be required for group events, commercial activities, and research projects. An application must be completed (call 707/465-7307 for more information).

Camping

The Redwood National and State Parks offer developed campgrounds and backcountry camping. Campgrounds fees are $35 at all campgrounds. **Reservations** (800/444-7275, www.reserveamerica. com) during the summer months are advised and should be made at least 48 hours in advance. However, Gold Bluffs Beach Campground never accepts reservation at any time during the year and is first-come, first-served.

Jedediah Smith Campground (800/444-7275, www.reserveamerica. com, $35) is in Crescent City within an old-growth redwood grove on the banks of scenic Smith River, offering a variety of recreational activities from swimming to fishing, and extensive hiking trails. There are 86 campsites that accommodate tents or RVs (hook-ups not available) and have full facilities with hot showers, fire pits and barbecues, food lockers, and a campfire center.

Mill Creek Campground (1111 2nd St., 800/444-7275, www.reserveamerica.

com, $35) in Crescent City offers 145 tent sites that sit amid large maple and alder trees, and young redwoods. A full-facility campground, it is only open May 15-October 31 and has access to Mill Creek and hiking trails.

Elk Prairie Campground (127011 Newton B. Drury Pkwy., 800/444-7275, www.reserveamerica.com, $35) in Orick offers easy access to 70 miles of hiking and biking trails, numerous opportunities for wildlife viewing, and seasonal ranger-led hikes all among ancient giant redwoods. There are 75 sites for tents or RVs (no hook-ups). The campground also offers hot showers, bathroom facilities, picnic tables, fire pits, barbecues, and food lockers.

Gold Bluffs Beach Campground (Davison Rd., 800/444-7275, www.reserveamerica.com, $35) is located in Orick near secluded beaches, hiking and biking trails, and wildlife viewing such as Roosevelt elk. There are campsites for tents or RVs (no hook-ups). Facilities include solar showers, restrooms, wind shelters, picnic tables, fire pits, barbecues, and food lockers.

Fires are allowed only in designated fire rings and grills provided by the parks. Dead and downed wood may be collected for burning (limit of 50 pounds) from within a quarter-mile of backcountry camps on national parkland. Wood collection is prohibited in developed campgrounds. State parklands allow up to 50 pounds of driftwood per person per day. It is imperative that you check with one of the local visitors centers to ensure that you are fully informed of permissible campfire activity.

Animal-proof food canisters are available free of charge at the **Redwood National State Park Information Center** (1111 2nd St., 707/465-7335).

Food and Supplies

There are no grocery stores or restaurants within the parks. You will find a collection of restaurants, full-service grocery stores, and a couple co-ops located in the nearby communities of Klamath (4.63 mi/7.46 km, north), Orick (3.42 mi/5.5 km, north), Crescent City (5.22 mi/8.4 km, southwest), Trinidad (16.67 mi/26.82 km, south), McKinleyville (25.18 mi/40.53 km, south), Arcata (31.15 mi/50.13 km, south), and Eureka (38.91 mi/62.62 km, south).

Sights

It's all about the trees! And there's plenty of them to see along US-101 from behind the wheel, but some of the most incredible sights are a short walk away. Rising an average of 300 feet, the **Stout Memorial Grove** (accessed via the east end of Howland Road and from Jedediah Smith Campground by way of a seasonal summer bridge) contains the tallest trees within the Jedediah Smith region. It's an easy 0.5-mile walk among sword ferns that carpet the forest floor, and the flow of the nearby Smith River is entrancing.

No doubt the giant coast redwoods are the cynosures of Redwood National and State Parks, but there is also an abundance of wildlife and stunning viewpoints that should not be overlooked. Possibly the best spot to spy migrating whales in the winter is from **Crescent Beach Overlook,** located less than two miles past Crescent Beach within the Del Norte section of the parks. The cliffside platform offers dominating views of the seascape that are simply hard to beat. A short trail leads down the bluffs to **Enderts Beach,** where driftwood, seashells, and the best tidepools are aplenty. The trail is part of the larger 70-mile-long Coastal Trail, which is a good way to explore—feet willing.

Farther south in Prairie Creek Redwoods State Park lies a beautiful natural landmark and popular destination, **Fern Canyon:** Water streams down its 50-foot steep walls, draped with thick emerald ferns. It's no wonder the site was used as a filming location for movies such as *The Lost World: Jurassic Park*

and the BBC's *Walking with Dinosaurs,* as the canyon exudes a prehistoric aura. Wear waterproof shoes or expect to get your feet wet!

To see **Big Tree,** a 304-foot-high redwood measuring 21 feet in diameter, follow Newton B. Drury Scenic Parkway. It's a short 100-yard walk from the Prairie Creek Visitor Center, and worth the 30-minute drive off US-101. Nearby, the **Ah Pah Trail** provides a glimpse into the past logging era, with interesting trailside exhibits.

A mile north of Orick on Bald Hills Road (watch for a sign at the junction of US-101) are two well-known groves: the regal **Lady Bird Johnson Grove,** where gathered giants create a cathedral-esque canopy, and **Tall Trees Grove,** whose star attraction is the soaring Howard Libbey Tree. The Lady Bird Johnson Grove is named in honor of the former first lady (wife of U.S. President Lyndon B. Johnson) in recognition of her efforts to help preserve America's natural beauty, which ultimately led to the bill that created Redwood National Park. But what really makes the trees here special is that in comparison to other groves, these trees are highlanders—sitting 1,200 feet above sea level.

To visit Tall Trees Grove, stop by Thomas H. Kuchel Visitor Center to pick up a free permit and combination to unlock the gate that leads to some of the most massive trees on the planet. There is a limit of 50 cars per day, and if you're one of the lucky ones (trailers and RVs are not permitted), it's a 45-minute drive to the trailhead up the narrow unpaved Bald Hills Road. The trail drops about 800 feet in elevation before arriving at Tall Trees Grove (2 miles) and the 367.8-foot former reigning giant, **Howard Libbey Tree.** Although larger redwoods have been discovered, Libbey continues to be popular among visitors due to its accessibility and the locations of rival giants never being revealed for their protection.

Beneath the lush green canopy,

majestic **Roosevelt elk** roam the northern redwood region; their noble antlers are observable in late summer through winter. In the 1920s, only 15 elk could be found here, but today, they are a common sight thanks to the protection of critical habitat. Safe viewing areas can be navigated by car at Elk Prairie along Newton B. Drury Scenic Parkway (34 miles south of Crescent City) and Elk Meadow via Davison Road (3 miles north of Orick). Another good viewpoint is less than five miles up the road from Elk Meadow at Gold Bluffs Beach. However, there is a day-use fee and trailers are not allowed, as this portion of the road is unpaved. As a gentle reminder, please *do not* approach Roosevelt elk. These wild animals need no introduction, and are perfectly hospitable—but from afar. It is also imperative that drivers respect speed limits and be attentive to wildlife along the roads and highways, as Roosevelt elk (or other forest critters) do not yield to drivers or look both ways.

Recreation

Before you set foot on a trail, it is always a good idea to pick up a map at any of the visitors centers. Backcountry hikers are encouraged to speak with the rangers to answer questions or just to pick their brains for good route advice.

More than 200 miles (322 km) of trails weave through old-growth forests, colorful meadows, prairies, and primeval beaches. Northern trails that start along US-199 near Hiouchi and end at the Klamath River include **Leiffer-Ellsworth Loop Trail,** a 2.6-mile loop in Jedediah Smith Redwoods State Park. The trailhead is off Walker Road, less than a half-mile from the US-199 junction. Head clockwise along Leiffer Loop to the Ellsworth Loop split-off, which bends around the south edge of Leiffer Loop. A less-traveled path, it passes through vine maple, California Hazel, and red huckleberries, before climbing 200 feet on a densely wooded hillside

to flatter land near the Smith River. Expect spectacular views and very little foot traffic.

Saddler Skyline Trailhead is located in Del Norte Coast Redwoods State Park between campsites 7 and 8 in the Mill Creek Campground. It's a 1.5-mile moderate hike with some steep grades and switchbacks. The trail is filled with numerous brush, wild ginger, huckleberry, California blackberry, and wildlife.

For an exhilarating adventure, **Little Bald Hills Trail** is a vigorous bike trail (and it's horse friendly), located in Jedediah Smith Redwoods State Park, offering a 3.3-mile primitive ride to the campsite and 4.8 miles to the park boundary. The trailhead is on the east end of Howland Hill Road. The trek is steep, rising 1,800 feet in elevation through a changing scenery of lush lowland redwoods, various shrubs, flowered meadows, and a few small ocean views before coming to the park boundary. Head back or continue through the Smith River National Recreation Area to Paradise Trail and on to South Fork Road; it's all downhill.

Although the redwoods are best known for towering trees, the nearly continuous **Coastal Trail** offers a 70-mile (142 km) journey along seaside bluffs, where on a clear day you can look out over endless blue waters, perhaps spotting spouting gray whales. Sea creatures hide in secluded tidepools and driftwood collects below the jagged sea cliffs. There are several access points such as Hidden Beach in Redwood National Park.

The Hidden Beach section of the Coastal Trail is 7.8 miles long, ascending approximately 1,390 feet above sea level. The trailhead is off US-101 at the north end of the Lagoon Creek parking lot, just before the Trees of Mystery attraction (via south). The trail is somewhat primitive as it climbs along spruce-covered bluffs; there are no redwoods on the Coastal Trail. At the first divide, a short loop curves to the left following the edge

NORTHERN CALIFORNIA COAST

of a lagoon (and the humming of the highway), or continue to the right toward a more scenic journey without highway interruption. Blackberry, bushels of ferns, tall red alder, and spruce border the pathway, offering peeks of the ocean, before you arrive at a nice open viewpoint. The trail culminates through a grassy hillside that gives way to views of the rushing Klamath River.

One of the best mid-spring to early summer hikes is on the Redwood National and State Parks' southern trail in Prairie Creek Redwoods State Park. The **Rhododendron Trail** is a colorful 6.8-mile wonderland filled with trees, bushes, red huckleberry, blackberry, and beautiful blooms of bright pink and red rhododendrons. It is the perfect landscape, favored among painters and photographers.

There are several access points from trails that traverse the pathway (Cathedral Trees Trail, the Brown Creek Trail, and South Fork Trail), but the main trailhead is located just off the east side of Newton B. Drury Scenic Parkway.

Patrick's Point State Park

Patrick's Point State Park (US-101, 25 miles north of Eureka, 707/677-3570, www.parks.ca.gov) is a rambling coastal park with campgrounds, trails, beaches, landmarks, and history. It's not the biggest of the many parks along the north coast, but it might be the best. The climate remains cool year-round, making it perfect for hiking and exploring, if not for ocean swimming. It's easy to get around Patrick's Point because it is tiny in comparison to the other parks. Request a map at the gate and follow the signs along the often-nameless park roads.

Sights

Prominent among the landmarks is the park namesake **Patrick's Point,** which offers panoramic Pacific views after a brief hike from a convenient parking lot. Another popular spot is **Wedding Rock,** adjacent to Patrick's Point in a picturesque cove. People truly do hike the narrow trail out to the rock to get married—you might even see a newly married couple stumbling along, holding hands on their way back from their ceremony.

Perhaps the most fascinating area in all of the park is **Sumeg Village.** This re-creation of a native Yurok village is based on an actual archaeological find that lies east of the "new" village. Visitors can crawl through the perfectly round hobbit-like hole-doors into semi-subterranean homes, meeting places, and storage buildings. Or check out the native plant garden, a collection of local plants the Yurok people used for food, basketry, and medicine. Today, the local Yurok people use Sumeg Village as a gathering place for education and celebrations, and request that visitors tread lightly and do not disturb this tranquil area.

For those who want to dip a toe in the ocean rather than just gaze at it from afar, Patrick's Point encompasses a number of accessible beaches. The steep trail leading down to **Agate Beach** deters few visitors. This wide stretch of coarse sand bordered by cliffs shot through with shining quartz veins is perfect for lounging, playing, and beachcombing. The semi-precious stones for which it is named really do cluster here. The best time to find good agates is in the winter, after a storm.

Recreation

Only six miles of trails thread their way through Patrick's Point. Choose from the **Rim Trail,** which will take you along the cliffs for a view of the sea and, if you're lucky, a view of migrating whales. On the other hand, tree-lovers might prefer the **Octopus Tree Trail,** which shows its walkers a great view of an old-growth Sitka spruce grove.

Camping

The campgrounds at Patrick's Point meander through the park. It can be difficult to determine the difference between **Agate Beach, Abalone,** and **Penn Creek,** so be sure to get good directions from the rangers when you arrive. Most campsites are pleasantly shaded by the groves of trees; all include a picnic table, a propane stove, and a food storage cupboard. You'll find running water and restrooms nearby, plus showers.

Information and Services

You can get a map and information at the **Patrick's Point State Park Visitors Center** (707/677-1945, usually 9am-4:30pm daily), immediately to the right when you get to the entry gate. Information about nature walks and campfire programs is posted on the bulletin board.

Arcata

Like its sister city Eureka, the pretty little town of Arcata has beautiful Victorian architecture. But as the home of Humboldt State University, it also has a reputation for its entrenched hippie culture, which today is more about progressive politics and a vibrant arts and music scene than tie-dyed T-shirts and psychedelia. You can also connect with nature here by visiting Arcata Marsh & Wildlife Sanctuary.

Getting There and Around

The best routes are from US-101, which runs north to south right through Arcata, and CA-299, which runs east to west.

If arriving by bus, **Amtrak** and **Greyhound** are both located at the **Arcata Transit Center** (925 E St., 707/825-8934).

A small airport, **Arcata-Eureka Airport** (3561 Boeing Ave., 707/839-5401) is located in McKinleyville, just six miles north of Arcata on US-101. Airline service is limited.

Walking and biking are the best modes of transportation. It's easy to check out a

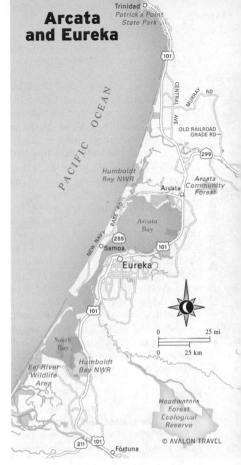

loaner bike at **Bike Library** (865 8th St., www.arcata.com/greenbikes, $20 refundable deposit), located in the North Coast Co-op parking lot.

Three local bus lines run through the city: **Humboldt Transit Authority** (707/443-0826, www.hta,org, $3.50 fare may vary); **Arcata and Mad River Transit** (707/822-3775, www.arcatatransit.org, $2.50 day-pass); and **Blue Lake Transit Authority** (707/668-5101, www.bluelake. ca.gov, $1.65 one-way pass).

Sights

The **Arcata Plaza** (808 G St., 707/822-2250, www.plazaarcata.com, 10am-6pm Mon.-Sat., noon-5pm Sun.) is one of the town's best features, with perfectly manicured lawns, regular events and activities, village shopping, music, and more.

Many 19th-century homes and buildings are beautifully maintained. Just nine blocks from Arcata Plaza, The **Pythian Castle** was built in 1885 to host the Knights of Pythias organization. Classic 1888 Victorian **The Lady Anne Inn** (902 14th St., 707/822-2797, www.ladyanneinn.com) sits on a hilltop overlooking Humboldt Bay.

Arcata also has the oldest movie theater in the United States, **The Minor Theater** (1001 H St., 707/822-3456, $6-9.50 per ticket), which shows all the newest releases. The Great Houdini performed his daring magic acts on the small theater stage; a trap door he used for his shows is still there.

Stroll downtown to see the **River Steps**, a 15-foot old-growth redwood carved by former college professor and artist, Bob Benson. The sculpture stands at the north end of the city, greeting passersby.

Food

A healthy and tasty choice is the ★ **Wildflower Café and Bakery** (1604 G St., 707/822-0360, wildflowercafebakery.com, 9am-3pm and 5:30pm-9:30pm Mon.-Tues. and Thurs.-Sun., 9am-3pm Wed., under $15), specializing in fresh and delicious vegetarian meals for breakfast, lunch, and dinner, with gourmet espresso and delicious house breads. Mouthwatering pizza and deli sandwiches is what **Arcata Pizza** (1057 H St., 707/822-4650, www.arcatapizza.com, 11am-midnight Sun.-Thurs., 11am-1am Fri.-Sat., under $18) creates with fresh ingredients. They have extended hours, so you can satisfy a late craving.

Nightlife

The **Humboldt Brewery** (856 10th St., 707/826-2739, www.humbrews.com, noon-11pm daily) offers a mix of rock and blues. **Cafe Mokka** (495 J St.,

707/822-2228, www.cafemokkaarcata.com, noon-11pm Sun.-Thurs., noon-1am Fri.-Sat.) is a great place to unwind while listening to live Celtic music, or meditating in a tranquil Finnish country sauna and soaking tub.

Two popular places to meet the locals or just have a drink with friends is **Sidelines Sports Bar** (732 9th St., 707/822-0919, 11am-2am daily), which features a jukebox and Thursday night DJs, and **The Alibi** (744 9th St., 707/822-3731, www.alibi.com, 8am-midnight daily), a lively venue with fabulous martinis, live bands, and a piano lounge.

Shopping

Discover beautiful beads from around the world and unique jewelry at **Heart Bead** (830 G St., 707/826-9577, www.heartbeads.com, 10am-6pm daily).

A couple great bookstores are **Northtown Books** (957 H St., 707/822-2834, www.northtownbooks.com, 10am-7pm Mon.-Thurs., 10am-9pm Fri., 10am-7pm Sat., 11am-5pm Sun.), a well-stocked independent bookstore with a wide range of genres; and, for used and rare books, **Tin Can Mailman** (1000 H St., 707/822-1307, www.tincanbooks.com, 10am-7pm Mon.-Sat., 11am-6pm Sun.), a short walk away.

Gear up with everything you need to explore the local rivers, trails, and beaches at **Adventure's Edge** (650 10th St., 707/822-4673, www.adventuresedge.com, 9am-6pm Mon.-Sat., 9am-5pm Sun.).

On Saturdays, the **Farmer's Market** (Arcata Plaza) is bustling with locals and out-of-towners shopping for fresh organic foods, artisan breads, and handcrafted art.

Recreation

Arcata Bay is the northern half of Humboldt Bay and part of the 300-acre Samoa Dunes Recreation Area, where you can hike or kayak. There are no fees to enter this area. Launch kayaks from the Arcata ramp or Hookton Slough in Humboldt Bay National Wildlife Refuge.

Fishing is also popular on Arcata Bay (New Navy Base Rd.) and many come seeking Pacific and California halibut. Mad River lies just north of Arcata, where steelhead, trout, king, and silver salmon are caught at the mouth of the river. The Mad River has also become known for its excellent winter steelhead, due to the **Mad River Fish Hatchery** (1660 Hatchery Rd., 707/822-0592, www.dfg.ca.gov/fish/Hatcheries/MadRiver). Contact the **California Department of Fish and Game** (707/445-6493, www.dfg.ca.gov/Fishing) for current regulations and license requirements.

The world-famous **Arcata Marsh & Wildlife Sanctuary** (569 S. G St., 707/826-2359, www.arcatamarshfriends.org, 9am-5pm Tues.-Sun., 1pm-5pm Mon., free) is a wetland preserve for over 150 bird species and other wildlife. Bird-watchers can enjoy walking trails, an interpretive center, and blinds (the best way to stay hidden).

Events

The annual **Arcata Main Street's Oyster Festival** (Main Street Plaza, June) has fast become a tradition as avant-garde culinary enthusiasts prepare oysters in every imaginable, but delicious, way.

On the second Friday of every month the phenomenon known as **Arts! Arcata** (Main Street Plaza, artsarcata.com) brings the community together with 60 visual artists and live musicians at 30 participating locations to celebrate the love of the Arts! It's a free event that everyone can enjoy.

Arcata is the starting point for the **Kinetic Grand Championship** (www.kineticgrandchampionship.com, Memorial Day weekend), when zany human-powered amphibious works of art take to the roads, beaches, and yes, the Humboldt Bay. The three-day race continues along California's northern coast through Eureka to Ferndale, offering participants a chance at numerous prizes, and everyone else even more laughs.

Accommodations

The cheapest place to stay is on the east side of US-101 at **Motel 6** (4755 Valley West Blvd., 707/822-7061, www.motel6.com, $40 and up). A couple other east-side hotel chains include the **Days Inn and Suites Arcata** (4975 Valley West Blvd., 707/822-4861, www.daysinnarcata.com, $80 and up), which provides an indoor swimming pool, hearty breakfast and dining at the hotel restaurant, and free WiFi; and the **Best Western Arcata Inn** (4827 Valley West Blvd., 800/568-8520 or 707/826-0313, www.book.bestwestern.com, $88 and up), which offers a good continental breakfast, pet-friendly service, and all the typical amenities you'd expect.

On the west side of US-101, the **Fairwinds Motel** (1674 G St., 707/822-4824, www.fairwindshotelarcata.com, $69) is cheap but clean and close to downtown. The most centrally located, **Hotel Arcata** (708 9th St., 707/826-0217 or 800/344-1221, $75 and up) is right on the plaza, close to shopping and sightseeing.

Information and Services

The **Arcata Chamber of Commerce** (1635 Heindon Rd., 707/822-3619, www.arcatachamber.com 9am-5pm Mon.-Fri.) operates the **California Welcome Center (CWC)** to provide valuable information and services to every traveler.

Eureka

The town of Eureka began as a seaward access point for the remote gold mines of the Trinity area. Almost immediately, settlers realized the worth of the redwood trees surrounding them and started building the logging industry. In the late 19th century, lumber barons built a wealth of lovely Victorian homes and downtown commercial buildings. Today, lumber is still a major industry in Eureka. But tourism is another draw, with people coming to enjoy the waterfront wharf and charming downtown shopping area. Active outdoors lovers can fish, whale-watch, and hike, while history buffs can explore museums, mansions, and even a working historic millworks.

Getting There and Around

Eureka is a short ride by vehicle from Arcata via southbound US-101. From San Francisco, it is a spectacular, scenic, six-hour drive north through Sonoma, Mendocino, and Humboldt Counties to reach Eureka.

The **Arcata-Eureka Airport** (3561 Boeing Ave., 707/839-5401) is located 10 minutes north of Eureka, and is served by three air carriers: Delta, Horizon Air, and United.

Bus service is provided by Amtrak, Greyhound, **Eureka Transit Service** (133 V St., www.eurekatransit.org, $3.95 day-pass), and **Humboldt Transit Authority** (707/443-0826, www.hta,org, $3.50 fare may vary). The Amtrak Thruway buses go from Eureka to the Capitol Corridor train at Martinez, northeast of San Francisco. Greyhound provides service nationally. Eureka Transit Service operates four weekday routes between downtown Eureka, Bayshore Mall, Henderson Center, Myrtletown, Cutten, and Pine Hill. Only three routes operate on Saturdays. Humboldt Transit Authority offers service within the county.

By foot is the best way to get around downtown Eureka to see its turn-of-the-century architectural charm and scenic flair.

Sights

Decorative Victorian-era buildings adorn **Old Town** (318 F St., 707/442-3235), creating an alluring village-esque feel for shopping, dining, or just taking a stroll. At the end of historic 2nd Street sits one of the most written-about and

photographed mansions, the **Carson Mansion** (143 M St., no tours). A masterpiece of Queen Anne architecture, it is considered the grandest Victorian home in America with renditions of the mansion found in amusement parks, including Disneyland's train station clock tower.

Take in the fresh air at the nearby New Fisherman's Plaza Boardwalk (C St.) and the views across the water of Woodley Island's Victorian seaport on **Humboldt Bay** (385 Startare Dr.); the **Table Bluff Lighthouse,** which was moved to the island in 1987; and **The Fisherman,** a memorial statue commemorating mariners lost at sea. To get the full perspective, hop on board the **Madaket** (C St. and 1st St., New Fisherman's Plaza Boardwalk, 707/445-1910, $18 adults, $10 children 5 and up) for a water tour of the bay, which offers an amazing look at the composition of the bustling harbor, and the variety of native marinelife, such as the Woodley Island godwits, pelicans, grebes, loons, and egrets. Across a small channel adjacent to Woodley Island sits **Indian Island** (or Duluwat Island), where the indigenous Wiyot people lived at an ancestral village known as Tolowot.

The town's rich history is proudly displayed at the **Clarke Historical Museum** (240 E St., 707/443-1947, www.clarkmuseum.org, 11am-4pm Wed.-Sat., donations accepted), with changing exhibits and rooms dedicated to vibrant Native American cultures, gold rush pioneers, the lumber and ranching empires, and farming and seafaring life.

The **Morris Graves Art Museum** (636 F St., 707/442-0278, www.humboldtarts.org, noon-5pm Wed.-Sun., $5 adults, free children under 17) houses seven galleries, a sculpture garden, and a museum store.

Food

The best places to enjoy a meal is in the historic downtown quarter at **Ramone's Bakery** (209 E St., 707/445-2923, www.

romanesbakery.com, 7am-6pm Mon.-Fri., 8am-5pm Sat., 8am-4pm Sun., $10-18), with baked goods like pumpkin scones and buttermilk coffeecake, herb breads, and espresso; the pub-like **Cafe Waterfront** (102 F St., 707/443-9190, www.upstairsatthewaterfront.com, 9am-9pm daily, $10-18), a choice spot for the season's best seafood; and the popular **Lost Coast Brewery** (617 4th St., 707/445-4480, www.lostcoast.com, 11am-10pm Sun.-Thurs., 11am-11pm Fri.-Sat., $8-20), which always serves up the classics, from burgers to Philly cheesesteak sandwiches, along with award-winning beers.

For family dining Italian-style, find a cozy table at **Mazzotti's Old Town** (301 F St., 707/445-1912, www.mazzottis.com, 11:30am-midnight Mon.-Fri., noon-midnight Sat., noon-9pm Sun., $12-24) or among the artful decor at **Gabriel's** (216 E St., 707/445-0100, lunch Tues.-Sat., $12-26).

If it's a good steak or fresh seafood you crave, head to the **Sea Grill** (316 E St., 707/443-7187, 11am-2pm Tues.-Fri., 5pm-9pm Mon.-Sat., $18-30).

The **Samoa Cookhouse** (511 Vance Rd., Samoa, 707/442-1659, www.samoa-cookhouse.net, breakfast, lunch, and dinner daily, $16) is a Eureka institution even though it's technically located in the little town of Samoa (take CA-255 over the water to get there). Red-checked tablecloths cover long rough tables to re-create a logging-camp dining hall atmosphere. Meals are served family-style from huge serving platters. Diners sit on benches and pass the hearty fare down in turn. Think big hunks of roast beef, mountains of mashed potatoes, and piles of cooked vegetables. This is the place to bring your biggest appetite!

Nightlife

The **Pearl Lounge** (507 2nd St., 707/444-2017, 4pm-2am Sun.-Thurs., 3pm-2am Fri.-Sat., no cover) has it all, micro-brews, organic beers, wine, live music, and a dance floor to get your groove. One block down, the **SpeakEasy** (411 Opera Alley, 707/444-2244, 4pm-11pm Sun.-Thurs., 4pm-2am Fri.-Sat., no cover) is a New Orleans-inspired bar located in a 120-year-old building that hosts live blues music, burlesque shows, and has an extensive drink menu.

A good Irish pub to stop in for Guinness, **Gallagher's** (139 2nd St., 707/442-1177, www.gallaghers-irishpub.com, 11am-9pm Mon.-Fri., noon-9pm Sat.-Sun.) has a friendly atmosphere with fun musical acts.

A stylish wine-and-beer-only venue, **2 Doors Down** (1626 F St., 707/268-8989, 4:30pm-9:30pm Sun.-Mon. and Wed.-Thurs., 4:30pm-10pm Fri.-Sat.) serves savory tapas and small Italian dishes to accentuate your drink.

Shopping

Old Town is a vibrant shopping area where you can find almost anything from antiques and books to gift boutiques and souvenirs.

Fine antique furniture, glassware, and memorabilia is found at **Antiques and Goodies** (1128 3rd St., 707/442-0445, 10am-5pm Wed.-Sat.). Collectibles from the 1920s to the 1950s are at **Annex 39** (610 F St., 707/443-1323, noon-5:30pm daily), located right next to the historic Eureka theater.

Find that book you've been looking for at **Eureka Books** (426 2nd St., 707/444-9593, www.eurekabooksellers.com, 10am-6pm daily), which offers new, used, and rare books, along with an extraordinary selection of vintage photographs, prints, and maps; or at **Booklegger** (402 2nd St., 707/445-1344, 10am-5:30pm daily), which carries over 50,000 volumes of literature in all genres.

A few fantastic places for unique gifts include **Many Hands Gallery** (438 2nd St., 877/445-0455, www.manyhandsgallery.net, 10am-9pm Mon.-Sat., 10am-6pm Sun.), a museum store featuring art and gifts from countries around the world and the art of 50 local artists; **Humboldt**

Herbals (300 2nd St., 707/442-3541, www. humboldtherbals.com, 10am-6pm Mon.-Sat., 11am-5pm Sun.), which offers over 400 organic, culinary, and medicinal herbs, bulk organic teas, locally crafted herbal products, aromatherapy, natural body care, books and gifts; and **Talisman Beads** (214 F St., 707/443-1509, www.talismanbeads.us, 11am-6pm Mon.-Sat., 11am-5pm Sun.), a remarkable treasure trove to beautiful Czech glass, Swarovski, African trade, sterling beads, and so much more.

Add to your wardrobe at **Alirose Boutique** (228 F St., 707/445-2727, www. aliroseboutique.com, 10am-6pm Mon.-Sat., 11am-5pm Sun.), which stocks everything from dresses to denim.

Recreation

Explore the rivers, bay, lagoons from a **kayak** by taking a guided tour or renting from **Humboats Kayak Adventures** (601 Startare Dr., 707/443-5157, www.humboats.com, $25 two-hour kayak, $40 two-hour paddleboard, $40 two-hour canoe).

A fun and romantic way to get around and experience the town of Eureka is by way of horse and carriage via **Old Town Carriage Co.** (2nd and F Sts., Old Town by the Gazebo, 646/591-2058, $28 for 20-25 minutes).

Stroll through a beautiful garden covered with varied shades of green and vibrant flowers at the **Humboldt Botanical Gardens** (7351 Tompkins Hill Rd., College of the Redwoods Campus, 707/442-5139, www.hbgf.corg, 10am-2pm Wed.-Sat., 11am-3pm Sun., $5 adults), where you can also explore trails that lead to surprising views of the bay and surrounding lands.

Events

Eureka's most unusual event is the **Kinetic Grand Championship** (http://kineticgrandchampionship.com), a race that starts in Arcata, continues through Eureka, and ends in Ferndale. During Memorial Day weekend each year, competitors create colorful, often ridiculous, human-powered locomotive sculptures. Be prepared for dinosaurs, donkeys, dung beetles, and other sublimely silly things not often seen in public. The sculptures cross pavement, sand, water, and mud over the course of the three-day race. While other towns now have their own kinetic sculpture races, the north coast is the origin of the event, and remains the grand championship of them all. For a great view, try to get a spot to watch Dead Man's Drop or the Water Entry.

Arts Alive (Old Town and downtown, 6pm-9pm first Sat. of the month) is a popular en-masse art browse, where lovers of art and artists mingle on the first Saturday of every month. About 80 galleries, museums, theaters, and cafés in Eureka's Old Town stay open late.

Accommodations

★ **Abigail's Elegant Victorian Mansion** (1406 C St., 707/444-3144, www.eureka-california.com, $225-300) is as Victorian as it gets. Originally built by one of the founders of Eureka, the inn has retained many of the large home's original fixtures. The owners took pains to learn the history of the house and town, and have added appropriate decor to create a truly Victorian mansion, right down to the vintage books in the elegant library. Each of the three rooms comes with its own story and astonishing collection of antiques. All rooms have private baths, though the bathroom might be just across the hall. Children are not encouraged at this romantic inn, but they can be accommodated.

The historic ★ **Cornelius Daly Inn** (1125 H St., 707/445-3638 and 800/321-9656, www.dalyinn.com, $130 and up) is draped in elegance with original turn-of-the-century antiques and lovely Victorian gardens.

A re-created Victorian manor, **Carter House Inn** (1033 3rd St., 800/404-1390 or 707/445-1390, www.carterhouse.com,

$159 and up) has spacious rooms and a big breakfast in the morning.

Standard but comfortable hotels in town are **Best Western Bayshore Inn** (3500 Broadway St., 707/268-8005 or 888/268-8005, $141 and up) and the slightly nicer **Best Western Humboldt Bay Inn** (232 W. 5th St., 707/443-2234 or 800/521-6996, $145 and up).

Information and Services
For further information, contact the **Eureka! Humboldt County Convention and Visitors Bureau** (1034 2nd St., 707/443-5097 or 800/346-3482).

✿ CA-211 to the Lost Coast

The Lost Coast stretches across 80 miles. Its rugged isolation, volcanic black sand, and wandering feral pathways attract backwoods meanderers, sandy-footed adventurers, and rugged explorers looking to be absorbed into its mysteries and untouched beauty.

The Lost Coast enigma is the work of the **King Range,** which rises 4,088 feet within a few miles of the coast and cuts it off from the main highway system; the state declared it impenetrable in the early 20th century. And the King Range is still rising at about 10 feet every 1,000 years. However, the Pacific Ocean is continually eroding its base, creating 700-foot cliffs, toppled trees, and miles of black sandy beaches.

The north section of the King Range is an exhilarating canvas of green meadows, spring wildflowers, and wind-blown shores, but even more inspiring is the central and southern reaches claimed by the **King Range National Conservation Area** and **Sinkyone Wilderness State Park.** These two areas also offer the best options for hiking and camping. In King Range NCA, the Lost Coast Trail from **Mattole Campground** traverses some of the coastline's best features from the old abandoned **Punta**

Gorda Lighthouse to abundant wildlife to rugged vistas to the famous **Black Sands Beach.**

Getting There
This side trip along the Lost Coast is roughly **100 miles,** but it's slow going along winding, sometimes rough coastal roads. Plan on at least **four hours** of driving, not including stops.

From US-101, head south on CA-211 toward Ferndale. You'll continue via Mattole Road, reaching the coast at Black Sands Beach. It takes another three hours driving along the King Range to reach Shelter Cove, which also offers coastal access. Head east to rejoin US-101 at Garberville.

A few tiny towns provide services not that far past Ferndale. **Petrolia** has a general store with the bare essentials and gasoline, and the slightly larger town of **Shelter Cove** offers a couple small inns and basic food services within a rural setting. But it is the remoteness that makes hiking and camping on this part of California's coastline remarkable.

Ferndale
Ferndale was built in the 19th century by Scandinavian immigrants who came to California to farm. Little has changed since the immigrants constructed their fanciful gingerbread Victorian homes and shops. A designated historical landmark, Ferndale is all Victorian, all the time. Just ask about the building you're in and you'll be told all about its specific architectural style, its construction date, and its original occupants. Main Street's shops, galleries, inns, and restaurants are all set into scrupulously maintained and restored late 19th-century buildings. Even the public restrooms in Ferndale are housed in a small Victorianesque structure.

Sights
The **Ferndale Museum** (515 Shaw Ave. at 3rd St., 707/786-4466, www.ferndale-museum.org, 11am-4pm Tues.-Sat. and

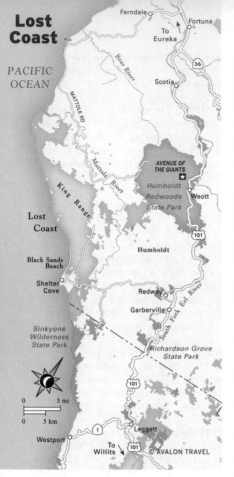

To Eureka

Lost Coast

PACIFIC OCEAN

Lost Coast

Black Sands Beach

Shelter Cove

Sinkyone Wilderness State Park

King Range

AVENUE OF THE GIANTS

Humboldt Redwoods State Park

Humboldt

Redway

Garberville

Richardson Grove State Park

Westport

To Willits

Leggett

© AVALON TRAVEL

0   5 mi
0   5 km

or two to get to the heart of downtown Ferndale. But the reward for staying outside of the town center is a spacious garden well worth a stroll of its own. In the heat of the afternoon, huge shade trees and perfectly positioned garden benches make a lovely spot to sit and read a book, hold a quiet conversation, or just enjoy the serene beauty of garden and town.

The beautiful **Victorian Inn** (400 Ocean Ave., 888/589-1808, www.victorianvillageinn.com, $115-480) is a vintage 1890 building constructed of local redwoods. The 13 rooms, all uniquely decorated, feature antique furnishings, luxurious linens, and pretty knickknacks.

Hotel Ivanhoe (315 Main St., 707/786-9000, www.ivanhoe-hotel.com, $95-145) is kitty-corner from the Victorian Inn. (Nothing in Ferndale is far from anything else in Ferndale.) In a town full of history, the Ivanhoe is the oldest hostelry still standing in town. The four guest rooms are done in rich colors that revive the western-Victorian atmosphere of the original hotel. The on-site **restaurant** is open for dinner only.

The **Gingerbread Mansion Inn** (400 Berding St., 800/952-4136, www.gingerbread-mansion.com, $175-340) has antiques, luxurious linens, and turn-down service.

Redwood Suites (332 Ocean Ave., 707/786-5000 or 888/589-1863, www.redwoodsuites.com, $115-145) is only a block off Main Street, with rooms that are simple yet comfortable. Suites with full kitchens are available, and the price is right.

Mattole Road

One of the few drivable routes to view the Lost Coast is via **Mattole Road.** Starting in Ferndale, this narrow, mostly paved two-lane road affords views of remote ranchland, unspoiled forests, and a few short miles of barely accessible cliffs and beaches. In good weather, the vista points from Mattole Road are spectacular. Lighthouse Road turns off Mattole

1pm-4pm Sun. June-Sept., $1) is a block off Main Street and tells the story of the town. Life-sized dioramas depict period life in a Victorian home, and antique artifacts bring history to life. Downstairs, the implements of rural coast history vividly display the reality that farmers and craftspeople faced in the pre-industrial era.

To cruise further back into the town's history, consider wandering out into the **Ferndale Cemetery** (on Ocean St.). Well-tended tombstones and mausoleums wind up the hillside that back the town.

Food and Accommodations

Guests of the **Shaw House B&B** (703 Main St., 707/786-9958, www.shawhouse.com, $125-275) must walk a block

Road south of Petrolia and runs west to Mattole, the northern end of the Lost Coast Trail.

Black Sands Beach

One of the most amazing and unusual—and accessible—sights on the Lost Coast is the ominous **Black Sands Beach,** composed of crumbly volcanic rock. It's roughly 20 miles south of Ferndale along Mattole Road. The dark sands of this wide beach also serve as the south end of the Lost Coast Trail.

Shelter Cove

Located on less than six square miles where the King Range meets the Pacific Ocean, **Shelter Cove** (pop. 592) hugs a secluded stretch of the California coast that looks like "the land that time forgot."

It was first inhabited by the Sinkyone Indians, possibly to escape the summer heat of the interior valleys. Then Spanish ships and seal traders arrived, and later ranchers settled into the area. A thriving tan bark industry followed, a wharf was built to ship the bark, and the little village quickly grew.

When the steep terrain surrounding Shelter Cove proved too difficult for highway builders to penetrate during the early 20th century construction of State Route 1 (referred to as California 1, Highway 1, and the Pacific Coast Highway), the long segment of what is now the Lost Coast was abandoned, and so was Shelter Cove when the tan bark industry met its end soon after.

The forsaken shoreline was deemed "The Lost Coast," but it wasn't truly forgotten. Three brothers who spent their summers here returned to see the village revived. The Machi brothers saw an opportunity for new industry development and tourism, promoting Shelter Cove as a vacation destination, and fishing as its bread and butter. City dwellers came from all over, including San Francisco (230 mi/370 km), and they never stopped coming.

Today, Shelter Cove is a community of fisherfolk, builders, and retirees. A nine-hole golf course encircles the single-runway Shelter Cove Airport at the heart of the commercial district. Most of the land belongs to the King Range National Conservation Area, which is managed by the Bureau of Land Management.

From Shelter Cove, head east to rejoin US-101 at Garberville (see page 165).

Food and Accommodations

The **Cove Restaurant** (10 Sea Ct., 707/986-1197, 5pm-9pm Thurs.-Sun., $6-20) is the best choice for a meal. If you'd like to stay the night, head for the clifftop **Inn of the Lost Coast** (205 Wave Dr., 707/986-7521 or 888/570-9676, www.innofthelostcoast.com, $150-275). Stock up on supplies at the small **general store** (7272 Shelter Cover Rd., 707/986-7733).

Scotia

The immaculate town of **Scotia** has been described by the *New York Times* as "equal parts Mayberry and Twin Peaks." The entire town was developed and constructed in the 1880s by the Pacific Lumber Company (known as PALCO), which maintained a uniquely positive relationship with conservationists until it became a wholly owned subsidiary of Texas mining company Maxxam, Inc., following a troubled stock market takeover in 1986. Unfortunately, the move proved injurious and after 145 years, PALCO filed for bankruptcy and became Humboldt Redwood Company. The Town of Scotia Company now manages the town as it progresses toward a self-governing community.

Sights

Scotia's transition from company town to growing independent community is a fascinating story. Stop first at the small **museum** (125 Main St., 707/764-2222, 9am-5pm Mon.-Fri. Memorial Day-Labor

Day, free) housed in the redwood Greek Revival former bank at the center of town to see old local artifacts, photographs, and exhibits about the town's past and future.

Food and Accommodations
A nice little historic B&B, the **Scotia Inn** (100 Main St., 707/764-5338, www.thes-cotiainn.com, $85-215), is beautifully maintained and features 22 rooms and a **restaurant** and **pub.**

Humboldt Redwoods State Park

Surprisingly, the largest stand of un-logged redwood trees anywhere in the world isn't on the coast and it isn't in the Sierra. It's right here in Humboldt, bi-sected by US-101. Come to this park to hike beneath 300-plus-foot old-growth trees that began their lives centuries be-fore Europeans knew California existed.

While it's more than worth the time to spend a weekend in the Humboldt Redwoods, you can also spend as little as an hour or two here. A drive through the Avenue of the Giants with a stop at the vis-itors center and a quick nature walk or pic-nic can give you a quick taste of this lovely south end of the coastal redwood region.

Visitors Center
The **visitors center** (17119 Ave. of the Giants/CA-254, 707/946-2263, www.parks.ca.gov, 9am-5pm daily Apr.-Oct., 10am-4pm daily Nov.-Mar.) for the park rests along the Avenue of the Giants, be-tween the towns of Weott and Myers Flat. Start here if you're new to the region or need hiking or camping information. You can also enjoy the theater, interpretive museum, and gift shop here.

★ Avenue of the Giants
The most famous stretch of redwood trees in the state, the **Avenue of the Giants** (look for signs on US-101 to turnoffs,

www.avenueofthegiants.net) paral-lels US-101 and the Eel River between Fortuna and Garberville. Visitors come from all over the world to gawk in won-der at the sky-high old-growth redwoods that line the pavement. Campgrounds and hiking trails sprout among the trees off the road.

The **Shrine Drive-Thru Tree** (13078 Ave. of the Giants, 707/943-1975, 6am-8pm daily, closed winter, $5 per vehicle) is near the town of Myers Flat at the south-ern end of the park. It's said that in the late 1800s teamsters pulled their coaches through the tree.

The Avenue's highest traffic time is July and August, when you can expect a bumper-to-bumper, stop-and-go traf-fic jam for almost the whole of the 31-mile stretch of road. If crowds aren't your thing, try visiting in the spring or fall, or even braving the rains of winter to gain a more secluded redwood experience.

Hiking
With all that fabulous forest, it's hard to resist parking the car and getting out to enjoy the world of the big trees up close and personal.

Many visitors start with the **Founders Grove Nature Loop Trail** (0.5 mile, easy), located at milemarker 20.5 on the Avenue of the Giants. This flat nature trail gives sedate walkers a taste of the big old-growth trees in the park. Sadly, the one-time tallest tree in the world (the Dyerville Giant) fell.

Right at the visitors center, you can enjoy the **Gould Grove Nature Trail** (0.5 mile, easy), a wheelchair-accessible in-terpretive nature walk that includes signs describing the denizens of the forest.

Camping
Few lodging options are really close to Humboldt Redwoods State Park other than the campgrounds in the park itself. Car and RV campers will find a few op-tions. The pleasant but not very private **Burlington Campground** (800/444-7275,

http://reserveamerica.com, $35 with one vehicle) is adjacent to the visitors center and is equipped with bathrooms and showers. Seasonal **Albee Creek** (Mattole Rd., 5 miles west of Ave. of the Giants, 800/444-7275, http://reserveamerica.com, $35 with one vehicle) has sites under redwoods and is very popular. The large and slightly more private **Hidden Springs Campground** (5 miles south of the visitors center, Ave. of the Giants, 800/444-7275, http://reserveamerica.com, $35 with one vehicle) is close to the Eel River. Reservations are strongly recommended for campsites, as this region is quite popular with weekend campers.

Garberville

Considered the gateway to both the Avenue of the Giants and the Lost Coast, the town of Garberville provides a few places to eat and sleep for those exploring redwood country.

Accommodations

The place to stay in the Humboldt Redwoods area is the **Benbow Inn** (445 Lake Benbow Dr., 707/923-2124 or 800/355-3301, www.benbowinn.com, $195-660). A swank resort backing onto Lake Benbow, this inn has it all: a gourmet restaurant, an 18-hole golf course, and a woodsy atmosphere that blends perfectly with the idyllic redwood forest surrounding it. Rooms glow with polished dark woods and jewel-toned carpets and decor. Wide king and comfy queen beds beckon to guests tired after a long day of hiking in the redwoods or golfing beside the inn.

The best deal is **Motel Garberville** (948 Redwood Dr., 707/923-2422, www.motelgarbervillecalifornia.com, $63 and up). At **Best Western Humboldt House Inn** (701 Redwood Dr., 707/923-2771, www.humboldthouseinn.com, $146-215), the rooms are clean and comfortable, the pool is sparkling and cool, and the

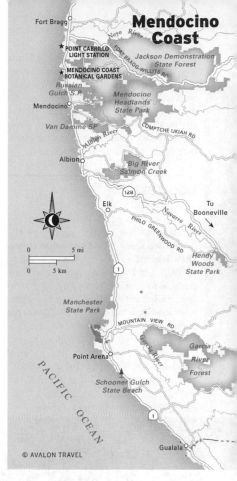

location is convenient to restaurants and shops in Garberville. Most rooms have two queen beds, making this motel perfect for families and couples traveling together on a budget.

Food

Enjoy a fresh, organic breakfast at the **Woodrose Café** (911 Redwood Ave., 707/923-3191, www.thewoodrosecafe.com, 8am-2pm daily, $9-16) or homemade bagels and espresso at **Bon Bistro & Bakery** (867 Redwood Dr., 707/923-2509, under $12).

The restaurant at the **Benbow Inn** (445 Lake Benbow Dr., 800/355-3301, www.benbowinn.com, breakfast, lunch, and dinner daily) matches the lodgings for superiority in the area. It serves upscale California cuisine and features an extensive wine list with many regional wineries represented. The white-tablecloth dining room is exquisite, and the expansive outdoor patio overlooking the water is the perfect place to sit as the temperature cools on a summer evening.

Leggett

The town of Legget is notable as the location of the southernmost of the drive-thru trees. The **Chandelier Drive-Thru Tree** (67402 Drive-Thru Tree Rd., 707/925-6464, www.drivethrutree.com, 8:30am-8pm daily June-Aug., 8:30am-5pm daily Sept.-May, $5) is at the junction of CA-1 and US-101. The tree opening is about six feet wide and a little over six feet high. And, of course, there's a gift shop. Leggett marks the point at which CA-1 splits off US-101 going south (and merges with US-101 going north).

Fort Bragg

A California Historical Landmark, Fort Bragg was established as a pre-Civil War military garrison, which was abandoned in the 1860s. The lumber and commercial fishing industries dominated the town's economic progress, leaving the tourist trade to its upscale neighbor, Mendocino. But since the 2002 closing of the Georgia Pacific lumber mill, Fort Bragg has slowly reinvented itself into a friendly destination for seaside travelers, with the old mill site becoming a topic of restoration and transformation.

These days visitors flock to Fort Bragg's northern end where multicolored glass paints the seashore at **Glass Beach** in **MacKerricher Park.** On the southern end of town lies **Mendocino Coast Botanical Gardens** and **Point Cabrillo Light Station State Historic Park,** where trails and stunning views abound!

the Chandelier Drive-Thru Tree in Leggett

Getting There and Around

State Route 1 (CA-1), California's Pacific Coast Highway, turns into Main Street as it passes through Fort Bragg. CA-20 heads east to west, running for several miles alongside and south of the Skunk Train route from Willits.

Rent a bicycle to get around at **Fort Bragg Cyclery** (221a N. Main St., 707/964-3509, www.fortbraggcyclery. com). **Mendocino Transit Authority** (Route 5, 707/462-1422 or 800/696-4682, www.4mta.org, $1.50 one-way) runs buses just south of Noyo Harbor and north of downtown on Elm Street.

Sights

The **Mendocino Coast Botanical Gardens** (18220 CA-1 N., 707/964-4352, www.gardenbythesea.org, 9am-5pm daily Mar.-Oct., 9am-4pm daily Nov.-Feb., $14 adults, $5 children) is a vast expanse of land bearing an astonishing variety of vegetation. Stretching 47 acres down to the sea, these gardens offer literally miles

of walking and hiking through careful plantings and wild landscapes. The gardens map is also a seasonal guide, useful for folks who aren't sure whether it's rhododendron season, or whether the dahlia garden might be in bloom. Butterflies flutter and bees buzz, and good labels teach novice botany enthusiasts the names of the plants they see.

Whether you're into scenery or history, nautical or otherwise, you won't want to miss a visit to the **Point Cabrillo Light Station State Historic Park** (12301 CA-1 N., 707/937-6122, www.pointcabrillo.org, 10am-4pm daily, $5). This 300-acre nature preserve, just south of Fort Bragg, features two museums, a marinelife exhibit, and walking trails. The beautiful **Point Cabrillo Lighthouse** (45300 Lighthouse Rd., 707/937-6122, 11am-4pm daily) has been functioning for more than 100 years. It was built in part to facilitate the movement of lumber and other supplies south to San Francisco to help rebuild the city after the massive 1906 earthquake. The site is currently being managed by a volunteer organization, the Point Cabrillo Lightkeepers Association. The trail that leads to the lighthouse from the parking lot is about 0.5 mile downhill, but remember you'll have to walk uphill to the parking lot.

Ride through the redwoods and into areas inaccessible by car on **The Skunk Train** (100 W. Laurel St., 866/457-5865, www.skunktrain.com, $34-74 round-trip), a line that runs 40 miles from Fort Bragg on the coast to Willits, traversing 30 bridges and trestles and two deep mountain tunnels. The name came from the pungent odor given off by the railbus. It's one of the best ways to see the local coast terrain, if not by foot.

Beaches

On the north edge of town, multicolored glass sparkles in the sand beneath the sun at **Glass Beach,** left over from its past as a garbage dump. Residents threw their trash over the cliffside to be burned in piles. After several decades, the pounding waves wore down the discarded broken bottles and jars into the pieces of small, smooth glass that have given the beach its name. Glass Beach is located on the southern end of **MacKerricher Park** (24100 MacKerricher Park Rd., 707/937-5804, www.parks.ca.gov), a pristine stretch of coastline that contains beaches, wildlife habitat, dunes, coves, tidepools, wetlands, forest, and Lake Cleone.

Food

The ★ **North Coast Brewing Company** (455 N. Main St., 707/964-3400, www.northcoastbrewing.com, from 2pm daily) opened in 1988, aiming at the then-nascent artisanal beer market. Come in, grab a classic brewpub meal, then check out the latest beers. Whether you choose an Acme, a Red Seal Ale, or an Old Rasputin (yes, really), you'll definitely enjoy.

The best pizza for miles can be found at **D'Aurelios** (438 S. Franklin St., 707/964-4227, 5pm-9pm daily, $8-12). Add some spice to your life with Mexican food at **La Playa** (542 N. Main St., 707/964-4074, 10am-9pm daily, $6-12).

For fresh seafood, **The Wharf** (780 N. Harbor Dr., 707/964-4283, www.wharf-restaurant.com, 11am-9:30pm daily, $10-28) serves a variety of cuisine from the sea along the Noyo River, while next door **Cap'n Flint's** (32250 N. Main St., 707/964-9447, 11am-9pm daily, $11-25) presents lighter prices.

Mendo Bistro (301 N. Main St., 707/964-4974, www.mendobistro.com, 5pm-9pm daily, $14-25) serves the finest local seafood, and offers a special menu that presents a selection of meats and sauces and lets you choose your own preparation style.

Cheap but great waffles and homemade goodies are at **Headlands Coffeehouse** (120 E. Laurel St., 707/964-1987, www.headlandcoffeehouse.com, 7am-10pm Mon.-Sat., 7am-7pm Sun., $4-8). **Egghead's Restaurant** (326 N. Main

St., 707/964-5005, www.eggheadsrestaurant.com, 7am-2pm daily, $8-13) has been serving an enormous menu of breakfast, lunch, and brunch items to satisfy diners for more than 30 years. The menu includes every imaginable omelet combination and "flying-monkey potatoes," derived from the *Wizard of Oz* theme that runs through the place.

Nightlife and Entertainment

Fort Bragg is not without its dive bars. Local favorite **Tip-Top Lounge** (321 N. Franklin St., 707/964-5448, 9am-2am daily) boasts cheap drinks, a pool table, and a jukebox. The **Welcome Inn** (148 E. Redwood Ave., 707/964-5491, 8am-2am daily) has a cool vibe and atmosphere, including several pool tables and shuffleboard.

Silver's at The Wharf (780 N. Harbor Dr., 707/964-4283, www.wharf-restaurant.com, 11am-9:30pm daily) is a sports bar setting with a large screen TV, a couple cozy couches, and a fantastic view of the Noyo River.

The best live music is at **Caspar Inn** (14957 Caspar Rd., 707/964-5565, www.casparinn.biz, 7pm-2am Fri.-Sat., 7:30pm-midnight Sun., $4-12 cover), where everything from hip-hop, rock, reggae, and even international acts come to play.

For a wide range of theater experiences, from musicals to operas to concerts, **Gloriana Musical Theater** (210 N. Corry St., 707/964-7469, $22 adults, $10 children) brings talented artists and actors together for fantastic performances that the whole family can enjoy.

Shopping

Antique shops and boutiques dot the lumber town. **Mendocino Vintage** (334 N. Franklin St., 707/964-5825, www.mendocinovintage.com, 11am-5pm Tues.-Sat.) has every old and unique object and treasure you could imagine: fine estate and costume jewelry, depression glass, paintings, candlesticks, collectible bottles, political buttons, and so much more.

Rubaiyat Beads (222 E. Redwood Ave., 707/961-0222, www.rubaiyatbeads.com, 10am-5pm Mon.-Sat.) is the place to discover beads, tribal jewelry, ethnic textiles, incense, and sacred treasures from around the world.

Be blown away by **Glass Fire Gallery** (18320 CA-1 N., 707/962-9420, www.glassforegallery.com, 11am-6pm Tues.-Sat., noon-5pm Sun.), where a large variety of gorgeous blown glass vessels, sea jellies, sculptures, and jewelry are displayed, or explore **Sacred Woods** (32281 N. Harbor Dr., 707/964-3507, www.sacredwoods.noyo.com, 10am-5pm daily), a garden collection of amazing sculptures and beautiful outdoor furniture from Thailand and Indonesia to the north coast.

Tons of used books and vintage records are found at **Windsong Used Books & Records** (324 N. Main St., 707/964-2050, 10am-5:30pm Mon.-Sat., 10am-4pm Sun.), which also has some gift items like candles, incense, and artwork. **The Bookstore & Vinyl Cafe** (353 N. Franklin St., 707/964-6559, 10am-5:30pm Mon.-Sat., 11am-4pm Sun.) is small but has a good selection of new and used books, with a great upstairs section filled with used records.

Stop by the **Lost Surf Shack** (319 N. Franklin St., 707/961-0889, www.lostsurfshack.com, 10am-6pm daily) for great beachwear. Surfers will love that they have everything to surf the waves, including board rentals.

For unique fashion items and gifts, go to **Toto Zaida** (137 E. Laurel St., 707/964-8686, 10am-5pm Mon.-Sat., 11am-3pm Sun.) or stop by **Tangents** (368 N. Main St., 707/964-3884, 9am-6pm daily), a mix of exotic and cool-funk fashion, including a nice selection of one-of-a-kind ethnic gifts.

Recreation
Go **abalone diving** or **kayak** the many caves and arches off the coast. You can rent gear and get all the information you need at **Sub-Surface Progression Dive Shop** (18600 CA-1 N., 707/964-3793, www.subsurfaceprogression.com, 9am-5pm daily), or observe over 150 species of birds at **Mendocino Coast Botanical Gardens** (18220 CA-1 N., 707/964-4352, www.gardenbythesea.com, $14 adults, $5 children 5-17).

Whale-watching is one of Fort Bragg's most popular attractions during the winter and spring, when gray and humpback whales migrate along the coast. They can be seen from several offshore points especially at **MacKerricher State Park** (24100 MacKerricher Park Rd., 707/937-5804, www.parks.ca.gov) and **Point Cabrillo Light Station State Historic Park** (south of Fort Bragg). Whale-watching charter boats, such as **Anchor Charter Boats** (32776 Park View Dr., 707/964-4550, www.anchorcharterboats.com, $35 pp), are located in Noyo Harbor.

Events
Taste local microbrews and wines and browse arts and crafts during the **Fort Bragg Whale Festival** (707/961-6300) held every third weekend in March, or celebrate the days of lumberjacks at **Paul Bunyan Days** (paulbunyandays.com, Labor Day weekend), which features a parade, logging show, and square dancing.

Accommodations
Although Fort Bragg lodgings may not be a bargain, they provide lower-priced alternatives to staying in Mendocino proper.

What really makes the **Beachcomber Motel** (1111 N. Main St., 707/964-2402, www.thebeachcombermotel.com, $109-259) worthwhile, besides its lower-than-B&B prices, is that it's right on the beach, offering many rooms with ocean views. Rooms are clean, with few amenities, but guests just need to walk out the back door to be on the sand.

The best bang for your buck is the **Grey Whale Inn** (615 N. Main St., 707/964-0640 or 800/382-7244, www.greywhaleinn. com, $100-195) on the northern end of town, which isn't fancy but is comfortable and conveniently located with good-sized rooms.

A popular little B&B in the heart of downtown, **Country Inn** (18725 CA-1 N., 707/964-3737, www.beourguests.com, $90-145) has a laid-back aura, friendly hosts, and a hot tub to unwind in at the end of a long day.

The **Old Coast Hotel** (101 N. Franklin St., 707/961-4488, $120 and up) is an ornate Victorian-era inn with a lively sports bar. The **Weller House Inn** (524 Stewart St., 707/964-4415 or 877/893-5537, www. wellerhouse.com, $130-195) is a restored 1886 mansion with a gorgeous ballroom and luxurious amenities.

Information and Services
The best source of information is the **Fort Bragg-Mendocino Coast Chamber of Commerce** (217 Main St., 707/961-6300, www.mendocinocoast.com).

Russian Gulch State Park

Some of the most popular hiking trails in coastal Mendocino County wind through **Russian Gulch State Park** (CA-1, two miles north of Mendocino, 707/937-5804, www.parks.ca.gov, $8). Russian Gulch has its own **Fern Canyon Trail** (three miles round-trip), winding into the second-growth redwood forest filled with lush green ferns. At the four-way junction, turn left to hike another 0.75 mile to the ever-popular 36-foot waterfall. Be aware that you're likely to be part of a crowd visiting the falls on summer weekends. To the right at the four-way junction, you can take a three-mile loop for a total hike of six miles that leads to the top of the attractive little waterfall. If you prefer the shore to the forest, hike west rather than east to take in the lovely wild headlands and see blowholes,

grasses, and even trawlers out seeking the day's catch.

Mendocino

Set on a bluff overlooking the ocean, the picturesque town of Mendocino is a favorite for romantic weekend getaways, with quaint bed-and-breakfasts, art galleries, and local sustainable dining. Art is especially prominent in the culture; from the 1960s onward, aspiring artists have found supportive communities here.

Sights
The town of Mendocino has long been an inspiration and a gathering place for artists of many varieties, and the **Mendocino Art Center** (45200 Little Lake St., 707/937-5818 or 800/653-3328, www.mendocinoartcenter.org, 10am-5pm daily, donation) is the main institution that gives these diverse artists a community, provides them with opportunities for teaching and learning, and displays the work of contemporary artists for the benefit of both the artists and the general public. Since 1959 the center has offered artist workshops and retreats. Today it has a flourishing schedule of events and classes, five galleries, and a sculpture garden. You can even drop in and make some art of your own. Supervised "open studios" in ceramics, jewelry making, watercolor, sculpture, and drawing take place throughout the year.

Mendocino Headlands State Park (Mendocino, 707/937-5804, www.parks. ca.gov, day-use only, free) occupies the waterfront land that surrounds the town of Mendocino. A few trails weave through the grassy bluffs and take you to cliffside water views or down to the beach. At the south end of the park, the historic **Ford House Museum and Visitor Center** (45035 Main St., 707/937-5394, 11am-4pm daily) has information about the town of Mendocino.

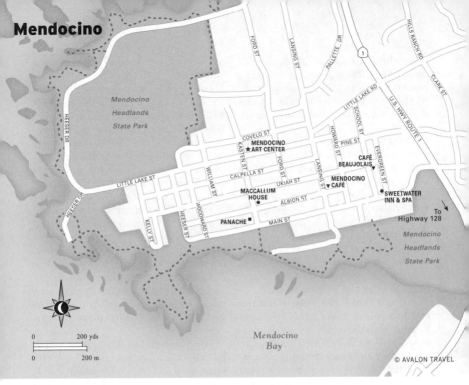

Mendocino

Mendocino Headlands State Park

COVELO ST
MENDOCINO ★ ART CENTER
CAFÉ BEAUJOLAIS
CALPELLA ST
UKIAH ST
MENDOCINO ▼ CAFÉ
MACCALLUM HOUSE
ALBION ST
SWEETWATER INN & SPA
PANACHE ■
MAIN ST
To Highway 128

Mendocino Headlands State Park

HEESER DR
FORD ST
LANSING ST
PALLETTE DR
HILLS RANCH RD
CLARK ST
LITTLE LAKE RD
SCHOOL ST
HOWARD ST
PINE ST
U.S. HWY ROUTE 1
EVERGREEN ST
KASTEN ST
WILLIAM ST
LITTLE LAKE ST
KELLY ST
HEESER ST
WOODWARD ST
LANSING ST

Mendocino Bay

0   200 yds
0   200 m

© AVALON TRAVEL

Food

One of the most appealing and dependable places to get a good meal any day of the week is the **Mendocino Café** (10451 Lansing St., 707/937-6141, www.mendocinocafe.com, 11am-9pm daily, $14-33). The café has good, simple, well-prepared food, a small kids menu, a wine list, and a beer list. Enjoy a Thai burrito, a fresh salmon fillet, or a steak in the warm, well-lit dining room. Or sit outside: The café is in the gardens of Mendocino Village, and thanks to a heated patio, you can enjoy outdoor dining any time of day.

Café Beaujolais (961 Ukiah St., 707/937-5614, www.cafebeaujolais.com, 11:30am-2:30pm Wed.-Sun., 5:30pm-9pm daily, $24-42) is a standout French-California restaurant in an area dense with great upscale cuisine. This charming out-of-the-way spot is a few blocks from the center of Mendocino Village in an older, creeper-covered home. Despite the white tablecloths and fancy crystal,

the atmosphere is casual at lunchtime and gets only slightly more formal at dinner. The giant salads and delectable entrées are made with organic produce, humanely raised meats, and locally caught seafood. Beware: The portions can be enormous, but you can get them half-size just by asking. Reservations are available on the website.

Shopping

Mendocino Village is a delightful place to browse. Not only are the galleries, bookstores, and boutiques welcoming and fun, the whole downtown area is beautiful. It seems that every shop in the Main Street area has its own garden, and each fills with a riotous cascade of flowers in the summertime.

Panache (45120 Main St., 707/937-0947, www.thepanachegallery.com) displays and sells beautiful works of art in all sorts of media. You'll find paintings and jewelry, sculpture and art glass. Much of the artistic focus reminds viewers of the sea crashing just outside the large multi-room gallery. The wooden furniture and boxes are a special treat: handmade treasures using rare woods combined and then sanded and polished to silk-smooth finishes.

Nothing makes a weekend getaway more enjoyable than a delicious book. Pick one up at the **Gallery Book Shop** (corner of Main and Kasten Sts., 707/937-2215, 9:30am-6pm Sun.-Thurs., 9:30am-9pm Fri.-Sat.).

Accommodations

Places to stay in Mendocino tend to be smaller, often luxury, properties. For lower-priced options, try Fort Bragg, about 10 miles and 20 minutes north.

Fun and funky, the **Sweetwater Inn and Spa** (44840 Main St., Mendocino Village, 800/300-4140, www.sweetwaterspa.com, $225-275) harkens back to the days when Mendocino was a starving artists' colony rather than a yuppie weekend retreat. A redwood water tower was converted into a guest room, joined by a motley connection of detached cottages that guarantee guests great privacy. Every room and cottage has its own style—you'll find a spiral staircase in the water tower, a two-person tub set in a windowed alcove in the Zen Room, and fireplaces in many of the cottages. Thick gardens surround the building complex, and a path leads back to the Garden Spa. The location, just past downtown on Main Street in Mendocino Village, is perfect for dining, shopping, and art walks.

With several properties in addition to the main hotel in Mendocino Village, **MacCallum House** (45020 Albion St., 800/609-0492, www.maccallumhouse.com, $150-350) is the king of luxury on the Mendocino coast. Choose from private cottages with hot tubs, suites with jetted baths, and regular rooms with opulent antique appointments. The woodwork gleams and the service pleases here. Note that a two-night minimum is required on weekends, and a three-night minimum goes into effect for most holidays.

For a perfect vantage point for sunset over the Pacific, stay at the **Sea Rock Bed & Breakfast Inn** (11101 Lansing St., 707/937-0926 or 800/906-0926, www.searock.com, $185-395). Located away from the Main Street area, this little village of cottages, junior suites, and suites sleep 2-4 people each. After you check in, you can sit outside on the Adirondack chairs to watch the lights change, or you can take the bottle of Husch Vineyard wine from your guest room, stroll across the street, and take it all in from the viewing platform right above the beach. The inn's breakfast room, where hot quiche and fresh fruit, included in the room rates, is served every morning, is also perfectly situated for optimal ocean views.

The **Stanford Inn** (Comptche Ukiah Rd., about 0.5 mile past the CA-1 intersection, 707/937-5615 or 800/331-8884, www.stanfordinn.com, $230-500) is one of the largest accommodations in the Mendocino area. This resort hotel sits up away from the beaches, surrounded by redwood forest. Gardens surround the resort (in fact, there's a nursery on the property), perfect for an after-dinner stroll. The location is convenient to hiking and only a short drive down to Mendocino Village and the coastline. Guest rooms have beautiful honey wood-paneled walls, pretty furniture, and puffy down comforters. You'll get the feel of an upscale forest lodge, whether you choose a basic Big River Room or one of the many varieties of suites. All rooms include breakfast at Ravens, a wood-burning fireplace, a TV with DVD player, a stereo, and Internet access.

Little River and Albion

Little River is about three miles south of Mendocino on CA-1. Tiny Albion is also along CA-1, about 8 miles south of

Mendocino and almost 30 miles north of Point Arena. Find a state park and several plush places to stay in this area.

Van Damme State Park

At **Van Damme State Park** (CA-1, three miles south of Mendocino, 707/937-5804, www.parks.ca.gov, free), take a walk to the park's centerpiece, the Pygmy Forest, on the wheelchair-accessible loop trail (0.25 mile, easy). Here, you'll see a true biological rarity: mature yet tiny cypress and pine trees perpetually stunted by a combination of always-wet ground and poor soil-nutrient conditions. You can get to the Pygmy Forest from this park's **Fern Canyon Trail** (six miles one-way, difficult), or drive Airport Road to the trail parking lot (opposite the county airport) directly to the loop.

Kayak Mendocino (707/813-7117, www.kayakmendocino.com) launches 1.5-hour Sea Cave Nature Tours (9am, 11:30am, 2pm, $60 pp) from Van Damme State Park. No previous experience is necessary, as the expert guides provide all the equipment you need and teach you how to paddle your way through the sea caves and around the harbor seals.

Camping (800/444-7275, www.parks.ca.gov, $35) is available in Van Damme State Park, and reservations are strongly encouraged.

Food and Accommodations

The **Little River Inn** (7901 CA-1 N., Little River, 707/937-5942 or 888/466-5683, www.littleriverinn.com, $189-375) appeals to coastal vacationers who like a little luxury. It has a nine-hole golf course and two lighted tennis courts, and all its recreation areas overlook the Pacific, which crashes on the shore just across the highway from the inn. The sprawling white Victorian house and barns hide the expanse of the grounds, which also has a great **restaurant** and a charming sea-themed bar. Relax even more at the in-house salon and spa.

The luxurious **Glendeven Inn** (8205

CA-1 N., 707/937-0083 or 800/822-4536, www.glendeven.com, $205-415) is situated in a historic farmhouse with ocean views. The hosts will help you settle in with a complimentary wine and hors d'oeuvres hour in the late afternoon, and they wake you in the morning with a three-course made-to-order breakfast, delivered to your guest room exactly when you want it.

The **Albion River Inn** (3790 CA-1 N., 707/937-1919 or 800/479-7944, www.albionriverinn.com, $195-355) is a gorgeous and serene setting for an away-from-it-all vacation. A full breakfast is included in the room rates, but pets and smoking are not allowed, and there are no TVs.

The **Ledford House Restaurant** (3000 CA-1 N., Albion, 707/937-0282, www.ledfordhouse.com, 5pm-close Wed.-Sun., $19-30) is beautiful even from a distance; you'll see it on the hill as you drive up CA-1. With excellent food and nightly jazz performances, it's truly special.

Information and Services

There is a **post office** (7748 CA-1, Albion, 707/937-5547, www.usps.com, 8:15am-1pm and 2pm-4:30pm Mon.-Fri.) in Albion.

❖ CA-128: Anderson Valley

To follow the Anderson Valley wine trail, head southeast on CA-128, about three miles south of Albion. The wine trail continues for roughly 60 miles (45 minutes) to Boonville. From Boonville, you can reverse the route to return to CA-1, or continue another 60 miles (90 minutes) to rejoin US-101 at Cloverdale.

Handley Cellars (3151 CA-128, 707/895-3876, www.handleycellars.com, 10am-5pm daily) offers a tasting of hand-crafted wines you probably won't see in your local grocery store.

The largest winery in the area is

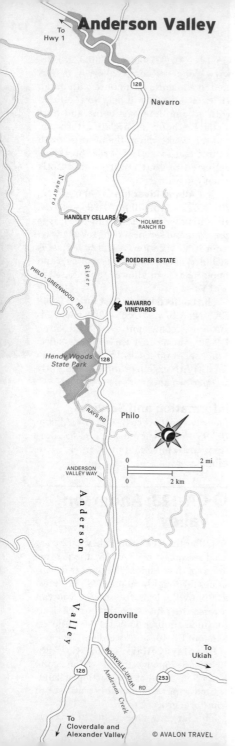

Navarro (5601 CA-128, Philo, 707/895-3686, www.navarrowine.com, 9am-5pm daily), which offers a range of tasty wines as well as some interesting specialty products such as verjus.

In a valley full of great wineries, **Roederer Estate** (4501 CA-128, 707/895-2288, www.roedererestate.com, 11am-5pm daily, tasting fee) creates some of the best sparkling wines in the state. Be sure to ask for a taste of Roederer's rarely seen still wines—you might find something wonderful.

For visitors who prefer a cold beer to a glass of wine, **Anderson Valley Brewing Company** (17700 CA-253, 707/895-2337, www.avbc.com, 11am-6pm Sat.-Thurs., 11am-7pm Fri., closed Tues.-Wed. in winter) serves up a selection of microbrews that changes each year and each season. The warehouse-sized beer hall has a bar, a number of tables, and a good-sized gift shop.

Elk

The town of Elk used to be called Greenwood, after the family of Caleb Greenwood, who settled here in about 1850. Details of the story vary, but it is widely believed that Caleb was part of a mission to rescue survivors of the Donner Party after their rough winter near Truckee.

Greenwood State Beach (CA-1, 707/937-5804, www.parks.ca.gov, visitors center 11am-1pm Sat.-Sun. Memorial Day-Labor Day) is an intriguing place to visit. From the mid-19th century until the 1920s, this stretch of shore was a stop for large ships carrying timber to points of sale in San Francisco and sometimes even China. The visitors center displays photographs and exhibits about Elk's past in the lumber business. It also casts light on the Native American heritage of the area and the natural resources that are still abundant.

A short hike demonstrates what makes

this area so special. From the parking lot, follow the trail down toward the ocean. You'll soon come to a fork; to the right is a picnic area. Follow the left fork to another picnic site and then, soon afterward, the beach. Turn left and walk about 0.25 mile to reach Greenwood Creek. Shortly past it is a cliff, at which point you have to turn around and walk back up the hill. Even in the short amount of time it takes to do this walk, you'll experience lush woods, sandy cliffs, and dramatic ocean overlooks.

Queenie's Roadhouse Café (6061 CA-1, 8am-3pm Thurs.-Sun.) is the place to go to fill up on American basics. The food is hot, the atmosphere is friendly, and the location is perfect—in the center of town and across the street from the ocean.

Point Arena Lighthouse

About 20 miles south of Elk is the **Point Arena Lighthouse** (45500 Lighthouse Rd., 707/882-2777 or 877/725-4448, www.pointarenalighthouse.com, 10am-4:30pm daily summer, 10am-3:30pm daily winter, $7.50 adults, $1 children). Although its magnificent Fresnel lens no longer turns through the night, it remains a Coast Guard light and fog station. But what makes this beacon special is its history. When the 1906 earthquake hit San Francisco, it jolted the land all the way up the coast, severely damaging the Point Arena Lighthouse. When the structure was rebuilt two years later, engineers devised the aboveground foundation that gives the lighthouse both its distinctive shape and additional structural stability.

Docent-led tours up to the top of the lighthouse are well worth the trip, both for the views of the lighthouse from the top and for the fascinating story of its destruction and rebirth through the 1906 earthquake as told by the knowledgeable staff.

Gualala

With a population of 585, Gualala ("wa-LA-la") feels like a metropolis along the CA-1 corridor in this region. It's located about 15 miles south of Point Arena. While it's not the most charming coastal town, it does have some of the services other places may lack.

If you're hungry when you hit town, try **Bones Roadhouse** (39080 CA-1, 707/884-1188, www.bonesroadhouse. com, 7:30am-10pm daily, $15-25) for barbecue and pulled pork in giant portions, served in a casual atmosphere with ocean views. Another popular option is **Trinks Café** (39140 CA-1 S., 707/884-1713, www. trinkscafe.com, 7am-5pm Mon.-Sat., 8am-4pm Sun., $12-22).

Surrounded by beautiful gardens, **North Coast Country Inn** (34591 CA-1, 707/884-4537 and 800/959-4537, www. northcoastcountryinn.com, $195-225) provides a country-style experience with rustic decor and fireplaces. **Gualala Point Regional Park** (42401 CA-1 S., 707/785-2377, $32 per night) has great year-round **camping.**

Salt Point State Park

Stretching for miles along the Sonoma coastline, **Salt Point State Park** (25050 CA-1, Jenner, 707/847-3221, www.parks. ca.gov, visitors center 10am-3pm Sat.-Sun. Apr.-Oct., day use $8 per vehicle) provides easy access to more than a dozen sandy state beaches. You don't have to visit the visitors center to enjoy this park and its many beaches—just follow the signs along the highway to the turnoffs and parking lots. To scuba dive or free dive, head for Gerstle Cove, accessible from the visitors center just south of Salt Point proper. The cove was designated one of California's first underwater parks, and divers who can deal with the chilly water have a wonderful time exploring the diverse undersea wildlife.

Fort Ross State Historic Park

There is no historic early American figure named Ross who settled here. "Ross" is short for "Russian," and this park commemorates the history of Russian settlement on the north coast. In the 19th century, Russians came to the wilds of Alaska and worked with native Alaskans to develop a robust fur trade, killing seals, otters, sea lions, and land mammals for their pelts. The hunters chased the animals as far as California. Eventually, a group of fur traders came ashore on what is now the Sonoma coast and developed a fortified outpost that became known as **Fort Ross** (19005 CA-1, Jenner, 707/847-3286, www.parks.ca.gov, Sat.-Sun. and holidays, parking $8). The area gradually became not only a thriving Russian American settlement but also a center for agriculture and shipbuilding and the site of California's first windmills. Learn more at the park's large visitors center, which provides a continuous film and a roomful of exhibits.

You can also walk into the reconstructed fort buildings and see how the settlers lived. (US-101 was originally built through the middle of the fort area, but it was moved to make way for the historic park.) The only original building still standing is the captain's quarters—a large, luxurious house for that time and place. The other buildings, including the large bunkhouse, the chapel, and the two cannon-filled blockhouses, were rebuilt using much of the original lumber used by the Russians. Be aware that a serious visit to the whole fort and the beach beyond is a level but long walk; wear comfortable shoes and consider bringing a bottle of water.

Jenner

Jenner is on CA-1 at the Russian River. It's a beautiful spot for a quiet honeymoon or a paddle in a kayak. **Goat Rock State Park** (Goat Rock Rd., 707/875-3483, www.parks.ca.gov, day-use $8) is at the mouth of the Russian River. A colony of harbor seals breed and frolic here, and you may also see gray whales, sea otters, elephant seals, and a variety of sea life. Pets are not allowed, and swimming is prohibited.

Both the food and the views are memorable at **River's End** (11048 CA-1, 707/865-2484, www.ilovesunsets.com, noon-3:30pm and 5pm-8:30pm Sun.-Mon. and Thurs. winter, noon-3:30pm and 5pm-8:30pm Sun.-Thurs., noon-3:30pm and 5pm-9pm Fri.-Sat. summer, $25-45). The restaurant is perched above the spot where the Russian River flows into the Pacific, and it's a beautiful sight to behold over, say, oysters or filet mignon. Prices are high, but if you get a window table at sunset, you may forget to think about it.

The cliff-top perch of the **Timber Coves Inn** (21780 CA-1 N., 707/847-3231, www.timbercoverinn.com, $195 and up) provides a spectacular view of the rugged Sonoma coast, making it one of the best places to stay.

Sonoma Coast State Park

Seventeen miles of coast are within **Sonoma Coast State Park** (707/875-3483, www.parks.ca.gov, day-use $8 per vehicle). The park's boundaries extend from Bodega Head at the south up to the Vista Trailhead, four miles north of Jenner. As you drive up CA-1, you'll see signs for various beaches. Although they're lovely places to walk, fish, and maybe sunbathe on the odd hot day, it is not advisable to swim here. If you go down to the water, bring your binoculars and your camera. The cliffs, crags, inlets, whitecaps, mini islands, and rock outcroppings are fascinating in any weather, and their looks change with the shifting tides and fog.

ᯤ CA-116: The Russian River

The Russian River meets the coast at Jenner. Turning inland onto CA-116 allows for a nice riverside drive. There are a few wineries in the **Guerneville** area, but most people come here to float, canoe, or kayak the gorgeous river. In addition to its busy summertime tourist trade, Guerneville is also a very popular gay and lesbian resort area. The rainbow flag flies proudly here, and the friendly community welcomes all.

CA-116 eventually ends, 30-plus miles inland from Jenner, at US-101, which can get travelers to San Francisco much more quickly than the winding but more beautiful CA-1.

Sights

Korbel Cellars (13250 River Rd., Guerneville, 707/824-7000, www.korbel. com, 10am-4:30pm daily), the leading producer of California sparkling wines, maintains a winery and tasting room on the Russian River, where visitors get to sample far more than the ubiquitous Korbel Brut that appears each New Year's. The facility also has a full-service gourmet deli and picnic grounds for tasters who want to stop for lunch.

Recreation

In summer, the waters of the Russian River are usually warm and dotted with folks swimming, canoeing, or simply floating tubes serenely downriver amid forested riverbanks and under blue skies. **Burke's Canoe Trips** (8600 River Rd., Forestville, 707/887-1222, www.burkescanoetrips.com, Memorial Day-mid-Oct., $60) rents canoes and kayaks on

the Russian River. The put-in is at Burke's beach in Forestville; paddlers then canoe downriver 10 miles to Guerneville, where a courtesy shuttle picks them up. Burke's also offers overnight campsites for tents, trailers, and RVs.

On the north bank, **Johnsons Beach & Resort** (16241 1st St., 707/869-2022, www.johnsonsbeach.com, 10am-6pm daily May-Oct.) rents canoes, kayaks, pedal boats, and inner tubes for floating the river. There is a safe kid-friendly section of the riverbank that is roped off for small children; parents and beachcombers can rent beach chairs and umbrellas for use on the small beach.

Accommodations

Guerneville offers a few nice little inns, like the intimate sanctuary **Applewood Inn** (13555 CA-116, 707/869-9093, www. applewoodinn.com, $195-335), with fine dining and a spa.

Bodega Bay

Bodega Bay is popular for its coastal views, whale-watching, and seafood, but it's most famous as the filming locale of Alfred Hitchcock's *The Birds*.

The best sight you could hope to see is a close-up view of Pacific gray whales migrating with their newborn calves. The whales head past January-May on their way from their summer home off Mexico back to their winter home in Alaska. If you're lucky, you can see them from the shore. **Bodega Head,** a promontory just north of the bay, is a place to get close to the migration route. To get to this prime spot, travel on CA-1 about one mile north of the visitors center and turn west onto Eastshore Road; make a right at the stop sign, and then drive three more miles to the parking lot. On weekends, volunteers from Stewards of the Coast and Redwoods (707/869-9177, ext. 1., www. stewardsofthecoastandredwoods.org) are available to answer questions. Contact

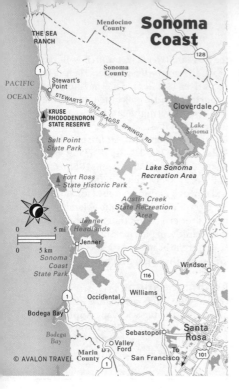

Sonoma Coast

THE SEA RANCH

Mendocino County

Sonoma County

128

PACIFIC OCEAN

Stewart's Point

STEWARTS POINT SKAGGS SPRINGS RD

KRUSE RHODODENDRON STATE RESERVE

Cloverdale

Lake Sonoma

Salt Point State Park

Fort Ross State Historic Park

Lake Sonoma Recreation Area

Austin Creek State Recreation Area

Jenner Headlands

Jenner

0   5 mi
0   5 km

Sonoma Coast State Park

Windsor

116

Occidental

Williams

Bodega Bay

Bodega Bay

Sebastopol

Santa Rosa

Valley Ford

To San Francisco

101

Marin County

© AVALON TRAVEL

them for organized whale-watching tours or to learn more about their various educational programs.

Food and Accommodations

Bodega Bay Lodge (103 CA-1, 707/875-4212 or 888/875-3525, www.bodegabaylodge.com, $215-450) is one of the more luxurious places to stay in the area. It is a large resort with long rows of semidetached cabins. The facility also has a spa, a pool, a fitness center, two fine restaurants, and a library. The lodge's **Duck Club Restaurant** (103 CA-1, 707/875-3525, www.bodegabaylodge.com, 7:30am-11am and 6pm-9pm daily, $18-36) offers a warm and elegant dining experience featuring hearty American entrées like steak, chicken, and halibut with seasonal vegetables. There's a fireside lounge overlooking the bay, and even some outdoor seating for warmer days.

One of the best restaurants in the area is **Terrapin Creek** (1580 Eastshore Dr., 707/875-2700, www.terrapincreekcafe.com, 4:30pm-9pm Thurs.-Sun., $22-29), where they make creative use of the abundance of fresh seafood available.

Gourmet au Bay (913 CA-1, 707/875-9875, www.gourmetaubay.com, 11am-7pm Sun.-Thurs., 11am-8pm Fri.-Sat.) is a shop and tasting bar in the coastal town of Bodega Bay with wines from a variety of different vintners.

Under 10 miles southeast of Bodega Bay on CA-1 is the town of Valley Ford ("town" feels like an overstatement). One of the few remaining 19th-century buildings houses the **Valley Ford Hotel** (14415 CA-1, 707/876-1983, www.vfordhotel.com, $115-122).

♦ CA-12: Sonoma and Napa

There's nothing like a drive through the Sonoma and Napa countryside, especially when there are grape-bearing vines that beckon a stop at a winery along the way. This side trip covers 60 miles (90 minutes of driving time). But plan for a full day, especially if you will be wine-tasting. Also plan on a designated driver to remain sober and safe on the road.

From Bodega Bay, take Highway 12 East (CA-12) to London Ranch Road in Sonoma County, where the historic **Benziger Family Winery** (1883 London Ranch Rd., Glen Ellen, 707/935-3000, 10am-5pm daily) sits alongside Jack London State Historic Park. The family vineyard was the first in the United States to go completely "green." Climb aboard the Biodynamic Vineyard Tram for a 45-minute tour ($25) to learn about the ecofriendly vineyard, then journey through the fermentation facility and crush pad and explore a hidden cave filled with treasured wine barrels, followed by a tasting of four wines.

Return to CA-12, head east, then hang left at West Napa Street (watch for Sonoma signs), which turns into Old Winery Road. Just five minutes from Sonoma's famous plaza square, **Buena**

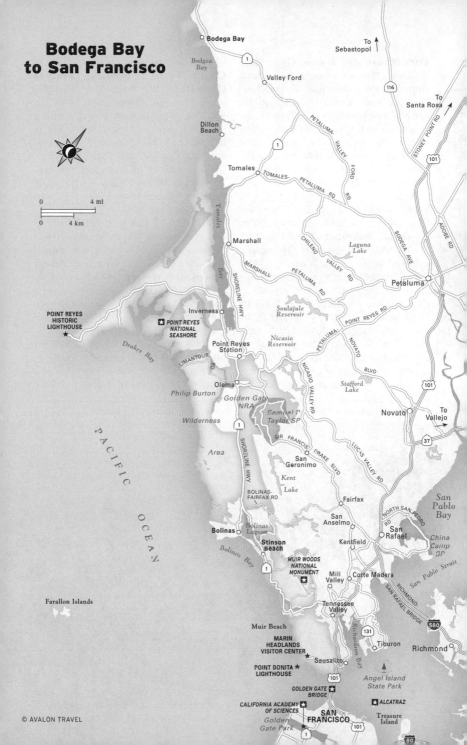

Bodega Bay
to San Francisco

Bodega Bay

Bodega Bay

To Sebastopol

Valley Ford

1

116

To Santa Rosa

Dillon Beach

PETALUMA-VALLEY FORD RD

STONEY POINT RD

101

Tomales

TOMALES-PETALUMA RD

ADOBE RD

BODEGA AVE

Marshall

CHILENO VALLEY RD

Laguna Lake

PETALUMA RD

Petaluma

MARSHALL-PETALUMA RD

SHORELINE HWY

Soulajule Reservoir

POINT REYES HISTORIC LIGHTHOUSE

Inverness

POINT REYES NATIONAL SEASHORE

POINT REYES RD

Drakes Bay

Point Reyes Station

Nicasio Reservoir

PETALUMA-POINT REYES RD

NOVATO BLVD

LIMANTOUR RD

Olema

Philip Burton

Golden Gate NRA

Samuel P. Taylor SP

Stafford Lake

Novato

To Vallejo

101

37

Wilderness

PACIFIC OCEAN

Area

SHORELINE HWY

1

SIR FRANCIS DRAKE BLVD

San Geronimo

LUCAS VALLEY RD

Kent Lake

BOLINAS-FAIRFAX RD

Fairfax

NORTH SAN PEDRO RD

San Pablo Bay

Bolinas

Bolinas Lagoon

San Anselmo

San Rafael

China Camp SP

Kentfield

Stinson Beach

1

MUIR WOODS NATIONAL MONUMENT

Corte Madera

RICHMOND-SAN RAFAEL BRIDGE

San Pablo Strait

Bolinas Bay

Mill Valley

Farallon Islands

Tennessee Valley

Richardson Bay

131

Tiburon

Richmond

Muir Beach

MARIN HEADLANDS VISITOR CENTER

POINT BONITA LIGHTHOUSE

Sausalito

Angel Island State Park

580

GOLDEN GATE BRIDGE

ALCATRAZ

CALIFORNIA ACADEMY OF SCIENCES

101

SAN FRANCISCO

Treasure Island

Golden Gate Park

1

101

80

0   4 mi
0   4 km

© AVALON TRAVEL

Vista Winery (18000 Old Winery Rd., 800/926-1266, www.buenavistawinery.com, $20 pp) is the oldest commercial wine producer in the state of California and a historic landmark. The Press House is open for tasting year-round and offers a chance to taste new releases, or if you'd rather, you can sample older wines in the library. There is also a Barrel Tour and Tasting (11am-2pm daily).

Backtrack via CA-29 South to CA-12 West/CA-121 South (follow signs for Sonoma) to the oldest family-owned winery, **Gundlach Bundschu** (2000 Denmark St., 707/938-5277, $50 tour). Owned and operated by six generations, since 1858, Gundlach Bundschu focuses on creating pinot noir, gewürztraminer, and chardonnay ultra-premium wines from its hand-farmed, 320-acre vineyard at the crossroads of the Sonoma Valley. Sample a selection of wines from the tasting room courtyard or enter the wine cave nearby through a tunnel, exiting into a view overlooking the vineyards and gorgeous lake.

Take the first right onto CA-12 West/CA-121 South to **Domaine Carneros** (1240 Duhig Rd., Napa, 800/716-2788, www.domainecarneros.com, $40 tour, $30 tasting pp) to taste award-winning sparkling wines or pinot noirs. Get a behind-the-scenes look at the magic of méthode champenoise sparkling winemaking with an intimate tour, or simply relax and enjoy a glass of wine while savoring the sweeping view of the south end of Napa Valley.

Take CA-12 East/CA-121 North to Henry Road in Napa County, winding through fields of wildflowers until you at last reach the entrance to **Artesa Vineyards & Winery** (1345 Henry Rd., Napa, 707/254-2126, www.artesawinery.com, tour 11am and 2pm daily, $30 tour, $20 tasting pp). Continue up the long driveway to the winery, built on the hillside. The facility is much like a modern museum with lots of hanging art, light-colored walls, and wood floors. Guided tours of the winemaking facility include

Napa Valley vineyards

a sparkling wine greeting and a reserve tasting of five wines at the end of the tour. Although Artesa's collection of wines is vast, they are most known for their estate pinot noir, which received high marks from *Wine Enthusiast*.

Return to the coast via CA-116 or Skillman Lane to CA-1 South in Marin County, culminating in Tomales Bay or continue south to Point Reyes.

Marshall

A quick stop for tourists heading to Tomales Bay and the Point Reyes Peninsula, the little community of **Marshall** (pop. 215) was built on the dairy industry in the 1850s but has since become a major center for oysters and clams. **The Marshall Store** (19225 CA-1, 415/663-1339, www.themarshallstore. com, 10am-4pm Mon. and Wed.-Fri., 10am-5pm Sat.-Sun. winter, 10am-5pm Mon. and Wed.-Fri., 10am-6pm Sat.-Sun.

summer, under $20) prepares them nearly 100 ways. You won't find many hotels in town, but it's a good place to grab a bite then move on.

For an upscale atmosphere, **Nick's Cove** (23240 CA-1, 415/663-1033, www. nickscove.com, 11am-9pm daily) serves a wide variety of wines and microbrews.

★ Point Reyes National Seashore

Point Reyes National Seashore (1 Bear Valley Rd., 415/464-5100, www.nps.gov/ pore, dawn-midnight daily) stretches for miles between Tomales Bay and the Pacific, north from Stinson Beach to the tip of the land at the end of the bay. The area boasts acres of unspoiled forest and remote, almost untouched beaches. The protected lands shelter a range of wildlife. In the marshes and lagoons, a wide variety of birds—including three different species of pelicans—make their nests. The pine forests shade shy deer and larger elk. Expect cool weather even in the summer, but enjoy the lustrous green foliage and spectacular scenery that result.

The Point Reyes area includes three tiny towns that provide services for the area: Olema, Point Reyes Station, and Inverness. You'll pass a few inns, restaurants, and shops in each. **Olema** (pop. 53) was once the main settlement in West Marin. Its name stems from the Miwok Indian word for "little coyote." The town grew around an old stagecoach road, leading to a Wild West era of card rooms, rough saloons, and obscene establishments. When the narrow-gauge railroad was laid to the north, it bypassed Olema for **Point Reyes Station** (pop. 871), which flooded with early settlers fired up by the gold rush. A few miles northwest of Port Reyes Station, the sleepy residential outpost of **Inverness** (pop. 1,304) is a destination for people trying to escape the big-city noise via romantic B&Bs and rental cottages amid its tranquil hills and beaches. Innumerable trails showcase glorious scenic and wildlife views.

Getting There and Around

Point Reyes Station is located along CA-1, which runs directly through downtown as Main Street. North of Olema, US-101 intersects with CA-1 via Sir Francis Drake Boulevard.

Transportation to Point Reyes from nearby San Rafael is available through the **West Marin Stagecoach** (415/526-3239, www.marintransit.org, $2).

Sights and Recreation

Located in Point Reyes Station, **The Bear Valley Visitor Center** (1 Bear Valley Rd., 415/464-5100, 10am-5pm Mon.-Fri., 9am-4:30pm Sat.-Sun. and holidays) is a popular starting point for visitors and offers nature trails and interpretive exhibits. It is also the access point to **Earthquake Trail,** which leads to a 16-foot crack in the ground caused by the 1906 shaker that is etched in the minds of San Franciscans. Another path connects to **Kule Loklo,** a reconstruction of a Miwok village.

It's a leisurely 25-minute drive to **Mt. Vision** for sweeping views of the national seashore. (Follow Sir Francis Drake Boulevard, then make a left onto Mt. Vision Road.)

Continue on Sir Francis Drake Boulevard and turn on Drakes Beach Road to reach **Kenneth C. Patrick Visitor Center** (1 Drakes Beach Rd., 415/669-1250, 10am-5pm Fri.-Tues.) and the **Tule Elk Preserve,** where a large herd of elk can often be seen roaming freely in the mist.

Continue to the end of Sir Francis Drake Boulevard to reach **Point Reyes Lighthouse** (27000 Sir Francis Drake Blvd., 415/669-1534, 10am-4:30pm Thurs.-Mon.). The jagged rocky shores of Point Reyes make for great scenery but dangerous maritime navigation. The lighthouse was constructed in 1870 and still stands today, accessed by descending a windblown flight of 300 stairs. It's worth the descent (and the uphill climb back). The Fresnel lens and original machinery all remain in place, but the tumultuous ocean views are the highlight. It's also the best place to view seasonal whale migrations in winter and spring (Dec.-June). From the lighthouse, a short hike past **Chimney Rock** reveals resident elephant seals. Migrating birds along the seashore bring **bird-watchers** during fall and spring, while gray whales can be seen making their annual journey from January through April.

Food

Start the morning at the 1950s-themed **Pine Cone Diner** (60 4th St., 415/663-1536, 8am-2:30pm daily, $9-13) for excellent chorizo scrambled eggs, or the divine **Bovine Bakery** (11315 CA-1, 415/663-9420, 6:30am-5pm Mon.-Thurs., 7am-5pm Sat.-Sun., under $8) with deliciously sweet delights and organic coffee.

The star of the Point Reyes Station restaurant scene is the ★ **Station House Café** (11180 CA-1, 415/663-1515, www.stationhousecafe.com, 8am-9pm Thurs.-Tues., $12-21), which is both casual and upscale. Since 1974, long before "organic" and "local" were foodie credos, the Station House Café has been dedicated to serving food with ingredients that reflect the agrarian culture of the area. More comfort food than haute cuisine, you'll find lots of familiar dishes and fantastic takes on old classics. The oyster stew is not to be missed.

For great deli sandwiches, **Whale of a Deli** (997 Mesa Rd., 415/663-8464, 9am-9pm daily, under $18) offers all kinds of meat and cheese combinations, including Mexican food and pizza. The all-Italian menu at **Osteria Stellina** (11285 CA-1, 415/663-9988, 11:30am-2:30pm and 5pm-9pm daily, $15-25) includes classic pasta dishes and pizza. Beer, music, and good, old-fashioned fun have made the 1906 **Old Western Saloon** (11201 CA-1, 415/663-1661, 10am-2am).

A historic 1876 building houses the **Sir and Star at the Olema** (10000 Sir Francis Drake Blvd., Olema, 415/663-1034, www.sirandstar.com, 5:30pm-10:30pm Wed.-Sun., under $22-30), with a memorable menu and a rustic motif. Sample fresh Tomales Bay oysters and dip into the extensive wine list at the **Farm House Restaurant** (10005 CA-1, 415/663-1264, 11:30am-9pm daily, $18-30), part of the Point Reyes Seashore Lodge.

The **Saltwater Oyster Depot** (12781 Sir Francis Drake Blvd., 415/669-1244, 5pm-9pm Mon. and Thurs.-Fri., noon-9pm Sat.-Sun., under $30), located on the southwest banks of the bay, is a good place to sample the local shellfish. Sample some local wines or margaritas while you're at it.

Shopping

Vita Collage (11101 CA-1, 415/663-1160, www.vitacollage.com, 11am-5pm Mon. and Wed.-Thurs., 11am-6pm Fri., 10am-6pm Sat.-Sun.) features fine jewelry, leather purses, and unique accessories, while next door the **Olema Trading Company** (9940 CA-1, 415/663-1547, 10am-5pm daily) sells locally handcrafted goods, including intricate stainedglass windows. For unique gifts of ethnic arts and crafts, **Zuma** (11265 CA-1, 415/663-1748, 10am-5pm daily) brings items around the world to one place. Gifts for the equestrian are at **Cabaline** (11313 CA-1, 415/663-8303, www.cabaline.com, 10am-5pm daily), which offers clothing, horse grooming tools, books, and toys for kids.

Natural luxury fibers is what **Coyuchi Outlet** (11101 CA-1 #201, 415/663-9149, www.coyuchi.com, 10am-5pm daily) uses to make soft bedding, loungewear, tablecloths, and more. For something truly

From top to bottom: Tule Elk at the Point Reyes National Seashore; distant view of elephant seals sun-bathing on Point Reyes Beach; trail heading toward Tomales Point.

one-of-a-kind, stop by **Shaker Shops West** (5 Inverness Way, 415/669-7256, www.shakershops.com, 10:30am-5pm Fri.-Sat.), creators of fine Shaker furniture and handcrafts.

Accommodations

The best place to stay, ★ **Olema Druids Hall & Cottage** (9870 Shoreline, 415/663-8727, www.olemadruidshall.com, $320 and up) is a beautifully restored 1885 meeting hall turned luxury inn. The beautiful **Olema Cottages** (9970 Sir Francis Drake Blvd., 415/663-1288, www.olemacottages.com, rooms $160-180, cottages $175-195) are surrounded by open space and pasture views. The **Bear Valley Inn** (88 Bear Valley Rd., 415/663-1777, www.bearvinn.com, $125-175) is a little bed-and-breakfast nestled in the rolling hills of west Marin. Another option is the 22-room **Point Reyes Seashore Lodge** (10021 CA-1, 415/663-9000, www.pointreyes-seashore.com, rooms $155 and up, cottages $195 and up).

Located just off Limantour Road, 8 miles from Point Reyes Station and 10 miles from the beach, the **Point Reyes Hostel** (1390 Limantour Spit Rd., 415/663-8811, www.norcalhostels.org/reyes, $24-120) is spare but comfortable, with dorm and private rooms, a communal kitchen, and three lounge areas. It is steps away from fantastic hiking and lush natural scenery.

Stinson Beach

The primary attraction at Stinson Beach is the tiny town's namesake: a broad 3.5-mile-long sandy stretch of coastline that's unusually (for Northern California) congenial to visitors. Although it's as plagued by fog as anywhere else in the San Francisco Bay Area, on rare clear days Stinson Beach is the favorite destination for San Franciscans seeking some surf and sunshine.

Recreation

To get out on the water, swing by **Stinson Beach Surf and Kayak** (3605 CA-1, 415/868-2739, www.stinsonbeachsurfandkayak.com, 10am-6pm Sat.-Sun., $20-40 per day). The owner, Bill, will set you up with a surfboard, kayak, boogie board, or stand-up paddle boat. Wetsuits, which you will certainly need, are available. He also offers surf lessons and is happy to give pointers to novices out on the lagoon about the general etiquette of paddling around wildlife.

Food

A few small restaurants dot the town; most of these serve seafood. Among the best is the **Sand Dollar Restaurant** (3458 CA-1, 415/868-0434, www.stinsonbeachrestaurant.com, lunch and dinner daily, $10-25). It actually serves more land-based dishes than seafood, but perhaps the fact that the dining room is constructed out of three old barges makes up the difference.

Accommodations

The Sandpiper Inn (1 Marine Way, 415/868-1632, www.sandpiperstinsonbeach.com, $120-170) has six guest rooms and four cabins, and you can choose between motel accommodations with comfortable queen beds, private baths, and gas fireplaces or the four individual redwood cabins, which offer additional privacy, bed space for families, and full kitchens.

The **Stinson Beach Motel** (3416 CA-1, 415/868-1712, www.stinsonbeachmotel.com, $150) features eight vintage-y, beach, bungalow-style guest rooms that sleep 2-4 guests each. Some guest rooms have substantial kitchenettes; all have private baths, garden views, TVs, and blue decor. The motel is a great spot to bring the family for a beach vacation.

🧭 Panoramic Highway: Mt. Tamalpais

To see the whole Bay Area in a single day, go to **Mount Tamalpais State Park**

(801 Panoramic Hwy., Mill Valley, 415/388-2070, www.parks.ca.gov, 7am-sunset daily, day-use parking $8). Known as Mount Tam, this park boasts stellar views of the San Francisco Bay Area—from Mount St. Helena in Napa down to San Francisco and across to the East Bay. The Pacific Ocean peeks from around the corner of the western peninsula, and on a clear day you can just make out the foothills of the Sierra Nevada mountains to the east. This park is the Bay Area's backyard, with hiking, biking, and camping opportunities widely appreciated for both their beauty and easy access. There are over 100 miles (160 km) of trails. Ample parking, interpretive walks, and friendly park rangers make a visit to Mount Tam a hit even for less outdoorsy travelers.

Although overnight backpacking isn't allowed, standard camping is available at the **Pantoll Ranger Station** (3801 Panoramic Hwy., 415/388-2070, 7am-sunset daily) and the historic 1920s Bootjack Campground. The ranger station can also set you up with maps and other information for your visit.

To reach Pantoll Ranger Station from Stinson Beach, take a right (east) on Panoramic Highway at the T intersection with CA-1 just south of town. The ranger station is about five miles inland on Panoramic Highway.

Muir Beach

Just off CA-1, Muir Beach is abundant with wildlife and picturesque scenery from colorful monarch butterflies fluttering through pine trees to fish splashing up rocky Redwood Creek. There are trails along the sandy beach, where boogie boarders and kayakers play in the crashing waves. A short hike on the trail to the left of the entrance leads to the top of a cliff, offering a spectacular view.

Food and Accommodations

A favorite follow-up for summertime beachgoers is grabbing a pint from the tavern at the **Pelican Inn** (10 Pacific Way, 415/383-6000, www.pelicaninn.com, $206-289) and enjoying it out front on the lawn. In winter, the cozy dining room has a true country pub feel. Each of the seven small guest rooms comes with a private bath and full English-style breakfast, but no TV or phone.

★ Muir Woods

Established in 1908 and named for naturalist and author John Muir, **Muir Woods National Monument** (Panoramic Hwy., off CA-1, 415/388-2596, www.nps.gov/muwo, 8am-sunset daily, $7 adults, free children under 15) comprises acres of staggeringly beautiful redwood forest nestled in Marin County. More than six miles of trails wind through the redwoods and accompanying Mount Tamalpais area, crossing verdant creeks and the lush forest. These are some of the most stunning and accessible redwoods in the Bay Area.

Begin your exploration at the **Muir Woods Visitor Center** (1 Muir Woods Rd., 9am-5:30pm daily, closing hours vary). In addition to maps, information, and advice about hiking, you'll also find a few amenities.

Muir Woods boasts many lovely trails that crisscross the gorgeous redwood forest. First-time visitors should follow the wheelchair- and stroller accessible **Main Trail Loop** (1 mile). Leading from the visitors center on an easy and flat walk through the beautiful redwoods, this trail has an interpretive brochure (pick one up at the visitors center) with numbers along the trail that describe the flora and fauna. Hikers can continue the loop on the Hillside Trail for an elevated view of the valley.

Getting There

Muir Woods is about 10 miles from Stinson Beach. Muir Woods Road comes off CA-1 about 6.5 miles south of Stinson Beach. Take Muir Woods Road for about 2.5 miles to reach the park entrance. To get back to CA-1, you don't need to go back the way you came. From the Muir Woods parking lot, turn left (east) onto Muir Woods Road, and in about 1.5 miles, it will hit Panoramic Highway, where you'll take a right. In about a mile, there will be a left turn to get back onto CA-1, which merges into US-101 through the rest of Marin County and over the Golden Gate Bridge.

Get to the Muir Woods parking areas early. They fill fast especially on holidays and weekends. To avoid the traffic hassle, ride the **Muir Woods Shuttle** (415/455-2000, http://goldengatetransit.org/services/muirwoods.php, Sat.-Sun. summer, $5 pp round-trip) that leaves from various points in southern Marin County, including the Sausalito ferry terminal.

Marin Headlands

The Marin Headlands lie north of San Francisco at the north end of the Golden Gate Bridge. The land here encompasses a wide swath of virgin wilderness, former military structures, and a historic lighthouse.

Going south, to access the Marin Headlands, take the Sausalito exit, which is the last exit before the Golden Gate Bridge. If you do nothing else in the headlands, visit the vista point on Conzelman Road. From the exit, make a left onto Alexander Avenue and then turn right (going uphill) on Conzelman Road. You'll see a few parking spaces on the left, usually filled up with multiple cars waiting; grab a spot if you can, and make the walk out to arguably the best view of the Golden Gate Bridge.

Start your exploration of the Marin Headlands at the **visitors center** (Field Rd. and Bunker Rd., 415/331-1540, www.nps.gov/goga, 9:30am-4:30pm daily), located in the old chapel at Fort Barry. It contains historical and natural history displays, a small gift shop, and details on hiking and biking routes.

Golden Gate Bridge National Recreation Area

A patchwork area that stretches from northern San Mateo County to southern Marin County, the **Golden Gate National Recreation Area** encompasses San Francisco Bay, welcoming more than 13 million visitors a year. The park offers visitors a monumental collection of attractions, such as the infamous Alcatraz, and the Presidio of San Francisco. It is also home to 1,273 plant and animal species, and has a half a dozen operational and shuttered military fortifications that go back through the centuries of California's history, from the Spanish conquistadors to the California Gold Rush to the still active Cold War-era Nike missile sites. There are miles of trails, and the 150-year-old Point Bonita Lighthouse.

★ Golden Gate Bridge

This icon of California is 1.7 miles across and joins southern Marin County to the city of San Francisco. Named after the gap in land that allows entry to San Francisco Bay from the Pacific, the **Golden Gate Bridge** is painted in magnificent "international orange." CA-1 blends with US-101 until you cross the bridge, and then splits off at the CA-1/19th Avenue exit. This route takes you through the Presidio of San Francisco and Golden Gate Park, but it's actually mostly a corridor through a few of the city's outer neighborhoods. To get to the heart of San Francisco, stay on US-101 as it follows Lombard Street and then Van Ness Avenue.

San Francisco

The beautiful city by its eponymous bay, San Francisco is famous for its ethnic diversity, liberal politics, and chilling, dense fog. Urban explorers can enjoy San Francisco's great art, world-class music, unique theater and comedy, and a laid-back club scene, not to mention the food. Many come to the city solely for its vibrant and innovative restaurant scene. Despite its reputation as being on the cutting edge of technology, San Francisco is not a city without history: Some of its most famous sights—Fisherman's Wharf, Alcatraz, Coit Tower—are reminders of its storied past.

Getting There and Around
Air
It's easy to fly into the San Francisco region. There are three major airports. Among them, you should be able to find a flight that fits your schedule. **San Francisco International Airport (SFO)** (www.flysfo.com) is 13 miles south of the city proper. **Oakland Airport (OAK)** (www.flyoakland.com) is 11 miles east of the city, but requires crossing the bay, either via the Bay Bridge or public transit. **Mineta San José Airport (SJC)** (www.flysanjose.com) is the farthest away, roughly 47 miles to the south. These last two airports are less than an hour away by car, with car rentals available. Some San Francisco hotels offer complimentary airport shuttles as well.

Public Transit
For getting around in dense and crowded downtown San Francisco, it's best to use public transportation. **BART** (www.bart.gov), or Bay Area Rapid Transit, connects San Francisco to other cities in the Bay Area, as well as to San Francisco International Airport. There are only eight BART stops within San Francisco proper, and aside from going to or from the airport ($8.50 to/from downtown), BART is most convenient for getting to the Mission district from downtown.

Within the city, **San Francisco Municipal Railway** (MUNI, 415/701-2311 or 311 within San Francisco, www.sfmta.com or 511.org, 6am-midnight daily with limited overnight service) runs a system of buses, light-rail, three cable cars, and one historic streetcar. MUNI can get you almost anywhere in San Francisco, but for destinations beyond downtown, it's debatable whether it's better to take a lumbering MUNI vehicle or drive and deal with the hassle of parking. Fares are $2.25 to ride anything except the cable cars for 90 minutes. Cable cars are $6 per ride. Unlimited ride Visitor Passports (one day $17, three days $26, seven days $35) are available and are valid on all MUNI vehicles, including cable cars, but they are not valid on BART.

Cable cars may be one of San Francisco's most recognizable icons, but they are not necessarily a great way to get around. While they are no slower than a bus, waiting to get on a cable car, especially on weekends, can take longer than the ride itself. Powell-Mason cable cars get you to Fisherman's Wharf in 30 minutes (not counting the wait); Powell-Hyde cable cars provide the scenic route; and the California line is the most historic and runs east to west, going over Nob Hill.

Sights
Union Square
Bordered by Geary, Powell, Post, and Stockton Streets, **Union Square** was named after the pro-Union rallies that took place there during the Civil War. Today, it is the city's premier shopping district with one of the largest collections of retail stores, department stores, art galleries, and bars in the western United States. At the center of Union Square stands a statue of Victoria, goddess of victory, a monument that commemorates admiral George Dewey's 1898 victory at Manila Bay during the Spanish American War. Views of the square are best from Harry Denton's Starlight Room in the Sir Francis Drake Hotel.

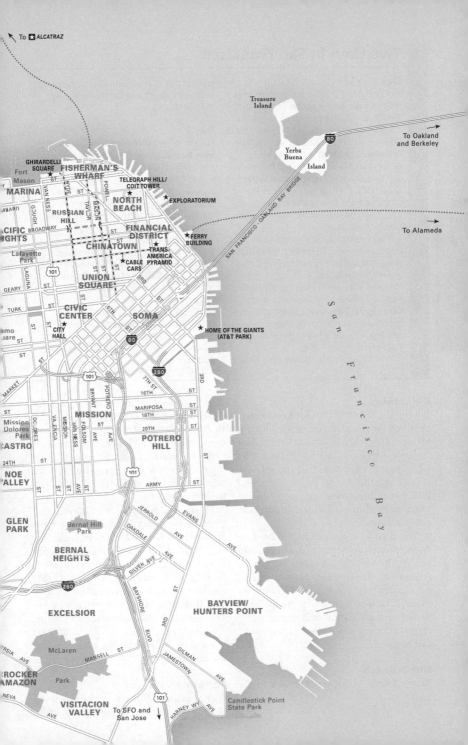

Two Days in San Francisco

Day 1

Start off with the famous French toast at **Mama's on Washington Square** (page 194). Then head to Union and Mason to climb aboard the only historical landmark on wheels in the United States: The **San Francisco cable car** will offer you a quick tour of the city. Take the Powell-Mason Line down to **Fisherman's Wharf** (page 190). Then continue west to Pier 33 to catch the ferry to **Alcatraz** (page 191). Tours sell out fast, so reserve your tickets in advance.

If your escape from Alcatraz built up an appetite, graze at the **Ferry Building** (page 191) or head to nearby **Fog City** (page 195) for lunch.

Spend the rest of your afternoon exploring North Beach. Be sure to stop at **City Lights Bookstore** (page 198), the legendary Beat Generation bookstore and enjoy an old-school cappuccino at **Caffe Greco** (page 194).

When evening hits, unwind at a cozy table at one of the best Italian restaurants in the city, **Trattoria Contadina** (page 195). Try the *vongole*.

Day 2

Start the day with pancakes at **Sears Fine Foods** (page 194). Then head for the **Dragon Gate** to begin your exploration of **Chinatown**. Once you've worked up an appetite, stop in **House of Xian Dumpling** (page 194) for lunch.

After lunch, head to Golden Gate Park. There are 1,017 acres to explore, including gardens, museums, lakes, picnic areas, and trails. Choose between the **California Academy of Sciences** (page 193), the **de Young Museum** (page 193), or the **Japanese Tea Garden** (page 193).

Splurge for dinner at **Farallon** (page 193) or **Alfred's Steakhouse** (page 195). End your stay with drinks and views of the city skyline at the **Starlight Room** (page 196).

Chinatown

A neighbor to North Beach, **Chinatown** is centered on Grant Avenue and Stockton Street. Established in 1848, it's the oldest Chinese district in the United States. The Chinese immigrants of that era were essential in building the Transcontinental Railroad. Chinatown remains an influential part of ethnic Chinese immigrant culture today.

The district is marked by the **Dragon Gate,** the only authentic Chinatown Gate in North America, located on Grant Avenue at Bush Street. More tourists pass under its green-tiled roof than pass over the Golden Gate Bridge. Once here, visitors become immersed in the many shops, temples, and dragon parades and celebrations.

North Beach

North Beach is San Francisco's Little Italy, dense with old-world cafés, restaurants, and delicatessens, but it was once an actual beach, filled in with landfill for warehouses, fishing wharves, and docks. In the late 1800s, thousands of Italians made the area their home. They are credited with saving the neighborhood during the 1906 fire by draping houses with blankets soaked in wine from the barrels in their cellars.

North Beach is also the birthplace of the Beat Generation. Many of the most famous Beat writers lived here, including Jack Kerouac, Allen Ginsberg, Gregory Corso, Neal Cassady, and poet Lawrence Ferlinghetti, who founded City Lights Bookstore, now a historic landmark. The **Beat Museum** (540 Broadway St., 415/399-9626, www.kerouac.com, 10am-7pm daily) features a collection of their works, including books and original manuscripts.

Fisherman's Wharf

Fisherman's Wharf encompasses the northern waterfront area from

Ghirardelli Square or Van Ness Avenue east to Pier 35 (Kearny Street). It is one of the city's busiest tourist attractions, likely attributed to its location on Pier 39, fresh seafood from the floating Forbes Island restaurant, and of course, the launching point of ferries headed to Alcatraz.

★ Alcatraz

Nicknamed "The Rock," **Alcatraz** (415/981-7625, www.alcatrazcruises. com, ferries depart from Pier 33 8:45am- 6:45pm daily, $30) was a military fortress turned maximum-security prison, and is today one of San Francisco's most popular attractions. The island became a prison in the 19th century while it still belonged to the military, which used it to house Civil War prisoners. The isolation of the island in the bay, as well as the frigid waters and strong currents, ensured that prisoners had little hope of escape, and risked death even in the attempt. In 1934, the military handed over the island to the Department of Justice, who used it to house a new style of prisoner: Depression-era gangsters. Honored maximum-security guests included Al Capone, George "Machine Gun" Kelly, and Robert Stroud ("the Birdman of Alcatraz"). The prison closed in 1963. During the 1960s, American Indians occupied Alcatraz, seeking to end a government policy of termination of Indian tribes.

Today, many of the buildings are gone. The barracks from its prior existence as a military base, the cell house, lighthouse, and a handful of other buildings remain.

A visit to Alcatraz involves a ferry ride to the island and an audio tour around the cell house. The tour lasts at least 2.5 hours, but tickets only specify departure times from Pier 33, so you can stay as long as you like until the last boat leaves the island. Buy tickets at least two weeks in advance; they often sell out, especially on summer weekends.

Coit Tower

Crowning the top of Telegraph Hill, **Coit Tower** (1 Telegraph Hill Blvd.) offers a 360-degree view of the bay, the city, and its bridges. Built in 1933, the 210-foot tower looks very much like a fire hose nozzle (whether or not by design is a subject of debate and local lore). Its interior features New Deal-era fresco murals. It's surrounded by 4.89-acre **Pioneer Park.**

Embarcadero

The skyscrapers of the Financial District create most of the San Francisco skyline, which extends out to the waterfront, locally called the **Embarcadero.** Hotels tend toward expensive tall towers, and the shopping here caters to folks with plenty of green. There's also a wealth of restaurants and bars, and foodie heaven at the Ferry Building.

Ferry Building

The restored 1898 **San Francisco Ferry Building** (1 Ferry Bldg., 415/983-8030, www.ferrybuildingmarketplace.com, 10am-6pm Mon.-Fri., 9am-6pm Sat., 11am-5pm Sun.) stands at the end of the Financial District at the edge of the water. Inside the handsome structure, it's all about the food, from fresh produce to high-end wine to cheese and gourmet eateries. Sample from local favorites like Cowgirl Creamery, Acme Bread Company, and Blue Bottle Coffee. For immediate gratification, a few incongruous quick-and-easy restaurants offer reasonable eats.

You can also actually catch a ferry here. Boats come in from Larkspur, Sausalito, Tiburon, Vallejo, and Alameda each day. Check with the **Blue and Gold Fleet** (www.blueandgoldfleet.com), **Golden Gate Ferry** (www.goldengate-ferry.org), and **Bay Link Ferries** (www.baylinkferry.com) for information about service, times, and fares.

Exploratorium

The innovative **Exploratorium** (Pier 15, 415/528-4420, www.exploratorium.edu,

North Beach and Fisherman's Wharf

© AVALON TRAVEL

MARITIME MUSEUM

RUSSIAN HILL

Aquatic Park

GHIRARDELLI SQUARE

THE ARGONAUT

FISHERMAN'S WHARF

FISH ALY

JEFFERSON ST

Reservoir

LOMBARD STREET

LOMBARD TERR

Fay Park

Michelangelo Playground

NORTH BEACH

Coolbirth Park

North Beach Playground

Washington Square

MAMA'S ON WASHINGTON SQUARE

TRATTORIA CONTADINA

Chestnut/ Kearny Park

PFEIFER ST

MIDWAY ST

CAFFE TRIESTE

HOTEL BOHÈME

CITY LIGHTS BOOKSTORE

VESUVIO

THE BEAT MUSEUM

'OLD VOGUE'

Pioneer Park

COIT TOWER

TELEGRAPH HILL

Walton Square

THE EXPLORATORIUM

PIER 39

Waterfront Park

🚢 ALCATRAZ

To Vallejo, Alameda, Oakland, Sausalito, Tiburon, and Angel Island

0   200 yds
0   200 m

10am-5pm Fri.-Wed., 10am-5pm and 6pm-10pm for 18 years and older Thurs., $29 adults, $24 children 13-17, $19 children 12 and under) makes science the most fun thing ever for kids; adults are welcome to join in, too. Learn about everything from frogs to the physics of baseball, sound, and seismology.

Golden Gate Park

Golden Gate Park (main entrance at Stanyan St. at Fell St., McLaren Lodge visitors center at John F. Kennedy Dr., 415/831-2700, www.golden-gate-park.com) was built on sand dunes in the late 1800s.

Today, in addition to walking and bike trails, the park encompasses gardens, cultural arts, and scientific museums. The **Japanese Tea Garden** is a place of solace to sit and sip tea while gazing at the remarkable 100-year-old trees and five acres of picturesque scenery. The **Conservatory of Flowers** offers a stroll through a Victorian greenhouse filled with vibrant flowers from all over the world, while the **San Francisco Botanical Garden at Strybing Arboretum** displays native blooms and plant life.

★ California Academy of Sciences

The **California Academy of Sciences** (55 Music Concourse Dr., 415/379-8000, 9:30am-5pm Mon.-Sat., 11am-5pm Sun., $35 adults, $30 children 12-17, $25 children 4-11) is a triumph of the sustainable scientific principles it exhibits. From its grass-covered roof to its underground aquarium, the award-winning design by architect Renzo Piano exemplifies environmental ideals. Visitors can wander through the steamy Rainforests of the World exhibit, contained inside a 90-foot glass dome, or travel through an all-digital outer space in the high-tech Morrison Planetarium. More studious nature lovers can spend hours examining exhibits like the 87-foot-long blue whale skeleton. The Steinhart Aquarium includes a display of coral reef, tidepool, and swamp habitats,

as well as a well-loved colony of African penguins. Kid-friendly, often interactive exhibits offer endless opportunities for learning.

de Young Museum

In Golden Gate Park, follow the artificial fault-line in the sidewalk to the **de Young Museum** (50 Hagiwara Tea Garden Dr., 415/750-3600, deyoung.famsf.org, 9:30am-5:15pm Tues.-Sun., open late on Fri. Apr.-Nov., $10 adults, $6 children 13-17, free children 12 and under), which showcases American art dating to the 17th century, international contemporary art, and art from the Americas, the Pacific, and Africa.

The Presidio

The Presidio (Montgomery St. and Lincoln Blvd., 415/561-4323, www.nps.gov/prsf, visitors center: 10am-4pm Thurs.-Sun., trails: dawn-dusk daily, free) is a sweeping stretch of land running along the San Francisco Headlands down to the Golden Gate. Established as a military installation by the Spanish in 1776, it was taken over by the U.S. Army in 1848, and became a national park in 1994. The Presidio had a role in every Pacific-related war from the Civil War through Desert Storm.

As you explore the huge park, you can visit the pioneering aviation area **Crissy Field,** Civil War-era fortifications at **Fort Point,** and the **Letterman Digital Arts Center** (Chestnut St. and Lyon St., www.lucasfilm.com), built on the site of a former army hospital. More recent additions include art installations by Andy Goldsworthy, who works with natural materials.

Food
Union Square
Make reservations in advance if you want to dine at the legendary **Farallon** (450 Post St., 415/956-6969, www.farallonrestaurant.com, 5:30pm-9:30pm Mon., 11:30am-3pm and 5:30pm-9:30pm Tues.-Thurs.,

11:30am-3pm and 5:30pm-10pm Fri.-Sat., 5pm-9:30pm Sun., $27-65). Seafood dominates the pricey menu, and the under-the-sea theme carries over into the decor—complete with jellyfish chandeliers.

Tucked away in a tiny alley that could have been transported from Paris, **Café Claude** (7 Claude Ln., 415/392-3505, www.cafeclaude.com, 11:30am-10:30pm Mon.-Sat., 5:30pm-10:30pm Sun., $21-28) serves classic brasserie cuisine.

Sears Fine Foods (439 Powell St., 415/986-1160, www.searsfinefood.com, 6:30am-10pm daily, under $28) is a good option for breakfast, with their famous dollar-sized pancakes.

Chinatown

If you like "hot," head to **House of Xian Dumpling** (925 Kearny St., 415/398-1626, www.houseofxiandumpling.com, 11am-10pm daily, $8-14) for fantastic Chinese food that's cheap and as spicy as you want it! Then walk a block to **Golden Gate Bakery** (1029 Grant Ave., 415/781-262, 8am-8pm daily, $10) to indulge in custard-filled confections or sugary lotus seed paste moon cakes.

North Beach

For a hearty breakfast, head to North Beach and look for the big green awning with little pink hearts at ★ **Mama's on Washington Square** (1701 Stockton St., 415/362-6421, www.mamas-sf.com, 11am-3pm Tues.-Sun., $8-13.50), which serves 10 types of French toast, to-die-for eggs Benedict, and the best Monte Cristo.

Just want a good cappuccino? **Caffe Greco** (423 Columbus Ave., 415/397-6261, www.caffegreco.com, 7am-11pm Sun.-Thurs., 7am-midnight Fri.-Sat., under $10) is known for precision and mastery in creating the perfect cappuccino and espresso.

No North Beach visit is complete without an authentic Italian meal, and

From top to bottom: the San Francisco Botanical Garden in Golden Gate Park; Chinatown; Fisherman's Wharf.

★ **Trattoria Contadina** (1800 Mason St., 415/982-5728, www.trattoriacontadina. com, 5pm-9pm daily, under $25) is the best; the proof is in the crowds at every meal.

Katsu Sushi House (745 Columbus Ave., 415/788-8050, www.katsusushi-house.com, 11:30am-2:30pm and 5pm-9:30pm Mon.-Thurs., 11:30am-2:30pm and 5pm-10pm Fri.-Sat., 5pm-9:30pm Sun., $5-9) is the local favorite for quality sushi with exceptional taste.

Fisherman's Wharf and Marina

Jump on board the floating **Forbes Island** (Pier 39's West Marina at Gate H, 415/951-4900, www.forbesisland.com, dinner daily, under $62, reservations required) at Fisherman's Wharf for a gourmet meal.

The culinary landmark **Swan Oyster Depot** (1517 Polk St., 415/673-1101 or 415/673-2757, 8am-5:30pm weekends only, under $25) serves the city's freshest shellfish and coldest Anchor Steam beer.

Embarcadero

Starving after a trip to Alcatraz? Stop by **Fog City** (1300 Battery St., 415/982-2000, www.fogcitysf.com, 11:30am-10pm Sun.-Thurs., 11:30am-11pm Fri.-Sat., $11-39) for its upscale American fare for lunch or dinner.

The landmark **Alfred's Steakhouse** (659 Merchant St., 415/781-7058, 5pm-9:30pm daily, $18-45) has been serving beef patrons for over 80 years with old-world charm.

Nightlife

San Francisco nightlife is buzzing and dynamic. New trends may flow in and out, but jazz, blues, and the "oldies but goodies" can still be found all over town. Several historic waterholes, from Prohibition to the Beatnik era, still welcome locals and tourists.

Bars and Clubs

Dating back to 1851, the **Old Ship Saloon** (298 Pacific Ave., 415/788-2222, www. oldshipsaloon.com, 11am-3pm and 4:30pm-midnight Mon.-Fri.) is made out of a ship's hull that ran aground during a storm off Alcatraz. An old polished mahogany bar that recalls the days of the Wild West, **Elixir** (3200 16th St., 415/552-1633, www.elixirsf.com, 3pm-2am Mon.-Fri., noon-2am Sat.-Sun.) claims the title of the city's second-oldest saloon, dating back to 1858.

A few other historic venues to grab a drink include **The Saloon** (1232 Grant St., 415/989-7666, noon-1:30am daily) and the **Bus Stop Saloon** (1901 Union St., 415/567-6905, 10am-2am Mon.-Fri., 9am-2am Sat.-Sun.), a bar that attracts a lively, young crowd and features several TVs and Pac-Man. At **Shotwell's** (3349 20th St., 415/648-4104, www.shotwellsbar.com, 4:30pm-2am Mon.-Sat., 4:30pm-1am Sun.), which first opened as a grocery store saloon in 1891 with a backroom for beer drinking, you can drink local microbrews and play pinball. The oldest bar in Chinatown, **Red's Place** (672 Jackson St., 415/956-4490, www.redsplacesf.com, 1pm-1am daily) is where local old-timers come for a drink in a low-key setting.

Slide (430 Mason St., 415/421-1916, www.slidesf.com, 9pm-3am Wed.-Sat.) is named for its serpentine entry, which is perfect for a dramatic entrance (wallflowers can use the door). It's a fun place to meet old friends or new ones. For quiet conversation, **Hotel Biron** (45 Rose St., 415/703-0403, www. hotelbiron.com, 5pm-2am daily) is the perfect date spot, and features rotating artwork and an immense wine list. A couple other great wine bars are **Café Nook** (1500 Hyde St., 415/447-4100, www.cafenook.com, 7am-10pm Mon.-Fri., 8am-10pm Sat., 8am-9pm Sun.), a charming little café by day and cozy wine bar by night, and the **Hidden Vine** (408 Merchant St., 415/674-3567, www. thehiddenvine.com, 4pm-10pm Mon., 4pm-midnight Tues.-Sat.), a unique place with red brick walls and an outdoor bocce ball court.

Live Music

Rising 21 stories above the Sir Francis Drake Hotel, the **Starlight Room** (450 Powell St., 415/395-8595, www.starlightroomsf.com, 6pm-midnight Tues.-Thurs., 6pm-1:30am Fri.-Sat., noon-2:30pm Sun. brunch, strict dress code) mixes classic glamour and chic sophistication into every cocktail, while presenting nightly music and entertainment, and the notorious Sunday's "A Drag" brunch.

For more than 100 years, the **Hotel Utah Saloon** (500 4th St., 415/546-6300, www.hotelutah.com, 11am-2am daily) has attracted all kinds of people, from gamblers and gold rush seekers to politicians and celebrities. Today, it plays host to some of the best live music and the longest-running open mics in town.

Though the Beatnik era of Jack Kerouac and Allen Ginsberg has faded, **Vesuvio Café** (255 Columbus Ave., 415/362-3370, www.vesuvio.com, 6pm-2am daily) continues to pay tribute to its jazz, art, and poetry roots, while **Caffe Trieste** (601 Vallejo St., 415/392-6739, www.caffetrieste.com, 6:30am-10pm Sun.-Thurs., 6:30am-11pm Fri.-Sat.) hosts poets, composers, and artists over some of the finest coffee in San Francisco.

Rita Hayworth got her start at **Bimbo's 365 Club** (1025 Columbus Ave., 415/474-0365, www.bimbos365club.com, $20 and up), a supper club and speakeasy in 1931. Today, everyone from up-and-coming indies to big headliners takes the stage.

For acoustic, piano, a mix of karaoke, big-screen TVs, or whatever you can handle, the **Gold Dust Lounge** (165 Jefferson St., 415/397-1695, www.golddustsf.com, 9am-2am daily) offers up great fun and entertainment, and serves classic cocktails.

Looking for high-quality performances? **Revolution Café** (3248 22nd St., 415/642-0474, www.revolution-cafe.com, 9am-midnight Sun.-Thurs.,

9am-2am Fri.-Sat.) is one of the best venues for free live music. From jazz to pop to world music, it's all good. **Ruby Skye** (420 Mason St., 415/693-0777, www.rubyskye.com, 9pm-2am Thurs., Fri.-Sat.9pm-4am Fri.-Sat.) is by far the top club in the heart of downtown, with a swanky lounge graced by celebrities and a killer sound system appreciated by top DJs. A thriller of a nightclub, **Vessel** (85 Campton Pl., 415/433-8585, www.vesselsf.com, 10pm-2am Thurs.-Sat.) boasts its award-winning Funktion One sound system, state-of-the-art LED lighting system, and world-class DJs all together in a luxury lounge setting.

Arts and Entertainment

San Francisco virtually oozes with culture, claiming great playwrights Sam Shepherd and Tom Stoppard and boasting avant-garde theater and internationally recognized symphony, opera, and ballet companies, not to mention the finest of classical and contemporary art galleries and museums.

Performing Arts

With a long and distinguished history, the prestigious **American Conservatory Theatre** is housed in the **Geary Theater** (415 Geary St., 415/749-2228, www.act-sf.org, $20 and up) and showcases diversely unique theater productions that are inspiring and thought-provoking.

Marvel at the magnificence and intricate beauty of the **Orpheum Theatre** (1192 Market St., 888/746-1799, www.shnsf.com, $69 and up), a dramatic, 12th-century Spanish palace with a vaulted ceiling and richly colored decor. It's been the setting for vaudeville, silent films, motion pictures, musical comedy, and other theatrical entertainment since it first opened in 1926. The illustrious **Golden Gate Theater** (1 Taylor St., 415/551-2050, www.shnsf.com, $35), which made its debut in 1922 during the vaudeville era with headliners like the Marx Brothers, presents Broadway shows like *Billy Elliot* and *Chicago*.

Other theaters include the **Curran Theatre** (445 Geary St., 888/746-1799, www.shnsf.com, $10-85), which hosts many traveling Broadway shows, and the **Lorraine Hansberry Theatre** (777 Jones St., 415/345-3980, lhtsf.org), which features productions written by African American playwrights.

Galleries

The **Xanadu Gallery** (140 Maiden Ln., 415/392-9999, www.xanadugallery.us, 10am-6pm Tues.-Sat.) has an extensive selection of Asian, African, and Oceanic works of art, housed in San Francisco's only Frank Lloyd Wright building, with an amazing Guggenheim-style interior.

Tucked away on the second floor of the Eureka Bank building, the **North Beach Museum** (1435 Stockton St., 415/391-6210, 9am-4pm Mon.-Thurs., 9am-6pm Fri., free) features changing displays and photo exhibits of the Chinese and Italian communities in the late 19th and early 20th centuries. The **Chinese Culture Center** (750 Kearny St. #3, 415/986-1822, www.c-c-c.org, 10am-4pm Tues.-Sat., $5 suggested donation) offers exhibitions of traditional and contemporary art, performances of Chinese opera and dance, tours, and workshops.

View artwork from emerging local artists at the **49 Geary Art Galleries** (49 Geary St., 888/470-9564, 9:30am-5:30pm Tues.-Fri., 10:30am-5:30pm Sat.). Visit **Robert Koch Gallery** (49 Geary St., 415/421-0122, www.kochgallery.com, 11am-5:30pm Tues.-Sat.) for photography. The **Haines Gallery** (49 Geary St. #540, 415/397-8114, www.hainesgallery.com, 10:30am-5pm Tues.-Sat.) showcases emerging and internationally established artists from all over the world.

Shopping

San Francisco has a large collection of retail stores, department stores, boutiques, galleries, and tourist shops, making it a premier city to shop. In Union Square you'll find many high-end retail shops; Chinatown is a destination for antiques and unique objects; North Beach caters to an eclectic crowd; while Fisherman's Wharf gives tourists mementos of the city to take home.

Union Square

Looking to make an impression? **Goyard** (345 Powell St., 415/398-1110, 10am-6pm Mon.-Sat., noon-5pm Sun.) French handbags and luggage is an ultra-luxury brand that most fine-tote carriers know by the signature, stenciled fabric with the distinctive chevron print. These babies are carried on many A-list arms, but be warned: they don't run cheap. And neither do the fine antiques at **333 Peking Arts Oriental Antiques & Furniture** (535 Sutter St., 415/433-6780, 10:30am-5:30pm Mon.-Sat.), where collectibles from the Han and Ming dynasties, including terra-cotta statues, porcelain figures, snuff bottles, and jade statues, are mesmerizing. **Farinelli Antiques** (311 Grant Ave., 415/433-4823, 9am-9pm Mon.-Sat., 10am-7pm Sun.) displays a breathtaking selection of 19th- and 20th-century European dining room sets, rare pianos, fine porcelain by Meissen and Sèvres, more than 100 chandeliers, marble and bronze statues, silk Persian carpets, rare jade and ivory...need I go on?

If whiskey is your passion, you've come to the right place when you step into the **Whisky Shop/Hector Russell Scottish Imports** (360 Sutter St., 415/989 5458). The shop sells more than 400 kinds of whiskeys, and if you take your whiskey the traditional Scottish way, the store imports and rents authentic hand-stitched kilts.

Aside from its many specialty shops, there are several big-name retail stores in Union Square, including **Gucci** (200 Stockton St., 415/392-2808, 10am-6pm Mon.-Sat., noon-6pm Sun.); **Giorgio Armani** (278 Post St., 415/434-2500, 10am-6pm Mon.-Sat.); **Neiman Marcus**

(150 Stockton St., 415/362-3900, 10am-7pm Mon.-Sat., noon-6pm Sun.); and **Prada** (201 Post St., 415/848-1900, 10am-7pm Mon.-Sat., 11am-6pm Sun.).

Chinatown

Asian Renaissance (662 Grant Ave., 415/397-2872) houses a vast selection of Asian imports, including bedspreads, Thai silk runners, kimonos, and books on feng shui. **Dragon House** (455 Grant Ave., 415/781-2351) sells authentic antiques and Asian fine arts, including jewelry that dates back 2,000 years. It's worth a stop at **Peter Pap Oriental Rugs** (470 Jackson St., 415/956-3300 and 888/581-6743, 10am-5pm Mon.-Sat.) just to run your fingers over the silken works of art.

Great China Herb Co. (857 Washington St., 415/982-2195) has a good selection and a Chinese doctor on-site. **Superior Trading Company** (835 Washington St., 415/982-8722, www.superiortrading.com, 9:30am-6pm daily) boasts the largest quantity of Oriental herbs and ginseng, with imports from China, Hong Kong, and Korea.

North Beach

No San Francisco shopping experience is complete without a visit to **City Lights Bookstore** (261 Columbus Ave., 415/362-8193, www.citylights.com, 10am-midnight daily), an iconic literary hub with the biggest and best collections of the written word.

An eclectic clothing store, **AB Fits** (1519 Grant Ave., 415/982-5726, www.abfits.com, 11:30am-6:30pm Tues.-Sat., noon-6pm Sun.) specializes in European and Asian designer jeans, seemingly made to fit each unique body.

Find a vintage favorite at **Old Vogue** (1412 Grant Ave., 415/392-1522, 11am-6pm Mon.-Tues., 11am-8pm Wed., 11am-10pm Fri.-Sat., noon-6pm Sun.), where old styles never go out of fashion.

Leather jackets and handmade sweaters are at **Knitz and Leather** (1429 Grant Ave., 415/391-3480, 11am-7pm Mon.-Sat.,

San Francisco skyline

noon-5pm Sun.), which offers unique designs and styles.

If sparkly is what catches your eye, **Macchiarini Creative Design & Jewelry** (1544 Grant Ave., 415/982-2229, 11am-6pm Tues.-Sat., noon-6pm Sun.) creates handmade jewelry that's modern, with tribal and African influences.

For something decorative for the home, **Biordi Arts** (412 Columbus Ave., 415/392-8096, 11am-5pm Mon.-Fri., 9:30am-5pm Sat.) imports handmade and painted majolica pottery from central Italy.

Fisherman's Wharf

Souvenir hunters will not be disappointed shopping at Fisherman's Wharf. **Only In San Francisco** (Pier 39 Concourse, 415/397-0143, www.onlyinsanfrancisco.net, 8:30am-10:30pm daily) is a souvenir superstore with gifts and memorabilia. The **Cable Car Store** (Pier 39, Beach St., and 2700 Taylor St., 415/397-0122 and 415/673-4165, www.

cablecarstore.com, 10am-9pm Mon.-Fri., 10am-10pm Sat.-Sun.) is a hot spot for anyone wanting to take a piece of San Francisco home with them. From cable car music boxes to magnets, T-shirts and sweatshirts to barking sea lions, it's all here. For fun games and puzzles, **Solve It! Think Out of the Box** (Pier 39 Concourse #251, 415/262-9924, www.solve-it-puzzles.com, 10am-9pm daily) offers brain-teasing gifts for everyone.

Recreation
Beaches

Ocean Beach is found where Golden Gate Park ends. The cold water and strong currents make it dangerous for swimming but popular among surfers who find the big waves worth the risk. Most visitors enjoy the beautiful seascape from the sand. It's a great place for a picnic or a bonfire. From time to time, debris from the 1800s shipwreck the *King Philip* reappears at low tide.

Below the cliffs on the Presidio's western shoreline, **Baker Beach** stretches a mile, offering magnificent views of Golden Gate Bridge and the Marin Headlands. **China Beach** is a tiny cove that got its name from the Chinese fishermen who anchored their small vessels nearby to camp on the beach. It lies between Baker Beach and Lands End and is part of the Golden Gate National Recreation Area. It offers a picnic area, sunbathing, and spectacular views of the Golden Gate. On the northwestern end of the city, the **Lands End** trail reveals hillsides of cypress and wildflowers, and the beautiful shoreline. It provides access to the old Sutro Baths, other beaches, and an observation site at the **visitors center** (680 Point Lobos Ave., 415/426-5240, 9am-5pm daily, donation).

The closest views of the Golden Gate Bridge in the city are from **Fort Point** (end of Marine Dr., 415/556-1693, 10am-5pm Fri.-Mon., free), a National Historic Site at the bridge's southern end. Although the

Civil War-era brick fort never saw action, there are tours and on-site reenactments.

Bicycling

Get around on a bike to see the parks, especially Golden Gate Park, which offers about a two-mile ride. On Sundays you can peddle around without traffic interruption when the city closes off the eastern half of JFK Drive in Golden Gate Park. **Golden Gate Park Bike and Skate** (3038 Fulton St., 415/668-1117, www.goldengateparkbikeandskate.com, 10am-6pm Mon.-Fri., 10am-7pm Sat.-Sun. summer, 10am-5pm Mon.-Fri., 10am-6pm Sat.-Sun. winter, $5-20 skates, $3-15 bikes) rents a variety of bike and skates.

Bike the 22-mile **Tiburon Loop,** which starts in San Rafael and goes through the Cal Park Hill Tunnel (no cars). The route offers glimpses of wildlife and gorgeous views of Richardson Bay and Angel Island. **Avenue Cyclery** (756 Stanyan St., 415/387-3155, www.avenuecyclery.com, 10am-6pm Mon.-Sat., 10am-5pm Sun., $8-30) rents bikes just outside Golden Gate Park.

Spectator Sports

San Franciscans love their **Giants** (AT&T Park, 24 Willie Mays Plaza at 3rd and King Sts., 415/972-2000 and 877/473-4849, www.sanfrancisco.giants.mlb.com, tickets $40 and up). Baseball games at AT&T Park swell restaurants, buses, and trains in the area to beyond capacity. This being San Francisco, the food options at the stadium range beyond hot dogs: Get Caribbean jerk chicken nachos, crab sandwiches, or garlic fries.

Events

The **North Beach Festival** (1630 Stockton St., 415/989-2220, June, free) celebrates the neighborhood's Italian heritage with live music, poetry readings, dancing, arts and crafts booths, and gourmet foods.

Chinatown's annual **Autumn Moon**

the Palace Hotel lobby

Festival (www.moonfestival.org, early Sept., free) continues the ancient Chinese tradition of celebrating the Harvest Moon, with colorful parades, local bazaars, entertainment, and divine mooncakes.

San Francisco has the biggest and arguably best **Pride Festival** (www.sfpride. org, June, free) in the nation, celebrating the city's groundbreaking, history-making lesbian, gay, bisexual, and transgender community. It kicks off with a well-attended parade down Market Street, ending at City Hall.

Accommodations

San Francisco is an expensive city, and room prices are no exception. The bulk of the hotels are either around Union Square or in the Fisherman's Wharf area. Staying around Union Square is convenient, with good access to public transportation, but will cost you, not only for the room, but for parking as well. Fisherman's Wharf proper is not much cheaper, and although the views may be more scenic, transit options are more limited than around Union Square. The lower-priced motels lining Lombard Street, west of Van Ness, often come with parking, but the location is inconvenient to most points of interest.

Under $150

For a budget room, Hostelling International's **Fort Mason Hostel** (240 Fort Mason, 415/771-7277, www.sfhostels. org, $28-119) has the advantage of beautiful views, owing to its perch on the north end of the city. Reservations far in advance are recommended. The HI **Downtown Hostel** (312 Mason St., 415/788-5604, www.sfhostels.org, $29-135) is more conveniently located at Union Square. Just outside Chinatown, the comfortable **Grant Plaza Hotel** (465 Grant Ave., 800/472-6899 or 415/434-3883, www.grantplaza.com, $140 and up) is close to many attractions and features colorful stainedglass windows and tasteful decor.

$150-250

Renovated with an eclectic mix of literary and visual motifs drawn from the Beat era, ★ **Hotel Boheme** (444 Columbus Ave., 415/433-9111, www.hotelboheme. com, $219-239) is an inviting and memorable experience for guests.

An upscale hotel with a Japanese theme, **Hotel Kabuki** (1625 Post St., 415/922-3200, www.jdvhotels.com, $224 and up) offers guests a relaxing stay with koi ponds, a Zen garden, and an on-site spa.

Experience the **Clift Hotel** (495 Geary St., 415/775-4700, www.morganshotel-group.com, $179 and up), a hip hotel with trendy furnishings in walking distance to shopping and the MUNI bus stops.

Over $250

The unique ★ **Argonaut Hotel** (495 Jefferson St., 415/563-0800, www.argo-naulthotal.com, $329 and up) has it all: history, classic style, prime location, elegant rooms, and superb service.

The iconic **Palace Hotel** (2 New Montgomery St., 415/512-1111, www.sfpalace.com, $249 and up) has remained a landmark for accommodations in San Francisco, with such timeless creations as the Garden Court's stainedglass dome, elegant decor and rooms, and revered restaurants.

San Francisco's first boutique hotel, **Hotel Union Square** (114 Powell St., 415/397-3000, www.hotelunionsquare.com, $269 and up) was built over 100 years ago and offers a fusion of art deco, beautiful brick walls, original 1915 Egyptian-motif mosaic murals, and classic San Francisco hospitality.

No list of San Francisco hotels would be complete without a representative from Nob Hill. **The Fairmont San Francisco** (950 Mason St., 415/772-5000, www.fairmont.com/san-francisco, $449-649) is often the choice of presidents and diplomats, and it is the picture of classic luxury.

Information and Services

The **San Francisco Visitor Information Center** (Hallidie Plaza Lower Level, 900 Market St., sanfrancisco.travel, 9am-5pm Mon.-Fri., 9am-3pm Sat.-Sun. May-Oct., closed Sun. Nov.-Apr.) is centrally located just outside the Powell Street BART and MUNI station. Free city maps, brochures, and sightseeing guides are available, as well as advice from knowledgeable locals.

CA-1 through San Francisco

In San Francisco, CA-1 does not run along the coast. It follows 19th Avenue south through some of the most gridded streets in the city until it joins I-280 near the border between San Francisco and its neighbor to the south, Daly City. CA-1 splits off from I-280 a few miles south, and you start getting glimpses of the ocean as you head toward Pacifica.

To drive along the coast in San Francisco, you would need to take the Great Highway, which starts at the very western end of Geary Avenue. It follows Ocean Beach until just past the San Francisco Zoo, when it hits CA-35, also known as Skyline Boulevard. Take CA-35 south for about five miles, where it meets up with CA-1.

Pacifica

Located about 15 miles south of San Francisco, this coastside community is best known to locals for its large and festive bowling alley **Sea Bowl** (4625 CA-1, 650/738-8190, www.seabowl.com, 10am-midnight Mon.-Thurs., 10am-12:30am Fri., 9am-1am Sat., 9am-midnight Sun.). For travelers, it has one of the closer RV parks to San Francisco. **San Francisco RV Resort** (700 Palmetto Ave., 650/355-7093 or 800/822-1250, www.sanfranciscorvresort.com, $69-82) can accommodate most RV sizes, and many sites have hook-ups.

Montara State Beach

Montara State Beach (2nd St. and CA-1, Montara, www.parks.ca.gov, 650/726-8819, 8am-sunset daily) is one of the most beautiful beaches in this area. It is as popular with tide-poolers, surfers, and anglers as it is with picnickers and beachcombers. The beach also remains relatively uncrowded compared to many of the other beaches to the south. It has a tendency to get windy, and there is limited parking. It is located off CA-1, about 20 miles south of San Francisco.

Moss Beach

Located 23 miles south of San Francisco, Moss Beach is one of several residential towns that line the coast. There is little here besides stunning scenery, a few small businesses, and the Fitzgerald Marine Reserve.

For tide-pooling near San Francisco, the **Fitzgerald Marine Reserve** (200 Nevada Ave., 650/728-3584, www.co.sanmateo.ca.us, sunrise-sunset daily) is the place to go. The 32-acre reserve extends from the Montara Lighthouse south to Pillar Point and is considered one of the most diverse intertidal zones in the Bay Area. On its rocky reefs, you can hunt for sea anemones, starfish, eels, and crabs—there's even a small species of red octopus. The reserve is also home to egrets, herons, an endangered species of butterfly, and a slew of sea lions and harbor seals that enjoy sunning themselves on the beach's outer rocks. For the best viewing, come at low tide (tide logs are available at most local bookstores, but for a quick reference, check out www.protides.com) and on weekdays, as this is a popular destination for families. For a more leisurely and drier experience, numerous trails crisscross the windswept bluffs and wind through sheltering groves of cypress and eucalyptus trees.

The **Moss Beach Distillery** (140 Beach Way, 650/728-5595, www.mossbeachdistillery.com, noon-8:30pm Mon.-Thurs., noon-9pm Fri.-Sat., 11am-8:30pm Sun., $15-38) has been featured on *Unsolved Mysteries* and *Ghost Hunters* and written up in countless publications not for its food but for its famous ghost: the Blue Lady. Rumor has it that a beautiful young woman walked the cliffs of Moss Beach from her home to a coastside speakeasy then known as Frank's Place, now Moss Beach Distillery, to meet her lover, a handsome piano player who worked in the bar. The Blue Lady, whose name has never been discovered, perished one night on the cliffs under suspicious circumstances, and her ghost is said to haunt the building. In addition to ghost stories and terrific ocean views, the restaurant offers something of a cross between traditional American food and California cuisine. Portions are

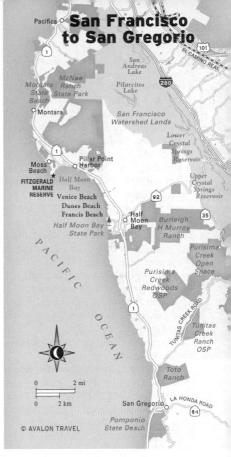

large and service is friendly, if occasionally slow during peak times.

Half Moon Bay

Located about 30 miles south of San Francisco on CA-1, Half Moon Bay is a charming small town with several shops and art galleries. Many of the local businesses line Main Street a block east of the CA-1 bypass. Half Moon Bay enjoys a beautiful natural setting and earns significant income from tourism, especially during the world-famous pumpkin festival each October.

Food
The quality of food in Half Moon Bay is superb. **Pasta Moon** (315 Main

St., 650/726-5125, www.pastamoon. com, 11:30am-2pm and 5:30pm-9pm Mon.-Thurs., 11:30am-2pm and 5:30pm-9:30pm Fri., noon-3pm and 5:30pm-9:30pm Sat., noon-3pm and 5:30pm-9pm Sun., $17-26) serves updated Italian cuisine with an emphasis on fresh, light dishes. Their wood-fired pizzas are particularly good and affordable, as are any of the pasta dishes, made with house-made noodles.

Cetrella (845 Main St., 650/726-4090, www.cetrella.com, 5:30pm-9:30pm Tues.-Thurs. and Sun., 5:30pm-10pm Fri.-Sat., $22-40) offers a range of Mediterranean-themed California cuisine in a big-beam space that looks like something out of the redwood forests up north. The chef uses local, often organic, ingredients to create stunning fare that varies by season. Look for Dungeness crab in winter and artichokes in spring.

For seafood, **Sam's Chowder House** (4210 N. Cabrillo Hwy., Pillar Point Harbor, 650/712-0371, www.samschowderhouse.com, 11:30am-9pm Mon.-Thurs., 11:30am-9:30pm Fri.-Sat., 11am-9pm Sun., $12-35) offers everything from a stiff drink at the bar to light appetizers and champagne on the deck, steaming plates of whole lobster, seafood paella, and seared tuna served in the ample yet cozy dining room.

When all you need is a quick bite or a casual lunch, the **Moonside Bakery & Café** (604 Main St., 650/726-9070, www.moonsidebakery.com, 7am-5pm daily, $10) can fix you up with breakfast pastries and espresso or sandwiches and wood-fired pizzas for lunch.

Recreation

The beaches of Half Moon Bay draw visitors from over the hill and farther afield all year long, despite the chilly fog during the summer. Perhaps the most famous beach in the area is one that has no name. At the end of West Point Avenue in the neighboring town of Princeton is the Pillar Point Marsh and a long stretch of beach that wraps around the edge of the point. This beach is the launch pad for surfers paddling out to tackle the infamous **Mavericks Break** (Pillar Point Marsh parking lot, past Pillar Point Harbor). Formed by unique underwater topography, the giant waves are the site of the legendary **Mavericks Surf Contest** (http://maverickssurf.com). The competition is always held in winter, when the swells reach their peak, and left until the last minute to ensure that they are the biggest of the year. When perfect conditions present themselves, the best surfers in the world are given 48 hours' notice to make it to Mavericks to compete. Unfortunately, you can't see the breaks all that well from the beach, but there are dirt trails that crisscross the point, where breathtaking views can be had. Walk up West Point Avenue past the yellow gate and catch any number of dirt trails heading west toward the bluffs. But for those eyeing the big waves, beware: Mavericks is not a beginner's break, especially in winter, and the giant breakers can be deadly.

Events

The biggest annual event in this small agricultural town is the **Half Moon Bay Art & Pumpkin Festival** (www.miramarevents.com). Every October, nearly 250,000 people trek to Half Moon Bay to pay homage to the big orange squash. The festival includes live music, food, artists' booths, contests, activities for kids, an adults lounge area, and a parade. Perhaps the best-publicized event is the pumpkin weigh-off, which takes place before the festivities begin. Farmers bring their tremendous squash on flatbed trucks from all over the country to determine which is the biggest of all. The winner gets paid per pound, a significant prize when the biggest pumpkins weigh over 1,000 pounds.

Accommodations

Half Moon Bay offers several lovely bed-and-breakfasts, like the elegant and affordable **Pacific Victorian Bed and Breakfast** (325 Alameda Ave., 888/929-0906, www.pacificvictorian.com, $150-195), which is only a block-and-a-half from the beach.

On the higher end, the **Ritz-Carlton Half Moon Bay** (1 Miramontes Point Rd., 650/712-7000, www.ritzcarlton.com, $500) looms large over the Pacific and resembles a medieval castle. Inside, guests enjoy the finest of modern amenities. The Ritz-Carlton has a top-tier restaurant (Navio), a world-class day spa, and posh guest rooms that really are worth the rates. Golf at the Ritz is second to none in the Bay Area.

Information and Services

Visit the **Half Moon Bay Chamber of Commerce** (235 Main St., 650/726-8389, www.halfmoonbaychamber.org, 9am-5pm Mon.-Fri., 10am-3pm Sat.-Sun.), in the red house just after you turn on Main Street from CA-92. The chamber also doubles as a visitors center, where you can find maps, brochures, and a schedule of events.

Central California Coast

The scenic coastline between San Francisco and Los Angeles holds some of California's most breathtaking vistas.

San Gregorio
Pescadero
San Jose
Merced
PIGEON PT. LIGHTHOUSE
Año Nuevo State Reserve
156
99
Santa Cruz ★ SANTA CRUZ BEACH BOARDWALK
Moss Landing
San Juan Bautista
5
Fresno
Monterey
★ MONTEREY BAY AQUARIUM
Carmel-by-the-Sea
101
BRIXBY BRIDGE ★
Big Sur
PFEIFFER BEACH ★
BIG SUR
1
★ HEARST CASTLE
46
San Simeon
Cambria
101
Cayucos
Morro Bay
San Luis Obispo
Pismo Beach
PACIFIC OCEAN
Santa Maria
101
1
Solvang
OLD MISSION SANTA BARBARA ★
CHUMASH PAINTED CAVE ★
Santa Barbara
To Channel Islands National Park ↓

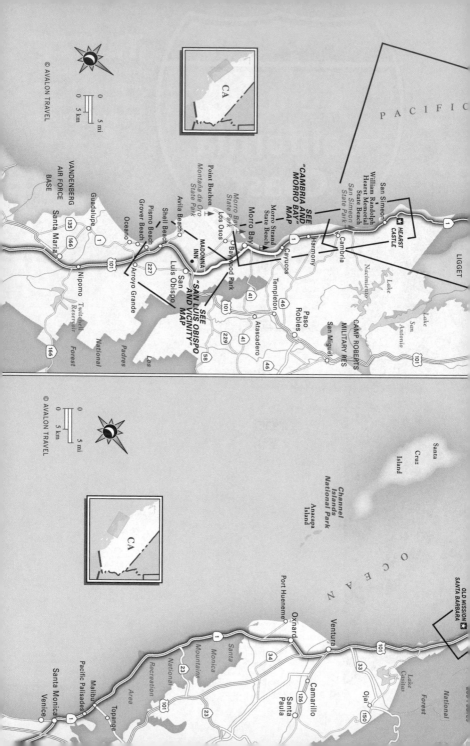

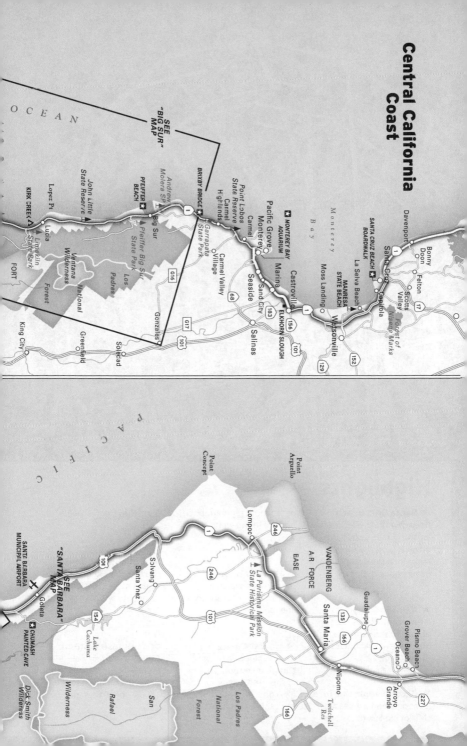

Central California Coast

O C E A N

P A C I F I C

SEE
"BIG SUR"
MAP

SEE
"SANTA BARBARA"
MAP

Monterey Bay

KIRK CREEK
Lopez Pt.
Lucia
Franklin
State Park
John Little
State Reserve
Ventana
Wilderness
National
Los Padres
Forest
FORT
King City
Greenfield
Soledad
Gonzales
Salinas
Andrew
Molera SP
PFEIFFER
BEACH
Big Sur
Pfeiffer Big Sur
State Park
Garrapata
State Park
Carmel Valley
Carmel
Highlands
Point Lobos
State Reserve
Carmel
Carmel
Village
Monterey
Pacific Grove
MONTEREY BAY
AQUARIUM
Seaside
Sand City
Marina
Castroville
Moss Landing
ELKHORN
SLOUGH
Watsonville
La Selva Beach
MANRESA
STATE BEACH
SANTA CRUZ BEACH
BOARDWALK
Santa Cruz
Capitola
Soquel
Scotts
Valley
Felton
Bonny
Doon
Davenport
Forest of
Nisene Marks
BRIXBY BRIDGE

G16
G17
101
68
183
156
129
152
1
17

Point
Concept
Point
Arguello
Lompoc
La Purisima Mission
State Historical Park
VANDENBERG
A I R   F O R C E
B A S E
Santa Ynez
Solvang
Santa Maria
Guadalupe
Nipomo
Pismo Beach
Grover Beach
Oceano
Arroyo
Grande
Twitchell
Res
Lake
Cachuma
Goleta
SANTA BARBARA
MUNICIPAL AIRPORT
CHUMASH
PAINTED CAVE
Dick Smith
Wilderness
San
Rafael
Wilderness
Los Padres
National
Forest

1
246
246
135
166
166
227
101
154
101

Highlights

★ **Santa Cruz Beach Boardwalk:** A roller coaster, arcade games, and all the carnival food you can eat make for a classic day at the beach (page 215).

★ **Monterey Bay Aquarium:** The vast array of sea life and exhibits at this mammoth aquarium is astonishing (page 223).

★ **Bixby Bridge:** Due to its location along the seaside cliffs of Big Sur, this is one of the most photographed bridges in the world (page 242).

★ **Pfeiffer Beach:** This is the place to watch the sun set along the Big Sur coastline (page 244).

★ **Hearst Castle:** No visit to the California coast is complete without a tour of this grand mansion on a hill, conceived and built by publishing magnate William Randolph Hearst (page 247).

★ **Old Mission Santa Barbara:** It's known as the queen of the missions for its beauty and lush setting (page 261).

★ **Chumash Painted Cave:** The artistry of these indigenous petroglyphs dates back at least to the 1600s—or farther (page 261).

Rolling green hillsides and towering redwoods descend to hidden coves and sea arches and the far-reaching coastline seems to extend into infinity.

CA-1 twists along the wild, rugged coast from the boardwalk and bohemia hub of Santa Cruz to Monterey, with its rich marinelife and renowned aquarium. The stunning stretch from Carmel to Big Sur boasts views of the Pacific bounded by jagged coastline and rock formations. The 320-foot concrete arch of the Bixby Bridge provides the perfect photo opportunity at its scenic overlook turnoff. Less than two hours south lie the blubbery elephant seals of Piedras Blancas and the grandiose Hearst Castle.

From here, CA-1 and US-101 engage a dance of merges and splits through farmlands that flourish from the cool climate, producing a bounty of crops, especially strawberries, artichokes, and, most recently, wine grapes. Put on the wine maps by the 2004 film *Sideways,* this wine country now competes with the best of them, with over 40,000 acres of grape-bearing vines.

Planning Your Time

Plan five days to a week to explore the Central Coast. It's easy to run yourself ragged trying to see and do everything. Instead, pick what interests you the most and leave everything else as an opportunity for an enhanced travel experience, if time allows.

Towns all along the coastline offer lodging, food, and fuel. Cities such as Santa Cruz, Monterey, San Luis Obispo, Santa Barbara, and Ventura offer more options, but smaller beach towns and resorts such as Carmel, Cambria, Morro Bay, and Pismo Beach may be more charming. Scenic Big Sur offers an interesting mix of campgrounds and upscale resorts.

It is just under 75 miles south from San Francisco to Santa Cruz via US-101, and 95 miles north from Los Angeles to Santa Barbara via US-101. If you plan to follow US-101 to California's Highway 1 (CA-1), the drive will prove much more scenic but longer.

Best Hotels

★ **West Cliff Inn:** The "Italianate Grand Dame" of Santa Cruz offers lavish amenities and commanding ocean views (page 221).

★ **Seven Gables Inn:** Every room has a view at this Monterey inn, considered one of the most romantic in America (page 229).

★ **Tradewinds Carmel:** Impeccable design makes this one of the most glamorous hotels on the coast (page 236).

★ **Post Ranch Inn:** This rustic yet luxurious resort blends right into the cliffside along Big Sur (page 245).

★ **Madonna Inn:** The famed road-trip stopover is kitschy, over the top, and excessively pink (page 256).

★ **Simpson House Inn:** Opulent rooms, a formal English garden, and evening wine-tastings are features of this Santa Barbara B&B (page 268).

Getting There

Car

The Central Coast is accessible by car via the scenic, two-lane CA-1, which winds along the entire stretch of the coastline.

US-101 is the primary highway that connects San Jose, Salinas, Paso Robles, San Luis Obispo, Santa Maria, Santa Barbara, Ventura, and on southward. Built along the railroad corridor, the highway at times runs parallel to CA-1, specifically through Ventura and Santa Barbara Counties.

Much of CA-1 is a two-lane road with winding turns around the coast. Some stretches are fairly isolated and it is always wise to make sure your tank is full before getting back on the road.

Air

Coastal international airports to access the Central Coast region from the south include **Los Angeles International Airport** (1 World Way, 310/646-5252, www.lawa.org/lax).

The major Northern California airport is **San Francisco International Airport** (650/821-8211, www.flysfo.com), on San Francisco Bay about 15 miles south of the city center.

Regional air service includes **Monterey Regional Airport** (200 Fred Kane Dr. #200, 831/648-7000, www.montereyairport.com), **San Luis Obispo Airport** (901 Airport Dr., 805/781-5205, www.sloairport.com), and **Santa Barbara Municipal Airport** (500 Fowler Rd., 805/683-4011, www.santabarbaraca.gov).

Train

Amtrak (800/872-7245, www.amtrak.com, $135 and up) offers service on the **Coast Starlight** to Seattle, Portland, Sacramento, Oakland, and Los Angeles. The **Pacific Surfliner** provides service from San Luis Obispo to Santa Barbara, Los Angeles, and San Diego. International visitors can buy an unlimited travel USA Rail Pass, good for 15, 30, or 45 days.

Bus

Greyhound (800/231-2222, www.greyhound.com) offers special discounts to students and seniors with routes and stops sticking to major highways and cities.

Fuel and Services

Gas stations are easy to find within beachfront towns, and the farther south you travel, the easier it gets. However, don't expect 24-hour service. If you pull into Big Sur at midnight with an empty tank, you'll find yourself stranded.

To receive reports on **road conditions,** call **511.** If your phone carrier does not support 511, call toll-free at 800/977-6368.

Best Restaurants

★ **Duarte's Tavern:** The olallieberry pie alone is worth a stop at this classic, James Beard-recognized road stop in tiny Pescadero (page 213).

★ **The Forge in the Forest:** This Carmel legend has been serving up perfect dishes for decades (page 233).

★ **Nepenthe:** The menu is short and tasty, but the real feast is the amazing view from the outdoor deck (page 238).

★ **Madeline's:** An exquisite menu and intimate setting make for a Parisian repast in Cambria (page 249).

★ **Stella Mare's:** French country dining and amazing desserts are on the menu in this historic Santa Barbara home (page 265).

For **emergency assistance** and services, call **911.**

San Gregorio

At the intersection of CA-84 and CA-1, **San Gregorio State Beach** (650/879-2170, www.parks.ca.gov, 8am-sunset daily, $10 per car) stretches farther than it seems. Once you're walking toward the ocean, the small-seeming cove stretches out beyond the cliffs that bound it to create a long stretch of beach perfect for contemplative strolling. San Gregorio is a local favorite in the summer, despite the regular appearance of thick, chilly fog over the sand. Brave beachgoers can even swim and bodysurf here, although you'll quickly get cold if you do so without a wetsuit. Picnic tables and restrooms cluster near the parking lot, but picnicking may be hampered by the wind.

The tiny town of San Gregorio is a picture of rolling rangeland, neat patches of colorful crops, and century-old homes, including a one-room schoolhouse and an old brothel. Its beating heart is the **San Gregorio General Store** (CA-84 and Stage Rd., 650/726-0565, www.sangregoriostore.com, 10:30am-6pm Mon.-Thurs., 10:30am-7pm Fri., 10am-7pm Sat., 10am-6pm Sun.). Open since 1889, the San Gregorio General Store has an eclectic book section and a variety of cast-iron cookery, oil lamps, and raccoon traps. In the back of the store are coolers stocked with juice, soda, bottled water, and deli sandwiches made in the back kitchen. The real centerpiece is the bar, serving beer, wine, and a large selection of spirits to ranchers and farmers out for a coffee break in the mornings and locals just getting off work. On the weekends the store is packed by mostly out-of-towners, and the live music keeps things moving. The deep picture windows out front make it a comfy place to watch the afternoon pass by with a cold beer. The San Gregorio General Store lives up to its name: You can even buy stamps or mail a letter at the full-service post office next door.

Pescadero

Pescadero is a tiny dot on the coastline, south of Half Moon Bay and well north of Santa Cruz, with one main street, one side street, several smallish farms, and, of course, the legendary Duarte's Tavern.

Pescadero State Beach (CA-1, north of Pescadero Rd., 650/879-2170, www.parks.ca.gov, 8am-sunset daily) is the closest beach to the town of Pescadero. It's a great spot to walk in the sand and stare out at the Pacific, but near-constant winds make it less than ideal for picnics or sunbathing. It does have some facilities, including public restrooms.

Food

★ **Duarte's Tavern** (202 Stage Rd., 650/879-0464, www.duartestavern.com, 7am-8pm daily, $13-25) has been honored by the James Beard Foundation as "An American Classic," and once you walk through the doors you'll see why. The rambling building features sloping floors and age-darkened wooden walls. The food is good, the service friendly, and the coffee plentiful. And while almost everybody comes to Duarte's eventually for a bowl of artichoke soup or a slice of olallieberry pie, it is really the atmosphere that is the biggest draw. Locals of all stripes—farmers, farmhands, ranchers, and park rangers—sit shoulder to shoulder with travelers from "over the hill," sharing conversation and a bite to eat, particularly in the dimly lit bar. The greatest assets are the outdated jukebox and excellent Bloody Marys, garnished with a pickled green bean.

Pigeon Point Lighthouse

South of Pescadero is **Pigeon Point Lighthouse** (210 Pigeon Point Rd., at CA-1, 650/879-2120, www.parks.ca.gov, 8am-sunset daily). First lit in 1872, Pigeon Point is one of the most photographed lighthouses in the United States. Sadly, visitors find the lighthouse itself in a state of disrepair, and recent earthquakes have made climbing to the top unsafe. Yet the monument stands, its hostel still shelters travelers, and visitors still marvel at the incomparable views from the point. Winter guests can look for migrating whales from the rocks beyond the tower.

For a budget place to stay in this area, try the **Pigeon Point Hostel** (210 Pigeon Point Rd., at CA-1, 650/879-0633, http://norcalhostels.org/pigeon, dorms $25-28, private rooms $76-168). This Hostelling International hostel has simple but comfortable accommodations, both private and dorm-style. Amenities include three kitchens, free WiFi, and beach access. But the best amenity of all is the cliff-top hot tub, which makes this hostel more than special.

Año Nuevo State Reserve

Año Nuevo State Reserve (1 New Years Creek Rd., CA-1, south of Pescadero, 650/879-2025, reservations 800/444-4445, www.parks.ca.gov, 8am-sunset daily, $10 per car) is world-famous as the winter home and breeding ground of the once-endangered elephant seals. The reserve also has extensive dunes and marshland. The beaches and wilderness are open year-round. The elephant seals start showing up in late November and stay to breed, birth pups, and loll on the beach until early March. Visitors are not allowed down to the elephant seal

Pigeon Point Lighthouse

habitats on their own and must sign up for a guided walking tour. Once you see two giant males crashing into one another in a fight for dominance, you won't want to get too close. Book your tour at least a day or two in advance since the seals are popular with both locals and travelers.

Santa Cruz

The seacoast city of Santa Cruz, with its ultra-liberal culture, redwood-clad university, and general sense of funky fun, prides itself on keeping things weird. The beach and the Boardwalk are its prime attractions. Hit the surf and soak up the sun!

Getting There and Around
Both US-101 and CA-1 provide access into Santa Cruz by car. The most picturesque route is CA-1 South through San Mateo County and Half Moon Bay to Santa Cruz.

Amtrak trains and Greyhound run to or near the downtown Santa Cruz Metro Center. The nearest major airports are in San Jose and San Francisco.

Santa Cruz is a walking and bicycling town. It's only a 20-minute walk from downtown to the beach. With 262 sunny days per year, why drive? But, if you do, there is plenty of parking. **Santa Cruz Metro** (920 Pacific Ave., 831/425-8600, www.scmtd.com, $6 day-pass) also provides service within the downtown and outer areas.

Sights
★ Santa Cruz Beach Boardwalk
The **Santa Cruz Beach Boardwalk** (400 Beach St., 831/423-5590, www.beachboardwalk.com, 11am-10pm Sun.-Thurs., 11am-11pm Fri.-Sat., ride hours vary by season, rides closed weekdays in winter, parking $15), or just "the Boardwalk" as it's called by the locals, has a rare appeal that beckons to young children, teenagers, and adults of all ages.

The amusement park rambles along each side of the south end of the Boardwalk; entry is free, but you must buy either per-ride tickets ($3-6) or an unlimited-rides wristband ($33). The Great Dipper boasts a history as the oldest wooden roller coaster in the state, still giving riders a thrill after all this time. In summer, a log ride cools down guests hot from hours of tromping around. The Boardwalk also offers several toddler and little-kid rides.

At the other end of the Boardwalk, avid gamesters choose between the lure of prizes from the traditional midway games and the large arcade. Throw baseballs at things, try your arm at skeeball, or take a pass at classic or newer video games. The traditional carousel actually has a brass ring to grab.

After you've worn yourself out playing games and riding rides, you can take the stairs down to the broad, sandy beach

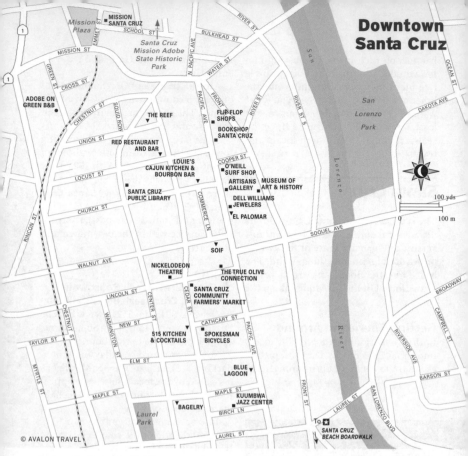

MISSION
SANTA CRUZ
Mission
Plaza
SCHOOL ST
BULKHEAD ST
RIVER ST
MISSION ST
Santa Cruz
Mission Adobe
State Historic
Park
WATER ST
San
GREEN ST
CROSS ST
ADOBE ON
GREEN B&B
CHESTNUT ST
SQUID ROW
N PACIFIC AVE
FRONT ST
RIVER ST
RIVER ST S
Lorenzo
Park
DAKOTA AVE
OCEAN ST
UNION ST
THE REEF
FLIP-FLOP
SHOPS
BOOKSHOP
SANTA CRUZ
RED RESTAURANT
AND BAR
PACIFIC AVE
L
o
r
e
n
z
o
LOCUST ST
LOUIE'S
CAJUN KITCHEN &
BOURBON BAR
COOPER ST
O'NEILL
SURF SHOP
ARTISANS
GALLERY
MUSEUM OF
ART & HISTORY
0   100 yds
CHURCH ST
SANTA CRUZ
PUBLIC LIBRARY
COMMERCE LN
DELL WILLIAMS
JEWELERS
0   100 m
EL PALOMAR
SOQUEL AVE
WALNUT AVE
SOIF
NICKELODEON
THEATRE
THE TRUE OLIVE
CONNECTION
R
i
v
e
r
BROADWAY
LINCOLN ST
CENTER ST
CEDAR ST
SANTA CRUZ
COMMUNITY
FARMERS' MARKET
CAMPBELL ST
WASHINGTON ST
NEW ST
CATHCART ST
PACIFIC AVE
RIVERSIDE AVE
TAYLOR ST
CHESTNUT ST
515 KITCHEN
& COCKTAILS
SPOKESMAN
BICYCLES
BARSON ST
ELM ST
MYRTLE ST
BLUE
LAGOON
MAPLE ST
MAPLE ST
KUUMBWA
JAZZ CENTER
BAGELRY
BIRCH LN
FRONT ST
LAUREL ST
SAN LORENZO BLVD
Laurel
Park
To
SANTA CRUZ
BEACH BOARDWALK
LAUREL ST
© AVALON TRAVEL

below the Boardwalk. It's a great place to flop down and sun yourself, or brave a dip in the cool Pacific surf. Granted, it gets crowded in the summertime.

Looking for something tasty to munch on or a drink to cool you off? You can definitely find it at the Boardwalk. An old-fashioned candy shop sells sweets to the sweet, while the snack stands offer corn dogs, burgers, fries, lemonade, and other generally unhealthy traditional carnival food.

Santa Cruz Surfing Museum

West of the Boardwalk, on Lighthouse Field State Beach, is the world's first surfing museum. Housed in the Mark Abbott Memorial Lighthouse, the **Santa Cruz Surfing Museum** (Lighthouse Point, West Cliff Dr., 831/420-6289, www.santacruzsurfingmuseum.org, 10am-5pm Wed.-Mon. July 4-Labor Day, noon-4pm Thurs.-Mon. rest of the year) relates the history of surfing through a collection of surfboards from different times and other ephemera of surf culture.

Seymour Marine Discovery Center

"Ms. Blue," one of the largest blue whale skeletons, rests across from **Seymour Marine Discovery Center** (100 Shaffer Rd., 831/459-3800, http://seymour-center.ucsc.edu, 10am-5pm Tues.-Sun., $8 adults, $6 children), where tours and exhibits let you dive into the latest ocean discoveries and where shark-petting is encouraged.

Food

You won't find much refined cuisine in Santa Cruz. A concentration of eating and drinking places can be found along Front Street and Pacific Avenue in downtown.

The original **Bagelry** (320 Cedar St., 831/429-8049, www.bagelrysantacruz.com, 6:30am-5:30pm Mon.-Fri., 7:30am-4pm Sat.-Sun., under $8) is the mecca of the perfect bagel. **Zoccoli's** (1534 Pacific Ave., 831/423-1711, www.zoccolis.com, 8am-6pm Mon.-Sat., 10am-6pm Sun., $6-8) is an Italian deli serving a wide array of sandwiches, along with soup and salad.

El Palomar (1336 Pacific Ave., 831/425-7575, www.elpalomarsantacruz.com, 11am-9:30pm Mon.-Wed., 11am-10pm Thurs., 11am-10:30pm Fri., 10am-10:30pm Sat., 10am-9:30pm Sun., $7-27) draws a line with Mexican food favorites like burritos and tacos. **Louie's Cajun Kitchen & Bourbon Bar** (110 Church St., 831/429-2000, www.louiescajunkitchen.com, 2pm-10pm Tues.-Sat., 10:30am-10pm Sun., $12-25) brings a little of New Orleans to the West Coast.

For the finer things, **Soif** (105 Walnut Ave., 831/423-2020, www.soifwine.com, 5pm-10pm Sun.-Thurs., 5pm-11pm Fri.-Sat., $5-28) offers a sophisticated ambiance and contemporary dishes.

Outside downtown, **Buttery** (702 Soquel Ave., 831/458-3020, www.butterybakery.com, 7am-7pm daily, $4-8) offers European-style baked goods. For pizza, **Engfer Pizza Works** (537 Seabright Ave., 831/429-1856, www.engferpizzaworks.com, 4pm-9:30pm Tues.-Sun., $8-23) creates wood-fired oven pizzas out of an old factory. Awesome tacos and fat burritos at **Tacos Moreno** (1053 Water St., 831/429-6095, 10am-10pm Mon.-Fri., 11am-7pm Sat.-Sun., under $6) mean a big line forms quickly at this popular place.

From top to bottom: the Santa Cruz Surfing Museum; surfing the waves; Capitola Wharf.

Nightlife

Several bars and lounges congregate in downtown, offering a variety of brewed concoctions to satisfy your palate and musical beats to keep your foot tapping, most without a cover charge. At the far end of the wharf, **Vino Prima** (55 Municipal Wharf, 831/426-0750, www.vinoprimawines.com, 2pm-10pm Mon.-Tues., 2pm-8pm Wed.-Fri., noon-10pm Sat., noon-8pm Sun.) pours California boutique wines, and even has a mimosa bar!

Your ticket to NFL games and cocktails, **Ideal Bar & Grill** (106 Beach St., 831/423-5271, www.idealbarandgrill.com, 8am-midnight Sun.-Thurs., 8am-2am Fri.-Sat.) has two big-screen TVs, a variety of mixed goods, and live music on Friday and Saturday nights. Enjoy live music, pub grub, and the outdoor patio at the **Seabright Brewery** (519 Seabright Ave. #107, 831/426-2739, www.seabrightbrewery.com, 11:30am-11:30pm daily), or hang out at **Blue Lagoon** (923 Pacific Ave., 831/423-7177, www.thebluelagoon.com, 4pm-2am daily) for beer and cocktails and live rock and roll!

Surf bar **The Reef** (120 Union St., 831/459-9876, 11am-10pm Sun.-Wed., 11am-11pm Thurs.-Sat.) hosts jazz jams and open mics. For a good old-fashioned pub, go to **Parish Publick House** (841 Almar Ave., 831/421-0507, www.polaro.com, 11am-2am daily), which has a great selection of draft beers and whiskey, savory fish-and-chips, and foot- stompin' music.

Mellow with a dash of hip, **515 Kitchen & Cocktails** (515 Cedar St., 831/425-5051, www.515santacruz.com, 4pm-1:30am daily) serves creative cocktails. Low lighting, music, and craft cocktails at **Red Restaurant and Bar** (200 Locust St., 831/425-1913, www.redsrestaurantand-bar.com, 3pm-1:30am daily) form an intimate setting. Santa Cruz's best kept secret, **Boccis Cellar** (140 Encinal St., 831/427-1795, 5pm-9pm daily) attracts locals and tourists not only because it's a

historical landmark (circa 1800s), but because it has some of the best wine, food, and musical entertainment around.

Arts and Entertainment

An eclectic city of art and entertainment, Santa Cruz's diversity gives it that uniquely captivating edge. Watch a Shakespearian production at the **Sinsheimer-Stanley Festival Glen** (UCSC Theater Arts Center, 1156 High St., 831/459-2159, $36-48 adults, $16 children under 18), an unforgettable venue set in a grove of massive redwoods beneath the starry sky.

Feel like a good movie and popcorn? **Nickelodeon Theatre** (210 Lincoln St., 831/426-7500, www.thenick.com, $10.50 general, $8 matinee) shows all the major blockbuster films, including a variety of foreign and indie productions. Don't pass up the snack bar's award-winning organic popcorn and locally made treats.

One of the oldest museums in the state of California, the **Santa Cruz Museum of Natural History** (1305 East Cliff Dr., 831/420-6115, santacruzmuseum.org, 10am-5pm Tues.-Sat., $4 adults, free children under 18) is where Ohlone Native American artifacts are preserved and visitors can learn about local flora and fauna. In the heart of downtown, **Museum of Art & History** (705 Front St., 831/429-1964, www.santacruzmah.org, 11am-5pm Tues.-Sun., $5 adults, $3 students and seniors) is a small facility with three floors of galleries, changing exhibits, and a gift shop.

Santa Cruz has a couple fantastic entertainment venues that feature class-act musicians. At **Kuumbwa Jazz Center** (320 Cedar St., 831/427-2227, $23 and up), local talent and internationally acclaimed jazz acts play to a packed house in a concert setting with food and drinks available. **Moe's Alley** (1535 Commercial Way, 831/479-1854, www.moesalley.com, up to $20) offers live performances from jazz and blues to reggae and salsa in a laid-back scene.

Shopping

The Clock Tower, the epicenter of Santa Cruz's downtown, is also the location of the Pacific Garden Mall. Further out you'll find Capitola Village, the Capitola Mall, and The Wharf.

Every Wednesday, the **Santa Cruz Community Farmers' Market** (corner of Cedar and Lincoln Sts., 831/454-0566, www.santacruzfarmersmarket.org, 1:30pm-6pm Wed. spring-fall) showcases the Central Coast's agricultural diversity with organic specialties that include sweet strawberries, artichokes, crafted goat cheeses, and vegetables. Closing hours change slightly with the winter winds; vendors pack up by 5pm.

To see artwork by a collection of other local artisans, **Artisans Gallery** (1368 Pacific Ave., 831/423-8183, www.artisanssantacruz.com, 10:30am-6:30pm Sun.-Thurs., 10:30am-8:30pm Fri.-Sat.), located downtown, features wall art, jewelry, ceramics, metal work, and woodworking.

On the east side of Soquel Creek, **Craft Gallery** (209 Capitola Ave., 831/475-4466) showcases pottery, clocks, candles, sea glass, sandcastles, and jewelry boxes. To put something in your new jewelry box, stop at **Dell Williams Jewelers** (1320 Pacific Ave., 831/423-4100 and 800/922-9592, www.dellwilliams.com, 10am-5:30pm Mon.-Sat.) for classic to contemporary jewelry.

Get a good book from **Bookshop Santa Cruz** (1520 Pacific Ave., 831/423-0900, www.bookshopsantacruz.com, 9am-10pm Sun.-Thurs., 9am-11pm Fri.-Sat.) to enjoy on the beach while working on your tan.

Surfers can find a huge selection of surfboards, sunglasses, and the famous O'Neill wetsuits at **O'Neill Surf Shop** (110 Cooper St., 831/469-4377, 10am-9pm Sun.-Thurs., 10am-10pm Fri.-Sat.).

Slip your feet into a pair of comfy sandals at **Flip Flop Shops** (1528 Pacific Ave., 831/316-0912, 10am-7pm Mon.-Thurs., 10am-8pm Fri.-Sat.) and take a stroll along the **Santa Cruz Wharf** (Beach St., 831/420-6025, www.santacruzwharf.com, 5am-2am daily) to shop for souvenirs or local vintage wines.

If you've tasted enough wine, discover **The True Olive Connection** (106 Lincoln St., 831/458-6457, www.trueoliveconnection.com, 10am-6pm Sun.-Thurs., 10am-7pm Fri.-Sat.), a family-owned retail boutique with over 35 delicious extra-virgin olive oils from around the world and 25 balsamic vinegars from Modena, Italy. Next door, let your hair down and go nuts over 120 different kinds of nuts, dried fruits, and other natural treats at **Nut Kreations** (104 Lincoln St., 831/431-6435, www.nutkreations.com, 10am-8pm Mon.-Sat., 11am-8pm Sun.).

Recreation

The Santa Cruz Wharf is known for fishing and viewing marinelife, while local parks and beaches offer many opportunities for surfing, bird- and butterfly-watching, kayaking, biking, golfing, and, of course, exploration of historic sites.

Santa Cruz Mission State Historic Park (144 School St., 831/425-5849, 10am-4pm Thurs.-Sun.) puts history buffs at the site of the oldest building in the city, founded by the Franciscans in 1791. This is the only remaining original building of the Mission Santa Cruz settlement. It's free to tour the mission, which has several good exhibits on local Native American life.

Both **Lighthouse Field State Beach** (740 W. Cliff Dr., 831/429-2850, 7am-sunset daily), well known to surfers for its great wave riding and the adjacent Surfing Museum, and **Natural Bridges State Beach** (2531 W. Cliff Dr., 831/423-4609, 8am-6pm daily, $10 parking), known for its natural sea arch, attract birders that gather for a rare glimpse of the black swift and colorful monarch butterflies, as well as to see offshore sea lions and the migrating whale population. Natural Bridges State Beach's remaining mudstone bridge (there were once three, two collapsed) was carved out by the Pacific Ocean through wind and water erosion. Arches are formed out of collapsed caves, the mouth becoming a gateway to the open sea.

Rent a kayak or paddleboard from **Kayak Connection** (413 Lake Ave., 831/479-1121, www.kayakconnection. com, 10am-5pm Mon.-Fri., 9am-6pm Sat.-Sun., $35 and up) to get a closer look at marine mammals or just a different perspective off the beach, or go scuba diving with **Aqua Safaris Scuba Center** (6896-A Soquel Ave., 831/479-4386, www. aquasafaris.com, 10am-6pm daily) and explore the world below the surface.

Take a three-mile walk or bike ride on **West Cliff Drive,** a path along the Pacific Ocean that provides a wonderful vantage point to see all the beachfront and offshore activity. Bike rentals and gear are available through several shops, including **Pacific Ave Cycles** (318 Pacific Ave., 831/471-2453, 10am-6pm daily, $20 and up), located right by the bike park off from the Boardwalk, or **Spokesman**

Bicycles (231 Cathcart St., 831/429-6062, www.spokesmanbicycles.com, 10am-6pm Mon.-Sat., noon-5pm Sun., $20 and up), just a few blocks from downtown.

Golf at the historic **Pasatiempo Golf Club** (20 Clubhouse Rd., 831/459-9169, www.pasatiempo.com, 9am-6pm daily, up to $260 green fees, $120 replay), designed by world-renown golf architect Alister MacKenzie. The club offers a beautiful course, daily tee times, a Tap Room, and the MacKenzie Bar & Grill, where you can have a bite to eat and kick back and relax after a long day on the green. Little golfers can test their skills at **Buccaneer Bay** (400 Beach St., 831/423-5590, www.beachboardwalk.com, 11am-pm Sun.-Fri., 10am-11pm Sat., $5), a two-story, 18-hole miniature golf course. But watch out for pirates!

Events

The second-largest gathering of "Woodies" in the world, **Woodies on the Wharf** (www.santacruzwoodies.com, late

Natural Bridges State Beach

June, free), features over 200 vintage and classic station wagons, and celebrates these beauties with music, food, prizes, and good old fashioned fun.

It just wouldn't be right if Santa Cruz wasn't host to some of the most recognized surf contests, such as the **O'Neill Coldwater Classic** (Steamer Ln., www. oneill.com, late Oct., free), an event that draws international boarders to Steamer Ln., a popular surfing spot in the West Cliff. **SCLU Longboard Invitational** (www.santa-cruz-longboard-union.com, free) rounds up nearly 200 longboarders from across the state each Memorial Day weekend to compete in the longest-running longboard surf contest. Hang out with the best surfers around, get some sun, and see who will win the title!

If it's music and food you enjoy, the **Mole & Mariachi Festival** (144 School St., 831/429-1840, www.thatsmypark.org, free) livens up downtown Santa Cruz with musical acts, local food, and family-friendly activities.

Every November is a celebration of sea glass, art, and ocean stewardship at **Santa Cruz Sea Glass & Ocean Art Festival** (400 Beach St., 831/332-7188, www.santa-cruzseaglass.com, free). November also hosts the **Santa Cruz Film Festival** (Del Mar and Rio Theaters, www.santacruz-filmfestival.com), which showcases a collection of independent films from all over the world.

Jump on board the **Santa Cruz Holiday Lights Train** (400 Beach St., 831/335-4484, www.roaringcamp.com, 5pm-8pm late Fri.-Sat. Nov.-Dec., $28 adults, $22 children) and sip hot cider as you go a-caroling for holiday fun Victorian-style. The train departs from the Santa Cruz Beach Boardwalk.

The premier way to see the best art in Santa Cruz, **Open Studios Art Tour** (831/475-9600 ext. 17, www.artscouncilsc.org) displays the works of more than 300 artists during the first three weekends in October. An events guide ($10) and the Open Studios Art Tour iTunes app ($5) are handy tools that provide a glimpse of an artist's work and exhibit location.

Accommodations

For a romantic getaway, the old-world charm of the "Italianate Grand Dame," ★ **West Cliff Inn** (174 W. Cliff Dr., 831/457-2200, www.westcliffinn.com, $175-400), embodies a lavish experience with gas fireplaces, deep soaking tubs, and commanding ocean views.

It just feels right to stay at a hostel in Santa Cruz. You can avail yourself of the **HI-Santa Cruz Hostel** (321 Main St., 831/423-8304, $27 dorms pp, $60-90 private rooms) with dorm beds in an immaculate 1870s cottage. There are also private rooms and cheaper rooms that share a bathroom.

Reasonably priced places include the **Beachview Inn** (50 Front St., 831/426-3575, www.beach-viewinn.com, $80 and up) and the **Seaway Inn** (176 W. Cliff Dr., 831/471-9004, $125 and up); both offer clean and comfortable rooms, and are close to the beach, wharf, and Boardwalk. Just three blocks from downtown and close to the warm sand and crashing waves, **Continental Inn** (414 Ocean St., 831/429-1221 and 800/343-6941, www.continentalinnsantacruz.com, $69-305) is comfortable and serves a great breakfast, while the **Carousel Beach Inn** (110 Riverside Ave., 831/425-7090 and 800/214-7400, www.santacruzmotels.com, $99-239) is just steps away from the excitement of the Boardwalk's rides and amusements.

For a room with a spectacular view, you really can't go wrong at **Beach Street Inns & Suites** (125 Beach St., 831/423-3031, www.beachstreetinn.com, $129 and up); most of their rooms overlook Monterey Bay. There's also an on-site gourmet café and free guest parking, which is a nice bonus in a location across from the Boardwalk.

A quaint little gem is the **Adobe on Green B&B** (103 Green St., 831/469-9866, www.adobeongreen.com, $149-199), with boutique accommodations and organic breakfasts in a quiet atmosphere. Stroll the garden grounds of **Babbling Brook** (1025 Laurel St., 831/427-2437 or 800/866-1131, $189 and up); the rooms are decorated in the French country style and feature featherbeds and fireplaces. Adorned in hardwoods, Tiffany lamps, and open hearths, the **Darling House** (314 W. Cliff Dr., 831/458-1958, www.darlinghouse.com, $145-325) is a 1910 oceanfront mansion with stunning views and grand rooms with private baths.

Walking distance to everything, **Pacific Blue Inn** (636 Pacific Ave., 831/600-8880, www.pacificblueinn.com, $170-240) is a quiet courtyard hotel with free loaner bikes and a breakfast you won't forget!

Information and Services

The **Santa Cruz Conference & Visitor Center** (1211 Ocean St., 9am-5pm Mon.-Fri., 10am-4pm Sat.-Sun.) provides brochures, maps, and useful information to point you in the right direction.

Moss Landing

Marked by the mammoth smokestacks of a power plant, Moss Landing is home to **Elkhorn Slough** (1700 Elkhorn Rd., 831/728-2822, www.elkhornslough.org, 9am-5pm Wed.-Sun., trail fee), a large wetland area full of birds and otters. One of a few remaining wetland areas of its kind on the Central Coast, it's home to nine species of fish and over 200 species of waterfowl. While you can access the wetlands and bird habitats from CA-1 in Moss Landing, to get to the visitors center you must drive several miles into the agricultural backcountry. But once you're there, knowledgeable and dedicated rangers can provide you with all the information you need to spot your favorite birds and animals, plus find a few you've never seen before.

CA-156: Castroville and San Juan Bautista

CA-156 passes through Monterey, San Benito, and Santa Clara Counties, overlapping US-101 for eight miles between Prunedale and San Juan Bautista. Considered to be the quickest route (along with US-101) from San Francisco Bay to the Monterey Peninsula, its westernmost two-mile stretch runs through the tiny town of Castroville, culminating at the CA-1 interchange.

Aside from the 1947 Artichoke Queen, a title bestowed on a young woman then named Norma Jean Baker (later better known as Marilyn Monroe), Castroville's claim to fame is growing the biggest artichokes. **The Giant Artichoke,** a resident 20-foot sculpture that has hovered over Merritt Street since the early 1960s, is a tribute to the town's farming talents and "artichoke thumb." Nearby, the **Giant Artichoke Restaurant** (11261 Merritt St., 831/633-3501, 7am-9pm daily) sells fried artichokes and other tasty green-layered creations.

The town lies 3 miles from the Pacific Ocean and 10 miles from Salinas in Monterey County. There is no direct access from CA-156 West to CA-1 North. Motorists heading west on CA-156 will need to exit at the CA-183 interchange to access CA-1. It is important to note that this is a highly traveled road that experiences delays due to congestion, and accidents are well documented along its meager length.

About 20 miles east of Castroville, past the US-101 junction with CA-156, is **San Juan Bautista.** This small town feels frozen in time—the buildings look like they could feature in an old western, and the state historic park at the center of town maintains four buildings from the 1800s. The town's most famous sight is one that never really existed. **Mission San Juan Bautista** (406 2nd St., 831/623-4528, www.oldmissionsjb.org, 9:30am-4:30pm Mon.-Sun., free) features prominently in Alfred Hitchcock's *Vertigo,* but the bell tower so central to the plot was fabricated for the movie.

Monterey

Originally inhabited by Native Americans who fished here, Monterey Bay became a fishing hub for the European settlers in the 19th century as well. Author John Steinbeck later immortalized its unglamorous fish-canning industry in his novel *Cannery Row.* It wasn't until the 20th century that the city began to lean toward gentrification. The bay became a wildlife preserve, the Monterey Bay Aquarium opened, and tourism became the mainstay of the local economy. Today, Monterey is the big city on the well-populated southern tip of its namesake bay.

It's plenty cosmopolitan, but a little more approachable than its high-class neighbor, Carmel.

The best days in Monterey are picture perfect: It's no wonder that so many artists have been inspired to paint this land-and seascape. Wandering the twisting coastline, you'll see boats, kayaks, and otters playing along the bay.

Getting There and Around

CA-1 runs through Monterey, providing access southward from Santa Cruz and northward through Big Sur. Southbound on US-101, at Prunedale, travel west on CA-156 to CA-1 South to Monterey.

The **Amtrak** (www.amtrak.com) Coast Starlight train stops in Salinas (30 minutes away) en route between Seattle, Washington, and Los Angeles, California. A free bus shuttles travelers from Salinas to the Monterey Transit Plaza.

Monterey Peninsula Airport (200 Fred Kane Dr., 831/648-7000, www.montereyairport.com) offers regular flights from San Francisco, Los Angeles, Phoenix, Denver, and Salt Lake City. Service providers include United, American, US Airways, and Allegiant Air.

Local bus service is provided by **Monterey-Salinas Transit** (888/678-2871, mst.org), with the towns of Carmel and Pacific Grove en route, as well as popular wineries. The Salinas **Greyhound** (www.greyhound.com) station also provides link service to Monterey.

Monterey's downtown operates a trolley service during the summer; however, you'll find many local area attractions, restaurants, and hotels are in walking distance.

Sights
★ Monterey Bay Aquarium
The first aquarium of its kind in the country, the **Monterey Bay Aquarium** (886 Cannery Row, 831/648-4800, www.montereybayaquarium.org, 9:30am-6pm

Monterey

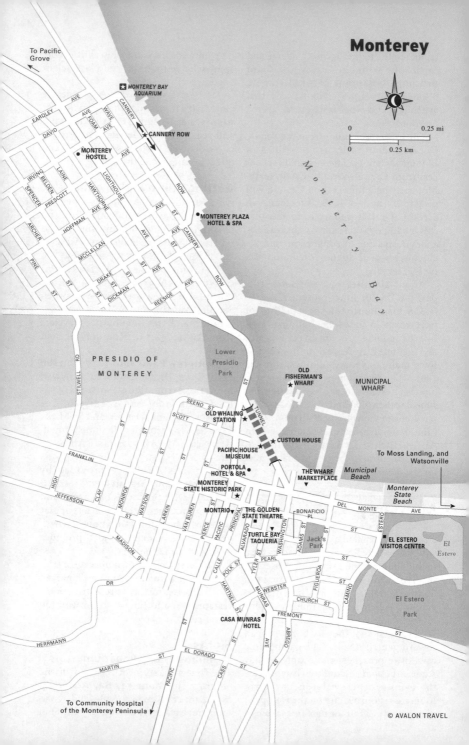

To Pacific Grove

★ Monterey Bay Aquarium

EARDLEY AVE
DAVID AVE
FOAM AVE
WAVE AVE
CANNERY ROW
★ CANNERY ROW

IRVING
SPENCER
BELDEN
LAINE
PRESCOTT
HAWTHORNE
LIGHTHOUSE AVE
ARCHER
HOFFMAN
MCCLELLAN
AVE
AVE
AVE
AVE

● MONTEREY HOSTEL

PINE ST
DRAKE AVE
DICKMAN AVE
REESIDE AVE
ROW ST
CANNERY ROW

● Monterey Plaza Hotel & Spa

Monterey Bay

0   0.25 mi
0   0.25 km

PRESIDIO OF MONTEREY

STILWELL RD

Lower Presidio Park

FRANKLIN

HIGH ST
JEFFERSON ST
CLAY ST
MONROE ST
WATSON ST
LARKIN ST
VAN BUREN ST
SCOTT ST
SEENO ST

★ OLD WHALING STATION
PACIFIC HOUSE MUSEUM
TUNNEL
★ CUSTOM HOUSE

OLD FISHERMAN'S WHARF ★

MUNICIPAL WHARF

To Moss Landing, and Watsonville

● PORTOLA HOTEL & SPA
★ MONTEREY STATE HISTORIC PARK

THE WHARF MARKETPLACE ▼

Municipal Beach

Monterey State Beach

MADISON ST

MONTRIO ▼

PIERCE ST
PACIFIC ST
PRINCIPAL ST
ALVARADO ST
WASHINGTON ST
CALLE PRINCIPAL
POLK ST
TYLER ST
PEARL ST
ADAMS ST
BONAFICIO PL
FIGUEROA ST
DEL MONTE AVE
CAMINO

■ THE GOLDEN STATE THEATRE
▼ TURTLE BAY TAQUERIA

Jack's Park

■ EL ESTERO VISITOR CENTER

El Estero

HERRMANN ST

DR

HARTNELL ST
MUNRAS ST
WEBSTER ST
CHURCH ST
FREMONT ST
ABREGO ST

● CASA MUNRAS HOTEL

El Estero Park

PACIFIC ST
CASS ST
EL DORADO ST
MARTIN ST

To Community Hospital of the Monterey Peninsula ↓

© AVALON TRAVEL

daily Memorial Day weekend-Labor Day weekend, 10am-5pm daily rest of year, $40 adults, $25 children) is still unique in many ways. From the very beginning, the aquarium's mission has been conservation. It has taken custodianship of the Pacific coastline and waters in Monterey County down to Big Sur, playing an active role in the conservation of at-risk wildlife in the area. Many of the animals in the aquarium's tanks were rescued; those that survive may eventually be returned to the wild. All the exhibits you'll see in this mammoth complex feature only local sea life.

The largest tank in the aquarium is a 1,200,000-gallon tank in the Open Sea galleries, which features one of the world's largest single-paned windows. In the peaceful jellyfish room, the balloon-like creatures drift through illuminated water. The highlight for many visitors, and often the most crowded area, is the sea otter experience. You can watch from two levels of windows to see the otters at play above water or below.

Cannery Row

Cannery Row (www.canneryrow.com) has American author John Steinbeck and his novel to thank for its name. The six blocks look much like as Steinbeck described them in his novel, though the canneries are long gone, replaced with seafood restaurants, shops, galleries, and wine-tasting rooms. The corrugated metal siding of the buildings is still here, as are the crossovers that connected them to the nearby railway. Now there's a bike and walking path where the trains once stopped to load up sardines for transport across the state.

Old Fisherman's Wharf

Watch sea lions and otters play in the harbor as working trawlers unload the catch of the day at **Old Fisherman's Wharf** (1 Old Fishermans Wharf, www.monterey-wharf.com), or explore sea life on a glass-bottom boat tour, go on a whale-watching tour, or just shop; it's all on the Wharf. Nearby, the **Wharf Marketplace** (290 Figueroa St., 831/649-1116, www.thewharfmarketplace.com, 7am-7pm daily) sits at the historic Standard Pacific Railroad Passenger Station, and is a pioneer in providing locally grown foods. It's the place to go for a firsthand look at the bounty produced by the surrounding farmlands.

Monterey State Historic Park

Probably the singularly most concentrated historic area in Monterey is **Monterey State Historic Park** (20 Custom House Plaza, 831/649-7118). The park encompasses the **Old Town Historic District,** a collection of historic buildings and intriguing features, such as the whalebone sidewalk in front of the **Old Whaling Station** (391 Decatur St., 831/375-5356). One of the most interesting ways to explore the grounds is to follow the two-mile **Path of History,** marked by yellow plaques in the sidewalk. It's a self-guided tour that leads to 55 historic sites, including adobes and the Royal Presidio Chapel, the oldest structure in Monterey. Maps and guidebooks are available at **Pacific House Museum** (10 Custom House Plaza, 831/649-2905, 10am-3pm Wed. and Fri.-Mon., $3), where you can also see interactive exhibits chronicling the past of early Native American life. Learn about the town's booming whaling era, displayed in the **Museum of Monterey** (5 Custom House Plaza, 831/372-2608, www.museumofmonterey.org, 11am-5pm Wed.-Sat., noon-5pm Sun., free), detailed through exhibits and old photographs.

The Royal Presidio Chapel

A striking example of 18th-century Spanish colonial architecture, **The Royal Presidio Chapel** played a pivotal role as an outpost for the Spanish military in North America, and is considered the most significant building in early California. Although the current structure was built in 1794, recent archaeology has revealed two previous structures, the oldest dating back to 1770, buried on the grounds and establishing the sight as the earliest Christian place of worship in the state of California. To the south of the chapel bell tower—which includes the oldest non-indigenous sculpture in the state, "Our Lady of Guadalupe"—granite and rock footings of the 1770 stone chapel still lie beneath the dirt unseen. The ornate stone-cut doors of the east chapel entryway were once the original doors to the baptistery, demolished in 1868.

Follow the path that leads to the San Carlos School and the Rectory of San Carlos Cathedral. To the right of the cathedral lies a statue of the Virgin Mary, and at the back of the building is a California landmark, the "Junipero Oak."

Food

In downtown Monterey, the selection of restaurants is more down to earth than those in the Fisherman's Wharf/Cannery Row area.

Chili egg puff stuffed with three cheeses, incredible omelets, and outrageously divine banana nut pancakes are the reasons **Rosine's** (434 Alvarado St., 831/375-1400, www.rosinesmonterey. com, 8am-9pm Sun.-Thurs., 8am-10pm Fri.-Sat., $8-24) should be your first morning stop in the historic center.

For fresh-off-the-boat seafood, head to **Monterey's Fish House** (2114 Del Monte Ave., 831/373-4647, 11:30am-2:30pm and 5pm-9:30pm daily, $12-21), west of downtown. Or, for food so delicious that "you'd be more than happy to consume them in a barn," the **Fishwife's Turtle Bay Taqueria** (431 Tyler St., 831/333-1500, www.turtlebay.tv, 11am-9pm Mon.-Fri., 11am-9:30pm Sat.-Sun., under $14) never disappoints with exceptional Mexican dishes, a wide selection of salsas, and a taco bar that you can enjoy in a tastefully decorated venue, not a barn!

Romantic **Epsilon** (422 Tyler St., 831/655-8108, www.epsilonrestaurant. com, 11am-2pm Mon.-Fri., 5pm-9:30pm

Old Fisherman's Wharf in Monterey

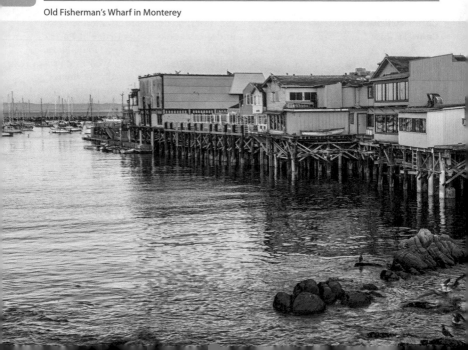

Tues.-Sun., $15-25) is a cozy Greek restaurant serving fantastic flavors of the Mediterranean. Another great date spot, **Alvarado Fish and Steak House** (481 Alvarado St., 831/717-4468, www.alvaradofishandsteakhouse.com, 4pm-9:30pm Mon.-Tues., 11:30am-9:30pm Wed., 11:30am-10pm Thurs.-Sun., $10-30) serves freshly caught seafood and choice steaks in an elegantly inviting atmosphere. **Montrio** (414 Calle Principal, 831/648-8880, www.montrio.com, 4:30pm-11pm daily, $16-30) is another entry in elegantly casual Monterey dining. The crab cakes are legendary.

The best place on the wharf is **Old Fisherman's Grotto** (39 Fisherman's Wharf, 831/375-4604, www.oldfishermansgrotto.com, 11am-10pm daily, $18 and up). For over 50 years, the Shake family has run the Wharf's premier restaurant as one of the most-sought-out restaurants, serving top seafood dishes, Angus steaks, and award-winning wines in style and with a beautiful view.

Cannery Row has a number of restaurants offering waterfront dining. **The Sardine Factory** (701 Wave St., 831/373-3775, www.sardinefactory.com, 5pm-9:30pm daily, $31-50) first opened in 1968 and helped to revitalize the Cannery Row area. World leaders and celebrities have enjoyed the seafood dishes here, served in elegant surroundings.

Nightlife

Alvarado Street is a concentrated area of lively bars and pubs like **Lallapalooza** (474 Alvarado St., 831/645-9036, www.lalla-palooza.com) for an endless list of martinis. Don't miss dinner, cocktails, and live jazz at **Cibo Ristorante Italiano** (301 Alvarado St., 831/649-8151, www.cibo.com, 5pm-2am daily). Taste artisanal cocktails in a vintage Parisian-style bar at **Hotel 1110** (1110 Del Monte Ave., 831/655-0515, www.hotel1110.com), which stays open late and has a rooftop lounge that overlooks the ocean. You just can't beat a good British pub, and Monterey has a couple. **Crown & Anchor** (150 W. Franklin St., 831/649-6496, www.crownandanchor.net, 11am-1:30am daily) is where over 20 of the best international brews hang out, all in good company, and the **Britannia Arms** (444 Alvarado St., 831/656-9543, 11am-2am daily) is a place where nothing goes better with a good ale than live music and soccer.

On Cannery Row, **Blue Fin** (685 Cannery Row, 831/717-4280, www.bluefinbilliards.com, 11am-2am daily) lets you let your hair down with live DJs, tournament pool tables, and karaoke, while nearby, **Sly McFly's** (700 Cannery Row, 831/649-8050, 11:30am-2am daily) is filled with the rhythms of jazz and blues.

In the Lighthouse District, **Carbone's** (214 Lighthouse Ave., 831/643-9169, www.lighthousedistrict.net, noon-2am Tues.-Sun., 2pm-2am Mon.) is a good old-fashioned neighborhood bar with pool, foosball, darts, live bands, and friendly people.

Arts and Entertainment

There are two **Monterey Museum of Art** (559 Pacific St., 831/372-5477, 11am-5pm Thurs.-Mon., $10) locations. One is in the heart of Old Monterey, which houses eight galleries filled with early American paintings, photography, and contemporary art. The other is located in **La Mirada** (720 Via Mirada, 831/372-3689, 11am-5pm Thurs.-Mon., $10), one of Monterey's oldest neighborhoods, and includes four contemporary galleries.

Catch a play or musical at **Unicorn Theatre** (320 Hoffman Ave., 831/649-0259, www.unicorntheatreinc.org, $12 and up), featuring new adaptations and rarely performed works. For soothing classics, **Monterey Symphony** (2560 Garden Rd., Ste. 101, 831/646-8511, www.montereysymphony.corg, $35 and up) performs the works of the great composers and their contemporaries with both public appeal and intellectual merit.

A world-class concert and live theater venue, **The Golden State Theatre** (417 Alvarado St., 831/649-1070, www.goldenstatetheatre.com, $35 and up) presents comedy, musicals, and more in a medieval-style castle.

Get a good laugh at Cannery Row's number one comedy club and bar, **Planet Gemini** (2110 N. Fremont St., 831/373-1449, www.planetgemini.com, 8pm-2am Tues.-Sat., 8pm-midnight Sun., $10-15), featuring nationally known comedians and major stars! An intimate theater on the Wharf, **Bruce Arris Wharf Theater** (Fisherman South Wharf #1, 831/649-2332, $25 and up) has become an icon for presenting classic plays and musicals to Monterey Bay, and is one of the most respected supporters of the arts.

Shopping

Shops line Fisherman's Wharf and Cannery Row, while, in downtown, independent stores dot Alvarado Street.

For the souvenir shopper, Fisherman's Wharf has several variety stores. **Balesteri's Wharf Front** (6 Fisherman's Wharf #1, 831/375-6411, 10am-7pm Mon.-Thurs., 10am-8pm Sat.-Sun.) sells ocean-themed gifts and jewelry, while **Pirates Cove Gifts & Things** (42 Fisherman's Wharf #1, 831/372-6688) has all kinds of fun pirate novelties, knickknacks, and clothing. Stop by the big pink building, better known as the **Harbor House Gifts** (1 Fisherman's Wharf #1, 831/372-4134), for truly unique gifts or just to see the world's largest hand-blown Venetian murano glass chandelier.

For something that sparkles, **Monterey Bay Silver Company** (95 Fisherman's Wharf #1, 831/373-1515) shines up beautifully jeweled wearables; **Splash** (95 Fisherman's Wharf #1, 831/373-3434) lets you show off Swarovski crystal fashion jewelry; and **Morning Star Pearl** (95 Fisherman's Wharf #1, 831/373-8105) strands together lovely pearls for that special someone.

Cutting-edge resort wear and fashion jewelry at **California Classics** (750 Cannery Row, 831/324-0528) or color-changing apparel and accessories at **Del Sol** (660 Cannery Row, Ste. 109, 831/375-4786) both make shopping the Cannery a unique experience. For those cool coastal evenings, **Pacific Coast Clothing & Gifts Company** (685 Cannery Row, 831/375-9822) keeps you warm with outerwear.

Two floors of antiques are packed into an old 1920s cannery building at **Cannery Row Antiques** (471 Wave St., 831/655-0264, www.canneryrowantiquemall.com, 10am-5:30pm Mon.-Fri., 10am-6pm Sat., 10am-5pm Sun.), or head to Alvarado Street where **Olio Vintage Fun** (380 Alvarado St., 831/375/6546, www.olio-vintagefun.com, 11am-4pm Tues., 10:30am-5:30pm Wed.-Sat.) houses a collection of cool, retro nostalgia. Nearby, **LeBlanc Gallery** (271 Alvarado Mall, 831/372-7756, www.leblancgallery.com, 10am-6pm daily) features sculptures, fountains, and beautiful wind chimes, while the local artist-owned **Venture Gallery** (260 Alvarado St., 831/372-6279, www.venturegallery.com, 10am-6pm daily) offers all original paintings, sculptures, ceramics, pottery, and jewelry by Monterey artisans.

Recreation

Cruise the bay and observe local marinelife, from sea lions to otters to migrating whales, on a tour provided by a number of charter companies, like **Princess Monterey Whale Watching** (96 Fisherman's Wharf #1, 831/372-2203 and 831/205-2370, www.montereywhale-watching.com, $45), or go deep-sea fishing for albacore, halibut, or sea bass with **Randy's Fishing Trips** (Old Fisherman's Wharf, 831/372-7440 and 800/251-7440, www.randysfishingtrips.com, $80-300). **Monterey Bay Sailing** (831/372-7245, www.montereysailing.com) offers sailing cruises and rentals. Get on board the **Little Mermaid Glass Bottom Boat Tours** (831/372-7151, www.monterey-whalewatching.com) for a window seat into the sea.

Land lovers can hike the waterfront **Monterey Bay Coastal Recreation Trail,** an 18-mile paved adventure, from Castroville to Pacific Grove, which follows the same route as the old Southern Pacific Railway, connecting the Monterey Bay Aquarium, Cannery Row, the Museum of Monterey, and Fisherman's Wharf. Go by bike from **Blazing Saddles Bike Rentals & Tours** (750 Cannery Row, 831/776-9577, $8-39), which has a great selection of bicycles for a fun adventure for the whole family.

If the life of a grape from vine to bottle sounds more intriguing, **Ag Venture Tours** (831/761-8463, www.agventure-tours.com, $75-125) specializes in wine-tasting, sightseeing, and agricultural education tours. The tasting room at **California Boutique Wines** (241 Alvarado St., 831/641-9463, 11am-8pm Tues. and Fri.-Sat., 11am-6pm Mon. and Wed.-Thurs., $10 and up) lets you simply relax and sample wines from throughout California.

Events

Get inspired by the largest mammals of the sea at the annual **Whalefest Monterey** (1 Old Fisherman's Wharf, www.montereywharf.com, Oct.) and get acquainted with the wonderful work of Monterey Bay marine groups, including the Monterey Bay National Marine Sanctuary. Celebrate the past at the **History Fest** (831/655-2001, www.historicmonterey.org, early Oct., free), which showcases Monterey's role in California's early history with art and cultural activities at Monterey's historical locations, including Custom House Plaza, Historic Monterey, the Presidio of Monterey, the Royal Presidio Chapel, and Cannery Row. Tap your foot to the beat of the **Monterey Jazz Festival** (2004 Fairground Rd., www.montereyjazzfestival.org, Sept., $50-360), one of the oldest jazz fests around, showcasing over 500 artists performing on eight stages spread over 20 acres.

The best poets, performers, and artisans come together every winter for the three-day **Cowboy Poetry and Music Festival** (93 Via Encanto, 831/649-5080, www.montereycowboy.com, Nov., $10 and up), featuring a Western dance night, art sale, "cowboy" church service, and many other festivities.

An eclectic mix of competitive events in the water and on the shore at **Monterey Beach Sportsfest** (831/383-8520, www.montereybeachsf.com, free) happens every October to celebrate wellness of the sea with a beer garden, food, lots of beach fun, and exciting sport competitions.

Accommodations

Lodgings in Monterey can be expensive, as it's a popular vacation spot, especially for weekending San Franciscans.

Spectacular views come with every guest room at ★ **Seven Gables Inn** (555 Ocean View Blvd., 831/372-4341, www.sevengablesinn.com, $219-689), considered to be "One of the 10 Most Romantic Inns in America" by American Historic Inns. This boutique hotel features more than views: ornately lavished rooms, a complimentary full breakfast, afternoon wine and cheese, and the fragrant scent of surrounding gardens carried on the breeze.

The **Monterey Hostel** (778 Hawthorne St., 831/649-0375, http://montereyhostel. com, $28 bunks, $62 private rooms) offers inexpensive accommodations within walking distance of the major attractions of Monterey, but the dorm rooms can be pretty crowded.

A cute, small, budget motel, the **Monterey Bay Lodge** (55 Camino Aguajito, 831/372-8057, www.monterey-baylodge.com, $135) brings a bit of the Côte d'Azur to the equally beautiful coastal town of Monterey. With small rooms decorated in classic yellows and blues, the lodge makes a good base for the budget-minded when traveling in the Monterey region.

Upscale guest rooms at a reasonable price and all the comforts of home makes **Hotel Abrego** (755 Abrego St., 831/373-1602, www.reservations@innsofmonterey.com, $125) a convenient place to put your feet up. Around the corner, **Casa Munras Hotel & Spa** (700 Munras Ave., 831/375-2411, hotelcasamunras. com, $169 and up) pampers guests in this adobe hacienda once owned by a 19th-century Spanish don. Next to the bay on Cannery Row, **Monterey Plaza Hotel and Spa** (400 Cannery Row, 831/646-1700 and 800/334-3999, www.montereyplazahotel.com, $179 and up) combines elegant European architecture, dramatic coastal views, and refined style for a supremely memorable stay.

A waterfront resort, **Portola Hotel & Spa** (2 Portola Plaza, 866/711-1534, www. portolahotel.com, $200) is located in the center of shopping, dining, and outdoor activities in Old Monterey.

A historic boutique B&B, **Old Monterey Inn** (500 Martin St., 831/375-8284 and 800/350-2344, www.oldmontereyinn.com, $199-449) features lavish rooms and suites on an estate surrounded by lush English gardens. A National Landmark, the **Centrella Inn** (612 Central Ave., 831/372-3372, www.centrellainn. com, $205 and up) oozes Victorian romance and charm, enchanting guests with luxurious bedding, antique decor, and the natural beauty of the nearby seashore.

Information and Services
The **Monterey Visitors Center** (401 Camino El Estero, 800/555-6290 and 888/221-1010, www.seemonterey.com, 9am-5pm daily) provides local information, maps, and brochures.

Pacific Grove

Monarch butterflies settle in Pacific Grove after their annual migration south, earning it the nickname Butterfly Town, U.S.A. Each October, a new generation of monarch butterflies arrives, clustering in the local eucalyptus trees.

Sights
See the migrant butterflies at the **Monarch Grove Sanctuary** (250 Ridge Rd. btwn. Lighthouse Ave. and Short St., 831/648-5716, dawn-dusk daily, free). Sanctuary docents are on-site noon-3pm daily to assist with monarch viewing and answer questions about the butterflies. There's no fee to get in, but donations are appreciated.

To learn more about the monarch butterflies as well as the birds, wildlife, plants, and geology of the area, visit the **Pacific Grove Museum of Natural History** (165 Forest Ave., 831/648-5716, www.pgmuseum.org, 10am-5pm Tues.-Sun., $9 adults, $6 children 4-18).

Pacific Grove is the site of the oldest continuously operating lighthouse on the West Coast: **Point Pinos Lighthouse** (80 Asilomar Ave., 831/648-3176, www.point-pinoslighthouse.org, 1pm-4pm Thurs.-Mon., $2 adults, $1 children).

A community gallery, **Pacific Grove**

Art Center (568 Lighthouse Ave., 831/375-2208, www.pgartcenter.org, noon-5pm Mon.-Sat., 1pm-4pm Sun., free) works to enhance art appreciation and encourage creative thinking, housing a large variety of art forms and exhibits.

Food and Accommodations

Pacific Grove's small-town feel extends to its eateries. A local favorite is **Peppers Mexicali Cafe** (170 Forest Ave., 831/373-6892, www.pepperspg.com, 11:30am-9pm Mon. and Wed.-Thurs., 11:30am-10pm Fri.-Sat., 4pm-9pm Sun., $13-18), where you'll see workers on their lunch breaks enjoying the fajitas and other south-of-the-border fare.

The Fishwife (1996 1/2 Sunset Dr., 831/375-7107, www.fishwife.com, 11am-9:30pm daily, $12-23) serves seafood for lunch and dinner.

Unassuming Pacific Grove has one landmark place to stay: **Asilomar** (800 Asilomar Blvd., 831/372-8016 or 888/635-5310, www.visitasilomar.com, $130-165), which was designed by architect Julia Morgan.

⟐ 17-Mile Drive

Hugging the coastline between Pacific Grove and Pebble Beach, **17-Mile Drive** ($9.50/vehicle, cash only, no motorcycles) offers an introduction to some of the most beautiful and representative land and seascapes on the Central Coast. But don't get too excited yet—long ago, the locally all-powerful Pebble Beach Corporation realized what a precious commodity they held in this road and began charging a toll. The good news is that when you pay your fee at the gatehouse, you'll get a map of the drive that describes the parks and sights that you will pass as you make your way along the winding coastal road. These include the much-photographed Lone Cypress,

the beaches of Spanish Bay, and Pebble Beach's golf course and resort. Stop at the many turnouts to take photos of the stunning ocean and the iconic cypress trees. You can picnic at many of the formal beaches, most of which have basic restroom facilities and ample parking lots. The only food and gas to be had are at the Inn at Spanish Bay and the Lodge at Pebble Beach. If you're in a hurry, you can get from one end of the 17-Mile Drive to the other in 20 minutes, but that would defeat the main purpose of taking 17-Mile Drive, which is to go slowly and stop often to enjoy the beauty of the area.

There are five entrance gates to 17-Mile Drive where you can pay the toll and receive the brochure (listed from north to south): **Pacific Grove Gate** (17-Mile Drive just past CA-68), **Country Club Gate** (Forest Lodge Rd. at Congress Ave.), **S.F.B. Morse Gate** (Morse Dr. at CA-68), **Highway 1 Gate** (17-Mile Drive at junction of CA-1 and CA-68), and **Carmel Gate** (N. San Antonio Dr. at 2nd Ave.).

Carmel

It's not unusual to find English cottages, Spanish motifs, and other European accents in this adorable village perched on the cliffs above the Pacific. It's worth a stop just to walk the cottage-lined streets and meander in and out of its art galleries (the highest number per capita in the United States). Carmel is also dog lover's central: Many hotels, shops, and even some restaurants allow them inside. It's worth staying longer to explore the golf courses and beach parks that surround the town.

Getting There and Around

CA-1 provides access to Carmel south from Monterey or north from Big Sur.

Amtrak (www.amtrak.com) runs a bus service to Carmel with stops to and

⚑ Side Trip to Pinnacles National Park

A 23-million-year-old geological phenomenon spewed into existence by a volcanic eruption that occurred 195 miles south in Southern California, **Pinnacles National Park** lies along the San Andreas Fault. Debris and erosion have formed the massive pillars and walls over time, but this majestic mountain's crowning glory is its two talus caves, composed from the large boulders that have fallen down into random piles.

The park was designated in January 2013, and hosts several healthy populations of smaller animals including bobcats, bats, the endangered California condor, and the highest bee variety in the world. Miles of hiking trails traverse the edges of an abundance of diverse habitat, offering ample wildlife viewing. Hike to Balconies Cave (9.4 miles round-trip) via Chalone Creek on the Bench and Old Pinnacles trails where you can explore the cave (a flashlight is required) and marvel at the views of the largest rock formations in the park. Or, opt for the shorter Balconies Cliffs-Cave Loop (a flashlight is required), which, after crossing up to Balconies Cave, heads down to the Old Pinnacles trail and through the cave. You may get wet, as wading may be necessary during winter months.

Other features of the park include Bear Gulch Cave, which is closed mid-May through mid-July to protect the park's colony of bats as they raise their young. The **campground** (reservations 877/444-6777, www.recreation. gov, $23 tents, $36 RVs) is located near the east entrance and is open to tents and RVs. It is outfitted with picnic tables, electrical hookups, water, showers, bathrooms, a swimming pool (Apr.-Sept.), and a **store** (831/389-4538, 3pm-5pm Sun.-Thurs., 2pm-5pm Fri., 10am-4pm Sat.).

There are two entrances to the park, one to the west off US-101 at Soledad and the other to the east on CA-146.

The **Pinnacles National Park Visitor Center** (5000 CA-146, 831/389-4485, www.nps.gov/pinn/planyourvisit, 9am-5pm daily, $10 parking fee) provides information on ranger-led programs, hiking trails, and rock-climbing routes, and it has several displays on the geologic history of the region.

from Monterey, as well as the Coast Starlight train, which provides coastline service.

The closest airline is **Monterey Peninsula Airport** (200 Fred Kane Dr., 831/648-7000, www.montereyairport. com), which provides flights from San Francisco, Los Angeles, Phoenix, Denver, and Salt Lake City, via United, American, US Airways, and Allegiant Air.

Carmel and its surrounding beaches are easily explored on foot. There is usually two-hour free parking. Bicycling is available, with visitors being reminded of the winding roads consisting of little to no shoulder space.

Local transit service is provided by **Monterey-Salinas Transit** (888/678-2871, mst.org) between Carmel and Monterey.

Sights

The **Carmel Mission** (3080 Rio Rd., 831/624-1271, 9:30am-5pm Mon.-Sat., 10:30am-5pm Sun., $6.50 adults, $2 children), just west of CA-1, a mile south of central Carmel, is considered the most beautiful mission of the 21 California missions. Formally named Mission San Carlos Borroméo del río Carmelhe, it served as home, headquarters, and final resting place of Father Junípero Serra, the Franciscan priest who founded the 21 California missions. Today, he is entombed under the chapel floor, southeast of the altar; the site is marked with an inscription. Explore the mission and museums, which house exhibits and displays of Spanish colonial liturgical art and artifacts, the elaborate travertine marble and bronze Serra memorial cenotaph, and a Native American cemetery. Plan to dress conservatively as Catholic Masses occur regularly. The gardens—where on weekends wedding parties alight from limos to take family photos—are beautiful, as is the facade with its photogenic bell tower. This is the mission to visit if you visit only one.

The famous stone home of poet Robinson Jeffers, the **Tor House** (26304 Ocean View Ave., 831/624-1840, tours 10am-3pm Fri.-Sat., $10) is the abode where Jeffers wrote all his most beloved poetical works, *The Women at Point Sur, Medea,* and others. Jeffers, who lived here between 1914 and 1962, built much of what you see here out of boulders he hauled up by hand from the beach. Both the house and the tower, known as Hawk Tower, reflect the genius of the man whose ashes were spread with his wife's beneath a nearby yew tree.

Created by the artist Jim Needham, **Gravity Garden** (97 Corona Rd., 831/625-3099, open daily, free) is an intriguing garden of sculpture rock, some stacked up to nine feet, without the use of supporting structures or bolts.

Food

Perfect dishes have attracted visitors and locals to ★ **The Forge in the Forest** (Junipero St. and 5th Ave., 831/624-2233, 11:30am-11pm daily, $14-34) for decades. The menu is overwhelming. Don't miss out on the stuffed portabello with crab, rosemary and Cajun spices, the lobster linguini with tarragon, or award-winning clam chowder.

For the best breakfast in town, **Em Le's Old Carmel Restaurant** (Dolores between 5th and 6th Aves., 831/625-6780, 7am-3pm Mon.-Tues., 7am-3pm and 4:30pm-8pm Wed.-Sun., under $15) is famous for their French toast and extensive breakfast menu, and don't miss out on great lunch and dinner options.

Breakfast at **Katy's Place** (Mission and 6th Aves., 831/624-0199, www.

katysplacecarmel.com, 7am-2pm daily, $12-22), a self-described "Carmel tradition" that can get quite crowded on weekend mornings. With a range of menu options, you're sure to find your favorite, whether you love heavy eggs Benedict or light Belgian waffles.

For a rare hole-in-the-wall locals' dining experience, seek out **Tommy's Wok** (Mission St. and Ocean Ave., 831/624-8518, www.tommyswokcarmel.com, 11:30am-2:30pm and 4:30pm-9:30pm Tues.-Sun., $10-20). All the veggies are fresh and organic, and the dishes taste reliably good whether you dine in or order takeout to enjoy elsewhere.

If you're just looking for a good burger, **R.G. Burgers** (201 Crossroads Shopping Village, 831/626-8054, www.rgburgers.com, 11am-8:30pm daily, under $13) is the best. Their shakes and sandwiches aren't bad either! For pizza with a perfect crust, **Allegro Gourmet Pizzeria** (Barnyard Shopping Village, 3770 The Barnyard, 831/626-5454, 11am-9pm daily, $15) offers fabulous gourmet pizza and a wide selection of classic Italian entrées.

For Mediterranean-inspired cuisine, dine at **Cafe Stravaganza** (241 Crossroads Blvd., 831/625-3733, www.thecrossroadscarmel.com, 8am-9pm daily, under $25), which serves generous portions and gourmet pizza you can't resist! Stylish and romantic, **PortaBella** (Ocean Ave., 831/624-4395, 11:30am-11pm daily, $16-36) has an undeniable ambience and fantastic dishes inspired by the Mediterranean countryside.

Nightlife

Carmel has a few traditional bars and pubs along with its handful of wine and cocktail bars.

Sade's (Lincoln St. btwn. Ocean and 7th Aves., 831/624-0787, 11am-2am daily) offers cocktails in a casual, friendly atmosphere. Located inside the Cypress Inn, **Terry's Lounge** (7th Ave. and Lincoln St., 831/624-3871,

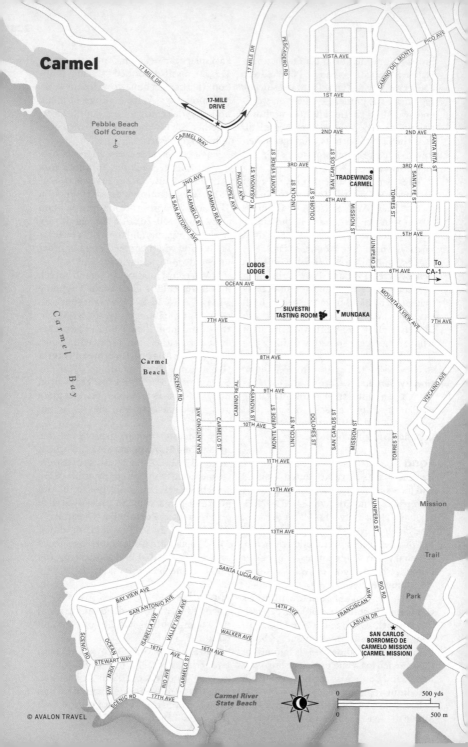

Carmel

17 MILE DR

17 MILE DR

17-MILE DRIVE

Pebble Beach Golf Course

CARMEL WAY

PESCADERO RD

VISTA AVE

PICO AVE

CAMINO DEL MONTE

1ST AVE

2ND AVE

2ND AVE

SANTA RITA ST

2ND AVE

N CARMELO ST

N CAMINO REAL

PALOU AVE

LOPEZ AVE

N CASANOVA ST

MONTE VERDE ST

3RD AVE

3RD AVE

SANTA FE ST

LINCOLN ST

DOLORES ST

SAN CARLOS ST

TRADEWINDS CARMEL

4TH AVE

TORRES ST

N SAN ANTONIO AVE

MISSION ST

JUNIPERO ST

5TH AVE

6TH AVE

To CA-1

LOBOS LODGE

OCEAN AVE

SILVESTRI TASTING ROOM

▼ **MUNDAKA**

MOUNTAIN VIEW AVE

7TH AVE

7TH AVE

7TH AVE

C a r m e l   B a y

8TH AVE

VIZCAINO AVE

Carmel Beach

SCENIC RD

CAMINO REAL

CASANOVA ST

9TH AVE

10TH AVE

MONTE VERDE ST

LINCOLN ST

DOLORES ST

SAN CARLOS ST

MISSION ST

TORRES ST

SAN ANTONIO AVE

CARMELO ST

11TH AVE

12TH AVE

JUNIPERO ST

13TH AVE

Mission

SANTA LUCIA AVE

Trail

BAY VIEW AVE

SAN ANTONIO AVE

VALLEY VIEW AVE

14TH AVE

FRANCISCAN WAY

RIO RD

Park

ISABELLA AVE

WALKER AVE

LASUEN DR

SCENIC RD

OCEAN VIEW AVE

16TH AVE

RIO AVE

CARMELO ST

16TH AVE

SAN CARLOS BORROMEO DE CARMELO MISSION (CARMEL MISSION)

STEWART WAY

SCENIC RD

17TH AVE

Carmel River State Beach

0   500 yds

0   500 m

© AVALON TRAVEL

11am-midnight daily) is a relaxing venue for drinks and live music. Referred to as one of Carmel's "Hidden Gems" by *Monterey Peninsula*, **Brophy's Tavern** (San Carlos St., 831/624-2476, www.brophystavern.com, noon-midnight Mon.-Sat.) offers a pub menu, which includes their popular Philly cheesesteak, beer, and drink specials.

For exceptional margaritas and a festive atmosphere, stop by **Baja Cantina & Grill** (7166 Carmel Valley Rd., 831/625-2252, 11:30am-midnight daily) and have a cocktail on their heated patio, or grab a beer and watch a sporting event. **Andre's Bouchee Bistro and Wine Bar** (Mission St., 831/626-7880, wine bar opens at 4:30pm daily) is a chic French restaurant that features a nice little wine bar with an exceptional selection. **Mundaka** (7th Ave. and San Carlos St., 831/624-7400, 5pm-10pm Sun. and Mon.-Thurs., 5pm-10:30pm Fri.-Sat.) offers wine, music, and Spanish-style tapas.

With over-sized chairs, a mahogany bar, and two large flat-screen TVs, **Fuse Lounge** (3665 Rio Rd., 831/624-1841, open daily) is a fusion of sophistication and casual ambience, featuring specialty cocktails, wine, and great live music.

Shopping

Carmel Plaza (Ocean Ave. and Mission St., 831/624-1385, http://carmelplaza.com, 10am-6pm Mon.-Sat., 11am-5pm Sun.) is a shopping must for elegant and fashionable items. A boutique with a Euro flare, **Pamplemousse** (Ocean Ave. btwn. Mission and San Carlos Sts., 831/624-1259, www.pamplemousseboutique.com, 10am-6pm Mon.-Sat., 11am-5pm Sun.) is an elegant find, offering contemporary clothing, accessories, and jewelry. **The Club** (Ocean Ave. btwn. San Carlos and Dolores Sts., 831/625-1645, www.theclubcarmel.com, 10am-6pm Mon.-Sat., 11am-5pm Sun.) is a premier designer clothing and accessories boutique. For the finest cashmere,

Carmel Cashmere & Co. (San Carlos St. and 6th Ave., 888/237-1581, www.carmelcashmere.com, 10am-6pm Mon.-Sat., 11am-5pm Sun.) sells the purest, high-quality cashmere in fashion and blankets. If your four-legged best buddy needs some new duds or a new toy for the beach, hop to **Diggidy Dog** (Mission St. btwn. Ocean and 7th Aves., 831/625-1585, www.diggidydog.com, 10am-6pm Mon.-Sat., 11am-5pm Sun.).

Exquisitely unique, the **Cayen Collection** (NW Mission St., btwn. 5th and 6th Aves., 831/626-2722, www.cayenjewelers.com, 10am-6pm Mon.-Sat., 11am-5pm Sun.) will make you want to drape yourself in jewels. There is just too much beauty in this one shop.

The Cheese Shop (Ocean Ave. and Mission St., Carmel Plaza, 831/625-2272, www.thecheeseshopinc.com, 10am-6pm Mon.-Sat., 11am-5pm Sun.) is filled with every deliciously cheesy gourmet treat and sophisticated wine imaginable.

Ooh and aah your way through **Conway of Asia** (Dolores btwn. Ocean and 7th Aves., 831/624-3643, www.conwayofasia.com, 10am-6pm Mon.-Sat., 11am-5pm Sun.), a world imports shop filled with beautiful antiques and contemporary Hindu, Buddhist, and Christian statuary, paintings, artifacts, furniture, carpets, and architectural antiquities.

Beaches

Friendly pets can run free along the 1.5 miles of **Carmel Beach** (bottom of Ocean Ave.). The **Scenic Bluff Path** follows along Scenic Road above Carmel Beach, which begins at 8th Avenue and meanders through rare Monterey cypress and landscaped gardens to Carmel Point, offering spectacular views of the rugged coastline. **Carmel River State Beach** offers bird-watchers the perfect opportunity to observe feathery residents at Carmel River Lagoon. Just north of Point Lobos, **Monastery Beach** is a popular diving area.

Events

The Annual **Carmel Mission Fiesta** (Carmel Mission Courtyard, Rio Rd. and Lasuen Dr., 831/624-8322, fall, free) celebrates the tradition of community with Mexican food, live music, and handmade arts and crafts.

From mermaids to castles and everything imaginable, Carmel's **Sand Castle Contest** (south of 10th Ave., 831/620-2020, Sept./Oct.) is an amazing event that takes over the shore each fall.

Accommodations

Accommodations in Carmel tend toward the quaint or luxurious.

Egyptian cotton linens, luxurious goose down feather beds, silk pillows, spa tubs, Japanese tansu wet bars and vanities, and antique and custom designed furniture from Bali and China are just a few reasons why ★ **Tradewinds Carmel** (Mission St. at 3rd Ave., 831/624-2776, www. tradewindscarmel.com, $250 and up) has been called one of the most glamorous hotels in *Architectural Digest* and voted as one of the world's top inns by *Coastal Living*, but isn't it better to experience the best for yourself?

Lobos Lodge (Monte Verde and Ocean Aves., 831/624-3874, www.loboslodge. com, $175-345) sits right in the midst of downtown Carmel-by-the-Sea, making it a perfect spot from which to dine, shop, and admire the endless array of art in this upscale town. Each of the 30 rooms and suites offers a gas fireplace, a sofa and table, a bed in an alcove, and enough space to stroll about and enjoy the quiet romantic setting. Do be aware that Lobos Lodge bills itself as an adult retreat. While families with children can stay here, expect to pay extra for more than two guests in your room, and there is little in the way of child-friendly amenities.

The historic **Pine Inn** (Ocean and Monte Verde Aves., 831/624-3851, www. pineinn.com, $179 and up) offers elegant,

Point Lobos State Reserve

boutique accommodations in downtown within walking distance to the ocean.

A pet-friendly B&B, **Carmel Country Inn** (Dolores St., 831/625-3263 and 800/215-6343, www.carmelcountryinn.com, $195-425) features intimate studios and large suites with luxury baths, and a daily breakfast buffet.

An exquisite mansion built in 1905, **La Playa Carmel** (8th Ave. and Camino Real, 831/624-6476 and 800/582-8900, www.laplayahotel.com, $317-678) offers a historic experience of elegant gardens and intimate patios and courtyards just steps from Carmel Beach.

A resort of splendor set among acres of bountiful beauty, **Carmel Valley Ranch** (1 Old Ranch Rd., 866/282-4745, www.carmelvalleyranch.com, $464-1,164) indulges guests with a cozy in-room fireplace, breakfast in bed, hot tubs throughout the property, an 18-hole golf course, access to hundreds of miles of hiking trails, mountain-top yoga, and so much more.

Information and Services

The **Carmel Chamber of Commerce & Visitor Center** (San Carlos btwn. 5th and 6th Aves., 831/624-2522 and 800/550-4333, 10am-5pm daily) is the best resource for local visitor information.

Point Lobos State Reserve

Three miles south of Carmel-by-the-Sea, **Point Lobos State Reserve** (CA-1, 831/624-4909, www.parks.ca.gov, 8am-sunset or 7pm, whichever is earlier, daily, $10 per car) is known as one of the most beautiful parks in the state park system, offering hikes through forestland and along the beach, scuba diving (831/624-8413) off the shore, picnic spots, and nature study. The dramatic scenery, resident marine and shore life, and one of the last groves of Monterey cypress in existence are just a few of the natural attractions here. Take a walk through unique ecosystems and observe the indigenous wildlife while strolling through the rugged landscape. Binoculars will help you see creatures offshore (such as otters!).

A small whaling cabin, first used by Portuguese whalers from the Azore Islands in 1861, is located at the southeast end of Whalers Cove. When whaling oil dropped in the 1880s due to kerosene lamps, the local industry dwindled but was briefly revived in 1897 when a Japanese company moved in; that operation lasted only a few years. The cabin is now the **Whalers Cabin Museum** (831/624-4909, 9am-5pm daily), which houses documents and equipment as well as old try pots used to boil whale blubber and the skeletal fragments of a 100-year-old fin whale.

Limits on the number of visitors in the park means that there may be a line to get in. Try to arrive early to avoid the wait. Be aware that from July through September fog often dims the summer sun at Point

Lobos, even midday. Spring and fall are the best times to visit, weather-wise.

Big Sur

Big Sur contains boundless wildernesses and 90 miles of staggeringly beautiful coastline. CA-1 twists around mountains and clings to rocky cliffs as it navigates the rugged coast between Carmel and San Simeon. The natural scenery and breathtaking vistas make this stretch one of the highlights of the entire Pacific Coast Highway.

Practicalities

The Big Sur region is sparsely populated and can feel remote. Less than 300 hotel rooms exist here, only three gas stations, and no supermarkets or fast-food restaurants. There is essentially one road in and one road out: CA-1 (California State Route 1, also known as Highway 1). The highway can be treacherous due to its winding character, but especially when fog sets in and visibility drops.

The biggest concentration of travel necessities, such as lodging, food, and gas, is in the town of Big Sur, about 25 miles south of Carmel. Otherwise, places to rest and fill up are few and far between until you reach Cambria.

Most options for food are provided by hotels and resorts, and many close by 9pm. Prices can be quite high for what you get (you won't find cheap here).

Accommodations are limited for an area that draws an estimated 3 million visitors each year, which explains the high room rates. There is little to no cell phone reception, and in some cases, no television network providers. **Big Sur Campground and Cabins** offers a wide range of camping options that put you right on the Big Sur River. There is no shortage of things to do, and the **Big Sur Chamber of Commerce** (47500 CA-1, 831/667-2100, www.bigsurcalifornia.

org, 9am-1pm Mon., Wed., and Fri.) has everything needed to help you decide.

Getting There and Around

Big Sur is a remote area accessible only by CA-1 via US-101 South to CA-156 West to CA-1; and US-101 North to CA-1. The easiest way to get there is by car, but gas stations are scarce (and expensive), so remember to fill up before entering the Big Sur region.

Monterey-Salinas Transit (888/678-2871, mst.org) route 22 bus runs from downtown Monterey to Nepenthe in Big Sur, and stops at several area state parks. Or take the convenient **Central Coast Day Tripper** (831/657-9442 and 831/241-2526), which runs along the Big Sur and Monterey Peninsula.

Bicycling CA-1 is common but can be dangerous due to the many turns and lack of shoulder space.

The nearest airport, **Monterey Regional Airport** (200 Fred Kane Dr. #200, 831/648-7000, www.montereyairport.com), is about 30 miles away.

Food

Most food choices are located inside resorts, hotels, and inns. Reservations are pretty much the norm or at least a necessity during peak season, and many places stop seating by 9pm.

★ **Nepenthe** (48510 CA-1, 831/667-2345, www.nepenthebigsur.com, 11am-10pm daily, $15-46) offers a short but tasty menu of meats, fish, and plenty of vegetarian dishes, but the real feast is the sweeping view—be sure to ask for a table outdoors. Located below Nepenthe, the seasonal **Cafe Kevah** (48510 CA-1, 831/667-2344, 10am-11pm Mon.-Fri., 11am-11pm Sat.-Sun., $8-18) offers a similar sampling of food at slightly lower prices. The view of the Pacific steals the show here, too.

Big Sur has some good breakfast spots. **Big Sur Bakery & Restaurant** (47540 CA-1, 831/667-0520, www.bigsurbakery.com, 8am-9pm daily, under $26) offers all

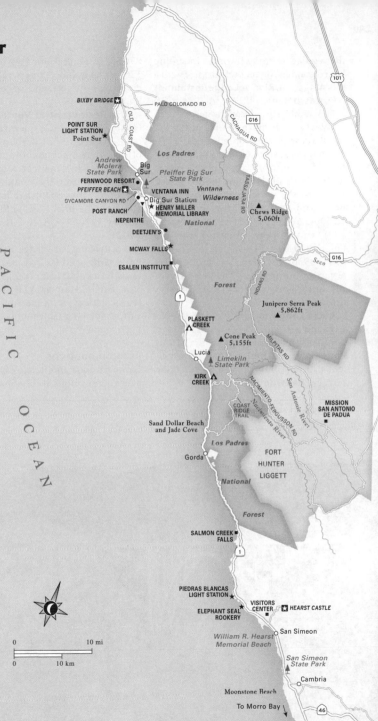

Big Sur

BIXBY BRIDGE ★
PALO COLORADO RD

POINT SUR
LIGHT STATION ★
Point Sur

Andrew
Molera
State Park

Big
Sur

Pfeiffer Big Sur
State Park

FERNWOOD RESORT ●
PFEIFFER BEACH ✚
SYCAMORE CANYON RD
Ventana Inn
Big Sur Station

POST RANCH ★ HENRY MILLER
NEPENTHE MEMORIAL LIBRARY

Ventana
Wilderness

DEETJEN'S ●

MCWAY FALLS ●

ESALEN INSTITUTE ■

Los Padres

National

Forest

Chews Ridge
5,060ft ▲

Junipero Serra Peak
5,862ft ▲

PLASKETT
CREEK △

Cone Peak
5,155ft ▲

Lucia ●
Limekiln
State Park

KIRK
CREEK △

COAST
RIDGE
TRAIL

Sand Dollar Beach
and Jade Cove

Los Padres

Gorda ●

FORT
HUNTER
LIGGETT

MISSION
SAN ANTONIO
DE PADUA ■

National

Forest

SALMON CREEK ■
FALLS

PIEDRAS BLANCAS
LIGHT STATION ★

VISITORS
CENTER ■ ✚ *HEARST CASTLE*

ELEPHANT SEAL
ROOKERY

San Simeon ●

William R. Hearst
Memorial Beach

San Simeon
State Park

Cambria ●

Moonstone Beach

To Morro Bay ↓

PACIFIC OCEAN

OLD COAST RD
CACHAGUA RD
TASSAJARA RD
INDIANS RD
MILPITAS RD
NACIMIENTO-FERGUSSON RD
San Antonio River
Nacimiento River
Seco

101
G16
G16
1
46

0   10 mi
0   10 km

© AVALON TRAVEL

the regular morning favorites including baked goodies. If you prefer a view with a morning meal, **Big Sur Lodge Restaurant & Espresso House** (47225 CA-1, 831/667-3111, www.bigsurlodge.com, 8am-9:30pm daily, $11-32) is on the banks of the Big Sur River with views of redwoods.

On the east side of the highway, one of the oldest and most atmospheric places is **Deetjen's Big Sur Inn** (48865 CA-1, 831/667-2377, www.deetjens.com, 8am-noon and 6pm-9pm Mon.-Fri., 8am-12:30pm and 6pm-9pm Sat.-Sun., under $43), a rambling and rustic redwood lodge built by a Norwegian immigrant in the 1930s and now a nonprofit, preservationist operation. Deetjen's serves Big Sur's best breakfasts and hearty dinners.

Lucia Lodge (62400 CA-1, 831/667-2391 and 866/424-4787, www.lucialodge.com, 11am-8pm Mon.-Fri., 11am-9pm Sat.-Sun., under $26) has excellent fish-and-chips. If you want a good burger, **Redwood Grill** (47200 CA-1, 831/667-2129, 11:30am-9pm daily, under $26) serves buffalo burgers, salmon burgers, veggie burgers, and, of course, beefy burgers.

The Restaurant at Ventana (48123 CA-1, 831/667-2331, www.ventanainn.com, 11:30am-9pm daily, under $48) offers a nice lunch and dinner menu of contemporary American food and gorgeous vistas from their outdoor terrace. For lunch with a Spanish flair and served at affordable prices, eat at **Ripplewood Resort** (47047 CA-1, 831/667-2242, $5-12).

North of Big Sur Village, the **Fernwood Bar & Grill** (47200 CA-1, 831/667-2422, www.fernwoodbigsur.com, 11am-11pm Sun.-Thurs., 11am-1am Fri.-Sat., $10-25) is a local hangout for meeting friends for a drink, playing table tennis, and listening to good music.

Accommodations
Campgrounds and hotel/resorts are the overnight options in Big Sur. Many do

Bixby Bridge

not have cell phone service, and reservations are required.

Just south of Lucia and Limekiln State Parks, **Kirk Creek Campground** (CA-1, 805/434-1996 and 877/444-6777, www.fs.usda.gov, $25 per night) is a reservation-only campsite located in Los Padres National Forest, offering campsites right on a bluff overlooking the ocean. Trails lead down to the dog-friendly beach, bluffs that overlook the beach, and coves in the area. Cross the highway from the campground to access the Vicente Flats Trailhead, which leads into the Ventana Wilderness. There are bathrooms but no running water. **Big Sur Campground and Cabins** (47000 CA-1, 831/667-2322, $50-65 tents, $120-165 tent cabins, $180-415 cabins) give you a choice between campsites, tent-cabins, or rustic cabins, in a quiet setting along the Big Sur River, which offers swimming, inner-tubing, or just drifting with the gentle flow.

Big Sur River Inn (46840 CA-1, 831/667-2700 and 800/548-3610, $125-270) offers

20 cabin-style guest rooms, a full-service restaurant, and a heated pool. About a mile south of Big Sur River Inn, **Fernwood Resort** (CA-1, 831/667-2422, www.fernwoodbigsur.com, $135-180) includes a 12-room motel, a small grocery-cum-convenience store, a restaurant, and a tavern that is, relatively speaking, the local nighttime hot spot. Farther down the small road, you'll find the campgrounds, which include a number of tent cabins as well as tent and RV sites.

Deetjens Big Sur Inn (48865 CA-1, 831/667-2377, www.deetjens.com, $100-270) is a rustic inn set among beautiful gardens, the redwoods, and the Castro Canyon waterfall. Overlooking the Pacific Ocean, **Ventana Inn & Spa** (48123 CA-1, 831/667-2331 and 800/628-6500, $550 and up) is a luxurious resort offering suites, villas, and cottages with everything you'll need to feel pampered, including pools, hot tubs, sauna, restaurant and bar, and stunning scenery.

Information and Services
Big Sur Chamber of Commerce (47500 CA-1, 831/667-2100, www.bigsurcalifornia.org, 9am-1pm Mon., Wed., and Fri.) provides local area information and travel brochures. For outdoor recreational information, **Big Sur Ranger Station** (47555 CA-1, 831/667-2315, 9am-4pm daily) offers maps, important area information, and services.

Check out **CalTrans** weather reports by calling the free hotline (888/836-0866), especially to avoid getting caught driving in morning fog.

Be aware that cell service is not reliable along the remote area of the coast. Gasoline is also limited, and those few stations that operate along the highway can be extremely expensive.

Garrapata State Park
Just off CA-1, seven miles south of Carmel, **Garrapata State Park** often goes unnoticed. It is marked with a single sign on the west side of the road and features

two miles of pristine coastline, colorfully diverse flora and fauna, and trails that run from the beaches and into groves of redwood. The Rocky Ridge Trail offers commanding views of the Pacific and Santa Lucia Mountains, as well as views of sea lions, sea otters, and gray whales.

The area was once the home of the Ohlone and Rumsien tribes and then became the residence of cows and sheep owned by Ezequiel Soberanes in the early 1900s, and later the Doud family. These names still live on within the park in Soberanes Point and Doud River.

★ Bixby Bridge

Eleven miles north of Big Sur Village, **Bixby Bridge** is an iconic landmark, spanning 713 feet in length. Like many bridges along CA-1, Bixby Bridge is a single-span concrete deck arch design, but it is considered one of the highest in the world. Concrete was chosen instead of steel because it was not only cheaper and reduced maintenance costs, but the

fact that concrete blended with the color and composition of the natural rock cliff made it all the more desirable.

Construction began in 1931; its many laborers were prisoners hoping to shave some time off their sentences. It was completed a year later.

Today the bridge is considered one of the most photographed due to its attractive design and, of course, its location. You can snap a photo from the north side of the bridge at the pull-off.

Andrew Molera State Park

The first "Big Sur" park you'll encounter is **Andrew Molera State Park** (CA-1, 20 miles south of Carmel, 831/667-2315, www.parks.ca.gov, day-use $10). Once home to small camps of Esselen Native Americans, then a Spanish land grant, this chunk of Big Sur eventually became the Molera ranch. Today, the **Molera Ranch House Museum** (831/667-2956, http://bigsurhistory.org/museum.html, 11am-3pm Thurs.-Sun.

Keyhole Arch on Big Sur's Pfeiffer Beach

mid-June-Labor Day) displays stories of the life and times of Big Sur's human pioneers and artists as well as the wildlife and plants of the region. Take the road toward the horse tours to get to the ranch house.

The park has numerous hiking trails that run down to the beach and up into the forest along the river; many of these are open to biking and horseback riding as well. Most of the park trails lie to the west of the highway. The beach is a one-mile walk down the easy, multi-use **Trail Camp Beach Trail.** From there, climb on the **Headlands Trail,** a 0.25-mile loop, for a beautiful view from the headlands. To get a better look at the Big Sur River, take the flat, moderate **Bobcat Trail** (5.5 miles round-trip) and perhaps a few of its ancillary loops. You'll walk right along the riverbanks, enjoying the local microhabitats. Just be sure to look out for bicycles and the occasional horse and rider. For an even longer and more difficult trek up the mountains and down to the beach, take

the eight-mile **Ridge Bluff Loop.** You'll start at the parking lot on the Creamery Meadow Beach Trail, then make a left onto the long and fairly steep Ridge Trail to get a sense of the local ecosystem. Then turn left again onto the Panorama Trail, which runs down to the coastal scrublands, and finally out to the Bluffs Trail, which takes you back to Creamery Meadow.

At the park entrance, you'll find bathrooms but no drinkable water and no food concessions. If you're camping here, be sure to bring plenty of your own water for washing dishes as well as drinking. If you're hiking for the day, pack in bottled water and snacks.

Pfeiffer Big Sur State Park

The biggest, most developed park in Big Sur is **Pfeiffer Big Sur State Park** (47225 CA-1, 26 miles south of Carmel, 831/667-2315, www.parks.ca.gov, day-use $10). It's got the Big Sur Lodge, a restaurant and café, a shop, an amphitheater, a softball field, plenty of hiking-only trails, and lovely redwood-shaded campsites. This park isn't situated by the beach; it's up in the coastal redwoods forest, with a network of roads that can be driven or biked up into the trees and along the Big Sur River.

Pfeiffer Big Sur contains **Homestead Cabin,** once the home of part of the Pfeiffer family, the first European immigrants to settle in Big Sur. Day-trippers and overnight visitors can take a stroll through the cabins of the Big Sur Lodge, built by the Civilian Conservation Corps during the Great Depression.

For a starter walk, take the easy 0.7-mile **Nature Trail** in a loop from Day Use Parking Lot 2. Grab a brochure at the lodge to learn about the park's plant life as you walk the trail. For a longer stroll, head out on the popular **Pfeiffer Falls Trail** (1.5 miles round-trip). You'll find stairs on the steep sections and footbridges across the creek, then a lovely platform at the base of the

60-foot waterfall, where you can rest and relax midway through your hike. For a longer, more difficult, and interesting hike deeper into the Big Sur wilderness, start at the Homestead Cabin and head to the **Mount Manuel Trail** (10 miles round-trip, difficult). From the Y-intersection with the Oak Grove Trail, it's four miles of sturdy hiking to Mount Manuel, one of the most spectacular peaks in the area.

This is one of the few Big Sur parks to offer a full array of services. Before you head out into the woods, stop at the Big Sur Lodge restaurant and store complex to get a meal and some water, and to load up on snacks and sweatshirts. Between the towering trees and the summer fogs, it can get quite chilly and somewhat damp on the trails.

★ Pfeiffer Beach

Some of the most dramatic views in Big Sur are seen at **Pfeiffer Beach** (accessed via Sycamore Canyon Rd., about 0.25 mile south of Big Sur), one of the most photographed spots, especially at sunset.

The stunning brilliance of **Keyhole Arch** at Pfeiffer Beach possesses a mystical power that captures the imaginations of those that see it. Professional and amateur photographers from all over the world try time and again to preserve the piercing beam of glory that radiates the cavern void, like a small door opening to heaven, just before the setting sun in the weeks surrounding winter solstice. The arch measures 20 feet by 20 feet and was not formed by human hands but by nature. The conditions for the awe-inspiring event are dependent on the sun's positioning directly behind the opening, a clear sky, and when the tide has aligned to a high enough position to reflect the natural light of ocean waters.

Hidden on an isolated stretch of CA-1 in Big Sur, and down an unmarked one-lane road (Sycamore Canyon Rd.), Pfeiffer Beach is not the easiest to find, but you'll kick yourself later if you miss

McWay Falls at Julia Pfeiffer Burns State Park

out on its impressive rock formations, sea caverns, and unusual purple sands, and most assuredly if you pass on the opportune moment to witness the natural phenomenon at Keyhole Arch.

Post Ranch Inn and Ventana

Two luxury properties sit essentially across the street from one another at the south end of Big Sur. ★ **Post Ranch Inn** (47900 CA-1, 800/527-2200, www.post-ranchinn.com, $825-1,225) is perched on the cliffs of Big Sur on the west side of CA-1. The unique design of the resort makes the structures seem like they are a part of the natural landscape, flowing around the curves, rather than leveling them off. Spa, yoga, and a rustic atmosphere are just a few of its perks.

On the other side of CA-1, **Ventana** (48123 CA-1, 831/667-2331 or 800/628-6500, www.ventanainn.com, $600-2,450) is a place where the panoramic ocean views begin in the parking lot. Picture home-baked pastries, fresh yogurt,

in-season fruit, and organic coffee delivered to your room in the morning, then imagine enjoying that sumptuous breakfast outdoors on your own private patio overlooking a wildflower-strewn meadow that sweeps out toward the blue-gray waters of the ocean. And that's just the beginning of an unbelievable day at the Ventana.

The guest rooms range from the "modest" standard rooms with king beds, tasteful exposed cedar walls and ceilings, and attractive green and earth tone appointments, all the way through generous and gorgeous suites to multi-bedroom houses. You'll reach your room by walking along the paved paths, which are crowded by lush landscaping, primarily California native plants that complement the wild lands of the trails behind the main hotel buildings.

The elegant Restaurant at Ventana is one way to get a bit of this luxury without committing to the price of a room.

Henry Miller Memorial Library

Henry Miller lived and wrote in Big Sur for 18 years, and one of his works is titled for the area. Today the **Henry Miller Memorial Library** (48603 CA-1, 831/667-2574, www.henrymiller.org, 11am-6pm daily) celebrates the life and work of Miller and his brethren in this quirky community center/museum/coffee shop/gathering place. The library is easy to find as you drive either north or south on CA-1—look for the hand painted sign and funky fence decorations. What you won't find is a typical lending library, bookshop, or slicked-up museum. Instead, you'll wander the lovely sun-dappled meadow, soaking in the essence of Miller's life here; come inside and talk to the docents about the racy novels Miller wrote; and maybe sit back with a cup of coffee to meditate on life, art, and isolated gorgeous scenery. The library offers a glimpse into Big Sur as an artists' colony that has inspired countless works by hundreds of people.

Julia Pfeiffer Burns State Park

One of the best-known and easiest hikes in all of the Big Sur region sits in **Julia Pfeiffer Burns State Park** (CA-1, 37 miles south of Carmel, 12 miles south of Pfeiffer Big Sur State Park, 831/667-2315, www.parks.ca.gov, $10/vehicle). The **Overlook Trail** runs only two-thirds of a mile round-trip, along a level wheelchair-friendly boardwalk. Stroll under CA-1, past the Pelton wheelhouse, and out to the observation deck and the stunning view of **McWay Falls**. The medium-sized waterfall cascades year-round off a cliff and onto the beach of a remote cove, where the water wets the sand and trickles out into the sea. The water of the cove gleams bright cerulean blue against the just-off-white sand of the beach. Anyone with an ounce of love for the ocean will want to build a hut right there beside the waterfall. But you can't—in fact, the reason you'll look down on a pristine and empty stretch of sand is that there's no way down to the cove that's even remotely safe.

The tiny Pelton wheel exhibit off the Overlook Trail describes what a Pelton wheel is and what it does. No other museums make their homes here, though there's a small visitors center adjacent to the parking lot.

If you want to spend all day at Julia Pfeiffer Burns State Park, drive north from the park entrance to the Partington Cove pullout and park along the side of the highway. On the east side of the highway, start out along the **Tanbark Trail** (6.4 miles round-trip, difficult). You'll head through redwood groves and up steep switchbacks to the top of the coastal ridge. Be sure to bring your camera to record the stunning views before you head back down the fire road to your car.

Esalen Institute

Visitors journey from all over the state and beyond to the **Esalen Institute** (55000 CA-1, 831/667-3000, www.esalen. org), sometimes called "The New Age Harvard." It's a forerunner and cutting-edge player in ecological living; a space to retreat from the world and build a new and better sense of self.

One of the biggest draws of the institute sits down a rocky path right on the edge of the cliffs overlooking the ocean. The clothing-optional bathhouse includes a motley collection of mineral-fed hot tubs looking out over the ocean—you can choose the Quiet Side or the Silent Side to sink into the water and contemplate the Pacific Ocean's limitless expanse, meditate on a perfect sunset or arrangement of stars, or (on the Quiet Side) get to know your fellow bathers.

Esalen is also the home of the California massage technique. If you are not staying at the retreat, a **massage** ($165 for those staying off-site) at Esalen will give you access to the baths for an hour before and after your treatment. You can also try to get one of the 20 **public access spots** (reservations 831/667-3047, $25) that are available nightly 1am-3am.

Piedras Blancas

Atop a rugged point, **Piedras Blancas Light Station** (15950 CA-1, 805/927-7361, Mon.-Sat. June 15-Aug. 31, Tues., Thurs., and Sat. Sept. 1-June 14, $10 adults, $5 children) first illuminated its light in 1875 to guide mariners along the rocky California coast. The lighthouse was built on indigenous land that was later claimed by Mission San Miguel, about 50 miles inland, and was eventually passed to the U.S. Coast Guard in 1937. Today, visitors can tour the lighthouse and explore the cultural and natural history.

About two miles south of the lighthouse, the **Northern Elephant Seal Rookery** (four miles north of Hearst Castle entrance on CA-1, 805/924-1628, www.elephantseal.org) is a spot where elephant seals have gathered since the 1990s. In the winter months, the seals come here to breed, and in the summer months they molt. Winter is the best time to view the males, females, and newborn pups. There is a large parking area with viewing spot signs, and a boardwalk where a guide is available 10am-4pm to provide information and answer questions.

San Simeon

Driving from north to south, San Simeon marks the end of the Big Sur coast. Although the most dramatic parts of the California coast are behind you, there are still plenty of sights to behold, including one of the most famous: Hearst Castle. In fact, the tiny town of San Simeon was founded to support the construction efforts up the hill at Hearst Castle. The town dock provided a place for ships to unload tons of marble, piles of antiques, and dozens of workers.

Sights
★ Hearst Castle
There's nothing else in California quite like **Hearst Castle** (750 Hearst Castle Rd., 800/444-4445, www.hearstcastle.com, 9am-close daily). Newspaper magnate William Randolph Hearst conceived of the idea of a grand mansion in the Mediterranean style, on the land his parents bought along the central California coast. His memories of camping on the hills above the Pacific led him to choose the spot on which the castle now stands. He hired Julia Morgan, the first female civil engineering graduate from UC Berkeley, to design and build the house for him. She did a brilliant job with every detail, despite the ever-changing wishes of her employer. By way of decoration, Hearst assisted in the relocation of hundreds of European medieval and Renaissance antiquities, from tiny tchotchkes to whole gilded ceilings. William Randolph also adored exotic animals, and created one of the largest private

zoos in the nation on his thousands of Central Coast acres. Though most of the zoo is gone now, you can still see the occasional zebra grazing peacefully along CA-1 to the south of the castle, acting as heralds to the exotic nature of Hearst Castle ahead.

The visitors center is a lavish affair with a gift shop, restaurant, café, ticket booth, and movie theater. Here you can see the much-touted film *Hearst Castle—Building the Dream,* which will give you an overview of the construction and history of the marvelous edifice, and of William Randolph Hearst's empire. Shuttles going up the hill to the castle board here; no private cars are allowed on the roads up to the castle proper. In order to get on the shuttle, you will need a ticket for a tour, which can be purchased at the visitors center, as long as spaces are available. Advance tickets (http://hearst.reserveamerica.com) are recommended, and tours can be purchased up to 56 days before the day of your visit.

There are four tours, each focusing on different spaces and aspects of the castle: Grand Rooms Tour, Upstairs Suites Tour, Cottages & Kitchen Tour, and the Evening Tour. The day tours ($25 adults, $12 children) are 45 minutes, and after the tour, you can walk around parts of the castle, such as the gardens and pools, before the shuttle back. The Evening Tour ($36 adults, $18 children), which is seasonal, is 100 minutes long, with volunteers dressed in 1930s fashion.

Beaches
The **William Randolph Hearst Memorial State Beach** (750 Hearst Castle Rd., San Simeon, 805/927-2020, www.parks.ca.gov, dawn-dusk daily) is located just across from the entrance to Hearst Castle, and offers beautiful coastline views off a 1,000-foot wooden pier, surrounded by sandy beaches. Fishing is permitted off the pier without a license, but limits are enforced. There are plenty of picnic areas and hiking and kayaking opportunities.

The park also encompasses the **Coastal Discovery Center** (San Simeon, 805/927-6575, www.montereybay.noaa.gov, 11am-5pm Fri.-Sun. and holidays, free), which offers educational and interactive exhibits that highlight the cultural and natural history of the area.

Food and Accommodations

San Simeon has a few places to stay that are convenient for visiting Hearst Castle. The **San Simeon Lodge** (9520 Castillo Dr., San Simeon, 805/927-4906, www.sansimeonlodge.net, $110-160) is a 60-unit motel near Hearst Castle and the beach. It's a very good value, though the accommodations are simple and basic. **Best Western Cavalier Oceanfront Resort** (9415 Hearst Dr., San Simeon, 805/927-6472 or 800/826-8168, www.cavalierresort.com, $270-340 d) was built in 1965 and makes for a comfortable stay. Of the 90 available, the best rooms face directly to the ocean, and each room has binoculars for admiring the landscape.

The **San Simeon Beach Bar & Grill** (9520 Castillo Dr., 805/927-4604, www.sansimeonlodge.net, 11am-midnight daily) has a pool table, TVs, and live music.

Cambria

Located roughly 10 miles south of Hearst Castle, Cambria owes much of its prosperity to that giant attraction. But this small beach town becomes surprisingly spacious when you start exploring it. Plenty of visitors come here to ply Moonstone Beach, peruse the charming downtown area, and just drink in the laid-back, art-town feel.

Getting There and Around

Traveling southbound via US-101, take the San Luis Obispo exit onto CA-1 Morro Bay/Hearst Castle and continue to Cambria. Traveling northbound via US-101, take CA-46 West to CA-1.

The closest **Amtrak** station is 35 miles south in San Luis Obispo (1011 Railroad Ave., 800/872-7245) and another is located in Paso Robles (800 Pine St., 800/872-7245), about 30 miles east.

San Luis Obispo Regional Transit Authority (179A Cross St., 805/781-4472, $1.25 one-way) runs between Morro Bay to Hearst Castle, stopping in Cayucos and Cambria via Route 15.

There is also a Cambria trolley, the **Otter Bus** (805/541-2228, 10am-6pm Fri.-Sun., free), which makes a loop around Cambria every half-hour.

Sights

While William Randolph Hearst built one of the most expensive homes ever seen in California, local eccentric Arthur Harold Beal (a.k.a. Captain Nit Wit or Der Tinkerpaw) got busy building the cheapest "castle" he could. **Nitt Witt Ridge** (881 Hillcrest Dr., 805/927-2690, tours free, by appointment only) is the result of five decades of scavenging trash and using it as building supplies to create a multi-story home like no other on the coast. Today, you can make an appointment with owners Michael and Stacey O'Malley to take a tour of the property. (Please don't just drop in.)

One of Cambria's oldest homes, the Guthrie-Bianchini House is the site of the **Cambria Historical Museum** (2251 Center St., 805/927-2891, http://cambriahistoricalsociety.com/museum.html, 1pm-4pm Fri.-Sun., 10am-1pm Mon.). Built in 1870, the house was later sold to Benjamin Franklin, rumored to be a relative of the Benjamin Franklin who helped draft the Declaration of Independence and the U.S. Constitution, among a number of other historic acts. Today, it preserves exhibits on Cambria's treasures of the past, including an oar from the lifeboat of the *S.S. Montebello,* which was sunk off the coast of Cambria on December 23, 1941.

A National Historic Registry

Landmark, **The Old Santa Rosa Chapel** (2353 Main St., 805/927-1175, 10am-3pm Fri.-Mon.) is one of the oldest churches in the county. It rests on a hilltop among a pine and oak forest near an old pioneer cemetery. Although the chapel's final Mass was in 1963, this pristine white church built of pine draws couples for wedding ceremonies, families for special celebrations, and curious visitors interested in the town's early settlement roots.

Food
Fine dining Parisian-style is what ★ **Madeline's** (788 Main St., 805/927-4175, 5pm-9pm daily, $22-46) is all about. An exquisite menu, local boutique wines, and an intimate setting make it the perfect evening out.

For the authentic flavors of Mexico, try **Medusa's Real Mexican Food** (1053 Main St., 805/927-0135, www.medusascambria. com, 7am-8pm Mon.-Sat., under $10) or **Las Cambritas** (2336 Main St., 805/927-0175, 11:30am-9pm daily, $11-24), which has all the spicy south-of-the-boarder dishes you love, plus mixed drinks and exceptional service.

Dragon Bistro (2150 Center St., 805/927-1622, 11am-9pm daily, $12-20) offers good Chinese food, large portions, and great prices. The widely known **Wild Ginger** (2380 Main St., Ste. G, 805/927-1001, www.wildginger.com, 11am-9pm daily, $14-20) offers popular dishes like prawn curry and Hunan beef.

The Sow's Ear (2248 Main St., 805/927-4865, www.thesowsear.com, 5pm-9pm daily, $19-31) does its best to create the proverbial "silk purse" dining experience, with upscale comfort foods and dim, romantic lighting.

A very popular stop, **Sea Chest Restaurant & Oyster Bar** (6216 Moonstone Beach Dr., 805/927-4514, 5:30pm-9pm Wed.-Mon., $18-42) is one of the best seafood restaurants around and offers beautiful waterfront views. The dining room fills up fast. It's cash only.

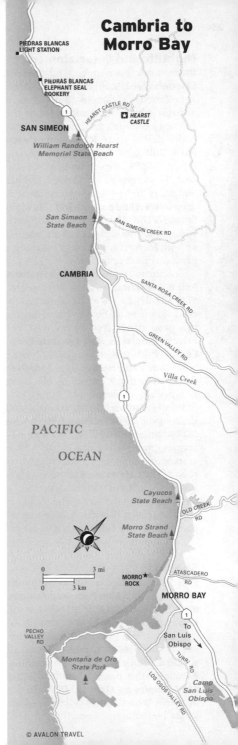

Cambria to Morro Bay

PIEDRAS BLANCAS LIGHT STATION

PIEDRAS BLANCAS ELEPHANT SEAL ROOKERY

HEARST CASTLE RD

HEARST CASTLE

SAN SIMEON

William Randolph Hearst Memorial State Beach

San Simeon State Beach

SAN SIMEON CREEK RD

CAMBRIA

SANTA ROSA CREEK RD

GREEN VALLEY RD

Villa Creek

PACIFIC

OCEAN

Cayucos State Beach

OLD CREEK RD

Morro Strand State Beach

0   3 mi

0   3 km

MORRO ROCK

ATASCADERO RD

MORRO BAY

To San Luis Obispo

TURRI RD

PECHO VALLEY RD

Montaña de Oro State Park

LOS OSOS VALLEY RD

Camp San Luis Obispo

© AVALON TRAVEL

Nightlife and Entertainment

Enjoy draft beer, pool, and **Mozzi's Saloon**'s (2262 Main St., 805/927-4767, 1pm-2am daily) famous $3 hot dogs in a historic building reminiscent of the cowboy days. For a good cocktail or specialty drink, go to **Moonstone Beach Bar & Grill** (6550 Moonstone Beach Dr., 805/927-3859, www.moonstonebeach. com, 11am-9pm daily), or for a full bar and one of the best Bloody Marys around, drop by **West End Bar and Grill** (774 Main St., 805/927-5521, www.westendcambria. com, 11am-9pm daily), a hub for meeting up with friends for a drink or watching a game on one of four TVs.

For music and $1 pints, **The Cambria Pub & Steakhouse** (4090 Burton Dr., 805/927-0782, www.thecambriapub. com, 11am-9pm Thurs.-Tues.) brings in a good-sized happy hour crowd. For eclectic entertainment, **Cambria Pines Lodge** (2905 Burton Dr., 805/927-4200, www.cambriapineslodge.com, 5pm-9pm daily) offers music including folk, rock, jazz, and even karaoke.

Immerse yourself in the dramatic and the comedic at **Pewter Plough Playhouse** (824 Main St., 805/927-3877, www.pewterploughplayhouse.org, $10), which casts outstanding stage productions year-round. The **Cafe-Piano Bar** (no cover) is just off the lobby of the theater, providing an intimate atmosphere with soft lights and featuring a Baldwin "parlor grand" piano. There is a full wine bar and a selection of premier beers.

Shopping

Filled with vintage treasures from over 30 dealers, **Rich Man Poor Man Antique Mall** (2110 Main St., 805/203-5350, www. richmanpoormanantiques.com, 10am-5pm daily) features furniture, glassware, rugs, tapestries, art, and jewelry, all within a unique two-floor, loft building. A couple other places to shop antiques are **Antiques on Main** (2338 Main St., 805/927-4292, 10am-5pm daily), where you're bound to find something to take home after browsing over 10,000 square feet of antique goods, and **Hidden Gate Antiques** (2261 Main St., 805/975-5140), which features collectible 18th- and 19th-century American antiques.

Dolce Yogurt & Boutique (801 B. Main St., 805/927-2638, 11am-6pm) offers delicious yogurt and women's fine clothing and accessories in one place. **The Gallery of Wearable Art** (4009 and 4015 West St., 805/927-1005, www.gowacambria.com, 11am-5pm daily) dresses you in one-of-a-kind fashions and unique accessories. **The Place** (2336 Main St., 805/927-1195, www.theplacecambria.com, 11am-6pm) is *the* place for classic clothing and accessories that are comfortable and affordable.

For specialty gifts and distinctive souvenirs, **A Matter of Taste in Cambria** (4120 Burton Dr., 805/927-0286, www. amatteroftastecambria.com, 10am-5pm daily) offers culinary delights for the gourmet cook, including jams and sauces, baking mixes, serving dishes, kitchen gadgets, and cookbooks. **Exotic Nature** (783 Main St., 805/927-8423 and 888/562-7903, www.exoticnature. com, 10am-5pm) is a wonder of gift options that include custom scented lotions, aromatherapy, soaps, candles, and clothing. For beautifully created jewelry, **Hauser Brothers Goldsmiths** (2060 Main St., 805/927-8315, www. hausergold.com, 10am-6pm) designs the "Joels Collection" and other fashionable treasures.

Recreation

For breathtaking views of seascapes, wildlife, and tidepools, stroll the **Moonstone Beach Boardwalk,** which follows along the cliffs; stairs take you down to the beach. Although you won't find moonstone here, you will find plenty of agates, and possibly jasper and California jade. On the northern end of Moonstone Beach, **Leffingwell Landing** (San Simeon-Monterey Creek Rd.) offers spectacular views for the amateur or professional photographer, and is a wonderful area to explore tidepools and marinelife.

Fiscalini Ranch Preserve (CA-1 to Windsor, past Shamel Park, 805/927-2856, www.ffrpcambria.org) offers one of the most popular trails, **Bluff Trail,** which is a continuation of the California Coastal Trail and offers awe-inspiring ocean views from almost every direction. It is a fairly easy walk, and includes both a paved pathway and boardwalk. Bikes are not allowed (but can be walked) and pets must be leashed.

Events

Over 420 lively and whimsical scarecrows decorate the streets of Cambria's West and East Villages every October during **Cambria Scarecrow Festival** (805/927-2597 and 805/909-9000, www.cambriascarecrows.com), a unique month-long event unlike anything else in the United States, with pie-eating contests, fun tours, and more.

Accommodations

A favorite even among the many inns of Cambria, the **Olallieberry Inn** (2476 Main St., 805/927-3222, www.olallieberry.com, $140-225) sits in a charming 19th-century Greek Revival home and adjacent cottage. Each of the nine rooms features its own quaint Victorian-inspired decor with comfortable beds and attractive appointments. A full daily breakfast (complete with olallieberry jam) rounds out the comfortable experience.

Sand Pebbles Inn (6252 Moonstone Beach Dr., 805/927-5600, www.cambriainns.com, $164 and up), a boutique hotel just a few steps away from the boardwalk, is among Cambria's mid-range lodgings with nice amenities.

Cambria Landing Inn & Suites (6530 Moonstone Beach Dr., 805/927-1619 and 800/549-6789, www.cambrialanding.com, $209 and up) provides ocean views, private balconies, and in-room fireplaces to make your stay a little more

cozy. A small hotel that offers sophistication and style, **El Colibri Boutique Hotel & Spa** (5620 Moonstone Beach Dr., 805/924-3003, www.elcolibrihotel.com, $219 and up) immerses guests in luxury with spa therapies and exclusive wines combined with rejuvenating rooms and atmosphere. Among beach cottages that offer unforgettable romantic escapes, **Fireside Inn** (6700 Moonstone Beach Dr., 805/927-8661 and 800/910-7100, www.pacificahotels.com, $119-263) is a good choice for couples that want to get away from the day-to-day bustle and relax on a private terrace, soak in a jet tub, and cozy up to a warm fireplace.

Moonstone Cottages (6580 Moonstone Beach Dr., 805/927-1366, www.cambriainns.com, $233-349) offers the perfect hideaway to enjoy a sunset from a quaint cottage, with lofted ceilings and Cape Cod-style furnishings. Set along the shores of the Central Coast, **Pelican Inn & Suites** (6316 Moonstone Beach Dr., 805/927-1500, www.pacifichotel.com, $299 and up) offers a quiet retreat with tailored guest services and comfortable accommodations.

Information and Services

Cambria Chamber of Commerce and Visitor Center (767 Main St., 805/927-3624, www.cambriachamber.org, 9am-5pm Mon.-Fri., noon-4pm Sat.-Sun.) offers extensive area information and visitor services.

Cayucos

Fifteen miles south of Cambria, the little town of Cayucos is often a stop for resort vacationers, and offers swimming, surfing, kayaking, and skin diving. There is a pier for rock fishing and surf fishing year-round at Estero Bay.

Most of the restaurants are located along Ocean Avenue. **Schooners** (171 N. Ocean Ave., 805/995-3883, 11am-9pm

Sun.-Thurs., 11am-10pm Fri.-Sat., $10-16) is a great spot for seafood. Charming **On The Beach Bed & Breakfast** (181 N. Ocean Ave., 805/995-3200, $249) has ocean views and easy access to the beach.

Morro Bay

Morro Bay is part of a coastal California that seems to be vanishing. It's not fancy or pretentious here, and hasn't been over-built with trendy shops and hotels. The atmosphere is languid; visitors can stroll along the Embarcadero to the call of sea lions, browsing the small shops and snacking on saltwater taffy. You're just as likely to see veteran fishermen walking around town as tourists.

The defining geographical feature of Morro Bay is the impressive ancient volcanic and sacred Chumash Indian site called Morro Rock, an unmistakable round formation rising out of the bay. You cannot climb on it since it's the home to endangered peregrine falcons.

Sights

The **Museum of Natural History** (20 State Park Rd., 805/772-2694, 10am-5pm daily, $3 adults, free children under 16) has a great location in the back bay, near the marina, with a view of the rock. It's a small, kid-friendly museum, with touch exhibits about sand, waves, and animals and a good assortment of stuffed birds, like the peregrine falcon. Best of all, there's an albatross dangling from the ceiling, its massive wingspan covering you like a shelter. There's also a full-sized skeleton of a minke whale on the outside deck overlooking the bay.

Food

Frankie and Lola's (1154 Front St., 805/771-9306, www.frankieandlolas.com, 6:30am-2:30pm daily, $8-13) serves breakfast and lunch in a small, deliberately low-key space. They are one of the few places to open early, should you need breakfast before you leave town. Like most everywhere, you can see the rock while you enjoy the creative food, like French toast that is dipped in crème brûlée and mixed with whole nuts. For seafood, try **The Galley** (899 Embarcadero, 805/772-7777, www.galleymorrobay.com, 11am-2:30pm and 5pm-close daily, $24-48), which offers dishes like pan-seared scallops, as well as simple presentations of swordfish, ahi tuna, and ono.

Accommodations

Morro Bay is a relaxing place to spend the night. The **Sundown Inn** (640 Main St., 805/772-7381, www.sundownmotel.com, $99) is a budget choice, with few amenities except for a coffeemaker in the room and a WiFi signal. The rooms are standard size and minimally decorated, but clean and comfortable. The eight-room **Estero Inn** (501 Embarcadero, 805/772-1500, www.esteroinn.com, $179-289) has well-appointed rooms and is conveniently located.

San Luis Obispo

Past Morro Bay, CA-1 turns inland and merges with US-101 at San Luis Obispo, known as SLO to locals. It's also known for its slow pace. But with a beautiful downtown fronted by Higuera Street and the accompanying river walk, San Luis Obispo is beginning to receive attention. Its idyllic way of life, proximity to the ocean and mountains, wide-open tracts of land, and nearly ideal weather make it a lovely place to stop.

Getting There and Around

Access by car is from US-101 and CA-1, which run through town. The two highways merge together at San Luis Obispo then split apart again to the south, in Pismo Beach.

San Luis Obispo County Regional Airport (901 Airport Dr., 805/781-5205) is the closest commercial airport, located about 35 miles south of Cambria. Flights to Los Angeles, San Francisco, and Phoenix are available. Car rentals are available.

Greyhound (150 South St., 805/543-2121, $18-45) runs daily buses to Los Angeles via Santa Barbara, and to San Francisco.

The **Amtrak** station is located downtown in San Luis Obispo (1011 Railroad Ave., 800/872-7245), with service from Seattle to Los Angeles via Coast Starlight.

San Luis Obispo Regional Transit Authority (179A Cross St., 805/781-4472, www.slorta.org, $1.25 one-way) operates bus routes throughout the region, including to Paso Robles, San Simeon, Cambria, Morro Bay, and Pismo Beach.

Most everything in San Luis Obispo's downtown area is within walking distance, and in cases where walking is not preferred, county bus lines run consistently throughout town.

Sights

Just west of US-101 at the foot of town, the **Madonna Inn** (100 Madonna Rd., 805/543-3000 and 800/543-9666, www.madonnainn.com, $189-599) is a remarkable example of what architecturally minded academic types like to call vernacular kitsch. Created by local contractor Alex Madonna, who died in 2004, the Madonna Inn offers over 100 unique rooms, each decorated in a wild barrage of fantasy motifs. Bright pink honeymoon suites are known as "Just Heaven" and "Love Nest." The "Safari Room" is covered in fake zebra skins above a jungle-green shag carpet. The name of the "Cave Man Room" speaks for itself (Yabba dabba doo!). *Roadside America* rates the Madonna Inn as "the best place to spend a vacation night in America." Even if you can't stay, at least stop for a look at the gift shop, which sells postcards of the different rooms. Guys should head down to the men's room, where the urinal trough is flushed by a waterfall.

Built in 1772, **Mission San Luis Obispo de Tolosa** (751 Palm St., 805/781-8220, www.missionsanluisobispo.org, 9am-4pm daily, $2 donation) is the fifth California mission founded by Junípero Serra, and is the only "L"-shaped mission in the state. An adjacent museum chronicles the daily lives of the Chumash tribal and Spanish colonial periods. Today, the mission church operates as a parish church of the Diocese of Monterey.

Located alongside the creek, **San Luis Obispo Museum of Art** (1010 Broad St., 805/543-8562, www.sloma.org, 11am-5pm daily, closed Tues. Labor Day-July 3, free) is a small gallery that showcases the work of local painters, sculptors, fine-art photographers, and special exhibitions.

Food

It's not all vegetarian at homey **Sally Loo's** (1804 Osos St., 805/545-5895, 6:30am-5:30pm Tues.-Sun., $7-10), but they certainly focus on healthy natural organic ingredients in dishes like goat cheese and asparagus quiche.

A popular stop, **Jaffa Café** (1212 Higuera St., 805/543-2449, www.jaffacafe.us, 11am-8pm daily, $8-10) whips up phenomenal Mediterranean dishes, including gyros, falafels, kebab, and excellent hummus! A hip spot with freshly baked goods, **Splash Cafe** (1491 Monterey St., 805/773-4653, 7am-8:30pm Sun.-Thurs., 7am-9:30pm Fri.-Sat., under $10) serves award-winning clam chowder. Beefy burgers are at **Eureka Burger** (1141 Chorro St., 805/903 1141, 11am-midnight daily, $10-15) and **Firestone Grill** (1001 Higuera St., 805/783-1001, 11am-10pm Sun.-Wed., 11am-11pm Thurs.-Sat., $6-13). Try a rib-eye sandwich or a great steak at **F. McLintocks Saloon** (686 Higuera St., 805/541-0686, 7am-9pm Sun.-Thurs., 7am-9:30pm Fri.-Sat., $10-24).

A hot spot for locals and an iconic dining experience, **Novo Restaurant and Lounge** (726 Higuera St., 805/543-3986, www.novorestaurant.com, 11am-9pm

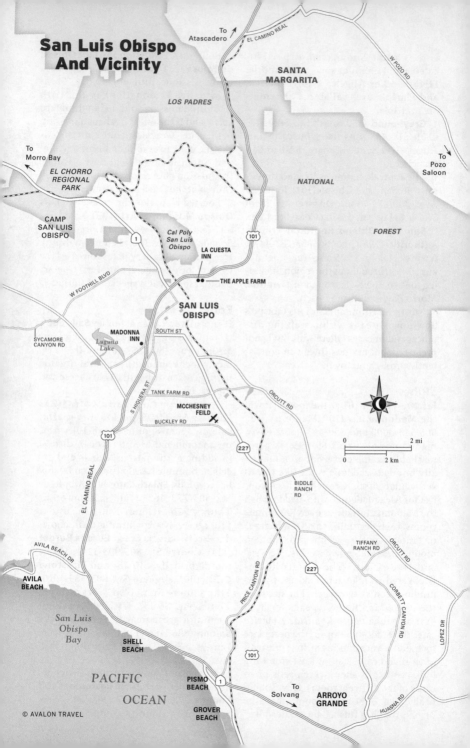

daily, $12-36) features a riverside patio, a flavorful array of international dishes, an endless selection of wine, and a full bar. Elegant with a touch of old-world sophistication, **Koberl at Blue** (998 Monterey St., 805/783-1135, www.epkoberl.com, 5pm-10pm daily, $23-50) is located in historic downtown and features "wine country cuisine to complement the Central Coast's wine region," including wonderful vegetarian dishes and delectable desserts.

Nightlife

Most of the bars are downtown, within walking distance from each other, and range from pubs to wine bars to martini lounges.

Pubs with a good selection of draft beer are **The Frog & Peach Pub** (728 Higuera St., 805/595-3764, www.frogandpeachpub.com, noon-2am daily), which also brings in live entertainment; **Spike's** (570 Higuera St., 805/544-7157, www.spikespub.com, 3pm-1am), which doesn't follow the beer fads and just serves exceptional imported beers; and **Pappy McGregor's Irish Pub** (1865 Monterey St., 805/543-5458, www.pappymcgregors.com, 11:30am-1am Mon.-Fri., 11am-1am Sat.-Sun.), which attracts a lively crowd and has amazing fiddle and banjo shows.

A couple inviting wine bars include **Luis Wine Bar** (1021 Higuera St., 805/762-4747, www.luiswinebar.com, 3pm-11pm Mon.-Thurs., 3pm-midnight Fri., noon-midnight Sat., noon-11pm Sun.), a relaxing atmosphere with an extensive wine list from San Luis Obispo County and the entire Central Coast, and **Luna Red** (1023 Chorro St., 805/540-5243, www.lunaredslo.com, 11am-close daily), a trendy place in a Spanish-style building with fine wines, cocktails, and tapas. Don't miss the **Silver Bar Cocktail Lounge** (100 Madonna Rd., 805/543-3000, www.madonnainn.com), located inside the Madonna Inn. It's decorated with *Alice in Wonderland* wingback chairs, pink retro bar stools, and a blooming fuchsia carpet.

Shopping

Downtown encompasses five streets of shopping. The most prominent is the main drag of Higuera Street and the streets of Monterey and Marsh, where you'll find big-name retailers, eclectic boutiques, and everything in between.

Cool, hip clothing is at **Ambiance** (737 Higuera St., 805/540-3380, www.ambianceslo.blogspot.com, 10am-8pm Mon.-Sat., 11am-7pm Sun.), with jewelry and accessories for every occasion. **HepKat Clothing & Beauty Parlor** (785 Higuera St., 805/547-0777, www.hepkatclothing.com, 10am-8pm daily) is a fashion-forward boutique that doubles as a beauty salon.

With many antiques dealers all under one roof, **The Antique Center** (1239 Monterey St., 805/541-4040, 11am-6pm Mon. and Wed.-Sat., 11am-5pm Sun.) houses immense collections of gorgeous turn-of-the-century and mid-century furniture and accessories, retro and vintage clothing, jewelry, antique bottles and pottery, and paintings. For artwork that's both witty and whimsical, **A Muse Gallery Fun** (845 Higuera St., 805/439-3000, www.amuseslo.com, 10:30am-6pm Mon.-Sat., 11am-5pm Sun.) features the "Art of Dr. Seuss" and "Snoopy," including contemporary works, jewelry, glass, and ceramics.

The Crushed Grape (319 Madonna Rd., Ste. 2, 805/544-4449, www.crushedgrape.com) sells a host of gourmet foods as well as gift baskets and unique wines. An open-air market, **Avila Valley Barn** (560 Avila Beach Dr., 805/595-2816) provides another opportunity for gift shopping, gourmet foods, and even hayrides. Stop by **The Secret Garden Herb Shop** (740 Higuera St., Ste. A, 805/544-4372, www.organicherbshop.com, 10:30am-5:30pm daily) and choose from rows and rows of fragrant organic teas.

Recreation

San Luis Obispo has several hiking and biking areas. Probably the most well known is **Bishop Peak,** the highest of the Nine Sisters (or Morros), a chain of volcanic peaks in the Santa Lucia Mountains that stretch east from Morro Bay. The peak can be accessed from two trailheads, from either Patricia Drive or Highland Drive. It's about a four-mile hike round-trip with several switchbacks through open oak woodlands, and up the west and east summits of the peak. There are plenty of oak trees, California blackberry, sage scrub, chaparral, monkeyflower, and poison oak, which you'll want to avoid. Bicycles are not allowed on the trail but are welcome at **Cerro San Luis,** another member of the Nine Sisters, which offers multiple biking trails. Located in the heart of downtown, **Wally's Bikes** (306 Higuera St., 805/544-4116, www.wallysbikes.com, $15 and up) offers bike and gear rentals at good prices.

San Luis Obispo is surrounded by beautiful vineyards that are worth exploring. Most vineyards are within a 15-minute drive in the Edna Valley, including **Stephen Ross Wine Cellars** (178 Suburban Rd., 805/594-1318, www.stephenrosswine.com, 11am-5pm Thurs.-Sun., $10 tasting) and **Filipponi Ranch Cellers** (1850 Calle Joaquin, 805/903-3567, noon-4pm Sat.-Sun., $10 tasting).

Accommodations

San Luis has a number of good places to stay, with reasonable rates that drop considerably after the summertime peak season. First on the list is the famed ★ **Madonna Inn** (100 Madonna Rd., 805/543-1800 and 800/543-9666, www.madonnainn.com, $235 and up), a whimsical hotel with eccentric taste and an excessively "pink" café.

The **La Cuesta Inn** (2074 Monterey

From top to bottom: Mission San Luis Obispo de Tolosa; Pismo Beach Butterfly Grove; Solvang.

St., 805/543-2777 and 800/543-2777, $80 and up) offers great pricing, although the place is average in appearance. **Avenue Inn Downtown San Luis Obispo** (345 Marsh St., 805/543-6443, $59-179) also offers affordable rates and is in walking distance to downtown restaurants and shopping. **La Cuesta Inn** (2074 Monterey St., 805/543-2777, $130) has large rooms, free continental breakfast, and free DVD rentals, a steal for the price.

Several hotels offer charming accommodations for a bit more cash. These include **Petit Soleil Bed & Breakfast** (1473 Monterey St., 805/549-0321, $170 and up), a charming European-style bed-and-breakfast that offers elegant morning meals, and evening complimentary wine-tasting; **Apple Farm** (2015 Monterey St., 805/544-2040, www.applefarm.com, $205 and up), an upscale country hotel with rooms that are smaller than average but cozy and tastefully decorated; and the **Garden Street Inn** (1212 Garden St., 805/545-9802, $180 and up), a little bed-and-breakfast right in the heart of downtown San Luis Obispo.

Information and Services

San Luis Obispo Visitor Center (1039 Chorro St., 805/781-2777, 10am-5pm Sun.-Wed., 10am-7pm Thurs.-Sat.) is a good resource for brochures and maps and provides information on available discounts for restaurants and events.

Pismo Beach

After passing through San Luis Obispo, US-101/CA-1 heads south back toward the coast, where CA-1 splits off from US-101 at Pismo Beach. This low-key, easygoing, touristy beach town is like a time machine that stops in 1960s California. Expect friendly people and great waves. Located at the end of Pomeroy Street, the pier is the focal point of the beach, with plenty of restrooms, food, and parking nearby.

Sights

Pismo Beach Butterfly Grove (CA-1 just south of North Pismo State Beach Campground, 805/473-7220, www.monarchbutterfly.org, docents available 10am-4pm daily Nov.-Feb., free) sees the return of monarch butterflies each November-February, when tens of thousands of butterflies migrate to this small grove of eucalyptus trees near the beach to mate. On average there are about 30,000 of these silent winged creatures, and the trees are often transformed into brilliant shades of orange after the butterflies' 2,000-mile journey to get here. This is the largest of the four gathering spots for the monarchs in California. Docents give talks about the butterflies and their very unique but short lives.

Food

Pismo is a good place to stop for a meal, especially for seafood.

Splash Cafe (197 Pomeroy, 805/773-4653, www.splashcafe.com, 8am-9pm daily, $8-15) is the place to go for cheap eats by the beach. This is classic Pismo—bright, airy, and rambunctious, with plastic chairs and tables and crudely painted walls with old surfing photos and other surfing paraphernalia. They are best known for their thick, chunky, and creamy clam chowder. The fish-and-chips and fish tacos are also worth trying. Burgers and shakes are also served. It does get crowded, so plan to get there early. There are also two locations in San Luis Obispo.

Steamers of Pismo (1601 Price St., 805/773-4711, www.steamerspismobeach.com, 11:30am-3pm and 4:30pm-9pm daily, $19-29) is all about seafood, with dishes like cioppino, Chilean sea bass, and a very good clam chowder. This is a popular spot for tourists because of the excellent views, and the service and food are equally good. For a table with an ocean view, make reservations.

The oft-crowded **Cracked Crab** (751 Price St., 805/773-2722, www.

crackedcrab.com, 11am-9pm Sun.-Thurs., 11am-10pm Fri.-Sat., $16-31) is *the* place to crack open crab, lobster, and other shellfish in a cafeteria-style environment. Old black-and-white photos of fishing days gone by line the walls. Perhaps it's the plastic bibs that give it away, but this is a hands-on joint. They will dump the shellfish right on your table so you can get to work.

For creative Latin American cuisine and gorgeous sunset views, dine at the **Ventana Grill** (2575 Price St., 805/773-0000, http://ventanagrill.com, Mon.-Thurs. 11:30am-10pm daily, $15-30). It's worth a visit for the margarita selection alone.

Accommodations
A few lower-priced chain hotels dot Pismo Beach and the surrounding communities of Avila Beach and Grover Beach. For a splurge, the **Dolphin Bay Resort and Spa** (2727 Shell Beach Rd., Pismo Beach, 805/773-4300 or 800/516-0112, www.thedolphinbay.com, $470-650) has one of the best locations on the entire Central Coast, perched just yards from the cliffs that drop dramatically down to the Pacific Ocean. The one-bedroom suites, at nearly 1,000 square feet, have full kitchens, fireplaces, and flat-screen plasma TVs, and bikes are provided for all guests.

Foxen Canyon Road: Santa Maria Valley

After CA-1 splits off from US-101 in Pismo Beach, the drive south along either highway is largely inland until it reaches Gaviota near Santa Barbara. Since you won't be missing any coastal scenery, you could take a detour even farther inland to the Santa Maria Valley to sample wines in the region made famous by the movie *Sideways*. Running roughly parallel to US-101, **Foxen Canyon Road** is a back road hugging the

foothills, with multiple wineries along the way.

From the north on US-101, take the East Betteravia Road exit and head east about three miles until it turns into Foxen Canyon Road. From this point, Tepusquet Road, where Kenneth Volk Winery is located, is about 10 miles away. From the south, take the Alisos Canyon Road turnoff from US-101, about 25 miles north of the CA-1-US-101 split in Gaviota. Take Alisos Canyon Road 6.5 miles and turn left onto Foxen Canyon Road. Foxen Canyon Road eventually turns into East Betteravia Road and connects back to US-101.

Located on a little road off Foxen Canyon Road, award-winning **Kenneth Volk Vineyards** (5230 Tepusquet Rd., 805/938-7896, www.volkwines.com, 10:30am-4:30pm daily, tasting $10) offers all the strange wines you've never tried. In addition to the standard offerings like chardonnay and cabernet sauvignon, Kenneth Volk is a champion of heirloom varieties like cabernet pfeiffer, négrette, verdelho, and aglianico. You won't regret the long trek to get to the tranquil 12-acre property along the Tepusquet Creek, surrounded by oak and sycamore trees.

Set in an old barn, **Rancho Sisquoc** (6600 Foxen Canyon Rd., 805/934-4332, www.ranchosisquoc.com, 10am-4pm Mon.-Thurs., 10am-5pm Fri.-Sun., tasting $10) makes a beautiful spot for a picnic. The wood-sided tasting room is rustic but comfortable, and the surrounding setting—a vast field with low hills in the distance—is perfect for some quiet wine-enhanced relaxation.

Foxen Winery (7600 Foxen Canyon Rd., 805/937-4251, www.foxenwinery.com, 11am-4pm daily, tasting $10) is known for its rustic wood tasting room: It looks like a rundown shed. But the wines are a far cry from rustic. In addition to the usual suspects, the winery is one of the few to produce the underappreciated chenin blanc. Foxen's longstanding reputation goes back six generations, and its

10 acres are the only dry-farmed vineyard in the area, meaning that irrigation is not used.

If you get a carnivorous craving between Pismo Beach and Foxen Canyon Road, stop by **Jocko's** (125 N. Thompson, Nipomo, 805/929-3565, 8am-10pm daily, $25). They're known for their oak-grilled steaks and their no-frills decor. The steaks and grilled meats are all prime quality, cooked and seasoned by people who know how to grill. On weekends, and often on weeknights as well, there are notoriously long waits. Make reservations, though that doesn't mean you won't still wait.

La Purisima Mission

Mission La Purisima Concepcion de Maria Santisima (2295 Purisima Rd., Lompoc, 805/733-3713, www.lapurisimamission.org, self-guided tours 9am-5pm daily, free one-hour guided tours daily at 1pm, $6 adults) is one of the best of the 21 California missions to visit. Its extensive restoration and wide grounds evoke the remoteness of the landscape during the mission period.

The mission was founded on December 8, 1787, but was destroyed by an earthquake in 1812. The fathers then rebuilt the mission in a different spot, and it is that mission that a quarter of a million visitors enjoy today as a state historic park. Sitting inside 2,000 acres are trails for simple hikes and walks, and when you visit you can examine the 5-acre garden that shows native and domestic plants typical of a mission garden, including fig and olive trees and a wide variety of plants like sage and Spanish dagger. Animals typical of the times, such as burros, horses, longhorn cattle, sheep, goats, and turkeys, are displayed in a corral in the main compound.

Wandering through the sleeping quarters, the weaving shop, candle-making room, chapel, and many other rooms on display, you can get a feel for daily life in the mission. You can also see few conical Chumash huts. This is one of the only missions that does not have church services now that it's a state park.

La Purisima is easily accessible from CA-1: In Lompoc, take Purisima Road east to the mission.

⚑ CA-246: Buellton and Solvang

The town of **Buellton,** a block west of US-101 at the Solvang exit, holds one of California's classic roadside landmarks, **Andersen's Pea Soup Restaurant** (376 Ave. of the Flags, 805/688-5581, www.peasoupandersens.net, 7am-10pm daily, $12), advertised up and down the coast. The **Hitching Post** restaurant (406 CA-246 E., 805/688-0676, www.hitchingpost2.com, 4pm-9:30pm Mon.-Fri., 3pm-9:30pm Sat.-Sun., $23-50) gained fame in the wine-loving road-trip movie *Sideways.*

Four miles east of Buellton and US-101 is America's most famous mock-European tourist trap, the Danish-style town of **Solvang** (pop. 5,332). Set up by a group of Danish immigrants in 1911 as a cooperative agricultural community, Solvang found its calling catering to passing travelers. The compact blocks of cobblestone streets and old-world architecture charms road-trippers and busloads of tourists with its Hans Christian Andersen museum, Little Mermaid statue, and the Round Tower windmill. **The Elverhoj Museum of Art & History** (1624 Elverhoy Way, 805/686-1211, www.elverhoj.org, 11am-4pm Wed.-Sun., $5 suggested donation) chronicles the cultural influence of the Danish people.

Just east of Solvang's windmills and gables, the brooding hulk of **Old Mission Santa Inés** (1760 Mission Dr., 805/688-4815, 9am-5pm daily, $5 guided tours) stands as a sober reminder of the region's Spanish colonial past. Built in

1804, it was once among the more prosperous of the California missions, but now it is worth a visit mainly for the gift shop selling all manner of devotional ornaments.

Pop singer Michael Jackson's Neverland Ranch lies in the foothills of the Santa Ynez Valley, southeast of Solvang via the truly scenic CA-254, which loops inland and continues south to Santa Barbara.

Gaviota State Park

CA-1 rejoins US-101 at Las Cruces, near the north end of **Gaviota State Park** (US-101, 33 miles west of Santa Barbara, 805/968-1033, www.parks.ca.gov, 7am-sunset daily, $10), which includes a beach, hiking trails, and hot springs. The trailhead to **Gaviota Peak** (six miles round-trip) is located at the parking area. The trail is mostly rugged and wide leading upwards, and the views of the ocean and the Channel Islands are fantastic. The trail that leads to the hot springs is shorter, only a mile, but there are still some beautiful scenic views along the way. Surfers and kayakers use a boat hoist on the west end of the beach to access the Santa Barbara Channel waters. At Gaviota Beach, US-101 turns east, hugging the coastline.

Refugio State Beach

Refugio State Beach (10 Refugio Beach Rd., Goleta, 805/968-1033, www.parks. ca.gov, 8am-sunset daily, $10) is a state park with a small strip of grass that abuts the water. It offers excellent coastal fishing, snorkeling, and scuba, as well as hiking, biking trails, and picnic sites. Palm trees planted near Refugio Creek give a distinctive look to the beach and camping area. With 1.5 miles of flat shoreline, Refugio is located 20 miles west of Santa Barbara on US-101 at Refugio Road.

El Capitán State Beach

El Capitán State Beach (off US-101, 17 miles west of Santa Barbara, 805/968-1033, www.parks.ca.gov, 8am-sunset daily, $10) offers visitors a sandy beach, rocky tidepools, and stands of sycamore and oak trees along El Capitán Creek. It's a perfect setting for swimming, fishing, surfing, picnicking, and camping. A stairway provides access from the bluffs to the beach area. Amenities include RV hookups, pay showers, restrooms, hiking and bike trails, a fabulous beach, a seasonal general store, and an outdoor arena. Many of the camping sites offer an ocean view. If you take US-101 north about 15 minutes from downtown you will see the El Capitán signs. At the bottom of the exit, turn left and go under the bridge. The road will take you right into the park.

Santa Barbara

It's called the American Riviera, with weather, community, and sun-drenched beaches reminiscent of the Mediterranean coast. In truth, Santa Barbara is all California. It has all the amenities of a big city, but the pace of life slows down just enough to make for a relaxing stay. In fact, many California natives consider it their favorite vacation spot. In town, you'll find world-class museums, shopping, and dining. Fabulous four-star resorts cluster along the beaches.

Getting There and Around

Sanata Barbara by vehicle is accessed via US-101. Take the Garden Street exit to go downtown and Cabrillo Boulevard for access to local beaches.

Santa Barbara Municipal Airport (500 Fowler Rd., 805/683-4011, www.santabarbaraca.gov) is the gateway for visitors via air travel with daily flights from

Los Angeles (LAX), San Francisco, Las Vegas, Phoenix, Denver, and other destinations. Car rentals are available from all major service providers.

The Santa Barbara **Amtrak** (www.amtrak.com) station is located in a historical landmark building and provides service from San Luis Obispo-San Diego on the Pacific Surfliner, and from Seattle-Los Angeles on the Coast Starlight.

The **Greyhound station** (800/231-2222, www.greyhound.com) is adjacent to the train station, providing service several times a day from Santa Barbara and Carpinteria to LAX, as well as other options. Car rental service providers are conveniently located near the Amtrak and Greyhound stations.

The **Santa Barbara Metropolitan Transit District** (SBMTD, www.sbmtd. gov) runs buses throughout the city, including the neighboring cities of Goleta and Montecito. SBMTD's route 11 bus links the airport with downtown Santa Barbara. A shuttle bus (9am-6pm fall-spring, 9am-10pm summer, $0.50) runs every 15 minutes along State Street between downtown Sola Street and along the waterfront; bus route 22 takes you right to the Museum of Art, Old Mission Santa Barbara, and more.

Walking, biking, even inline skating is popular along the waterfront, and there are businesses that rent gear.

Sights
★ Old Mission Santa Barbara
Old Mission Santa Barbara (2201 Laguna St., 805/682-4713, www.santabarbaramission.org, 9am-5pm daily, self-guided tours $7 adults, $5 seniors, $2 children 5-15), with its coral pink facade, is considered the prettiest of all the California missions, albeit one of the least authentic. A self-guided tour takes you through the interior courtyard, where a center fountain is encircled by palm trees, and the cemetery where a beautiful Moreton Bay fig tree planted around 1890 still stands. From there it is a few steps into

the church. It has the most decorated of the mission interiors, with lots of vibrant stenciling surrounding the doors and altar and a complete painted wainscoting. Large paintings flank both walls. Near the formal entrance, a small gated room houses the only original altar and tabernacle in the California mission chain, dating from 1786. After leaving the church, you'll enter the museum section, which houses old photographs and artifacts from the early services.

★ Chumash Painted Cave
Mysterious red, black, and white images are concealed in a small sandstone cave at **Chumash Painted Cave State Historic Park** (CA-154, right on Painted Cave Rd., 805/733-3713, www.parks.ca.gov). Launch your expedition and navigate the steep path leading to the cave entrance, where Delphian-like images date to the 1600s and earlier. Although the images are known to be the artistry of ancient Chumash ancestors, the subjects depicted in the rock art are open to speculation and interpretation. Many believe the petroglyphs created using mineral pigments depict Chumash cosmology, possibly representing a solar eclipse that happened in November 24, 1677, but some images are thought to date back 1,000 years or more. The cave was discovered in the 1870s. The iron gate that blocks passage was placed at the cavern mouth in 1908 for the purpose of preservation.

The cave is accessed from the very narrow and winding Painted Cave Road (north) off of CA-154, about 11 miles (18 km) northwest of Santa Barbara. Look to the left side of the road for the cave. There is a small parking shoulder and an interpretive sign about the site. Flash cameras will harm the images and are prohibited.

Stearns Wharf
Stearns Wharf (intersection of State St. and Cabrillo Blvd., www.stearnswharf. org) is Santa Barbara's most visited

Santa Barbara

To
Santa Barbara
Botanic Garden

192

MISSION CANYON RD

PUESTA DEL SOL RD

STATE ST

192

MISSION RIDGE RD

FRANCHESCHI
PARK

ALAMEDA PADRE SERRA

OLD MISSION
SANTA BARBARA

SANTA BARBARA
GOLF CLUB

LAGUNA ST

SANTA BARBARA ST

ANACAPA ST

STATE ST

CHAPALA ST

DE LA VINA ST

MISSION ST

101

E ARRELLAGA ST

E MICHELTORENA ST

SANTA BARBARA
BOWL

N MILPAS ST

SIMPSON
HOUSE
INN

Alice Keck
Park Memorial
Gardens

STATE
STREET

THE SANTA BARBARA
COUNTY COURTHOUSE

El Presidio
de Santa Bárbara
State Historic Park

W ISLAY ST

W VALERIO ST

W BATH ST

W SOLA ST

W VICTORIA ST

W ANAPUMA ST

W FIGUEROA ST

W CARRILLO ST

W CANON PERDIDO ST

STATE ST

E COTTA ST

E COTTA ST

E HALEY ST

E GUTIERREZ ST

W DE LA
GUERRA ST

W ORTEGA ST

101

AMTRAK

TY WARNER
SEA CENT

STEARNS
WHARF

MEIGS RD

To
Arroyo Burro
Beach

225

CLIFF DR

CLIFF DR

WEST BEACH

SHORELINE DR

Leadbetter
Beach

© AVALON TRAVEL

192

COLD SPRINGS RD

ASHLEY RD

192

HOT SPRINGS RD

OUR LADY OF
MOUNT CARMEL
CATHOLIC CHURCH

192

E COTA ST

E MONTECITO ST

HOT SPRINGS RD

OLIVE MILL RD

COAST VILLAGE RD

101

*Andre Clark
Bird Refuge*

101

S MILPAS ST

NINOS DR

E CABRILLO BL

Chase Palm
Park

Cabrillo
Park

EAST BEACH

CHANNEL DR

E CABRILLO BL

PACIFIC
OCEAN

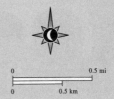

0   0.5 mi

0   0.5 km

landmark. Santa Barbara has no natural harbor, and the wharf was built in 1871 to allow ships to off-load supplies for the bourgeoning town. The current iteration is a favorite for tourists. Frankly, there are a lot of typical tourist shops selling seashells, small, personalized license plates, and gift items you can find most anywhere, but if you walk to the end, you get some of the best views back to the city. There are no railings at the end of the wharf, so keep an eye on little ones.

In addition to the views, there are a few restaurants, an ice cream store, and the **Ty Warner Sea Center** (211 Stearns Wharf, 805/962-2526, www.sbnature.org, 10am-5pm daily, $8 adults, $7 seniors and teens 13-17, $5 children 2-12). A branch of the Santa Barbara Museum of Natural History, this two-story building is devoted to giving you a better understanding of how our oceans work. There are touch tanks on the lower level and staff to answer questions.

El Presidio de Santa Bárbara State Historic Park

Founded on April 21, 1782, **El Presidio de Santa Bárbara State Historic Park** (123 E. Canon Perdido St., 805/965-0093, www.sbthp.org, 10:30am-4:30pm daily, $5 adults, $4 seniors, admission includes Casa de la Guerra) can rightfully be called the birthplace of Santa Barbara. The presidio was the last in a chain of four military fortresses built by the Spanish along the coast of California. The whitewashed buildings were constructed of sun-dried adobe bricks laid upon foundations of sandstone boulders. Timbers from the Los Padres forest supported roofs of red tile. The buildings of the presidio form a quadrangle enclosing a central parade ground. Today, only two sections of the original presidio quadrangle remain: El Cuartel (the second-oldest building in California, dating from 1782), the family residence of the soldier assigned to guard the western gate into the Plaza de Armas; and the Canedo Adobe, named after the

Old Mission Santa Barbara

presidio soldier to whom it was deeded when the presidio became inactive. El Cuartel is small, with tiny doors and windows reflective of the time, but the massively thick walls still stand as they have for more than 200 years, with only cosmetic touch-ups to the plaster that covers the original adobe bricks. The presidio is just a block off State Street downtown and can easily be worked into your downtown sightseeing plans.

Santa Barbara County Courthouse

Covering an entire city block, the still-functioning **Santa Barbara County Courthouse** (1100 Anacapa St., 805/962-6464, www.sbcourts.org, 8am-5pm Mon.-Fri., 10am-4:30pm Sat.-Sun., free docent-led tours 10:30am and 2pm Mon.- Fri., 2pm Sat.-Sun.) is a stunning example of Spanish and Moorish design. William Mooser designed this courthouse to replace the earlier 1872 version, a colonial-looking thing with a massive domed cupola. When the courthouse was

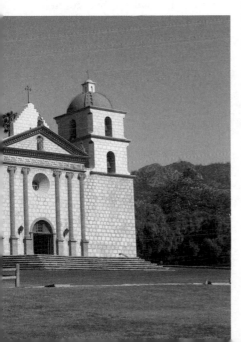

completed in 1929, it was unlike anything in the city. Lush grounds, including the copious lawn and Sunken Gardens, lay the foundation for the sandstone building with arabesque windows, archways, hand-painted wood ceilings, walls with intricate designs, and pueblo tile inlays nearly everywhere flashing brilliant colors and native designs. Of particular note is the Mural Room, once used by the county board of supervisors. The huge room is covered in a mural depicting the early Chumash Indians and following the history of the area leading up to California statehood. All tours of the building meet in the Mural Room and are approximately one hour.

The clock tower, known as **El Mirador,** juts out of the top of the courthouse, making it one of the tallest structures in the city, though the tower is a mere 85 feet tall. But it is here that you'll get the best views of downtown, the mountains, and the ocean from a downtown perspective—it's a must for photo ops.

Santa Barbara Museum of Art

See the power of the visual arts at the **Santa Barbara Museum of Art** (1130 State St., 805/963-4364, www.sbmuseart.org, 11am-5pm Tues.-Sun., $10 adults, $6 seniors and students, free children under 6, free Sun.). Santa Barbara has one of the most impressive art museums and best collections for a community of its size and showcases pieces in many styles and from various eras. Their notable Asian holdings contains more than 2,600 objects representing 4,000 years of history and include Japanese woodblock prints and the 19 Chinese robes that started the collection.

Food

An upscale establishment inside a historic 1872 house, ★ **Stella Mare's** (50 Los Patos Way, 805/969-6705, www.stellamares.com, 11:30am-2:30pm Tues.-Fri., 5pm-close Tues.-Sun., 10am-2:30pm brunch Sun., under $25) offers the perfect

Santa Barbara Urban Wine Trail

Catering to the affections of crushed-grape aficionados, the **Santa Barbara Urban Wine Trail** (www.urbanwinetrailsb.com, $10-20 for 4-8 wines) leads to about 25 premium tasting rooms, all within blocks of downtown and the beach. Most are open 10am-6pm, with some last pours offered as late as 8pm. Most belong to the Santa Barbara County Vintners' Association, whose membership is made up of only licensed growers with a winery facility in the Santa Barbara County and at least 75 percent annual production in Santa Barbara County. Seventeen tasting rooms are located in Santa Barbara's up-and-coming **Funk Zone neighborhood** (funkzone.net), which offers plenty to see and do beyond wine, including galleries and shops.

table for two for romantic, French country-style dining. For something light, share one of their delicious small plates. Under no circumstances should you pass on desserts like chocolate ganache-filled cream puffs and lavender and vanilla creme brulee.

The Habit (www.habitburger.com, 10:30am-9pm Mon.-Sat., 11am-8pm Sun., under $10) has locations downtown (628 State St., 805/892-5400) and near the beach (216 S. Milpas St., 805/962-7472), both serving burgers so thick you have to open your mouth pretty wide.

Vegans and vegetarians will find happiness at **Natural Café & Juice Bar** (508 State St., 805/962-9494, www.thenaturalcafe.com, 11am-9pm Mon.-Sun., under $10), with outdoor sidewalk dining. In contrast, **Woody's BBQ** (5112 Hollister Ave., 805/967-3775, www.woodysbbq.com, 11am-9pm Sun.-Thurs., 11am-10pm Fri.-Sat., under $18) will keep meat-lovers contentedly licking their fingers.

Expect a wait at **Arigato Sushi** (1225 State St., 805/965-6074, 5:30pm-10pm daily, under $20), but good sushi is worth it! Fresh seafood with an unpretentious dash of sophistication keeps the dining rooms at **Arch Rock Fish** (608 Anacapa St., 805/845-2800, www.archrocksantabarbara.com, 11:30am-10pm daily, under $26) and **Enterprise Fish Company** (225 State St., 805/962-3313, 11:30am-10pm Sun.-Thurs., 11:30am-11pm Fri.-Sat., under $26) busy.

One of the best restaurants in town, **Downey's Restaurant** (1305 State St., 805/966-5006, www.downeyssb.com, 5pm-9pm daily, $30-45), and the local favorite **Wine Cask** (813 Anacapa St., 805/966-9463, www.winecask.com, 11am-9pm Tues.-Sun., $24 and up) both feature excellent California cuisine and perfect wine pairings. Reservations are recommended.

Nightlife

Many of the bars and nightclubs are on or around the main drag of State Street, much of which caters to the college students from the nearby university.

Bars with strong, cheap drinks are **Joe's Cafe** (536 State St., 805/966-4638), which packs a pretty potent punch, and **Sharkeez** (525 State St., 805/845-9572), not as strong as Joe's but Thursday $1 drink nights make it a popular hangout.

Well-known pubs are **The James Joyce** (513 State St., 805/962-2688, 10am-2am daily), a traditional Irish watering hole with weekend bands, and **Dargan's Irish Pub & Restaurant** (18 E. Ortega St., 805/568-0702), which serves some good Irish stew, Guinness, and Irish music.

Play a few rounds of pool or sit back with a beer or glass of wine and listen to rock bands at **Elsie's Tavern** (117 De La Guerra, 805/963-4503, noon-2am Mon.-Fri., 4pm-2am Sat.-Sun.). If you're into the jazz scene, check out **SOhO Restaurant and Music Club** (1221 State St., 805/962-7776, www.sohosb.com,

6:30pm-11pm, $10 and up). To dance the night away, **Wildcat Lounge** (15 W. Ortega St., 805/962-7970, 4pm-2am daily) is "the" dance club in Santa Barbara and offers a full bar.

Serving light food and cocktails, **Blush Restaurant & Lounge** (630 State St., 805/957-1300, www.blushsb.com, 11am-close daily, 3pm-7pm happy hour) has a chic modern feel, with signature drinks and a primo happy hour. Voted the "best" Santa Barbara happy hour, **Sandbar Mexican Restaurant and Tequila Bar** (514 State St., 805/966-1388, www.sandbarsb.com, 11am-2am daily, 3pm-7pm daily happy hour) features superb drinks, half-off appetizers, and a lively outdoor patio.

Les Marchands Wine Bar & Merchant (131 Anacapa St., Ste. B, 805/284-0380, 11am-10pm Sun.-Thurs., 11am-midnight Fri.-Sat.) offers a vast selection of wine by the glass, and excellent international beer and cider.

Arts and Entertainment

The **Arlington Theatre** (1317 State St., 805/963-9589, $35 and up) hosts many of the Santa Barbara International Film Festival events as well as big-name performers. It's worth the price of admission to admire its Spanish colonial and Mission Revival architecture, which features a covered courtyard with a fountain. Elaborate Spanish balconies, staircases, and houses are built out from the walls, creating the illusion of a Spanish colonial town.

Catch a fabulous musical comedy, theatrical play, or musical performance at the **Ensemble Theatre Company** (33 W. Victoria St., 805/965-5400, www.etcsb.org, $25 and up), or for cirque, aerial, burlesque, and cabaret, **The Savoy** (409 State St., 805/957-4111, www.savorysb.com, $30 and up) showcases an "extraordinary blend of contemporary entertainment." Housed in a historic landmark building dating back to 1889, the venue itself offers almost as many features on its three floors as it does variety shows,

including a restaurant, three bars, a patio, and multiple stages.

Exclusively filled with original works, the Santa Barbara Art Association's **Gallery 113** (1114 State St. #8, 805/965-6611, www.sbartassoc.org/gallery-113) hosts numerous exhibitions.

Shopping

Plenty of open-air shopping centers house the usual retail chains, but **La Arcada** (1114 State St., 805/966-6634, www.laarcadasantabarbara.com) offers unique local boutiques, galleries, and specialty shops. Parking is free for the first 75 minutes, but don't expect easy or free beach parking.

Treasures abound at **Santa Barbara Arts** (1114 State St., 805/884-1938, www.sbarts.com, 11am-6pm Mon.-Sat., 11am-5pm Sun.), with an eclectic mix of artist-made creations from handmade jewelry to ceramics to paintings. For fine oil paintings and sculptures, explore the **Waterhouse Gallery** (1114 State St., 805/962-8885, 11am-5pm Mon.-Sat., 11am-4pm Sun.) and **Oliver & Espig** (1108 State St., 805/962-8111 or 805/585-5257, http://oliverandespig.com, 11am-5:30pm Tues.-Sat.), known for their handcrafted jewelry.

Browse artisanal food at **Isabella Gourmet Foods** (5 E. Figueroa St., 805/585-5257, 9am-6pm Mon.-Fri., 10am-6pm Sat., 11am-5pm Sun.) or French handmade chocolates at **Chocolats du CaliBressan** (1114 State St. #25, 805/568-1313, www.chococalibressan.com, 10am-6pm Tues.-Fri, 10:30am-5pm Sat., 11:30am-5pm Sun.).

The Italian Pottery Outlet (929 State St., 877/496-5599, www.italianpottery.com, 10:30am-6pm daily) carries the biggest collection of Italian pottery and ceramics at affordable prices.

Mystique Sonique (1103 State St., 805/568-0473, www.mystiquesonique.com, 10am-7pm daily) has a great selection of all things vintage, hip, and chic for both men and women. **Fuzion Gallery**

& Boutique (1115 State St., 805/687-6401, www.fuzionsb.com, 11am-7pm Sun.-Thurs., 11am-8pm Fri.-Sat.) stocks cutting-edge clothing from around the world, as well as from local start-ups. Hidden gem **Lovebird Boutique & Jewelry Bar** (7 E. De La Guerra St., 805/568-3800, www.lovebirdsb.com, 10am-6pm Mon.-Thurs., 10am-8pm Fri.-Sat., 10am-7pm Sun.) has beautiful unique adornments.

Recreation

Long, flat **Leadbetter Beach** (Shoreline Dr. and Loma Alta Dr., sunrise-10pm daily) is the best in Santa Barbara. Sheer cliffs rise from the sand, trees dot the point, and the beach is protected by the harbor's breakwater, making it ideal for swimming.

Named because it is east of Stearns Wharf, **East Beach** (Cabrillo Blvd. at S. Milpas St., sunrise-10pm daily) is all soft sand, with a dozen volleyball nets, a snack bar, a children's play area, and a bike path.

Known locally as Hendry's, dog-friendly **Arroyo Burro Beach** (Cliff Dr. and Las Positas Rd., sunrise-10pm daily) is a popular spot for surfers and kayakers. Far removed from downtown, it's very popular with locals.

Santa Barbara is also home to numerous private and public golf courses. **Hidden Oaks** (4760 Calle Camarada, 805/967-3493, 8:30am-8pm, $12) and **Twin Lakes** (6034 Hollister Ave., 805/964-1414, www.twinlakesgolf.com, 7am-7pm daily, $13-14) are both affordable nine-hole courses. The **Santa Barbara Golf Club** (3500 McCaw Ave., 805/687-7087, 6am-8:30pm daily, $40 and up) and the world-class **Rancho San Marcos** (4600 CA-154, 805/683-6334, www.rsm1804.com, 6am-7pm daily, $40-80) offer the complete 18-hole golf experience.

Events

The biggest event of the year, **Fiesta** or **Old Spanish Days** (downtown Santa Barbara, 805/962-8101, www.oldspanishdays-fiesta.org, late July or early August, tickets: Carriage Museum, 129 Castillo St., $25) is a week-long celebration of the city's Spanish, Mexican, and Native American history. Events feature Folklorico, flamenco, and Aztec music and dance, fantastic foods, and the amazing El Desfile Histórico (Historical Parade).

The Santa Ynez Band of Chumash Indians host the annual **Intertribal Pow-Wow** (Live Oaks, Los Padres National Forest, www.santaynezchumash.org/culture.html, 10am-5pm fall, free, $3 parking), where hundreds of tribes gather in honor of culture and heritage, with drummers from the United States and Canada, a variety of foods, and authentic handmade native crafts.

Hollywood notables gather for the annual **Santa Barbara International Film Festival** (805/963-0023, www.sbiff.org, $60-75 tickets), which includes tributes, movie screenings, and a gala.

The first Thursday of each month, the Santa Barbara Arts Collaborative curates **Art Crawl** (Del La Guerra and Anacapa Sts., www.sbartsblog.com, 5:30pm first Thurs. of the month, free), focusing on the best of the local art scene.

Accommodations

Santa Barbara is an expensive place to stay, regardless of time of year, weather, or even economic downturns. Most properties require a two-night minimum stay during the summer.

The ★ **Simpson House Inn** (121 E. Arrellaga, 805/963-7067, www.simpsonhouseinn.com, $375-610) features opulent rooms on an 1874 estate with a well-manicured and formal English garden. A vegetarian breakfast starts the day, afternoon tea and desserts are available at midday, and an evening wine-tasting brings the day to a close. It's a short walk to State Street.

The inexpensive **Santa Barbara Tourist Hostel** (134 Chapala St., 805/963-0154, $25-45 dorm, $69-125 private with shared bath, $79-139 private room and bath) is only two blocks from the beach and one block from State Street. The **Avania Inn** of Santa Barbara (128 Castillo St., 805/963-4472, $129 and up) features pillow top beds, a complimentary hot breakfast, free parking, and a steamy redwood sauna.

Hotel Milo (202 W. Cabrillo Blvd., 805/965-4577 and 800/965-9776, www.hotelmilosantabarbara.com, $209 and up), a stone's throw from the beach, features beautiful outdoor gardens, views of the wharf and harbor, and complimentary bikes for guests.

The mission-style **Fess Parker** (633 E. Cabrillo Blvd., 805/564-4333, www.fessparkersantabarbarahotel.com, $219 and up) sits right on the beach and offers wine-tasting and five restaurants.

Intimate and elegant, the **Brisas del Mar Inn** (223 Castillo St., 805/966-2219, $197 and up) is a Mediterranean-style villa just two blocks from the beaches and downtown, with spacious, comfortable rooms and complimentary bikes.

The nicest B&B for the price is **A White Jasmine Inn** (1327 Bath St., 805/966-0589, $161-327), composed of three cottages, with richly decorated rooms and fragrant surrounding gardens.

The refined **Santa Ynez Inn** (3627 Sagunto St., 805/688-5588 and 800/643-5774, www.santaynezinn.com, $285 and up) rests in the foothills of wine country, offering a quiet retreat filled with luxury and warm hospitality.

Information and Services
The **Santa Barbara Visitors Center** (1 Garden St., 805/965-3021 and 805/568-1811, 9am-5pm daily) staff are available to assist visitors by answering questions and providing local area and service information. The center is centrally located in downtown inside a traditional adobe building.

Channel Islands National Park

Channel Islands National Park is made up of a total of eight islands, though only five of those (Anacapa, Santa Cruz, Santa Rosa, San Miguel, and Santa Barbara) are within sight of the mainland. For just over 30 years these areas have been federally protected. Long before they were tourist spots, they were ranch lands. And even longer before that, some 13,000 years ago, archaeological evidence suggests that they there were inhabited by indigenous people. Today, they're one of the last remaining wilderness spots in California.

Visiting the Park
Channel Islands National Park (1901 Spinnaker Dr., 805/658-5700, free) is one of the least visited national parks in the United States, but it offers an array of outdoor activities, including backpacking, camping, scuba diving, kayaking, and surfing. The islands are most known for their high number of mysterious sea caves, arches, and abundant wildlife. A trip to the islands is an adventure into a solitary world, and a hidden paradise for every outdoor adventurer.

The National Park Service authorizes a small number of guides and outfitter services. It is important to check with the visitors center and national park service to plan your trip accordingly.

Getting There and Around
From Santa Barbara Harbor, **Truth Aquatics** (301 W. Cabrillo Blvd., 805/962-1127, $50 and $75 round-trip pp) provides access by boat to the islands. From Ventura, **Island Packers** (1691 Spinnaker Dr., Ventura, 805/642-1393, www.islandpackers.com) provides day trips ($59-82 adults, $41-65 children) and overnight ($79-114 adults, $57-90 children) transportation to four of the islands, as well as whale-watching cruises.

Air travel is possible from Camarillo Airport via **Channel Islands Aviation** (305 Durley Ave., Camarillo, 805/987-1301, $150-160 adults round-trip, $125-135 children) to Santa Rosa Island only.

Plan to walk or kayak your way around. There's no public transportation on any of the islands, and biking is not allowed.

Seasons

Temperatures average in the mid-60s°F to the low-50s year-round, but this is the coast, so be prepared for high winds and fog. The outer islands of Santa Rosa and San Miguel experience more frequent high winds, at times 30-knot winds. Other islands have more moderate winds. However, during the late spring and summer months, fog thickens, causing challenging visibility.

Park Entrances

Boaters must access Santa Barbara Island via the landing cove; dock access is limited. Access to Santa Rosa Island is permitted via coastline or beaches, and piers are available at Bechers Bay. Access to San Miguel Island is through Cuyler Harbor (beach only) or Tyler Bight. Access to

Anacapa Island is at East Anacapa or Frenchy's Cove, however, a permit is required at Middle Anacapa and visitors must be accompanied by a park ranger (access to West Anacapa is not allowed). Access to Santa Cruz Island is available via the pier at Scorpion Anchorage or Prisoners Harbor.

Check with **The Nature Conservatory** (805/964-7839, www.nature.org) for information regarding any necessary boat landing permits, and for a full list of regulatory information.

Visitors Centers

Channel Islands National Parks Mainland Visitor Center (1901 Spinnaker Dr., 805/658-5700, 8am-5pm Mon.-Fri., 8am-5:30pm Sat.-Sun.) is located in Ventura and provides interpretive programs, tidepool displays, a bookstore, and island exhibits.

The **Outdoors Santa Barbara Visitor Center** (113 Harbor Way 4th Fl., 805/884-1475, 11am-5pm daily) offers visitors

Channel Islands National Park

exhibits and information about Channel Islands National Park and Channel Islands National Marine Sanctuary.

The small visitor contact stations on Santa Barbara and Anacapa Islands include resource displays and information on each island. Scorpion Ranch on Santa Cruz Island also houses information.

Information and Services

All information can be obtained via the visitors centers and through the **National Recreation Reservation Service** (805/658-5711 and 877/444-6777, www.recreation.gov). There are no entrance fees, but a permit is required for camping and backcountry camping.

Boaters should check with **The Nature Conservancy** (805/964-7839, www.nature.org) for landing information and permits. Private boaters must receive permission to land on certain islands, including Santa Cruz Island.

Overnight **camping and backcountry camping reservations** (805/658-5711 and 877/444-6777, www.recreation.gov) can be made no more than five months in advance. Information required includes camping dates, transportation information, and number of campers.

For weather reports, check the **Channel Islands Internet Weather Kiosk** (www.channelislands.noaa.gov/news/kiosk.html).

Sights and Recreation

Go sea cave kayaking with **Santa Barbara Kayak Tours** (next to the Launch Ramp, 805/962-2826, $10 and up rental, $50 and up for tours), which offers guided tours on several of the islands, as well as multiday trips.

All the islands offer hiking, water activities, and camping. Trails range from relatively flat trails to steep, rugged, mountainous trails. It is important to remember to stay within park boundaries and not hike on The Nature Conservancy property, which is clearly marked by a fence line.

On **Santa Cruz Island,** Scorpion Beach offers some of the best areas for water sports with easy beach access, and nearby sea caves for adventure exploration. Prisoners Harbor and Smugglers Cove also provide beach access; however, snorkeling and diving are not allowed. To access kelp beds, snorkelers and divers should explore near the pier and at the bay's eastern end.

Santa Rosa Island offers sandy beaches, with easy access, and great opportunities for surfing. The north shore is best in winter and spring and the south shore is best in summer and fall.

Aggressive winds at **San Miguel Island** make water activities dangerous for the inexperienced. However, there is an exceptional 16-mile guided hike to Point Bennett, where you can see one of the largest ensemble of wildlife gather.

Santa Barbara Island is a great place to see seals and sea lions from Landing Cove and from the overlook points of Sea Lion Rookery and Elephant Seal Cove. There

are incredible stands of native vegetation and wildflowers. Kayakers can explore Sea Lion Rookery to the south, which offers a wonderland of wildlife, sea caves, and ocean arches.

The Landing Cove on **Anacapa Island** provides excellent swimming, diving, and snorkeling, but remember there are no lifeguards. Kayakers can head east toward Arch Rock or west toward Cathedral Cove for marine and wildlife viewing and sea caves. Hiking is limited on the island to only about two miles of trail.

There is no fishing allowed on any of the islands, and visitors are asked to stay on the trails and not disturb the flora or fauna. Visitors are asked to avoid animal nesting areas and to stay out of caves if not professionally guided. The park website contains a detailed list of restrictions.

Camping

Camping is available by **reservation only.** Campsites are primitive, with basic picnic tables and pit toilets. Trash containers are not provided; campers are expected to pack out their own garbage. Campsites are all close together, so don't expect a lot of privacy during high season. **Water** is available at the Scorpion Anchorage on Santa Cruz, at the Santa Rosa campground, and nowhere else. Due to the wind, San Miguel and Santa Rosa campgrounds have **windbreaks** for each campsite.

There are **no food venues, stores, or restaurants** on the islands. Santa Rosa Island campground and Scorpion Anchorage on Santa Cruz are the only sites for water. Plan accordingly and bring your own food and water.

Fires are not permitted except on eastern Santa Cruz Island, where there are fire pits and wood provided.

Camping on Santa Rosa Island beaches is for experienced kayakers and boaters on a seasonal basis, and a permit is required ($10-15 per night).

A **40-pound weight limit** restriction is imposed by the boat concessionaire. Bring the necessities, keeping in mind what is available on-site. With exception of Santa Rosa and San Miguel, which are both 1 mile to 1.5 miles, campgrounds are 0.5 mile from the landings. The eastern Santa Cruz site is an easy flat walk, while San Miguel and Santa Barbara are an uphill trek. Anacapa is uphill as well and includes stairs—a lot of stairs (approximately 156).

Ventura

About 35 miles southeast of Santa Barbara, Ventura sits sandwiched between the American Riviera and Los Angeles. Ventura has long been the middle child, going about its own business, seemingly unaffected by the passage of time, a beach town best known to local surfers. But today, its walkable Main Street, just three blocks from the beach, is undergoing a renaissance. Eclectic buildings include art deco facades next to turn-of-the-20th-century structures next to polished tile-and-glass designs. New and trendy restaurants are opening up, and nightlife offerings are worth seeking out.

Sights

At the west end of Main Street, **Mission San Buenaventura** (211 E. Main St., 805/648-4496, 10am-5pm Mon.-Fri., 9am-5pm Sat., 10am-5pm Sun., $4 adults, $1 children) was the ninth mission in California, established in 1782. It is one of the few missions to still have wooden bells on display. From the gift shop, where the self-guided tour begins, the door opens to the courtyard, a beautifully landscaped area with a fountain in the center, surrounded by a few benches and interlocking short pathways. The church is across the courtyard. The church itself is long and narrow, a neoclassical-looking arch over the altar giving a more modern feel to the interior. The area behind

273

the church is part of the original brick reservoir.

Recreation

Whatever your taste, Ventura has the beach for you. **San Buenaventura State Beach** (San Pedro St. and US-101, 805/968-1033, www.parks.ca.gov, dawn-dusk daily) offers two miles of sea and sand for swimming, surfing, and picnicking. Accessed off Main Street, **Emma Wood State Beach** (W. Main St. and Park Access Rd., recorded information 805/585-1850, www.parks.ca.gov, www. reserveamerica.com, dawn-dusk daily, day-use $10 per vehicle) can be rocky but is a great spot for windsurfing. Families flock to **Harbor Cove Beach** (1900 Spinnaker Dr., dawn-dusk daily), where the harbor's breakwaters provide relative safety from the ocean currents. Food and other amenities can be found across the street at Ventura Harbor Village. Farther north, **Faria Beach** (4350 W. US-101, at State Beach exit, 805/654-3951, dawn-dusk daily) is available for tent camping and has 15 RV hookups.

Ventura is also known for **surfing,** with **The Rincon** (Bates Rd. and US-101) its most famous landmark. Located between Santa Barbara and Ventura, The Rincon is a small cliffside cove between US-101 and the ocean. The intense swells make it a surfer's dream. Near the pier,

C-Street is the nickname for another popular surfing spot, a mile-long stretch of sand at the end of California Street. Spectators gather along the concrete boardwalk to see wave-riders in action.

Food and Accommodations

One of the best examples of Ventura's burgeoning culinary scene is **Watermark on Main** (589 E. Main St., 805/643-6800, www.watermarkonmain.com, 5pm-9pm Tues.-Thurs., 5pm-10pm Fri.-Sat., $18-48), housed inside a stunningly and lovingly restored 1928 bank building. Steak and seafood are served under vintage art deco light fixtures and a hand-painted plaster ceiling. **Yolanda's Mexican Cafe** (2753 E. Main St., 805/643-2700, www. yolandasmexicancafe.com, 11am-9:30pm Mon.-Thurs., 11am-10pm Fri.-Sat., 10am-9pm Sun., $10-20) serves some of the best Mexican food in Ventura; they're noisy, colorful, and very good food for the price.

Ventura is full of chain hotels and motels. For something different, downtown's **Bella Maggiore Inn** (67 S. California St., 805/652-0277 or 800/523-8479, www. bellamaggioreinn.com, $95-180) has a definite European feel. Just three blocks from the beach, the 32 rooms in this charmingly peculiar spot are all configured differently, and the inn almost feels more like a large bed-and-breakfast than a hotel.

Southern California Coast

When most people think of Southern California, the images that come to mind are white sands, sun-kissed beach bodies, Disneyland, and, of course, Hollywood.

Barstow

14

5

15

126

101

TCL CHINESE THEATRE
HOLLYWOOD WALK OF FAME
GRIFFITH PARK

RODEO DRIVE
THE GETTY
CENTER

215

Ventura

10

Malibu

Santa
Monica

1

Los Angeles

10

VENICE BEACH
BOARDWALK

91

Long Beach

5

15

Huntington
Beach

Dana Point
Laguna Beach
Newprt Beach

Catalina
Island

1

Oceanside

Carlsbad

PACFIC
OCEAN

LA JOLLA
COVE

La Jolla

San Clemente
Island

1

San Diego

San Diego

BALBOA PARK

Tijuana

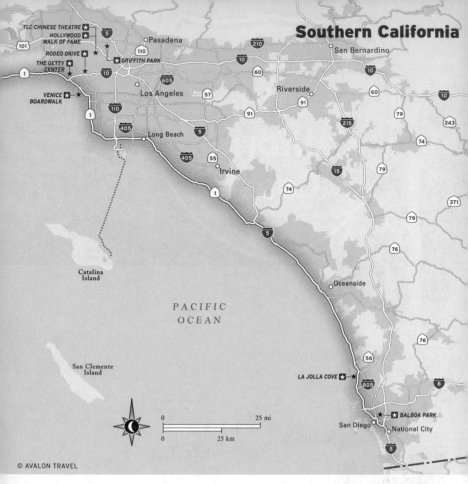

Southern California

TLC CHINESE THEATRE
HOLLYWOOD WALK OF FAME
RODEO DRIVE
THE GETTY CENTER
GRIFFITH PARK
Pasadena
San Bernardino
VENICE BOARDWALK
Los Angeles
Riverside
Long Beach
Irvine
Catalina Island
PACIFIC OCEAN
San Clemente Island
Oceanside
La Jolla Cove
Balboa Park
San Diego
National City

0   25 mi
0   25 km

© AVALON TRAVEL

The SoCal megalopolitan area is blessed with a car-crazy culture, soft sandy beaches, and the "happiest place on Earth."

It's also inhabited by movie stars. You'll see their names embedded in the ground beneath your feet in the Hollywood Walk of Fame—and you may even catch them shopping in Beverly Hills or clubbing in Hollywood.

Drive Southern California's coast via PCH (that's what cool people call CA-1)

and you'll encounter some of the best beaches and most fashionable hubs in the state, from Malibu's glorious El Matador Beach to Venice Beach and its boardwalk spectacle.

Continue south past vibrant seaside towns that lap up the Orange County sunshine. Join the mix of locals and tourists surfing, snorkeling, and kayaking in places like Newport, Laguna, and La Jolla. You reach the end of the road—or at least CA-1—in San Diego, which boasts sparkling waters, historical sites, and a rich cultural scene.

Planning Your Time

Though seven days is adequate, give yourself extra time to journey down the

Highlights

★ **Venice Beach Boardwalk:** From the freaky to the fantastic, the Venice Boardwalk has it all. Prepare yourself for people-watching of fantastic proportions (page 287).

★ **TCL Chinese Theatre:** This Hollywood icon opened in 1927 and hosts the footprints of the stars, along with premieres of their movies (page 293).

★ **Hollywood Walk of Fame:** Since 1960, entertainment legends have wished for a spot on this iconic three-mile sidewalk of the stars (page 293).

★ **Griffith Park:** A welcome expanse of greenery, "L.A.'s Central Park" includes the Griffith Observatory and the L.A. Zoo (page 295).

★ **Rodeo Drive:** Though the price tags along this famed Beverly Hills boulevard may be bigger than your zip code, window-shopping and celebrity-spotting is free (page 297).

★ **The Getty Center:** High on a hilltop above L.A., this free museum is home to eclectic art pieces and stunning views of the skyline (page 297).

★ **La Jolla Cove:** With its white sand and deep blue water, this beach north of San Diego is a refuge from the road, and its sea caves are a refuge for diverse marinelife (page 322).

★ **Balboa Park:** This sprawling urban park includes Spanish colonial architecture, lush gardens, multiple museums, and the world-famous San Diego Zoo (page 329).

splashy Southern California coast. The plethora of sights and activities combined with a warm, sunny disposition is best experienced in a state of flexibility.

SoCal has vast overnight options, but it is necessary to make reservations at popular hotels at least a month in advance during late spring and summer. This is especially important in areas with concentrated attractions such as Los Angeles and San Diego. In off-season months, two-weeks prior to stay is sufficient.

It's just over 60 miles from Oxnard to Los Angeles, and another 125 miles to San Diego. Driving times are dependent on the infamous Southern California traffic. Following scenic CA-1 is typically a much slower drive, but keep in mind that traffic can grind to a halt on the major freeways (US-101 and I-5) as well.

Getting There
Car
Southern California seems built for car travel. Major highways from the north include I-5 (southbound from Sacramento to San Diego), US-101 (southbound from Santa Barbara), and the coast hugger better known as Highway 1 (CA-1). From the east, I-15 connects Las Vegas to San Diego, and I-10 connects Phoenix to Los Angeles.

Air
Major airports are **Los Angeles International Airport (LAX)** (1 World Way, 310/646-5252, www.lawa.org/lax) and **San Diego (SAN)** (3225 N. Harbor Dr., 619/400-2404, www.san.org). The Los Angeles metropolitan area also offers several smaller, often less congested airports: Bob Hope in Burbank (BUR), John Wayne in Orange County (SNA), and Long Beach (LGB).

Train
Amtrak (800/872-7245, www.amtrak. com, $135 and up) offers service on the **Coast Starlight** to Seattle, Portland, Sacramento, Oakland, and Los Angeles. The **Pacific Surfliner** provides service from San Luis Obispo to Santa Barbara, Los Angeles, and San Diego. The **Sunset Limited** travels east-west between Tennessee and Los Angeles. International visitors can buy an unlimited travel USA Rail Pass, good for 15, 30, or 45 days.

Bus
Greyhound (800/231-2222, www.

Best Hotels

★ **Viceroy Hotel:** This ecofriendly Santa Monica hotel is a trendsetter (page 286).

★ **Ace Hotel:** This hip up-and-comer includes vibrant lounges, a cozy coffee shop, and an ornate theater—that's Hollywood style (page 305).

★ **Beverly Wilshire Hotel:** Even in Beverly Hills, this Italian Renaissance masterpiece stands out (page 305).

★ **Crystal Cove Beach Cottages:** Enjoy a peaceful retreat in a rustic cabin on one of the last undeveloped beaches in Southern California (page 315).

★ **La Valencia:** This La Jolla villa is almost as beautiful as its views of the shimmering Pacific (page 323).

★ **Hotel Indigo:** This eco-chic hotel is at the center of the action in San Diego's Gaslamp Quarter (page 336).

★ **Hotel del Coronado:** This grand Victorian resort in San Diego is famous for celebrity guests like Marilyn Monroe and its resident ghost (page 337).

greyhound.com) offers special discounts to students and seniors with routes and stops sticking to major highways and cities.

Fuel and Services

Cars, and subsequently **gas stations** and other services, are ubiquitous in high-population Southern California. Compared to most of the country, California typically has substantially higher gasoline prices because of its high taxes. Avoid fueling up in downtown L.A. or along Olympic and San Vicente Boulevards.

To receive reports on **road conditions,** call **511.** If your phone carrier does not support 511, call toll-free at 800/977-6368.

For **emergency assistance** and services, call **911.**

Oxnard

Where Pacific Coast Highway 1 (CA-1) splits from US-101, Oxnard is the gateway to California's southern coast, with wide sandy beaches and the **Channel Islands Harbor,** an exceptional place for diving, sea kayaking, sport fishing, and whale-watching. It's been ranked as one of the wealthiest and safest cities in America.

Downtown bursts with activity in historic **Heritage Square** (715 South A St.), a hub for shopping, community events, and wine-tasting at Rancho Ventavo Cellars Tasting Room. The open-air plaza features 15 restored Victorian mansions, fountains, and surrounding gardens. Guided **walking tours** (805/483-7960 ext. 3, 10am-4pm Sat., 1pm-4pm Sun., $5) provide an overview of the city's early farming roots and booming growth, attributed to the sugar beet industry.

Oxnard hosts the **California Strawberry Festival** (Strawberry Meadows of College Park, 3250 S. Rose Ave., $12 adults, $5 children, $10 parking), on the third weekend in May, featuring appropriately themed food items such as strawberry nachos, strawberry pizza, strawberry funnel cake, strawberry sundaes, and strawberry champagne.

At the **California Welcome Center** (2786 Seaglass Way, 805/988-0717, 9am-9pm daily), you'll find the most informative regional and state maps and brochures, as well as concierge services, souvenirs, food items, and special offers and attraction discounts.

Best Restaurants

★ **Neptune's Net:** After a day riding waves, Malibu surfers sate their appetites with fresh seafood at the coastside spot (page 280).

★ **Valentino's:** This chic Italian eatery in Santa Monica is legendary (page 284).

★ **Original Pantry:** This L.A. breakfast spot is "never closed—never without a customer." Taste the food and you'll see why (page 298).

★ **Yuca's:** This tiny taqueria serves the best Mexican food in L.A. and has the James Beard Award to prove it (page 299).

★ **Bouchon Bistro:** Celebrity chef Thomas Keller's L.A. outpost showcases the elegant French cuisine that made him famous (page 300).

★ **Porkyland Restaurant:** This La Jolla grill serves authentic Mexican cuisine with a kick (page 319).

Malibu

When many people think of "L.A.," they're really picturing the beach communities to the west of Los Angeles proper. It all begins with Malibu, which stretches for more than 20 miles, hugging the coastline the whole way. It doesn't look like a town or a city in the conventional sense. Don't search for the town center; there isn't one. Instead, the "town" is a mix of beaches and multi-million-dollar homes, perched precariously on the mountains rising up over the coastline and occupied by superstars you would recognize from movie screens. For road-trippers, Malibu offers a gradual introduction to Los Angeles, with its odd mix of beautiful natural scenery and luxurious excess.

Point Mugu State Park

Right around **Point Mugu State Park** (9000 CA-1 W., 310/457-8143, www. parks.ca.gov, 8am-10pm daily, $8-12), 15 miles south of Oxnard, CA-1 comes back to the coast and stays there as it passes through Malibu and Santa Monica. In addition to the beach, there are hiking trails, dunes, and campsites.

Food

A few miles down the highway, ★ **Neptune's Net** (42505 CA-1, 310/457-3095, www.neptunesnet.com, 10:30am-7pm Mon.-Thurs., 10:30am-8pm Fri., 10am-7:30pm Sat.-Sun., $8-18) catches all kinds of seafood to serve to hungry diners, often in a fried form. Because it's situated adjacent to the County Line surf break, salt-encrusted local surfers often satisfy their enormous appetites here after hours out on the waves.

Leo Carrillo State Park

The beach at **Leo Carrillo State Park** (35000 CA-1 W., 310/457-8143, www. parks.ca.gov, 8am-10pm daily, $12) offers more than just sunbathing and

view of Malibu from the Pacific Coast Highway

swimming. Caves, reefs, and tidepools make for an interesting stop. There is also a **visitors center** (10am-2pm Fri.-Sat.).

Nicholas Canyon County Beach

Less crowded than other nearby beaches, **Nicholas Canyon** (33850 CA-1, http:// beaches.lacounty.gov, $3-10) offers one of the few good point breaks in Los Angeles County, making it a good spot for bodysurfing, bodyboarding, wind-sailing, and scuba diving. (It's often referred to as "Zeros" or "Point Zero.") Families enjoy nearly a mile stretch of sandy beach, with picnic tables and full bathroom facilities.

After exploring the beach, visit the fascinating **Chumash Discovery Village** (33904 CA-1, 424/644-0088) that lies on a bluff overlooking the Pacific. Eight prehistoric (4000-6000 BC) sites have been found within a half-mile of the current replicated village. Guided tours and presentations are available by appointment.

El Pescador State Beach

El Pescador State Beach (32860 CA-1, 310/457-1324, 8am-sunset daily) (the name means "the fisherman" in Spanish) is a well-known spot for surf fishing, surfing, and bodyboarding. It also offers good beachcombing, including tidepools rich with colorful sea anemones and starfish and small caves that can be explored at low tide.

El Matador State Beach

A rugged strip of white sand, steep cliffs, sea stacks, and incredible swells makes **El Matador State Beach** (32215 CA-1, 8am-sunset daily, parking $8 all day) a favorite among surfers and bodyboarders. The natural splendor has made it a favorite backdrop for photo shoots as well. Park at the top of the bluff and follow the long staircase down the cliffside and onto the beach.

Zuma Beach

If you've ever seen the cult classic film *Earth Girls Are Easy,* you'll recognize legendary **Zuma Beach** (30000 CA-1, http://beaches.lacounty.gov, $3-12.50). This popular surf and boogie boarding break fills up fast on summer weekends. Crystal-clear water (unusual for the L.A. area) makes it good for swimming. Grab a spot on the west side of CA-1 for free parking, or pay a little for one of the more than 2,000 spots in the beach parking lot. Amenities include a snack bar, board-walk, and volleyball courts, as well as restrooms and showers.

Point Dume State Beach

The crystal-clear water at **Point Dume State Beach** (Westward Beach Rd., 310/457-8143, sunrise-sunset daily), just two miles off of CA-1, makes it one of the best places in Southern California to scuba dive. The views from atop the coastal bluff are outstanding. It's named in honor of Padre Francisco Dumetz of Mission San Buenaventura by explorer George Vancouver, who made a spelling error.

Malibu Lagoon State Beach

In a row of private beaches fronting mansions, **Malibu Lagoon State Beach** (23200 CA-1, 310/457-8143, www.parks.ca.gov, 8am-sunset daily, $12) offers public access. Malibu Creek runs into the ocean here, creating a unique wetlands ecosystem that's well worth exploring. The ancillary **Malibu Surfriders Beach** is a pretty stretch of sugar-like sand, offering a wealth of activities. Other park attractions include the 1929 **Adamson House and Malibu Lagoon Museum** (23200 CA-1, 310/456-8432, www.adamsonhouse.org, $7 adults, $2 children).

Malibu Pier

Malibu Pier (23000 CA-1, www.malibupiersportfishing.com) is busy in the summertime and lonely in the winter, when only die-hard surfers ply the adjacent three-point break and a few fisherfolk brave the chilly weather (which in Malibu means under 70°F). The pier hosts board rentals, sport fishing, and whale-watching charters, restaurants, and food stands. Interpretive signs describe local history.

The Getty Villa

Perched on the cliffs just east of Malibu in Pacific Palisades, the **Getty Villa** (17985 CA-1, Pacific Palisades, 310/440-7300, www.getty.edu, 10am-5pm Wed.-Mon., free but reservations required, $15 parking) is a lush estate, styled in the manner of an ancient Roman country home. The museum's immense, if at times controversial, collection of Etruscan, Greek, and Roman antiquities includes 44,000 pieces; only a small fraction are on display in its 23 galleries.

Santa Monica

Born as a seaside retreat in the 1900s, Santa Monica was at one time home to silver-screen giants like Greta Garbo and Cary Grant. By the late 1960s, the Santa Monica Freeway brought new growth, and an eclectic mix of families, free-spirited surfers, and business professionals. Today, Santa Monica comes as close to a community of moderate means as you'll find along the L.A. coastline. With its fun-but-not-fancy pier, its inexpensive off-beach motels, and a variety of delicious inexpensive dining options, Santa Monica is a great choice for a road-trip stop.

Getting There and Around

CA-1 runs north and south along the coast traveling right through Santa Monica. The often congested I-10 Freeway (also known as the Santa Monica Freeway and the San Bernardino Freeway) runs to the Santa Monica Pier from downtown Los Angeles; it's a rare day when traffic moves at the posted MPH. If you are driving from Los Angeles, I-5 and US-101 join I-10 around downtown L.A. This can be confusing if you're unaware, so keep your eye on the signs.

Not many places in Los Angeles can be accessed without a car, but Santa Monica is an exception. Many of the city's tourist destinations are within walking distance of each other. **Santa Monica's Bike Transit Center** (www.bikesm.com) provides bike rentals and two secured parking sites: at 320 Broadway and at 215 Colorado Avenue. A U-lock is recommended.

The **Big Blue Bus** (310/451-5444, www.bigbluebus.com, $1, free transfers) provides service both locally and throughout the Greater Los Angeles area.

Sights
Santa Monica Beach

Santa Monica Beach embodies the city's history, scenic beauty, and active lifestyle with 3.5 miles of wide, sandy beach, perfect for sunbathing, biking, or roller blading. Known as "The Strand," this well-traveled path connects Santa Monica Beach to Will Rogers State Beach to the north and Redondo Beach to the south. Lifeguards keep watch over surfers, swimmers, and beach bunnies (much of the hit TV show *Baywatch* was filmed here). There are plenty of picnic areas and playgrounds.

Santa Monica Pier

The landmark **Santa Monica Pier** (Colorado Ave., 310/458-8900, www.santamonicapier.org) has welcomed generations of families and out-of-towners since 1909. Today, highlights include a historic carousel, solar-paneled Ferris wheel, arcade games, and thrill rides at **Pacific Park** (310/260-8744, www.pacpark.com, $4-6 per ride, unlimited rides $29). Tucked beneath the carousel, the **Santa Monica Pier Aquarium** (1600 Ocean Front Walk, 310/393-6149, www.healthebay.org, 2pm-5pm Tues.-Fri., 12:30pm-5pm Sat.-Sun., $5 adults, free children 12 and under) includes touch tanks that allow for exploration of sea creatures like urchins, snails, and sea cucumbers, and worthwhile exhibits dedicated to jellyfish, leopard sharks, and stingrays. During the summer, the boardwalk becomes a stage for weekly outdoor concerts and free events. Historical **walking tours** (11am or noon Sat.-Sun., free) start at the **Pier Shop & Visitor Center** (310/458-8066); look for the tour guide in the blue shirt.

Palisades Park

Virtually nothing can escape the view of **Palisades Park** (851 Alma Real Dr., 310/454-1412, dawn-dusk daily), which lies atop sandstone cliffs overlooking Santa Monica Beach. Photographers, tourists, joggers, and yoga practitioners make use of the manicured lawns, benches, and pathway, appreciating the obscurely twisted trees, rose garden, artworks, and historic structures along the way. At the northern end of the park is a Chilkat Tlingit totem pole featuring a fish, raven, bear, and wolf. At the

---

From top to bottom: Santa Monica Pier; Santa Monica Beach; lifeguard tower on Venice Beach.

southern end, two cannons installed in 1908 point directly at the Santa Monica Pier, and a stone monument marks the 400th anniversary of explorer Juan Rodriguez Cabrillo's 1542 encounter of the bay. If you don't mind the park's resident homeless, who generally keep to themselves, Palisades is a good spot for watching the sunset.

Annenberg Community Beach House

In the 1920s, publishing bigwig William Randolph Hearst built the beachfront 100-room mansion that later became the **Annenberg Community Beach House** (415 CA-1, 310/458-4904, www.annenbergbeachhouse.com, tours as well as cultural and art programs and recreational activities, free) for his mistress, actress Marion Davies. Today, modern additions to the historic estate include a play area, art gallery, and an array of recreational activities, including swimming in the historic marble and tile pool (June-Sept., $10 adults, $4 children 1-17).

Food

Two fine restaurants are worth the splurge and the reservations that are required. Elegant ★ **Valentino's** (3115 Pico Blvd., 310/829-4313, www.valentinosantamonica.com, 5pm-10pm Tues.-Thurs., 5pm-10:30pm Fri.-Sat., under $50) is a local legend for its contemporary Italian dishes with farm-to-table ingredients and an extensive wine list. With two Michelin stars, **Melisse** (1104 Wilshire Blvd., 310/395-0881, 6pm-9:30pm Tues.-Thurs., 6pm-10pm Fri., 5:45pm-10pm Sat., $125 pp minimum) offers an exclusive experience, following in the French tradition of table-side carving, with multiple seasonal courses and world-class wines. The creation of chef Josiah Citrin, Melisse has received the highest marks in Zagat and Michelin. The ambience is chic, the tastes incomparable.

Enjoy a meal with your toes in the sand at **Back on the Beach** (445 CA-1, 310/393-8282, www.backonthebeachcafe.com, 8am-3pm Mon.-Thurs., 8am-8pm Fri.-Sun., under $16), which features tasty breakfast omelets and great fish tacos and burgers for lunch.

Tacos Por Favor (1406 Olympic Blvd., 310/392-5768, www.tacosporfavor.net, 8am-8pm Mon.-Sat., $7) makes fresh Mexican favorites like chicken mole burritos and chorizo taquitos, and they deliver (11am-3pm Mon.-Sat.).

Bay Cities Italian Deli & Bakery (1517 Lincoln Blvd., 310/395-8279, www.bcdeli.com, 9am-7pm Tues.-Sat., 9am-6pm Sun., under $10) has been whipping up authentic Italian pasta and sandwiches since 1925. Take a number; it's worth the wait.

The famed burger at the **Father's Office** (1018 Montana Ave., 310/736-2224, www.fathersoffice.com, 5pm-10pm Mon.-Wed., 5pm-11pm Thurs., 4pm-11pm Fri., noon-11pm Sat., noon-10pm Sun., $5-14), dubbed one of the best in the world by *Esquire* magazine, pulls in patty connoisseurs to enjoy its dry-aged beef topped with caramelized onions, gruyère and Maytag cheeses, bacon, and arugula. Don't ask for substitutions—why mess with modifying perfection?

Though local favorite **Santa Monica Seafood** (1000 Wilshire Blvd., 310/393-5244, www.smseafoodmarket.com, 11am-9pm Mon.-Sat., 11am-8pm Sun., under $25) is a retail fish market, it includes a café and oyster bar that serves fresh seafood with an Italian twist.

With a history dating back to the 1940s, **Snug Harbor** (2323 Wilshire Blvd., 310/828-2991, www.snugharbor.us, 6am-3pm daily, under $12) is every local's favorite breakfast diner, serving everything from bacon and eggs to biscuits to the Captain's Wafflewich.

Nightlife and Entertainment

A half-block south of the pier, **Chez Jay** (1657 Ocean Ave., 310/395-1741, www.chezjays.com) doesn't look like much, but the little nautical dive bar has been serving locals and celebrities for almost

50 years. Jay's peanuts are as famous as its clientele—ask them about the nut that made it to the moon! Open since 1934, **The Galley** (2442 Main St., 310/452-1934, www.thegalleyrestaurant.net, happy hour 5pm-7pm daily) is a local landmark. Classic movie memorabilia decorate the walls, including the steering wheel from the *Mutiny on the Bounty*. The drinks are generous and the food fantastic, especially the salad dressing, which is the secret of the success of the owner, long-time comedian Captain Ron.

Two well-established Brit pubs, **Ye Olde Kings Head** (116 Santa Monica Blvd., 310/451-1402, www.yeoldkingshead.com) and **Cock N Bull Pub** (2947 Lincoln Blvd., 310/399-9696), fill up for soccer and rugby games. Both offer a good range of brews and spirits, as well as fish and chips.

Welcoming **Obrien's Pub** (2941 Main St., 310/396-4725, www.obriensonmain.com) has live music, comedy, and televised sports events and a menu with a mix of Irish and American dishes. Get your groove on at **Main on Main** (2941 Main St., 310/396-6678, www.mainonmain.com, $5 after 11pm weekends), a sleek nightclub featuring great cocktails to accompany the booming music. Doors open at 10pm on weekends and there's no cover charge until 11pm.

DJs spin all the top tunes at **V Lounge** (2020 Wilshire Blvd., 310/829-1933, www.vloungela.com, no cover), where clubbers bounce around the sunken dance floor. The dress code is enforced, so no muscle shirts or speedos!

Shopping

Shopping on **Main Street** (www.mainstreetsm.com) may have you seeing stars (Julia Roberts, Owen Wilson, and David Letterman have been spotted here). If you don't spot a celeb, you can settle with window-shopping. Main Street is the greenest street in Santa Monica with earth-conscious boutiques like **Vital Hemp** (2305 Main St., 310/450-2260,

10am-7pm daily), a producer of quality hemp clothing for men and women that's friendly to the planet, and **Natural High Lifestyle** (2510 Main St., 323/691-1827, www.naturalhighlifestyle.myshopify.com), which features clothing and products made from hemp, organic cotton, buckwheat hulls, and FSC-certified plywood.

M Hanks Gallery (3008 Main St., 310/392-8820, mhanksgallery.com, by appointment only) specializes in African American artworks. The eclectic **Mindfulness** (2711 Main St., 310/452-5409, www.mindfulnest.com, 10:30am-6:30pm Mon.-Sat., noon-5pm Sun.) features the works of nearly 100 contemporary artists. On Sundays, Main Street hosts the widely popular **Farmer's Market** (2640 Main St., at Heritage Square, 9:30am-1pm every Sun.), which features food booths, local retailers, arts and crafts, live music, and fun activities for the little ones, like face-painting. Parking is free at the John Muir lot and Santa Monica Alternative Schoolhouse (SMASH) located on Ocean Park Boulevard (between 5th and 6th Sts.). Validated parking is also available at 2600 Barnard Way in lot 5S.

From Main Street, take the TIDE shuttle to **Third Street Promenade,** a vibrant pedestrian-only shopping center with dozens of vendor carts sprinkled throughout, selling anything from souvenirs to jewelry. You'll also find great restaurants, movie theaters, street performers, and popular chain stores like Abercrombie & Fitch, Express, and Pottery Barn, with a few independent art galleries and specialty and vintage shops.

Adamm's Stained Glass Studio & Art Gallery (1426 4th St., 310/451-9390, www.adammsgallery.com, 10am-6pm Mon.-Fri., 11am-5pm Sat.) has built its reputation for creating the finest stained and leaded glass, beveled glass, and etched and carved glass windows, doors, and houses with a collection of some of the best emerging artists.

Owned by a Tibetan transplant, **Tibetan Arts** (704 Santa Monica Blvd., 310/458-6304, www.tibetan-arts.com, 10am-7pm daily) offers beautiful and authentic Himalayan art, pashmina shawls, bags, jewelry, clothing, and rugs.

With stores in San Francisco, Los Angeles, and Studio City, **Wasteland Vintage** (1330 4th St., 310/395-2620, www.shopwasteland.com) is hardly a big-chain retailer, but it has created a name for itself. Wasteland is a self-defined trendsetter with independent collections that express the multiple personalities of each wearer.

Adjacent to the Promenade, **Santa Monica Place** (4th St. and Broadway, 310/394-5451) is an open-air mall, stocked with a collection of high-end retailers like Tiffany, Bloomingdales, and Kenneth Cole.

Recreation

Beach volleyball is said to have been born in Santa Monica. A number of courts located north and south of the pier are available daily for public play on a first-come, first-served basis. Courts may be reserved in advance by calling 310/458-8300 and paying a required permit fee ($10-32).

Bike "The Strand" (40 miles), a popular and easily accessible bike path that gets busy in the summer; make sure to check with the local visitors center or bike rental shop for any safety requirements. You can ride to Will Rogers State Beach to the north and Redondo Beach to the south. There are many coastal communities in between, like Venice Beach (3 miles south) and Pacific Palisades (2.8 miles north). The bike path runs parallel to the **Oceanfront Walk** (a pedestrian walkway), until Bicknell Avenue (south of the pier) when it veers west, following the coastline north passing under the Santa Monica Pier, and on to Will Rogers State Beach. The Santa Monica portion of The Strand runs from Temescal Canyon in the north to Washington Boulevard in Venice in the south (8.5 mi/13.7 km). **Blazing Saddles** (320 Santa Monica Pier, 310/393-9778, 9am-6:30pm Mon.-Fri., 8am-8pm Sat.-Sun.) rents bikes right off the pier.

Santa Monica Beach Surf Lessons (Ocean Ave. and Bicknell St., 310/962-7873, www.surflessonswithkatie.com, from $109 for 2-hour lesson) offers private instruction packages to wannabe surfers (board, wet suit, and bottle water included). Rent a surfboard ($20-50), roller blades ($10-30), or even a beach chair and umbrella ($11-20) at **Perry's Beach Rentals** (2600 Ocean Front Walk, 310/584-9306, www.perryscafe.com).

Events

Bring a blanket, find a spot on the beach, and watch the sun set while listening to Santa Monica Pier's summer **Twilight Dance Series** (7pm-10pm Thurs. in summer). In the fall, the pier hosts **Front Porch Cinema** (Fri. nights), with music, films, and food and drinks. Rent a lawn chair for a few bucks or bring your own.

Accommodations

Ecofriendly trendsetter ★ **Viceroy Hotel** (1819 Ocean Ave., 310/260-7500 and 800/670-6185, www.viceroyhotelsandresorts.com, $300 and up) has been one of the top 50 hotels by *Conde Nast Traveler*, among others. Large airy cabanas with comfy couches and fluffy pillows provide shade from the sun and access to the pool. It's a block from the beach and a few blocks from downtown.

The green-certified **Ambrose Hotel** (1255 20th St., 310/315-1555, www.ambrosehotel.com, $175 and up) has a positive impact on its guests and the environment. Elegant rooms include cotton robes, bath linens, and natural bath products. Some have balconies and terraces; all come with a complimentary breakfast.

In the course of its history, the art deco 1933 **Georgian Hotel** (1415 Ocean Ave.,

310/395-9945 and 800/538-8147, www.
georgianhotel.com, $200 and up) has
hosted stars and starlets. Today, it continues to please with stylish guestrooms
and suites, boutique amenities, and a
contemporary restaurant. It's just steps
from the sand and close to shopping and
restaurants.

Shutters on the Beach (Pico Blvd.,
310/458-0030 and 800/334-9000, $575
and up) is a luxury hotel set right on the
sand. Guest rooms are bright with hard-
wood floors, Tibetan rugs, spacious bathrooms, and balconies. The hotel houses a
café, bar, and fine dining, as well as a spa.

HI Los Angeles/Santa Monica (1436
2nd St., btwn. Santa Monica Blvd. and
Broadway, 310/393-9913, www.reserve@
HILosAngeles.org, $30 and up) offers
clean dorm-style and private rooms,
and facilities that feature daily movies,
Internet access, kitchen, laundry, and
breakfast.

Information and Services

Free brochures and information on area
attractions are available at the **Pier Shop
& Visitor Center** (200 Santa Monica Pier,
310/393-7593, 11am-5pm Mon.-Thurs.,
11am-7pm Fri.-Sun.). There is also a
walk-in **Visitor Information Center** (2427
Main St., 310/393-7593 and 800/544-
5319, 9am-5:30pm Mon.-Fri., 9am-5pm
Sat.-Sun.) that provides information resources, three computers with high-speed
Internet access, and souvenirs. Tickets
to area attractions are also available for
purchase.

★ Venice Beach Boardwalk

Ever wondered what it would be like to
visit another planet? Go to Venice Beach.
You'll witness every walk of life: Zany
street performers, oiled-up body builders, psychics, preachers, and self-proclaimed freaks all make an appearance

at the 2.5-mile-long boardwalk. It's the
best people-watching in the world!

The beachfront counterculture
here is unmatched in the bizarre and
strange; not even Ripley's Believe It or
Not! comes close. After an afternoon
on the boardwalk, nothing will surprise
you. Not convinced? For $5 you can see
"One-Eyed Jack," the cyclops chihua-
hua, a two-headed turtle, and "Itty and
Bitty," the two-headed kitty. Live shows
feature fire-eaters and appearances by
"Larry the Wolf Boy," who's listed in the
Guinness Book of World Records. All this
and more is part of Ray Todd's **"Venice
Beach Freakshow"** (909 Ocean Front
Walk), which has gained a huge following. "Freakshow" even has its own televised spot on AMC.

If you're approached by a giant (about
6'3") wearing spring-loaded shoes and
a black shirt imprinted with a capital
"V," don't run away! His name is Jeffrey
Solomon. In the 1960s, he walked his
pet tiger on a 50-foot chain down Rose
Avenue. Today, he walks tourists (minus
the chain), while giving fascinating accounts of Venice past and present, including little-known facts like how an
amusement park became a part of the
underwater ecosystem. His **Venice Beach
Walking Tours** (310/433-8453, www.ven-
icebeachwalkingtours.com, $40-60) are
worth the cost just for the interesting
characters Solomon introduces you to
along the way.

Aside from the usual freaks, you'll
find cafés, souvenir shops, and recreational activities. For $4 you can pump
iron at Muscle Beach. At 10:30am on
Saturdays, take a free yoga class on the
beach. There's also an outdoor roller rink
and skate park.

The best time to visit is in the summer, mid-morning through the late afternoon. At night, the Venice Beach
Boardwalk can feel more like *Creep Show,*
with the crowd morphing from eccentric
to spooky.

Los Angeles

Los Angeles (pop. 10 million and counting) has had its share of facelifts over the past two centuries, reinventing itself from Spanish military outpost to seaside playground to cinematic dream factory to super-suburbia. It's a city built on dreams, schemes, and intrigues, so it's no surprise that the movie industry found its home here.

L.A. is always looking to the future and is not much for nostalgia. Little of the city's early beginnings remain, except on Olvera Street, the very spot where the Pueblo de Los Ángeles was founded in 1781. California became a U.S. state in 1850 and the railroad opened up the West to the rest of the country, which prompted enthusiastic advertisements by L.A. big shots selling the "American Dream." And that's what the city has been doing ever since.

As L.A. races into its future, the city has given itself another facelift, reviving many landmark buildings amid construction of several shiny new ones. But that's not all—L.A.'s car-centered culture may evolve as plans for a more pedestrian-friendly city are made. Will Angelenos really trade in their beloved automobiles for a pair of sneakers? Only time will tell . . . as the reinvention continues. . . .

Getting There and Around
Car

Los Angeles is crisscrossed with freeways, providing numerous yet congested access points into the city. From the north and south, I-5 provides the most direct access to downtown L.A. From I-5, US-101 South leads directly into Hollywood; from here, Santa Monica Boulevard can take you west to Beverly Hills. Connecting from I-5 to I-210 will take you east to Pasadena. The best way to reach Santa Monica, Venice, and Malibu is via CA-1, also known as the Pacific Coast Highway. I-10 can get you there from the east, but it will be a long, tedious, and trafficked drive.

Traffic can be awful any time, even outside of typical rush hours. Local drivers accustomed to the conditions aren't always polite. Expect to be cut off by drivers paying attention to everything in the world but the road. Most road signs use numbers, but locals, including the radio traffic reporters, use names (e.g., Santa Ana Freeway, Santa Monica Freeway, etc.). There's no visible name-to-number translation on most maps, and names can change depending on which section of freeway you're driving.

Parking in Los Angeles can be challenging and expensive. You will find parking lots and structures included with many hotel rooms, but parking on the street can be difficult or impossible, parking lots in sketchy areas (like the Flower and Jewelry Districts) can be dangerous, and parking structures at popular attractions can be expensive.

Air

L.A. is one of the most airport-dense metropolitan areas in the country. **Los Angeles International Airport (LAX)** (1 World Way, Los Angeles, 310/646-5252, www.lawa.org) has the most flights, which makes it the most crowded of the L.A. airports, with the longest security and check-in lines. If you can find a way around flying into LAX, do so. One option is to fly into other local airports, including **Bob Hope Airport (BUR)** (2627 N. Hollywood Way, Burbank, 818/840-8840, www.burbankairport.com) and **Long Beach Airport (LGB)** (4100 Donald Douglas Dr., Long Beach, 562/570-2600, www.lgb.org). It may be a slightly longer drive to your final destination, but it can be well worth it. If you use LAX, arrive a minimum of two hours ahead of your domestic flight time, three hours on busy holidays.

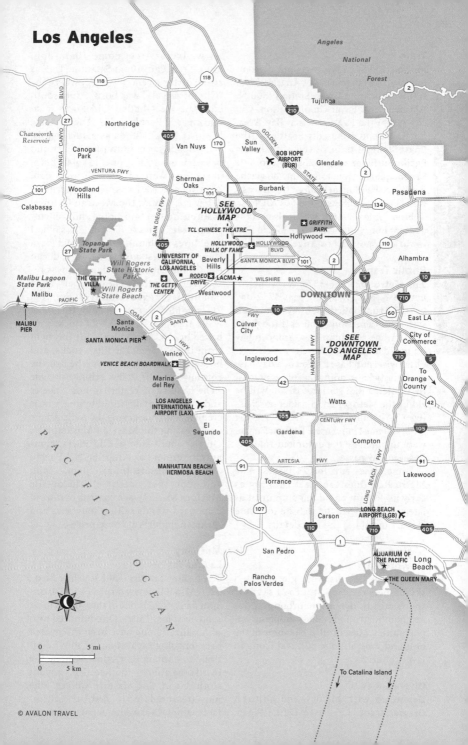

Los Angeles

Angeles
National
Forest

Tujunga

Chatsworth
Reservoir

Northridge

Van Nuys

Sun
Valley

BOB HOPE
AIRPORT
(BUR) ✈

Glendale

Pasadena

Canoga
Park

VENTURA FWY

Sherman
Oaks

Burbank

SEE
"HOLLYWOOD"
MAP

★ GRIFFITH
PARK

Woodland
Hills

Calabasas

TCL CHINESE THEATRE

HOLLYWOOD
WALK OF FAME

HOLLYWOOD
BLVD

Hollywood

SANTA MONICA BLVD

Alhambra

Topanga
State Park

UNIVERSITY OF
CALIFORNIA,
LOS ANGELES ★

Beverly
Hills

Malibu Lagoon
State Park

THE GETTY
VILLA ★

Will Rogers
State Historic
Park

THE GETTY
CENTER ★

RODEO
DRIVE ■

LACMA ★

WILSHIRE   BLVD

Malibu

PACIFIC

Will Rogers
State Beach

Westwood

DOWNTOWN

MALIBU
PIER ★

Santa
Monica

SANTA
MONICA

FWY

Culver
City

SEE
"DOWNTOWN
LOS ANGELES"
MAP

East LA

City of
Commerce

SANTA MONICA PIER ★

Venice

Inglewood

To
Orange
County

VENICE BEACH BOARDWALK ★

Marina
del Rey

Watts

LOS ANGELES
INTERNATIONAL
AIRPORT (LAX) ✈

El
Segundo

CENTURY FWY

Gardena

Compton

MANHATTAN BEACH/
HERMOSA BEACH ★

ARTESIA   FWY

Lakewood

Torrance

Carson

LONG BEACH
AIRPORT (LGB) ✈

San Pedro

ALIQUARIUM OF
THE PACIFIC ★

Long
Beach

Rancho
Palos Verdes

★ THE QUEEN MARY

PACIFIC   OCEAN

0   5 mi

0   5 km

To Catalina Island

© AVALON TRAVEL

Train

Amtrak (800/872-7245, www.amtrak.com) has an active rail hub in Los Angeles. Most trains come in to **Union Station** (800 N. Alameda St.). From Union Station, you can get to the San Francisco Bay Area, Portland, and eventually Seattle on the **Coast Starlight** train, or you can take the **Pacific Surfliner** south to San Diego. The **San Joaquin** runs out to Sacramento via the Bay Area. The **Sunset Limited** travels east-west between Tennessee and Los Angeles.

From Union Station, which also acts as a Metro hub, you can take the Metro Rail to various spots in Los Angeles.

Public Transit

The **Metro** (323/466-3876, www.metro. net, cash fare $1.75, day pass $7, 7-day pass $25) runs both the subway Metro Rail system and a network of buses throughout the L.A. metropolitan area. You can pay on board a bus if you have exact change. Otherwise, purchase a ticket or a day pass from the ticket vending machines present in all Metro Rail stations. If you will be riding the Metro often, consider purchasing a TAP refillable card ($1 plus regular fare); you must purchase a TAP card if you want to purchase the unlimited-ride day or seven-day passes.

Some buses run for 24 hours. The Metro Rail lines can start running as early as 4:30am and don't stop until as late as 1:30am. See the website for route maps, timetables, and fare details.

Sights
Downtown

Downtown L.A. has tall, glass-coated skyscrapers creating an urban skyline, sports arenas, rich neighborhoods, poor neighborhoods, and endless shopping opportunities. Most of all, it has some of the best and most unique cultural icons in L.A. County.

Olvera Street

Bejeweled with history and culture, **Olvera Street** (125 Paseo De La Plaza,

www.olvera-street.com, 10am-8pm Mon.-Fri., 10am-10pm Sat.-Sun., free) is at the historic center of L.A., where the "City of Angels" was born. At its south end, the tree-shaded Old Plaza (also known as El Pueblo de Los Ángeles State Historic Park) stands as a small gathering space for community events and pays tribute to the pueblo's 44 *pobladores* who were of Spanish, Mexican, African, and Native American heritage. A few steps away, the Mexican Cultural Institute houses traditional and contemporary Mexican art. Two of L.A.'s oldest structures are found here. The Old Plaza Church was first built in 1784 but, due to floods and earthquake damage, was reconstructed in 1861. The oldest surviving building is the **Avila Adobe** (10 Olvera St., 213/485-6855, 9am-4pm daily, free). The walls are made of 2.5-3-foot thick, sun-baked bricks. A mixture of tar (brought from the La Brea Tar Pits), rocks, and horsehair was used to weatherize the cottonwood roof. A few exhibits include "The History of Water" in Los Angeles and a Tribute to Christine Sterling, who is credited with preserving the Avila Adobe and creating the Mexican Marketplace. On the south side of Old Plaza, community group Las Angelitas del Pueblo offers 50-minute **tours** (10am, 11am, and noon Tues.-Sat., free). The on-site Mexican Marketplace consists of rows of clapboard stands selling souvenirs and Mexican imports at cheap prices.

Mid-City
La Brea Tar Pits

The **La Brea Tar Pits** (5801 Wilshire Blvd., 323/857-6300, www.tarpits.org, 9:30am-5pm daily, free) is one of the world's most renowned fossil sites. One-hundred tons of fossilized bone have been discovered here; ongoing excavations of Pit 91 continue to unmask its victims. Among the fossils are a saber-toothed tiger, a giant sloth, bison, and six dire wolves. The most treasured find is "Zed," a nearly intact mammoth skeleton. A partial human

Two Days in Los Angeles

Day 1

Go Hollywood—Hollywood Boulevard, that is. Check out star footprints outside the **TCL Chinese Theatre** (page 293) and wander the **Hollywood Walk of Fame** (page 293). Poster and memorabilia shops abound, so pick up a still from your favorite movie.

For lunch, enjoy award-winning Mexican fare at **Yuca's** (page 299). Then head to **Griffith Park** (page 295) to enjoy the green space and the view of the **Hollywood Sign** from the Griffith Observatory.

If you're more interested in high culture, spend the afternoon at **The Getty Center** (page 297). (Reserve free tickets in advance.) Take in dizzying ocean views, wander through the gardens, and tour the museum's small but outstanding collections.

For dinner, sample the slices at **Pizzeria Mozza** (page 300) or dine on pasta at sister restaurant **Osteria Mozza**. After dinner, cruise the **Sunset Strip** (page 293), where revelers flock to legendary music clubs like the **Whisky a Go Go** and **The Viper Room** (page 301); or

grab some laughs at **The Comedy Store** (page 302).

Day 2

After breakfast at **Original Pantry** (page 298), head to the birthplace of L.A.: **Olvera Street** (page 290). Tour the city's oldest structure, the Avila Adobe, and stroll the colorful marketplace. To explore much deeper into the city's past, spend the morning with the famous fossils at the **La Brea Tar Pits** (page 290).

Then it's off to Beverly Hills for an afternoon of star-spotting and window-shopping on **Rodeo Drive** (page 297). If you're hungry, stop in at **The Grill on the Alley** (page 300), site of many entertainment power lunches. As long as you're in Beverly Hills, splurge for dinner at one of two restaurants founded by celebrity chefs: Thomas Keller's **Bouchon Bistro** (page 300) or Wolfgang Puck's **Spago Beverly Hills** (page 300).

After dinner, toast the city with a cocktail at **The Rooftop** (page 301) in the Standard Hotel. Watch the sun set over the city skyline and wait for the stars to come out.

---

skeleton, estimated to be 10,000 years old, has also been found.

Pit 91 has a viewing station, where docents explain how and why the bubbling asphalt has risen to the surface. The **George C. Page Museum** (5801 Wilshire Blvd., 323/857-6300, www.tarpits.org, 9:30am-5pm daily, $12 adults, $5 children, tours are free with admission) features several excavated skeletons and other fascinating exhibits. Giant-sized sculptures of mammoths and other prehistoric animals are often draped with climbing children. Wear a pair of cheap shoes—it isn't unusual to leave with tar in your footprints!

Los Angeles County Museum of Art
The 20-acre **Los Angeles County Museum of Art** (LACMA, 5905 Wilshire Blvd.,

323/857-6000, www.lacma.org, 11am-5pm Mon.-Tues. and Thurs., 11am-8pm Fri., 10am-7pm Sat.-Sun., $15 general admission, $10 parking) holds the city's most impressive collections—120,000 works spanning human history. Covering three floors, The Broad Contemporary Art Museum displays a selection of modern American art by artists that include Andy Warhol, Jasper Johns, and Robert Rauschenberg. The Art of the Americas Building includes an astounding display of 2,500 pre-Columbian objects, many excavated from burial chambers in Jalisco, Mexico. At the main level, the Ahmanson Building features a large staircase, reminiscent of Rome's Spanish Steps, while the plaza holds African art and modern works by greats like Picasso and Kandinsky. Classical Greek and

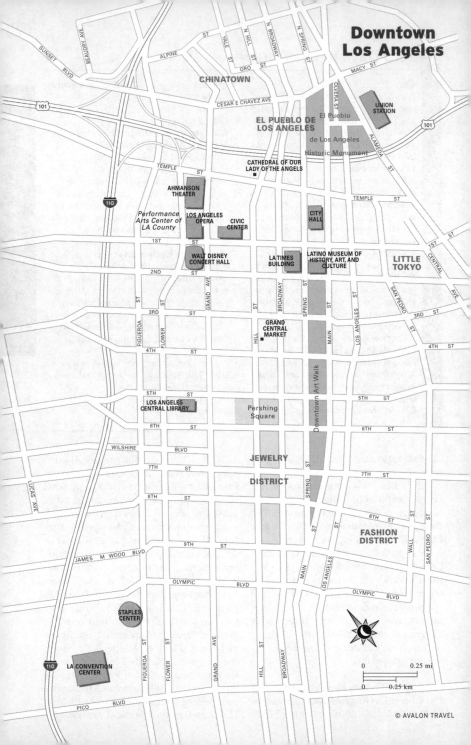

Downtown Los Angeles

CHINATOWN

EL PUEBLO DE LOS ANGELES

El Pueblo de los Angeles Historic Monument

UNION STATION

CATHEDRAL OF OUR LADY OF THE ANGELS

AHMANSON THEATER

Performance Arts Center of LA County

LOS ANGELES OPERA

CIVIC CENTER

CITY HALL

WALT DISNEY CONCERT HALL

LA TIMES BUILDING

LATINO MUSEUM OF HISTORY, ART, AND CULTURE

LITTLE TOKYO

GRAND CENTRAL MARKET

Downtown Art Walk

LOS ANGELES CENTRAL LIBRARY

Pershing Square

JEWELRY DISTRICT

FASHION DISTRICT

STAPLES CENTER

LA CONVENTION CENTER

0   0.25 mi

0   0.25 km

© AVALON TRAVEL

Roman works are found on the second level. Admission is free every second Tuesday of the month.

Hollywood

The world's movie capital earned its reputation during the boom of the 1920s when the entertainment industry cast Hollywood in its own opulent image. Today, the only "real" movie businesses remaining are the blockbuster premieres at the major movie theaters here. Paramount Studios, at Melrose and Gower, is the last of the big five studios still active in Hollywood proper. But some of the old Tinseltown glitz remains. Fine restaurants draw glamorous crowds after dark, and celebrities still attend blockbuster premieres at the iconic movie theaters in Hollywood.

★ TCL Chinese Theatre

The most famous movie theater in the world literally made its mark with the handprints and footprints of silver-screen stars. Although official accounts say actress Norma Talmadge sparked a Hollywood tradition when she accidentally stepped into the wet concrete, the theater's owner, Sid Grauman, took credit for the idea. Today, millions of tourists visit **TCL Chinese Theatre** (6925 Hollywood Blvd., 323/464-8111, www. tclchinesetheatres.com) to ogle the 200 celebrity prints and autographs immortalized in concrete. The first footprints belong to Mary Pickford and Douglas Fairbanks (1927); more recent additions include Robert De Niro and Sandra Bullock.

The theater's ornate architecture features a large dragon across the front, two stone Chinese guardian lions at the entrance, and etched shadow dragons along the copper roof. Inside, wall murals greet movie ticket holders. A glass case in the west wing displays three wax figures outfitted in authentic Chinese costumes.

★ Hollywood Walk of Fame

Fame is what Hollywood is all about, so it's no surprise that it's home to the world's most famous sidewalk. Each year 10 million people visit the **Hollywood Walk of Fame** (Hollywood Blvd. from La Brea Ave. to Vine St., 323/469-8311, www. walkoffame.com), a 1.3-mile stretch that commemorates the entertainment industry's elite. Inspired by the handprints at Sid Grauman's Chinese Theatre, five-pointed terrazzo and brass stars are embedded into a charcoal background along Hollywood Boulevard and three blocks of Vine Street. To find a specific star, check the directory online map (www.walkof-fame.com).

Though official groundbreaking did not occur until 1960, eight inaugural stars were temporarily planted on the northwest corner of Hollywood and Highland in 1958 to gain public attention. Contrary to popular belief, Joanne Woodward was not the first to be immortalized. The first permanent star is found at the intersection of Hollywood and Gower, and belongs to Stanley Kramer, director of *Guess Who's Coming to Dinner* and *It's a Mad, Mad, Mad, Mad World,* among others. Ms. Woodward, however, was the first to be photographed with her star. A circular, bronze emblem symbolizes one of five categories: motion pictures, broadcast television, music or audio recording, broadcast radio, and theater. Gene Autry is the only recipient with stars in all five categories.

Who deems Walk of Fame hopefuls "worthy" enough to join the more than 2,500 deified legends? A special committee bound by rules, procedures, and financing selects the honoree. The price of a star is about $30,000 and is usually paid by the representing movie company or record label.

Sunset Strip

It's been the playground of mobsters, Hollywood celebrities, and rock stars: **The Sunset Strip** has a long colorful

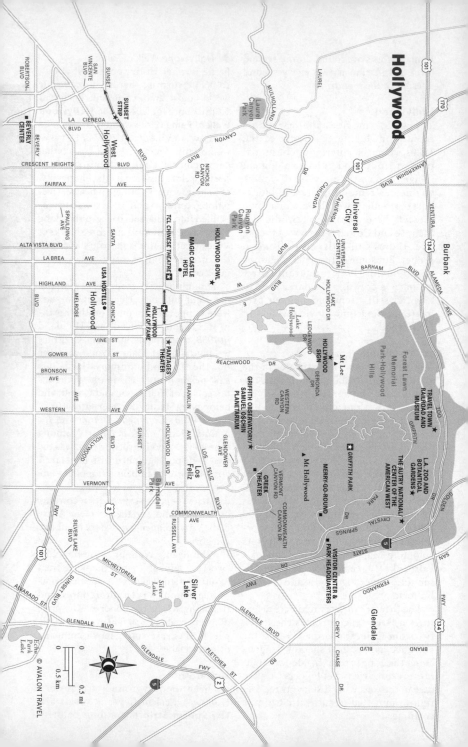

Hollywood

ROBERTSON BLVD

SAN VINCENTE BLVD

SUNSET

■ BEVERLY CENTER

LA CIENEGA BLVD

SUNSET STRIP ★

West Hollywood

SUNSET BLVD

BEVERLY

CRESCENT HEIGHTS

BLVD

FAIRFAX

AVE

SPAULDING AVE

ALTA VISTA BLVD

LA BREA

SANTA

AVE

USA HOSTELS ● Hollywood

HIGHLAND

AVE

MONICA

MELROSE

BLVD

GOWER

VINE ST

ST

BRONSON AVE

WESTERN

AVE

AVE

Laurel Canyon Park

MULHOLLAND

LAUREL

101

170

LANKERSHIM BLVD

VENTURA

Burbank

134

NICHOLS CANYON RD

CANYON BLVD

Runyon Canyon Park

LAUREL CANYON BLVD

CAHUENGA BLVD

CAHUENGA BLVD

Universal City

UNIVERSAL CENTER DR

BARHAM

BLVD

ALAMEDA AVE

HOLLYWOOD BOWL ★

TCL CHINESE THEATRE ★

MAGIC CASTLE HOTEL ●

W

E

HOLLYWOOD DR

Lake Hollywood

Lake Hollywood

LEDGEWOOD DR

BLVD

Forest Lawn Memorial Park–Hollywood Hills

TRAVEL TOWN RAILROAD AND MUSEUM ★

Hollywood Walk of Fame

HOLLYWOOD WALK OF FAME ★

FRANKLIN

HOLLYWOOD

SUNSET

PANTAGES THEATER ★

BEACHWOOD

DR

HOLLYWOOD SIGN ★

● Mt Lee

DERONDA DR

GRIFFITH OBSERVATORY & SAMUEL OSCHIN PLANETARIUM ★

WESTERN CANYON RD

GRIFFITH

ZOO DR

GOLDEN STATE

L.A. ZOO AND BOTANICAL GARDENS ★

THE AUTRY NATIONAL CENTER OF THE AMERICAN WEST ★

AVE

GLENDOWER AVE

Los Feliz

HOLLYWOOD BLVD

LOS FELIZ BLVD

Barnsdall Park

VERMONT

▲ Mt Hollywood

GREEK THEATER ■

VERMONT CANYON RD

MERRY-GO-ROUND ■

✚ **GRIFFITH PARK**

PARK

CRYSTAL SPRINGS DR

SAN FERNANDO

FWY

134

Glendale

COMMONWEALTH AVE

RUSSELL AVE

COMMONWEALTH DR

STATE DR

5

VISITOR CENTER & PARK HEADQUARTERS ■

CHEVY CHASE DR

BRAND BLVD

SILVER LAKE BLVD

SUNSET BLVD

101

ALVARADO ST

MICHELTORENA ST

Silver Lake

Silver Lake

FLETCHER ST

GLENDALE BLVD

2

Echo Park Lake

GLENDALE BLVD

GLENDALE

FWY

© AVALON TRAVEL

0   0.5 km

0   0.5 mi

5

2

Welcome to Hollywood!

You'll know you've arrived when you see the **Hollywood Sign** (www.hollywoodsign.org). When it was erected in 1923 atop Mt. Lee, it read "Hollywoodland." Twenty-six years later, "land" was removed and the 50-foot-tall letters that remained became a permanent feature of the Los Angeles landscape. Like all Hollywood stars, a bit of maintenance is required (the sign was made of wood). To ensure the sign's longevity, the original letters were auctioned off to the highest bidder (Hugh Hefner bought the "y" and Alice Cooper bought the "o" in memory of comedian Groucho Marx) and replaced with shiny new 45-foot-tall letters made of sheet metal; the refurbishment was completed in 2010. Access to the sign ain't what it used to be due to problems with vandalism and complaints from local residents. The area is now outfitted with high-security motion detectors, closed-circuit cameras, razor-sharp barbed wire, and "Restricted Entry" warning signs. Try to climb the fence and Los Angeles Police will have you cuffed quicker than you can say "tourist."

You can get a good look at the sign from the **Griffith Observatory** (Griffith Park, 4730 Crystal Springs Dr., noon-10pm Tues.-Fri., 10am-10pm Sat.-Sun., free), the **Hollywood and Highland Visitors Center** (6801 Hollywood Blvd., 323/467-6412, 9am-10pm Mon.-Sat., 10am-7pm Sun.), or **Lake Hollywood Park** (Canyon Lake Dr., 323/666-5046, 5am-sunset daily, free).

history. The 1.5-mile portion of Sunset Boulevard stretches from Havenhurst Drive in West Hollywood to Sierra Drive near Beverly Hills. Infamous gangsters Bugsy Siegel, Micky Cohen (who was shot at what today is called the Key Club), Johnny Roselli, and Tony Comero were regulars at The Melody Room (a.k.a. The Viper), using it as a gambling den. Nightclubs and upscale restaurants attracted stars such as Clark Gable, Cary Grant, Fred Astaire, Jean Harlowe, and Lana Turner. Famed writers Dorothy Parker and F. Scott Fitzgerald lived at the Garden of Allah apartments that once stood between Crescent Heights and Havenhurst. Howard Hughes lived in the penthouse of the Argyle Hotel (known as the Sunset Tower Hotel, 8358 Sunset Blvd.), as did John Wayne, who kept a cow on his apartment balcony.

Decades worth of up-and-coming rock acts first made their names on the Strip and lived at the "Riot Hyatt." Today, you'll still find many of the Strip's legendary rock clubs here, such as **The Roxy,** the **Whisky a Go Go,** and **The Rainbow Bar &** Grill. At night, especially on weekends, no one is alone on the Strip. Don't plan to drive quickly or park on the street after dark; the crowds get big, complete with celebrity hounds hoping for a glimpse of their favorite star out for a night on the town.

★ Griffith Park

The 4,210-acre **Griffith Park** (4730 Crystal Springs Dr., 323/913-4688, 6am-10pm daily) is the largest municipal park in the country, with numerous opportunities for mingling with nature while enjoying some of the city's iconic sights. It's also recognizable from its role as the backdrop for many films, including *Rebel Without a Cause* and *Back to the Future*.

The cosmos come alive at **Griffith Observatory** (2800 E. Observatory Rd., 213/473-0800, noon-10pm Tues.-Fri., 10am-10pm Sat.-Sun., free), the park's most popular sight. Experienced stargazers help visitors explore the galaxies through demonstrations of powerful telescopes. At the entrance, a Foucault pendulum demonstrates the rotation of the Earth, while other displays focus on the moon and ocean tides. Planetarium shows ($7) occur daily.

The park has several fun activities for kids, including the **L.A. Zoo and Botanical Gardens** (5333 Zoo Dr., 10am-5pm daily, $19 adults, $14 children), the **Travel Town Railroad** (5200 Zoo Dr., 323/662-5874, www.traveltown.org, 10am-4pm Mon.-Fri., 10am-6pm Sat.-Sun., $3), pony rides, and a swimming pool. Educational sights include the **Autry National Center of the American West** (4700 Western Heritage Way, 323/667-2000, 9am-4pm Tues.-Fri., 9am-5pm Sat.-Sun., $10 adults, $6 students, $4 children 3-12, free children under 3), which holds an impressive collection of more than 500,000 Western and Native American artworks and artifacts.

A 53-mile network of hiking trails offers chances to spot local wildlife such as deer, coyotes, wild quail, and foxes. Many trails lead to viewpoints that include the Hollywood Sign; the most spectacular is from the observatory parking lot to Mount Hollywood. In a wooded canyon, the **Bird Sanctuary** (323/666-5046, 2900 N. Vermont Ave., 10am-5pm daily) provides the perfect spot for bird-watching, while the **Ferndell Nature Museum** (Fern Dell Dr., at the Western Canyon entrance to the park, 6am-10pm daily), an outdoor exhibit, lets visitors explore native species of ferns, flowers, and plants. There is a snack stand and picnic area nearby to enjoy in the cool shade along a babbling brook.

Beverly Hills

Thousands flock to Beverly Hills to get a glimpse of the stars and to browse the exorbitantly priced boutiques on Rodeo Drive. Five-star restaurants and chic hotels offer only the crème de la crème.

The three-block stretch of Wilshire Boulevard that runs through Beverly Hills from Downtown to the ocean is known as "Museum Row," which includes the Los Angeles County Museum of Art at its far southeast corner. To the east,

Griffith Observatory

Beverly Hills links to West Hollywood via the Sunset Strip at Sierra Drive. At its northwest side, the world-famous Getty Center sits atop the Santa Monica Mountains.

★ Rodeo Drive

In the well-to-do neighborhood of Beverly Hills, the biggest celeb in town is the three-block hotshot known as **Rodeo Drive** (pronounce ro-DAY-o, not like the bronco-riding cowboy event). Impressive boutiques and stylish shops abound with more than 100 of the most elite hotels and prestigious fashion retailers touting their "best in show" wearables. Though price tags may be bigger than your zip code, not everything is for sale. Take a walk along the palm tree-lined drive to see the historic, iconic, and spectacular!

At the base of Rodeo Drive, the **Beverly Wilshire Hotel** (famous for the movie *Pretty Woman*) has been a fixture for over 100 years, lavishing the rich and famous in luxury. A newer addition,

Rodeo Drive **Walk of Style** puts a twist on the Hollywood Walk of Fame by honoring fashion legends with bronze plaques (personal quote and signature included) embedded into the sidewalk. The first honoree inducted was high-fashion guru Giorgio Armani, whose quote reads: "Fashion and cinema together for life." Along the "Walk," look for other past winners, which include Princess Grace of Monaco, Salvatore Ferragamo, and Gianni and Donatella Versace.

Other sights include artist Robert Graha's *Torso*, a 14-foot aluminum sculpture that glistens under the Southern California sun at the intersection of Rodeo Drive and Dayton. Nearby stands Frank Lloyd Wright's last Los Angeles building project, The Anderton Court, a four-level shopping complex with an exposed, angular ramp, several circular windows, and a large geometric mast.

Although you won't see *The Beverly Hillbillies'* Oldsmobile spewing exhaust down Rodeo Drive, designer Bijan Pakzad's (founder of the exclusive House of Bijan) black and yellow Bugatti Veyron and custom yellow Rolls-Royce have become big photo ops. To step into the House of Bijan ("the world's most famous store"), pay up. It's open by appointment only, catering to celebrities, movie moguls, and anyone willing to spend $15,000 or more on a single suit.

★ The Getty Center

High on a hilltop overlooking both Hollywood and Beverly Hills—the whole of the city, really—**The Getty Center** (1200 Getty Center Dr., 310/440-7300, 10am-5:30pm Tues.-Fri. and Sun., 10am-9pm Sat., free admission, $5 audio tour, $15 parking) is a fortress of travertine- and aluminum-clad pavilions, built to house the eclectic art collection of billionaire J. Paul Getty, which includes everything from Renaissance-era paintings to pop art. Getty opened a museum at his Malibu estate in the 1950s (the Getty Villa can still be visited today). After his death in 1976, an endowment was established to preserve his beloved collection and make it accessible to the public. The center opened in 1998, welcoming visitors by way of a three-car, cable-pulled hover-train funicular (a large parking garage is at the base of the hill). Steps lead up to the main entrance of the rotunda building, which links all five of the art pavilions. Richard Meier's striking design includes fountains, glass windows several stories high, and an open plan that permits intimate vistas of the city below. A separate west building includes a cafeteria and restaurant. Stairs from the terrace lead down to outdoor terraces and gardens designed by Robert Irwin. The gardens and the views are as inspiring as the art. On a clear day, you can see the entire city skyline as it moves west to the Pacific.

Admission is free; however you'll have to pay to park or take Metro bus 761. To take the free tram from the parking structure, ride the elevators up to the Lower Tram Station. The center is also accessible by way of the 0.75-mile pedestrian path that is about a 20-minute walk from the parking structure.

Food

L.A. is the birthplace of the drive-thru and numerous fast-food chains litter the roadsides. The list of notable places to eat is never-ending, but foodies should focus their attention in Downtown and Hollywood. Old-time diners are still local favorites. Hollywood restaurants have the most diversity of flavors. Beverly Hills wins for upscale dining; it's where you are most likely to see celebrity chefs. The more famous the name and the more upscale the menu, the more essential the reservation.

Downtown

Serving breakfast 24 hours a day, the ★ **Original Pantry** (877 S. Figueroa St., 213/972-9279, www.pantrycafe.com, 24 hours daily, $8-22 cash only) has been a

view of the Los Angeles skyline from the Getty Center

fixture in Downtown L.A. for 90 years. Join the lines under the red-and-white awnings. The classic American fare, served in huge portions, is worth it.

No L.A. visit is complete without a stop at **Tommy's** (2575 Beverly Blvd., 213/389-9060, www.originaltommys.com, 24 hours daily, under $10). Its unrivaled chili burger is so good that it's made the tiny burger shack a local institution. Imitators don't measure up, so "Look for the shack" on the Tommy's logo to be sure you've arrived at the *original*. There are other locations throughout L.A., including a Hollywood location (5873 Hollywood Blvd.) with great people-watching.

Philippe the Original (1001 N. Alameda St., 213/628-3781, www.philippes.com, 6am-10pm daily, under $10) proclaims itself "Home of the French Dip Sandwich." Everyone comes to this sawdust-floored eatery to sit along communal wooden tables and enjoy the classic roasted meat sandwich.

A food truck that grew up to be a

standalone restaurant, **Mexicali Taco & Co** (702 N. Figueroa St., 213/613-0416, 11am-10pm Mon.-Thurs., 11am-midnight Fri.-Sat., $4-10) features tasty Baja-style grub. The headliner is the vampire: a half-taco half-quesadilla made with your choice of meat, slathered with garlic sauce and cheese.

Busy **Bottega Louie** (700 S. Grand Ave., 213/802-1470, www.bottegalouie. com, 8am-11pm Mon.-Thurs., 8am-midnight Fri., 9am-midnight Sat., 9am-11pm Sun., under $32) serves classic Italian pizza and pasta in its 255-seat café. The attached gourmet market is known for its sweet confections.

The 100-year-old **Grand Central Market** (317 S. Broadway, 213/624-2378, www.grandcentralmarket.com, 8am-6pm Sun.-Wed., 8am-9pm Thurs.-Sat.) is the oldest open-air market in the city, offering a wide variety of authentic dishes from around the world, from Mexican to Middle Eastern delights to Asian favorites. The market is often packed with locals grabbing a bite to go (Eggslut wins for longest line ever!) and tourists strolling about the food and gift shops. There is a parking garage ($2 for 90 minutes) on Hill Street (a one-way road).

Hollywood

With two locations, ★ **Yuca's** (4666 Hollywood Blvd., 323/661-0523 and 2056 Hillhurst Ave., 323/662-1214, 11am-6pm Mon.-Sat., $3-10) serves the best Mexican fare in L.A. and that's saying something. They have the James Beard Award to prove it. There's not much dining space (the Hillhurst Ave. location is just a hut), but there's plenty of room for carnitas burritos, tacos, and tortas.

The top dog in Hollywood can be found at **Pink's Hot Dogs** (709 N. La Brea Ave., 323/931-4223, www.pinkshollywood.com, 9:30am-2am Sun.-Thurs., 9:30am-3am Fri.-Sat., $4). Celebs like Jay Leno and Bruce Willis are aficionados of Pink's signature chili dog. Orson Welles reputedly ate 18 in a single sitting!

For a truly delicious lunch, **Zankou Chicken** (7851 Sunset Blvd., 323/882-6365, www.zankouchicken.com, 10am-11pm daily, $8-14) slowly cooks chicken to perfection Armenian-style. Order a whole or half chicken, falafel, kebabs (your choice of meat), and enjoy with fresh pita, hummus, and garlic sauce.

The wood-fired oven at **Pizzeria Mozza** (641 N. Highland Ave., 323/297-0101, www.pizzeriamozza.com, noon-midnight daily, $11-29) turns out rustic, blistered pizzas with luxurious toppings. Reservations are tough to get, but bar seats are available for walk-ins. Just as popular, **Osteria Mozza** (6602 Melrose Ave., 323/297-0100, www.osteriamozza.com, noon-midnight daily, $19-38) next door has a larger menu of luscious pastas and adventurous meat dishes.

Beverly Hills

A favorite of celebrity diners like Reese Witherspoon and Ryan Seacreast, the swanky ★ **Bouchon Bistro** (235 N. Canon Dr., 310/271-9910, 11:30am-10:30pm daily, $27-62) is known for its celebrity chef Thomas Keller. The seasonal menu includes some standbys: roast chicken, steak frites, and croque madame. The atmosphere is vibrant, with an open terrace, mosaic flooring, and murals painted by French artist Paulin Paris. Reservations are wise.

Wolfgang Puck's **Spago Beverly Hills** (176 North Canon Dr., 310/385-0880, www.wolfgangpuck.com, noon-2:30pm Tues.-Sat., 6pm-10pm Mon.-Fri., 5:30pm-10:30pm Sat., 5:30pm-10pm Sun., $35-100) has earned its iconic status. The open kitchen crafts inspired dishes with the best locally grown ingredients and the wine list is mind-boggling. Outside, the romantic patio is centered on a fountain etched with the word "passion" and two imported 100-year-old olive trees.

Walter's Café (153 S. Beverly Dr., 310/275-5505, 7:30am-7:45pm Mon.-Fri., 8:30am-3:45pm Sat., 9am-2:45pm Sun., $8-15) has been providing exceptional food and service to Beverly Hills since 1949. The menu is big and the prices reasonable.

Entertainment bigwigs conduct business meetings at **The Grill on the Alley** (9560 Dayton Way, 310/276-0615, 11:30am-9pm Mon., 11:30am-10pm Tues.-Thurs., 11:30am-10:30pm Fri.-Sat., 5pm-9pm Sun., $22 and over), which pleases with all-American comfort food like meatloaf, its signature chicken pot pie, and generously portioned shortcake. Reservations are wise.

West Side

The **Apple Pan** (10801 W. Pico Blvd., 310/475-3585, 11am-midnight Tues.-Sun., under $10) is best known for slinging some of the best hamburgers on the planet.

The huge sandwiches and heart-warming soups at **Canter's Deli** (419 N. Fairfax Ave., 213/651-2030, www.cantersdeli.com, 24 hours daily, $8-15) draw night owls to the heart of the predominantly Jewish Fairfax District.

Food Trucks

Don't knock L.A.'s food trucks; they're fast, cheap, and serve tasty fare that rivals even the best restaurants and cafés.

Ricky's Fish Tacos (1400 N. Virgil, 323/906-7290, 11am-4pm Wed.-Fri., 11am-5pm Sat.-Sun., $5) are stuffed with lightly battered and fried catfish. You may also see Ricky's Fish Tacos food trucks in parking lots; when owner Ricky Pina tweets his location (@RickysFishTacos) lines are sure to follow.

You've never tasted grilled cheese until you've had one made by **The Grilled Cheese Truck** (323/522-3418, @GCTLosAngeles, $5). Choose from six types of cheeses (American cheese, sharp cheddar, gruyere, double cream brie, habanero Jack, and sun-dried tomato goat cheese) and add extras like caramelized onions, smoked pork, and even Fritos!

The **Pudding Truck** (www.roaming-hunger.com/the-pudding-truck, $3-6) is a ginormous step up from the old semi-creepy neighborhood ice cream truck. This treat-mobile serves gourmet pudding cooked the old-fashioned way for a creamier, decadent dessert complete with artisanal toppings. It's organic and naturally gluten-free; there are even vegan options so everyone can enjoy a little puddin'.

Nightlife

Whether you prefer the hip dive bars or glitzy lounges of Downtown and Hollywood, or hobnobbing at chichi clubs in Beverly Hills, Los Angeles leaves nothing out for the bacchanal.

Bars and Clubs

The "sky party" at **The Rooftop** (550 S. Flower St., 213/892-8080, www.standardhotels.com/downtown-la) in The Standard hotel comes complete with DJs, waterbeds, a heated pool, and let's not forget the stunning panoramic view. Non-hotel guests are welcome, but it's not so easy to get in. Even if you don't make it onto the roof, you can get a drink at the trendy ground-level bar—minus the pool, waterbeds, and view, of course.

The no-frills **Golden Gopher** (417 W. 8th St., 213/614-8001, 5pm-2am Tues.-Fri., 8pm-2am Sat.-Mon.) is the perfect Downtown pit stop for a reasonably priced beer, but it isn't a typical dive bar; there's a dress code. If you prefer a frou-frou drink, they'll mix, shake, and blend it up. Low-key entertainment options like a jukebox and Pac-Man arcade game are here.

Down the street, **Pattern Bar** (100 W. 9th St., 213/627-7774, noon-midnight Mon.-Thurs., noon-2am Fri., 6pm-2am Sat., 6pm-midnight Sun.) attracts a trendier crowd with its chic-meets-funky decor (vintage sewing stools line the bar). Tapas and cocktails named in honor of top designers lure in weekday fashionistas, but come the weekend, DJs draw a mixed crowd for dancing.

Cheap drinks and no fancy-schmancy business seem to be the motto at **The Dime** (442 N. Fairfax Ave., 323/651-4421, www.thedimela.net, 7am-1:30am daily). Nightly DJs spin a mix of old-school, hip-hop, and indie beats attracting unpretentious, hip crowds, and the occasional celebrity. Just north of The Dime, **The Woods** (1533 N. La Brea Ave., 323/876-6612, 6pm-2am Mon.-Fri., 8pm-2am Sat.-Sun.) lives up to its name, decked out with rustic furnishings like antler chandeliers and tree stump tables.

Speakeasy survivor **Boardner's** (1652 N. Cherokee Ave., 323/462-9621, www.boardners.com, $3-20 cover) gives the fortysomething crowd a place to relive the 1980s every Monday night. "Bar Sinister" on Saturday nights lures Goths (black is required!). The rest of the week you'll find anything from aerialists and ribbon dancers twirling beneath the cathedral ceilings to *Beavis and Butthead* headbangers. Control freaks and minions take over the second floor for S&M role playing.

Bar Centro (465 S. La Cienega Blvd., 310/246-5555, 5:30pm-midnight Mon.-Thurs. and Sun., 5:30pm-1am Fri. Sat.) vibrates with the silk-stocking, upper crusters of Beverly Hills, nibbling caviar and sipping the latest martini concoction. The centerpiece is a long table with aqua orbs. There is plenty of seating to socialize and curtained hideaways to get cozy.

Live Music

Two Sunset Strip legends mix celebrity with infamy. **The Viper Room** (8852 Sunset Blvd., 310/358-1881, www.viper-room.com, 9pm-2am daily, $8-25 cover charge) is where gangster Bugsy Siegel hung out in the 1940s, country giant Johnny Cash recorded his comeback album, and River Phoenix collapsed. Iconic bands like The Doors and The Byrds got their start at the **Whisky a Go Go** (8901 Sunset Blvd., 310/652-4202, www.whiskyagogo.com, no cover Mon.). These days, both venues welcome live local bands that play for boisterous young crowds each night, with occasional special appearances by famed artists like Prince and Aerosmith.

A great date spot, **Catalina Bar & Grill** (6725 W. Sunset Blvd., 323/466-2210, www.catalinajazzclub.com, $10-30) boasts a long list of famed jazz musicians such as Max Roach, Dizzy Gillespie, and Carmen McRae. Unless you plan to have dinner, there is a two-drink minimum.

El Floridita (1253 N. Vine St., 323/871-8612, www.elfloridita.com, $10 cover) sizzles with salsa dancing every Monday, Friday, and Saturday. Skip the cover charge and order an entrée of Cuban delights.

Don't be put off by the location of **Villains Tavern** (1356 Palmetto St., 213/613-0766, 7pm-2am Tues., 5:30pm-2am Wed.-Sat.) down by the L.A. River. It has a happenin' live music scene with everything from jazz to swing. A collection of colorful apothecary bottles ornament the wall at the entrance, and a huge gothic mirror frames the bar, where mixologists serve cocktails in mason jars.

Laugh out loud at the **Groundlings Theater** (7307 Melrose Ave., 323/934-4747, www.groundlings.com, $13-20), which has been a fixture of L.A.'s improv and sketch comedy scene for 40 years. It's known as a proving ground for future *Saturday Night Live* stars (Will Ferrell, Kristen Wiig, and Phil Hartman all started here). Other comedy stalwarts **The Improv** (8162 Melrose Ave., 323/651-2583, www.improv.com, $11-21), **The Comedy Store** (8433 Sunset Blvd., 323/650-6268, www.thecomedystore.com, free-$20), and **Laugh Factory** (8001 Sunset Blvd., 323/656-1336, www.laughfactory.com, $20-45 plus 2-drink minimum) also get big laughs, compliments of both up-and-comers and famed comedians (Chris Rock, Adam Sandler, Jerry Seinfeld, George Lopez, and Jon Stewart).

Arts and Entertainment

Downtown and Hollywood hold the bulk of galleries, theaters, and performance centers.

The glittering **Geffen Playhouse** (10886 Le Conte Ave., 310/208-5454, www.geffenplayhouse.com, $24-46) is home to a good-sized main stage, the Gil Cates Theater, and the cozier Skirball Kenis Theater. The company offers a mix of new work and local premieres, frequently with big-name talent. Special nights include Wine Down Sundays, Lounge Fridays, and Talk Back Tuesdays, where a special drinks or coffee reception is held before the performance. Saturday mornings often feature great kid-oriented shows.

Downtown's beloved 3,200-seat **Dorothy Chandler Pavilion** (135 N. Grand Ave., 213/972-7211, www.musiccenter.org) is a landmark performance center that boasts curving staircases, sparkling chandeliers, and grand halls draped in red and gold. The Pavilion is home of the Los Angeles Opera from September through June, and the Glorya Kaufman Presents Dance series.

A multitude of Latin productions, as well as better-known commercial work like *Jesus Christ Superstar* and *A Night Without Monty Python,* are featured at the **Montalban Theatre** (1615 N. Vine St., 323/871-2420, www.themontalban.com), named for actor Ricardo Montalbán *(Star Trek II: The Wrath of Khan, Fantasy Island).*

The 2,600-seat art deco **Pantages Theatre** (6233 Hollywood Blvd., 323/468-1770, www.broadwayla.org) hosts celebrated Broadway musicals like *Wicked* and *The Lion King.*

Shopping

Where do people in L.A. go to shop? Downtown offers a multi-ethnic open-air market and entire streets lined with vendors that can exhaust even a shopaholic; Hollywood has everything from designer shops and lingerie boutiques to record stores and a farmers market; while Beverly Hills reigns as the queen of luxury shopping—for those with deep enough pockets.

Downtown

The 90 blocks of the **Fashion District** (110 E. 9th St., 213/488-1153, 9am-5pm daily) offer the best places to shop for wholesale clothing, shoes, accessories, and cosmetics. Among the crowded walkways and energetic price bargaining, the country's largest flower market stocks scores of fresh-cut bouquets.

Offering big discounts on precious stones and metals, the **Jewelry District** (Hill St., Olive St., and Broadway) gives those with an obsession for shiny things endless opportunities to hold on and not let go! Parking is available on Broadway.

The marketplace on **Olvera Street** (125 Paseo De La Plaza, 10am-7pm daily) includes dozens of vendor stalls selling leather items, sombreros, pottery, puppets, and handcrafted gifts.

Hollywood

Amoeba Records (6400 W. Sunset Blvd., 323/245-6400) holds an impressive collection of new and used CDs, DVDs, and vinyl records covering a multitude of genres. When you're done browsing, stay for a live musical performance; a variety of bands and artists play here regularly.

Fred Segal (8118 Melrose Ave., 323/651-4129, 10am-7pm Mon.-Sat., noon-6pm Sun.) is well stocked with everything from hip sportswear and sunglasses to high-end beauty products and the latest in foot fashion. Big price tags are reduced at sales in late September and early January. Park in the free lot at the rear of the store. A second store is located in Santa Monica (500 Broadway, 310/458-6365, 10am-7pm Mon.-Sat., noon-6pm Sun.).

The **Original Farmers Market** (6333 W. 3rd St., 323/933-9211, www.farmersmarketla.com, 9am-9pm Mon.-Fri., 9am-8pm Sat., 10am-7pm Sun.) packs in over 70 vendors, selling everything from gourmet foods to toys and gifts. Directly across from the market, **The Grove** (189 The Grove Dr., 10am-9pm Mon.-Fri., 10am-10pm Sat., 11am-8pm Sun.) provides a 575,000-square-foot "shop til you drop" experience, with both boutiques and high-end department stores. A beautifully landscaped park features a "dancing" water fountain choreographed to music.

Beverly Hills

The five floors of **Barneys New York** (9570 Wilshire Blvd., 310/276-4400, www.barneys.com, 10am-7pm Mon.-Wed. and Fri.-Sat., 10am-8pm Thurs., noon-6pm Sun.) are filled with enough designer clothing, cosmetics, and jewelry to put any fashion diva in a Prada coma. Get some air and a glass of wine at the rooftop restaurant.

MAC (133 N. Robertson Blvd., 310/271-9137) supplies beauty products that you can't find anywhere else. Displays of eye shadows and lipsticks are arranged like works of art and professional make-up artists offer private lessons.

The eight-level **Beverly Center** (8500 Beverly Blvd., 310/854-0070, www.beverlycenter.com, 10am-9pm Mon.-Fri., 10am-8pm Sat., 11am-6pm Sun.) includes a multitude of stores ranging from boutiques to big retailers. All together you'll find about 160 stores to spend your hard-earned dollars.

The rich and famous head to **Rodeo Drive** (between Santa Monica and Wilshire Blvds. and Beverly Dr.) to pick up their necessities, while everyone else settles for window-shopping. More than 100 boutiques along the three-block stretch include flagship stores for Chanel, Hermes, and Harry Winston.

Recreation
Beaches

Sunset Beach (along CA-1) doesn't have concessions, fire pits, parking lots, or really any of the extra amenities (concessions, on-site bike rentals, boardwalk, etc.) you find at most other beaches. However, it is worth a visit, especially if you want to avoid L.A.'s parade of oiled-up beach bodies. Wild winds provide the perfect fuel for windsurfing, kayaking, and paddle boarding, and good waves for bodysurfing. The beach lies along CA-1 with Seal Beach Street to the north and Warner Avenue to the south. Street parking is free and limited.

Southeast of Sunset Beach, three-mile-long **Bolsa Chica State Beach** (CA-1 in Huntington Beach, 6am-10pm daily, parking lot closes at 9pm) has smaller waves, making it a popular spot for beginning surfers. Amenities include fire rings, volleyball courts, restrooms and showers, picnic ramadas (714/377-9422 for reservations), barbecue grills, basketball courts, and a paved bike path.

Thirty miles south from Bolsa Chica State Beach, **Torrance Beach** (387 Paseo de la Playa, Torrance, parking $7) offers 40 acres of soft sand at the foot of craggy cliffs that stretch south to the Palos Verdes Peninsula. Popular activities are swimming, skin diving, surfing, volleyball, and fishing. Multiple parking spaces, bathrooms and showers, lifeguards, and a concession stand make it easy to stay the entire day.

Bicycling

One of Griffith Park's best features is the nine-mile **bike loop.** The route follows a tree-lined pathway and parts of the L.A. River Bike Path via Riverside Drive, forming a loop inside the park. Route information and bikes are available at **Griffith Park Bicycle Rental** (4730 Crystal Springs Dr., 323/662-6573, $8-25).

The seven-mile ride along the **Ballona Creek Trail** connects Ballona Creek in Culver City west to the Coast Bike Path in Marina Del Rey. Access is at Syd Kronenthal Park (behind the ballfield). North of Inglewood the path is rough and you'll be working against the wind, but picturesque ocean views make it

worthwhile. The path ends at Fisherman's Village in Marina del Rey, but links to the beachfront **South Bay Trail,** which continues 22 miles along Santa Monica State Beach, north to Malibu and south to Torrance.

Expect twists, turns, and uphill insanity via **The Donut.** (The trail started 50 years ago at a donut shop.) This intense trail stretches 42 miles from Redondo Beach to Palos Verdes. Competitive cyclists train on the route. The views of Point Vice, Point Fermin, and Catalina Island are remarkable.

Spectator Sports

The **Los Angeles Dodgers** (1000 Elysian Park Ave., 323/224-1471, www.dodgers.com) are the hometown baseball team. With L.A.'s perfect climate, Dodger Stadium hosts some of the most beautiful outdoor games in the country.

Staples Center (1111 S. Figueroa St., 213/742-7100, www.staplescenter.com) doubles as a sports and entertainment venue. It's home to the L.A. Kings hockey team, Lakers, Sparks, and Clippers basketball teams, while also hosting big-name performers like Katy Perry, Taylor Swift, and Madonna.

Events

On New Year's Day, the **Tournament of Roses Parade** (www.tournamentofroses.com/RoseParade.aspx) takes place just northeast of Downtown in Pasadena, with marching bands from all over the world, equestrians, over 40 rose-covered floats, and the crowning of the Rose Queen and her court. Bleacher seats are available and run $50-100. It's not unusual for people to camp out overnight for free curbside seating. If that doesn't sound appealing, try finding a spot early in the morning east of Lake Avenue.

The slightly twisted **Doo Dah Parade** (Raymond Ave. and Holly St., Pasadena, 626/440-7379, http://pasadenadoodah-parade.info, free) is a parody of the Rose Parade that takes place each November.

Some of the tongue-in-cheek highlights have included the Shopping Cart Drill Team, the Bastard Sons of Lee Marvin, the Men of Leisure Synchronized Nap Team, Claude Rains, and the 20-Man Memorial Invisible Man Marching Drill Team.

Every second Thursday of the month, more than 25,000 visitors roam the **Downtown Art Walk** (between 4th and 7th Sts. and Spring and Main Sts., www. downtownartwalk.org), when local galleries open their doors. Maps are available online.

Accommodations
Under $150
Affordable Downtown's **Stay on Main Hotel** (636 Main St., 213/213-7829, www. stayonmain.com, $35 dorms, $50 suites, $80 and up for rooms with private bath) is a boutique hotel and hostel that provides comfort with cool, retro-style touches, and iPod docks. **USA Hostels Hollywood** (1624 Schrader Blvd., 323/462-3777 and 800/524-6783, www.usahostels.com, $30-40 dorms, $70-85 suites, includes breakfast) puts you right in the center of Hollywood's happening nightlife.

$150-250
Located in the historic 1927 United Artists building, the hip ★ **Ace Hotel** (929 S. Broadway, 213/623-3233, www. acehotel.com/losangeles, $199 and up) includes an ornate theater, vibrant lounges, and a cozy coffee shop.

With a retro-1960s vibe, **The Standard Downtown** (550 S. Flower St., 213/892-8080, www.standardhotels.com/down-town-la, $195 and up) features platform beds, roomy tubs, peek-a-boo showers, and the world's coolest rooftop poolside bar.

On Hollywood's west side, **Farmer's Daughter Hotel** (115 S. Fairfax Ave., 323/937-3930, www.farmersdaughter-hotel.com, $179-269, $18 parking) hosts *American Idol* contestants. In addition to urban cowboy decor, rooms feature rain showerheads, refrigerator, hair dryer, and mini-bar. Strange but fun mutant-sized rubber duckies hang out at the pool.

A hideaway in the heart of West Hollywood, **San Vicente Bungalows** (845 N. San Vicente Blvd., 310/854-6915, www. sanvicentebungalows.com, $169-205) is in walking distance to shopping, restaurants, and top clubs, like Whisky a Go Go, yet offers a serene oasis away from the bustle. An additional $10 fee gets you a continental breakfast and WiFi.

The 1927 art deco **Crescent Hotel** (403 N. Crescent Dr., 310/247-0505, www. crescentbh.com, $224 and up) is just two blocks from famed Rodeo Drive. Rooms range from the 130-square-foot "Itty Bitty" to the 400-square-foot "Grand King." Beds are triple-sheeted in Turkish cotton. The Terrace offers classic breakfast and dinner menus, while The Lounge serves evening cocktails and small plates.

The intricate design at Spanish-inspired **Figueroa Hotel** (939 S. Figueroa St., 213/627-8971 and 800/421-9092, www.figueroahotel.com, $148 and up) includes elegant arches and richly colored rooms. Its central location is close to great restaurants, clubs, and Downtown attractions.

Just off Sunset Boulevard, the **Magic Castle Hotel** (7025 Franklin Ave., 323/851-0800, www.magiccastlehotel. com, $149 and up) is two blocks from the Hollywood Walk of Fame and TCL Chinese Theatre. Choose from standard, one-room, or two-room suites, each with complimentary breakfast and guest robes and cozy slippers. Guests also get free tickets to the historic Magic Castle, a private magic club.

Over $250
Even steps away from Rodeo Drive, the exquisite Italian Renaissance architecture of the ★ **Beverly Wilshire Hotel** (9500 Wilshire Blvd., 310/275-5200, www. fourseasons.com, $475 and up) stands out. Inside, marble crown moldings, dark woods, and crystal chandeliers continue

the elegance. Three restaurants and two bars offer an array of dishes and drinks.

In the heart of West Hollywood, **Mondrian Hotel** (8440 Sunset Blvd., 323/650-8999, $295-495) demonstrates luxury from the moment you open its mahogany doors and step into its modish lobby. Rooms feature 300-thread-count sheets, rain showerheads, bamboo floors, and floor-to-ceiling windows. The Lobby Bar offers a café menu, while the Herringbone restaurant serves fine seafood. The Skybar is an open-air poolside lounge, fully equipped with world-class DJs, celebrity appearances, and stunning city views.

The glamorous **Montage Beverly Hills** (225 N. Canon Dr., 888/860-0788, www.montagehotels.com, $595 and up) pampers its guests with Hollywood style, with every whim satisfied. Guest rooms ensure comfort with electronically controlled lighting, temperatures, and draperies. A 20,000-square-foot spa, award-winning dining, and a shimmering rooftop pool with sweeping views complete the picture.

Information and Services

The **Los Angeles Convention and Visitors Bureau** (www.discoverlosangeles.com) maintains visitor information centers adjacent to two Metro stations. One of these is in Hollywood, **Hollywood and Highland Visitors Center** (6801 Hollywood Blvd., 323/467-6412, 9am-10pm Mon.-Sat., 10am-7pm Sun.), and the other is in Downtown, **Union Station Visitors Center** (800 N. Alameda St.). Maps, brochures, information, and advice about visiting the greater Los Angeles area are all available.

The South Bay

South of Venice, CA-1 takes a turn through the workaday streets of western Los Angeles, even passing LAX airport, before hitting the three beach cities that

the *Queen Mary* in Long Beach Harbor

make up what is locally known as the South Bay: Manhattan Beach, Hermosa Beach, and Redondo Beach. All three are destinations for beach recreation, particularly surfing and volleyball. Every August, Manhattan Beach is the site of the **Manhattan Beach Open volleyball tournament** (www.themanhattanbeachopen.com), while the cities take turns hosting the **International Surf Festival** (www.surffestival.org).

Home to wealthy sports and entertainment notables, **Manhattan Beach** is among the most desirable places to live in California, with homes selling for $1 million and up. It's also considered one of the top beaches in the nation (*GQ Magazine*, 2014), its smooth sand attracting over 3.8 million visitors each year.

CA-1 runs down the middle of **Hermosa Beach,** which extends 15 blocks from east to west and 40 blocks from north to south. The beach is a hot spot for sunbathers, surfers, paddle boarders, and beach volleyball. At the end of Pier

Avenue is an entourage of shops and eateries, as well as lively surf bars, clubs, and music venues.

Redondo Beach's stretch of sand gets crowded in the summertime, particularly near its pier, so if rubbing elbows with your fellow sun-worshippers doesn't work for you, you should head elsewhere. Surfers favor Manhattan and Hermosa, so there's more room for swimming in the water at Redondo. You'll also find the usual volleyball and other beach games, as well as restaurants on the pier.

Long Beach

CA-1 heads east and inland at the Palos Verdes Peninsula (sadly bypassing some beautiful coastline there) and continues into Long Beach. Despite its name, it's not as much a beach town as a working port, the point of entry for much of the commercial shipping coming into Los Angeles. All the action—including the tourist action—is in Long Beach Harbor, at the south end of I-710.

Sights

One of the most famous ships ever to ply the high seas, the magnificent **Queen Mary** (1126 Queens Hwy., 877/342-0738, www.queenmary.com, $28-75) now sits at permanent anchor in Long Beach Harbor, where it acts as a hotel, a museum, and an entertainment center with several restaurants and bars. You can book a stateroom ($109-489) and stay aboard, come for dinner, or just buy a regular ticket and take a self-guided tour. Explore many of the decks at the bow, including the engine room that still boasts much of its massive machinery, and see exhibits that describe the ship's history. The ship is also one of the most famously haunted places in California. Over its decades of service, a number of unfortunate souls lost their lives aboard the *Queen Mary,* and apparently some of them stuck around even after their deaths. To learn more, book

a spot on one of the evening events, such as the Paranormal Ship Walk (8pm Sun.-Thurs., $39).

On the other side of Long Beach Harbor, the **Aquarium of the Pacific** (100 Aquarium Way, 562/590-3100, www.aquariumofpacific.org, 9am-6pm daily, adults $29, children $15) hosts animal and plant life native to the Pacific Ocean, from the local residents of SoCal's sea up to the North Pacific and down to the tropics. This large aquarium has far more than the average number of touch-friendly tanks, including the Shark Lagoon where you can "pet" a few of the sharks the aquarium cares for.

Accommodations
For a unique place to stay in Long Beach Harbor, try the **Dockside Boat and Bed** (316 E. Shoreline Dr., Dock 5A, Rainbow Harbor, 562/436-3111, www.boatandbed.com, $235-330). You won't get a regular old hotel room—instead, you'll get a whole yacht. The yachts run 38-54 feet and can sleep 2-4 people. Unfortunately, you can't take your floating accommodations out for a spin; these yachts are permanent residents of Rainbow Harbor.

Catalina Island

For a slice of Greece in Southern California, take a ferry or a helicopter out to **Catalina Island** (www.catalina.com). You can see Catalina from the shore of Long Beach on a clear day, but for a better view you've got to get out there. The port town of Avalon welcomes visitors with plenty of European-inspired hotels, restaurants, and shops. But the main draw of Catalina lies outside the walls of its buildings. With its Mediterranean climate, Catalina is a good spot for outdoor recreation on land or water.

Getting There and Around
Most folks take the ferry over from the mainland coast. The **Catalina Express**

(310/519-1212 or 800/481-3470, www.catalinaexpress.com) serves as the major carrier, with multiple departures every day, even in the off-season. Although boats depart from Long Beach (320 Golden Shore, $74.50 adults round-trip, $59 children round-trip) and Dana Point (34674 Golden Lantern St., $76.50 adults round-trip, $61 children round-trip), San Pedro Port (Berth 95 at Swinford and Harbor Blvd., $74.50 adults round-trip, $59 children round-trip) has the most departures to Avalon. The trip to the island takes about one hour.

You can also get to Catalina by air. **Island Express Helicopter Service** (310/510-2525 or 800/228-2566, www.islandexpress.com, $250-390 round-trip per person) can fly you from Long Beach, San Pedro, or Santa Ana to Catalina in about 15 minutes.

Once you're on the island, the easiest way to get around is to walk. Some locals and visitors prefer golf carts, which can be rented at any number of outlets, including **Island Rentals** (125 Pebbly Beach Rd., 310/510-1456, www.catalinagolfcartrentals.com, $40/hr), near the ferry dock. Taxis hover near the ferry dock when the ferries are due in each day, and it's customary to share your ride with as many people as can fit. To get a cab back to the ferry or the helipad when it's time to leave, call 310/510-0025.

Sights
When approaching Catalina on the ferry, you'll notice a round, white, art deco building on one end of town. This is the **Casino** (1 Casino Way, theater 310/510-0179). It's not a gambling hall, but rather harks back to the older Italian meaning of the word, "place of entertainment." It's used for movies and events.

Outside town, the coolest place to visit is the **Wrigley Memorial and Botanical Garden** (Avalon Canyon Rd., 1.5 miles west of town, 310/510-2897, 8am-5pm daily, $5 adults, free children). Stroll through serene gardens planted with flowers, trees, and shrubs native to California—or even to Catalina specifically. At the center of the garden is the Wrigley Memorial, dedicated to the memory of the chewing-gum magnate who adored Catalina and used his sticky fortune to improve it. Most notably, he funded the building of the Avalon Casino.

Food

So where do the locals go? Many of them crowd into **El Galleon** (411 Crescent Ave., 310/510-1188, 11am-9pm daily, $18-33), which features hearty American dishes with lots of aged steaks, chicken, and fresh fish. It's part of the pedestrian-only stretch of Crescent Avenue, and the porch has a fabulous view of the harbor.

Steve's Steakhouse (417 Crescent Ave., 310/510-0333, www.stevessteakhouse. com, 11:30am-2pm and from 5pm daily, $16-35) offers more than just steak; there are plenty of seafood options, too.

Recreation

You'll find plenty of places to kick off into the water. The most popular spot is the **Avalon Underwater Park** (Casino Point). This protected area at the north end of town has buoys and markers to help you find your way around the reefs and keep safe. Not only will you see the famous bright-orange garibaldi fish, you'll get the opportunity to meet jellyfish, anemones, spiny lobsters, and plenty of other sea life. Out at the deeper edge of the park, nearly half a dozen wrecked ships await your examination.

Diving Catalina (34 Middle Terrace Rd., 310/510-8558, www.divingcatalina. com) offers guided snorkel tours of the Casino Point Dive Park that include all equipment with the fees. Certified scuba divers can book a two-hour guided tour of Avalon Underwater Park. **Snorkel Catalina** (310/510-3175 or 877/218-9156, www.snorkelingcatalina.com) specializes in deeper water excursions farther away from shore, taking guests out on a

custom pontoon boat. Standard tours run 2-4 hours and let you check out the prettiest fish, sleekest seals, and friendliest dolphins around the island.

Kayaking is one of the most popular ways to see otherwise unreachable parts of Catalina. Rent a kayak, or if you're not confident in your own navigation abilities, take a tour with a reputable company. **Descanso Beach Ocean Sports/ Catalina Island Kayak & Snorkel** (310/510-1226, www.kayakcatalinaisland.com) offers several kayak tours to different parts of the island for a range of experience levels. All trips start north of Avalon and the Casino at Descanso Beach Club.

To rent kayaks, snorkel gear, or stand-up paddleboards, try **Wet Spot Rentals** (Avalon Boat Landing, 310/510-2229, www.catalinakayaks.com, 9am-5pm daily Apr.-Aug.).

A great way to get around and beyond Avalon is on a bicycle. You can bring your own bike aboard the ferries that travel to and from the island. Rent a bicycle right on the island at **Brown's Bikes** (100 yards from the ferry dock, 310/510-0986, www. catalinabiking.com, $8-18/hr, $20-45/day).

Catalina Adventure Tours (1 Cabrillo Mole, 562/432-8828, www.catalinaadventuretours.com, tours $28-84 adults) offers both land and sea tours, including underwater views from the semi-submersible Nautilus.

Accommodations

For inexpensive accommodations, your best bet is the **Hermosa Hotel & Cottages** (131 Metropole St., 310/510-1010 or 800/668-5963, www.hermosahotel.com, $150-350), which offers simple rooms about a block from the harbor beaches and a short walk from the Casino, shops, and restaurants.

The bright yellow **Hotel Mac Rae** (409 Crescent Ave., 310/510-0246 or 800/698-2266, www.hotelmacrae.com, $129-349) has been in the Mac Rae family for four generations, and they've been running the hostelry since 1920. The rooms are right on the waterfront and have a Mediterranean flavor.

🔶 Disneyland Resort

The "Happiest Place on Earth" lures millions of visitors of all ages each year with promises of fun and fantasy. During high seasons, waves of humanity flow through **Disneyland Resort** (1313 S. Disneyland Dr., Anaheim, 714/781-4565, www.disneyland.disney.go.com, 8am-midnight daily Disneyland Park, 8am-10pm daily Disney California Adventure Park, one-day ticket for one park $99 ages 10 and up, $93 ages 3-9, additional $56 for both parks), moving slowly from Land to Land and ride to ride. Even the most cynical and jaded visitors can't quite keep their cantankerous scowls set once they're ensconced inside Uncle Walt's dream. It really *is* a happy place.

Disney's rides, put together by the park's "Imagineers," are better than those at any other amusement park in the state. The technology of the rides isn't more advanced than other parks, but it's the attention to detail that makes a Disneyland ride experience so enthralling. Even the spaces where you stand in line match the theme of the ride you're waiting for, from the archaeological relics of Indiana Jones to the tombstones of the Haunted Mansion. If you've got several days in the park, try them all! But if you don't, pick from the best of the best in each Land.

The Disneyland Resort is made of up of three main areas: Disneyland Park, the original amusement park that started it all in 1955; Disney California Adventure Park, a California-themed park that opened in 2001 with faster rides meant to appeal to older kids and adults; and Downtown Disney, a shopping and eating district outside the two parks.

Getting There

Disneyland is located in Anaheim about 25 miles south of downtown Los Angeles and is accessible from I-5 South. Exit on Disneyland Drive toward Ball Road; stay in the left three lanes for **parking** (1313 S. Disneyland Dr., $17). From Long Beach, Disneyland can be reached via CA-22 East.

Disneyland Park

There are eight areas, or "Lands," of Disneyland Park: Main Street, U.S.A.; Tomorrowland; Fantasyland; Mickey's Toontown; Frontierland; Critter Country; New Orleans Square; and Adventureland.

Upon entering, you'll be in Main Street, U.S.A., which has a few shops, information booths, and other practicalities. Your first stop inside the park should be one of the information kiosks near the front entrance gates. Here you can get a map, a schedule of the day's events, and the inside scoop on what's going on in the park during your visit.

Due north of Main Street is Sleeping Beauty's Castle and Fantasyland, with Mickey's Toontown beyond. To the east is Tomorrowland. Adventureland and Frontierland lie to the west of Main Street, with New Orleans Square to the west of Adventureland, and Critter Country in the far western reaches of the park.

The magical **FastPasses** are free with park admission. The newest and most popular rides offer FastPass kiosks near the entrances. Feed your ticket into one of the machines, and it will spit out both your ticket and a FastPass with your specified time to take the ride. Come back during your window and enter the always-much-shorter FastPass line, designated by a sign at the entrance. If you're with a group, be sure you all get your FastPasses at the same time, so you all get the same time window to ride the ride.

Adventureland

Adventureland is home to **Indiana Jones**

Adventure, arguably one of the best rides in all of Disneyland. Even the queue is interesting: Check out the signs, equipment, and artifacts in mock-dusty tunnels winding toward the ride. The ride itself, in a roller-coaster style variant of an all-terrain vehicle, jostles and jolts you through a landscape that Indy himself might dash through, pursued by booby-traps and villains. Hang on to your hat—literally! It's also home to the kitschy, classic **Jungle Cruise,** where you'll encounter angry, angry hippos.

New Orleans Square

Next to Adventureland lies New Orleans Square and the **Pirates of the Caribbean** ride. Look for Captain Jack Sparrow to pop up among the other disreputable characters engaged in all sorts of debauchery. For a taste of truly classic Disney, line up in the graveyard for a tour of the **Haunted Mansion.** Concentrating more on creating a ghoulish atmosphere, rather than speed or twists and turns, it's less of a ride than an experience.

Critter Country

Splash Mountain, Disney's take on the log ride, is the main attraction in Critter Country. The ride culminates in a long drop fashioned as if going over a waterfall. As the name suggests, it is possible that you'll get wet on this ride.

Frontierland

Take a ride on a Wild West train on the **Big Thunder Mountain Railroad.** This older roller coaster whisks away passengers on a brief but fun thrill-ride through a "dangerous, decrepit" mountain's mine shafts. As you stand in line, be sure to read the names of the locomotives as the trains come rushing by.

Fantasyland

Fantasyland sits behind **Sleeping Beauty's Castle,** which itself is not a ride, but a walk-through attraction. Many of the rides here cater to the younger set,

like the **carousel** and the flying **Dumbos.** The crazy fun of **Mr. Toad's Wild Ride** has appeal to all ages. Even though it's not really a roller coaster, this ride entertains with its wacky scenery, from a sedate library to the gates of hell.

Tucked back in Fantasyland is what to many is Disneyland's quintessential ride: **It's a small world.** With a constant soundtrack of the famous song in the background, the ride slowly tours an idealized vision of the world and introduces some favorite Disney characters.

If it's a faster thrill you're seeking, head for one of the most recognizable landmarks at Disneyland. The **Matterhorn Bobsleds** roller coaster looks like a miniature version from its namesake in the Swiss Alps. Inside it, you'll board a bobsled coaster car and plunge down the mountain on a twisted track that takes you past rivers, glaciers, and the Abominable Snowman.

Mickey's Toontown

Set behind Fantasyland, Mickey's Toontown is the company town where Mickey, Donald Duck, Goofy, and other classic Disney cartoon characters make their residences. Wandering through it, you'll feel like you're inside a cartoon yourself. The main ride here is **Roger Rabbit's Car Toon Spin.**

Tomorrowland

Located toward the front of the park, Tomorrowland, despite its futuristic theme, is home to many classics, like **Star Tours** and perennial favorite, **Space Mountain,** a fast roller coaster that whizzes through an almost entirely darkened world.

Food

The best areas of the park to grab a bite are Main Street, New Orleans, and Frontierland as they offer the most variety in concessions. But you can find at least a snack almost anywhere in the park.

For a sit-down restaurant meal inside the park, make reservations in advance for a table at the **Blue Bayou Restaurant** (New Orleans Square, 714/781-3463, $30-48). The best part about this restaurant is its setting, in the dimly lit swamp overlooking the Pirates of the Caribbean ride. The Cajun-ish cuisine matches the setting, though if you're looking for authenticity you'd do better looking elsewhere. You will get large portions, and tasty sweet desserts make a fine finish to your meal.

Disney California Adventure Park

Disney California Adventure Park (8am-10pm daily) celebrates much of what makes California special. Like Disneyland Park, it's divided into themed areas. Rides in California Adventure tend toward the thrills of other major amusement parks, but include the great Disney touches that make the Mouse special.

You'll find two information booths just inside the main park entrance, one off to the left as you walk through the turnstile and one at the opening to Sunshine Plaza. This is where you'll get your park guide, Time Guide, and more information about what's going on in the park that day.

Hollywood Pictures Backlot

Celebrating SoCal's famed film industry, the Backlot holds the ultimate thrill ride inside: **The Twilight Zone Tower of Terror.** Enter the creepy "old hotel," go through the "service area," and take your place inside an elevator straight out of your worst nightmares on this free-fall ride.

Less extreme but also fun, **Monsters, Inc. Mike & Sully to the Rescue!** invites guests into the action of the movie of the same name. You'll help the heroes as they chase the intrepid Boo. This ride jostles you around a bit, but can be suitable for smaller kids as well as bigger ones.

a bug's land

Wanna live like a bug? Get a sample of the world of tiny insects on **It's Tough to Be a Bug!** This big-group, 3-D, multi-sensory ride offers fun for little kids and adults alike. You'll fly through the air, scuttle through the grass, and get a good idea of what life is like on six little legs. When they say this ride engages *all your senses,* they mean it.

Paradise Pier

Paradise Pier mimics the Santa Monica Pier and other waterfront attractions like it, with thrill rides and an old-fashioned midway. Most of the extreme rides cluster in the Paradise Pier area. The extra-long **California Screamin',** a high-tech roller coaster designed after the classic wooden coasters of carnivals past, includes drops, twists, a full loop, and plenty of screaming fun.

Golden State

For a glimpse into other parts of the state, with attractions styled after the Bay Area, Wine Country, and Cannery Row, head to the aptly named Golden State. Want a bird's-eye view of California? Get on board **Soarin' Over California.** This combination ride and show puts you and dozens of other guests on the world's biggest "glider" and sets you off over the hills and valleys of California. You'll feel the wind in your hair as you see the vineyards, mountains, and beaches of this diverse state. If you prefer water to wind, take a ride down the **Grizzly River Run,** a Disney version of one of the many wild California rivers that rafters love to run.

Cars Land

The high-powered characters from the hit 2006 film *Cars* populate rides like **Luigi's Flying Tires** and **Mater's Junkyard Jamboree.** The **Radiator Springs Racers** has park visitors racing through the film's Route 66-inspired setting in six-person vehicles.

Food

Most of the food is clustered in the Golden State area. For a Mexican feast, try **Cocina Cucamonga Mexican Grill** (Pacific Wharf, $10.50-14). If you're just dying for a cold beer, get one at the **Bayside Brews** (Paradise Pier, $6-8). If your thirst is for California wines, head for the **Mendocino Terrace** (Pacific Wharf, $9-15).

Downtown Disney

You don't need an admission ticket to take a stroll through the shops of Downtown Disney. In addition to the mammoth World of Disney Store, you'll find a Build-a-Bear Workshop and a LEGO Store, among mall staples like Sephora. You can also have a bite to eat or take in some jazz or a new-release movie at Downtown Disney.

Accommodations
Disney Hotels

For the most iconic Disney resort experience, you must stay at the **Disneyland Hotel** (1150 Magic Way, 714/778-6600, http://disneyland.disney.go.com, $450-500). This nearly 1,000-room high-rise monument to brand-specific family entertainment has themed swimming pools, themed play areas, and even character-themed guest rooms that allow the kids to fully immerse themselves in the Mouse experience. The monorail stops inside the hotel, offering guests the easiest way into the park proper without having to deal with parking.

It's easy to find the **Paradise Pier Hotel** (1717 S. Disneyland Dr., 714/999-0990, http://disneyland.disney.go.com, $340-450); it's that high-rise thing just outside of the parks. This hotel boasts what passes for affordable lodgings within walking distance of the parks. Rooms are cute, colorful, and clean. You'll find a (possibly refreshing) lack of Mickeys in the standard guest accommodations at the Paradise, which has the feel of a beach resort motel.

Disney's Grand Californian Hotel and Spa (1600 S. Disneyland Dr., 714/956-6425 or 714/635-2300, http://disneyland.disney.go.com, $540-660) lies inside Disney California Adventure Park, attempting to mimic the famous Ahwahnee Lodge in Yosemite. The hotel is surrounded by gardens and has restaurants, a day spa, and shops attached on the ground floors; it can also get you right out into Downtown Disney and thence to the parks proper. Guest rooms at the Californian offer more luxury than the other Disney resorts, with dark woods and faux-Craftsman detailing creating an attractive atmosphere.

Outside the Parks

The massive park complex is ringed with motels, both popular chains and more interesting independent hotels. **The Anabella** (1030 W. Katella Ave., Anaheim, 714/905-1050, www.anabella-hotel.com, $110-130) is a three-block walk to the parks. Guest rooms are furnished with an eye toward modern, stylish decor. You can get limited room service at the Anabella, and you can leave your car in their parking lot to avoid the expense of parking at Disneyland.

The **Desert Palms Hotel & Suites** (631 W. Katella Ave., 714/535-1133 or 888/521-6420, www.desertpalmshotel.com, $160-250) is in walking distance of Disneyland. Regular rooms have one king or two queen beds, a TV, a phone, Internet access, and not a ton of room to walk around after all your luggage is crowded in with the furniture.

Huntington Beach

South of Long Beach, CA-1 enters Orange County, where the coastline returns to beaches that are wide, flat, sandy, and often crowded in the summer.

Huntington City Beach (103 CA-1 from Beach Blvd. to Seapoint St., 714/536-5281, 5am-10pm daily) runs the length of the south end of town, petering out as the oil industry gets going at the north end. Known as Surf City, USA, it's the home of the **International Surfing Museum** (411 Olive Ave., 714/960-3483, www.surfing-museum.org, noon-5pm Wed.-Fri. and Sun., noon-8pm Tues., noon-7pm Sat., free), with classic surfboards and other memorabilia, as well as the **U.S. Open of Pro Surfing** (www.vansusopenofsurfing. com). But even average beachgoers can catch a wave at this famous surf break. Anglers prefer the Huntington Beach Pier, while cyclists, inline skaters, and joggers take to the beachside cement walkway.

Food and Accommodations

For a quick bite to eat, stop at the **Bodhi Tree Café** (501 Main St., Ste. E, 714/969-9500, 11am-10pm daily, $10-20) for vegetarian soups, salads, and sandwiches. **Sugar Shack Café** (213 1/2 Main St., 714/536-0355, www.hbsugarshack, 6am-2pm Mon.-Tues. and Thurs.-Fri., 6am-8pm Wed., 6am-3pm Sat.-Sun., $10) is a great place for breakfast.

You can have an almost beachfront room at the **Sun 'N Sands Motel** (1102 CA-1, 714/536-2543, www.sunnsands. com, $189-289). This tiny place is across the highway from Huntington Beach, so only a few lanes of asphalt separate you from the sand. Expect a standard motel king or double-queen guest room, with a private bathroom, TV with movie channels, and WiFi.

Newport Beach

After passing over the Santa Ana River, CA-1 enters Newport Beach, the affluent community that served as the setting for the TV show *The O.C.* Most of the activity in Newport Beach centers around the Balboa Peninsula, which is accessed via Newport Boulevard off CA-1. Newport Boulevard merges with Balboa

Boulevard, which is the main thoroughfare on the peninsula. Parking is limited all over the Balboa Peninsula.

Stretching southeast from the Newport Beach Pier (off 21st St.), **Newport Municipal Beach** is a beautiful and popular place to stretch out on the sand.

There's also a bike path that runs along nearly the entire peninsula. You can rent a bike at **Balboa Bikes 'n' Beach Stuff** (601 E. Balboa Blvd., 949/723-1516, www.balboabikes.com, 9am-sunset daily summer, 10am-sunset daily winter), where you can rent a bike all day for $10 and pick up some saltwater taffy treats to take along for the ride.

Food and Accommodations

Local institution **The Crab Cooker** (2200 Newport Blvd., 949/673-0100, 11am-9pm Sun.-Thurs., 11am-10pm Fri.-Sat., $17-24) serves up seafood in a surprisingly not-fried form. Looking for gourmet French cuisine with a hint of romance? **Pescadou Bistro** (3325 Newport Blvd., 949/675-6990, www.pescadoubistro. com, 5:30pm-close Tues.-Sun., $21-35) fits the bill.

Check into **The Island Hotel Newport Beach** (690 Newport Center Dr., 949/759-0808, www.islandhotel.com, $259-379) for perhaps the ultimate O.C. experience. The high-rise luxury hotel is situated in a giant shopping mall, a few minutes' drive from the beach. Expect cushy beds with white linens, private bathrooms, and all the best amenities.

Crystal Cove State Park

Crystal Cove State Park (8471 CA-1 N., 949/494-3539, www.crystalcovestatepark. com, 6am-sunset daily, $15) preserves one of the few stretches of undeveloped coastline in Orange County. Hiking through rolling hills, tide-pooling, and bird-watching are a few of the activities that can be enjoyed here.

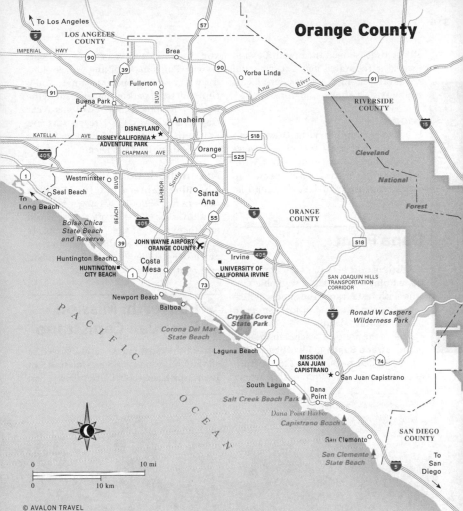

Accommodations

Restored historic cabins are available for overnight stays at the ★ **Crystal Cove Beach Cottages** (www.crystalcovebeach-cottages.com or www.reserveamerica.com, $169-249). The rustic accommodations are very popular; reservations can be made seven months prior to the time of your stay.

Laguna Beach

Farther south, the town of Laguna Beach has some of the nicest sands in the county. With more than a dozen separate beaches, you'll find it hard to choose your favorite. **Heisler Park** and **Main Beach Park** are connected, so you can walk from one to the other. Both offer protected waterways, tidepools, and water-based playground equipment. Local art is displayed in the form of benches and sculptures. You can scuba dive at several reefs right off the beach. You'll find all the facilities and amenities you need, from picnic tables to lawns to restrooms. You can park on the street if you find a spot, but be aware that the meters get checked all the time, so feed them well! Beyond the beach, there are shops, galleries, and restaurants along CA-1, or South Coast Highway, as it's known on this stretch.

Food

If you get hungry, try the **Orange Inn** (703 CA-1, 949/494-6085, www.orange-inncafe.com, 6:30am-7pm daily, $5-10), which serves breakfast, burgers, and smoothies in a casual, surf shack-like space.

Dana Point

A bustling port between 1830 and 1840, **Dana Point** today offers a walkable marina with restaurants and shops. It also serves as departure point for visitors to Santa Catalina Island.

One of the prettiest beaches in the area is **Capistrano Beach** (35005 Beach Rd., 949/923-2280 or 949/923-2283, http://ocparks.com, 6am-10pm daily), where

you can catch a wave or a game of volleyball. Paths make biking, inline skating, and walking popular pastimes. You'll find a metered parking lot adjacent to the beach, plus showers and restrooms. Near Capistrano Beach, CA-1 reaches its end as it joins up with the I-5 freeway for the 40-mile drive into San Diego.

Accommodations

The **Blue Lantern Inn** (34343 Blue Lantern St., 949/661-1304, www.bluelanterninn.com, $200-350) offers beachfront elegance. Each of the 29 rooms boasts soothing colors, charming appointments, and lush amenities, including a spa tub in every bathroom.

I-5 North: Mission San Juan Capistrano

One of the most famous and beloved of all the California missions is **Mission San Juan Capistrano** (26801 Ortega Hwy., San

Mission San Juan Capistrano

Juan Capistrano, 949/234-1300, http://missionsjc.com, 8:30am-5pm daily, $9 adults, $6 children). From Dana Point, it's a quick 2.5-mile trip up I-5 to the mission.

This was the only mission church where Father Serra presided over Sunday services. Today, this mission has a beautiful new Catholic church on-site, extensive gardens and land, and an audio tour of the museum, which was created from the old mission church and buildings. Inside the original church, artifacts from the early time of the mission tell the story of its rise and fall. The graveyard outside continues that narrative, as do the bells and other buildings of the compound. In late fall and early spring, monarch butterflies flutter about in the flower gardens and out by the fountain in the courtyard.

These days, the mission may be most famous for the swallows that return every spring to the little town of San Juan Capistrano and the celebrations that take place in their honor. These celebrations began during the mission's heyday in the 18th century and may have been started by Native Americans centuries before that.

Outside the mission, you'll find the town's main street, Camino Capistrano, which positively drips Spanish colonial history. Each old adobe building boasts a brass plaque describing its history and use over the years.

Oceanside and Carlsbad

As I-5 makes its run toward the border with Mexico, it enters San Diego County at Camp Pendleton. Two charming beach towns offer beaches and sights worth stopping at along the way.

Oceanside sits about 20 miles south of the Orange County/San Diego County border. It's home to the **California Surf Museum** (312 Pier View Way, 760/721-6876, http://surfmuseum.org, 10am-4pm daily, $5 adults, free children under 12), where you can admire and appreciate the ancient sport and art of surfing through exhibits on board-shaping to photo essays about legendary surfers.

Just south of Oceanside lies Carlsbad and its main attraction: **Legoland** (1 Legoland Dr., 760/918-5346, http://california.legoland.com, 10am-6pm daily, $87 ages 13 and up, $81 ages 3-12). This amusement park showcases what can be made from the iconic Danish building blocks, from dragons and pharaohs to miniature versions of major U.S. cities. An aquarium and water park are also part of this resort complex and cost an extra admission fee.

Torrey Pines State Reserve

In addition to walks on the beach, the **Torrey Pines State Reserve** (12600 N.

Wine-Tasting by Horseback

Horses and wine? Who knew these two would make a perfect pairing! In the **Temecula Valley,** renowned wineries and horse ranches share the rolling countryside, so wine-tasting via horseback makes perfect sense.

Saddle Up Tours (951/297-9196, www.saddleuptours.com) and **Wine Country Trails** (951/506-8706, www.winecountrytrailsbyhorseback.com) both offer packages that include tastings at 1-5 wineries and a gourmet meal ($115-415), with local wine history along the trail. Rides take place in the early morning when the air is crisp and in the evening just as the sun is setting, and generally last 90 minutes. If you've never been on a horse, don't worry. Rides are always led by a professional who provides instruction and horses are well-seasoned, so you don't have to be an experienced bronco-buster.

Out on the trail, you'll ride through open country, dotted with shrubbery and grapevines, with commanding views of the valley. Though you won't be sampling wine while riding through the vineyards (that's the reward at the end!), your horse will likely make a few stops to partake of the fruit.

The final destination is a tasting at some of the valley's best winemakers. **Wilson Creek Winery** (35960 Rancho California Rd., 951/699-9463) is home of the famous almond sparkling wine and lush 30-year-old cabernet grapevines. **Lorimar Vineyards** (39990 Anza Rd., 951/240-5177) features premium wines, live music, and a revolving art gallery. **Baily Vineyard** (33440 La Serena Way, 951/676-9463) is a master of the Bordeaux varieties. **Danza del Sol Winery** (39050 De Portola Rd., 951/302-6363) offers an incredible selection of both whites and reds.

Getting There

Temecula lies 44 miles northeast of Oceanside. To get there, follow CA-76 East, then take I-15 North to Temecula Parkway. Take the CA-79 South exit toward Old Town Front Street.

Torrey Pines Rd., 858/755-2063, www.torreypine.org, 7:15am-sunset daily, $15) offers some unusually beautiful wilderness trails. Be sure to look for *Pinus torreyana,* the rarest species of pine tree in the United States. The shortest walk is the High Point Trail, only 100 yards up to views of the whole reserve, from the ocean to the lagoon to the forest and back. For an easy, under one-hour walk, take the Guy Fleming Trail for a level two-thirds of a mile through forest, wildflower patches, and views of the ocean.

Enjoy a picnic at **Torrey Pines State Beach,** which rests right below the reserve. At low tide, you can walk south to Black's Beach, at the northernmost point of La Jolla.

Torrey Pines is located on Coast US-101, west off the Carmel Valley Road exit on I-5.

La Jolla

True to it name, La Jolla is "the jewel" of a coastline awash in scenic beauty. Its grandeur couldn't be more obvious than at its famous beaches: striking La Jolla Cove, lively La Jolla Shores, and secluded Black's Beach. Once a well-to-do San Diego suburb, it's grown into a destination in its own right, in part because it's home to the prestigious University of California at San Diego, which draws not only students and faculty, but admirers of its Renaissance architecture and 1,200 acres of gorgeous landscape.

Getting There and Around
Car

La Jolla is located off the I-5 freeway, just south of Del Mar and north of Downtown San Diego. Northbound, take La Jolla Parkway to Torrey Pines Road via I-5

North. Southbound, take I-5 South and Torrey Pines Road to Fay Avenue. Parking is challenging and expensive ($12-15).

Bus

San Diego's **Metropolitan Transit System** operates Route-30, connecting to Pacific Beach, Old Town, and Downtown to the south, and University of California, San Diego and University City to the east, stopping within walking distance of many local attractions. **North County Transit District**'s (760/966-6500) Route-101 also serves University of California, San Diego and University City, running north on Torrey Pines Road to North San Diego County.

Sights

University of California, San Diego

The **University of California, San Diego** has earned its prestigious reputation as one of the nation's top public institutions and research facilities, but its 1,200 acres of sprawling lawns, eucalyptus, and treasured sights have also contributed to its notoriety. A walk around the campus showcases a number of famous artworks and interesting architectural structures.

Undoubtedly the most beloved structure is the postmodern **Geisel Library,** named for author Theodore Geisel, a.k.a. Dr. Seuss, creator of classic kid books *Cat in the Hat* and *Green Eggs and Ham.* The library first opened in 1970 and was renamed after Geisel following his 1991 death. A collection of the author's manuscripts, audio recordings, drawings, photographs, and other memorabilia are displayed. At night, the UFO-like building is aglow with lights, as though it is ready for liftoff.

Artworks from the **Stuart Collection** surround the library. On the east side of the library, the winding 560-foot-long *Snake path,* created by artist Alexis Smith, circles a small garden, then continues on past a marble bench with a quote from English poet Thomas Gray

and a monumental granite book carved with a quote from John Milton's *Paradise Lost. Stonehenge* replicates the prehistoric monument in Wiltshire, England. Other pieces include Niki de Saint Phalle's bright *Sun God* statue and Bruce Nauman's giant neon letters, titled *Vices & Virtues.*

Museum of Contemporary Art San Diego

The **Museum of Contemporary Art San Diego** (MCASD, 700 Prospect Ave., 858/454-3541, www.mcasd.org, 11am-5pm Thurs.-Tues., $10, free with military ID) has a small branch in La Jolla. The building was redesigned by Philadelphia architect Robert Venturi, whose mantra was "less is boring." Its 4,000 multifaceted artworks include painting, sculpture, photography, and video, with work by surrealist Joseph Cornell, minimalist Frank Stella, and pop artist Andy Warhol. The 1960s and '70s conceptual art collection includes art from Latin America, with an emphasis on the San Diego/Tijuana region. There is a beautiful sculpture garden outside the museum.

Food

For lunch with a kick, try ★ **Porkyland Restaurant** (1030 Torrey Pines Rd., 858/459-1708, www.goporkyland.com, 9am-8pm daily, under $10), serving award-winning Mexican dishes, made fresh daily.

Lines gather outside **Konos Café** (704 Garnet Ave., 858/483-1669, www.konoscafe.com, 7am-3pm Mon.-Fri., 7am-4pm Sat.-Sun., under $8) for hearty morning fare and good prices.

Also known for great breakfasts, **Brockton Villa** (1235 Coast Blvd., 858/454-7393, www.brocktonvilla.com, 8am-3pm Mon., 8am-9pm Tues.-Sun., under $15) serves classic dishes along with ocean views from its dining room and outdoor patio.

La Jolla's **Burger Lounge** (1101 Wall St., 858/456-0196, www.burgerlounge.com,

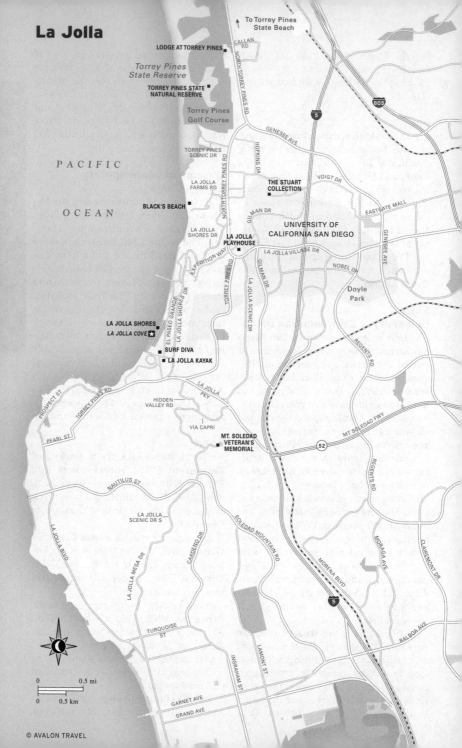

10:30am-9pm Sun.-Thurs., 10:30am-10pm Fri.-Sat., $5-10) isn't the usual counter-service beef chain. Expect healthy grass-fed beef with organic cheese and condiments. Albacore, lamb, and panko-crusted chicken round out the menu.

Cafe Japengo (8960 University Center Ln., 858/450-3355, www.cafe-japengo.com, 11:30am-2:30pm Sat.-Sun., 6pm-10pm Sun.-Wed., 6pm-10:30pm Thurs.-Sat., $12-46) offers a hip, urbane atmosphere and a menu of Asian-fusion dishes, including great sushi.

Located inside the La Jolla Shores Hotel, **Shores Restaurant** (8110 Camino del Oro, 858/456-0600, www.theshores-restaurant.com, 7am-10pm daily, $12-28) offers seasonal cuisine, a wide selection of wines, and beautiful oceanfront views.

Enjoy a villa-by-the-sea dining experience at La Valencia Hotel's **The Med** (1132 Prospect St., 858/454-0771, www.lavalencia.com, 7am-5:30pm daily, under $45). Dining areas include a casual patio, main dining room, and oceanview terrace, each offering fresh seafood, like locally caught swordfish. A fantastic weekend brunch (10:30am-2:30pm Sat.-Sun, $28) is served. Reservations are recommended.

Nightlife and Entertainment

Sports bars and trendy lounges dot Prospect Street, which runs parallel to Coast Boulevard. A cantina that doubles as a busy sports bar, **Jose's Court Room** (1037 Prospect St., 858/454-7655) offers a lively atmosphere, great drinks, and taco Tuesdays! Come in for happy hour (4pm-7pm Mon.-Fri.) for $5 appetizers, $3 beers, $4 margaritas, wine, and cocktails.

Prospect Bar & Grill (1025 Prospect St., 858/454-8092, www.prospectbar.com) features expertly crafted drinks, daily happy hours, live music and DJs every weekend, and great house specials. Relax with a drink, watch sports in action on a wide-screen television, play a game of pool, or mingle in the glass-enclosed patio.

Located in the Grande Colonial Hotel, **Nine-Ten** (910 Prospect St., 858/964-5400, www.nine-ten.com) features imaginative cocktails and martinis, and organic liqueurs amidst chic decor.

Beaumont's Eatery (5662 La Jolla Blvd., 858/459-0474, www.beaumont-seatery.com) has a casual vibe, live weekend music, and happy hours (3pm-6:30pm daily) with $6 mojitos and margaritas, $3 off specialty drinks, and $1 off microbrews.

Big-name performers still deliver punch lines at the **La Jolla Comedy Store** (916 Pearl St., 858/454-9176, www.lajolla.thecomedystore.com, $5 cover after 8pm). Even newcomers try to be funny on Sunday's Mic Night (7pm, free).

Plays and musicals grace the stage of the **La Jolla Playhouse** (2910 La Jolla Village Dr., 858/550-1010, www.lajollaplayhouse.org, $20 and up), including Broadway shows like *Jersey Boys* and Pulitzer Prize winners like *I Am My Own Wife*.

Shopping

La Jolla offers upscale shopping at one-of-a-kind boutiques along the blocks of Prospect Street and Girard Avenue.

Chic and unique, **Pomegranate Boutique** (1152 Prospect St., 858/459-0629, www.pomegranatelajolla.com, 10am-6pm Mon.-Sat., 11am-6pm Sun.) lets small designers and artists from around the world showcase their style. A sophisticated store with savvy and elegant women's designer wear, **Robina Boutique** (1261 Prospect St., 858/454-2964, 10am-6pm daily) also carries great handbags and jewelry. The wearable designs at **Rica Boutique** (7456 Girard Ave., 858/459-0208, www.shop-rica.com), where "surfer girl meets bohemian gypsy," are quintessential California.

The **Ascot Shop** (7750 Girard Ave., 858/454-4222, www.ascotshop.com, 10am-6pm Mon.-Sat., 11am-5pm Sun.) carries a large collection of top men's brands like Eton, Peter Miller, and Remy.

Browsing at **Barry Lawrence Ruderman Antique Maps** (7463 Girard Ave., 858/551-8500, 9am-4pm Mon.-Fri., weekends and evenings by appointment) is like visiting a museum of antiquities. With topographical maps from around the world, it's a haven for collectors. **Ark Antiques** (7620 Girard Ave., 858/459-7755, 10am-4:30pm Mon.-Sat.) offers a wide range of heirloom items from fine furniture and paintings to jewelry and china.

Warwick's (7812 Girard Ave., 858/454-0347, 9am-6pm Mon.-Sat., 10am-5:30pm Sun.) is the country's oldest family-owned bookstore with an eclectic collection of great reads, and high-profile signings by beloved authors and entertainers like Cary Elwes *(The Princess Bride)* and singer Sheila E.

Beaches and Recreation
★ La Jolla Cove

Set against beautiful sea cliffs, small **La Jolla Cove** is just south of La Jolla Shores.

Its white sand and deep blue water is a refuge for those wanting to relax surrounded by natural beauty. Above the sea cliffs, a grassy park looks out into the horizon, a perfect place to picnic or watch the sunset. Beneath the water's surface, colorful fish, coral, and sea kelp are plentiful and protected—the cove is part of the La Jolla Underwater Reserve. You'll often see scuba divers and snorkelers bobbing around the surface before descending into the water for a closer look at the rich marinelife. Kayaks, boards, and rafts of any kind are not allowed in the area. Underwater snorkeling tours ($35 and up) and equipment rentals are provided by companies like **La Jolla Kayak** (858/459-1114).

Access to the cove is from the park atop the cliffs via steps and a climb over rocks. There are bathrooms, outdoor showers (one indoor shower), and a changing area with benches. A "gallery" and lifeguard station is also found at the park, where you can get updated

La Jolla Sea Caves

on current beach conditions. Lifeguards look after the public 9am-sunset.

At 100 years and counting, **La Jolla Cove Rough Water Swim** (ljrws@att.net) reigns as the oldest ocean swim in the world. More than 2,100 swimmers participate in the open swim as an estimated 9,000 spectators gather on the shore every summer.

La Jolla Sea Caves

At the northern end of La Jolla Cove are seven mysterious and intriguing sea caves: The Clam's Cave, Sunny Jim Cave, Arch Cave, Sea Surprize, Shopping Cart, Little Sister, and White Lady. The best way to see them all is from the ocean on a guided tour ($39 and up) with **La Jolla Kayak** (858/459-1114). If that sounds too adventurous, you can access **Sunny Jim Cave** via an artificially constructed tunnel from **The Cave Store** (1325 Coast Blvd., 858/459-0746, 10am-5:30pm daily, $5 adults, $3 children 16 and under). It's 145 steep steps down (much more fun going down than climbing back up).

There's a handrail if you need to hold on or catch your breath.

La Jolla Shores

Lively **La Jolla Shores** has the widest stretch of sand and the widest range of activities, including swimming, surfing, diving, and volleyball. Gentle and predictable waves make it popular with beginning surfers. A park and playground make it family-friendly.

There are plenty of parking spots and full bathroom facilities. If you need to brush up on your skills or you're just learning, there are local surf schools like **Surf Diva** (2160 Avenida de la Playa, 858/454-8273, $93 and up) to help out.

Black's Beach

The best surfing is at **Black's Beach,** but you'll have to hike down the cliffside with surfboard in tow, or take the long way around from La Jolla Shores. The beach is less populated, though you're likely to get an eyeful (nudists hang out here). The breaks are top-of-the-line and the waves are rough enough to toss you around. But if you lose your shorts, don't worry; no one will care. Its seclusion is makes it a popular sunbathing spot for nudists.

Accommodations

Cheap rooms don't come easy in La Jolla, even in the off-season.

A local fixture since 1926, ★ **La Valencia** (1132 Prospect St., 858/454-0771, www.lavalenica.com, $380 and up) is reminiscent of a Mediterranean villa, complete with palm trees waving in the breeze and oceanfront views. Dining on-site includes Cafe la Rue, a modern bistro, and upscale restaurant The Med. The heated pool overlooks the shimmering Pacific.

The Bed & Breakfast Inn at La Jolla (7753 Draper Ave., 888/988-8481, www.innlajolla.com, $210-459) offers 13 uniquely styled rooms and two suites, some with fireplaces and ocean views but all elegant and comfortable.

The Origin of Sunny Jim Cave

Back in the day (around 1898), San Diego-La Jolla Railway Co. sponsored gimmicks to attract tourists. Some of the crazy stunts involved cliff-jumping while set ablaze (remarkably the jumper lived). When the mayor's son got in on the act and died from his injuries, the mayor shut the stunt down. The railroad didn't linger long before coming up with another gimmick. The sandstone caverns carved out by wind and wave erosion were difficult to enter because of the harsh, crashing surf. But with a long enough rope, a visitor could be lowered off the cliffside and dangled in front of the mouth of a cave to peer inside. Enter German entrepreneur and geologist Gustauf Shultz, who employed two Chinese men to dig a tunnel from the cliff into the largest cavern, with the idea of charging visitors for the descent. The idea worked, and news of the cave spread, eventually reaching *The Wizard of Oz* author L. Frank Baum, who named the cave "Sunny Jim" after a *Force Wheat Cereal* cartoon character. Apparently Baum thought the mouth of the cave resembled Sunny Jim's noggin. The cave continues as a tourist attraction, but the rope has been replaced by 145 steps (handrail included). At the bottom, colorful mineral deposits and the ocean are visible. Reservations are not necessary, but hours of operation change due to weather and season.

It's just a block from La Jolla Cove's cliffs and beaches and the Museum of Contemporary Art San Diego.

La Jolla Residence Inn (8901 Gilman Dr., 858/587-1770, $250 and up) offers extended stay suites with full kitchens near the University of San Diego. The hotel includes a pool and hot tub, and a small commons patio with barbecue grills.

The rustic alpine **Lodge at Torrey Pines** (11480 N. Torrey Pines Rd., 858/453-4420, $400 and up) rests on a bluff with commanding ocean views, spacious rooms (520-1,500 square feet), and luxuries like Egyptian cotton linens. There's also a full-service spa and the 36-hole Torrey Pines Golf Course. Dining on-site includes a casual grill and A.R. Valentien, a high-end restaurant with exceptional cuisine and elegant decor.

Information and Services

On the corner of Prospect Street, **Find It La Jolla** (7966 Herschel Ave., 858/729-5307, 11am-4pm Mon.-Sat.) provides visitor information to local activities, dining, and shopping.

San Diego

San Diego is the ideal destination for anyone whose idea of the perfect vacation is lying on a white-sand beach, looking out over the Pacific Ocean, and sipping the occasional cocktail. Resort hotels and restaurants perch along the seaside, beckoning visitors to the friendliest city in California.

Even though its physical area is small compared to other California metropolises, San Diego can't be beat for the density and diversity of attractions. With a world-famous zoo, dozens of museums, a thick layer of military and mission history, and unmatched recreation, San Diego offers education, enlightenment, and fun. Urban explorers will enjoy the bar and club scene, as well as a thriving theater community.

Across the bay, the enclave of Coronado beckons beach bums and film aficionados to the grandly historic (and reputedly haunted) Hotel del Coronado, where the Marilyn Monroe film *Some Like It Hot* was filmed.

Getting There and Around
Car
Most visitors drive into San Diego via the heavily traveled I-5 from the north or south. I-805 runs parallel to I-5 at La Jolla and leads south into Mission Valley. To drive between the North County and San Diego, take I-15, which runs north-south farther inland. Be sure to avoid rush hour, as the backup on I-15 can become extensive after Poway. Both I-805 and I-15 cross I-8, which runs east-west through Mission Valley. The smaller yet surprisingly pretty CA-163 runs north-south from I-5 in Balboa Park north to I-15 in Miramar.

Parking is the hardest at the beaches in the summertime. In the various downtown areas, you'll find fairly average city parking issues. Happily, San Diego's major attractions and event venues tend to be accompanied by large parking structures. Just be prepared to pay a premium if you're doing something popular.

Air
The major-league **San Diego International Airport** (3665 N. Harbor Dr., www.san.org), a.k.a. Lindbergh Field, is stuffed right along San Diego Bay, convenient to Downtown, Coronado, and almost every major San Diego attraction.

Train
Amtrak (800/872-7245, www.amtrak. com, $135 and up) runs the **Pacific Surfliner** a dozen times a day from San Luis Obispo to San Diego, with stops in Santa Barbara, Los Angeles, and Anaheim. Check into transfers from the **Coast Starlight** and the **Capitol Corridor** routes as well. Amtrak services the Santa Fe Depot (1050 Kettner Blvd.) and the Old Town Transit Center (4005 Taylor St.).

A reliable local commuter train, **The Coaster** (www.sdcommute.com, $4-5.50 adults one-way, $2-2.75 seniors, free for children under 6) runs from Oceanside into Downtown San Diego and back a dozen times a day Monday-Friday, with five trains running Saturdays, plus special event and holiday service. Purchase tickets from the vending machines in every train station. In the North County, NCTD Coaster Connecter bus routes can connect to the train station. In San Diego proper, catch the trolley or the bus from either the Old Town Transit Center or the Santa Fe station.

Bus and Trolley
In Downtown San Diego, Coronado, and La Jolla, the **MTS** (www.sdcommute.com or www.sdmts.com) operates both an extensive bus system and trolley routes. Trolley tickets cost $2.50. Bus fares are $2.25 for local routes and $2.50-5 for express routes. Use the vending machines at trolley stations to get a day pass ($5 regular day pass, $12 Rapid Express Routes day pass). If you plan to pay for your fare for buses or trolleys on board, have exact change available.

Sights
Downtown
San Diego's Downtown stretches to Coronado Island and the bay on one side and Old Town and Balboa Park on the other. Its core is the entertaining Gaslamp Quarter.

Gaslamp Quarter
Perhaps the best-known area of Downtown San Diego, the **Gaslamp Quarter** (4th, 5th, and 6th Aves. and Broadway) has exuded atmosphere since its earliest inception in the 19th century. The 5th Avenue Pier led sailors right to the area, where saloons and brothels flourished. Today, the brothels are gone, but the Gaslamp Quarter bustles with traffic, as visitors and locals crowd into the popular and sometimes quirky restaurants, dance like mad at the many bars and clubs, and spend their cash in the shops and boutiques. In the evenings, the gaslamp-shaped streetlights illuminate the sidewalks and the historic

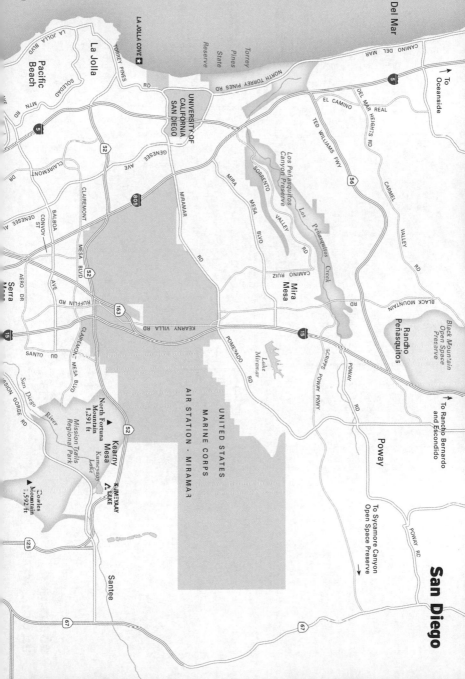

Downtown San Diego

SAN DIEGO INTERNATIONAL AIRPORT

San Diego Bay

San Diego Bay

COMMERCIAL FISHING PIER

★ USS MIDWAY

■ SAN DIEGO-CORONADO FERRY

Tuna Harbor Park

Tuna Harbor

■ CRUISE SHIP TERMINAL

MARITIME MUSEUM OF SAN DIEGO ★

Embarcadero

SEAPORT VILLAGE

Ferry

W BROADWAY

■ VISITOR INFORMATION

■ AMTRAK

W ASH ST

W LAUREL AVE

N HARBOR DR

PACIFIC HWY

Amtrak

JUNIPER ST

KETTNER BLVD

INDIA ST

LITTLE ITALY

I-5 SAN DIEGO FREEWAY

La Pensione Hotel ■

W DATE ST

Amtrak Pkwy

COLUMBIA ST

W BEECH ST

FIR ST

STATE ST

UNION ST

FRONT ST

MARKET ST

SAN DIEGO CONVENTION CENTER

San Diego Trolley (orange)

1ST AVE

2ND AVE

3RD AVE

4TH AVE

5TH AVE

6TH AVE

7TH AVE

8TH AVE

Horton Plaza Park ▲

Horton Plaza

GASLAMP QUARTER

e F G J K

San Diego Trolley (blue and orange)

BROADWAY

A ST

B ST

C ST

ST

W CEDAR ST

3RD ST

5TH ST

ELM ST

FIR ST

GRAPE ST

HAWTHORNE ST

IVY ST

PARK WEST

AVE

PETCO PARK

EAST VILLAGE

ST

10TH AVE

11TH AVE

PARK BLVD

13TH ST

14TH ST

15TH ST

16TH ST

17TH ST

ISLAND

MARKET

SAN DIEGO CITY COLLEGE

I-5

★ BALBOA PARK

163

PARK

FLORIDA DR

PERSHING DR

GOLDEN HILL

B ST

C ST

e F G ST

BROADWAY

SHERMAN HEIGHTS

K ST

25TH ST

26TH ST

94

ST

ST

GOLF COURSE DR

N

0
0.25 km
0.25 mi

© AVALON TRAVEL

architecture of some of the structures, especially along Fifth Avenue.

Maritime Museum of San Diego

The impressive collection of historic, restored, and replica vessels at the **Maritime Museum of San Diego** (1492 N. Harbor Dr., 619/234-9153, 9am-8pm daily, $12 adults, $8 children) is a must-see for seafaring enthusiasts. The prized relic is *Star of India,* the world's oldest active sailing ship. Built in 1863, of iron in a time when ships were made of wood, the *Europa* made 21 rugged voyages around the world, some lasting a year. The *Berkeley* is an 1898 steam ferryboat that operated for 60 years on San Francisco Bay. Purchased in 2004, the *HMS Surprise* is a 24-gun Royal Navy frigate built for the Academy Award-winning *Master and Commander: The Far Side of the World.* Other vessels include the *Medea,* a 1904 steam yacht, the *Californian,* a replica of a gold rush-era patroller, and the *B-39 Soviet,* one of the largest conventionally powered submarines ever built.

USS *Midway*

Follow the footsteps of the 225,000 sailors who served aboard **USS *Midway*** (910 N. Harbor Dr., 619/544-9600, 10am-5pm daily, $20), America's longest-serving aircraft carrier. First launched in 1945, the ship today serves as a museum, offering an up-close look at life at sea. Real *Midway* sailors narrate a self-guided audio tour and docents are available to answer questions. Explore the crew's sleeping quarters, the galley, engine room, even the ship's jail. The museum is also home to 29 restored aircraft and two flight simulators ($8 double, $16 single), which roll, spin, and loop during mock aerial combat missions.

Museum of Contemporary Art San Diego

Although its main branch is in La Jolla, the Downtown branch of the **Museum of Contemporary Art San Diego** (MCASD, 1100 and 1001 Kettner Blvd., 858/454-3541, www.mcasd.org, 11am-5pm Thurs.-Tues., $10) is worth a visit for its collection of conceptual works and pop art, and hosts exhibitions of works by up-and-coming artists. Admission is free the third Thursday of the month (5pm-7pm).

★ Balboa Park

A sprawling 1,200-acre urban park with numerous open spaces, gardens, theaters, and the world-famous San Diego Zoo, **Balboa Park** (1549 El Prado, 619/239-0512) is the cultural center of Downtown. Many of the city's museums are found along Balboa Park's Prado, inside Spanish colonial revival buildings, built for the 1915-1916 Panama-California Exposition. The multicultural tapestry includes the Centro Cultural de la Raza, the World Beat Center (dedicated to African culture), the Spanish Village Art Center (home to 30 artists), the Mingei Museum of International Folk Art, the Museum of Man anthropological museum, and the Japanese Friendship Garden.

Balboa's gardens are a cultivated wonder of 350 species of plants and an estimated 1,500 trees, many selected by "the Mother of Balboa Park," Kate Sessions, who is credited with the park's rise to enchantment.

The most photographed park sight, the historic **Botanical Building** (1549 El Prado, 619/239-0512, 10am-4pm Fri.-Wed., free) captivates with its magical dome and serene lily pond. Walking paths meander through the colorful landscape of the ambrosial **Inez Grant Memorial Rose Garden,** with 130 species of the fragrant flower, and the fascinating **Desert Garden,** with 1,300 succulents and desert plants from around the world.

Ride the historic **Carousel** (11am-5pm Sat.-Sun., $2.50) built in 1910. Grab the brass ring and your ride is free! All but two of the intricately hand-carved animals are original pieces. The model G16 **Miniature Railroad** (11am-4:30pm Sat.-Sun., 11am-6:30pm daily in summer,

Two Days in San Diego

Day 1

Start your day at the cluster of culture in **Balboa Park** (page 329). Explore the diverse museums and art galleries, wander the gardens, admire the exquisite **Botanical Building**, or get acquainted with exotic animals at the **San Diego Zoo** (page 330)—where animal lovers can easily spend the whole day. For lunch, get a gourmet pie at **La Pizzeria Arrivederci** (page 332).

After lunch, head to California's first mission, **Mission San Diego de Alcala** (page 331). An hour is enough time to spend exploring its museum and beautiful gardens.

Continue your journey through the city's past in historic Old Town. Take a walking tour or pay a visit to the ghouls at **The Whaley House** (page 331), America's most haunted house. Return to the land of the living with dinner and margaritas at **El Agave** (page 332).

End your evening in the lively **Gaslamp Quarter.** Choose between music at the **House of Blues** (page 333) or rooftop cocktails at **Float** (page 333).

Day 2

Head to the harbor and the **Maritime Museum of San Diego** (page 329), with one of the largest historic sea vessel collections in the nation. A half-mile south (just past the Broadway Pier), the **USS Midway** (page 329) is anchored in the harbor, waiting to be boarded and explored.

Drive across the two-mile San Diego-Coronado Bridge, or take the foot ferry from the Broadway Pier to the Coronado Ferry Landing (the ferry takes 15 minutes). After arriving in Coronado, grab lunch at one of the many cafés. Rent a bicycle from **Bikes & Beyond** (page 336) and glide along the **Bayshore Bikeway** (page 336), just over two miles to **Hotel del Coronado** (page 332). (MTS Route 904 also runs from the ferry landing to the hotel.) Put in some more serious beach time or spend your afternoon strolling the Del's ornate lobby and grand decks, which look out across the Pacific—perfect for watching the sunset. End your day at the Del, or head back across the bridge for a seafood dinner at **Searsucker** (page 332) and a farewell toast at **Rooftop600** (page 333).

$2.50) takes a half-mile trip through four acres of the park.

San Diego Zoo

The biggest family attraction in Balboa Park, **San Diego Zoo** (2920 Zoo Dr., 619/231-1515, 9am-5pm daily Nov.-Feb., 9am-6pm daily Mar.-May and Sept.-Oct., 9am-9pm daily June-Aug., $48 adults, $38 children) showcases more than 4,000 endangered and exotic animals from around the world, including one of the largest populations of giant pandas. Activities include the "African Rain Forest," "Tiger River," and "Reptile Mesa." Walking paths connect all areas of the park; guided bus tours, express buses, and an aerial tram provide faster transportation as well.

The San Diego Museum of Art

The San Diego Museum of Art (1450 El Prado, 619/232-7931, www.sdmart.org, 10am-5pm Mon.-Tues., Thurs., and Sat., 10am-9pm Fri., noon-5pm Sun., $12) in Balboa Park is renowned for Renaissance works by legendary painters, such as Goya and Rubens. It also holds a large collection of Asian and contemporary art, as well as an outdoor sculpture courtyard and garden.

Old Town and Mission Valley

Old Town encompasses the first Spanish settlements in what would eventually become California. It's the perfect place to get started on a historic tour of the city or a good ghost-hunting tour.

The Whaley House

Where is America's most haunted abode? According to Travel Channel's *America's Most Haunted*, it's in San Diego. Since its construction in 1857 on the site of the town's public gallows, **The Whaley House** (2482 San Diego Ave., 619/297-7511, 10am-10pm daily summer, 10am-5pm Mon.-Tues., 10am-10pm Thurs.-Sun. winter, $6 adults, $4 children) has been the scene of many tragic events. Ominous footsteps on the second floor and ghostly apparitions have been reported. Several Whaley family members died in the house, including the 22-year-old Violet Whaley, who shot herself in the summer of 1885 after discovering her husband was a con artist. A passage from poet Thomas Hood's *Bridge of Sighs,* her suicide note is preserved at the museum and reads: *"Mad from life's history, Swift to death's mystery; Glad to be hurled, Anywhere, anywhere, out of this world."* Special evening tours ($10 adults, $5 children) are offered.

Mission San Diego de Alcala

Just under 10 miles west of Old Town, Mission Valley is named for the first of 21 California missions established by Father Junípero Serra. **Mission San Diego de Alcala** (10818 San Diego Mission Rd., 619/281-8449, 9am-4:45pm daily, $3 adults, $1 children) remains an active Catholic parish while offering a small museum. First built on Presidio Hill in 1769, it was moved in 1774 to its present location in Mission Valley to make way for a Spanish military outpost. Prior to World War II, the crumbling buildings underwent reconstruction; their preservation continues today. Tour the bougainvillea-filled garden near a 46-foot-high bell tower and the museum, which holds old photographs and relics unearthed during excavations of the site.

From top to bottom: the Botanical Building at Balboa Park; Mission San Diego de Alcala; The San Diego Museum of Art.

Coronado

The long, blue Coronado Bridge connects Downtown San Diego to Coronado, an island-like enclave that beckons beach bums and film aficionados alike to the historic Hotel del Coronado. While the Del dominates the Coronado scenery, the island town also offers an array of other accommodations and restaurants.

Hotel Del Coronado

For more than 125 years, **Hotel del Coronado** (1500 Orange Ave., 800/468-3533) has illuminated the shores of the Pacific Ocean with its majestic beauty. The "Grand Lady by the Sea" draws thousands each year to admire its pristine white Victorian architecture, crowned with a red roof and soaring towers. Notable guests have included Thomas Edison, Charlie Chaplin, Babe Ruth, Charles Lindbergh, and Marilyn Monroe (during filming of *Some Like It Hot*). *Wizard of Oz* author L. Frank Baum is said to have based the Emerald City on the hotel.

As with many old-world structures, Hotel del Coronado is haunted. In 1892, a young woman named Kate Morgan checked in and never checked out. She was found dead on a staircase leading to the beach and no one ever claimed her body. Today, many believe Kate still occupies her former guest room.

Though the more lavish rooms cost a pretty penny, the hotel offers more affordable accommodations with no frills. You don't have to be a hotel guest to explore the property or enjoy its exquisite views.

To get there, drive across the two-mile San Diego-Coronado Bridge, or take the foot ferry from the Broadway Pier to the Coronado Ferry Landing. The ferry takes only 15 minutes and departs every hour on the hour (9am-9pm Sun.-Thurs., 9am-10pm Fri.-Sat.).

Food

San Diego cuisine benefits from its proximity to Mexico, with excellent south-of-the-border dishes, but you'll also find a pleasant diversity of flavors throughout the city, as well as some of the freshest seafood.

Downtown

At **Searsucker** (611 5th Ave., 619/233-7327, www.searsucker.com, 11:30am-2pm and 5:30pm-10pm Mon.-Thurs., 11:30am-2pm and 5:30pm-11pm Fri., 10am-2pm and 5:30pm-11pm Sat., 10am-2pm and 5:30pm-10pm Sun., $30), in the Gaslamp Quarter, celebrity chef Brian Malarkey offers a diverse menu focusing on creative American and freshly caught seafood.

In Old Town San Diego, **El Agave** (2304 San Diego Ave., 619/220-0692, www.elgave.com, 11am-10pm daily, $30) offers delicious Mexican fare, with mole and other sauces made from scratch.

The Oceanaire Seafood Room (400 J St., 619/858-2277, www.theoceanaire.com, 5pm-10pm Sun.-Fri., 5pm-11pm Sat., $24-40) also features the freshest bounty from the sea, including an exceptional oyster bar. The service and sophisticated atmosphere are worth the price.

The Mission (1250 J St., 619/232-7662, www.themissionsd.com, 7am-3pm daily, under $14) is a popular breakfast spot with great vegetarian and low-calorie choices.

Balboa Park

You'll find pizza heaven inside **La Pizzeria Arrivederci** (3789 4th Ave., 619/542-0293, 5pm-10pm Mon.-Thurs., 11:30am-11pm Fri.-Sat., 11am-10pm Sun., $10-22). In addition to the city's best gourmet pies, there are other classic Italian dishes.

The Afghani cuisine at **Khyber Pass** (523 University Ave., 619/294-7579, 11:30am-10pm daily, $14-30) includes fabulous curries, kebobs, hummus, and garlic naan.

Point Loma-Ocean Beach

Old Townhouse Restaurant (4941 Newport Ave., 619/222-1880, 6am-2pm daily, $5-11) has been greeting early risers for 35 years and counting. It's famous for its mimosas and cups of bottomless coffee.

Pork lovers head to **Phil's BBQ** (3750 Sports Arena Blvd., 619/226-6333, 11am-10pm Tues.-Thurs. and Sun., 11am-11pm Fri.-Sat., under $25) for their signature mesquite-barbecued ribs. Try them with a side of colossal onion rings.

Tender Greens (2400 Historic Decatur Rd., 619/226-6254, 11am-9pm daily, under $12) offers a number of vegetarian dishes, all made with the freshest ingredients.

Nightlife
Downtown comes alive after dark with trendy rooftop and spacious warehouse bars. The Gaslamp District's DJs pump up the volume while Hillcrest offers a Beatnik vibe. Beachside watering holes are more laid-back.

Bars and Clubs
San Diego's best rooftop bars and best poolside bars are one and the same. Hard Rock San Diego's **Float** (207 5th Ave., 619/764-6924, www.hardrockhotelsd.com, 11am-2am daily) is a rooftop oasis with day beds, VIP cabanas, DJs, fire pits, and amazing views. You can also raise a glass poolside at **Rooftop600** (600 F St., 619/814-2055, www.rooftop600.com), a premier lounge for the fashionable crowd. DJs entertain Thursday-Saturday.

A state-of-the-art venue boosting a classic design, **Omnia San Diego** (454 6th Ave., 619/544-9500, www.omnianightclub.com) adds to the vibrant nightlife in the Gaslamp Quarter. **Croce's Park West** (2760 5th Ave., 619/233-4355) has an open patio bar with an extended list of beers on tap, award-winning wines, and great happy hour specials. Right off I-5 at the Washington Street exit, **57 Degrees Warehouse** (1735 Hancock St., 619/234-5757) pours local brews and boutique wines.

In Hillcrest, **The Wine Lover** (3968 5th Ave., 619/294-9200) serves exceptional wines in a comfortable outdoor and indoor setting. For more great wine, head to **Wine Steals** (1243 University Ave., 619/295-1188), which offers daily specials; there's another location in Point Loma (2970 Truxtun Rd., 619/221-1959). Festive **Baja Betty's** (1421 University Ave., 619/269-8510, www.bajabettyssd.com) is a gathering place for the gay community. Expect 100 brands of tequila, fancy cocktails, and friendly service.

Point Loma gastropub **Sessions Public** (4204 Voltaire St., 619/756-7715) has a laid-back vibe and a unique beer selection, including local craft beers and Belgian brews on tap. **Shades** (5083 Santa Monica Ave., 619/222-0501) specializes in bar bites, half-price specials, and, best of all, a beachfront view!

Live Music
With three different stages and music every night of the week, the Gaslamp Quarter's **House of Blues** (1055 5th Ave., 619/299-2583, www.houseofblues.com/sandiego) attracts famed entertainers like Snow Patrol and Deadmau5. "Gospel Lunch" (11am on select Sundays) features local talent belting out traditional and contemporary hymns.

The hip **Casbah** (2501 Kettner Blvd., 619/232-4355, www.casbahmusic.com) is famous for showcasing rising stars, hosting the likes of Nirvana and Smashing Pumpkins.

In the heart of Ocean Beach, **Winstons** (1921 Bacon St., 619/222-6822, www.winstonsob.com) hosts local and touring bands. Summer weekends are packed; Wednesday is open mic night and Thursday and Friday are devoted to comedy.

Arts and Entertainment
With beauty and grace, **California Ballet Company** performs classic productions from Shakespeare's *A Midsummer Night's Dream* to Tchaikovsky's *Nutcracker,* September-May at the Civic Center (1100 3rd Ave., 619/570-1100,

www.californiaballet.org). The historic **Balboa Theatre** (868 4th Ave., 619/570-1100, www.sandiegotheatres.org) is a multi-performance venue featuring ballet, modern dance, plays, and comedy acts.

The San Diego Symphony Orchestra takes the stage at the dazzling 2,200-seat **Copley Symphony Hall** (750 B St., 619/235-0804, www.sandiegosymphony.org). First opened in the 1920s, it's built in the French Renaissance style, with superb acoustics.

The Old Globe (1363 Old Globe Way, 619/234-5623, www.oldglobe.org) is the site of the popular Shakespeare Festival, as well as classics and Broadway productions.

Shopping

The Gaslamp Quarter offers an eclectic combination of trendy and vintage treasures. Balboa Park is peppered with museum gift shops and tourist souvenirs. Beachfront communities provide the typical bikini boutiques and surf shops.

Downtown

Rising five levels above Downtown, **Westfield Horton Plaza** (324 Horton Plaza, 619/238-1596, www.westfield.com/hortonplaza, 10am-9pm Mon.-Fri., 10am-8pm Sat., 11am-6pm Sun., parking $8/hr) offers top department stores and retail chains.

Colorful gift shops abound at Old Town's **Bazaar del Mundo Shops** (4133 Taylor St., 619/296-3161, www.bazaardelmundo.com), a world market filled with international crafts and gifts. Shops include **The Gallery,** with authentic Native American jewelry, **Ariana** (619/296-4989) for women's fashion, and **The Kitchen Shop** with handcrafted Guatemalan pottery and carved kitchenware.

Over 50 shops at **Seaport Village** (849 W. Harbor Dr., 619/235-4014, 10am-9pm daily Sept.-May, 10am-10pm daily

Coronado Central Beach

...

June-Aug.) offer a diversity of items from clothing to art and toys.

Balboa Park

Located in a turn-of-the-century carriage house, **Marston** (3525 7th Ave., 619/297-9327, 10am-5pm Fri.-Mon.) has everything from arts and crafts to books and home furnishings. The **San Diego History Center Gift Store** (1649 El Prado, 619/232-6203, 10am-5pm Tues.-Sun.) features vintage reproductions of jewelry, pottery, and lamps, as well as art by local artists.

Books, candles, T-shirts, beaded curtains, key chains, and novelties are all at **Babette Schwartz** (421 University Ave., 619/220-7048, 11am-9pm Mon.-Thurs., 11am-9pm Fri.-Sat., 11am-5pm Sun.), located between 4th and 5th Avenues.

Shoe junkies will delight in **Mint**'s (525 University Ave., 619/291-6468, 10am-8pm Sun.-Fri., 10am-9pm Sat.) wall-to-wall selection of stylish fashion for the feet.

Point Loma-Ocean Beach

The Humble Hippie (4896 Newport Ave., 619/501-5091, www.thehumblehippie.com, 11am-8pm Mon.-Sat., noon-5pm Sun.) means comfortable clothing, hemp products, and colorful tapestries, while more hippie styles along with belts and cute purses are found nearby at **Sunshine Daydreams** (4979 Newport Ave., 619/225-0708).

You'll find surf gear and surfwear at **South Coast Surf Shop** (5023 Newport Ave., 619/223-7017, www.southcoast.com, 10am-7pm Mon.-Sat., 10am-6pm Sun.).

With swimwear, towels, and more, **Wings** (4948 Newport Ave., 619/224-2165, www.wingsbeachwear.com) has everything you need for the beach.

Recreation
Beaches

Between the San Diego River and the hills of Point Loma, laid-back **Ocean Beach** is popular among surfers, swimmers, sunbathers, and even dogs. At its north end, pets can run free along the sand and crashing waves at **Dog Beach.** At the foot of Newport Avenue, you can fish without a license off Ocean Beach Pier (size and catch limits still apply).

Point Loma Beach (1424 Sunset Cliffs Blvd.) is one of the best places in San Diego to explore tidepools, which are plentiful with marinelife. Drive to **Sunset Cliffs Natural Park** (700-1300 block of Sunset Cliffs Blvd.) to look out among the sandstone bluffs that rise above the sparkling sea. On the southwest tip of Point Loma lies the **Old Cabrillo Lighthouse** (1800 Cabrillo Memorial Dr., 619/557-5450, 9am-5pm daily), as well as ample opportunities for hiking, exploration of tidepools, and surfing.

Coronado Central Beach (along Ocean Blvd.) is a 1.5-mile stretch of sand set against the backdrop of the legendary Hotel del Coronado. The beach is free to visit; parking is free along Ocean Boulevard.

Bicycling

The **Ocean Beach Bike Path** is a five-mile section of the **San Diego River Trail**, which runs parallel to the south bank of the San Diego River from Dog Beach to Hotel Circle Place in Mission Valley. Access is at Robb Field Skate Park, and at Dog Beach, via a steep sidewalk.

A 25-mile ride along San Diego Bay, the **Bayshore Bikeway** begins at the Embarcadero in Downtown and loops around the bay, running along separate bike lanes. It passes numerous attractions, parks, and beaches, including Coronado, where riders have the option of turning around and following the trail back or taking the Coronado Ferry back into Downtown. At the Coronado Ferry Landing, **Bikes & Beyond** (1201 1st St., 619/435-7180, www.bikes-and-beyond.com, bikes $22/hr) rents bikes that can get you on your way.

Spectator Sports

The San Diego Chargers play at Qualcomm Stadium (9449 Friars Rd., 858/874-4500) in the heart of Mission Valley, just minutes from Downtown. The **San Diego Padres** take the field at Petco Park (100 Park Blvd., 619/795-5000 and 877/374-2784, www.sandiego.padres.mlb.com, $10-15 pass), in the heart of Downtown.

Events

In the heart of Old Town, **Latin American Festival** (first weekend in Aug., 10am-8pm, free) celebrates San Diego's Mexican heritage with folk art, traditional clothing, colorful imports, handcrafted jewelry, live entertainment, and delicious cuisine.

Every July, Hillcrest comes alive with the three-day San Diego **Pride Festival** (619/297-7683, www.sdpride.org), which features a parade, 5k run, and an enormous block party, and attracts nearly 300,000 people.

Downtown's **Spirits Festival** (858/551-1605, www.sandiegospiritsfestival.com, $45 and up) celebrates the end of summer with cocktails and culinary delight at the Broadway Pier.

Accommodations

San Diego has acres of hotels. Prices are at their lowest between September and June. Accommodations in glorious Coronado are pricy, but you can't beat the town's beachside charm.

Under $150

Clean and stylish, **La Pensione Hotel** (606 W. Date St., 800/232-4683, www.lapensionehotel.com, $100 and up) is a four-story hotel in Little Italy offering a frescoed courtyard and good old-fashioned quiet.

The Pearl Hotel (1410 Rosecrans St., 619/226-6100, www.thepearl.com, $139 and up) is a retro-style abode with comfortable rooms.

Vintage Queen Anne beauty **Keating House** (2331 2nd Ave., 619/239-8585, www.keatinghouse.com, $129 and up) is within walking distance of all of the attractions in Balboa Park and the Gaslamp Quarter.

Budget accommodations begin with the **HI-San Diego** (521 Market St., 619/525-1531, www.sandiegohostels.org, $40-130), located in the middle of the Gaslamp Quarter. You can get just about anywhere from this almost-elegant youth hostel.

$150-250

Eco-chic ★ **Hotel Indigo** (509 9th Ave., 619/727-4000, www.hotelinsd.com, $146 and up) is the first LEED-certified hotel in the city with ecofriendly features, spacious rooms, floor-to-ceiling windows, and spa baths.

President Benjamin Harrison, King Kalakaua of Hawaii, and even Babe Ruth stayed in Downtown's **Horton Grand Hotel** (311 Island Ave., 619/544-1886, www.hortongrand.com, $149-269), but its most famed guest was lawman Wyatt Earp, who took up residence for seven years! Its Victorian-era architecture and furnishings have been updated with all the modern comforts and conveniences to create a timeless experience.

A great bang for your buck, **The Declan Suites** (701 A St., 866/716-8130, www.declansuitessandiego.com, $169-229) has some of the largest rooms in San Diego. Two-room suites feature living rooms, pullout sofa beds, and a wet bar.

A contemporary hotel in the Gaslamp Quarter, **The Omni** (675 L St., 619/231-6664, www.omnihotels.com, $179-249) is close to boutiques, galleries, and nightclubs. It also connects to Petco Park via sky-bridge.

With spa service and a rooftop pool lounge, **Hotel Solamar** (435 6th Ave., 877/230-0300, www.hotelsolamar.com, $209-249) touts itself as Downtown's hip luxury hotel. Its location near the Gaslamp Quarter provides easy access to nightlife.

Over $250
Even in swanky Southern California, ★ **Hotel del Coronado** (1500 Orange Ave., 619/435-6611 or 800/468-3533, www.hoteldel.com, $300-500) wins the prize for grandiosity. The white-painted, red-roofed mammoth sprawls for acres from the road to the sand. Inside, the Del is at once a historical museum, shopping mall, food court...and a hotel.

It offers almost 700 rooms, plus another 70-plus individual cottages. Room sizes and decor vary, from smaller Victorian-decorated guest rooms to expansive modern suites.

W Hotel (421 W. B St., 619/398-3100 or 877/946-8357, $264-530) is sleek, chic, and oh-so sophisticated. With 350-thread-count linens, pillow-top mattresses, a rooftop lounge with private cabanas, and five-star dining, it's the perfect place to indulge.

The romantic **1906 Lodge at Coronado Beach** (1060 Adella Ave., 619/437-1900 and 866/435-1906, www.1906lodge.com, $309 and up) lavishes couples in luxury in quaint beachside suites featuring whirlpool tubs, cozy fireplaces, and patios.

Information and Services
The **San Diego Convention and Visitors Bureau** (SDCVB, www.sandiego.org) operates the **International Visitor Information Center** (1140 N. Harbor Dr., 619/236-1212, 9am-4pm daily Oct.-May, 9am-5pm daily June-Sept.), located Downtown. Here you can get help with everything from flight information to restaurant coupons to hotel reservations. To get a feel for the town before you arrive, check out the SDCVB web site. Friendly folks can answer emails and phone calls about most anything pertaining to San Diego County.

Essentials

Getting There

Air

Seattle-Tacoma International Airport (SEA) (17801 International Blvd., 800/544-1965, www.portseattle.org/sea-tac) is Washington state's main airport and is the gateway to the Pacific Northwest, served by all major domestic and international airlines.

Portland International Airport (PDX) (7000 Northeast Airport Way, 877/739-4636, www.flypdx.com) is a joint civil-military airport and Oregon's largest airport. It is served by all major domestic airlines and two international providers (Japan and the Netherlands).

San Francisco International Airport (SFO) (800/435-9736, www.flysfo.com) is California's major northern hub, largest airport in the Bay Area, and the second busiest in California.

Los Angeles International Airport (LAX) (1 World Way, 424/646-5252, www.airport-la.com) is Southern California's biggest and one of the world's busiest airports.

San Diego International Airport (SAN) (3225 N. Harbor Dr., 619/400-2404, www.san.org) is a regional, single-runway commercial airport with domestic flights and limited international providers.

To get through security checkpoints, a photo ID (valid driver's license or current passport) and boarding ticket is required. Depending on the time of year you travel, security wait times can take 30 minutes or more. Always check ahead to make sure your flight is on time (delays and cancellations do happen). Confirm your departure gate, as this can change even after you've arrived to the previously reported gate of departure. In such cases, an announcement usually occurs, but be vigilant or you could find yourself attempting to board a flight headed for Timbuktu, while your flight has already left the gate!

All airports provide assistance to the elderly and individuals with disabilities. Food, restrooms, rental car companies, and taxi and shuttle services are located on-site.

Train

Amtrak (800/872-7245, www.amtrak. com) offers service throughout the West Coast on several lines. The **Coast Starlight** runs along the West Coast, connecting Seattle, Portland, San Francisco, Los Angeles, and San Diego. The Talgo train, also called the **Cascade,** is a high-speed option that travels from Vancouver, British Columbia, to Seattle in 4 hours, and from Seattle to Portland in about 3.5 hours. The **Pacific Surfliner** provides service from San Luis Obispo to Santa Barbara, Los Angeles, and San Diego.

Trains arrive and depart from Seattle's **King Street Station** (303 S. Jackson St.); Portland's **Union Station** (800 NW 6th Ave.); San Francisco's **Caltrain Station** (1149 22nd St.); Los Angeles's **Union Station** (800 N. Alameda St.); and San Diego's **Santa Fe Depot** (1050 Kettner Blvd.).

Bus

Greyhound Express (800/231-2222, www. greyhound.com) serves major cities in Washington, Oregon, and California, with nationwide connections. Buses travel main interstates in both north and south directions (US-101, I-5), stopping in many small towns, including points along the coast. Buses do not stop in state or national parks or at tourist attractions.

The Bolt Bus (877/265-8287, www. boltbus.com) is a fast and cheap way ($21 or less) to travel I-5 (northbound and southbound) from Seattle to Portland, or San Francisco to Los Angeles. Both Greyhound Express and Bolt buses feature comfortable seating with extra legroom, WiFi, and plug-in outlets. Bolt buses allow travelers to reserve their

The Pacific coastline offers one of the most scenic Amtrak routes.

seats; however, Express travelers should arrive early, as it is first-come, first-served. The best seats are from mid-center to the front, away from the bathroom. Buses can be cold, so bring a sweater!

Stations are generally located in less-than-desirable downtown nooks. To ensure safety, do not walk to your hotel from a bus station; instead, take a taxi. Small towns generally do not have bus stations. Know exactly when and where the bus will drop you, and make sure your connecting ride (taxi or other) is there on arrival or shortly after.

Tickets may be purchased online with a credit card, or at a station ticket window, using credit, debit, travelers checks, or cash. Be sure to bring photo ID.

A convenient high-tech feature, Greyhound's mobile app allows smartphone users to manage trips, search schedules, access Road Rewards, use discounts, and find terminal locations right from their phone. iPhone and Android users can download the app. Check the website (www.greyhound.com) for details.

Car Rental

Major international rental car companies are easily found at international airports, such as Sea-Tac, PDX, SFO, LAX, and SAN, and in and around larger cities. Most require drivers to be at least 25 years of age (some allow 21 years of age with an extra fee), possess a valid driver's license, and have a major credit card (debit cards are not acceptable). Expect to pay around $30 per day and up, plus taxes, fees, and insurance (optional). If you are in the military or a member of AAA, AARP, or Costco, discounts may apply. Airports have lower rates, but fees run higher. Hybrid and biofuel rental cars are available at a few companies, such as Hertz, Enterprise, Avis, Thrifty, and Budget; however, expect to pay more to be environmentally responsible.

Rental car companies include:

- **Avis** (800/331-1212, www.avis.com)

- **Budget** (800/527-0700, www.budget.com)

- **Dollar** (800/800-3665, www.dollar.com)

- **Enterprise** (800/261-7331, www.enterprise.com)

- **Hertz** (800/654-3131, www.hertz.com)

- **National** (877/222-9058, www.nationalcar.com)

- **Thrifty** (800/847-4389, www.thrifty.com)
  Zipcars (866/494-7227, www.zipcar.com) rent by the hour or day; gas and insurance is usually included in the rate, but there is a mileage limit. This is a membership-based service with fees starting at $7.

Driving Directions

The Pacific Coast Highway stretches 1,700 miles north to south, tracing most of the coastal regions of Washington, Oregon, and California. However, a quicker albeit less scenic north-south route is via I-5 (roughly 1,300 miles, 20 hours between Seattle and San Diego). If you want to drive the entire coastal highway, you can plan on returning to your starting point more quickly via I-5. You can also divert from the coast to I-5 at various points along the way to make up time. Keep in mind that I-5 and US-101 run parallel at the southern end of the route, near San Diego.

Two routes travel west to the north Washington coast: from Seattle via the Seattle-Bainbridge Island Ferry (801 Alaskan Way, 888/808-7977 or 206/464-6400, www.wsdot.wa.gov/ferries, $15.30 vehicle one-way, $8 for walk-ons) and from Olympia via I-5 to the US-101 exit, where the highway runs along the Olympic Peninsula's southern edge and up the northern coast (49 mi, 52 min). The southern portion is also accessed via Olympia following the same route but taking WA-8 to US-101 South at Montesano.

Oregon's north coast can be accessed from Portland, via US-30 West to Astoria (97.46 mi, 2 hrs), and to Cannon Beach (80 mi, 1.5 hrs) via US-26 West. The southernmost access point is Eugene to Reedsport via US-38 West. Here, the highway connects with US-101, which travels south to Brookings (230 mi, 4 hrs) near the Northern California border.

Northern California coastal access is from Redding to Arcata via US-299 West (142 mi, 3 hrs), where the highway traverses US-101, and from Sacramento to San Francisco via US-80 West (90 mi), which merges with US-101. Another option is from Grants Pass, Oregon, via US-199 South, which merges with US-101 then heads south to Crescent City, California (100 mi, 2 hrs).

San Diego provides direct access to the south coast, where I-5 briefly runs through the city and parallel to CA-1.

Road Rules

Here are a few of the important rules of the road. Drivers and all passengers are required by law to wear a seat belt. Infant and child safety seats are required for children weighing less than 60 pounds and/or under the age of six. It is illegal to operate a vehicle and a handheld device at the same time. All motorcyclists must wear a helmet. Don't litter; there are severe penalties ($1,000 or more) for throwing garbage of any kind from a vehicle. No drinking and driving; driving while intoxicated is extremely dangerous and highly illegal. Always abide by posted speed limits and other road signs.

Highway Safety

The highway has many sharp curves, steep ledges, and high cliffs that do not have guardrails. Drive as slowly as road conditions demand, even if that's slower than the posted speed limit. Take your time and enjoy the coastal scenery; after all, that's what you came for!

This road is quite isolated, especially in areas on Washington state's Olympic Peninsula and just south of Carmel in California, where there are no connecting routes to the interior for more than 90 miles. Make sure you have a full tank of gas, plenty of water, warm clothing, and snacks before traveling these sections of the coastal route.

Many sections of Pacific Coast Highway are not lit by streetlights, making visibility difficult at night, especially when encountering the blinding headlights of oncoming cars. If you are not comfortable driving at night, plan your itinerary accordingly, driving only by day.

Like George of the Jungle, "Watch out for that tree!"…a redwood tree, that is. Some of these beauties sit on the edge of the highway and at dramatic curves, making it very easy to lose a side mirror if you drift too far to the right.

In case of an emergency, always carry flares, a spare tire, and a jack and wrench. Though in some parts of the road you may not receive cell phone service, carry a phone with you. Only pull over when absolutely necessary! Otherwise, wait until you reach a pullout or other safe area. When pulling over, get as far onto the shoulder as you can.

Weather Considerations

With exception to Southern California, weather conditions change rapidly along the Pacific Coast. Be prepared for weather extremes, from blustery rains to windstorms and hot sunny days. In some areas, snow can also be a factor in winter. Be prepared with chains, and know how to use them. If bad weather persists and is deemed unsafe for travel, highways can be closed abruptly with some sections impassable. This typically occurs when heavy rains create mudslides. Know alternative routes in the event of a road closure.

Fog! It's like something out of a horror flick when you're caught in it. Fog is the most likely hazardous condition that you are bound to run into at some point on your trip. When warm inland air mixes with cool coastal temperatures, shazam! Fog appears, and can linger awhile. Use the pullouts if needed; otherwise, use low beams and drive *very* slowly.

For road conditions and weather reports, check **Washington State Department of Transportation** (800/695-7623, www.wsdot.com/traffic/weather); **Oregon Department of Transportation** (www.oregonlive.com/roadreport/wide/index.ssf?statewide); and **California Department of Transportation** (www.dot.ca.gov/cgi-bin/roads.cgi). You can also use the 511 hotline for updates and reports when traveling in Washington, Oregon, and California's San Francisco Bay Area.

Wildlife on the Road

You may not meet up with Wile E. Coyote or the Roadrunner, but it is highly likely that you will cross paths with deer, elk, fox, raccoon, and other animals. Warning signs are usually posted in areas with higher animal crossing activity. If you come upon wildlife standing in the road, come to a stop and honk your horn, but do not attempt to veer to the side to pass. Deer especially are known to dart in random directions, and headlights can confuse them. Do not get out of the car and approach wild animals. Wait until the road is clear, then be on your way.

Road Etiquette

The majority of the Pacific Coast Highway is two lanes. This can pose a problem when "speed racer" comes up from behind, seemingly out of nowhere. The law requires slower vehicles to use turnouts or safely pull over when five or more cars pile up. If one car makes it clear that they want to get by, let them pass. Do not jeopardize your safety by trying to navigate a winding, unfamiliar highway at an uncomfortable speed. It is imperative that you always leave at least three feet between your car and another vehicle, especially motorcyclists and bicyclists!

Parking

Most attractions, museums, parks, and beaches offer on-site parking, though many require a fee. When booking a hotel, ask if there is a secured parking garage or an open lot, and if there is a daily fee (parking fees can be up to $30 per day). Some hotels offer free parking.

The Pacific Coast Highway serves as the major route of access to the many beaches and beachside towns. On-street parking within these communities can be hard to find during peak season when much of the road is clogged up with traffic. Parking garages, lots, and metered off-street parking is offered in just about every town. Parking suggestions are offered for various cities and towns throughout this book with current fee information included.

Fuel

Gasoline is difficult to come by on the more rural segments of the road, especially the farther north you are. Even in California, there can be long stretches where you may not see a gas station for miles. Know your mpg (miles per gallon) and fuel up whenever you have the opportunity. Prices on the coast may be considerably higher. GasBuddy.com is a great resource that allows users to check for fueling stations in your area and look for the cheapest rates.

Motorcycles

Motorcyclists are common along the coast, especially during the summer. You can't beat the gorgeous scenery, twists and turns of the highway, and slower-paced lifestyle of coastal communities as compared to the bustle and traffic of big cities. As with traveling any road, always follow rules of the road, wear a helmet, and keep at least three car lengths between you and other vehicles. Never use the shoulder (or fog line) to pass another vehicle! When necessary use pullouts, and watch for wildlife. Windstorms and rains can create difficult road conditions, such as fallen tree branches, debris, and standing water.

Bicycles

Experienced cyclists will find the Pacific Coast Highway a great way to travel. The shoulder (known as the fog line) can be hazardous due to gravel and road debris. Bicyclists are not legally required to stay on the shoulder, but many do as a courtesy to road vehicles.

Take advantage of pullouts along the highway to allow vehicles to pass. Be cautious when riding cliffside in Big Sur. This part of the highway is extremely windy and rises high above the Pacific. To avoid peddling against the wind,

travel from north to south. Two other precautions: Watch for parked cars on the side of the road where the highway passes through coastal towns and watch out for redwood trees. As you wind your way through the redwood forest, you'll find that some trees sit very close to the edge of the road. Stay alert to avoid accidents. The Adventure Cycling Association offers resources at www.adventurecycling.org.

Visas and Officialdom

Passports and Visas

Visitors from other countries must have a **valid passport** and a **visa.** Visitors with current passports from one of the following countries qualify for the **visa waivers:** Andorra, Australia, Austria, Belgium, Brunei, Chile, Czech Republic, Denmark, Estonia, Finland, France, Germany, Greece, Hungary, Iceland, Ireland, Italy, Japan, Latvia, Liechtenstein, Lithuania, Luxembourg, Malta, Monaco, the Netherlands, New Zealand, Norway, Portugal, San Marino, Singapore, Slovakia, Slovenia, South Korea, Spain, Sweden, Switzerland, Taiwan, and the United Kingdom. They must apply online with the Electronic System for Travel Authorization at www.cbp.gov and hold a **return plane ticket** to their home countries less than 90 days from their time of entry. Holders of **Canadian passports** don't need visas or waivers. In most countries, the local U.S. embassy can provide a **tourist visa.** Plan for at least two weeks for visa processing, longer during the busy summer season (June-Aug.). More information is available online: http://travel.state.gov.

Customs

Foreigners and U.S. citizens age 21 or older may import (free of duty) the following: 1L of alcohol; 200 cigarettes (one carton); 50 cigars (non-Cuban); and $100 worth of gifts.

International travelers must declare

amounts that exceed $10,000 in cash (U.S. or foreign), travelers checks, or money orders. Meat products, fruits, and vegetables are prohibited due to health and safety regulations.

Drivers entering California stop at **Agricultural Inspection Stations.** They don't need to present a passport, visa, or even a driver's license, but should be prepared to present fruits and vegetables, even those purchased within neighboring states just over the border. If you've got produce, it could be infected by a known problem pest or disease; expect it to be confiscated on the spot.

International Drivers Permits

International visitors need to secure an **International Driving Permit** from their home countries before coming to the United States. They should also bring the government-issued driving permit from their home countries. They are also expected to be familiar with the driving regulations of the states they will visit. More information is available online: www.usa.gov/Topics/Motor-Vehicles.shtml.

Travel Tips

Conduct and Customs

The legal **drinking age** in the United States is 21. Expect to have your ID checked not only in bars and clubs, but also before you purchase alcohol in restaurants, wineries, and markets.

Smoking is banned in many places. Don't expect to find a smoking section in restaurants or an ashtray in bars. Some establishments allow smoking on outdoor patios. Many hotels, motels, and inns are also nonsmoking. Smokers should request a smoking room when making reservations.

Money

The currency is the **U.S. dollar ($).** Most businesses accept the **major credit cards** Visa, MasterCard, Discover, and American Express. ATM and debit cards work at many stores and restaurants, and ATMs are available throughout the region. You can **change currency** at any international airport or bank. Currency exchange may be easier in large cities and more difficult in rural and wilderness areas.

Banking hours tend to be 8am-5pm Monday-Friday, 9am-noon Saturday. Never count on a bank being open on Sunday. There are **24-hour ATMs** not only at banks but at many markets, bars, and hotels. A **convenience fee** of $2-4 per transaction may apply.

Internet Access

While many hotels and B&Bs offer free WiFi, some charge a fee of $6-12 per hour. Free WiFi is becoming more and more available at cafés and public libraries as well. Do not expect to find WiFi-friendly locations within rural areas, parks, or campgrounds.

Cell Phones

Several spots along the winding Pacific Coast Highway are dead zones. Cell service is simply unreliable even from the best carrier. Check your phone and make your calls on arrival or before leaving a travel hub or large town along the route.

Hotel and Motel Chains

Hotel and motel chains like **Best Western** (800/780-7234, www.bestwestern.com), **Motel 6** (800/557-3435, www.motel6.com), **Days Inn** (800/225-3297, www.daysinn.com), and **Super 8** (800/454-3213, www.super8.com) are easy to find along the coast. Many offer discount rates (depending on season) and reasonable amenities. Expect higher rates during the summer (June-Sept.).

High season is from June to August (although, in spring rates rise too) and you may find better deals as a walk-in guest during the off-season. The best tactic is to shop for deals and use any

346

ESSENTIALS

discount cards and auto-memberships that give you lower rates at participating hotels and motels. Stop at local vistors centers or pick up a complimentary ad magazine (which includes hotel and motel discount coupons) at local restaurants, convenience stores, and businesses.

Mid-week rates are lower, unless there is a special event taking place. Be sure to ask if the quoted rate includes tax, as this can add 10 percent or more to your final bill. If you find yourself without accommodations, many online travel services, including **www.hotels.com,** offer last-minute reservations.

Traveling with Children

Children will enjoy aquariums, amusement parks, and, perhaps most of all, the beach. Many beaches and parks are equipped with bathrooms. You'll also find several good family-friendly restaurant and hotel options. Generally hotels allow up to four in a room, so be sure to inquire about a suite if necessary.

The main concerns when traveling the highway with children is that the long drive can make them antsy and the twists and turns can cause nausea, even for moms and dads. Make plenty of stops to allow your young ones to burn off some energy and for everyone to use the bathroom, stretch their legs, and breathe in the fresh air. Bring plenty of car-fun activities to keep your kids busy, like books and travel games.

It's always a good idea to set some simple travel rules with your children before heading out on the road and remind them along the way. I cannot emphasize enough the importance of children staying close to their parents at lookout points and on trails. Many scenic pullouts do not have guardrails; gravel can make it easy to slip and fall off the cliffside. This is especially true at Big Sur.

Senior Travelers

If you are over 60 years of age, ask about potential discounts. Nearly all attractions, amusement parks, theaters, and museums offer discount benefits to seniors. Be sure to have some form of valid identification on hand or you'll end up having to pay full price. A driver's license or current passport will do.

Accessibilty

Most public areas are equipped to accommodate travelers with disabilities, including hotels, restaurants, museums, public transportation, and several state and national parks where you'll find paved trails. That said, there are still some attractions that will pose challenges, such as certain historic sights and wildlife areas.

For those with permanent disabilities, including the visually impaired, inquire about a free **Access Pass** (888/275-8747, ext. 3) from the National Parks Service. It is offered as part of the America the Beautiful-National Park and Federal Recreational Lands Pass Series. You can obtain an Access Pass in person at any federal recreation site or by submitting a completed application (www.nps.gov/findapark/passes.htm, $10 processing fee may apply) by mail. The pass does not provide benefits for special recreation permits or concessioner fees.

Environmental Concerns

Each state has environmental concerns that involve water pollution, disruption of fish and wildlife habitat, and emissions. Washington, Oregon, and California have poured resources into conservation and preservation efforts, and have moved forward with renewable energy, recycling, and composting campaigns.

You can do your part as a visitor and protect the natural environment by doing the following: stay on trails and do not stomp on plantlife; utilize pet waste receptacles in pet-friendly campgrounds; protect water sources by camping at least 150 feet from lakes and streams; leave rocks and plants as you find them;

light fires only where permitted and use only established fire pits; pack it in, pack it out—check your campsite for garbage and properly dispose of it or take it with you.

Health and Safety

If immediate help is needed, always **dial 911;** otherwise, go to the nearest 24-hour hospital emergency room.

Carry your **medical card** and a list of any **medications** you are taking. Keep a **first-aid kit** in your car or luggage, and take it with you when hiking. A good kit should include sterile gauze pads, butterfly bandages, adhesive tape, antibiotic ointment, alcohol wipes, pain relievers for both adults and children, and a multi-purpose pocketknife.

Do not ignore **health or safety warnings!** Some beaches within California have health warning signs posted due to potential bacteria in the water. If you see such a sign, stay out of the water or risk getting sick!

Whether you're in a large city, resort area, small town, or even wilderness area, take precautions against **theft.** Don't leave any valuables in the car. If you must, keep them out of sight in the trunk or compartment with a lock if available. Keep wallets, purses, cameras, mobile phones, and other small electronics on your person if possible.

Crime is more prevalent in large cities. Be alert to your surroundings, just as you would in any unfamiliar place. Avoid using ATMs at night or walking alone after dark. Carry your car keys in your hand when walking out to your car. Certain **urban neighborhoods** are best avoided at night. Call a taxi to avoid walking too far to get to your car or waiting for public transportation.

Keep a safe distance from **wildlife.** Stay at least 300 feet away. Bring binoculars if you want an up-close view. If you encounter a bear or cougar, do not run or turn your back! Try to appear larger and bring pepper spray and a walking stick to use in defense. Stay in a group when hiking, as these animals typically target lone prey. Keep children close and where you can see them.

Be cautious at **viewpoints,** especially along coastal cliffs. Losing your footing can be fatal. Keep children from sitting on or climbing over railings.

Resources

Organizations
Washington

Northwest Tribal Tourism (www.explorepacificnwtribes.com): An online resource that highlights Native American cultures, historic sights, scenic points of interest, recreational activities, and more. A travel-friendly published guide is distributed at local vistors centers and chambers of commerce.

Olympic Peninsula Visitor Bureau (800/942-4042, www.olympicpeninsula.org): A regional organization that offers a synopsis of local destinations, things to do, and transportation information. The bureau is also considered the primary contact for travel writers, film scouts, and tour operators.

Seattle B&B Association (206/547-1020, www.lodginginseattle.com): A member-based organization that provides a directory of local bed-and breakfast venues.

Washington Lodging Association (877/906-1001, www.stayinwashington.com): A complete listing of member hotels, motels, lodges, and B&Bs.

Washington Tourism Alliance (800/544-1800, www.experiencewa.com): Due to state budget cuts, Washington state no longer supports a tourism department, but instead, state tourism activity is run by a group of tourism professionals, aptly named the Washington Tourism Alliance. The website is rich with everything Washington—a "must see" when planning a trip.

Oregon

Astoria Travel (www.travelastoria.com): The official website for the Oregon seaside community of Astoria, with online visitor maps and events calendar.

Oregon Bed & Breakfast Guild (www. obbg.org): The professional association of Oregon's individually operated bed-and-breakfast inns, which provides a B&B directory and trip planner.

Southern Oregon (www.southernoregon. org): A noteworthy website with outdoor activities, festivities, and suggested itineraries.

Travel Oregon (www.traveloregon.com): The state's main tourism entity that offers complete resource information for visitors.

Travel Portland (www.travelportland. com): The city's official online guide to local art, food, hotels, and lifestyle.

California

Access Northern California (www.accessnca.com): The organization helps individuals with disabilities navigate their way through Northern California by providing wheelchair-friendly trails and locations for a better experience.

California Bed & Breakfast (www.cabbi. com): The state's only association of member B&Bs from the redwood coast to San Diego.

Los Angeles Convention Bureau (www. discoverlosangeles.com): The official guide to the Los Angeles areas where you can browse the entire caboodle of what L.A. has to offer.

San Diego (www.sandiego.org): The city's web-based travel guide, where local area information and special offers on area attractions and activities are provided, including trip planners.

San Diego Professional Tour Guide Association (www.sdtourguides.com): A nonprofit organization composed of local tour guides, some with over 25 years of travel industry experience and many who are multilingual.

San Francisco Travel (www.sanfrancisco. travel): Features trip ideas, tickets to area attractions, and downloadable visitor guides.

Visit California (www.visitcalifornia. com): This is a California Tourism Industry-run site that offers detailed information on northern, central, and southern California travel offerings.

Newspapers and Magazines
Washington

Queen Anne News (www.queenannenews. com): Founded in 1919, this is a weekly community newspaper that is a good resource for local community arts and events.

Seattle Magazine (www.seattlemag. com): This sophisticated publication keeps readers in the know of the sparkly Emerald City's hip restaurants and hangouts.

Seattle Weekly (www.seattleweekly.com): Filled with local events and reviews of local eateries and nightlife venues, the paper is available at no cost.

The Stranger (www.thestranger.com): A free weekly paper filled with "things to do" in Seattle, including great suggestions on restaurants, bars, and music venues.

Washington Festivals & Events Calendar (www.wfea.org): A complete and free guide to Washington state's many year-round celebrations.

Oregon

Northwest Coast Magazine (www.nwcmagazine.com): Interesting stories about people, culture, and the landscape of northern Oregon.

Oregon Coast Magazine (www.oregoncoastmagazine.com): A colorful and engaging resource with local area history, photos, and highlighted information about area sights, such as lighthouses.

Oregon Coast Today (www.oregoncoast-today.com): Published in Lincoln City, this free weekly features current information on arts, entertainment, and activities.

The Oregonian (www.oregonianlive.com): This is Portland's daily newspaper, which has an entertainment section and events calendar.

California

Los Angeles Times (www.latimes.com): A longstanding news publication with a fantastic *Arts & Culture* section.

Monterey County Weekly (www.montereycountyweekly.com): Gives visitors local information on food, wine, and fun.

San Diego CityBeat (www.sdcitybeat.com): The guide to San Diego's eclectic mix of food, music, art, and culture.

San Diego Reader (www.sandiegoreader.com): This weekly provides focused arts and culture coverage.

San Diego Union-Tribune (www.utsandiego.com): This is the daily newspaper for the San Diego metro area.

The San Francisco Chronicle (www.sfgate.com): This is the daily news for the City by the Bay.

San Francisco Weekly (www.sfweekly.com): A good resource for news, art, film, and local happenings.

Santa Barbara Independent (www.independent.com): Packed with information on visual arts, galleries, theater, food venues, and hotels.

Travel Guidebooks
Washington

Alden, Peter, and Paulson, Dennis. *National Audubon Society Field Guide to the Pacific Northwest.* Knopf Doubleday Publishing Group, 1998. A pocket field guide that covers habitats of more than 1,000 of the most common species found in the Pacific Northwest, with additional coverage on the region's topography and geology.

Burlingame, Jeff. *Moon Olympic Peninsula.* Avalon Travel Publishing, 2015. An extensive journey through the mountain meadows and temperate rain forests of Washington state's magnificent Olympic Peninsula, with recommendations on hiking, birding, camping, and exploration.

Oregon

McRae, W. C., and Jewell, Judy. *Moon Coastal Oregon.* Avalon Travel Publishing, 2014. Filled with information on dining, accommodations, and recreation along Oregon's coastal beaches.

Nelson, Dan. *Day Hiking Oregon Coast.* Mountaineers Books, 2007. A user-friendly trail guide with grids, charts, and useful information.

California

Brown, Ann Marie. *Moon Bay Area Biking: 60 of the Best Rides for Road and Mountain Biking.* Avalon Travel Publishing, 2012. The perfect complement to a coast trip for avid cyclists, *Moon Bay Area Biking* is filled with rides in and around the Bay Area and alongside the Pacific Coast, outlining a wide variety of scenic roads and trails.

Linhart Veneman, Elizabeth. *Moon Napa & Sonoma.* Avalon Travel Publishing, 2013. An immersion into Northern California's wine country from the coastal mountains of Santa Cruz to the hot, windy hills of Sonoma.

Thornton, Stuart. *Moon Coastal California.* Avalon Travel Publishing, 2013. A focus on California's diverse coastline, with information on hiking trails, surfing spots, and recommended stops along the way.

History and Culture
Washington

Frye Bass, Sophie, and Clark, Florenz. *Pig-Tail Days in Old Seattle.* Binford & Mort Publishing, 1973. A fascinating account of Seattle's early days as told by the granddaughter of Seattle founder Arthur A. Denny, with stories about some of the city's famous streets.

Halliday, Jan, and Chehak, Gail. *Native Peoples of the Northwest.* Sasquatch Books, 2002. The only guide that introduces readers to contemporary Northwest Native cultures.

Mapes, Lynda. *Native Peoples of the Northwest.* Mountaineers Books, 2013. An exploration into one of the largest dam removal projects in the world, and the efforts to save the Northwest ecosystem.

McNulty, Tim. *Olympic National Park: A Natural History.* University of Washington Press, 2009. A look at the heart of the Olympic Peninsula's ecosystems, wildlife, and current archaeological discoveries.

Oregon

Blakely, Joe R. *Building Oregon's Coast Highway 1936-1966: Straightening Curves and Uncorking Bottlenecks.* CreateSpace Independent Pub, 2014. An epic journey of how Oregon's spectacular coast highway was built across a steep basalt cliff, through Arch Cape, bridging Thomas Creek gorge and leveling mountains.

Clark, Ella E. *Indian Legends of the Pacific Northwest.* University of California Press, 2003. Native American myths that tell the story of their link to the mountains, lakes, and rivers, and of the creation of the world.

Gulick, Bill. *Roadside History of Oregon.* Mountain Press Publishing Company, 1991. The book follows Lewis and Clark's journey along the Columbia River to pioneer town-builders at the end of the Oregon Trail, from the lighthouses off the storm-ridden coast to the Chinese who helped shape Oregon's early fishing and mining industries.

California

Estrada, William D. *Los Angeles' Olvera Street.* Arcadia Publishing, 2006. A historical look at the El Pueblo de La Reina de Los Angeles—where the city was born in 1781, and its evolution.

Henson, Paul, and Usner, Donald. *The Natural History of Big Sur.* University of California Press, 2007. An ecological look at the diversity of Big Sur's many species of marine wildlife, and the impact by developers. The book provides excellent information for visitors, bringing greater awareness to the importance of preserving the region's natural resources.

Scheffler Innis, Jack. *San Diego Legends: Events, People, and Places That Made History.* Sunbelt Publications, 2004. Everything you'd want to know about San Diego—a fantastic historical account of the rise of the seaside city, including stories about the infamous "nudist invasion" of the 1935 California-Pacific Exposition, the murder of the first mayor, and more.

Outdoor Recreation

National Park Service (360/565-3130, www.nps.gov/olym): Provides detailed information, which includes fees, hours, trails, fishing regulations, and more.

Recreation.gov (www.recreation.gov): Provides national parks and forests campground information with options to reserve campsites.

U.S. Forest Service—Pacific Northwest Region (503/808-2468, www.fs.usda.gov/r6): Information on Oregon and Washington National Forests with external links and resources.

Washington

The Mountaineers (206/521-6000 main line, 206/521-6030 emergency line, www.mountaineers.org): A Seattle-based nonprofit organization that helps people explore, conserve, and learn about the lands and waters of the Pacific Northwest through sponsored excursions, books, and magazines.

Washington Department of Fish & Wildlife (360/902-2200, http://wdfw.wa.gov): A complete online guide to fishing and hunting regulations, including seasonal and permit information.

Washington State Parks & Recreation Commission (360/902-8844, www.parks.wa.gov): Details Washington's diverse parks, and provides access to campground information and reservations.

Oregon

Oregon Birding Association (www.orbirds.org): A resource for avid bird-watchers that includes a species checklist, field trips options, and the *Oregon Birds Journal,* printed twice a year.

Oregon Ocean Paddling Society (www.oopskayak.org): Provides NOAA charts, weather conditions, and paddling locations, including organized trips, classes, and other activities.

Oregon State Parks Information Center (www.oregon.gov/oprd/parks): Provides camping information within Oregon State Parks.

Portland Hikers (www.portlandhikersfieldguide.org): A great website provided by Trailkeepers of Oregon with a list of winter, spring, and backpacking trails to explore.

California

California Coast Birding Trail (http://caccbt.info): An Audubon-California supported website that offers habitat information in the areas of Monterey, San Luis Obispo, Santa Barbara, and Ventura.

California Department of Parks & Recreation (www.parks.ca.gov): Provides camping, off-highway vehicles, and boating information, including fees and regulations.

Redwoods National and State Parks (www.nps.gov/redw): Complete information on visiting the largest trees on Earth, such as park fees, hours, seasons, transportation, trails, and available campgrounds.

Surfline (www.surfline.com): A fantastic website that provides current surfing conditions along the entire California coast.

Sports
Washington

Seattle Mariners (http://seattle.mariners.mlb.com): Official Mariners Baseball website, providing schedules, stats, ticket information, and an online fan store.

Seattle Seahawks (www.seahawks.com): Schedules, stats, tickets, and a "Worldwide 12" interactive fan locator that allows you to pinpoint 12th men and their locations around the world.

The Sounders (www.soundersfc.com): Seattle's Major League Soccer team's official website lets users view players and schedules, and access information on Team Camps and partners.

Oregon

Portland Timbers and Thorns (www.timbers.com): The site contains seasonal schedules for both Portland's professional soccer clubs: men's Timbers and women's Thorns.

Portland Trail Blazers (www.nba.com/blazers): Blazer basketball fans can check for game information and ticket availability.

California

Los Angeles Angels of Anaheim (www.losangeles.angels.mlb.com): The official team site provides highlights, insider news, and game clips.

Los Angeles Dodgers (www.losangeles.dodgers.mlb.com): The website is a resource for fans of the four-time world champion Dodgers and baseball lovers with news, stats, schedules, and player highlights.

San Francisco Giants (www.sanfrancisco.giants.mlb.com): The official team site, offering video streaming, game roster, park location, and ticketing.

INDEX

C

INDEX

LIST OF MAPS

LIST OF MAPS

PHOTO CREDITS

MAP SYMBOLS

▬▬▬ Expressway	○ City/Town	✈ Airport	⚓ Golf Course		
▬▬▬ Primary Road	◉ State Capital	✈ Airfield	P Parking Area		
▬▬▬ Secondary Road	⊛ National Capital	▲ Mountain	≜ Archaeological Site		
⋯⋯ Unpaved Road	★ Point of Interest	✛ Unique Natural Feature	⛪ Church		
▬▬ Feature Trail	• Accommodation		Gas Station		
------ Other Trail	▾ Restaurant/Bar	Waterfall	Glacier		
⋯⋯⋯ Ferry	▪ Other Location	⚑ Park	Mangrove		
▭▭ Pedestrian Walkway	Λ Campground	⊓ Trailhead	Reef		
▭▭ Stairs		Skiing Area	Swamp		

CONVERSION TABLES

°C = (°F - 32) / 1.8
°F = (°C x 1.8) + 32
1 inch = 2.54 centimeters (cm)
1 foot = 0.304 meters (m)
1 yard = 0.914 meters
1 mile = 1.6093 kilometers (km)
1 km = 0.6214 miles
1 fathom = 1.8288 m
1 chain = 20.1168 m
1 furlong = 201.168 m
1 acre = 0.4047 hectares
1 sq km = 100 hectares
1 sq mile = 2.59 square km
1 ounce = 28.35 grams
1 pound = 0.4536 kilograms
1 short ton = 0.90718 metric ton
1 short ton = 2,000 pounds
1 long ton = 1.016 metric tons
1 long ton = 2,240 pounds
1 metric ton = 1,000 kilograms
1 quart = 0.94635 liters
1 US gallon = 3.7854 liters
1 Imperial gallon = 4.5459 liters
1 nautical mile = 1.852 km

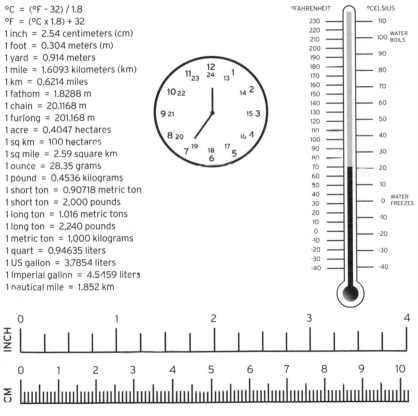

MOON PACIFIC COAST HIGHWAY ROAD TRIP

Avalon Travel
a member of the Perseus Books Group
1700 Fourth Street
Berkeley, CA 94710, USA
www.moon.com

Editor: Kevin McLain
Series Manager: Leah Gordon
Copy Editor: Naomi Adler Dancis
Graphics and Production Coordinator: Darren Alessi
Cover Design: Erin Seaward-Hiatt
Interior Design: Darren Alessi
Moon Logo: Tim McGrath
Map Editor: Albert Angulo
Cartographer: Brian Shotwell
Proofreader: Alissa Cypher
Indexer: Rachel Kuhn

ISBN: 978-1-63121-029-7
ISSN: 2380-5625

Printing History
1st Edition — January 2016
5 4 3 2 1